Junior Cycle Maths

# Text & Tests

## Ordinary Level Maths

**2**

**Paul Cooke • O.D. Morris • Deborah Crean**

 The Celtic Press

Available FREE as an
eBook
www.cjf.ie/code

The paper stock used in this publication comes from managed forests. This means that at least one tree is planted for every tree felled. The inks used for printing are environmentally friendly and vegetable based.

*Acknowledgements*
We would like to express our deep appreciation to Paul Behan for his contribution to the Geometry sections of this text.

First Published in April 2019 by
The Celtic Press
Ground Floor – Block B
Liffey Valley Office Campus
Dublin 22

This Reprint May 2022

ISBN: 978-0-7144-2751-5

# Contents

1. **Number 1** .......................................................................................... **1**
   1.1   Natural numbers   1
   1.2   Integers and order of operations   4
   1.3   Fractions   8
   1.4   Decimals and percentages   14
   1.5   Revision of ratio   20
        Test Yourself 1   24
        Assignment   26

2. **Algebra 1** ....................................................................................... **27**
   2.1   Dealing with algebraic expressions   27
   2.2   Removing brackets   30
   2.3   Evaluating expressions   32
   2.4   Solving linear equations   34
   2.5   Writing and solving equations   37
   2.6   Algebraic division   40
        Test Yourself 2   42
        Assignment   44

3. **Sets** ............................................................................................... **45**
   3.1   Revision of sets terminology   45
   3.2   Set difference   51
   3.3   Using Venn diagrams to solve problems   54
        Test Yourself 3   59
        Assignment   62

4. **Factors** .......................................................................................... **63**
   4.1   Factorising with common factors   63
   4.2   Factorising by grouping terms   66
   4.3   Differences of two squares   67
   4.4   Factorising quadratic expressions   69
   4.5   Quadratic expressions: Third term negative   71
        Test Yourself 4   73
        Assignment   74

5. **Applied Arithmetic** ..................................................................... **75**
   5.1   Household bills   75
   5.2   Applying percentages   81
   5.3   Interest   86
   5.4   Compound interest   87
   5.5   Income tax   90
   5.6   Currency transactions   93
        Test Yourself 5   95
        Assignment   98

6. **Perimeter, Area, Volume** .................................................... **99**
   - 6.1  Review of perimeter and area .................................... 99
   - 6.2  Area of parallelogram ............................................ 104
   - 6.3  Rectangular solids ................................................ 107
   - 6.4  Scale drawing ..................................................... 114
   - Test Yourself 6 .................................................. 119
   - Assignment ...................................................... 122

7. **Statistics 1** ..................................................................... **123**
   - 7.1  Statistical questions ............................................ 123
   - 7.2  Sampling ......................................................... 131
   - Test Yourself 7 .................................................. 135
   - Assignment ...................................................... 137

8. **Probability** .................................................................... **138**
   - 8.1  Listing outcomes ................................................ 138
   - 8.2  Chance and the probability scale .............................. 142
   - 8.3  Probability and equally likely outcomes ...................... 146
   - 8.4  Two events: Use of sample spaces, tree diagrams, two-way tables ... 151
   - 8.5  Estimating probability from experiments ...................... 155
   - Test Yourself 8 .................................................. 161
   - Assignment ...................................................... 164

9. **Statistics 2** ................................................................... **165**
   - 9.1  Summary statistics .............................................. 165
   - 9.2  The mean ......................................................... 169
   - 9.3  The range: variability .......................................... 173
   - 9.4  Which average to use ........................................... 176
   - 9.5  Frequency tables ................................................ 179
   - Test Yourself 9 .................................................. 184
   - Assignment ...................................................... 187

10. **Geometry 1: Triangles and Quadrilaterals** ....................... **188**
   - 10.1  Revision of lines and angles ................................. 188
   - 10.2  Angles of a triangle .......................................... 192
   - 10.3  Quadrilaterals ................................................. 196
   - 10.4  The theorem of Pythagoras .................................. 202
   - Test Yourself 10 ................................................. 208
   - Assignment ...................................................... 211

11. **Time and Speed** .......................................................... **212**
   - 11.1  Time and timetables .......................................... 212
   - 11.2  Speed, distance, time ........................................ 218
   - Test Yourself 11 ................................................. 222
   - Assignment ...................................................... 224

**12. Simultaneous Equations** ........................................................................ **225**

12.1 Simultaneous equations ..................................................................... 225
12.2 Solving simultaneous equations ......................................................... 226
12.3 Problems leading to simultaneous equations ....................................... 229
Test Yourself 12 ............................................................................... 233
Assignment ...................................................................................... 234

**13. Quadratic Equations** ............................................................................ **235**

13.1 Solving quadratic equations using factors ........................................... 235
13.2 Problems leading to quadratic equations ............................................ 238
Test Yourself 13 ............................................................................... 242
Assignment ...................................................................................... 243

**14. Coordinate Geometry: The Line** ........................................................ **244**

14.1 The coordinated plane ....................................................................... 244
14.2 Revision of midpoint of a line segment ............................................... 247
14.3 Distance between two points .............................................................. 250
14.4 Revision of slope of a line segment .................................................... 253
14.5 The equation of a line ....................................................................... 258
14.6 The equation of a line containing $(x_1, y_1)$ with slope m ..................... 262
14.7 Graphing lines .................................................................................. 265
14.8 Intersection of lines .......................................................................... 268
Test Yourself 14 ............................................................................... 271
Assignment ...................................................................................... 273

**15. Statistics 3** ......................................................................................... **274**

15.1 Revision of line plots and bar charts .................................................. 274
15.2 Pie charts ........................................................................................ 279
15.3 Stem and leaf plots .......................................................................... 286
15.4 Histograms ...................................................................................... 291
15.5 Misleading graphs ............................................................................ 296
Test Yourself 15 ............................................................................... 300
Assignment ...................................................................................... 303

**16. Number 2: Indices and Standard Form** ............................................. **304**

16.1 The laws of indices ........................................................................... 304
16.2 Numbers in standard form ................................................................. 309
16.3 Using the calculator .......................................................................... 313
16.4 Significant figures: Approximation ...................................................... 315
Test Yourself 16 ............................................................................... 318
Assignment ...................................................................................... 320

**17. Circles and Cylinders** ......................................................................... **321**

17.1 The circumference of a circle ............................................................. 321
17.2 The area of a circle ........................................................................... 326
17.3 Cylinders .......................................................................................... 330
Test Yourself 17 ............................................................................... 334
Assignment ...................................................................................... 336

## 18. Geometry 2: Triangles and Circles ................................. 337

| | | |
|---|---|---|
| 18.1 | Congruent triangles | 337 |
| 18.2 | Similar triangles | 344 |
| 18.3 | Angles and circles | 349 |
| | Test Yourself 18 | 355 |
| | Assignment | 357 |

## 19. Patterns and Sequences ................................. 358

| | | |
|---|---|---|
| 19.1 | Sequences | 358 |
| 19.2 | Repeating patterns | 363 |
| 19.3 | Linear sequences | 366 |
| 19.4 | Finding the nth term Tn, of a linear sequence | 370 |
| 19.5 | Linear sequences formed from shapes | 373 |
| 19.6 | Other sequences | 376 |
| 19.7 | Graphing linear sequences | 379 |
| | Test Yourself 19 | 383 |
| | Assignment | 385 |

## 20. Algebra 2: Inequalities, Algebraic Fractions ................................. 386

| | | |
|---|---|---|
| 20.1 | Plotting numbers on the number line | 386 |
| 20.2 | Solving inequalities | 390 |
| 20.3 | Adding algebraic fractions | 393 |
| 20.4 | Solving equations involving fractions | 394 |
| 20.5 | Solving problems involving fractions | 397 |
| 20.6 | Simplifying algebraic fractions | 398 |
| | Test Yourself 20 | 401 |
| | Assignment | 402 |

## 21. Functions ................................. 403

| | | |
|---|---|---|
| 21.1 | Functions | 403 |
| 21.2 | Mapping diagrams | 406 |
| 21.3 | Notation for functions | 411 |
| | Test Yourself 21 | 413 |
| | Assignment | 415 |

## 22. Graphing Functions ................................. 416

| | | |
|---|---|---|
| 22.1 | Graphing linear functions | 416 |
| 22.2 | Graphs of quadratic functions | 421 |
| 22.3 | Using quadratic graphs | 425 |
| | Test Yourself 22 | 432 |
| | Assignment | 434 |

23. **Trigonometry** 435

23.1 The theorem of Pythagoras 435
23.2 Sides of a right-angle triangle 439
23.3 Sine, cosine and tangent ratios 440
23.4 Using your calculator to find ratios 443
23.5 Finding sides and angles of a triangle 445
23.6 Using trigonometry to solve problems 450
Test Yourself 23 455
Assignment 457

24. **Drawing and Interpreting Real-life Graphs** 458

24.1 Distance-time graphs 458
24.2 Directly proportional graphs 463
24.3 Real-life graphs 469
Assignment 474

25. **Geometry 3: Transformations, Constructions, Proofs** 475

25.1 Transformation geometry 475
25.2 Symmetries 479
25.3 Constructions 1 485
25.4 Constructing triangles and rectangles 491
25.5 Revision of theorems 496
Assignment 500

**Answers** 501

# Preface

This book is written as a complete two-year course in mathematics, responding to the new specification for Junior Cycle Ordinary Level students.

It revisits the topics covered in *Text & Test 1* (new edition) and encourages the further development of the student's mathematical knowledge and skills. Each chapter of this book contains:

- Chapter outlines
- Clear explanations and examples
- A large number of well-structured graded questions
- Detailed diagrams
- Test Yourself revision exercises

The book emphasises discussion, cooperation and communication in acquiring the understanding of the fundamental concepts in the mathematics specification by using:

- Investigations
- Assignments

The free online resources contain Reviews of each chapter.

While retaining many successful features of the previous *Text & Tests* series, this book is designed to help students prepare for final exams and classroom-based assessments by being numerate; working with others; being creative; communicating; collecting and managing information.

Paul Cooke
Deborah Crean
O.D. Morris

# Number 1

*From first year, you will recall how to:*

- identify the set of Natural Numbers, N,
- find factors, multiples, HCF and LCM,
- identify the set of Integers, Z,
- use BIRDMAS,
- identify the set of Rational Numbers (fractions), Q,
- add, subtract, multiply and divide fractions,
- change between fractions, decimals and percentages,
- use ratios and proportions,
- identify commutative, associative and distributive properties.

*In this chapter, you will learn to:*

- identify the set of Real Numbers, R,
- categorise numbers into their correct sets.

## Section 1.1  Natural numbers

The **natural numbers** are the counting numbers  1, 2, 3, 4, 5, 6, …
Since there is no largest number, we say that the set is **infinite**.

The natural numbers are represented on the number line by dots :

The set of natural numbers is denoted by the letter **N**.

The **factors** of a natural number are all the whole natural numbers which divide into it, leaving no remainder.

The factors of 12 are  1, 2, 3, 4, 6 and 12.

The **HCF (highest common factor)** of two or more natural numbers is the largest factor that is common to all of them.

## Example 1

Find the HCF of 24 and 40.

The factors of 24 are: 1, 2, 3, 4, 6, 8, 12, 24.
The factors of 40 are: 1, 2, 4, 5, 8, 10, 20, 40.
The HCF of 24 and 40 is 8.

## Multiples

The **multiples** of a number are obtained by multiplying it by 1, 2, 3, 4, ... .
The multiples of 8 are 8, 16, 24, 32, 40, 48, ...
The multiples of 10 are 10, 20, 30, 40, 50, 60, ...

As seen above, the **lowest common multiple (LCM)** of 8 and 10 is 40.
The lowest common multiple of any two numbers is the **smallest** multiple which is common to both of them.

## Prime numbers

A **prime number** is a natural number which has only two factors, itself and 1.
The first seven prime numbers are: 2, 3, 5, 7, 11, 13, 17, ...

**Note:** The number 4, for example, is not prime as it has three factors, 1, 2 and 4.

## Example 2

Express 72 as a product of its prime factors.

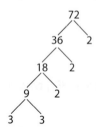

72 expressed as a product of its prime factor is
$2 \times 2 \times 2 \times 3 \times 3$.
This can be written as $2^3 \times 3^2$.

## Exercise 1.1

**1.** State whether each of these numbers is a natural number:

(i) 6      (ii) $-4$      (iii) $3\frac{1}{2}$      (iv) 0.5      (v) 0      (vi) 23

2. Write the first six multiples of 5.

3. (i) Write the first eight multiples of 6.
   (ii) Write the first eight multiples of 7.
   (iii) What is the lowest common multiple of 6 and 7?

4. Write down all the factors of each of these numbers:
   (i) 28     (ii) 30     (iii) 45     (iv) 60     (v) 72.

5. Find the highest common factor (HCF) of
   (i) 12 and 18     (ii) 24 and 30     (iii) 36 and 64     (iv) 20, 24 and 36.

6. Write down the three multiples of 6 that are between 50 and 70.

7. (i) Write down the first ten prime numbers.
   (ii) Explain why there is only one even prime number.

8. Which of these numbers are prime?
   (i) 13     (ii) 21     (iii) 23     (iv) 31     (v) 39     (vi) 53

9. Write each of these numbers as a product of its prime factors:
   (i) 24     (ii) 36     (iii) 42     (iv) 66     (v) 100

10. Write three two-digit prime numbers which, when their digits are reversed, are also prime. (Exclude 11.)

11. Find two prime numbers with a sum of 46 and a difference of 12.

12. Peter and Jane compared the number of euro each had.
    Peter said that the lowest common multiple of their money was €24.
    How much money could each have?

13. The lowest common multiple of the ages of Jack, Sarah and Colm is 36 years.
    Find their ages.

14. Three bells chime at intervals of 4, 5 and 6 seconds respectively. If they all chime at the same instant, how long before they all chime together again?

## *Investigation:*

If **n** is any whole positive number, investigate why:

   (i)   $n + 1$ **might** be an even or odd number.

  (ii)   $2n$ **must always** be an even number.

 (iii)   $2n + 1$ **must always** be an odd number.

## *Investigation:*

A four-digit number is written as PQRS. Find
two possible numbers given the following clues:

**1.** All the digits are different

**2.** The product of the digits R and S equals the digit P.

**3.** Digit Q is one more than digit P.

**4.** The sum of all the digits is 18.

| P | Q | R | S |
|---|---|---|---|
|   |   |   |   |
|   |   |   |   |
|   |   |   |   |
|   |   |   |   |

# Section 1.2  Integers and order of operations

The set of natural numbers, zero and negative whole numbers together form the set of integers, i.e.,

$$\ldots, -5, -4, -3, -2, -1, 0, 1, 2, 3, 4, 5, \ldots$$

We use the letter **Z** to represent integers.

When we show the set of integers on the number line, it will look like this:

## Adding integers

**1.** When the signs are the same, add the numbers and retain the sign.

**2.** When the signs are different, retain the sign of the numerically bigger number and take the smaller number from the bigger number.

Examples:   (i)  $3 + 8 - 3 - 4 = 11 - 7 = 4$

   (ii)  $-3 + 7 - 9 + 2 = 7 + 2 - 3 - 9$

$$= 9 - 12 = -3$$

   (iii)  $-6 + 13 = 7$

## Multiplying and dividing integers

The rules for multiplying and dividing integers are highlighted on the right.

When multiplying or dividing integers,
> like signs give plus
> unlike signs give minus

**Example 1**

Write each of these as a single integer:

(i) $6 \times (-4)$

(ii) $-3 \times (-10)$

(iii) $\dfrac{-9 \times (-8)}{-12}$

(i) $6 \times (-4) = -24$

(ii) $-3 \times (-10) = 30$

(iii) $\dfrac{-9 \times (-8)}{-12} = \dfrac{72}{-12}$
$$= -6$$

## Order of operations

When a calculation involves more than one operation **BIRDMAS** represents the order of operations that enables us to do the calculation correctly.

When a calculation involves brackets as well as other operations, this is the correct order to work out the answers.

| First | Second | Third | Fourth |
|-------|--------|-------|--------|
| ( ) | $\square^2$ or $\boxed{\sqrt{\phantom{x}}}$ | $\times$ or $\div$ | $+$ or $-$ |

**B** – brackets
**I** – index/power
**R** – roots
**D** – division
**M** – multiplication
**A** – addition
**S** – subtraction

**Example 2**

Evaluate:  $6 \times (2 + 7) - 2 \times 7$

$6 \times (2 + 7) - 2 \times 7 = 6 \times (9) - 14$
$$= 54 - 14 = 40$$

**Note :**  If a calculation involves a combination of multiplications and divisions, work across the line from left to right.

## Exercise 1.2

**1.** Write each list of temperatures in order, lowest first:
   (i) −4°C, 3°C, 10°C, −7°C, 0°C,
   (ii) 7.5°C, −5°C, 6°C, −4.5°C, −1°C.

**2.** Work out the finishing temperature in each of these:
   (i) Start at 2°C, fall 6 degrees.     (ii) Start at −5°C, fall 4 degrees.
   (iii) Start at −10°C, rise 8 degrees.     (iv) Start at 2°C, fall 12 degrees.

**3.** Work out each of these:
   (i) $8 − 2 − 1$     (ii) $5 − 2 − 4$     (iii) $−10 + 3 − 2$     (iv) $3 − 4 − 7$
   (v) $−3 + 10 − 9$     (vi) $−5 − 4 − 10$     (vii) $3 − 14 + 9$     (viii) $−2 − 5 + 11$

**4.** Work out the answers and write them in order, lowest first:
   The letters will spell the name of a car.

R $12 − 7$     U $−4 − 2$     A $−2 + 5$     S $−5 − 4$     B $6 − 8$     U $10 − 4$

**5.** From the numbers in the loop,
   find two numbers which add up to
   (i) 3          (ii) −5          (iii) −16          (iv) 5.

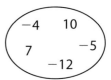

**6.** Write down the answer to each of these:
   (i) $4 × (−3)$     (ii) $−3 × 6$     (iii) $−2 × (−3)$     (iv) $−4 × 10$
   (v) $6 × (−20)$     (vi) $7 × (−8)$     (vii) $2 × 3 × (−4)$     (viii) $−2 × (−4) × (−6)$

**7.** Copy and complete these:
   (i) $? × (−6) = −12$     (ii) $4 × ? = −20$     (iii) $8 × ? = −24$
   (iv) $−6 × ? = 42$     (v) $−7 × ? = −56$     (vi) $? × (−6) = −30$

**8.** Find the value of each of these:
   (i) $−14 ÷ 2$     (ii) $−28 ÷ (−7)$     (iii) $36 ÷ −4$     (iv) $−72 ÷ (−8)$

9. Work out the answers to the questions below.
   Use the code to change them to letters.
   Re-arrange the letters to spell some animals.

| A | B | C | E | G | H | I | M | O | P | R | S | T | W |
|---|---|---|---|---|---|---|---|---|---|---|---|---|---|
| $-12$ | $-24$ | $-28$ | $-36$ | $24$ | $30$ | $-18$ | $48$ | $20$ | $-20$ | $36$ | $28$ | $-60$ | $-48$ |

(i)  $4 \times -5$
     $3 \times 10$
     $-6 \times 6$
     $4 \times 7$
     $-9 \times 4$

(ii)  $-6 \times 4$
      $9 \times -2$
      $3 \times -8$
      $-10 \times 6$
      $-2 \times 6$
      $4 \times 9$

(iii)  $12 \times 4$
       $6 \times -6$
       $2 \times 14$
       $5 \times 6$
       $2 \times 18$
       $-3 \times 4$
       $15 \times -4$

10. Evaluate each of the following :
    (i)  $14 \div 2 + 3 \times 4$
    (ii)  $60 \div 3 \div 4 + 2$
    (iii)  $(16 + 4) \div 5 \times 3$
    (iv)  $5 \times (4 - 3) + 9$
    (v)  $6 \times (2 + 7) - 2 \times 7$
    (vi)  $5 + 7 - 3 \times 2$
    (vii)  $3 \times 15 - 6 \times 5$
    (viii)  $18 \div 2 \times 10 - (7 \times 8)$
    (ix)  $6 \times 9 + 4$

11. Insert brackets where necessary to make the following equations true :
    (i)  $6 + 8 - 1 = 13$
    (ii)  $54 \div 6 + 3 + 2 = 8$
    (iii)  $6 + 34 \div 2 + 3 \div 2 = 13$
    (iv)  $42 \div 5 + 2 \times 5 = 30$
    (v)  $15 + 4 \times 5 - 5 = 15$
    (vi)  $81 \div 9 \div 2 + 1 = 3$

12. State whether each of the following is true or false :
    (i)  $16 \div (3 + 1) \times 3 + 6 = 36$
    (ii)  $(2 + 3 \times 5) - (3 + 16 \div 4) = 18$
    (iii)  $5 \times 10 + 3 \times 8 \div 4 = 56$
    (iv)  $44 \div 4 + 7 \times 2 - 3 = 5$

13. Insert the symbols $\times, \div, +, -$ to make the following equations true :
    (i)  $(2 \boxed{\phantom{x}} 8) \boxed{\phantom{x}} 5 = 2$
    (ii)  $(14 \boxed{\phantom{x}} 5) \boxed{\phantom{x}} 9 = 81$
    (iii)  $6 \boxed{\phantom{x}} (8 \boxed{\phantom{x}} 3) = 30$
    (iv)  $(21 \boxed{\phantom{x}} 5) \boxed{\phantom{x}} 2 = 13$
    (v)  $12 \boxed{\phantom{x}} 8 \boxed{\phantom{x}} 5 = 9$
    (vi)  $40 \boxed{\phantom{x}} (14 \boxed{\phantom{x}} 7) = 38$

14. Simplify each of the following :
    (i)  $\dfrac{53 - 21}{9 - 5}$
    (ii)  $\dfrac{3 \times 8 + 6}{6}$
    (iii)  $\dfrac{57}{7 - (2 \times 3)}$
    (iv)  $\dfrac{(3 + 8) - 5}{3 + (8 - 5)}$

**15.** (i) Choose three numbers from this
set to make the highest product:

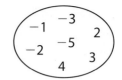

$$\square \times \square \times \square$$

(ii) Choose three numbers from the set to
make the lowest product.

**16.** In the morning at 8 o'clock the temperature of a fridge
was measured at −6°C. Over the next hour the fridge door
is opened and closed and the temperature rises and
falls.

(i) If the temperature increases by 4°C, then reduces by
2°C, increases again by 5°C and finally reduces
by 3°C. Find the final temperature of the fridge
at 9 o'clock.

(ii) The fridge temperature decreases by 1.5°C every
hour (if the fridge door is kept closed), at what time
will the fridge temperature return to its lowest value
of −6°C assuming the fridge door is kept closed?

# Section 1.3 Fractions

A **fraction** consists of two whole numbers
– a **numerator** and a **denominator**
– separated by a bar symbol, as shown

$\dfrac{4}{5}$ ← numerator
← denominator

## Types of fractions

$\frac{4}{5}$ is a **proper fraction**       … as the numerator is less than the denominator

$\frac{7}{6}$ is an **improper fraction**       … as the numerator is greater than the denominator

$2\frac{3}{4}$ is a **mixed number**       … as it is really $2 + \frac{3}{4}$

$\frac{1}{2}, \frac{3}{6}$ are **equivalent fractions**    … as both fractions represent equal portions

## Adding and subtracting fractions

To add (or subtract) two fractions, we convert them to two fractions with the same denominator, and then add (or subtract) the new numerators.

> **Example 1**
>
> Find  (i) $\frac{5}{6} + \frac{3}{4}$      (ii) $1\frac{4}{5} - 1\frac{1}{3}$
>
> (i) $\frac{5}{6} + \frac{3}{4} = \frac{10}{12} + \frac{9}{12} = \frac{19}{12} = 1\frac{7}{12}$ ... the LCM of 6 and 4 is 12
>
> (ii) $1\frac{4}{5} - 1\frac{1}{3} = \frac{9}{5} - \frac{4}{3} = \frac{27}{15} - \frac{20}{15} = \frac{7}{15}$

## Multiplying and dividing fractions

To multiply two fractions, multiply the numerators together and multiply the denominators together, and then simplify.

**Examples :**  (i) $\frac{2}{3} \times \frac{1}{4} = \frac{2}{12} = \frac{1}{6}$

(ii) $4\frac{2}{3} \times 1\frac{1}{2} = \frac{14}{3} \times \frac{3}{2} = \frac{42}{6} = 7$

To **divide** by a fraction, multiply by its reciprocal.

> The reciprocal of $\frac{2}{3}$ is $\frac{3}{2}$.

**Examples :**  (i) $2 \div \frac{3}{4} = \frac{2}{1} \times \frac{4}{3} = \frac{8}{3} = 2\frac{2}{3}$

(ii) $2\frac{1}{3} \div \frac{2}{3} = \frac{7}{\cancel{3}_1} \times \frac{\cancel{3}^1}{2} = \frac{7 \times 1}{1 \times 2} = \frac{7}{2} = 3\frac{1}{2}$

**Note :** $\frac{7}{2}$ is called a Rational number.

Real – number – line

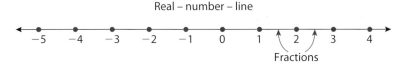

Fractions

The set of **Real numbers** contain the sets of natural, integer and rational numbers

---

**Example 2**

If $\frac{7}{8}$ of a number is 56, find the number.

$\frac{7}{8}$ of the number = 63

$\frac{1}{8} = \frac{63}{7} = 9$  ... ÷ by 7

$\frac{8}{8} = 9 \times 8 = 72$

∴  the number is 72

---

## Exercise 1.3

**1.** Copy and complete each statement :

(i) $\frac{1}{2} = \frac{\square}{10}$     (ii) $\frac{1}{4} = \frac{\square}{12}$     (iii) $\frac{2}{5} = \frac{\square}{20}$     (i) $\frac{2}{3} = \frac{4}{\square}$

**2.** Write these fractions in their simplest form :

(i) $\frac{4}{8}$     (ii) $\frac{10}{15}$     (iii) $\frac{21}{28}$     (iv) $\frac{15}{25}$     (v) $\frac{15}{21}$

**3.** Convert these mixed numbers to improper fractions :

(i) $1\frac{2}{3}$     (ii) $2\frac{5}{8}$     (iii) $3\frac{3}{4}$     (iv) $5\frac{3}{5}$     (v) $7\frac{5}{8}$

**4.** Convert these improper fractions to mixed numbers, simplifying where possible :

(i) $\frac{8}{5}$     ii) $\frac{23}{4}$     (iii) $\frac{16}{7}$     (iv) $\frac{26}{8}$     (v) $\frac{39}{6}$

**5.** Which of these fractions is the largest?    $\frac{17}{4}$   $\frac{13}{10}$   $\frac{18}{5}$   $\frac{9}{2}$

**6.** Arrange these fractions in order of size, smallest first.

$\frac{11}{4}$     $\frac{15}{5}$     $\frac{17}{10}$     $\frac{10}{3}$     $\frac{8}{7}$

**7.** Add each of these, giving your answer in its lowest terms :

(i) $\frac{4}{7} + \frac{2}{7}$     (ii) $\frac{2}{9} + \frac{4}{9}$     (iii) $\frac{8}{15} - \frac{2}{15}$     (iv) $\frac{13}{24} - \frac{7}{24}$

**8.** Find the lowest common denominator for each pair of fractions :

(i) $\frac{5}{6}$ and $\frac{2}{3}$     (ii) $\frac{3}{4}$ and $\frac{5}{6}$     (iii) $\frac{1}{6}$ and $\frac{4}{9}$     (iv) $\frac{7}{12}$ and $\frac{3}{8}$

9. Work out each of these, simplifying your answers where possible :

   (i) $\frac{1}{5} + \frac{7}{10}$     (ii) $\frac{3}{8} + \frac{1}{4}$     (iii) $\frac{5}{12} + \frac{1}{6}$     (iv) $\frac{3}{4} + \frac{2}{3}$

   (v) $\frac{1}{6} + \frac{5}{9}$     (vi) $\frac{2}{5} + \frac{2}{3}$     (vii) $\frac{6}{7} + \frac{1}{4}$     (viii) $\frac{4}{9} + \frac{5}{12}$

10. Work out each of these. Express each answer in its simplest form :

    (i) $\frac{11}{12} - \frac{5}{6}$     (ii) $\frac{4}{5} - \frac{3}{8}$     (iii) $\frac{5}{6} - \frac{3}{5}$     (iv) $\frac{6}{7} - \frac{4}{21}$

11. Arrange these fractions in order, starting with the smallest each time :

    (i) $\frac{1}{2}$   $\frac{1}{4}$   $\frac{2}{5}$   $\frac{1}{10}$   $\frac{3}{5}$         (ii) $\frac{5}{8}$   $\frac{3}{4}$   $\frac{5}{6}$   $\frac{2}{3}$   $\frac{7}{12}$   $\frac{17}{24}$

12. Simplify each of these :

    (i) $2\frac{2}{3} + 1\frac{1}{4}$     (ii) $2\frac{4}{5} + 1\frac{1}{2}$     (iii) $5\frac{1}{2} + \frac{7}{10}$     (iv) $2\frac{5}{6} + 1\frac{3}{4}$

    (v) $2\frac{4}{5} - 1\frac{1}{2}$     (vi) $2\frac{2}{3} - \frac{3}{5}$     (vii) $1\frac{3}{8} - \frac{3}{4}$     (viii) $5\frac{5}{6} - 3\frac{2}{3}$

13. Work these out, simplifying your answer where possible :

    (i) $\frac{5}{6} \times \frac{3}{4}$     (ii) $\frac{4}{7} \times \frac{1}{2}$     (iii) $\frac{2}{3} \times \frac{9}{14}$     (iv) $\frac{5}{6} \times \frac{2}{15}$

14. Simplify each of these :

    (i) $\frac{2}{7} \times 14$     (ii) $\frac{5}{7} \times 35$     (iii) $1\frac{1}{9} \times 18$     (iv) $\frac{7}{12} \times 36$

15. Work out each of these :

    (i) $2\frac{1}{4} \times \frac{2}{3}$     (ii) $2\frac{1}{2} \times 1\frac{5}{7}$     (iii) $1\frac{2}{3} \times \frac{6}{11}$     (iv) $3\frac{2}{3} \times 2\frac{1}{4}$

16. Simplify each of these :

    (i) $\frac{5}{6} \div \frac{2}{3}$     (ii) $\frac{7}{12} \div \frac{1}{6}$     (iii) $\frac{9}{10} \div \frac{3}{4}$     (iv) $\frac{7}{10} \div \frac{4}{5}$

    (v) $3\frac{1}{2} \div \frac{3}{4}$     (vi) $10 \div 1\frac{2}{3}$     (vii) $4\frac{1}{2} \div 3$     (viii) $\frac{6}{7} \div 1\frac{2}{3}$

17. Work out each of these :

    (i) $1\frac{1}{8} \div 2\frac{1}{4}$     (ii) $8\frac{1}{4} \div 1\frac{3}{8}$     (iii) $3\frac{1}{8} \div 3\frac{3}{4}$     (iv) $4\frac{2}{3} \div 1\frac{7}{9}$

18. Which is the larger in each pair? Show your working.

    (i) $\frac{2}{3}$ of 81 or $\frac{11}{12}$ of 60         (ii) $\frac{3}{4}$ of 24 or $\frac{2}{3}$ of 27.

**19.** (i) Match each calculation to a diagram.

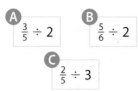  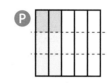    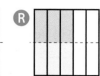

(ii) Work out the result of each calculation.

**20.** Work out each answer and use
the code to change it to a letter.
Then rearrange the letters to spell
a city.

| S | G | R | I | O | A | D | P | W | L | E | M |
|---|---|---|---|---|---|---|---|---|---|---|---|
| $\frac{1}{12}$ | $\frac{1}{10}$ | $\frac{1}{9}$ | $\frac{1}{8}$ | $\frac{1}{6}$ | $\frac{3}{16}$ | $\frac{1}{5}$ | $\frac{1}{4}$ | $\frac{3}{8}$ | $\frac{1}{2}$ | $\frac{2}{5}$ | $\frac{3}{4}$ |

$\frac{1}{2}$ of $\frac{3}{4}$    $\frac{1}{2}$ of $\frac{1}{5}$    $\frac{1}{3}$ of $1\frac{1}{2}$    $\frac{1}{8}$ of $\frac{2}{3}$    $\frac{1}{4} \times \frac{2}{3}$    $\frac{1}{4} \times \frac{3}{4}$    $\frac{1}{5} \times \frac{1}{2}$

**21.** Jan uses $\frac{1}{4}$ litre of milk to make a milkshake.

Which calculation gives how much milk she would need to make 10 milkshakes?

**A** $\frac{1}{4} + 10$     **B** $10 - \frac{1}{4}$     **C** $\frac{1}{4} \times 10$     **D** $\frac{1}{4} \div 10$

**22.** A year-group of 72 students was asked how they travelled to school one morning.
$\frac{1}{4}$ of the year-group travelled by bicycle, $\frac{2}{9}$ by bus, $\frac{1}{3}$ on foot, and the rest by car.
How many of the students travelled by car?

**23.** Alec's dog eats $\frac{2}{3}$ of a tin of *Butch* each day.

What is the least number of tins Alec needs to
buy to feed his dog for 7 days?

**24.** (i) If $\frac{3}{4}$ of a number is 36, find the number.

(ii) The difference between $\frac{1}{3}$ and $\frac{1}{2}$ of a number is 14; find this number.

**25.** A bottle contains $1\frac{1}{2}$ litres of detergent.

Each load of washing needs $\frac{1}{20}$ of a litre.

How many loads of washing can be done using one bottle?

**26.** In a bag of 28 coloured counters, $\frac{1}{4}$ are red, $\frac{2}{7}$ are blue and the rest are yellow.
How many of the counters are yellow?

**27.** Adam spent $\frac{5}{9}$ of his money. If he had €36 left, how much had he at first?

**28.** Which of these two rectangles has the greatest length?
Express the difference between the lengths as a fraction of a metre.

(i)
Area
$2\frac{3}{4}$ m²    $1\frac{4}{7}$ m

(ii)
Area
$4\frac{2}{3}$ m²    $3\frac{1}{3}$ m

**29.** Jane has a chocolate bar.
Jane eats $\frac{1}{3}$ of it and a friend eats $\frac{1}{4}$ of the bar.
The remaining chocolate is shared between Jane's two brothers.
What fraction of the bar does each brother get?

**30.** What is the largest and smallest answer that you
can make using two of the numbers from the box?
You can either multiply or divide the numbers.

$\frac{3}{5}$     $1\frac{3}{4}$

$\frac{1}{10}$     $3\frac{5}{6}$

$\frac{1}{8}$     $2\frac{2}{3}$

**31.** A farmer has 360 ewes and each ewe has either 1 or 2
new born lambs.
If there are 495 lambs in total, what fraction of the ewes
had twins?

**32.** A tree loses $\frac{2}{3}$ of its leaves in the first week of November.
Then $\frac{2}{3}$ of the remaining leaves in the second week and
$\frac{2}{3}$ of those remaining in the third week.
If there are 45 leaves remaining on the tree, how many
leaves did the tree have originally?

# Section 1.4 Decimals and percentages

The number $1\frac{3}{10}$ may also be written as the decimal 1.3.

A decimal point in a number separates the whole number part from the fractional part.

The decimal $4.85 = 4 + \frac{8}{10} + \frac{5}{100}$

$$= 4 + \frac{80}{100} + \frac{5}{100} = 4\frac{85}{100}$$

Here are some more decimals converted to fractions:

(i)  $0.4 = \frac{4}{10} = \frac{2}{5}$

(ii)  $0.65 = \frac{65}{100} = \frac{13}{20}$

(iii)  $0.125 = \frac{125}{1000} = \frac{1}{8}$

## Adding and subtracting decimals

When adding or subtracting decimals, line up the decimal points directly beneath one another.

$$\begin{array}{r} 38.42 \\ + 6.08 \\ \hline 44.50 \end{array} = 44.5 \qquad \begin{array}{r} 15.06 \\ -3.465 \\ \hline 11.595 \end{array}$$

## Fractions to decimals

If the denominator of a fraction contains 10, 100, 1000 …, it can easily be converted to a decimal.

(i)  $\frac{7}{10} = 0.7$      (ii)  $\frac{67}{100} = 0.67$      (iii)  $\frac{135}{1000} = 0.135$

To convert a fraction such as $\frac{3}{8}$ to a decimal, we divide 3 by 8 as shown.

$$\begin{array}{r} 8\overline{)3.000} \\ 0.375 \end{array}$$

$\therefore \quad \frac{3}{8} = 0.375$

 When using a calculator to convert $\frac{3}{8}$ as a decimal,

Key in ⊟ then 3, ⇓, 8, ⇨ and finally ⌷=⌷.

The screen displays $\frac{3}{8}$ in the bottom right hand corner.

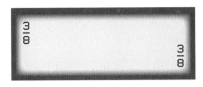

Pressing the **S ⇔ D** key the fraction is converted to a decimal. ➡

## Multiplying and dividing decimals

To **multiply** 23.24 by 1.2, we first multiply 2324 by 12

$$
\begin{array}{r}
2324 \\
\times\ \ 12 \\
\hline
27888
\end{array}
$$

Since we have increased one number by a factor of 100 and the second by a factor of 10, the answer must be reduced by a factor of 1000

Thus $23.\underset{2}{24} \times 1.\underset{1}{2} = 27.\underset{3}{888}$

When **dividing** a number by a decimal, change the denominator into a whole number as follows:

(i) $\dfrac{28}{0.4} = \dfrac{28 \times 10}{0.4 \times 10} = \dfrac{280}{4} = 70$

(ii) $\dfrac{115.2}{0.09} = \dfrac{115.2 \times 100}{0.09 \times 100} = \dfrac{11\,520}{9} = 1280$

## Percentages

**Percent** means 'out of every hundred'.

$\dfrac{20}{100} = 20\%$      $\dfrac{80}{100} = 80\%$      $\dfrac{35}{100} = 35\%$      $\dfrac{6}{100} = 6\%$

To convert a **fraction to a percentage**, multiply the fraction by 100 and add the % symbol.

(i) $\frac{1}{5} = \frac{1}{5} \times \frac{100}{1}\% = 20\%$

(ii) $\frac{3}{4} = \frac{3}{4} \times \frac{100}{1}\% = \frac{300}{4}\% = 75\%$

The diagram below shows the close relationship between decimals and percentages:

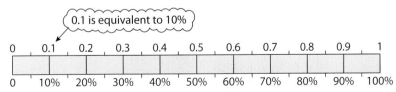

---

**Example 1**

(i) Express 0.46 as a percentage.

(ii) Express $\frac{11}{20}$ as a percentage.

(i) $0.46 = \frac{46}{100} = 46\%$

(ii) $\frac{11}{20} = \frac{11}{20} \times \frac{100}{1}\% = \frac{1100}{20}\% = \frac{110}{2}\% = 55\%$

---

Here are some useful conversion facts you should know, as they are used very frequently.

| Percentage | Decimal | Fraction |
|:---:|:---:|:---:|
| 1% | 0.01 | $\frac{1}{100}$ |
| 5% | 0.05 | $\frac{1}{20}$ |
| 10% | 0.1 | $\frac{1}{10}$ |
| $12\frac{1}{2}\%$ | 0.125 | $\frac{1}{8}$ |
| 20% | 0.2 | $\frac{1}{5}$ |
| 25% | 0.25 | $\frac{1}{4}$ |
| $33\frac{1}{3}\%$ | 0.333 … | $\frac{1}{3}$ |
| 50% | 0.5 | $\frac{1}{2}$ |
| 75% | 0.75 | $\frac{3}{4}$ |
| 100% | 1 | 1 |

To change a fraction or decimal to a percentage, multiply by 100 and add the % sign.

## Percentages of a number

To find the percentage **of** a number, change the percentage to a fraction or a decimal and then multiply this by the number.

e.g. Find 5% of €65 $= 0.05 \times €65 = €3.25$

$\qquad$ or $= \frac{5}{100} \times €65 = €\frac{325}{100} = €3.25$

Using a calculator, key in **5**, **SHIFT**, **(** , $\times$, 65, = to produce 5% $\times$ 65, $\frac{13}{4}$ appears on the screen.

Again pressing **S $\Leftrightarrow$ D** key the fraction is changed to a decimal 3.25 as above.

---

**Example 2**

Find the difference in value between 25% of €226 and 30% of €180.

25% of €226 $= 0.25 \times €226 = €56.50$

30% of €180 $= 0.3 \times €180 = €54.00$

$\therefore €56.50 - €54.00 = €2.50$

---

## Exercise 1.4

(Do not use a calculator for this exercise.)

1. Express each of these decimals as a fraction in its simplest form:
   (i) 0.8          (ii) 0.25          (iii) 0.75          (iv) 0.35          (v) 0.05

2. Express each of these fractions as a decimal:
   (i) $\frac{7}{10}$     (ii) $\frac{65}{100}$     (iii) $\frac{87}{100}$     (iv) $\frac{5}{100}$     (v) $\frac{35}{1000}$

3. Write down the answer to each of these:
   (i) 1.6 × 10          (ii) 1.34 × 100          (iii) 1.04 × 100          (iv) 0.2 × 100

4. Work out each of these:
   (i) 74 ÷ 10          (ii) 345 ÷ 100          (iii) 1.5 ÷ 100          (iv) 184 ÷ 1000

5. Work out each of these:
   (i) $\frac{1.8}{2}$     (ii) $\frac{3.6}{0.6}$     (iii) $\frac{2.16}{0.3}$     (iv) $\frac{61.5}{5}$     (v) $\frac{8.15}{0.5}$

6. Given that 12.7 × 7.5 = 95.25, without doing any further multiplication, write down the answer to each of these:
   (i) 1.27 × 7.5          (ii) 0.127 × 7.5          (iii) 12.7 × 0.075

7. Work out each of these:
   (i) 20 × 0.6          (ii) 0.3 × 90          (iii) 0.04 × 30          (iv) 0.6 × 500
   (v) 0.3 × 400          (vi) 0.2 × 15          (vii) 0.3 × 0.7          (viii) 2.1 × 0.4

8. What decimal number does each arrow point to?

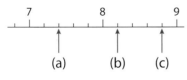 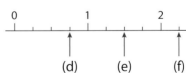

9. Change each of these percentages to a fraction in its simplest form:
   (i) 60%          (ii) 25%          (iii) 75%          (iv) 65%          (v) $12\frac{1}{2}$%

10. Work these out:
    (i) 20% of 70          (ii) 30% of 80          (iii) 75% of 36          (iv) 40% of 60

**11.** This pie chart shows how 120 first-year pupils travel to school.

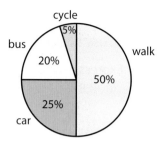

    (i)  How many children walk to school?

    (ii)  How many come by car?

    (iii)  How many come by bus?

    (iv)  How many cycle?

**12.** Work out each of these:

    (i)  Increase 60 by 25%        (ii)  Increase 140 by 15%

    (iii)  Decrease 75 by 20%      (iv)  Decrease 240 by $12\frac{1}{2}$%

**13.** Find four matching pairs that give the same answer.

| 10% of 40 | 20% of 50 | 50% of 6 | 5% of 80 |
|---|---|---|---|

| 30% of 10 | 30% of 50 | 25% of 40 | 75% of 20 |
|---|---|---|---|

**14.**  (i)  What fraction of this shape is shaded?

    (ii)  What percentage of the shape is shaded?

    (iii)  Copy the shape and shade in more squares so that $\frac{4}{5}$ of the shape is shaded.

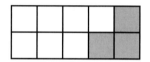

**15.**  (i)  Write 15% as a decimal.

    (ii)  Write $\frac{2}{5}$ as a decimal.

    (iii)  Use your answers to (i) and (ii) to help you write these in order, smallest first:

          0.2    15%    0.09    $\frac{2}{5}$

**16.** Write each of these lists in order of size, smallest first.

    (i)  0.3  28%  $\frac{1}{4}$  0.18      (ii)  8%  0.6  $\frac{7}{10}$  0.55

    (iii)  78%  $\frac{3}{4}$  0.09  0.8      (iv)  $\frac{1}{2}$  48%  0.4  0.19

**17.** Copy and complete this table.

| Percentage | Fraction | Decimal |
|---|---|---|
| 21% | $\frac{21}{100}$ | |
| | $\frac{57}{100}$ | |
| | | 0.41 |
| 9% | | |
| | $\frac{3}{100}$ | |
| | | 0.08 |

**18.** Ronan's test scores are given in the table.

(i) Copy and complete the table by working out Ronan's percentage score for each subject.

| Subject | Score | Percentage |
|---------|-------|------------|
| English | $\frac{70}{80}$ | |
| Maths | $\frac{34}{40}$ | |
| Geography | $\frac{28}{35}$ | |
| Business | $\frac{54}{60}$ | |
| Science | $\frac{56}{64}$ | |

(ii) In which subject did Ronan achieve his best result?

**19.** Dermot's garden is a rectangle measuring 15 metres by 5 metres.

(i) What is the total area of the garden?

(ii) The lawn takes up 55% of the garden. What is the area of the lawn?

(iii) A flower bed is a rectangle measuring 3 m by 2 m.
What percentage of the garden is this?

**20.** House prices increased by 4% in June.
In November it was reported that house prices had fallen by 4%.
A house was valued at €240 000 in May.
Work out the value of this house in December.

## Investigation:

Investigate what happens if a piece of card (of any length) is first increased in length by 50% and then the new piece of card is reduced in length by 50%.

Original piece of card

(i) increased by 50%, new length = ?

(ii) and then reduced by 50%, new length = ?

What conclusion can you make based on this investigation?

# Section 1.5 Revision of ratio

## 1. Ratio

We use ratio to compare two or more quantities.
In the given figure, the ratio of green squares to yellow squares is $8:4$.
The ratio $8:4$ can be simplified by dividing each term by 4.
Thus, $8:4 = 2:1$.
$2:1$ is called the **simplest form** of the ratio.

To express the ratio $15$ minutes $: 1\frac{1}{2}$ hours as a ratio without units, we express both parts in the same units.
Thus, $15$ minutes $: 1\frac{1}{2}$ hours $= 15$ minutes $: 90$ minutes $= 1:6$.
A ratio is normally expressed in whole numbers.
The ratio $\frac{1}{2}:\frac{3}{4}$ can be expressed in whole numbers by multiplying each term by 4, the LCM of 2 and 4.
Thus, $\frac{1}{2}:\frac{3}{4} = \frac{2}{4}:\frac{3}{4} = 2:3$

---

**Example 1**

Divide €720 between Alan and Beth in the ratio $5:4$.

We divide €720 into nine parts, since $5 + 4 = 9$.
€720 ÷ 9 = €80
Alan gets 5 parts and Beth gets 4 parts.
Alan's share $= €80 \times 5 = €400$;　Beth's share $= €80 \times 4 = €320$.

---

## 2. Proportion

While ratios compare one part to another part, proportion compares a part to the total.
The proportion of the given circle that is shaded red is $\frac{2}{6}$ or $\frac{1}{3}$.
Proportion is generally expressed as a fraction, decimal or percentage.

If 1 litre of petrol cost €1.60, 2 litres cost €3.20 and 3 litres cost €4.80.
Here the costs of 1 litre, 2 litres and 3 litres are in **direct proportion**.

---

**Example 2**

A car travels 78 km on 9 litres of petrol.
  (i) How far is it likely to travel on 21 litres of petrol?
 (ii) How many litres would be required for a journey of 390 km?

  (i) Here we are looking for **distance**, so we keep distance last.

   9 litres do 78 km

   1 litre does $\frac{78}{9}$ km

   21 litres do $\left(\frac{78}{9} \times \frac{21}{1}\right)$ km $= 182$ km.

 (ii) Here we are looking for **litres**, so we keep litres last.

   78 km require 9 litres

   1 km requires $\frac{9}{78}$ litres

   390 km require $\left(\frac{9}{78} \times \frac{390}{1}\right)$ litres $= 45$ litres

   $\therefore$   A 390 km journey would require 45 litres.

## Exercise 1.5

**1.** For this pattern of coloured squares, write down these ratios :
  (i)  green : yellow    (ii)  pink : white
 (iii)  blue : green    (iv)  white : yellow.

Now write down as a fraction in its simplest form
  (v)  the proportion of the whole figure that is coloured blue
 (vi)  the proportion of the whole figure that is coloured yellow
(vii)  the percentage of the whole figure that is coloured white.

**2.** Give each of these ratios in its simplest form :
  (i)  3 : 6     (ii)  4 : 12     (iii)  20 : 25     (iv)  16 : 28
  (v)  60 : 48     (vi)  30 : 75     (vii)  35 : 63     (viii)  24 : 36

**3.** Fill in the missing numbers so that the ratios are equivalent :
  (i)  $1 : 3 = 3 : \square$     (ii)  $3 : 5 = 9 : \square$     (iii)  $2 : \square = 6 : 18$
 (iv)  $\square : 7 = 4 : 14$     (v)  $12 : \square = 36 : 9$     (vi)  $7 : 3 = \square : 12$

**4.** Express these ratios in their simplest terms :
  (i)  15 mins : 1 hour     (ii)  3 days : 2 weeks     (iii)  30c : €1.50.

**5.** Express the following ratios as whole numbers:

    (i) $\frac{1}{2}:2$         (ii) $\frac{3}{4}:1\frac{1}{2}$         (iii) $\frac{1}{2}:\frac{1}{3}$         (iv) $\frac{3}{4}:\frac{7}{8}$

**6.** The line below is divided into ten equal parts.

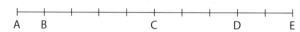

Find the ratios:

    (i) $\dfrac{|AB|}{|AE|}$       (ii) $\dfrac{|AB|}{|BC|}$       (iii) $\dfrac{|AE|}{|AB|}$       (iv) $\dfrac{|CD|}{|CB|}$

Now write down which point divides $|AD|$

    (v) in the ratio $5:3$       (vi) in the ratio $1:7$.

**7.** Express these ratios in their simplest form:

    (i) length of rectangle A to length of rectangle B

    (ii) width of rectangle A to width of rectangle B

    (iii) area of rectangle A to area of rectangle B.

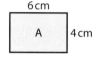
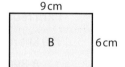

**8.** A pink-coloured paint is made by mixing red and white in the ratio of $1:5$.
If the red and white paints were mixed in the ratio $1:8$, would the paint be lighter or darker than the original?

**9.** A school consists of boys and girls in the ratio $4:3$.
If there are 560 students in the school, find how many boys and girls are in the school.

**10.** Two brothers, Tom and Gerry, are to divide €1890 between them in the ratio $5:4$.
How much does each receive?

**11.** Divide €200 in the ratio $2:3:5$.

**12.** Sand and cement are mixed together in the ratio $4:1$.
If there are 375 kg in the mixture, how many kg of cement are in it?

**13.** A sum of money is divided between A and B in the ratio $3:2$.
If A receives €840, find the sum of money.

14. This is a recipe for pastry to make 16 mince pies.

    (i) To make 24 mince pies what weight would you
        need of
        (a) flour   (b) sugar   (c) butter?

    (ii) How many egg yolks would you need for
        40 mince pies?

    (iii) If a quantity of pastry contained 135 g of brown
        sugar, how many mince pies could be made?

> **Pastry for Mince Pies**
> (makes 16 pies)
>
> 500 g wholeweat flour
> 180 g brown sugar
> 240 g of butter (chopped)
> 4 egg yolks
> 2–3 drops of vanilla

15. If nine copies of a book cost €165.60, find the cost of four copies.

16. A car travels 40 km in 30 minutes. How far would it travel in
    (i) 10 minutes   (ii) 45 minutes   (iii) $2\frac{1}{2}$ hours?
    How long would it take to do a journey of 100 km?

17. A car travels 144 km on 16 litres of fuel.
    (i) How far will it travel on 1 litre?
    (ii) How far will it travel on 14 litres?
    (iii) How many litres of fuel would be needed for a journey of 90 km?

18. Adam is 12 years old and Emer is 8 years old.
    €5400 is divided between them in the ratio of their ages.
    How much does each receive?

    In eight years time, another €5400 will be divided between them in the ratio of
    their ages at that time. How much will they each receive then?

19. Three quarters of the pupils in a class are boys and the rest are girls.
    What is the ratio of boys to girls in the class?

20. A square has the same area as a rectangle.
    The sides of the rectangle are in the ratio 9 : 4.
    The perimeter of the rectangle is 130 cm.
    (i) Calculate the lengths of the sides of the
        rectangle.
    (ii) Calculate the area of the rectangle.
    (iii) Calculate the side length of the square.
    (iv) Write down the ratio of the perimeters of the two shapes in the form
        perimeter of square : perimeter of rectangle.
        Give your answer in its simplest form.

# Test yourself 1

1. (i) Find the lowest common multiple of 8 and 12.
   (ii) Find the highest common factor of 12 and 30.

2. (i) Copy this shape and
      shade 20% of it.

   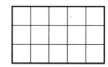

   (ii) Arrange these fractions in order, starting with the largest:

   $$\frac{3}{4} \qquad \frac{4}{5} \qquad \frac{7}{10} \qquad \frac{3}{5} \qquad \frac{9}{10} \qquad \frac{13}{20}$$

3. A prize fund is divided between $A$, $B$ and $C$ in the ratio $4:3:2$ respectively.
   If $C$'s share is €1224, find the total fund.

4. Put these in
   three matching
   groups.

   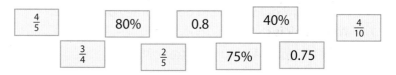

5. State whether each of the following is TRUE or FALSE:
   (i) $(16 + 3 \times 2) \div 11 - 1 = 1$
   (ii) $15 \times 3 \div (6 + 3) + 1 = 6$
   (iii) $100 \div 25 \times (6 + 2) = 26$
   If the result is false, give the correct answer.

6. Find the value of each expression when $n = -4$.
   Use the code to change to letters.
   Rearrange the letters to make a European country.
   $4n + 2 \qquad 3n + 10 \qquad 2n \qquad n - 2$
   $-6 - n \qquad n - 1 \qquad n + 2$

   | A | B | C | E | G |
   |---|---|---|---|---|
   | $-2$ | $-14$ | $-12$ | $-9$ | $-26$ |

   | I | L | M | N | U |
   |---|---|---|---|---|
   | $-8$ | $-5$ | $1$ | $-6$ | $-11$ |

7. A recipe uses 12 onions to make $1\frac{1}{2}$ litres of chutney.
   (i) How much chutney can be made with 48 onions?
   (ii) How many onions are needed for $4\frac{1}{2}$ litres of chutney?

8. Write each list in order, starting with the smallest:
   (i) $\frac{1}{2} \qquad \frac{1}{4} \qquad \frac{2}{5} \qquad \frac{3}{10} \qquad \frac{3}{5}$
   (ii) $60\% \qquad \frac{3}{4} \qquad \frac{1}{2} \qquad \frac{4}{5} \qquad 0.65 \qquad \frac{2}{3}$

**9.**
A · B · C · D · E · F · G · H · I · J · K

Which point divides the line [AK] in the ratio:
    (i)  9 : 1      (ii)  7 : 3      (iii)  3 : 7      (iv)  4 : 1      (v)  1 : 4?

**10.** This is a recipe for 4 servings.
How much of each ingredient would
be needed for 10 servings?

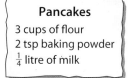

**Pancakes**
3 cups of flour
2 tsp baking powder
$\frac{1}{4}$ litre of milk

**11.** Work out these percentages:
    (i)  40c as a percentage of €5.
    (ii)  18 minutes as a percentage of 4 hours.

**12.** In a town, the ratio of adults to children is 2 : 5.
If there are 2400 adults in the town, find its population.

**13.** Which pair is the larger? Show your working.

        $\frac{3}{4}$ of 32   or   $\frac{2}{3}$ of 36

**14.** A woman walks 9 km in 2 hours.
If she walks at the same pace, how far can she walk in 5 hours?

**15.** An expedition company has lists of suggested meals.
This is a list of food for one meal for five people.

20 veggie sausages
750 g rice
5 litres of water

      Make a list of food they would need for seven people.

**16.** For each pair of equations below, write down which is the correct equation,
(a) or (b):
    (i)  (a)  $16 \div 4 + 4 = 8$        (b)  $16 \div (4 + 4) = 8$
    (ii)  (a)  $(13 + 8) \div (3 + 4) = 3$    (b)  $13 + 8 \div 3 + 4 = 3$
    (iii)  (a)  $81 \div 9 + 1 = 9$       (b)  $81 \div 9 + 1 = 10$

**17.** A rectangle is divided into four triangles, as shown.
Find the ratio of

      Area of smallest triangle : Area of largest triangle.

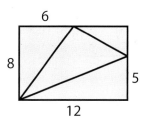

# Assignment:

**A:** Make a chart of the table below.

Using only the numbers 1, 2, 3, 4, 5, 6, 7, 8 and 9 place one number in each box.

|  | Prime number | Multiple of 3 | Factor of 16 |
|---|---|---|---|
| **Number greater than 5** |  |  |  |
| **Odd number** |  |  |  |
| **Even number** |  |  |  |

**B:** Make a chart of the mathematical sentences below. Place one of the words commutative, associative, distributive (all terms from **book 1**) after each one to describe the property of the operation shown:

|  | Property |
|---|---|
| $3 \times (4 + 5) = 3 \times 4 + 3 \times 5$ |  |
| $6 \times 7 = 7 \times 6$ |  |
| $5 + (4 + 9) = (5 + 4) + 9$ |  |

# Algebra 1

## From first year, you will recall how to:

- use symbols for unknown quantities,
- identify terms and expressions,
- add and subtract like terms,
- multiply out expressions containing brackets,
- multiply different terms,
- substitute values for variables in an expression,
- find an expression for the area of a rectangle,
- form and solve equations,
- use algebra to solve word problems.

## In this chapter, you will learn to:

- solve perimeter and area problems involving algebraic expressions,
- perform algebraic division.

## Section 2.1  Dealing with algebraic expressions

$2x^2 + 3x - 4$  is called an **expression**.

It consists of three **terms**.

The terms are separated by a plus $(+)$ or a minus $(-)$ sign.

The letter $x$ is called a **variable**.

A **coefficient** is a number before a variable.

In  $2x^2$, the coefficient is 2; in  $3x$, the coefficient is 3.

The term  $-4$  is known as a **constant**; it does not change.

In the expression  $2x^2 + 5x - 2 + 3x + 4x^2$,

> $2x^2$  and  $4x^2$  are called **like terms**;
> $5x$  and  $3x$  are also like terms.

The expression  $2x^2 + 5x - 2 + 3x + 4x^2$  may be simplified by combining the like terms as follows:

$$2x^2 + 5x - 2 + 3x + 4x^2$$
$$= 2x^2 + 4x^2 + 5x + 3x - 2$$
$$= 6x^2 + 8x - 2$$

> Like terms only may be added or subtracted.

---

**Example 1**

Simplify  (i) $4a + 6b + 6 - 2a + b - 3$   (ii) $2x^2 - 3x - 7 - x^2 - 5x + 3$

(i)  $4a + 6b + 6 - 2a + b - 3$
  $= 4a - 2a + 6b + b + 6 - 3$
  $= 2a + 7b + 3$

(ii)  $2x^2 - 3x - 7 - x^2 - 5x + 3$
  $= 2x^2 - x^2 - 3x - 5x - 7 + 3$
  $= x^2 - 8x - 4$

---

## Exercise 2.1

Simplify each of the following expressions by adding like terms:

**1.** $5x + 3x + 2x$

**2.** $4a + 5a - 2a$

**3.** $2a + 3b + 3a + 5b$

**4.** $2x + 3y + 4x - y$

**5.** $12a + b + 3a + 5b$

**6.** $3x + 2y + 3 + 4x + 3y + 1$

**7.** $5x - 4 + 2x + 8$

**8.** $7x - 4 - 3x + 7$

**9.** $6a + b + 3 + 2a + 2b - 1$

**10.** $3x + 4 + 2x - 6 + x + 3$

**11.** $3a - b + 4a + 5b - 2a$

**12.** $2ab + 4 + 3ab - 2$

**13.** $2p + 3q - r + p - 4q + 2r$

**14.** $5k + 3 - 4k + 6 + k - 4$

**15.** $2ab + c + 5ab - 4c$

**16.** $3xy + 2z + xy + 9z$

**17.** $6ab + 2cd - ab + 3cd$

**18.** $6x - xy + 5x - 7xy$

**19.** $10 + 13a - 7a \mid 2a$

**20.** $3x^2 + 2x + 7x^2 - x$

**21.** $10t + 2w - 11t - 6w$

**22.** $7 + 4h - 10h - 16$

**23.** $5m^2 + 7m + 3 - 2m^2 - 5m$

**24.** $6a^2 + 9a - 1 + 5a^2 - 10a$

**25.** $9a^2 + 6a^2 - a^2 - 10a - a$

**26.** $5ab - 4bc + 2ab + 3bc$

**27.** Write down a simplified expression for the perimeter of each shape:

(i)
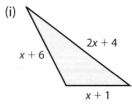

(ii)
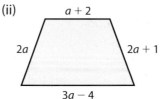

(iii)
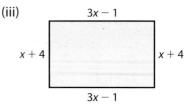

**28.** The number in each box is found by adding the numbers in the two boxes under it. Find the missing expressions $a, b, c, d, e, f$ and $g$. Write each expression in its simplest form.

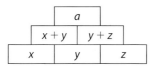 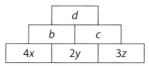 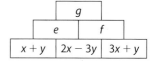

**29.** Work out an expression for each length marked **?**.

(i)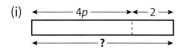

(ii)

(iii)

(iv)

**30.** Here are six cards with expressions written on them:

(i) $2x$  (ii) $x - 5$  (iii) $7 - x$  (iv) $3x + 1$  (v) $x + 3$  (vi) $4 - 2x$

(i) Which two cards total $4x + 4$?
(ii) Which two cards total $x + 5$?
(iii) Which two cards total 4?
(iv) Which two cards total 10?
(v) Which three cards total 12?
(vi) Which three cards total $3x + 11$?
(vii) What is the total of all of the expressions on the cards?

**31.** Write out each of these with the question marks filled in:
(i) $2a - ? + b + 2a = 4a - 2b$
(ii) $2w + x - ? + 3x = 4x - 3w$
(iii) $3k - ? - j - k = 2k - 5j$
(iv) $10 - 2k + ? - k - 8j - ? = 6 - ? - 5j$

**32.** Work out an expression for the missing length.

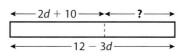

**33.** The number in each box is found by adding the numbers in the two boxes under it. Find the missing expressions $a, b$ and $c$.

**34.** $2x^2 + 3xy - 4x + 6$ is an expression.

(i) Name two variables in this expression.

(ii) What is the coefficient of $x$ in the expression?

(iii) How many variables are in the expression?

(iv) Which term contains two variables?

(iv) What is the constant in the expression?

# Section 2.2  Removing brackets

To write $3x \times 4y$ as a single term, we multiply the coefficients 3 and 4 and then multiply the variables $x$ and $y$.

Thus,   $3x \times 4y = 3 \times 4 \times x \times y = 12xy$.

Similarly,   (i) $3a \times 6b = 18ab$      (ii) $-3p \times 4q = -12pq$.

In your study of algebra so far, you will have learned how to remove brackets as follows:

$a(b + c) = ab + ac$      Here each term inside the bracket is multiplied by $a$.

**Remember**:   $3(a + 2) = (a + 2) + (a + 2) + (a + 2) = a + a + a + 2 + 2 + 2 = 3a + 3(2)$
$$= 3a + 6$$

Similarly,   (i) $5(2x + 6) = 10x + 30$

(ii) $-4(5a - 2) = -20a + 8$

(iii) $-(6x - 4) = -6x + 4$

(iv) $-(-9a + 6) = 9a - 6$.

> If there is a minus outside the brackets, the sign of each term inside the brackets is changed when the brackets are removed.

## Multiplication involving indices

As $5 \times 5$ can be written as $5^2$, similarly $x \times x$ is written as $x^2$.

Also, $a \times a \times a = a^3$

and   $a^2 \times a^2 = a \times a \times a \times a = a^4$

$a^2 \times a^3 = a \times a \times a \times a \times a = a^5$

$3x(2x^2 - x + 4) = 6x^3 - 3x^2 + 12x$.

> When multiplying powers of the same number, add the indices.

## Multiplying two expressions

Here is a reminder of how to multiply two expressions, each containing two terms:

$(2x + 3)(3x - 5) = 6x^2 + 9x - 10x - 15$
$$= 6x^2 - x - 15$$

|     | $3x$ | $-5$ |
| --- | --- | --- |
| $2x$ | $6x^2$ | $-10x$ |
| $+3$ | $9x$ | $-15$ |

## Example 1

Remove the brackets and simplify:

$$(2x - 3)(3x + 4)$$

$$(2x - 3)(3x + 4) = 6x^2 - 9x + 8x - 12$$
$$= 6x^2 - x - 12$$

|      | $3x$    | $+4$   |
|------|---------|--------|
| $2x$ | $6x^2$  | $+8x$  |
| $-3$ | $-9x$   | $-12$  |

## Exercise 2.2

**1.** Express each of the following as a single term by removing the multiplication sign:

(i)  $3 \times 4a$      (ii)  $3x \times 7$      (iii)  $8 \times 2m$      (iv)  $12a \times 4$

(v)  $3m \times 2m$      (vi)  $2p \times 3q$      (vii)  $k \times 6k$      (viii)  $3a \times 2b$

**2.** Simplify each of these:

(i)  $ab \times a$      (ii)  $2ab \times b$      (iii)  $3ab \times 2ab$      (iv)  $5cd \times 2de$

(v)  $2b \times 3a$      (vi)  $9a \times 2bc$      (vii)  $a \times b \times c$      (viii)  $2x \times 3y \times 2x$

**3.** Simplify these products:

(i)  $(-3x) \times 5$      (ii)  $7 \times (-2m)$      (iii)  $(-4) \times (-3a)$

(iv)  $9m \times (-3)$      (v)  $(-5) \times (-6k)$      (vi)  $(-7a) \times (-2)$

(vii)  $(-a) \times 2b$      (viii)  $(-p) \times (-q)$      (ix)  $5n \times (-2m)$

(x)  $(-6t) \times (-w)$      (xi)  $(-8x) \times 7y$      (xii)  $10m \times (-3m)$

Remove the brackets and simplify each of these:

**4.** $3(2x - 1) + 5(x + 2)$        **5.** $2(x - 4) + 3(2x + 5)$

**6.** $5(3x - 2) - 2(x - 1)$        **7.** $3(3x + 2) - 4(2x + 1)$

**8.** $6(2x - 3) + 2(3x - 1)$        **9.** $5(x - 2) - (2x + 4)$

**10.** $3(2a - 7) - 5(a - 4)$        **11.** $2(3a - 4) - (5a - 3)$

**12.** $2(x^2 - 3x + 1) + 2(x^2 + x - 4)$        **13.** $5(x^2 - x - 4) - 2(2x^2 - 3x + 2)$

**14.** Copy and complete the diagram to find the product of each of the following:

(i)  $(2x + 1)(x + 3) =$

|      | $x$     | $+3$   |
|------|---------|--------|
| $2x$ | $2x^2$  |        |
| $+1$ |         | $+3$   |

(ii) $(3x + 3)(x - 5) =$

|  | $x$ | $-5$ |
|---|---|---|
| $3x$ |  | $-15x$ |
| $+3$ | $+3x$ |  |

Find the product of each of these:

**15.** $(2x + 3)(x + 4)$

**16.** $(x + 5)(2x + 1)$

**17.** $(3x + 2)(x - 4)$

**18.** $(x + 3)(2x - 3)$

**19.** $(2x - 2)(x + 4)$

**20.** $(2x - 3)(x + 1)$

**21.** $(x - 3)(x - 2)$

**22.** $(2x - 3)(x - 2)$

**23.** $(4x - 5)(x + 3)$

**24.** $(2x + 1)(x - 6)$

**25.** $(3x + 2)(x - 5)$

**26.** $(x - 5)(2x - 3)$

**27.** $(5x - 2)(2x + 3)$

**28.** $(2x - 1)(x + 4)$

**29.** $(2x - 2y)(x - 3y)$

**30.** $(3x - y)(4x + 3y)$

**31.** $(4x - 5y)(x + y)$

**32.** $(x + 4)^2$

**33.** $(2x + 3)^2$

**34.** $(2x - 1)^2$

**35.** Find an expression, in its simplest form, for
   (i) the perimeter of this rectangle
   (ii) the area of the rectangle.

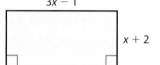
$3x - 1$

$x + 2$

## Section 2.3 Evaluating expressions

When $x = 3$, the value of $2x + 5$ is $2(3) + 5 = 6 + 5 = 11$.
When $x = 2$, the value of $3x^2 - 6x$ is $3(2)^2 - 6(2) = 3(4) - 12 = 12 - 12 = 0$.

---

**Example 1**

If $a = 2, b = 3$ and $c = -4$, find the value of
(i) $a + b$       (ii) $2a - b$       (iii) $3a^2 - 2c$       (iv) $2c^2 - 4ab$

(i) $a + b = 2 + 3$          (ii) $2a - b = 2(2) - 3$
$\qquad = 5$                  $\qquad\qquad = 4 - 3 = 1$

(iii) $3a^2 - 2c = 3(2)^2 - 2(-4)$          (iv) $2c^2 - 4ab = 2(-4)^2 - 4(2)(3)$
$\qquad\qquad = 3(4) + 8$                  $\qquad\qquad\qquad = 2(16) - 4(6)$
$\qquad\qquad = 12 + 8 = 20$                  $\qquad\qquad\qquad = 32 - 24 = 8$

---

> *Remember*
>
> When evaluating an expression,
> (i) multiply and divide before you add or subtract
> (ii) any number multiplied by zero is zero, e.g. $6 \times 0 = 0$.

## Exercise 2.3

**1.** If $x = 3$ and $y = 2$, find the value of each of these:
   (i) $5x$      (ii) $4x - 3$      (iii) $x + 2y$      (iv) $2x - y$

**2.** If $a = 4$ and $b = 2$, find the value of each of these:
   (i) $2a + b$      (ii) $a + 2b$      (iii) $b - 3a$      (iv) $3a - 2b$

**3.** If $x = 2, y = 3$ and $z = -1$, evaluate each of these:
   (i) $x + 2y$      (ii) $3x + z$      (iii) $2y + 3z$      (iv) $4x + 5z$

**4.** Work out the value of each of these when $a = -3$:
   (i) $a + 8$      (ii) $6a$      (iii) $7 - a$      (iv) $3a - 5$

**5.** Work out the value of each of these when $x = 2$:
   (i) $x^2 + 5$      (ii) $2x^2 - 3$      (iii) $x^2 + 2x$      (iv) $3x^2 - 4x + 2$

**6.** If $a = 4$ and $b = -3$, evaluate each of these:
   (i) $2a + b$      (ii) $a - 4b$      (iii) $2a^2 - b$      (iv) $b^2 - 2a$
   (v) $2(a + b)$      (vi) $3(a^2 + 3b)$      (vii) $2b^2 - a$      (viii) $b^2 - 2b + a$

**7.** If $x = 4$, find the value of each of these:
   (i) $2x^2 - 3$      (ii) $\dfrac{x^2 + 4}{x + 1}$      (iii) $\dfrac{3x - 2}{9 - x}$      (iv) $\dfrac{2x^2 - 2}{2x + 2}$

## *Investigation:*

| A | B | C | E | G | H | I | M | O | P | R | S | T | U | W |
|---|---|---|---|---|---|---|---|---|---|---|---|---|---|---|
| $-2$ | $-5$ | $8$ | $3$ | $-3$ | $0$ | $-6$ | $2$ | $-1$ | $5$ | $1$ | $-4$ | $7$ | $6$ | $-9$ |

Copy each list and by working out the value of the expressions in each list, change the numbers to **letters** using the code above. Then rearrange the letters to spell an animal

**List A**

| | | letter |
|---|---|---|
| $p + 4$ | when $p = -5$ | |
| $r - 1$ | when $r = 9$ | |
| $t - 11$ | when $t = 2$ | |

Animal A = _____

**List B**

| | | letter |
|---|---|---|
| $2 - p$ | when $p = -1$ | |
| $3q + 8$ | when $q = -2$ | |
| $15 + 3r$ | when $r = -3$ | |
| $2d + 4$ | when $d = -4$ | |
| $9 + 5e$ | when $e = -2$ | |

Animal B = _____

**List C**

| | | letter |
|---|---|---|
| $-1 - u$ | when $u = -8$ | |
| $6 + v$ | when $v = -3$ | |
| $15 + 4w$ | when $w = -2$ | |
| $\frac{x}{2} + 4$ | when $x = -6$ | |
| $1 + \frac{y}{2}$ | when $y = -4$ | |

Animal C = _____

**8.** If $a = 3, b = 2$ and $c = 1$, find the value of each of these:

(i)  $a(b + c)$   (ii)  $ab$   (iii)  $3bc$   (iv)  $2ab - 3c$

(v)  $2abc$   (vi)  $a^2 - bc$   (vii)  $2b^2 - a$   (viii)  $2ab - 5c$

## Section 2.4  Solving linear equations

An **expression** $3x + 2$ can have many values depending on the value of $x$.

If $x = 1$, then $3x + 2 = 3(1) + 2 = 5$
If $x = 6$, then $3x + 2 = 3(6) + 2 = 20$

If $3x + 2 = 14$, to find the value of $x$ that resulted in 14 we must **solve the equation** $3x + 2 = 14$ for $x$.

The three scales below will help you recall the steps needed to solve $3x + 2 = 14$

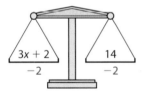
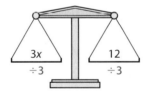
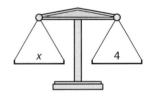

Take 2 from both sides    Divide both sides by 3    $x = 4$ is the solution

The scales above illustrate that solving an equation requires us to change the equation into a simpler one. This is done by adding, subtracting, multiplying or dividing **both sides** of the equation by the **same number**.

**Example 1**

Solve the equation $3x - 5 = 16$.

$$3x - 5 = 16$$
$$3x - 5 + \mathbf{5} = 16 + \mathbf{5} \quad \text{... add 5 to both sides}$$
$$3x = 21$$
$$x = 7 \quad \text{... divide both sides by 3}$$

**Example 2**

Solve the equation $3(2x - 6) = 2(2x + 1)$.

$$3(2x - 6) = 2(2x + 1)$$
$$6x - 18 = 4x + 2 \quad \text{... remove the brackets}$$
$$6x - \mathbf{4x} - 18 = 4x + 2 - \mathbf{4x} \quad \text{... take 4x from each side}$$
$$2x - 18 = 2$$
$$2x - 18 + \mathbf{18} = 2 + \mathbf{18} \quad \text{... add 18 to each side}$$
$$2x = 20$$
$$x = 10 \quad \text{... divide each side by 2}$$

## Exercise 2.4

**1.** Each symbol stands for a number. Find its value.

  (i)  ◀ $+ 1 = 7$        (ii)  ■ $- 2 = 12$        (iii)  ★ $\times 3 = 21$        (iv)  $5 +$ ▮ $= 14$

  (v)  $8 -$ ◆ $= 3$        (vi)  $4 \times$ ♣ $= 32$        (vii)  ⬡ $\div 3 = 11$        (viii)  ✳ $+$ ✳ $= 30$

**2.** Write down the missing numbers to make these equations true:

  (i)  $\Box + 8 = 15$        (ii)  $12 - \Box = 8$        (iii)  $\Box \times 3 = 30$

  (iv)  $\Box \times 6 + 2 = 26$        (v)  $27 \div \Box + 1 = 10$        (vi)  $7 + 5 + \dfrac{\Box}{2} = 15$

**3.** Solve each of these equations:

  (i)  $2x = 8$        (ii)  $3x = 27$        (iii)  $5x = 35$        (iv)  $6x = 42$        (v)  $9x = 63$

Solve these equations:

**4.** $x - 2 = 5$        **5.** $x - 7 = 9$        **6.** $x + 5 = 12$

**7.** $2x - 1 = 7$        **8.** $3x - 1 = 8$        **9.** $3x - 5 = 16$

**10.** $4x + 2 = 26$        **11.** $2x + 5 = 13$        **12.** $5x - 3 = 22$

**13.** $3x - 2 = x + 4$      **14.** $3x + 3 = 2x + 7$      **15.** $4x - 2 = 3x - 1$

**16.** $6x - 2 = 4x + 10$      **17.** $7x + 10 = 4x - 2$      **18.** $7x - 12 = 4x$

Remove the brackets and then solve the following equations:

**19.** $4(2x - 3) = 36$             **20.** $5x + 5 = 2(2x + 5)$

**21.** $3(2x + 1) = 2x + 11$         **22.** $5(2x - 1) = 8x + 7$

**23.** $5(x - 2) = 4(x - 1)$         **24.** $5(x - 5) = 3(x + 1)$

**25.** $4(x + 5) = 2(x + 1)$         **26.** $4(3x + 6) = 3(5x - 2)$

**27.** $3(2x + 1) = 2x + 11$         **28.** $3(x - 2) = 5x - 12$

**29.** $3(x - 9) - 3 = x - 2$        **30.** $2(5 + x) - 12 = 4$

**31.** $4(2x - 3) = 2(3x - 5)$       **32.** $3(5x - 2) = 4(3x + 6)$

**33.** $3(x + 3) - 7 = 5(x - 4) + 18$      **34.** $4(x - 2) - 6 = 6 - (x + 5)$

**35.** Work out the value of $x$ for each strip:

    (i)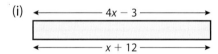

    (ii)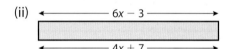

**36.** Work out what $x$ stands for in each of these:

    (i)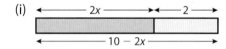

    (ii)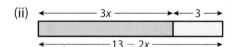

**37.** The perimeter of the given triangle is 36 cm.
Form an equation and solve it to find the value of $x$.

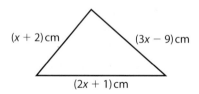

**38.** Solve each of these equations:
    (i)   $3(a + 2) - 2(a + 1) = 6$          (ii)   $5(m + 3) - 4(m + 2) = 10$
    (iii)   $5(n + 4) - 3(n - 2) = 30$       (iv)   $6(a + 2) - 4(a - 1) = 20$

# Section 2.5 Writing and solving equations

The ability to change a problem expressed in words into a mathematical equation and then to solve it is very important in mathematics.

The following example will show how equations can be formed from word problems.

## Example 1

When 3 is taken from five times a certain number, the result is the same as adding 6 to twice the number. Find the number.

Let $x$ be the required number.
$\therefore$ five times a certain number is $5x$ and twice the number is $2x$.

Equation:

$$5x - 3 = 2x + 6$$
$$5x - 3 + 3 = 2x + 6 + 3 \quad \ldots \text{ add 3 to each side}$$
$$5x = 2x + 9$$
$$5x - 2x = 2x + 9 - 2x \quad \ldots \text{ take } 2x \text{ from each side}$$
$$3x = 9$$
$$x = 3$$

The required number is 3.

## Exercise 2.5

1. Write an equation for each of the following and solve it.
   Let $x$ be the unknown number in each case.

   (i) I think of a number.
   When I multiply it by 3 and then add 2, the answer is 17.
   What is the number?

   (ii) I think of a number.
   When I multiply it by 4 and then add 1, the answer is 13.
   What is the number?

   (iii) I think of a number.
   When I multiply the number by 3 and then subtract 4, the answer is the same as twice the number.
   What is the number?

   (iv) I think of a number.
   When I add 2 to the number and multiply my answer by 4, the result is 20.
   What is the number?

**2.** If I multiply a number by 4 and then add 3, the result is the same as adding 8 to three times the number.
Form an equation in $x$ and solve it to find the number.

**3.** I think of a number, multiply it by 8, and then subtract 2.
I get the same result as when I multiply this number by 2 and add 10.
What is this number?

**4.** A number is multiplied by 3 and 5 is then added.
If the result is 17, find the number.

**5.** When 3 is added to a number and the result is doubled, the result is 24.
Write an equation in $x$ and solve it to find the number.

**6.** 9 is subtracted from a certain number and the result is multiplied by 4.
If the answer is 24, what is the number?

**7.** One number is 4 bigger than another number.
If $x$ is the smaller number, what is the larger one?
When twice the smaller number is added to the larger, the result is 16.
Find the two numbers.

**8.** Martin is three times as old as Eoin.
If Eoin is $x$ years old, find in terms of $x$:
  (i) Martin's age
  (ii) Martin's age in three years time
  (iii) Eoin's age in three years time.
  (iv) In three years time the sum of their ages will be 26. Write an equation to represent this information.
  (v) Solve the equation to find Martin and Eoin's age

**9.** A restaurant has a special price for groups of more than 10 given by the formula
Price = fixed charge + €18 × number in the group.
Calculate the number in the group if the fixed charge was €55 and the guests paid a total of €307.

**10.** One number is 5 greater than another number.
If the smaller number is added to twice the larger number, the answer is 28.
Find the two numbers.

**11.** (i) Find an expression for the perimeter of this triangle.
  (ii) What value of $x$ gives a perimeter of 55?

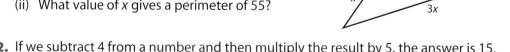

**12.** If we subtract 4 from a number and then multiply the result by 5, the answer is 15.
Find the number.

**13.** (i) Find an expression, in terms of $x$, for the perimeter of this rectangle. Give your answer in its simplest form.

(ii) The perimeter of the rectangle is 44 cm. Write down an equation and solve it to find the value of $x$.

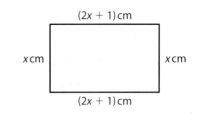

**14.** (i) Write an expression for the sum of the angles marked in this triangle. Give your answer in its simplest form.

(ii) The angles of a triangle add up to 180°. Write down an equation in $x$ and use it to find the value of $x$.

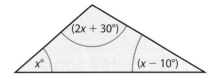

**15.** In a furniture store, a chair costs €$x$ and a stool costs €10 less than a chair. If 2 stools and 3 chairs cost €230, find the cost of a chair and the cost of a stool.

**16.** In this diagram, the number in each box is found by adding the two numbers above it. Find the value of $x$.

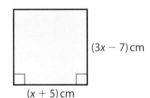

**17.** The given figure is a square. Form an equation in $x$ and solve it. Hence, find the length of the side of the square.

$(3x - 7)$ cm

$(x + 5)$ cm

**18.** Emer is 4 years older than Leah. If twice the sum of their ages is 48 years, how old is Leah?

**19.** 166 people live in an apartment block and of these, $x$ are women. There are 8 fewer men than women, and there are 30 more children than women. How many women live in the block?

**20.** A triangle and rectangle are shown below:

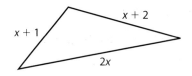

Find the value of $x$ which
   (i)   gives a triangle with a perimeter of 63
  (ii)  gives a triangle and rectangle with equal perimeters
 (iii)  makes the rectangle into a square.

# Section 2.6  Algebraic division

We have already learned how to multiply two algebraic expressions such as $(x + 4)(x - 3)$.

In this section, we will learn how to divide an expression such as $x^2 + x - 12$ by $(x + 4)$

$$x^2 + x - 12 \div (x + 4)$$

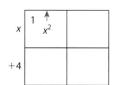 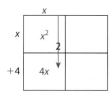 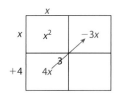 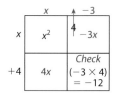

**1.** Divide $x^2$ by $x$      **3.** Work out what needs to be added to $4x$ to get $x$.

**2.** Multiply $x$ by 4      **4.** Divide $-3x$ by $x$

$$\therefore x^2 + x - 12 \div x + 4 = x - 3$$

---

**Example 1**

Divide $2x^2 - 5x + 3$ by $x - 1$.

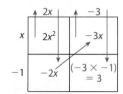

1.   $2x^2 \div x = 2x$
2.   $2x \times -1 = -2x$
3.   $(-2x) + (-3x) = -5x$
4.   $-3x \div x = -3$

The answer is $2x - 3$.

## Exercise 2.6

By completing the grid, divide each of the following:

**1.** (a)  $x^2 + 5x + 6 = x + 3$

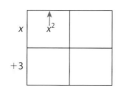

(b)  $x^2 + 8x + 15 = x + 5$

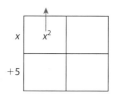

**2.** $x^2 + 8x + 16 \div x + 4$

**3.** $x^2 + 9x + 14 \div x + 2$

**4.** $2x^2 + 9x + 4 \div x + 4$

**5.** $6x^2 + 5x + 1 \div 2x + 1$

**6.** $2x^2 + x - 10 \div 2x + 5$

**7.** $6x^2 - 10x - 4 \div 3x + 1$

**8.** $2x^2 - 7x - 4 \div x - 4$

**9.** $3x^2 - 22x + 7 \div 3x - 1$

**10.** $6x^2 + 11x - 35 \div 2x + 7$

**11.** $\dfrac{10x^2 - 7x - 12}{2x - 3}$

**12.** $\dfrac{15x^2 - 26x + 8}{5x - 2}$

## Test yourself 2

1. Simplify each of these expressions:

   (i) $4x + 5 - 2(x + 1)$      (ii) $6(y + 4) - 2(y + 3)$      (iii) $4(3 + k) - 2(k - 5)$

2. Find the value of each of these when $x = 3$ and $y = -2$:

   (i) $2x + y$      (ii) $xy$      (iii) $x + 3y$      (iv) $2x^2 + y^2$

3. (i) By forming an equation
   work out what $x$ stands for.
   (ii) What is the length of the plank?

   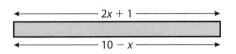

4. Simplify each of these:

   (i) $3x + 4 + 5x - 1$      (ii) $5x - 3 - 2x + 4 + 3x - 6$

5. **A** $\boxed{17 + (a + b)}$      **B** $\boxed{20 - (b + c)}$      **C** $\boxed{20 - (a + c)}$

   When $a = 3$, $b = 4$ and $c = 5$, which of the expressions above is the biggest?

6. Solve each of these equations:

   (i) $9x + 10 = 5x - 2$      (ii) $2(5 + x) - 14 = 4$

7. If $x = 3$ and $y = -2$, find the value of

   (i) $4x$      (ii) $2x + y$      (iii) $2x - 3y$      (iv) $2(x + y)$

8. Look at these rods:
   Write an expression for each length marked **?**

   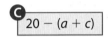

9. If I add 3 to a number and multiply the result by 4, the answer is 48.
   Write an equation in $x$ and solve it to find the number.

10. Remove the brackets and simplify each of these:

    (i) $3(2x - 6) + 2(x - 2)$      (ii) $3x(x + 4) - 2x(x - 3)$

11.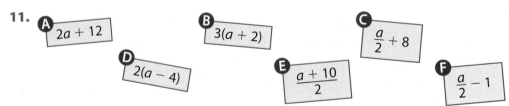

    (i) Work out the value of each expression when $a = 20$.
    (ii) Which expression has the value 0 when $a = 4$?

    (iii)  Which expression has the smallest value when $a = 10$?

    (iv)  Which two expressions have the same value when $a = 6$?

**12.** Simplify each of these:

    (i)  $6a + 3b - 2a + b$               (ii)  $6p - 2q + 4 - 4p + 3q - 2$

**13.** What expression does the question mark (**?**) stand for in each of these shapes?

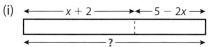

    (i)  $x + 2$    $5 - 2x$         (ii)  $k + 4$    **?**

           **?**                       $10 - 3k$

**14.** In the given triangle, the two marked sides are equal in length.

Find the value of $x$.

Now find the total length of the three sides.

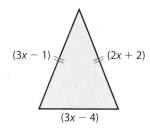

$(3x - 1)$    $(2x + 2)$

$(3x - 4)$

**15.** Divide each of the following:

    (i)  $x^2 + 5x + 6 \div x + 2$          (ii)  $2x^2 + 8x - 24 \div x + 6$

**16.** In a magic square, each row, column and diagonal add up to the same number.

Show that this is a magic square when $a = 7, b = 2$ and $c = 3$.

| $a - b$ | $a + b - c$ | $a + c$ |
|---|---|---|
| $a + b + c$ | $a$ | $a - b - c$ |
| $a - c$ | $a - b + c$ | $a + b$ |

**17.** Which of the expressions in the boxes has the highest value when $x = 5$?

Which of the expressions has the lowest value when $x = 5$?

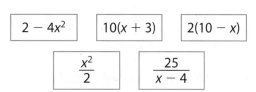

$2 - 4x^2$    $10(x + 3)$    $2(10 - x)$

$\dfrac{x^2}{2}$    $\dfrac{25}{x - 4}$

**18.** *Temporary Work* hires out workers to companies.

For each worker you hire, they charge a fee of €$a$ and then €$b$ per hour worked.

    (i)  For a lorry driver, the fee is €30 and the hourly rate €15.

        How much would it cost to hire a lorry driver for 8 hours?

    (ii)  A worker works for 6 hours.

        If T is the total hire fee for the worker in euro, write down a formula connecting $T, a$ and $b$.

# Assignment:

Simplify each part and put the letter for that part in the box above the correct answer.

The sequence of letters should answer this question.

Why didn't the boy drink his milk after his bath?

| | | |
|---|---|---|
| **F** $10x + 7x$ | **H** $6m - 5m$ | **E** $3a + 2a + 6a$ |
| **B** $2p \times 9$ | **M** $20b \div b$ | **R** $2a \times a$ |
| **T** $6m - 10m$ | **I** $(-3) \times 6q$ | **E** $(-40n) \div (-10)$ |
| **H** $12k - 6l + 2k$ | **O** $8t \times 7t$ | **T** $36pq \div 9q$ |
| **N** $15y \div (-3y)$ | **A** $5x^2 + 2x - 3x^2$ | **D** $7m - (-3m)$ |
| **H** $-12k + 10k$ | **A** $9a - 7a - a$ | **T** $9a \times 7b$ |
| **E** $(-18ab) \div 9b$ | **F** $ab \times ac$ | **S** $2x \times \frac{1}{2}x$ |
| **H** $3x - 7x$ | **I** $-3m + 10m$ | **K** $9p - 2q - 7p$ |
| **A** $16mn \div 8$ | **M** $(-6a) \times (-3b)$ | **O** $7m - 3m + 2n$ |
| **H** $8x \times 3xy$ | **R** $14m^2 \div (-7m)$ | **G** $5ab + 7ba$ |
| **D** $8pq + 7pq - 3p$ | **N** $4m \times 2n \times 5$ | **R** $16x \div 4x \times 2x$ |
| **O** $13k \times 2k \div k^2$ | **R** $3m^2 + m^2 - 6m^2$ | **T** $3x + 7y - 2y + x$ |
| **I** $-m + n + m - n$ | **F** $3a \times 4b \times 5c$ | **I** $100bc \div 20b$ |
| **K** $(-2x) \times 5x \times (-3)$ | **L** $24ab \div 6a \times 2b$ | **O** $6y^2 + 7y - 8y^2 + 2y$ |
| **E** $(-6m) \times (-6m)$ | **L** $5ab + (6a \times 2b)$ | **N** $(32x^2 \div 4x) - 7x$ |

| $a$ | $a^2bc$ | $-4m$ | $-2a$ | $-2m^2$ | $10m$ | $-2m$ | $-18q$ | $x$ | $30x^2$ | $7m$ | $-5$ | $12ab$ | $-4x$ | $0$ | $x^2$ | $18p$ | $2mn$ | $4p$ | $m$ | $-2k$ | $11a$ |
|---|---|---|---|---|---|---|---|---|---|---|---|---|---|---|---|---|---|---|---|---|---|
| | | | | | | | | | | | | | | | | | | | | | |

| $14k - 6l$ | $2x^2 + 2x$ | $15pq - 3p$ | $40mn$ | $-2y^2 + 9y$ | $2a^2$ | $56t^2$ | $4m + 2n$ | $18ab$ | $8b^2$ | $36m^2$ | $60abc$ | $4x + 5y$ | $17x$ | $26$ | $8x$ | $63ab$ | $24x^2y$ | $4n$ | $20$ | $5c$ | $17ab$ | $2p - 2q$ |
|---|---|---|---|---|---|---|---|---|---|---|---|---|---|---|---|---|---|---|---|---|---|---|
| | | | | | | | | | | | | | | | | | | | | | | |

# Sets

*From first year, you will recall how to:*

- define a set and an element,
- identify a null set,
- identify the universal set,
- use the symbols, $\in$, $\notin$, $\cup$, $\cap$,
- identify equal sets,
- find subsets of a given set,

- draw and interpret two set Venn diagrams,
- find the cardinal number, #, of a set,
- find the complement of a set,
- define the difference between the number sets $N, Z, Q$ & $R$.

*In this chapter, you will learn to:*

- generate rules to define a given set,
- find the set difference, using the symbol $/$,

- use Venn Diagrams to solve word problems,
- place the number sets, $N, Z, Q$ and $R$ into a Venn Diagram.

## Section 3.1  Revision of sets terminology

In this section we will revise the sets operations that you will have met in first-year.

1. **Equal sets**

   Two sets are **equal** if they contain exactly the same elements.

   If $A = \{2, 4, 6, 8\}$ and $B = \{4, 6, 8, 2\}$, then **$A = B$**.

2. **Union of two sets ($A \cup B$)**

   The **union** of two sets $A$ and $B$ is the set of elements that are in $A$ **or** $B$.

   It is found by putting together all the elements of $A$ and $B$ into a new set without repeating any element. The new set is written as **$A \cup B$**.

   If $A = \{1, 2, 3, 4\}$ and $B = \{3, 4, 5, 6\}$, then $A \cup B = \{1, 2, 3, 4, 5, 6\}$.

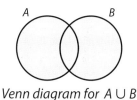

*Venn diagram for $A \cup B$*

## 3. Intersection of two sets (A ∩ B)

The **intersection** of two sets $A$ and $B$ is the set of elements that are in both $A$ **and** $B$.

It is found by putting all the elements common to both $A$ and $B$ into a new set.

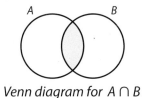

*Venn diagram for A ∩ B*

The new set is written as **A ∩ B**.

In the given Venn diagram, $A \cap B$ is shaded.

If $A = \{1, 3, 5, 7, 9, 11\}$ and $B = \{6, 7, 8, 9, 10, 11, 12\}$, then $A \cap B = \{7, 9, 11\}$.

## 4. Subsets (B ⊂ A)

Set $B$ is a **subset** of set $A$ if all the elements of $B$ are contained in $A$.

It is written $B \subset A$.

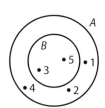

If $A = \{1, 2, 3, 4, 5\}$ and $B = \{3, 5\}$, then $B \subset A$.

Since all the elements of (any) set $A$ are in $A$, $A$ is a subset of itself.

Also the null set is a subset of all sets.

For all sets $A$
$A \subset A$ and $\emptyset \subset A$

## 5. The universal set (U)

The set from which all other sets being considered are taken is called the **universal set**.

It is denoted by the capital letter **U** and is represented by a rectangle.

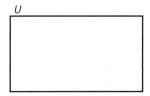

## 6. The complement of a set (A′)

The complement of a set $A$ is the set of elements in the universal set $U$ which are not in $A$.

It is written as **A′** and is illustrated by the shaded area in the given Venn diagram.

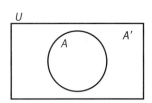

If $U = \{1, 2, 3, 4, 5, 6, 7, 8, 9, 10\}$

and $A = \{2, 3, 5, 7\}$, the set of prime numbers between 1 and 10.

then $A' = \{1, 4, 6, 8, 9, 10\}$, the set of non-prime numbers between 1 and 10.

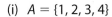

**Example 1**

Use the given Venn diagram to list
the elements of each of these sets:

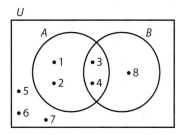

  (i)  $A$          (ii)  $A \cup B$      (iii)  $A'$

(iv)  $A \cap B$    (v)  $(A \cap B)'$.

  (i)  $A = \{1, 2, 3, 4\}$

 (ii)  $A \cup B = \{1, 2, 3, 4\} \cup \{3, 4, 8\} = \{1, 2, 3, 4, 8\}$

(iii)  $A' = \{5, 6, 7, 8\}$

(iv)  $A \cap B = \{1, 2, 3, 4\} \cap \{3, 4, 8\} = \{3, 4\}$

 (v)  $(A \cap B)' = \{1, 2, 5, 6, 7, 8\}$

## 7. The cardinal number of a set (#)

The number of elements in a set is called the **cardinal number** of the set.

The symbol **#** is used to denote the cardinal number.

From the given Venn diagram,

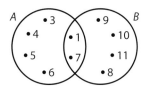

  $\#A = 6$          $\#B = 6$

  $\#(A \cap B) = 2$    $\#(A \cup B) = 10$.

## 8. Rules for Sets

Sets are defined by (a) listing the elements or

                 (b) a rule.

If $A = \{2, 4, 6, 8, 10, 12, 14, 16, 18, 20, 22, 24, 26, 28\}$

We could write the rule, $A = \{$whole, positive, even numbers less than 30$\}$

Also, using algebra and mathematical symbols,

$A = \{x \mid x$ is an even number $< 30, x \in N\}$

**Example 2**

List the elements in each of the following sets:

  (i)  $C = \{$factors of 24$\}$

 (ii)  $D = \{$multiples of 3 less than 30$\}$

(iii)  $E = \{x \mid 4 < x < 20, x \in N\}$

(i) the factors of 24 = C = {1, 2, 3, 4, 6, 8, 12, 24}
(ii) multiples of 3 less than 30 = D = {3, 6, 9, 12, 15, 18, 21, 24, 27}
(iii) natural numbers between 4 and 20 =
   E = {5, 6, 7, 8, 9, 10, 11, 12, 13, 14, 15, 16, 17, 18, 19}

## Exercise 3.1

**1.** What is the diagram on the right
called?
Now list the elements of A.
What is #A?

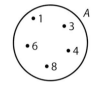

**2.** On the right, set $X$ is represented
by a Venn diagram. Say if each
of the following is true or false:

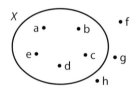

   (i) $d \in X$        (ii) $g \in X$
   (iii) $e \in X$       (iv) $f \in X$.

**3.** What do the symbols $\in$ and $\notin$ stand for?
   $A = \{1, 2, 3, 4\}$    $B = \{a, b, c, d\}$    $C = \{x, y, z\}$
   Copy and insert the correct symbol $\in$ or $\notin$ in each of the following:
   (i) $3 \dots A$    (ii) $2 \dots B$    (ii) $c \dots B$    (iv) $d \dots C$    (v) $z \dots C$.

**4.** Which two of the following sets are equal?
   $A = \{2, 3, 4, 6\}$    $B = \{6, 4, 3, 1\}$    $C = \{6, 3, 4, 2\}$.
   Explain why they are equal.

**5.** From the given Venn diagram, list the elements
of each of these sets:

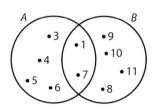

   (i) $A$            (ii) $B$
   (iii) $A \cap B$       (iv) $A \cup B$.

**6.** $A = \{1, 2, 3, 4, 5, 6\}$    $B = \{4, 5, 6, 7, 8\}$    $C = \{7, 8, 9, 10\}$
   List the elements of each of these sets:
   (i) $A \cap B$    (i) $B \cup C$    (i) $B \cap C$    (i) $A \cap C$.

**7.** From the Venn diagram on the right, write down

    (i) #A             (ii) #B

    (iii) #(A ∩ B)    (iv) #(A ∪ B).

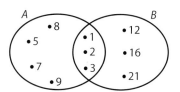

**8.** Given  U = {1, 2, 3, 4, 5, 6, 7, 8, 9}

         A = {1, 3, 5, 7}

         B = {5, 6, 7, 8}.

Copy the Venn diagram on the right and illustrate the given information on it.

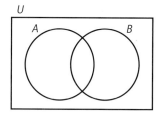

**9.** From the given Venn diagram, list the elements of

    (i) P             (ii) Q

    (iii) P ∩ Q      (iv) P ∪ Q.

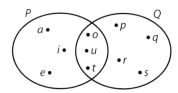

**10.** From the given Venn diagram, list the elements of each of these sets:

    (i) U      (ii) A      (iii) A′.

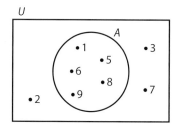

**11.** Use the given Venn diagram to list the elements of each of these sets:

    (i) A      (ii) B        (iii) A′

    (iii) B′     (iv) A ∪ B    (vi) (A ∪ B)′.

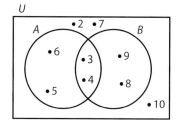

**12.** In the given Venn diagram, each dot represents an element.

Write down

    (i) #A        (ii) #B       (iii) #U

    (iv) #(A ∪ B)   (v) #(A ∩ B)  (vi) #(A ∪ B)′.

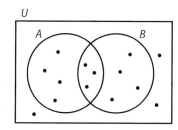

**13.** If $U = \{1, 2, 3, 4, 5, 6, 7, 8, 9, 10\}$
   $A = \{1, 3, 5, 7\}$
   $B = \{3, 4, 5, 6\}$, list the elements of

   (i) $A'$     (ii) $B'$     (iii) $A \cup B$     (vi) $(A \cup B)'$.

**14.** Given $U = \{1, 2, 3, \ldots, 12\}$
   $A = \{1, 2, 3, 4, 5, 6\}$
   $B = \{3, 5, 7, 9, 11\}$.

   Make a copy of the given Venn diagram
   and fill in the information provided.

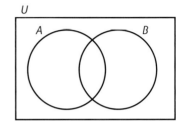

**15.** Using the Venn diagram on the right,
   say if each of the following is true or
   false:

   (i) $7 \in (A \cup B)$     (ii) $3 \in B$
   (iii) $6 \in (A \cap B)$     (iv) $9 \in A'$
   (v) $9 \in U$     (vi) $8 \in (A \cup B)$.

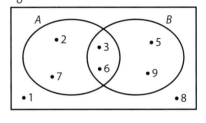

**16.** Given $U = \{a, b, c, d, e, f, g\}$
   $X = \{a, b, c, d\}$
   $Y = \{b, e, f\}$.
   (i) Place the letters $a, b, c, d, e, f, g$ in
       the Venn diagram on the right.
   (iii) List the elements of $X'$.
   (v) What is $\#(X \cup Y)'$?

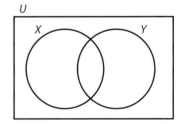

**17.** What do the symbols $\subset$ and $\not\subset$ stand for?
   Now state which of the two symbols should be inserted in the space provided in
   each of the following to make the statement true:
   (i) $\{a, b\} \ldots \{a, b, c, d\}$           (ii) $\{2, 3\} \ldots \{2, 3, 4, 5\}$
   (iii) $\{1\} \ldots \{2, 4, 6, 8\}$           (iv) $\{d, e, f\} \ldots \{a, b, c, d, e\}$

**18.** If $A = \{3, 4, 5\}$ list all the subsets with:
   (i) 1 element only
   (ii) 2 elements only
   List all other possible subsets.

**19.** List the elements in each of the following sets.

(i)  $A = \{$Integers between $-3$ and $3\}$

(ii)  $B = \{$Multiples of 4 less than $24\}$

(iii)  $C = \{x \mid 2 \leq x \leq 11, x \in N\}$

**20.** Draw a Venn diagram of the following sets.

(i)  $R = \{$Multiples of 8 less than $40\}$

(ii)  $S = \{$Multiples of 6 less than $40\}$

**21.** List the elements in $A \cap B$ if $A = \{x \mid 5 \leq x \leq 10, x \in N\}$, $B = \{x \mid -3 \leq x < 8, x \in Z\}$

**22.** List the elements in $C \cap D$ if $C = \{x \mid -4 < x \leq 9, x \in Z\}$, $D = \{x \mid -2 \leq x < 2, x \in Z\}$

**23.** In the diagram over;

$U = \{$Natural numbers from 1 to 10 inclusive$\}$

$A = \{$Factors of 6$\}$

$B = \{$Even numbers$\}$

Copy and complete the Venn diagram and use it to answer True or False to each of the following:

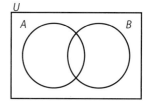

(i)  $A \cap B = \{\}$            (ii)  $A \neq B$            (iii)  $A \cup B = U$

# Section 3.2 Set difference

In this section we introduce a new term called **set difference**.

To illustrate set difference, we take two sets $A$ and $B$, where

$$A = \{1, 2, 3, 4, 5, 6\} \quad \text{and} \quad B = \{4, 6, 8, 10\}.$$

If we remove from set $A$ all the elements which are in set $B$, we have **$A$ less $B$ ($A \setminus B$)**.

$\therefore \quad A \setminus B = \{1, 2, 3, 5\}$

*Set difference*      $A \setminus B$  is the set of elements of $A$ which are not in $B$.

Set difference can be illustrated by Venn diagrams as follows:

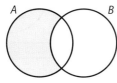                 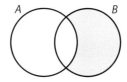

Shaded area is $A \setminus B$               Shaded area is $B \setminus A$

Note: In practical terms, $A \setminus B$ is the set of elements that are in **$A$ only.**

It is obvious from the diagram that $A \setminus B$ is not equal to $B \setminus A$.

---

**Example 1**

If $A = \{a, b, c, d, e, f, g\}$ and $B = \{e, f, g, h, i\}$, find

   (i) $A\backslash B$           (ii) $B\backslash A$           (iii) $(A \cup B)\backslash(A \cap B)$

  (i) $A\backslash B$ is the set of elements of $A$ which are not in $B$.

      $\therefore$   $A\backslash B = \{a, b, c, d\}$

  (ii) $B\backslash A = \{h, i\}$

  (iii) $A \cup B = \{a, b, c, d, e, f, g, h, i\}$ and $A \cap B = \{e, f, g\}$

      $\therefore$   $(A \cup B)\backslash(A \cap B) = \{a, b, c, d, h, i\}$

---

$U = \{$students in my class$\}$
$C = \{$students who have cats$\}$
$D = \{$students who have dogs$\}$
$C \backslash D = \{$students who have cats **only**$\}$
$D \backslash C = \{$students who have dogs **only**$\}$
$C \cup D = \{$students who have cats **or** dogs$\}$
$C \cap D = \{$students who have cats **and** dogs$\}$
$(C \cup D)' = \{$students who **do not** have cats
         **or** dogs$\}$

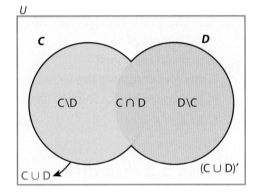

## Exercise 3.2

**1.** $A = \{1, 2, 3, 4, 5, 6, 7, 8\}$, $B = \{3, 6, 9, 10\}$ and $C = \{2, 4, 6, 8\}$.
List the elements of the following sets.

    (i) $A\backslash B$         (ii) $B\backslash C$         (iii) $A\backslash C$         (iv) $C\backslash A$

**2.** From the given Venn diagram, list the elements of

    (i) $A\backslash B$
    (ii) $B\backslash A$
    (iii) $U\backslash A$
    (iv) $U\backslash(A \cap B)$

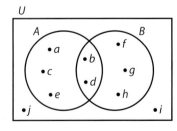

3. Based on the given Venn diagram, say if each of the following is true or false:

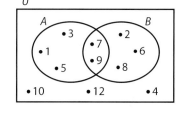

   (i)   $3 \in A \setminus B$
   (ii)  $7 \in B \setminus A$
   (iii) $\#(B \setminus A) = 3$
   (iv)  $\#U = 12$
   (v)   $\#(A \cap B) = 2$
   (vi)  $6 \in U \setminus A$
   (vii) $\#(U \setminus A) = 6$
   (viii) $\#(U \setminus B) = 8$

4. Given  $X = \{2, 4, 6, 8, 10, 12\}$  and  $Y = \{3, 6, 9, 12, 15\}$.
   Find   (i) $X \setminus Y$   (ii) $Y \setminus X$.
   Is  $X \setminus Y = Y \setminus X$ ?

5. Given   $A = \{4, 5, 6, 8, 10, 12\}$      $B = \{1, 2, 3, 4, 5, 6\}$
            $C = \{2, 4, 10, 14\}$            $D = \{0, 5, 10, 15\}$

   List the elements of the following sets:

   (i)   $A \setminus C$
   (ii)  $B \setminus D$
   (iii) $D \setminus A$
   (iv)  $A \setminus (B \cap C)$
   (v)   $B \setminus (C \cup D)$
   (vi)  $(A \cup B) \setminus (A \cap B)$

6. $U = \{a, b, c, d, e, f, g, h, i\}$, $A = \{d, f, g, e, i\}$ and $B = \{b, e, h, i\}$.
   Draw a Venn diagram to illustrate these sets.
   Use the Venn diagram to write down

   (i)   $\#(A \setminus B)$
   (ii)  $\#(U \setminus A)$
   (iii) $\#[U \setminus (A \cup B)]$
   (iv)  $\#[U \setminus (A \cap B)]$

7. Make two copies of this Venn diagram.

   (i)   On the first, shade in $P \setminus Q$.
   (ii)  On the second, shade in $Q \setminus P$.

8. Based on the given Venn diagram, say whether each of the following is true or false:

   (i)   $A \setminus B = \{9, 7, 3\}$
   (ii)  $\#(B \setminus A) = 3$
   (iii) $\#(U \setminus A) = 6$
   (iv)  $\#(A \cup B) = 6$
   (v)   $\#[U \setminus (A \cap B)] = 9$
   (vi)  $(A \cap B) \subset U$.

9. There are 20 players on a basketball panel. 16 can shoot with the right hand but 4 can shoot with both left and right hands as shown in the Venn diagram. By copying and completing the following Venn diagram find:

   (a) How many players can shoot with the right hand only?
   (b) How many players can shoot with their left hand?
   (c) How many players can shoot with their left hand only?

53

**10.** James made a poster entitled "Sets of numbers"

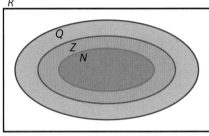

    (i) Write down the name of the sets marked
       $N, Z, Q, R$

    (ii) Copy the diagram and add one number
       into each of the sections:

       (a) $N$              (c) $Q \backslash Z$

       (b) $Z \backslash N$        (d) $R \backslash Q$

**11.** In the diagram, $A = \{$Students who like apples$\}$
           and $B = \{$Students who like bananas$\}$.

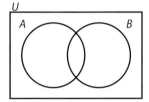

    Describe the set of students in

    (i) $A \cup B$          (ii) $A \backslash B$

    Copy the diagram and shade in the region
    $(A \cup B) \backslash (A \backslash B)$

## Section 3.3 Using Venn diagrams to solve problems

Venn diagrams are very useful when solving problems involving two or more sets.
In these problems we are interested in the **number** of elements in the set rather than the
elements themselves.

Consider the given Venn diagram.

$U$ represents a class of students.
$A$ represents those who study Art.
$B$ represents those who study Biology.

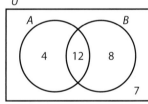

| Note: | |
|---|---|
| 12 study both Art **and** Biology | |
| 4 study Art **only** | $\therefore 12 + 4 = 16$ study Art |
| 8 study Biology **only** | $\therefore 12 + 8 = 20$ study Biology |
| | $\therefore 12 + 4 + 8 = 24$ study Art **or** Biology |
| 7 study **neither** of these subjects | $\therefore 12 + 4 + 8 + 7 = 31 =$ the number of students in the class. |

## Example 1

In a class of 30 pupils, 17 study German, 16 study Spanish and 5 study both German and Spanish.

Represent this information on a Venn diagram.

Use the Venn diagram to write down the number of pupils who study

(i) German only (ii) Spanish only (iii) neither German nor Spanish.

We use the given information to fill in the Venn diagram.

First place 5 in the set $G \cap S$ ... 5 study both German and Spanish

(i) German only $= 17 - 5 = 12$

(ii) Spanish only $= 16 - 5 = 11$

(iii) Neither $= 30 - 12 - 5 - 11$
     $= 2$

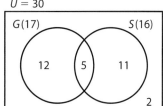

## Example 2

All of the 30 students in a class have either a mobile phone, or an iPad or both.
If 27 students have a mobile phone and 15 have an iPad, how many students have

(i) both items

(ii) a mobile phone only

(iii) an iPad only?

In the Venn diagram,
$M$ = mobile phone and $P$ = iPad.

Since $27 + 15 = 42$, which is more than the 30 in the class, there is an 'an overlap' of 12. Therefore, 12 have both a mobile phone and an iPad.

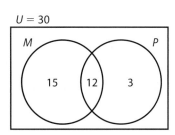

Now, we fill in the three regions shown:

(i) 12 students have both items

(ii) 15 students have a mobile phone only ... $27 - 12 = 15$

(iii) 3 students have an iPad only. ... $15 - 12 = 3$

## Exercise 3.3

**1.** In the given Venn diagram,

   *U* is the set of pupils in the class
   *B* is the set of pupils who play basketball
   *F* is the set of pupils who play football.

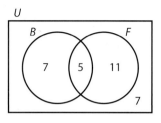

   (i) How many pupils play both games?
   (ii) How many pupils are there in the class?
   (iii) How many pupils play football only?
   (iv) How many pupils play neither of the two games?

**2.** 30 pupils were asked which of the television
   programmes P and Q they watch. Some of
   the information obtained is represented
   in the Venn diagram shown.

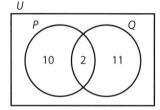

   (i) How many pupils watched programme P?
   (ii) How many pupils watched programme Q only?
   (iii) How many pupils watched both programmes?
   (iv) How many watched neither?

**3.** In the given Venn diagram,
   *U* is the set of teenagers in a
   Youth Club.
   *P* is the set of teenagers who use
   PlayStation.
   *X* is the set of teenagers who use Xbox.

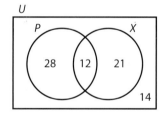

   (i) How many teenagers use PlayStation?
   (ii) How many teenagers use Xbox?
   (iii) How many teenagers use PlayStation only?
   (iv) How many teenagers use neither of these games?

**4.** In a class of 30 students,
   12 study Biology (*B*), 16 study
   French (*F*), and 5 study both subjects.
   Copy the Venn diagram and represent
   the given information on it.

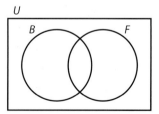

   (i) Write down the number of students who study
       Biology but not French.
   (ii) How many students study neither of these two subjects?
   (iii) How many students study only one of these subjects?

**5.** Copy the Venn diagram shown and fill
in the number of elements in each region,
given that
$\#(A) = 10$, $\#(B) = 16$ and $\#(A \cap B) = 4$.

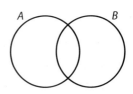

**6.** The Venn diagram shows two intersecting
sets $A$ and $B$ and the number of elements
in each region.
Find  (i) $\#A$        (ii) $\#B$
      (iii) $\#(A \cap B)$    (iv) $\#(A \cup B)$.

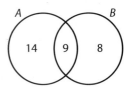

**7.** Copy the given Venn diagram and fill in
the four regions, given that

$$\#U = 42, \#A = 21, \#B = 18, \text{ and } \#(A \cap B) = 6.$$

Now write down

(i) $\#(A \cup B)$      (ii) $\#B'$      (iii) $\#(A \cup B)'$.

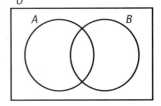

**8.** In a survey of 40 households, 22 had a dog and 16
had a cat.
If 8 households had both a cat and a dog, represent
this information on a Venn diagram and write down
how many households had neither.

**9.** In the given Venn diagram,
$U$ = the students in Class 2L,
$H$ = the students in 2L who study
    Home Economics,
$G$ = the students in 2L who study
    German.

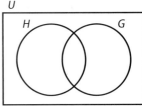

If 20 students study Home Economics, 12 study German, 8 study both these
subjects, and 9 study neither, show this information on a copy of the Venn diagram.

  (i)  How many students are there in the class?
 (ii)  How many students study Home Economics but not German?
(iii)  How many students study just one of these subjects?

**10.** Copy the Venn diagram shown and fill
in the three regions given that
#A = 12, #B = 14 and #(A ∪ B) = 22.

Write down  (i)  #(A ∩ B)  (ii)  #(B\A).

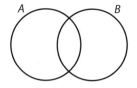

**11.** The tennis club and cricket club joined to form one club.
There were 55 people in the tennis club and 45 people in
the cricket club but only 84 people in the combined club.
  (i)  Explain why there were not 100 people in
       the combined club.
 (ii)  How many people belonged to both the tennis
       and cricket club?
(iii)  How many people belonged to the tennis club
       but not to the cricket club?

**12.** In a class of 32 girls, 16 play hockey and
12 play tennis.
If 10 girls play neither of these sports,
represent this information on a Venn
diagram.
Use the Venn diagram to write down
  (i)  the number of girls who play both sports
 (ii)  the number of girls who play hockey but not tennis
(iii)  the number of girls who play at least one of these sports.

**13.** In a survey of 80 people, 56 had watched RTE1 on the previous night and 34 had
watched TV3.
If 22 people had watched neither of these stations, how many people had watched
both?

**14.** Copy the Venn diagram and fill in the
number of elements in each region
given that
#A = 21, #B = 16, #(A ∪ B) = 30 and
#U = 43.
Find  (i)  #(A ∩ B)  (ii)  #(B\A)  (iii)  #(A ∪ B)'.

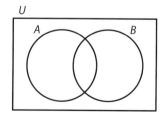

## *Investigation:*

**A:** Draw a large poster of the universal set below and complete the chart describing the seven regions.

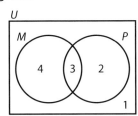

| Region | In set notation (in terms of M and P) | In words (in terms of M and P) |
|--------|---------------------------------------|--------------------------------|
| 1 | | |
| 2 | | |
| 3 | | |
| 4 | | |
| 3 + 4 | | |
| 2 + 3 | | |
| 2 + 3 + 4 | | |

**B:** Consider your class as a Universal set. Collect data using a simple questionnaire to draw a Venn diagram of two particular sets of students in your class.

E.g.   (i)  students who sometimes walk / get the bus to school.
     (ii)  students who intend to study Biology / Chemistry in 5th year.
    (iii)  students who play Football / Basketball.
    (iv)  students who like pizza / pasta etc.

Describe in words the number of students in your class who belong in each region of the Venn diagram.

## Test yourself 3

1. Based on the given Venn diagram, write down the elements of these sets:

   (i)  $A$           (ii)  $A \backslash B$

   (iii)  $A'$        (iv)  $\#(A \cup B)'$.

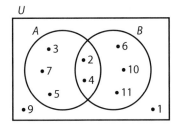

2. In the given diagram, each dot
   represents an element.
   Now write down
   (i) #A            (ii) #(A ∪ B)
   (iii) #U          (iv) #(A ∩ B)'.

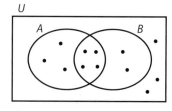

3. From the given Venn diagram, list the
   elements of each of these sets:
   (i) P             (ii) Q
   (iii) P ∪ Q       (iv) P\Q.

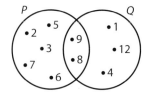

4. U is the set of pupils in a class.
   T is the set of pupils who play tennis.
   H is the set of pupils who play hurling.
   (i) How many pupils are there in the class?
   (ii) How many pupils play tennis?
   (iii) How many pupils play both games?
   (iv) How many pupils play neither of the two games?
   (v) How many pupils play one game only?

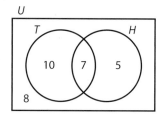

5. Given A = {1, 2, 3, 4}, B = {4, 5, 6} and C = {1, 4, 8}.
   Write down the element(s) of these sets:
   (i) A ∩ B     (ii) A\C     (iii) A ∪ C     (iv) (A ∪ C)\B.

6. In the Venn diagram on the right, which **one**
   of the following statements is true?
   (i) 6 ∈ (A\B)
   (ii) #A = 2
   (iii) #(A ∪ B) = 2
   (iv) #(A ∪ B)' = 2.

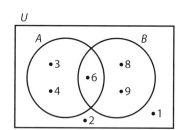

7. From the given Venn diagram, list
   the elements of each of these sets:
   (i) X          (ii) Y          (iii) U
   (iv) X ∩ Y     (v) X'          (vi) (X ∪ Y)'.

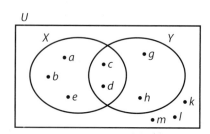

8. Forty students took a mathematics examination consisting of two parts.
   Thirty students passed in Part 1 and twenty eight students passed in Part 2.
   If twenty four students passed in both parts, how many students passed in neither part?

9. Examine the given Venn diagram
   and list the elements of these sets:
   (i) $B$           (ii) $A \cup B$
   (iii) $A \setminus B$      (iv) $A'$.

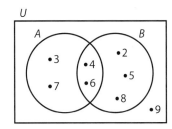

10. Copy the Venn diagram on the
    right and fill in the four
    regions, given that
    $\#U = 40$, $\#A = 19$, $\#B = 16$ and $\#(A \cap B) = 7$.
    Now write down
    (i) $\#(A \cup B)$  (ii) $\#(A \setminus B)$  (iii) $\#(A \cup B)'$

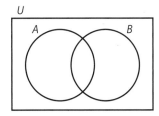

11. In the given Venn diagram,

    $A \cup B = \{4, 9, 12, 15, 18, 20\}$.

    Copy this Venn diagram.
    In the set $A$, put numbers divisible by 2.
    In set $B$, put numbers divisible by 3.
    Now use the Venn diagram to write down
    the numbers divisible by both 2 and 3.

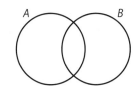

12. In a survey, 100 people were asked if they
    had been on a sun holiday or on a skiing
    holiday the previous year.
    60 had been on a sun holiday, 15 had
    been on a skiing holiday and 30 had
    been on neither.
    Copy the given Venn diagram and
    insert the appropriate numbers in the brackets.

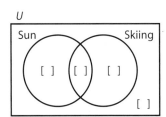

## Assignment:

Revise the idea of a subset and then make a poster of the sets below, shading the areas indicated:

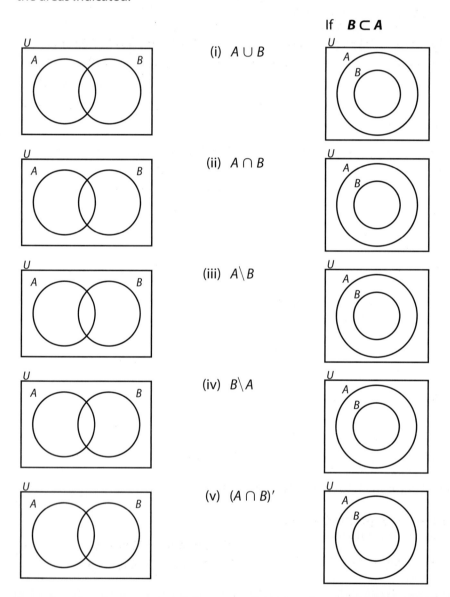

If **B ⊂ A**

(i) $A \cup B$

(ii) $A \cap B$

(iii) $A \setminus B$

(iv) $B \setminus A$

(v) $(A \cap B)'$

By comparing the two sets of diagrams, if **B ⊂ A**, what conclusions can you make about:

    (i) $A \cup B =$           and (ii) $A \cap B =$

# Factors

*From first year, you will recall how to:*

- Identify terms and expressions,
- find factors,
- find the Highest Common Factor (HCF) of a group of numbers.

*In this chapter, you will learn to:*

- find the HCF of an algebraic expression,
- factorise by grouping terms,
- factorise the difference of two squares (DOTS),
- factorise a quadratic expression.

## Section 4.1  Factorising with common factors

Since $9 \times 5 = 45$, we say that 9 and 5 are **factors** of 45.
15 and 3 are also factors of 45.

The factors of 24 are  1, 2, 3, 4, 6, 8, ⑫, 24.
The factors of 36 are  1, 2, 3, 4, 6, 9, ⑫, 18, 36.
The **highest common factor** is 12.

Here are two algebraic terms:  $6xy$  and  $12x$.
The highest common factor of the numbers is 6.
The highest common factor of the variables is $x$.
So the highest common factor of the two terms is  $6 \times x$, i.e. $6x$.

Similarly, the highest common factors of

  (i)  $3a$  and  $6a^2 = 3a$
(iii)  $5a^2b$  and  $-15ab = 5ab$

 (ii)  $6x^2$  and  $-12xy = 6x$
(iv)  $4x^2$  and  $+16xy^2 = 4x$

Take the expression  $5x + 10$.
     $5x + 10 = 5(x + 2)$
     5  and  $(x + 2)$  are called the factors of  $5x + 10$.

| | $x$ | $+2$ |
|---|---|---|
| 5 | $5x$ | $+10$ |

To factorise an algebraic expression:

> Find the highest common factor and write it outside the brackets or outside the array.
> Divide each term by this factor and write the results inside the brackets or on top of the array.
> Check your result by expanding the brackets.

Here are some expressions that have been factorised:

(i)  $x^2 + 7x = x(x + 7)$

(ii)  $3x^2 - 9x = 3x(x - 3)$

(iii)  $3xy - 12x = 3x(y - 4)$

(iv)  $12x^2y^2 - 6xy = 6xy(2xy - 1)$

Using the array method we have:

|     | $x$ | $+7$ |
| --- | --- | --- |
| $x$ | $x^2$ | $+7x$ |

|     | $x$ | $-3$ |
| --- | --- | --- |
| $3x$ | $3x^2$ | $-9x$ |

|     | $y$ | $-4$ |
| --- | --- | --- |
| $3x$ | $3xy$ | $-12x$ |

|      | $2xy$ | $-1$ |
| --- | --- | --- |
| $6xy$ | $12x^2y^2$ | $-6xy$ |

## Exercise 4.1

**1.** Write down the highest common factor of each of these:

    (i)  9 and 12      (ii)  12 and 18      (iii)  14 and 21      (iv)  21 and 35

**2.** Write down the highest common factor of each of these:

    (i)  $4x$ and $12x$      (ii)  $3n$ and $9n$      (iii)  $10x$ and $15x$

    (iv)  $3a^2$ and $6a$      (v)  $3xy$ and $12x^2$      (vi)  $2a^2b$ and $6ab$

Copy and complete numbers (**3–16**).

**3.** $4x + 8 = 4($      )      **4.** $6a + 12b = 6($      )

**5.** $7x + 14y = 7($      )      **6.** $22a + 33b = 11($      )

**7.** $12x - 24y = 12($      )      **8.** $ab + bc = b($      )

**9.** $2ax + 4ay = 2a($      )      **10.** $x^2 + x = x($      )

**11.** $5x^2 - 10x = 5x($      )      **12.** $3a^2 + 6a = 3a($      )

**13.** $4x^2 - 12x = 4x($       $)$       **14.** $6ab - 12bc = 6b($       $)$

**15.** $7x^2y - 14xy = 7xy($       $)$       **16.** $6x^2y - 15x^2 = 3x^2($       $)$

Factorise each of the following using brackets or the array model.

**17.** $4x + 16$       **18.** $6x + 18y$       **19.** $10a - 40b$

**20.** $ab + ay$       **21.** $3ab + 3bc$       **22.** $2xy - 2xz$

**23.** $7xy + 14xz$       **24.** $5ab - 15bc$       **25.** $6ax - 12ay$

**26.** $x^2 + 4x$       **27.** $3x^2 + 9x$       **28.** $5x^2 + 10x$

**29.** $6a^2 - 12a$       **30.** $7a^2 - 21a$       **31.** $10x^2 + 40x$

**32.** $25x^2 - 15x$       **33.** $7x^2 - 28x$       **34.** $12x^2 + 18x$

**35.** $15x^2 + 25xy$       **36.** $3x^2 - 6x^2y$       **37.** $x^3 + x^2 + x$

**38.** $3ab^2 - 6ab$       **39.** $12xy - 24x^2y$       **40.** $15x^3 - 35x^2$

## *Investigation:*

Fully factorise each of the following expressions

| | | | |
|---|---|---|---|
| (i) $3a^2 - 15ab$ | $2a^3 - a^2b$ | $7ab - 35b^2$ | |
| (ii) $4a^2 - 2ab$ | $2a^2b + 2a$ | $2ab - 10b^2$ | |
| (iii) $7ab + 7b^2$ | $5a - 25b$ | $2ab^2 + 2b$ | |
| (iv) $4ab - 2b^2$ | $3b^2a + 3b^3$ | $a^3 - 5a^2b$ | $2a^2b + 3ab^2$ |

Use the code below to find a letter for **each** factor.
Code

| E | H | P | S | O | A | I | L | G | R | T | U | N |
|---|---|---|---|---|---|---|---|---|---|---|---|---|
| 5 | $2a$ | $3a$ | $2b$ | $7b$ | $a^2$ | $ab$ | $3b^2$ | $a+b$ | $a-5b$ | $2a-b$ | $ab+1$ | $2a+3b$ |

Rearrange each set of letters to spell a bird:

(i) _____       (ii) _____

(iii) _____       (iv) _____

Note: $3b^2a + 3b^3 = 3b^2(a + b)$

# Section 4.2 Factorising by grouping terms

Some four-termed expressions do not have an overall common factor, but can be factorised using the array method or by using pairs of brackets.

$ab + ac + bd + dc =$

$= (b + c)(a + d)$

| | $b$ | $+c$ |
|---|---|---|
| $a$ | $ab$ | $ac$ |
| $+d$ | $bd$ | $dc$ |

$\underbrace{ab + ac}\ \underbrace{+ bd + dc}$

**or** $= a(b + c) + d(b + c)$

$= (b + c)(a + d)$

---

**Example 1**

Find the factors of (i) $2ab + 2ac + 3bx + 3cx$

(ii) $3ax - bx - 3ay + by$

(i) $2ab + 2ac + 3bx + 3cx =$

| | $b$ | $+c$ |
|---|---|---|
| $2a$ | $2ab$ | $+2ac$ |
| $+3x$ | $3bx$ | $+3cx$ |

$= (b + c)(2a + 3x)$

**Or** $2ab + 2ac + 3bx + 3cx$

$= 2a(b + c) + 3x(b + c)$

$= (b + c)(2a + 3x)$

(ii) $3ax - bx - 3ay + by =$

| | $3a$ | $-b$ |
|---|---|---|
| $x$ | $3ax$ | $-bx$ |
| $-y$ | $-3ay$ | $+by$ |

Note:

$-3ay$ is factorised as $3a(-y)$ and $+by$ is factorised as $-b(-y)$

$3ax - bx - 3ay + by = x(3a - b) -y(3a - b)$

$= (3a - b)(x - y)$

---

**Example 2**

Factorise $6x^2 + 2a - 3ax - 4x$.

$6x^2 + 2a - 3ax - 4x =$

| | $2x$ | $-a$ |
|---|---|---|
| $3x$ | $6x^2$ | $-3ax$ |
| $-2$ | $-4x$ | $+2a$ |

Note:

Rearrange the terms so that an $x$ can be factorised horizontally and vertically.

Note:

$-4x$ is factorised as $2x(-2)$ and $+2a$ is factorised as $-a(-2)$

$= (2x - a)(3x - 2)$

## Exercise 4.2

Using the array method factorise each of the following:

**1.** $a(x + 4) + b(x + 4)$

**2.** $x(2a + 3) + 4(2a + 3)$

**3.** $x(y + z) + y(y + z)$

**4.** $a(b + 2c) + 3(b + 2c)$

Write down the factors of each of the following:

**5.** $a(x - 6) + 3(x - 6)$

**6.** $2a(x + y) - 3b(x + y)$

**7.** $3x(2x - 3) + (2x - 3)$

**8.** $2a(3b - c) - (3b - c)$

**9.** $ax + ay + bx + by$

**10.** $ab + bc + ad + cd$

**11.** $ac + bc + 3a + 3b$

**12.** $mp + np + mq + nq$

**13.** $2ab + 2bc + 3ad + 3cd$

**14.** $7ax - 7bx + 3a - 3b$

**15.** $ac - bc + 2a - 2b$

**16.** $ac - bc + 2ad - 2bd$

**17.** $2ax + 3ay + 2bx + 3by$

**18.** $4x - 4y + ax - ay$

**19.** $3a - 3b + ax - bx$

**20.** $ax - 2a + 4x - 8$

**21.** $2ab - bc + 2ad - cd$

**22.** $2ax - ay + 2bx - by$

**23.** $x^2 + ax + bx + ab$

**24.** $a^2 - 2ab + ac - 2bc$

**25.** $4ay + xy - 4az - xz$

**26.** $3mx - am + 3nx - an$

**27.** $x^2 - xy + xz - yz$

**28.** $2x - 2y - cx + cy$

**29.** $3x + 3y - bx - by$

**30.** $5a + 5b - ac - bc$

**31.** $x^2 - 2x + xy - 2y$

**32.** $a^2 - 3a + ab - 3b$

**33.** $ax - a - bx + b$

**34.** $ay - 2by - az + 2bz$

**35.** $x(2a - 3b) + 2a - 3b$

**36.** $a(x + 2y) - x - 2y$

**37.** $ab - bc + ac - b^2$

**38.** $ab - 2cd - bc + 2ad$

**39.** $3a - 3b + ab - 9$

**40.** $3ax - 4by + 2bx - 6ay$

# Section 4.3  Difference of two squares

Numbers such as  1, 4, 9, 16, 25, … are called **perfect squares** as they are obtained by multiplying some whole number by itself, e.g.  $4 = 2^2, 9 = 3^2, …$

Expressions such as  $10^2 - 4^2$,  and  $x^2 - 9$  are known as the **difference of two squares**.

When you multiply $(x + a)(x - a)$, you get $x^2 - a^2$.
Thus, the factors of $x^2 - a^2$ are $(x + a)(x - a)$.

|  | $x$ | $+a$ |
|---|---|---|
| $x$ | $x^2$ | $+ax$ |
| $-a$ | $-ax$ | $-a^2$ |

$$(x + a)(x - a) = x^2 + ax - ax - a^2$$
$$= x^2 - a^2$$

$$x^2 - a^2 = (x + a)(x - a)$$

In words:   $(\text{first})^2 - (\text{second})^2 = (\text{first} + \text{second})(\text{first} - \text{second})$

---

**Example 1**

Factorise     (i)  $x^2 - 9$        (ii)  $a^2 - 25$

(i)  $x^2 - 9 = (x)^2 - (3)^2 = (x + 3)(x - 3)$

(ii)  $a^2 - 25 = (a)^2 - (5)^2 = (a + 5)(a - 5)$

---

## *Investigation:*

(i)  By using the array method show that,
$a^2 - b^2 = (a - b)(a + b)$

|  | $a$ | $-b$ |
|---|---|---|
| $a$ |  | $-ab$ |
| $+b$ | $ab$ |  |

(ii)  Using this result evaluate (without using a calculator)

| $51^2 - 49^2$ | ( | )( | ) | ( | )( | ) = |  |
|---|---|---|---|---|---|---|---|
| $76^2 - 24^2$ | ( | )( | ) | ( | )( | ) = |  |
| $293^2 - 7^2$ | ( | )( | ) | ( | )( | ) = |  |
| $27^2 - 3^2$ | ( | )( | ) | ( | )( | ) = |  |
|  |  |  |  |  |  |  |  |

Noting the pattern in the differences above add a difference of two
squares into the last line. Compare results with other students in the class.

(iii)  Using a calculator verify each result.

## Exercise 4.3

Factorise each of the following:

**1.** $x^2 - 4$ **2.** $x^2 - 16$ **3.** $y^2 - 36$ **4.** $y^2 - 100$ **5.** $a^2 - 9$

**6.** By first taking out the highest common factor, factorise fully each of the following.
(The first one is done for you.)
(i)  $3a^2 - 12 = 3(a^2 - 4) = 3(a - 2)(a + 2)$
(ii)  $5c^2 - 5d^2$ (iii)  $3a^2 - 27$ (iv)  $3x^2 - 75$ (v)  $12a^2 - 48$

Use factors to find the value of each of these:

**7.** $96^2 - 4^2$ **8.** $27^2 - 26^2$ **9.** $101^2 - 99^2$ **10.** $55^2 - 54^2$

# Section 4.4 **Factorising quadratic expressions**

An expression of the form $ax^2 + bx + c$ – where $a$, $b$ and $c$ are numbers – is called a
**quadratic expression** since the highest power of $x$ is 2.

$6 \times 4 = 24$, therefore 6 and 4 are factors of 24.

Similarly in algebra, since $(x + 5)(x + 2) = x^2 + 7x + 10$, we say that $(x + 5)$ and
$(x + 2)$ are the factors of $x^2 + 7x + 10$.

The product $(x + 5)(x + 2) =$

|     | $x$     | $+5$ |
|-----|---------|------|
| $x$ | $x^2$   | $5x$ |
| $+2$| $2x$    | $10$ |

$= x^2 + 7x + 10$

 (i)  $x^2$ is obtained from the product $x \times x$
 (ii)  10 is the product of 5 and 2, the two number
     terms
(iii)  $7x$ is obtained by adding the $x$-terms.
     i.e.  $5x$ and $2x = 7x$

We factorise a quadratic expression by 'trial and error' to find numbers such that the
terms in $x$ added give the middle term.

---

**Example 1**

Factorise $x^2 + 8x + 15$.

The factors of $x^2 + 8x + 15$ will take
the form $(x + ?)(x + ?)$.

We are looking for factors of 15
whose sum is 8.

These factors are 3 and 5.
the factors are $(x + 3)(x + 5)$.

|       | $x$    | $+5$  |
|-------|--------|-------|
| $x$   | $x^2$  | $+5x$ |
| $+3$  | $+3x$  | $+15$ |

| 15 | |
|----|----|
| 3  | 5  |
| 15 | 1  |

**Note:** To verify that the factors are correct $3x + 5x =$ middle term $= 8x$.

## Third term positive, middle term negative

If the third term of a quadratic expression is positive and the middle term is negative,
e.g. $x^2 - 8x + 15$, then the factors will take the form

$(x - ?)(x - ?)$

---

**Example 2**

Find the factors of $x^2 - 11x + 28$.

The factors of 28 which add up to
$-11$ are $-7$ and $-4$.

|       | $x$    | $-7$   |
|-------|--------|--------|
| $x$   | $x^2$  | $-7x$  |
| $-4$  | $-4x$  | $+28$  |

| 28 | |
|-----|------|
| $-1$ | $-28$ |
| $-4$ | $-7$  |
| 1    | 28    |
| 4    | 7     |

the factors are $(x - 7)(x - 4)$.

**Note:** $(-4x) + (-7x) =$ middle term $= -11x$.

## Exercise 4.4

Find the factors of each of the following:

1. $x^2 + 3x + 2$
2. $x^2 + 4x + 4$
3. $x^2 + 8x + 7$

4. $x^2 + 5x + 6$
5. $x^2 + 8x + 12$
6. $x^2 + 9x + 14$

7. $a^2 + 7a + 12$
8. $x^2 + 4x + 3$
9. $a^2 + 6a + 8$

10. $a^2 + 9a + 18$
11. $a^2 + 10a + 16$
12. $a^2 + 10a + 24$

13. $x^2 + 11x + 24$
14. $x^2 + 12x + 20$
15. $x^2 + 12x + 27$

16. $x^2 + 13x + 22$
17. $x^2 + 13x + 30$
18. $x^2 + 11x + 30$

19. $x^2 + 14x + 33$
20. $x^2 + 15x + 36$
21. $x^2 + 15x + 44$

22. $x^2 + 9x + 20$
23. $x^2 + 18x + 17$
24. $x^2 + 18x + 32$

25. $x^2 - 4x + 3$
26. $x^2 - 5x + 6$
27. $x^2 - 6x + 8$

28. $x^2 - 5x + 4$
29. $x^2 - 7x + 12$
30. $x^2 - 7x + 10$

31. $x^2 - 9x + 14$
32. $x^2 - 11x + 24$
33. $p^2 - 8p + 15$

34. $x^2 - 9x + 18$
35. $x^2 - 9x + 20$
36. $x^2 - 12x + 20$

37. $x^2 - 12x + 35$
38. $x^2 - 10x + 24$
39. $x^2 - 14x + 24$

40. $x^2 - 12x + 27$
41. $x^2 - 11x + 30$
42. $x^2 - 13x + 30$

43. $x^2 - 17x + 30$
44. $x^2 - 13x + 36$
45. $m^2 - 15m + 36$

46. $x^2 - 14x + 45$
47. $x^2 - 14x + 40$
48. $x^2 - 13x + 40$

# Section 4.5  Quadratic expressions – Third term negative ──

Take the expression $x^2 - 2x - 8$.
Here the final term is negative.
When the final term is negative, the factors will be
of the form $(x + ?)(x - ?)$   **or**   $(x - ?)(x + ?)$

|     | $x$ | $+2$ |
|-----|-----|------|
| $x$ | $x^2$ | $+2x$ |
| $-4$ | $-4x$ | $-8$ |

| $-8$ | |
|------|------|
| $-1$ | $+8$ |
| $-2$ | $+4$ |
| $-4$ | $+2$ |
| $-8$ | $+1$ |

Since we need $-2x$ when we add the
middle terms the factors are, $-4x, 2x$.

In this case, the factors are $(x + 2)(x - 4)$.  $\ldots -4x + 2x = -2x$

## Exercise 4.5

Factorise each of the following:

**1.** $x^2 - x - 2$  **2.** $x^2 - 2x - 3$  **3.** $x^2 - 3x - 4$

**4.** $x^2 + 2x - 3$  **5.** $x^2 - x - 12$  **6.** $x^2 + x - 12$

**7.** $x^2 - 4x - 12$  **8.** $x^2 - 3x - 10$  **9.** $x^2 - 9x - 10$

**10.** $x^2 - 5x - 14$  **11.** $x^2 - 2x - 15$  **12** $x^2 + 7x - 18$

**13.** $x^2 + 3x - 18$  **14.** $x^2 + 4x - 21$  **15.** $x^2 - 2x - 24$

**16.** $x^2 + 5x - 24$  **17.** $x^2 - 10x - 24$  **18.** $x^2 - x - 30$

**19.** $x^2 + 7x - 30$  **20.** $x^2 - 13x - 30$  **21.** $x^2 + 3x - 28$

**22.** $x^2 - 12x - 28$  **23.** $x^2 + 5x - 36$  **24.** $x^2 - 9x - 36$

**25.** $x^2 + 6x - 40$  **26.** $x^2 - 3x - 40$  **27.** $x^2 - 18x - 40$

**28.** $x^2 - 4x - 45$  **29.** $x^2 + 6x - 16$  **30.** $x^2 - 8x - 48$

Factorise each of the following which contain examples of the three types we have met so far:

**31.** $p^2 + 9p + 14$  **32.** $m^2 - 12m + 27$  **33.** $x^2 + 2x - 24$

**34.** $x^2 - 8x + 7$  **35.** $x^2 - 9x + 14$  **36.** $x^2 - 4x - 32$

**37.** $x^2 + 14x + 24$  **38.** $x^2 + x - 42$  **39.** $x^2 + 5x - 50$

**40.** $x^2 - 11x + 28$  **41.** $x^2 - 4x - 60$  **42** $s^2 - 17s + 60$

# Test yourself 4

1. Copy and complete each of the following:
   (i) $9x^2 + 36x = 9x($    $)$
   (ii) $5ab + 15bc = 5b($    $)$
   (iii) $6ax - 12ay = 6a($    $)$
   (iv) $6x^3 - 18xy = 6x($    $)$

2. Factorise each of these:
   (i) $7a + 7b + xa + xb$
   (ii) $a^2 - 5ab + ac - 5bc$

3. Factorise each of these:
   (i) $x^2 - 16x + 55$
   (ii) $16x^2 - 16$

4. Find the missing expressions in these statements:
   (i) $3p^2 - 6p = 3p($    $)$
   (ii) $20n^2 + 5n = 5n($    $)$
   (iii) $9x^2 - 3x = 3x($    $)$
   (iv) $5d^2 - 15d = 5d($    $)$

5. ① 
   | | $n$ | $+3$ |
   |---|---|---|
   | $($    $)$ | $n^2$ ② | |
   | ④ $($    $)$ | ③ | $3$ |

   By completing the array in the order 1, 2, 3, 4, find the second factor of $n^2 + 4n + 3$.
   i.e. complete the following
   $(n + 3)($    $) = n^2 + 4n + 3$

6. Using an array complete each of these:
   (i) $(n + 4)($    $) = n^2 + 8n + 16$
   (ii) $(n - 2)($    $) = n^2 + 4n - 12$
   (iii) $(n - 3)($    $) = n^2 - 11n + 24$

7. (i) Factorise $144 - b^2$.
   (ii) Use the difference of two squares to evaluate $53^2 - 47^2$.

8. Complete the following:
   (i) $2xy - 6yz = 2y($    $)$
   (ii) $3x^2y - 9xyz = 3xy($    $)$

9. Factorise each of these:
   (i) $6ax - 3bx + 2ay - by$
   (ii) $x^2 - 15x + 54$

10. (i) Factorise $6x^2 - 24$.
    (ii) Use factors to find the value of $93^2 - 87^2$.

11. Factorise each of these:
    (i) $8a + 12b - 16c$
    (ii) $6x^2 - 18x$

12. Factorise the following:
    (i) $5x + xy + y^2 + 5y$
    (ii) $x^2 - 13x + 22$

13. (i) Factorise $16 - a^2$.
    (ii) Find the factor that is common to $x^2 - x - 20$ and $x^2 - 25$.

## Assignment:

Using the array method twice, find the expression whose factors are:

**(a)** $(x + 2)(x + 4)(x + 5)$

**Step 1.**

$(x + 2)(x + 4) =$

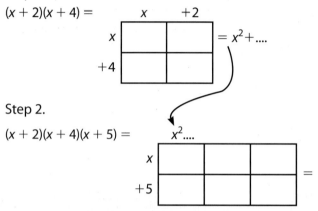

$= x^2 + ....$

**Step 2.**

$(x + 2)(x + 4)(x + 5) =$

$x^2 ....$

$=$

**(b)** Using the array method, expand $(x + 1)(x + 6)(x - 4)$

# Applied Arithmetic

*chapter* **5**

## From first year, you will recall how to:

- find the percentage of a quantity,
- increase or decrease a quantity by a percentage,
- calculate VAT,
- calculate percentage profit or loss.

## In this chapter, you will learn to:

- calculate household bill charges,
- apply standard rate income tax charges,
- evaluate net pay after deductions,
- convert between different currencies,
- apply compound interest to investments and loans,
- find the rate or principal of an investment or loan,
- calculate deprecation.

## Section 5.1  Household bills

In this section we will deal with various household bills such as electricity, gas and telephone bills. We will also deal with the cost of postage, holidays and insurance as well as car hire and mobile phone charges.

Each utility bill shows:

❯ how many units of energy were used,

❯ the cost of each unit,

❯ extra charges e.g. standing charges, levies,

❯ VAT

---

**Example 1**

Calculate the electricity bill from
the information given opposite:

| | |
|---|---|
| Standing charge: | €23.80 |
| Number of units used: | 1025 |
| Cost per unit: | 23 cent |
| VAT on total bill at 10%. | |

1025 units @ 23c per unit = 1025 × 23c

| | | |
|---|---|---|
| | = | €235.75 |
| Standing charge | = | 23.80 |
| Total | = | €259.55 |
| VAT @ 10% | = | 25.96 |
| Total (including VAT) | = | €285.51 |

[€259.55 ÷ 10 = €25.96]

---

## Exercise 5.1

**1.** Find the total of this garage bill:

| | |
|---|---|
| 7 litres of oil at €8.30 per litre | = |
| 20 litres of petrol at €1.65 per litre | = |
| 4 brake pads at €35.40 each | = |
| 3 hours labour at €21 per hour | = |
| 4 tyres at €74.80 each | = _____ |

Total: €

**2.** Find the total amount of this bill, including VAT:

| | |
|---|---|
| 9 litres of paint @ €10.50 a litre | = |
| 3 brushes at €8.30 each | = |
| 6 rolls of wallpaper at €14.25 each | = |
| 3 packets of paste at €6.90 each | = |
| 10 sheets of sandpaper at 95c each | = _____ |
| | = € |
| VAT at 20% | = |
| Total: | = € |

**3.** Find the total of this bill from a garden centre:

| | |
|---|---|
| 7 rose bushes at €9.30 each | = |
| 5 shrubs at €14.40 each | = |
| $4\frac{1}{2}$ dozen bulbs at €8.40 per dozen | = |
| 2 spades at €35.50 each | = |

800 grams of grass-seed at €4.80 per 100 g =

12 kg of fertiliser at €4.55 per kg          =  _____

VAT at $12\frac{1}{2}\%$ =

Total = €

**4.** A plumber goes to a builders' providers and buys the following items:

30 metres of copper piping at €6.80 a metre

12 taps at €28.30 each

16 copper fittings at €7.30 each

5 radiators at €184 each

Find the amount he has to pay if he is given a discount of 20%.

**5.** An electricity bill shows the following:

| Meter Readings | |
|---|---|
| **Present Reading** | **Previous Reading** |
| 87642 | 86971 |

(i) How many units were used?

(ii) Each unit costs 21c. Find the total cost of the units used.

**6.** A householder's electricity bill is charged in the following way:
- A standing charge of €26.80
- 1256 units at 23c per unit
- VAT at 10% on the total bill.

Find the total amount of the electricity bill.

**7.** Mrs Heaton received a bill of €130.80 for the electricity she used in a two-month period. The bill included a standing charge of €25.20. If each unit of electricity cost 22 cent, find how many units were used.

**8.** An electricity bill contains the following information:

Present meter reading:     38429 units

Previous meter reading:     36738 units

Standing charge €18.40

Find the total amount of the bill, including the standing charge, if each unit of electricity costs 23 cent.

**9.** A supplier charges for electricity supplied in the following way:

    *Day rate*: 24c per unit     *Night rate*: 10.5c per unit

Calculate the electricity bill for each of the following users based on the unit rates given above:

| Name | No. of units used at *day rate* | No. of units used at *night rate* | Standing Charge |
|---|---|---|---|
| D. Maher | 420 | 130 | €28.90 |
| G. O'Gorman | 560 | 370 | €25.60 |

**10.** A refrigerator uses 1.2 units of electricity a day (24 hours).
What does it cost to operate a refrigerator for a year (365 days) if each unit of electricity costs 15c?

**11.** Rachel's gas meter was read on 1 March.
The reading was | 1 | 7 | 4 | 2 |

92 days later, the meter was read again.
The reading was | 1 | 9 | 5 | 6 |

Calculate the total gas bill that Rachel will have to pay for the 92 days from 1 March, using the charges given on the right.

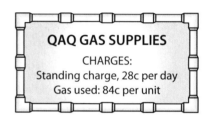

**QAQ GAS SUPPLIES**
CHARGES:
Standing charge, 28c per day
Gas used: 84c per unit

**12.** A householder is charged for the gas that he uses in the following way:
Standing charge: €26.30.
Reducing rate for therms used:
    0–20 therms: €1.40 per therm
    21–40 therms: €1.26 per therm
    over 40 therms: €1.06 per therm.
Calculate the householder's bill for a period in which he uses 54 therms.

**13.** The table on the right gives the postage rates for parcels to any part of Ireland.
Find the total cost of sending the following parcels.
> 2 parcels weighing 3.4 kg each
> 4 parcels weighing 1.6 kg each
> 1 parcel weighing 7.1 kg
> 2 parcels weighing 4.8 kg each.

| Weight not over | Cost |
|---|---|
| 1 kg | €6.50 |
| 3 kg | €9.80 |
| 5 kg | €12.60 |
| 10 kg | €17.60 |

**14.** John hired this car for 8 days and drove 850 kilometres. How much did the hire of the car cost him?

**SPEEDY'S CAR HIRE**

€70 per day & 40c per kilometre

**15.** Alan earns €12.80 per hour for working a basic week of 38 hours.
Overtime is paid at 'time and a half'.
The table below shows the hours Alan worked last week.

| Day | Monday | Tuesday | Wednesday | Thursday | Friday |
|---|---|---|---|---|---|
| Hours | 10 | 8 | 7 | 9 | 12 |

   (i)   How many hours overtime did he work last week?
   (ii)  Calculate his total pay for last week.
   (iii) If Alan earned €582.40 in a particular week, how many hours overtime did he work that week?

**16.** The charges for Olivia's bill-pay phone per month are as follows.

   Fixed charge:      €15
   Call charges:      First 50 minutes free
                      Additional minutes, 18 cent per minute
   Text messages:     First 100 text messages free
                      Additional text messages, 14 cent each.

During June, Olivia used 120 minutes call-time and sent 128 text messages.
   (i)  Calculate the total charge for all her phone calls.
   (ii) Find the total amount of her bill for the month.

**17.** *Eircom* charges 15c for each metered unit used. If each local telephone call uses 1 unit every 3 minutes (or part thereof) during peak time, calculate the cost of each of these local calls made at peak time:

|       | Starting time | Finishing time |
|---|---|---|
| (i)   | 9.07 a.m.     | 9.12 a.m.      |
| (ii)  | 12.49 p.m.    | 1.04 p.m.      |
| (iii) | 11.54 a.m.    | 12.16 p.m.     |

**18.** A telephone call to Australia is charged in the following way:

   €5.40 for the first 3 minutes, and
   €1.75 for each minute (or part of minute) over 3 minutes

Find the cost of a call to Australia which lasts $8\frac{1}{2}$ minutes.

**19.** The table below gives the cost per adult for a two-week holiday in a hotel, apartment or villa:

| Accommodation | May | June | July | August |
|---|---|---|---|---|
| *Hotel Loredo* | €1120 | €1280 | €1390 | €1470 |
| *Vista Apartments* | €760 | €850 | €930 | €1020 |
| *Centra Villas* | €830 | €900 | €970 | €1080 |
| Children under 16 years of age: Half price | | | | |

Find the total cost of each of the following holidays:
   (i)   two adults in *Hotel Loredo* for 2 weeks in July
  (ii)   four adults in *Centra Villas* for 2 weeks in August
 (iii)   two adults and two children aged 8 years and 12 years in *Vista Apartments* for 2 weeks in May
 (iv)   two adults and three children aged 10, 11 and 17 years in *Hotel Loredo* for 2 weeks in August

**20.** The table below gives the premiums for insuring buildings and contents as quoted by the *Coverall Insurance Company*.

| | Buildings per €1000 | Contents per €1000 |
|---|---|---|
| Area 1 | €2.80 | €7.40 |
| Area 2 | €3.20 | €8.50 |
| Area 3 | €3.60 | €10.25 |
| Area 4 | €3.84 | €11.10 |

Based on the table above, calculate the premium for insuring each of the following:
   (i)   a house worth €320,000 in Area 3
  (ii)   a house worth €260,000 with contents worth €25,000 in Area 4
 (iii)   a house worth €220,000 with contents worth €42,000 in Area 1
 (iv)   a house worth €180,000 with contents worth €32,000 in Area 2.

An insurance company charges €5.40 per €1000 value to insure a premises against fire. If the owner of a premises pays €1404 to the insurance company, find the value of this premises.

**21.** Jane's electricity bill is shown below.

Copy and complete to find the total bill for May / June.

| Current reading | Previous reading | Unit usage | Unit price | Amount |
|---|---|---|---|---|
| 14305 | 13445 | | 0.17 | |
| Savings | (Dual fuel /DD/ Online Billing) | | | €20 |
| Standing charge  65 days | | @ €0.4 / day | | |
| PSO Levy | May / June | | | €15 |
| Sub-total | | | | |
| Vat @ 13.5% | | | | |
| Total | | | | |

## Investigation:

Special Offer
3 lunches for €25

Jill, Nadia and Alan went for lunch.

They each paid the waiter €10 for their lunch.
€30 in total.

When the waiter went to the till he realised that he had forgotten the special offer and took €5 out of the till to pay Jill and her friends. Since €5 does not divide evenly by 3 he put €2 in his pocket and returned €1 to each of the friends. So each paid €9 for their meal.

$3 \times €9 = €27 + €2$ in the waiter's pocket $= €29$.

Where is the missing €1?

# Section 5.2  Applying percentages

Although in most cases we will use a calculator to find a percentage of a number it is important to understand the mathematical processes involved.

The calculator first changes the percentage into a decimal and then multiplies the decimal by the required number.

**Changing percentages to decimals.**

To find 4% multiply by 0.04

To find 12% multiply by 0.12

To find 87% multiply by 0.87

To find 104% multiply by 1.04

To find 187% multiply by 1.87

Using a calculator to find **104% of 80**

**104 … shift … ( … × … 80 … =  83.2**

**1.04 × 80 = 83.2**

## 1. Value-added tax (VAT)

**Value-added tax** or **VAT** is a government tax which is added to many of the things that we buy. In most shops, the marked price of an item includes VAT and so we do not have to calculate it.

Sometimes, the prices of more expensive items such as television sets, commercial vehicles and furniture are given without VAT. In these cases, the shopkeeper calculates the VAT amount and adds it to the price of the item.

If an article is priced at €280 plus VAT at 23%, the full price can be worked out as follows:

1% of €280 = €2.80

23% of €280 = €2.80 × 23 = €64.40

∴  the full price = €280 + €64.40

= €344.40

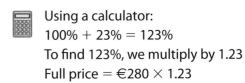 Using a calculator:

100% + 23% = 123%

To find 123%, we multiply by 1.23

Full price = €280 × 1.23

= €344.40

---

**Example 1**

The rate of VAT on bicycles is 23%.

(i)  Find the selling price of a bicycle priced at €360 + VAT.

(ii)  Another bicycle is advertised at €615 which includes VAT. Find the price of this bicycle before VAT was added.

(i)  23% of €360 = €360 × 0.23 = €82.80

∴   the selling price of the bicycle = €360 + €82.80

= €442.80

Or

Adding 23% gives 123%

123% of €360 = €360 × 1.23 = €442.80  ... as above.

(ii)  €615 represents 123% of the price before VAT is added.

$$123\% = €615$$

$$1\% = €\frac{615}{123}$$

$$100\% = €\frac{615}{123} \times \frac{100}{1}$$

$$100\% = €500$$

∴   the price of the bicycle before VAT was added was €500.

## 2. Percentage profit or loss

When dealing with percentage profit or loss, we base this percentage on the **cost price**, unless otherwise stated.

$$\text{Percentage profit} = \frac{\text{Profit}}{\text{Cost price}} \times \frac{100}{1}\%; \quad \text{Percentage loss} = \frac{\text{Loss}}{\text{Cost price}} \times \frac{100}{1}\%$$

## Example 2

(i)  A hardware store buys lawnmowers for €480 and sells them for €576. Calculate the percentage profit the store makes on the lawnmowers.

(ii)  By selling washing machines for €650, an electrical store makes a profit of 25%. What did the store pay for these washing machines?

(i)  Profit = €576 − €480 = €96

$$\text{Percentage profit} = \frac{\text{Profit}}{\text{Cost Price}} \times \frac{100}{1}\%$$

$$= \frac{96}{480} \times \frac{100}{1} = 20\%$$

The percentage profit = 20%.

(ii)  €650 represents 125% of the cost price  ... 25% profit margin.

$$\therefore \quad 125\% = €650$$

$$1\% = \frac{€650}{125}$$

$$100\% = \frac{€650}{125} \times \frac{100}{1}$$

$$= €520$$

$\therefore$  the store paid €520 for the washing machines.

## Exercise 5.2

**1.** Express each of the percentages as decimals:
   (i)  6%          (ii)  8%          (iii)  $7\frac{1}{2}\%$          (iv)  $9\frac{1}{2}\%$          (v)  10%
   (vi)  13%        (vii)  $12\frac{1}{2}\%$        (viii)  106%        (ix)  112%        (x)  84%

**2.**  (i)  Increase 200 by 10%.                    (ii)  Increase 120 by 20%.
       (iii)  Increase 250 by 4%.                    (iv)  Decrease 120 by 15%.

**3.**  (i)  Find 80% of 400.                         (ii)  Find 5% of 360.
       (iii)  Find 185% of 600.                       (iv)  Find $12\frac{1}{2}\%$ of 120.

**4.** Find the selling price of each of the following:
   (i)  An iPad costing €650 + VAT at 23%.
   (ii)  A games console costing €120 + VAT at 21%.
   (iii)  A set of tyres costing €300 + VAT at $13\frac{1}{2}\%$.
   (iv)  A patio furniture set costing €1200 + VAT at 15%.

**5.** A meal for 4 people cost €110 + VAT at 9%.
   Find the cost of the meal after VAT is added.

**6.** An hotel bill amounts to €220 after VAT at 10% is added.
   Find the amount of the bill before VAT is added.

**7.** The selling price of a television set is €984.
   If this includes VAT at 23%, find the price before VAT is added.

**8.** An electricity bill amounts to €135 after VAT at $12\frac{1}{2}\%$ is added.
   Find the amount of the bill before VAT is added.

**9.** Write out the amounts that should go in the highlighted boxes marked A to G.

| Cost price | Profit or loss | Selling price |
|---|---|---|
| €176 | €8.80 profit | A |
| €460 | €92 loss | B |
| €1.80 | €0.63 profit | C |
| D | €5000 loss | €25 000 |
| E | €4.20 profit | €42 |
| F | €2560 loss | €8000 |
| €3680 | G | €4800 |

**10.** A greengrocer buys oranges for 80c and sells them for €1. Find his percentage profit.

**11.** Jack bought a painting for €600 and sold it for €660. Find
  (i) his profit      (ii) his percentage profit.

**12.** A menswear store buys jackets for €320 and sells them for €400. Find the percentage profit the store makes.

**13.** A jeweller bought an engagement ring for €1200 and sold it at a profit of 15%. Find the sale price of the ring.

**14.** By selling television sets for €720, a store makes a profit of 20%.
  (i) What did the store pay for the television sets?
  (ii) If the store sold the television sets for €690, what percentage profit would it make?
  (iii) If the store sold the television sets for €570, what percentage loss would it make?

**15.** A shop owner marks everything up by 30%. If she sells an article for €78, find both the cost price and the profit on the article.

**16.** A garden centre buys azaleas for €11.50 and sells them for €14.95. Calculate the percentage profit it makes.

**17.** In a sale, the marked prices are reduced by 30%.
  (i) Calculate the sale price of a jacket if the marked price is €350.
  (ii) Find the marked price of a dress if the sale price is €168.

**18.** By selling a laptop for €1150, a store makes a profit of 25%.
  (i) What did the store pay for the laptop?
  (ii) At what price should the laptop be sold to make a profit of 20%?

**19.** When an item is sold for €176, the profit is 10% on the cost price. When the selling price is increased to €192, calculate the percentage profit on the cost price.

**20.** A greengrocer buys 30 boxes of strawberries at €5.25 each and sells 28 of them at a profit of 30%. If the remaining two boxes are unsaleable, find his percentage profit on the deal.

**21.** By selling a jacket for €416, a store makes a profit of 30%.
   (i)   Find the cost price of the jacket.
   (ii)  If the selling price of the jacket is reduced by 10% in a sale, calculate the percentage profit the store now has on the cost price.

**22.** Philip wants to buy an i-pad. He tries three different stores.

Which store offers the best price for the i-pad?

## Section 5.3  Interest

If we invest money in a bank, building society or credit union, we are paid for the use of this money.

The money we receive is called **interest**.

The sum of money we invest is called the **principal**.

If we are paid 6% interest, we receive €6 each year for every €100 we invest.

The percentage interest that we receive is called the **rate**.

If you invest €100 for 1 year at 8%, you will receive €8 interest.

You will then have €108 in your account at the end of the year.

The sum of money you have in your account at the end of any year is called the **amount**.

> Amount = Principal + Interest

---

**Example 1**

€350 is invested for 1 year at 6% per annum (year).
Find the amount at the end of the year.

$$\text{Amount} = 106\% \text{ of } €350$$
$$= €350 \times 1.06$$
$$= €371$$

---

## Exercise 5.3

1. Without using a calculator, write down,
   - (i) 6% of €100
   - (ii) 8% of €100
   - (iii) 4% of €200
   - (iv) 7% of €300

2. Use your calculator to find
   - (i) 4% of €600
   - (ii) 7% of €750
   - (iii) 9% of €950
   - (iv) 11% of €1200

3. Use your calculator to find
   - (i) $4\frac{1}{2}$% of €600
   - (ii) $8\frac{1}{2}$% of €1500
   - (iii) $7\frac{1}{2}$% of €1380
   - (iv) $12\frac{1}{2}$% of €2400

4. Use your calculator to find
   - (i) 108% of €300
   - (ii) 106% of €900
   - (iii) 104% of €1600
   - (iv) 112% of €1750
   - (v) 115% of €1050
   - (vi) 110% of €680.

5. Find the interest earned on each of the following:
   - (i) €300 after 1 year at 3%
   - (ii) €700 after 1 year at 6%
   - (iii) €1200 after 1 year at 8%
   - (iv) €1400 after 1 year at 4%
   - (v) €600 after 1 year at 2%
   - (vi) €2000 after 1 year at 6%.

## Section 5.4 Compound interest

Jack invested €500 in a credit union at 6% per annum

His interest for the first year was €30

At the end of the first year, he then had €530 in his account

For the second year, €530 earned interest at 6%

$$6\% \text{ of } €530 = €530 \times 0.06$$
$$= €31.80$$

Notice that the interest (€31.80) for the second year is greater than the interest (€30) for the first year.

This happened because the interest for the first year itself earned interest during the second year.

∴ the amount at the end of the second year is

$$€530 + €31.80 = €561.80$$

This kind of interest is called **compound interest**.

The basic method for calculating compound interest is illustrated in the following example.

## Example 1

€1200 is invested for 3 years at 4% per annum compound interest.
What will the investment amount to?

| | |
|---|---|
| Principal for the first year | $= €1200$ |
| Interest for the first year | $= 4\% \text{ of } €1200$ |
| | $= 1200 \times 0.04 = €48$ |
| Principal for the second year | $= €1200 + €48 = €1248$ |
| Interest for the second year | $= 4\% \text{ of } €1248$ |
| | $= 1248 \times 0.04 = €49.92$ |
| Principal for the third year | $= €1248 + €49.92 = €1297.92$ |
| Interest for the third year | $= 4\% \text{ of } €1297.92$ |
| | $= 1297.92 \times 0.04$ |
| | $= 51.9168 = €51.92$ |
| $\therefore$  Amount at end of third year | $= €1297.92 + €51.92$ |
| | $= €1349.84$ |

When calculating compound interest it is very useful to use a table format as the next example shows.

## Example 2

€1800 is invested for 3 years at 3% per annum.
Calculate (i) the compound interest earned and (ii) the final amount.

| Year | Principal | Rate | Interest | Final Amount |
|:---:|:---:|:---:|:---:|:---:|
| 1 | €1800 | 3% | $(1800 \times 0.03) = €54$ | €1854 |
| 2 | €1854 | 3% | $(1854 \times 0.03) = €55.62$ | €1909.62 |
| 3 | €1909.62 | 3% | $(1909.62 \times 0.03) = €57.29$ | €1966.91 |

(i)  Compound interest earned $= €54 + €55.62 + €57.29 = €166.91$
   Note; we can also calculate the compound interest by
   €1966.91 $-$ €1800 $= €166.91$.
(ii)  The final amount $= €1966.91$

## Exercise 5.4

**1.** By copying and completing the following chart, find (i) the compound interest (ii) the final amount when €400 is invested for 2 years at 6%. Give your answer correct to the nearest cent.

| Year | Principal | Rate | Interest | Final Amount |
|------|-----------|------|----------|--------------|
| 1 | €400 | 6% | (400 × 0.06) = | € |
| 2 | | 6% | | € |

**2.** Using the following chart find the compound interest on €800 invested for 2 years at 8%.

Give your answer correct to the nearest cent.

| Year | Principal | Rate | Interest | Final Amount |
|------|-----------|------|----------|--------------|
| 1 | €800 | 8% | | € |
| 2 | | 8% | | € |

Find the compound interest on each of the following.

Give your answers correct to the nearest cent, where necessary.

**3.** €900 for 2 years at 5%

**4.** €1000 for 2 years at 9%

**5.** €700 for 2 years at 4%

**6.** €850 for 2 years at 10%

**7.** €800 for 3 years at 5%

**8.** €1200 for 2 years at 12%

**9.** €700 for 2 years at 11%

**10.** €1800 for 3 years at 4%

**11.** Find, correct to the nearest euro, the compound interest on €840 for 2 years at 7% per annum.

**12.** Find what €1200 will amount to if invested for two years at 12% per annum compound interest.

**13.** A woman invests €1500 in a building society for three years at 5% per annum compound interest. How much has she in the society at the end of the three years?

**14.** €1400 was invested for two years at compound interest.

The rate of interest for the first year was 8% and the rate for the second year was 10%.

Calculate the amount at the end of the two years.

**15.** A farmer borrowed €12 000 from a bank at 9% per annum compound interest. What did he owe the bank at the end of three years?

**16.** Ella invested her savings of €12 000 in a bank for 3 years. For the first year the interest rate was 3%. For the second year the rate increased to 4% and for the third year it increased further to 6%. At the end of the second year Ella withdrew €500 to pay for a holiday.

By copying and completing the chart below find how much Ella had in the bank at the end of the three years.

| Year | Principal | Rate | Interest | Final Amount | Withdrawal |
|------|-----------|------|----------|--------------|------------|
| 1 | €12 000 | 3% | | € | |
| 2 | | 4% | | € | €500 |
| 3 | | 6% | | € | |

**17.** (i) What percentage of €2000 is €15?

(ii) €20 is the interest earned on €3000 in the local credit union for 1 year, find the rate of interest.

**18.** (i) Find €30 as a percentage of €2500,

(ii) €12 000 invested for 1 year earns €45 in interest. What rate of interest was used?

**19.** Copy and complete the chart of Tom savings over 3 years as shown below:

| Year | Principal | Rate | Interest | Final Amount |
|------|-----------|------|----------|--------------|
| 1 | €1200 | | | €1236 |
| 2 | €1236 | | | €1273.08 |
| 3 | €1273.08 | | | €1311.27 |

# Section 5.5  Income tax

Most wage and salary earners pay a portion of their wages or income to the state.

The money is deducted from their wages by their employers and passed on to the Revenue Commissioners.

Money paid to the state in this way is called **income tax**.

Workers pay income tax on **all** their income at one of two rates.

These rates are called the **Standard Rate** and the **Higher Rate**.

The Standard Rate is generally around 20% and the Higher Rate is around 40%.

In this chapter we will deal only with the standard rate.

At the beginning of the year every worker gets a **tax credit** certificate.

This gives the amount of money that a person can deduct from his **gross tax** every week or month. The employer subtracts the tax credit from the gross tax to get the **tax payable**.

**Take-home pay** = Gross pay − Tax payable

**Tax payable** = gross tax − tax credit

## Example 1

A printer has a weekly wage of €860.
He pays income tax on all his wage at the standard rate of 21%.
If he has a tax credit of €66 a week, find how much income tax he pays.

Gross tax  = 21% of €860
      = €860 × 0.21 = €180.60
Tax payable  = gross tax − tax credit
      = €180.60 − €66
      = €114.60
The printer pays €114.60 income tax each week.

## Exercise 5.5

**1.** Aaron's weekly wage is €800.
His tax credit is €90 a week.
He pays income tax at the rate of 20%.
Copy and complete the table on the right
to find Aaron's take-home pay.

| Gross pay | €800 |
|---|---|
| Tax @ 20% | …… |
| Tax credit | €90 |
| Tax payable | …… |
| Take-home pay | …… |

**2.** Helen's gross pay for the year is €34 800.
Her tax credit is €2585.
She pays income tax at the rate of 22%.
Copy and complete the table on the right.

| Gross pay | |
|---|---|
| Tax @ 22% | |
| Tax credit | |
| Tax payable | |
| Take-home pay | |

**3.** Copy and complete the following:

Weekly wage       = €600
Tax @ 20% on all income = €600 × 0.2 = €…
Tax credits       = €42
Tax payable       = €… − €42 = €….

4. Leah has a weekly wage of €770.
   Her weekly tax credit is €72 and the standard rate of tax is 25%.
   How much income tax does she pay each week?

5. Conor has a monthly wage of €3200.
   His monthly tax credit is €280 and the standard rate of tax is 22%.
   Find how much income tax he pays each month.

6. Elaine has a weekly wage of €920.
   Her weekly tax credit is €84 and the standard rate of tax is 24%.
   How much income tax does she pay each week?

7. Jill has an annual salary of €42 000.
   Her annual tax credit is €3600 and the standard rate of tax is 22%.
   How much income tax does she pay for the year?

8. A carpenter has a weekly wage of €1050.
   His weekly tax credit is €78 and the standard rate of income tax is 24%.
   (i)  Calculate how much income tax he pays each week.
   (ii) What is his net pay (i.e. take-home pay) for the week?

9. Emma is paid €10.40 per hour for a 35-hour working week.
   For each hour over 35 hours, she is paid $1\frac{1}{2}$ times the normal hourly rate.
   Her tax credit for the week is €68 and the standard rate of tax is 26%.
   If in a particular week she worked 45 hours, find
   (i)   her gross wage for the week
   (ii)  the amount of income tax she pays
   (iii) her take-home pay for the week.

10. John White is a factory manager and he earns €54 000 a year.
    His yearly tax credit is €4300 and the standard rate of income tax is 24%.
    He also makes a pension contribution of 6% of his salary.
    (i)   Find his pension contribution for the year.
    (ii)  How much income tax does he pay for the year?
    (iii) Find his net pay after income tax and pension contribution have been deducted.

11. Padraic's yearly salary is €48 000.
    Using the information on his salary
    card find:
    (i)  Total monthly deductions,
    (ii) Monthly take home pay.

    **P. Sweeney**
    Tax rate 20%
    Yearly tax credit = €2600
    Fixed monthly pension deductions of €120

**12.** Jeanne earns €46 000 a year. Her yearly tax credit is €3800 and the standard rate of tax is 20%. She is paid in 26 fortnightly payments and has fixed deductions of €140 per fortnight.
Find her take home pay per fortnight.

## Section 5.6 Currency transactions

When we visit a country that does not use the euro, we generally change our euro into the currency of that country.

In Britain, their money is pounds sterling (£).

In the USA, money is in US dollars (US$).

If you visit a foreign exchange counter, you will generally see displayed the amounts of other currencies that you will receive for €1. An example of such a table is shown on the right.

| €1 = | |
|---|---|
| Sterling | 0.85 |
| US dollar | 1.40 |
| Japanese yen | 110 |
| Swiss franc | 1.3 |

When working out how much of one currency you should get in exchange for another, always put the currency you **require** on the **right-hand side**.

---

**Example 1**

If €1 = $1.4 and €1 = 110 yen, find
  (i)  how many dollars you would get for €400
  (ii) how many euro you would get for 5000 yen.

(i)  €1 = $1.4
  $\therefore$  €400 = $1.4 × 400          You require dollars; have
           = $560          dollars on the right.

(ii) 110 yen = €1
        1 yen = €$\frac{1}{110}$
     5000 yen = 5000 × $\frac{1}{110}$ = $\frac{5000}{110}$ = €45.4545

           = €45.45          Note: All currency answers are
  $\therefore$  5000 yen = €45.45          rounded to 2 decimal places.

---

## Exercise 5.6

**1.** If €1 = $1.45 and €1 = 115 yen,
  (i)  how many dollars would you get for €300
  (ii) how many yen would you get for €750?

2. If €1 = 1.3 US dollars, find
   (i) how many dollars you would get for €450
   (ii) how many euro you would get for 800 dollars.

3. If €1 = 120 yen, find
   (i) how many yen you would receive for €900
   (ii) how many euro you would receive for 9000 yen.

4. Given that €1 = £0.80 sterling, find
   (i) how many pounds sterling you would get for €1200
   (ii) how many euro you would get for £600.

5. On a visit to Switzerland, a person bought a leather jacket
   for 560 Swiss francs.
   If €1 = 1.4 Swiss francs, find the cost of the jacket in euro.

6. If €1 = 1.4 Canadian dollars,
   (i) how many Canadian dollars would you get for €3500?
   (ii) how many euro would you get for 5600 Canadian dollars?

7. If €1 = $1.4 and €1 = £0.85 sterling,
   (i) find in euro the cost of a camera which is priced in New York at $350
   (ii) find in euro the cost of a watch in London priced at £360.

8. If €1 = 9.2 Swedish krona, find
   (i) how much in Swedish krona would you get for €750?
   (ii) how much in euro you would get for 1500 krona?

9. A Swiss visitor exchanged 4200 Swiss francs for euro at a bureau de change.
   The rate of exchange was €1 = 1.45 Swiss francs.
   Find, correct to the nearest euro, what the visitor received if the bureau charged
   1% commission.

10. If €1 = 9.5 South African rand, find
    (i) the price in euro of a car in South Africa with a marked price of 64 000 rand
    (ii) the cost in rand of a flight from Dublin to Cape Town if the quoted price is €840.
        Give your answer to part (i) correct to the nearest euro.

11. A bank displays the following sign
    above the foreign currency desk.
    Tom changed €800 for his trip to
    Japan. How many yen did he receive?
    He changed 2080 yen back into euro
    when he returned. How many euro did he receive?

    Foreign Exchange:

    |      | We buy | We sell |
    |------|--------|---------|
    | Yen  | 130    | 127     |

## Test yourself 5

1. Karen is arranging a picnic lunch for 8 people.
   She spends €36.20 on sandwiches, €8.40 on crisps and €15.40 on drinks.
   - (i) What is the total cost of the picnic?
   - (ii) The 8 people agree to share the total cost equally.
     How much does each person pay?

2. Caroline buys a painting for €800 and sells it for €1040.
   What is her percentage profit?

3. A householder's electricity bill is charged in the following way:
   - › A standing charge of €23.40
   - › 1256 units at 22c per unit
   - › VAT at 10% on the total bill.

   Find the total amount of the electricity bill.

4. Find the gross wage of each of the following workers if they all receive *time and a half* after 40 hours work:
   - (i) A van driver who works 45 hours at €15.40 per hour
   - (ii) A plumber who works 48 hours at €18 per hour

5. Mrs Moore received a bill for €176.24 for the electricity used during a two-month period. This included a fixed charge of €22.40. If each unit of electricity cost 24c, find how many units of electricity she used.

6. Here is the menu at the *Red Robin Cafe*.
   - (i) Jack bought 3 burgers, 3 french fries and 2 soft drinks.
     How much did he pay?
   - (ii) Jill bought 3 cheeseburgers and 3 soft drinks.
     What change did she get out of €30?

   | The Red Robin Cafe | |
   | --- | --- |
   | Burger | €4.20 |
   | Cheese burger | €5.10 |
   | French fries | €2.70 |
   | Soft drinks | €1.95 |

7. Barry has a weekly wage of €620. He has a tax credit of €34 and he pays income tax on all his wages at the standard rate of 22%.
   Find how much income tax he pays each week.

**8.** A gas company charges the following *reducing rate* for the gas used by domestic consumers:

| | |
|---|---|
| First 585 kWh per two months | 12c per kWh |
| Next 585 kWh per two months | 8c per kWh |
| All other gas each two months | 6c per kWh |

In a two-month period, Mrs O'Leary used 1476 kWh of gas.
If the standing charge on her bill was €45.20, calculate the amount of her bill after VAT at 15% was added.
Give your answer correct to the nearest euro.

**9.** Find the compound interest earned on €900 for 2 years at 6% per annum.

**10.** A car may be rented by either of the following methods:

    A:  €85 per day with no extra charges
    B:  €35 per day and 60c for each km travelled.

A man wanted to rent a car for 2 weeks and travel 1200 km. Find
(i)  how much he would pay by each method
(ii)  how much he would save by taking the cheaper method.

**11.** If €1 = 40 Thai baht, find
(i)  how many baht can be exchanged for €1800
(ii)  how much 2200 baht are worth in euro.

**12.** €4500 was invested for 2 years at compound interest.
The rate for the first year was 8% and for the second year 6%.
Find the total interest earned.

**13.** Find the percentage increase in each of these:
(i)  From €25 to €28.50          (ii)  From 2 metres to 2.14 metres.

**14.** Jean has an annual income of €42 000.
Her tax credit for the year is €3200.
She pays income tax at the rate of 24%.
(i)  Find how much income tax she pays in the year.
(ii)  Find her take-home pay for the year.

**15.** Every percentage increase or decrease corresponds to a multiplier.
Match these percentage changes to their multipliers.

**A** Increase by 76%     **B** Decrease by 24%

$\times$ 1.24     $\times$ 0.76

**C** Increase by 24%     **D** Decrease by 76%

$\times$ 0.8     $\times$ 1.76

**E** Increase by 20%     **F** Decrease by 20%

$\times$ 0.24     $\times$ 1.2

**16.** To hire a car, a person has to pay €390 per week, plus 22 cent for each kilometre travelled.
  (i)  Find the cost of hiring the car for 2 weeks if 960 km were travelled.
  (ii) A tourist hired a car for two weeks and paid €1275.
       How many kilometres did she travel?

**17.** Neil and nine of his friends plan a game of golf followed by a set meal.
The prices are as set out below:

Golf

€30 per person
20% off for groups of 10 or more

Set meal

€25 per person    or
€60 for a group of 3 people

Neil has €480 to pay for all the golf and the meals. The money left over is to be given as a tip.
How much will be left for the tip?

# Assignment:

In Applied Arithmetic, many terms are used in discussing different problems. It is very important to have a clear understanding of these terms.

Research each of the following terms and make a list of the agreed definitions from your group.

| | |
|---|---|
| **Salary** | |
| **Wages** | |
| **Income** | |
| **Commission** | |
| **Overtime** | |
| **Piece work** | |
| **Income tax** | |
| **Tax credit** | |
| **Tax payable** | |
| **Net pay** | |
| **Take-home pay** | |
| **Discount** | |
| **Budget** | |
| **Profit** | |
| **Loss** | |
| **Investment** | |
| **Principal** | |
| **Interest rate** | |
| **Compound interest** | |
| **VAT** | |
| **Final amount** | |
| **Loan** | |
| **Repayment** | |
| **Loan term** | |
| **Depreciation** | |

# Perimeter – Area – Volume

# chapter 6

## *From first year, you will recall how to:*

- convert between different units of measurement,
- find the perimeter of straight edged shapes,
- find the area of rectangles, triangles and compound shapes,
- calculate the surface area and volume of rectangular solids.

## *In this chapter, you will learn to:*

- find the area of a parallelogram,
- draw the net of a rectangular solid,
- draw and interpret scaled diagrams,
- measure the capacity of containers.

## Section 6.1  Review of perimeter and area

In Book 1, you found the perimeter and area of squares, rectangles and triangles.

The box below summarises what you learned.

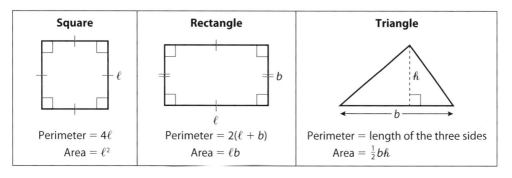

| Square | Rectangle | Triangle |
|---|---|---|
| Perimeter $= 4\ell$<br>Area $= \ell^2$ | Perimeter $= 2(\ell + b)$<br>Area $= \ell b$ | Perimeter $=$ length of the three sides<br>Area $= \frac{1}{2}bh$ |

Here are three triangles which all have different shapes.

In each triangle, the base (*b*) and perpendicular height (*h*) are shown.

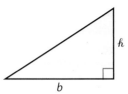 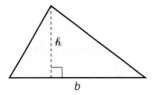 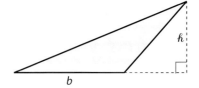

For each triangle, the area $= \frac{1}{2}bh$.

---

**Example 1**

Find the area of the shaded region of this figure.

Shaded area = area of rectangle − area of triangle

$$= (20 \times 16) - \left(\frac{1}{2} \times 12 \times 9\right)$$
$$= 320 - 54$$
$$= 266 \text{ cm}^2$$

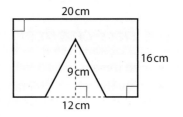

---

**Example 2**

The area of the given triangle is 56 cm².
Find the perpendicular height, *h*.

$$\text{Area} = \frac{1}{2} \times 14 \times h \quad \ldots \text{base} = 14 \text{ cm}$$
$$\therefore \frac{1}{2} \times 14 \times h = 56$$
$$7h = 56$$
$$h = 8 \text{ cm}$$

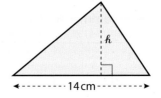

---

## Exercise 6.1

**1.** Work out the perimeter of each of these rectangles:

(i)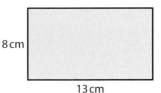

9 cm

14 cm

(ii)

8 cm

13 cm

(iii)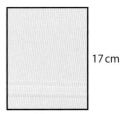

17 cm

11 cm

**2.** Find the area of each of the rectangles in Question **1.** above.

**3.** Find (i) the perimeter
(ii) the area
of the given figure

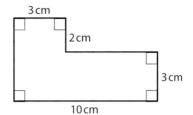

**4.** Work out the area of each of these floors.

(i)

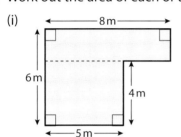

(ii)

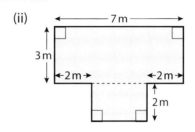

**5.** Find the areas of the following triangles:

(i)

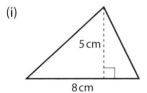

(ii) (iii)

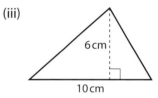

**6.** Find the areas of the following triangles:

(i) (ii)

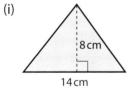

(iii)

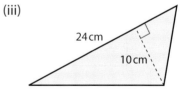

(iv) (v)

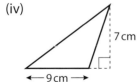

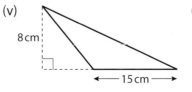

(vi)

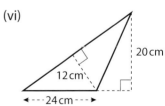

**7.** Find the areas of the following shapes which are composed of rectangles and triangles.

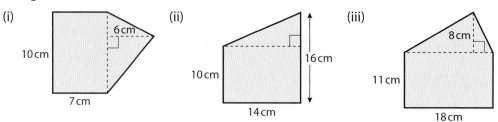

(i)  10 cm  6 cm  7 cm

(ii)  10 cm  16 cm  14 cm

(iii)  8 cm  11 cm  18 cm

**8.** Calculate the area of each of the coloured figures shown below:

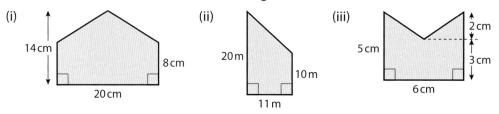

(i)  14 cm  8 cm  20 cm

(ii)  20 m  10 m  11 m

(iii)  5 cm  2 cm  3 cm  6 cm

**9.** Find the area of the border in each of these rectangles:

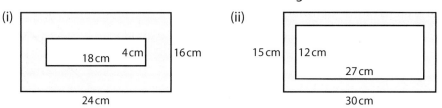

(i)  18 cm  4 cm  16 cm  24 cm

(ii)  15 cm  12 cm  27 cm  30 cm

**10.** Find the length of the missing side in each of these rectangles; the area is given in each case:

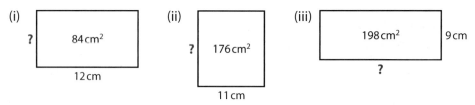

(i)  ?  84 cm²  12 cm

(ii)  ?  176 cm²  11 cm

(iii)  198 cm²  9 cm  ?

**11.** Find the length of the side of each square shown below:

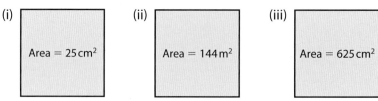

(i)  Area = 25 cm²

(ii)  Area = 144 m²

(iii)  Area = 625 cm²

**12.** Find the height $h$, in centimetres, of each of these triangles:

(i)

8 cm

Area = 24 cm²

(ii)

6 cm

Area = 21 cm²

(iii)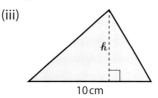

10 cm

Area = 45 cm²

**13.** Find the length of the line segment marked $x$ in each of these triangles:

(i)

$x$

⟵------- 18 cm -------⟶

Area = 90 cm²

(ii)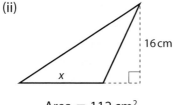

16 cm

$x$

Area = 112 cm²

(iii)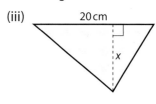

20 cm

$x$

Area = 120 cm²

**14.** Work out the perimeter of each of these shapes, where all the angles are right angles:

(i)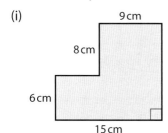

9 cm

8 cm

6 cm

15 cm

(ii)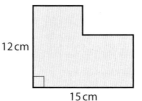

12 cm

15 cm

(iii)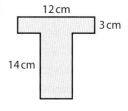

12 cm

3 cm

14 cm

(You have sufficient dimensions to find these perimeters.)

**15.** Triangle $B$ is double the area of triangle $A$.
The height of both triangles is 6 cm.

  (i)  Find the area of triangle $A$.
  (ii)  Find the area of triangle $B$.
  (iii)  Work out the value of $x$.

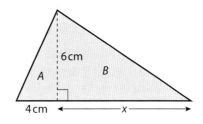

6 cm

$A$      $B$

4 cm  ⟵—— $x$ ——⟶

**16.** Find the area of the shaded portion of the
diagram on the right.

Hence find the area of the unshaded part.

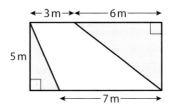

⟵3 m⟶⟵—— 6 m ——⟶

5 m

⟵—— 7 m ——⟶

**17.** Find the area of the shaded part of each triangle:

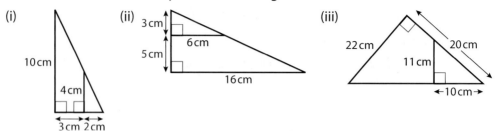

(i)       (ii)       (iii)

**18.** This is an abstract painting in which white rectangles are painted over a coloured background. Each white rectangle measures 15 cm by 24 cm and the painting is 102 cm by 60 cm.

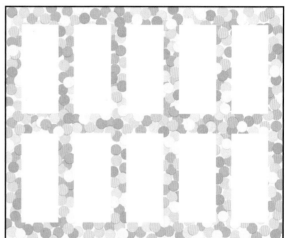

  (i)  Find the area of the white paint showing.

 (ii)  Find the area of the coloured paint showing.

(iii)  If the rectangles are evenly spaced, both across the painting as well as from top-to-bottom, find the widths of the coloured parts of the painting.

## Section 6.2  Area of a parallelogram

A parallelogram is a figure in which the opposite sides are both equal in length and parallel.

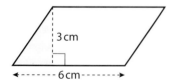  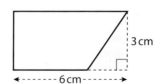

By cutting the parallelogram on the left above along the dotted line and then placing the blue triangle at the other end, a rectangle is formed.

Area of rectangle = 6 cm × 3 cm = 18 cm²

∴   area of parallelogram is also 18 cm², i.e., 6 cm by 3 cm

Area of parallelogram is
     base × perpendicular height.

Area = $b \times h$

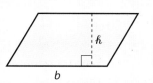

Area of this parallelogram

    = base × perpendicular height
    = 12 cm × 8 cm
    = 96 cm²

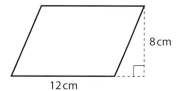

## Exercise 6.2

**1.** Find the area of each of these parallelograms:

(i)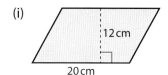

(ii)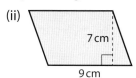

(iii)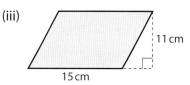

**2.** Work out the area of each of these parallelograms:

(i)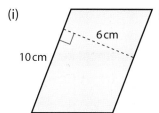

(ii)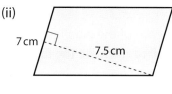

(iii)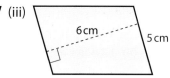

**3.** Write down the value of $h$ in each of these parallelograms:

(i)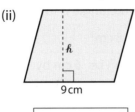

(ii)

(iii)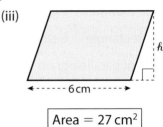

(i) 5 cm    Area = 30 cm²

(ii) 9 cm    Area = 63 cm²

(iii) 6 cm    Area = 27 cm²

**4.** Select the correct measurements to find the area of each of these parallelograms:

(i) 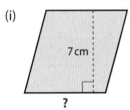  (ii) 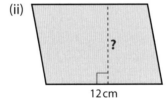  (iii)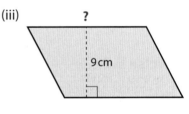

(i) 10 cm  9 cm  14 cm

(ii) 11 cm  14 cm  18 cm

(iii) 15 cm  8 cm  10 cm

**5.** Calculate the missing length in each parallelogram:

(i)

7 cm

?

Area = 35 cm²

(ii)

?

12 cm

Area = 78 cm²

(iii)

?

9 cm

Area = 108 cm²

**6.** Work out the area of the white parallelogram inside the given rectangle.
Hence find the area of the shaded region of the figure.

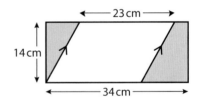

23 cm

14 cm

34 cm

**7.** (i) Work out the area of each of the parallelograms below.
(ii) Use the area you found to calculate the missing measurement in each figure.

(a)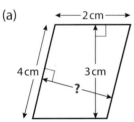

2 cm

4 cm    3 cm

?

(b)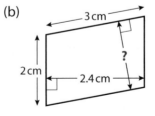

3 cm

2 cm

?

2.4 cm

(c)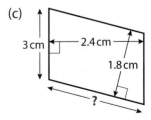

15 cm

3 cm  2.4 cm

1.8 cm

?

# Section 6.3 Rectangular solids

The volume of any rectangular solid is given by;

Volume = Length × Width × Height.

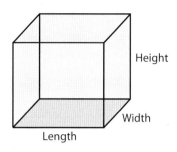

Volume is a measure of the space occupied by the solid.

From the diagram it can be seen that
Length × Width = Area of the base.

∴ Volume = Area of base × Height

The units of volume are; m × m × m = m³ (cubic metres) e.g. used for containers on ships,
or cm × cm × cm = cm³ (cubic centimetres) e.g. used for packets of food,
or mm × mm × mm = mm³ (cubic millimetres) e.g. used for tablets, medicines.

## Surface area of rectangular solid

Each rectangular solid has three pairs of rectangular faces.

∴ Surface area = $2\ell w + 2\hbar w + 2\ell \hbar$

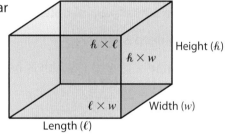

**Volume of rectangular solid** = $\ell \times w \times \hbar$

**Surface area of rectangular solid**
= $2(\ell w + \hbar w + \ell \hbar)$

$\ell$ = length, $w$ = width, $\hbar$ = height

Volume of **cube** = $\ell \times \ell \times \ell = \ell^3$
Surface area of cube = $6(\ell \times \ell) = 6\ell^2$

for a cube; $\ell = w = \hbar$

---

**Example 1**

Find (i) the volume (ii) the surface area of the given rectangular solid.

Length($\ell$) = 15 cm
Width($w$) = 12 mm = 1.2 cm
Height($\hbar$) = 8 mm = 0.8 cm

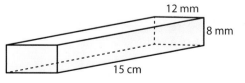

(i)  Volume = $\ell \times w \times h$
$$= 15 \text{ cm} \times 1.2 \text{ cm} \times 0.8 \text{ cm} = 14.4 \text{ cm}^3$$

Remember:
1 cm = 10 mm

(ii)  Surface Area = $2\ell w + 2\ell h + 2wh$
$$= 2(15 \text{ cm} \times 1.2 \text{ cm}) + 2(15 \text{ cm} \times 0.8 \text{ cm}) + 2(1.2 \text{ cm} \times 0.8 \text{ cm})$$
$$= 61.92 \text{ cm}^2$$

---

### Example 2

The volume of the rectangular pool shown is 500 m³.
Find the depth of the pool marked $h$ m in diagram.

If the tank is $\frac{4}{5}$ full of water, how deep is the water?

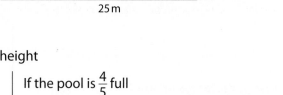

Volume = length × width × height

$$500 \text{ m}^3 = 25 \text{ m} \times 8 \text{ m} \times h \text{ m}$$

$$500 \text{ m}^3 = 200 \, h \text{ m}^3$$

$$200 \, h = 500$$

$$\therefore h = \frac{500}{200} = 2.5 \text{ m}$$

If the pool is $\frac{4}{5}$ full

then the depth of water $= \frac{4}{5} \times 2.5 \text{ m} = 2 \text{ m}$

---

## Nets of solids

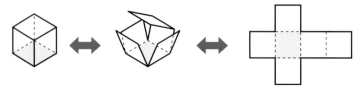

If the surface of a solid is cut along its edges and laid flat, a plan of the surface is formed. This plan (above right) is called a **net** of a solid and is very useful in calculating the surface area of a solid.

## *Investigation:*

There are 11 possible nets of a cube.
Three have been given to you.

Using a large sheet of squared paper, copy and complete the 8 remaining **different** nets.

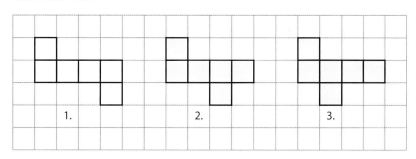

1.   2.   3.

**Note:** If you are unsure if it is a net, cut it out and crease it along fold lines, then fold it to see if it makes a cube.

---

**Example 3**

(i)  By drawing a net for this open box, calculate the (external) surface area of the box.

(ii)  A large sheet of card [AB × BC] is needed to make each box.

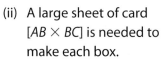

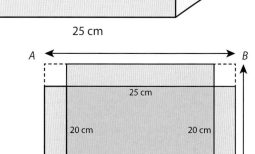

(a)  Find the length of *AB* and *BC*.

(b)  Calculate the cost of manufacturing 10 boxes if the material needed to manufacture the box cost €0.10 per 100 cm².

(i)  The total surface area = 25 cm × 20 cm = 500 cm²
    + 2(5 cm × 25 cm) = 250 cm²
    + 2(5 cm × 20 cm) = 200 cm²
    ─────────────────────────────
    Total surface area = 950 cm²

(ii) $|AB| = (25 + 2 \times 5)\text{cm} = 35 \text{ cm}$
$\quad |BC| = (20 + 2 \times 5)\text{cm} = 30 \text{ cm}$

To make a 1 box a sheet measuring 35 cm × 30 cm = 1050 cm² is needed.

To manufacture 10 boxes 10 × 1050 cm² = 10 500 cm² is needed.

∴ cost for 10 boxes $= \dfrac{10\,500}{100} \times €0.10 = €10.50$

## Capacity – The Litre

The capacity of a container is the amount of liquid it can hold.
The most commonly-used metric measure of capacity is the **litre**.
A cube with edge of length 10 cm contains 1 litre.

∴ 1000 cm³ = 1 litre

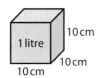

*Remember*    To convert cubic centimetres (cm³) to litres, divide by 1000.

## Exercise 6.3

**1.** Find the volume of each of these rectangular solids:

(i) 4 cm, 2 cm, 3 cm

(ii) 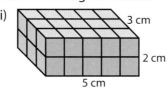 3 cm, 2 cm, 5 cm

(iii) 3 cm, 4 cm, 6 cm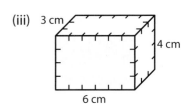

**2.** Find the surface area of each of the solids in Question **1.** above.

**3.** Find  (a) the volume  (b) the surface area of these solid cuboids:

(i) 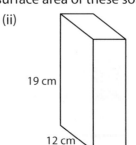 3 cm, 4 cm, 10 cm

(ii) 19 cm, 12 cm, 6 cm

(iii) 6 cm, 6 cm, 6 cm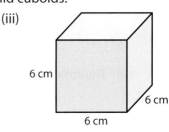

**4.** By drawing the net of each of the following, find the surface area of the open boxes shown.

(i)

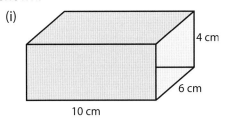

10 cm · 6 cm · 4 cm

(ii)

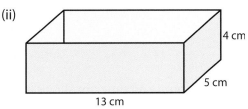

13 cm · 5 cm · 4 cm

**5.** Each of the solid shapes below can be broken into two or more rectangular solids. The dotted lines indicate how the figures may be divided.
Now find the total volume of each of these shapes:

(i)

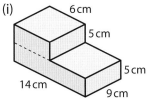

6 cm · 5 cm · 5 cm · 14 cm · 9 cm

(ii)

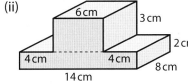

6 cm · 3 cm · 2 cm · 4 cm · 4 cm · 8 cm · 14 cm

(iii)

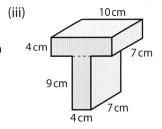

10 cm · 4 cm · 7 cm · 9 cm · 7 cm · 4 cm

**6.** Eight cubes of side 2 cm are glued together as shown to make a solid. Find:

(i) the volume

(ii) the surface area of the solid.

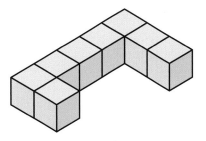

**7.** The volume of each of the following rectangular solids is given.
Find the length of the side marked with a letter.

(i)

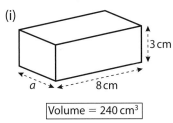

3 cm · a · 8 cm

Volume = 240 cm³

(ii)

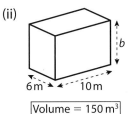

b · 6 m · 10 m

Volume = 150 m³

(iii)

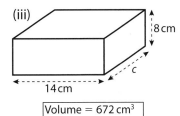

8 cm · 14 cm · c

Volume = 672 cm³

**8.** The volume of a cube is 125 cm³.
Find (i) the length of the side of the cube
(ii) the surface area of the cube.

**9.** The surface area of this cube is 96 cm².
   Find  (i)  the length of the side of the cube
         (ii)  the volume of the cube.

**10.** The figure on the right shows a stack of cubes of side 2 cm.
   (i)   How many cubes are in the stack?
   (ii)  What is the volume of the stack?
   (iii) How many faces are visible? (include the base)
   (iv)  What is the surface area of the stack?

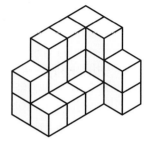

**11.** How many bricks each measuring
   2 cm × 3 cm × 5 cm will fit into a box
   measuring 15 cm × 30 cm × 10 cm?

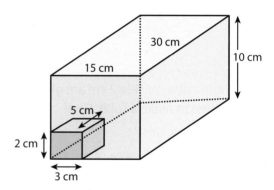

**12.** A tank has a capacity of *3* litres.
   The height of the tank is 4 cm and the
   length of the tank is 30 cm as shown.
   Find the width, *w*, of the tank.

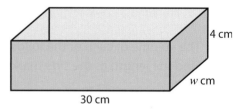

**13.** Ten rectangular slabs of
   insulation measuring
   1.1 m × 2.2 m × 10 cm
   are stacked in a
   cardboard box. Find:

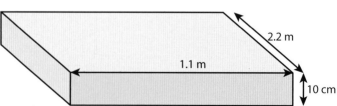

   (i)  the capacity of the box in   (a)  m³   (b) litres,
   (ii) the external surface area of the box.

**14.** 36 bars of gold each measuring
18 cm × 7 cm × 6 cm are melted
down made into cubes.
Each cube has a side of 3 cm.
Each cube is worth €40 000.
Calculate the total value of all the gold.

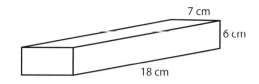

**15.** Peter has 70 rectangular packets each
with a base of area 25 cm × 25 cm
and a height of 10 cm.
He puts as many packets as
possible into a box with dimensions
100 cm × 75 cm × 55 cm.
 (a) Draw the base of the box and
    mark in how many boxes will
    fit along the bottom of the box.
 (b) The lid of the outer box must close.
    How many packets will Peter
    have left over?

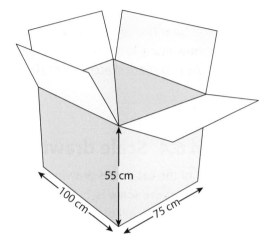

**16.** This large cube is made by stacking smaller cubes together.
Calculate the volume of each small cube.

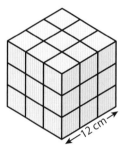

**17.** The two boxes shown have the same volume.
Find the ratio $\frac{a}{b}$ of the two unknown sides.

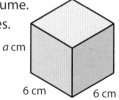
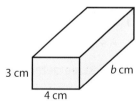

**18.** If 1 litre = 1000 cm³, find the capacity of these rectangular containers in litres.

(i)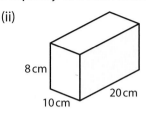

20 cm
15 cm
20 cm

(ii)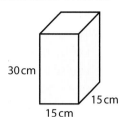

8 cm
20 cm
10 cm

(iii)

30 cm
15 cm
15 cm

**19.** The dimensions of a closed rectangular box
are shown on the right.
Draw an accurate sketch of the net for this box.

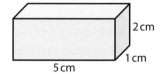

2 cm
1 cm
5 cm

## Section 6.4  Scale drawing

The height of the cat in this drawing is 4 cm.
We are told that the **scale** is 1 : 10.
This means that the real cat is 10 times as tall as the
cat shown in the drawing.
The height of the 'real cat' is 4 cm × 10 = 40 cm.
The picture shown is an example of a scaled drawing.

In everyday life, people such as architects and
engineers make scale drawings of buildings and bridges.
Builders must then be able to read and understand
them so that the structures can be built properly.

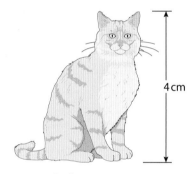

4 cm

Scale = 1 : 10

> Scale drawings have the same shapes as the objects that they represent but they are
> of different sizes.

> The scale of a drawing is length of drawing : real length.
> A scale of 1 : 100 means that the real size is 100 times the size of the drawing.

> The scale determines the size of the drawing.
> A 1 : 10 scale drawing of an object would be bigger than a 1 : 100 scale drawing of the
> same object.

Here is a scale drawing of a clock.

The scale is 1 : 6.

The drawing is 5 cm by 5 cm.

The actual length of the clock is 5 cm × 6

$$= 30 \text{ cm.}$$

Accordingly, the actual dimensions of the clock are 30 cm by 30 cm.

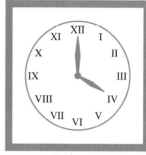

Scale 1 : 6

---

**Example 1**

Part of a house plan drawn to a scale of 1 : 100 is shown.

Bedroom 1 is a square of sides 5 cm.

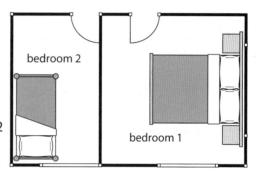

(i) Find the actual length of this bedroom in metres.

(ii) Measure the width of bedroom 2 on the plan and hence write down its width in metres.

(iii) The kitchen in the house is 6.5 metres by 4.8 metres. What are the dimensions of the kitchen in the plan?

(i) On the plan, 1 cm = 100 cm  ... 1:100 scale

∴   5 cm = 500 cm

= 5 metres

The length of bedroom 1 is 5 metres.

(ii) The width of bedroom 2 is 3 cm.

3 cm = (3 × 100) cm  in real width

= 300 cm = 3 metres

The width of bedroom 2 is 3 metres.

(iii) The kitchen is 6.5 m by 4.8 m or 650 cm by 480 cm.

Since the scale is 1 : 100, we divide both 650 cm and 480 cm by 100 to find the dimensions in the plan.

Dimensions in the plan $= \dfrac{650}{100}$ cm  by  $\dfrac{480}{100}$ cm

= 6.5 cm  by  4.8 cm

---

**Example 2**

The scale on a map is 1 : 100 000.
(i) Find the distance in kilometres between two towns which are 7 cm apart on the map.
(ii) Two train stations are 25 km apart.
How many centimetres apart are they on the map?

(i) Scale = 1 : 100 000

$$\therefore \quad 1\,\text{cm} = 100\,000\,\text{cm}$$

$$7\,\text{cm} = 700\,000\,\text{cm}$$

$$= \frac{700\,000}{100}\,\text{metres} = 7000\,\text{m} = 7\,\text{km}$$

The towns are 7 km apart.

(ii) $25\,\text{km} = \dfrac{25}{100\,000}\,\text{km on the map}$

$$= \frac{25 \times 1000}{100\,000}\,\text{metres}$$

$$= \frac{25}{100}\,\text{m} = 0.25\,\text{m} = 25\,\text{cm}$$

The train stations are 25 cm apart on the map.

---

## Exercise 6.4

**1.** The scale on a building plan is 1 : 50.
Find the actual length if the length of the line on the plan is:
(i) 3 cm      (ii) 7 cm      (iii) 18 cm      (iv) 6.5 cm      (v) 12.8 cm

**2.** The scale on a map is 1 cm = 10 km.
(i) Find the distance between two towns if they are 8 cm apart on the map.
(ii) If two train stations are 60 km apart, how far are they apart on the map?

**3.** Find the actual lengths of the following lines on a building plan for which the scale is given:
(i) 2 cm – scale is 1 : 300          (ii) 6 cm – scale is 1 : 400
(iii) 8 cm – scale is 1 : 500         (iv) 7.5 mm – scale is 1 : 1000

**4.** Use the scales given to find the actual heights of the animals below:

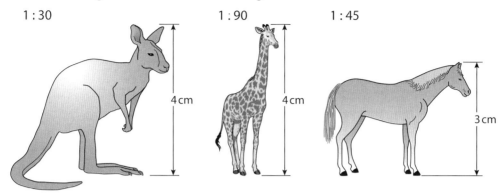

1 : 30                    1 : 90                    1 : 45

4 cm                     4 cm                     3 cm

**5.** This is the scale drawing of a lorry.
The scale is 1 : 100.
If the line segment beneath the lorry
measures 6.2 cm write down the actual
length of the lorry.
Find also the maximum height of the
lorry.

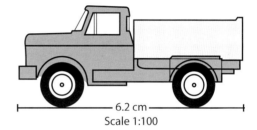

6.2 cm
Scale 1:100

**6.** A walking map has a scale of 1 : 20 000.

  (i) Find the actual distance for each of these scaled distances:
      (a) 2 cm          (b) 5 cm          (c) 8.5 cm          (d) 12.5 cm

  (ii) Find the distances on the map for these actual distances:
      (a) 10 km          (b) 4 km          (c) 40 km          (d) 27 km

**7.** A map has a scale of 1 : 500 000.
  (i) The distance between two service stations
      on the map is 3.4 cm.
      What is the actual distance?
  (ii) The next emergency phone is 22 km away.
      How many centimetres would this be on the map?

EMERGENCY
22 km

**8.** From the drawing,
by measurement
and calculation, find:
  (i) the maximum
      length of the bus
  (ii) the maximum
      height of the bus.

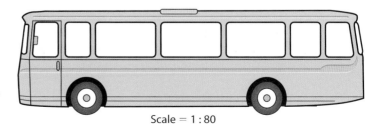

Scale = 1 : 80

9. A surveyor needs to draw an accurate
   plan of this awkwardly-shaped field.
   The scale he will use is 1 cm = 10 m.

   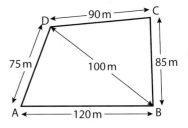

   (i) What lengths will these lines have on the plan?
      (a) [AB]          (b) [BC]
   (ii) Construct an accurate scale drawing of this
        field using the given scale.

10. The scale on a map is 5 cm to 2 km. Express this in the form 1 : $n$.
    Now find the distance, in cm, on the map between two towns, A and B, which are in
    reality 30 km apart.

11. A girl made this scale drawing to calculate
    the height, |AB|, of a triangular wall.
    (i) Measure the distance |CB| on the scale
        drawing and calculate the scale of the
        drawing.
    (ii) By measurement and calculation,
         find the real height |AB|.
    (iii) Find the area of this triangular wall.

    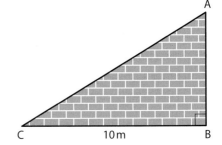

12. (i) A 1:50 scale model of a yacht is to be built.
        If the yacht is 25 metres long, how long will the model yacht be?
    (ii) A scale drawing is to be made of a car.
         If the car is 6.25 m long, and the model is to be 25 cm long, what should the
         scale be?
         Give your answer in the form 1:?.

# Test yourself 6

**1.** Find the area of the figure shown on the right.

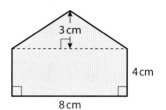

**2.** Find (i) the volume
(ii) the total surface area
of the given rectangular solid.

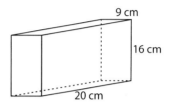

**3.** Find the area of the shaded region of the given figure.

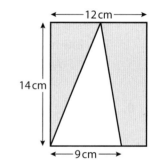

**4.** This rectangular solid has a square base and a volume of 864 cm³. Find the length $\ell$ of the solid.

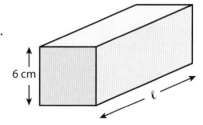

**5.** The area of the given triangle is 49 cm². Find the perpendicular height $h$.

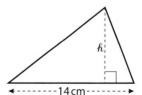

**6.** When this net is folded a rectangular
box is formed.

    Find   (i)  the value of the lengths $a$, $b$,

           (ii)  the capacity of the box in litres,

         (iii)  the surface area of the box

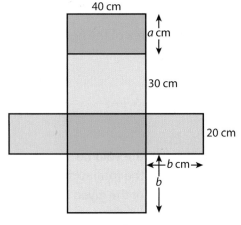

**7.** A rectangular petrol tank has dimensions as
shown on the right.

    (i)  Find the volume of the tank in $cm^3$.

   (ii)  How many litres of petrol would fit in
the tank?

**8.** Here is the net of a cube.
Which face would be opposite face 1
when folded?

| | | | | |
|---|---|---|---|---|
| 5 | | | | |
| 4 | 1 | 2 | 3 | |
| 6 | | | | |

**9.** Denise has a rectangular garden that
measures 10 m by 13 m.

Her garden has a lawn, a square patio of
side length 5 m and a vegetable patch that
is 4 m by 1.5 m.

What is the area of the lawn?

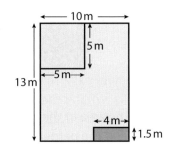

**10.**  (i)  Find the volume of the figure shown.

    (ii)  How many faces does this solid have?

   (iii)  Find the surface area of the solid.

   (iv)  A model of the figure is built with straws
as shown. What is the total length of straw needed.

    (v)  If straws are 20 cm long, how many straws are
needed to build the model?

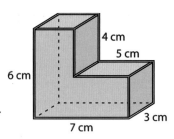

**11.** To find the area of the given parallelogram, only two of the given measurements are necessary.
By selecting the correct two, find its area.

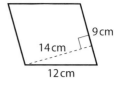

**12.** In the given diagram, equal lengths are marked.
   (i)   Find the area of △ABE.
   (ii)  Find the area of △ACD.
   (iii) Hence find the area of BCDE.

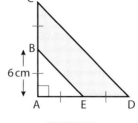

**13.** Here is the net of a rectangular box.
The shaded rectangle is the base of the box.
   (i)   What is the height of the box?
   (ii)  Find the volume of the box.
   (iii) Find the surface area of the box.

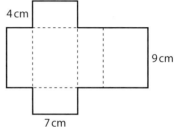

**14.** The diagram on the right shows a room 5 m long and 4 m wide.
A carpet is placed in the room so that there is a uniform border $\frac{1}{2}$ m in width left all round.

Find   (i)   the area of the carpet in m²
         (ii)  the area of the border in m²
         (iii) the cost of the carpet if 1 m² costs €80
         (iv)  the cost of staining the border at €14 per m².

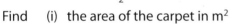

**15.** A map has a scale of 1 : 25 000.
   (i)  What is the actual distance if the scaled distance is 4 cm?
   (ii) What is the scaled distance if the actual distance is 3.5 km?

**16.** The volume of the stack of cubes shown in 216 cm³.
   (i)  Find the volume of one cube.
   (ii) Find the length of the edge of each cube.

## Assignment:

Copy this diagram of a 3-D solid.

Using arrows label a face, an edge and a vertex.

Copy and complete a large chart of the following 3-D solids:

Count the number of   (i)  Vertices (V)   (ii)  Edges (E)
(iii)  Faces (F),

then find the value of V − E + F for each of the solids.

Write a conclusion from your research.

| | V | E | F | V − E + F | Solid |
|---|---|---|---|---|---|
| A | 8 | 12 | 6 | 2 | Cube |
| B | | | | | |
| C | | | | | |
| D | | | | | |
| E | | | | | |
| F | | | | | |

**Conclusion:**

# Statistics 1

# chapter 7

## From first year, you will recall how to:

- plan a survey,
- collect data,
- identify numerical and categorical data,
- understand populations and bias,
- write suitable questionnaires,
- get a simple random sample,
- gather representative samples.

## In this chapter, you will learn to:

- identify data collected through primary and secondary sources,
- use frequency tables to organise collected data,
- understand how social media can cause bias in data collection,
- identify the limitations of sample data.

## Section 7.1  Statistical questions

The purpose of statistics is to answer questions and provide information on relevant topics.

In most countries the government is the biggest collector of statistics. A **census** is carried out every five years to collect statistics.

Governments provide information about:

> The numbers out of work
> Inflation
> The number of visitors to Ireland
> The number of students sitting examinations per year etc.

Other organisations are interested in statistical questions such as;

> The average rainfall per month etc.
> The change in the value of shares
> The most popular models of car etc.

Companies do **market research** to find out what customers like/dislike about certain products or services.

Having statistics helps us to plan for the future.

## Investigation:

Carefully listen to or read news reports;

  (i)   on a radio or television
  (ii)   in a newspaper or magazine
 (iii)   on the internet.

Make a list of 3 sets of statistics that are mentioned.

Write down the statistical question that is being asked by each statistical report.

## Types of data

All statistics start with a question.
e.g. How long did people spend watching the world cup?
To answer each question, we need **data**.

**Data** is another name for the facts and pieces of information that we collect.
Data that is not in an organised form is called **raw data**.
Data can be divided into two broad categories, namely **categorical data** and **numerical data**.

## Categorical data

Data which fits into a group or category is called **categorical data**.
It is generally described using words such as colour, favourite sport or country of birth.

## Numerical data

Data which can be counted or measured is called **numerical data** because the answer is a number.

Here is a summary of data types:

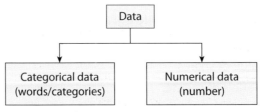

---

**Example 1**

For each of the following, write down whether it is numerical or categorical data:
  (i)   the number of goals scored in a hockey match
  (ii)   the temperature in an oven
  (iii)   people's hair colours
  (iv)   countries where cars were manufactured
  (v)   star ratings of the quality of hotels
  (vi)   time taken for athletes to run 400 metres.

  (i)   numerical          (ii)   numerical          (iii)   categorical
  (iv)   categorical        (v)   categorical        (vi)   numerical

---

## Collecting data

Data can be collected by any of these methods:

> **Surveys;** doing a survey by means of a questionnaire and recording what people say

> **Experiments;** carrying out an experiment which may involve the use of technology such as a computer or data logger

> **Research;** researching sources such as reference books, websites, databases, newspapers and historical records.

When stating conclusions based on data collected it is very important to note whether the data came from a **primary source** i.e. a survey or an experiment carried out by yourself or a **secondary source** i.e. data obtained by researching other sources e.g. newspapers, magazines or internet sources e.g. Facebook, Wikipedia etc.

The reliability of data, particularly secondary data, is essential when making conclusions based on that data.

Before you collect data, you need to have a clear question in your mind that you want answered. You then need to decide what sort of data to collect and the most suitable and efficient method of collecting it.

## Surveys

The main survey methods are:

> personal interviews in which people are asked questions; this is generally done by means of a **questionnaire**.

> telephone surveys; here the interview is conducted by phone

> **observation**; this involves monitoring behaviour

## Experiments

Experiments are particularly useful for collecting scientific data; drug companies carry out experiments to test the benefits and the side-effects of new drugs; car companies, testing batteries for electric cars.

## Questionnaires

A **questionnaire** is a set of questions designed to obtain data from individuals.

People who answer questionnaires are called **respondents**.

There are two ways in which the questions can be asked.

› An interviewer asks the questions and fills in the questionnaire

› People are given a questionnaire and asked to fill in the responses themselves.

**When you are composing questions for a questionnaire,**

› be clear what you want to find out and what data you need

› ask short, concise questions

› start with simple questions to encourage the person who is giving the responses

› provide response boxes where possible:     Yes ☐        No ☐

› avoid leading questions such as

      'Don't you agree that there is too much sport on television?'

  or   'Do you think that professional footballers are overpaid?'

› avoid personal questions such as those which involve name, exact age or weight.

## Avoiding bias

Social media sites are now being used to **source data** for research purposes. Technology is used to analyse this information.

**Benefits**: hundreds of millions of users.

**Dangers**: selection bias can occur by excluding large sections of the population with little or no access to social media.

When you are collecting data, you need to make sure that your survey or experiment is **fair** and avoids **bias**. If bias exists, the data collected might be unrepresentative.

Here are some questions which should be avoided because they suggest a particular answer or because they may cause embarrassment or shame.

Have you ever stolen money from your parents?

Yes ☐          No ☐

Few students are likely to answer this question honestly if they have already stolen.

Do you agree that the Minister for Finance should resign because of the poor state of the economy?

Yes ☐          No ☐

The wording of this question suggests that the right answer is 'yes'. It is a leading question and therefore likely to be **biased**.

## Organising data in a frequency table

Since most surveys result in the collection of a lot of data we need to organise this data so as it makes sense.

A frequency table is a useful and efficient way of grouping and counting data.

The **frequency** of a piece of data is the number of times it appears in the set of data.

### Example 2

Twenty hockey matches were surveyed, and the number of goals scored noted. This is the data collected.

2  2  1  2  0  3  2  1  1  4
1  1  1  2  2  0  3  2  1  2

Use a tally table to make a frequency table for this data.

For each score in the list we draw a tally mark in the tally column.

The first score is a 2, so a "|" is placed in the tally column beside the 2. We continue until we have made a tally mark for each score.

| Score | Tally | Frequency |
|-------|-------|-----------|
| 0 | || | 2 |
| 1 | ||||| || | 7 |
| 2 | ||||| ||| | 8 |
| 3 | || | 2 |
| 4 | | | 1 |
| | Total | 20 |

**Note 1**; ||||| represents five.

**Note 2**; Always check that the total of the frequencies is equal to the total number of the given data.

## Exercise 7.1

**1.** State whether each of the following is numerical or categorical data:
  (i) The number of cars sold by a certain garage last month
  (ii) The favourite soccer teams of pupils in your class
  (iii) The continent of birth of people who came to Ireland in the past year
  (iv) The number of horses in a race
  (v) The time taken by the winning horse to complete the race
  (vi) The blood-types of the teachers in your school
  (vii) The types of trees in a wood
  (viii) The length of time taken to complete a sudoku puzzle.

**2.** State whether each of the following is an example of primary data or secondary data:
  (i) Conor tossed a coin 100 times and recorded the result to investigate if the coin was fair.
  (ii) Brenda counted the number of SUVs that passed the school gate between 9 a.m. and 10 a.m..
  (iii) Shane used the internet to check the number of medals Ireland won in boxing in the last four Olympic Games.
  (iv) Emer checked the Central Statistics Office website to check the number of people on the Live Register for each of the last twenty four months.

**3.** A brewery wants to produce a new type of beer.
  Suggest how they might use both primary and secondary data to do market research.

**4.** Niamh wants to find out how often adults go to the cinema.
  She uses this question on a questionnaire.

  'How many times do you go to the cinema?'

  ☐      ☐      ☐

  Not very often    Sometimes    A lot

  (i) Write down **two** things wrong with this question.
  (ii) Design a better question for her questionnaire to find out how often adults go to the cinema.
  You should include some response boxes.

5. Eamonn is trying to find out what people think of the *FFG Political Party*.
   He is trying to decide between these two questions for his questionnaire.
   Which question should he use? Explain your answer.
   (i) How do you rate the *FFG Party's* economic policies?

   Strongly
   agree ☐    Agree ☐    Don't
   know ☐    Disagree ☐    Strongly
   disagree ☐

   (ii) Do you agree that the *FFG Party* has the best economic policies?

   Yes ☐         No ☐

6. Explain what is wrong with each of the following survey questions.
   Suggest a better alternative for each question.
   (i) What age are you?
   (ii) Would you describe yourself as being well-educated?
   (iii) Normal people like animals.
       Do you like animals?
   (iv) Would you agree that top actors are paid too much?
   (v) Have you ever taken illegal drugs?
   (vi) Where exactly do you live?
   (vii) In view of the huge numbers of road accidents outside this school, do you
       think the speed limit should be reduced?

7. Aidan wants to find out what students think about the library service at his college.
   Part of the questionnaire he has written is shown.

   **Q1.** What is your full name? .................................................................

   **Q2.** How many times a week do you go to the library?
   ☐ Often      ☐ Sometimes      ☐ Never

   (i) Why should Q1 not be asked?
   (ii) What is wrong with the choices offered in Q2?

8. This question was included in a questionnaire.

   How old are you?    Young ☐    Middle-aged ☐    Elderly ☐

   (i) What is wrong with the question and responses?
   (ii) Rewrite the question and responses in a better way.

**9.** Valerie is the manager of a supermarket.
She wants to find out how often people shop at her supermarket.
She will use a questionnaire.

Design a suitable question for Valerie to use on her questionnaire.
You must include some response boxes.

**10.** Give a reason why questions A and B below should be re-worded before being
included in a questionnaire.
Rewrite each one showing exactly how you would present it in a questionnaire.

**Question A:** Do you live in a working-class or middle-class area?
**Question B:** The new supermarket seems to be a great success. Do you agree?

**11.** Susan is trying to find out opinions about the local soccer club. She posts a
question to their Facebook page. Give some reasons why the data collected might
be biased.

**12.** Alex has decided to do a project on social media use in his class.
Write a question he might use that would give numerical data.

**13.** Natalia writes the following question in a survey.
"Normal people sleep eight hours a night. Do you sleep eight hours a night?"
Give a reason why the question is unsuitable and rewrite it in a suitable form.

**14.** The ages of the members of the school drama club are as
follows:

12, 13, 12, 14, 15, 18, 13, 15, 16, 14, 15, 17, 13, 14, 15, 14, 16,
17, 15, 15, 16, 12, 13, 14, 15, 17, 16, 14, 15, 13, 16, 14, 15, 13.

(i) Create and complete a frequency table to display
the data.
(ii) What is the difference in age between the eldest and youngest student
in the club?
(iii) What is the most common age of students in the club?
(iv) What is the least common age of students in the club?
Can you suggest a reason for this?

**15.** Ethan did a traffic survey by observation at the gates of his school between 9.00 – 9.30 am. on a Monday. His results were as follows:

| bus | lorry | bus | car | lorry | bus | lorry | bus | car |
|------|-----------|------|-----------|------|-----------|------|-----------|------|
| van | motorbike | bus | lorry | car | motorbike | car | motorbike | van |
| van | bus | car | motorbike | bus | lorry | bus | lorry | car |
| bus | car | van | car | car | van | van | car | car |
| car | lorry | bus | car | bus | motorbike | car | bus | lorry |
| lorry | car | car | car | van | bus | lorry | car | car |
| bus | motorbike | car | lorry | lorry | car | car | van | car |
| car | car | lorry | motorbike | car | bus | car | motorbike | bus |

(i) Copy and complete the tally / frequency chart.
(ii) Which vehicle passed the gate most frequently?
(iii) Explain why it was important for Ethan to write the day and time on his chart?

| Vehicle type | Tally | Frequency |
|------|------|------|
| Bus | ЖЖ ЖЖ ЖЖ l | |
| Car | | |
| Lorry | | |
| Van | | |
| Motorbike | | |
| | Total | |

# Section 7.2  Sampling

If you were asked to investigate the claim,

'Rugby players in Ireland are taller than Gaelic football players',

do you measure the heights of all rugby players and all Gaelic football players in the country?
This would be an enormous task as there are thousands of players in these categories.

In this study, we use the word **population** to describe **all** the rugby and Gaelic footballers in the country.

When a population is too large for a study, we collect data from some members of the population only. In statistics, this group is called a **sample**. The purpose of a sample is to collect data from some of the population and use it to draw conclusions about the whole population.

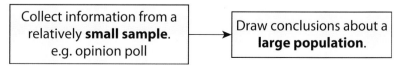

## Bias

The sample you select for your study is very important. If the sample is not properly selected, the results may be **biased**. If **bias** exists, the results will be distorted and so will not be properly representative of the population as a whole.

The **size** of a sample is also important. If the sample is too small, the results may not be very reliable. If the sample is too large, the data may take a long time to collect and analyse.

**Note:**   Raw data can be collected from a whole population in the case of a small village. However a sample of the population is needed to collect data from the inhabitants of a city.

## Random sample

One of the ways to avoid bias in a survey is to take a **random sample**.

In a random sample, every member of the population being considered has an equal chance of being selected. Random samples need to be carefully chosen.

Methods for choosing a **random sample** could involve giving each member of the population a number and then selecting the numbers for the sample in one of these ways:

> putting the numbers into a hat and then selecting however many you need for the sample

> using a random number table

> using a random number generator on your calculator or computer.

Electronic calculators are very useful for generating random numbers.

If you want to generate 3-digit numbers, press ⎡SHIFT⎤, and then press ⎡Ran #⎤.

Now press ⎡=⎤ and disregard the decimal point.

If the number displayed is   0.107, write 107.

Press ⎡=⎤ repeatedly to get more random numbers.

## Exercise 7.2

1. A school has 820 students and an investigation concerning the school uniform is being conducted.

   40 students from the school are randomly selected to complete the survey on their school uniform. In this situation,
   - (i) what is the population size
   - (ii) what is the size of the sample?

2. Would you collect data from the whole population or just a sample in each of the following cases?

   | Population | Data required |
   |---|---|
   | (i) Students in your class | Birthdays |
   | (ii) Trees in school grounds | Circumference of trunk |
   | (iii) Trees in a forest | Circumference of trunk |
   | (iv) Shoppers in local supermarket | Daily spend |
   | (v) Cars in local car dealership | Price of second hand cars |

3. Jack wanted to find information on how much pocket money the 900 hundred students in his school got each week. He planned to have a sample size of (i) 4 **or** (ii) 40 **or** (iii) 400.

   Which sample size should he pick?

   Explain why you did not choose the remaining two options.

4. Melanie wants to find out how often people go to the cinema.
   She gives a questionnaire to all the women leaving a cinema.

   Her sample is biased.
   Give **two** possible reasons why.

5. Amy wants to find out how often people play sport.
   She went to a local sports shop and questioned the people she met.
   Explain why this sample is likely to be biased.

6. Dara wants to find out how people get to work each day.
   Which of the following is the most appropriate group to question?
   - A: Every fourth person at a bus stop.
   - B: A group of people at lunch break.
   - C: People arriving late for work.

**7.** Jennifer wants to investigate if people want longer prison sentences for criminals.
Which of the following is the most appropriate group to question?
A:  Members of the gardaí.
B:  People at a football match.
C:  People who have been in prison.
Explain your answer.

**8.** Amanda wants to choose a sample of 500 adults from the town where she lives.
She considers these methods of choosing her sample:

Method 1:    Choose people shopping in the town centre on Saturday mornings.
Method 2:    Choose names at random from the electoral register.
Method 3:    Choose people living in the streets near her house.

Which method is most likely to produce an unbiased sample?
Give a reason for your answer.

**9.** Comment on any possible bias in the following situations:
  (i)  Sixth-year students only are interviewed about changes to the school uniform.
  (ii)  Motorists stopped in peak-hour traffic are interviewed about traffic problems.
  (iii)  Real estate agents are interviewed about the prices of houses.
  (iv)  A 'who will you vote for?' survey at an expensive city restaurant.

**10.** A research company is canvassing peoples'
opinions on whether smoking should be
banned in all public places.

They canvass people standing outside
buildings in the city during office hours.
Explain why the data collected is likely to
be biased.

**11.** Use the ⎡Ran #⎤ key on your calculator to choose a sample of 8 pupils from a
year-group of 100.

**12.** Which of the following samples are likely to be representative samples?
For those that are not representative, give a reason why they are not.

(A) Survey task: To test the effectiveness of a new drug for migraines.
Sample: Chosen by giving the drug to all patients, of just one doctor, who suffer from migraines.

(B) Survey task: To survey opinion about fresh bread baked in a local supermarket.
Sample: Chosen by interviewing every 20th shopper at the supermarket checkout on a Saturday

(C) Survey task: To survey the voting intentions of residents of a particular constituency in the coming election.
Sample: A random sample of people at the local train station between 7 a.m. and 9 a.m. are surveyed.

## Test yourself 7

**1.** State whether each of the following sets of data is numerical or categorical:
   (i) Favourite type of apple.
   (ii) The head-count at a small protest rally.
   (iii) The weights of three-year-old children.
   (iv) The brands of dog-food on sale in a supermarket.
   (v) County of birth.
   (vi) The amount of rainfall in each month of the year.

**2.** State whether each of the following is primary data or secondary data:
   (i) Counting the number of hatchback cars passing the school gate.
   (ii) Looking at records to see how many people passed through Shannon Airport each day in June one year.
   (iii) Examining tourist brochures to find the average weekly snowfall at a skiing resort.
   (iv) Checking *Wikipedia* to see how many gold medals each country won at the London Olympics.

3. Which of the two questions and responses below are the more suitable for inclusion in a questionnaire?
Give a reason for your selection.

(i)
     Do you agree that having a lovely, warm, relaxing bath at night helps you go to sleep?
     Yes ☐     No ☐

(ii)
     Does a warm bath at night help you go to sleep?
     Yes ☐     No ☐     Not sure ☐

4. To gather information about the public's opinion on whether money should be spent upgrading the local library, a questionnaire form is placed in the library for members of the public to fill out. Explain why this sample is likely to be biased.

5. The data table below shows the percentage unemployment figures for 1999 to 2005.

| Year | 1999 | 2000 | 2001 | 2002 | 2003 | 2004 | 2005 |
|---|---|---|---|---|---|---|---|
| **Male** | 5.2 | 4.7 | 4.0 | 3.6 | 3.7 | 3.4 | 3.3 |
| **Female** | 4.7 | 4.1 | 3.8 | 3.0 | 3.0 | 2.7 | 2.5 |

(i) What was the male unemployment rate in 2003?
(ii) Which year had the (a) highest    (b) lowest percentage total unemployment
(iii) Between which two years did the female unemployment rate fall the most?

6. Elizabeth surveyed 30 students in her year to determine the number of children in each family.
This resulted in the following data.    2 3 1 3 4 2 1 3 2 5
                               1 3 2 5 6 2 1 2 1 4
                               4 2 2 3 1 1 2 3 1 2

(i) Draw a frequency table for this data.
(ii) In what % of homes were there 3 children?
(iii) Why did the number 0 not appear in the data?

**7.** Explain what is wrong with each of the following survey questions and suggest better alternatives.

  (i)  How many phones are there in your home?
 (ii)  What type of car do you own?
(iii)  What is your email address?

**8.** A county engineer is carrying out a traffic survey.
He is trying to find out how busy a particular road is.
Each day, he counts the number of cars passing a particular point between 2 p.m. and 3 p.m..
He uses this information to write a report.
State why his sample is likely to be biased.

**9.** What is wrong with the following examples of collecting information?

  (i)  I phoned 1000 people and discovered that 92 per cent of people have a telephone.
 (ii)  I interviewed 100 people who came out of *Zac's Discount* and found that 63 per cent of people use *Zac's Toothpaste*.
(iii)  I asked 50 people to answer Yes or No to the question "Have you stopped insulting your neighbours?", and found that 80 per cent of people have stopped insulting their neighbours

## Assignment:

Using a random sample of at least 30 students from 1$^{st}$ year and 6$^{th}$ year, carry out the following survey;

To compare the number of siblings, 1, 2, 3, 4 or $> 4$, in the 1$^{st}$ year group, with the number of siblings in 6$^{th}$ year of your school.

Present your results in percentages in the form of a frequency table.
Write any conclusions about the changes, if any, in the size of families you can deduce from your data over the 6 years.

## From first year, you will recall how to:

- list the outcomes of an experiment,
- use the Fundamental Principle of Counting,
- link chance with probability,
- check for equally likely outcomes,
- use fractions to measure probability,
- identify favourable outcomes,
- make a probability scale,
- understand fair / biased experiments,
- apply probability to the tossing of coins, the rolling of dice, spinning of spinners, picking of cards from a deck of cards etc.

## In this chapter, you will learn to:

- draw and use two-way tables,
- draw and use tree diagrams,
- estimate probability from experiments,
- use probability to answers word problems,
- make connections between probability and sets.

## Section 8.1  Listing outcomes

Here is a spinner with 8 sectors.
It has 8 different numbers and 3 different colours.
If the spinner is spun, you may get any of the numbers
1, 2, 3, 4, 5, 6, 7 or 8.
These are called **outcomes**.
If we are interested in colours only, then the possible
outcomes are green, blue and yellow.

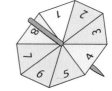

For the spinner above, we **listed** all the **possible outcomes** for numbers and for colours.

We will now consider the outcomes when this spinner is spun and a coin is tossed.

Here is the list of the possible outcomes:

1H, 2H, 3H, 4H, 5H, 6H, 7H, 8H, 1T, 2T, 3T, 4T, 5T, 6T, 7T, 8T,

where H stands for head and T stands for tail.
Notice that there are **16** possible outcomes.

The number of outcomes can be found much more easily by multiplying **8** (number of outcomes for the spinner) and **2** (number of outcomes for the coin), i.e. $8 \times 2 = 16$.

The preceding example illustrates the **Fundamental Principle of Counting** which is given on the right.

> If one event has **m** possible outcomes and a second event has **n** possible outcomes, the two events have **m** × **n** possible outcomes.

## Investigation:

Draw a chart, listing the number of outcomes for different events. Some suggestions are given below:

| | Event / Experiment | Number of outcomes |
|---|---|---|
| | (a) Tossing a coin <br> (b) Tossing two coins | (a) <br> (b) |
| | (a) Rolling a die <br> (b) Rolling a die and tossing a coin | (a) <br> (b) |
| | (a) Picking a suit of cards <br> (b) Picking a spade from a deck <br> (c) Picking a king <br> (d) Picking a red card. | (a) <br> (b) <br> (c) <br> (d) |
| | (a) Picking a colour <br> (b) Picking a number <br> (c) Picking a number greater than 200 | (a) <br> (b) <br> (c) |
| | (a) Selecting a student from your class <br> (b) Selecting a girl from your class | (a) <br> (b) |

## Two-way tables

When the two spinners on the right are spun, the possible outcomes can be shown in an organised way by means of a **two-way table**, as shown below.

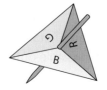 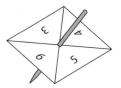

Numbers

|   | **3** | **4** | **5** | **6** |
|---|---|---|---|---|
| **R** | 3R | 4R | 5R | 6R |
| **B** | 3B | 4B | 5B | 6B |
| **G** | 3G | 4G | 5G | 6G |

Colours

Number of possible outcomes is

$$4 \times 3 = 12$$

## Tree diagrams

Tree diagrams can also be used to work out the number of outcomes when two or more events occur. Each possibility is written at the end of a branch.

Using the spinners above the following tree diagram shows all 12 possible outcomes.

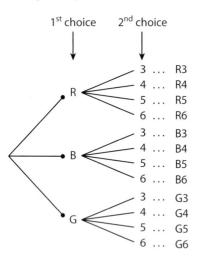

Number of possible outcomes is $3 \times 4 = 12$

The **Fundamental Principle of Counting** can be extended to any number of events.

If a businessman has to choose a shirt, a tie and a jacket from 5 shirts, 3 ties and 4 jackets, he has

$$5 \times 3 \times 4 \text{ choices} = 60 \text{ choices}$$

A tree diagram is very suitable to **list** all the combinations in this case.

## Exercise 8.1

1. An 'early-bird' menu consists of 3 starters and 4 main courses.
   How many different 2-course meals can you have?

2. Two coins are tossed.
   List all the possible outcomes using H for head and T for tail.

3. This spinner is spun and the die is thrown.
   (i) How many different outcomes of colour
   and number can you have?
   (ii) How many of these outcomes will have
   the colour yellow?
   (iii) How many of the outcomes will have the number 3?

4. A code consists of one of the letters A, B, C or D followed by a digit from 1 to 9.
   How many different codes are possible?

5. A lunch menu consists of 3 starters, 4 main courses and 2 desserts.
   How many different 3-course meals can a person have?

6. A car manufacturer produces different types of cars as follows:
   › the model can be Saloon, Estate or Hatchback
   › the colours can be silver, black or red
   › the style can be Standard, Deluxe or Premium.
   How many different choices of car does a buyer have?

7. A game consists of spinning the given
   spinner and throwing a die.
   (i) If the outcome of the game is a
   letter and a number, how many
   different outcomes are possible?
   (ii) If the game consists of a colour
   and a number, how many different
   outcomes are possible?

8. A pupil must choose one subject out of each of the following subject groups:
   › Group A has 3 modern languages $L_1$, $L_2$, $L_3$.
   › Group B has 2 science subjects $S_1$, $S_2$.
   › Group C has 2 business subjects $B_1$, $B_2$.
   Draw a tree diagram to show the different subject selections that are possible.

9. A restaurant advertises its lunch menu using the sign shown on the right.

   (i) The menu has a choice of five starters and nine main courses.
   How many items must appear on the dessert menu to justify the claim of 180 different lunches?

   (ii) On a particular day, one of the starters and one of the main courses were not available.
   How many different three-course lunches was it possible to have on that day?

> **Lunch Menu**
>
> **3 courses for €18**
>
> Choose from our range of starters, main courses and desserts.
>
> 180 different lunches to choose from.

10. The 5 class prefects Eimear(E), Samantha(S), Mia(M), Paul(P) and Neil(N) had to supervise in the morning or afternoon.
    The year-head in charge insisted that two students, a boy and a girl, must supervise at the same time.
    Using a tree diagram list out all 12 combinations(outcomes) possible.

11.

|  | Swimming | Tennis | Football | Totals |
|---|---|---|---|---|
| **Boys** | 12 | ( ) | ( ) | 46 |
| **Girls** | 16 | ( ) | 11 | 40 |
| **Totals** | ( ) | 22 | ( ) | 86 |

The two-way table above shows the sport preference of $2^{nd}$ year students in a school.

   (i) Copy the table and fill in the missing numbers
   (ii) How many students are in second year?
   (iii) Which is the least popular sport?
   (iv) Which is the most popular sport among girls?
   (v) What fraction of the students prefer tennis?
   (vi) What percentage of girls prefer swimming?

# Section 8.2  Chance and the probability scale

You will already be familiar with words such as

   **Impossible    Unlikely    Even chance    Likely    Certain**

to describe the **chance** or **probability** of something happening.

If we want to be more specific, we use numbers to describe how likely something is to happen.

An event which is **certain to happen** has a **probability of 1**.

An event which **cannot happen** has a **probability of 0**.

All other probabilities will be a number greater than 0 and less than 1.

The more likely an event is to happen, the closer the probability is to 1.

The line shown below is called a **probability scale**.

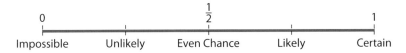

There is an **even chance** that the next person you meet on the street will be a male.

It is **certain** that the sun will rise in Ireland tomorrow.

It is **impossible** to get 7 when a normal die is rolled.

## *Investigation:*

Probabilities that are written in fraction form can easily be converted to percentage / decimal form and vice versa.

Make a poster of events A, B, C, D, E and F, completing the chart below, showing the probability of these events in fraction / percentage / decimal form.

Plot each of the events on a probability scale as shown below.

| Event | Probability | | |
|:---:|:---:|:---:|:---:|
| | **Fraction** | **Percentage** | **Decimal** |
| A | $\frac{1}{4}$ | 25% | 0.25 |
| B | | 50% | |
| C | $\frac{3}{5}$ | | 0.6 |
| D | | 75% | |
| E | $\frac{3}{10}$ | | |
| F | | | 0.01 |

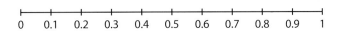

## Exercise 8.2

1. Which of these labels best describes the likelihood of each of the events below occurring?

| Impossible | Unlikely | Even Chance | Likely | Certain |

(i) A coin will show 'tails' when you toss it.

(ii) You are more than ten years old.

(iii) The sun will not set in Ireland tomorrow.

(iv) You will win an Olympic medal.

(v) The next person you meet on the street will be Irish.

(vi) You will get an even number when an ordinary dice is thrown.

(vii) You will get less than 5 winning numbers when playing the *Euromillions* some Friday.

(viii) It will snow later today.

(ix) I draw a red card from a standard pack of playing cards.

(x) You will get homework tonight.

2. For each of the events given below, choose one of these words:

**impossible**   **unlikely**   **even chance**   **likely**   **certain**

(i) A die is to be thrown.
Event 1:   A 6 will be thrown.
Event 2:   A number less than 4 will be thrown.
Event 3:   A number greater than 3 will be thrown.
Event 4:   A zero will be thrown.
Event 5:   A natural number less than 7 will be thrown.

(ii) One card is to be chosen at random from these five.
Event 1:   The card will be a *heart*.
Event 2:   The card will be less than 8.
Event 3:   The card will be a *diamond*.
Event 4:   The card will be a 2.
Event 5:   The card will not be a 3.

**3.** Here are four spinners with different colours:

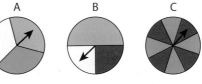

All the spinners are spun.
 (i) Which spinner has an even chance of showing blue?
 (ii) Which spinner has an even chance of showing red?
 (iii) Which spinner has the least chance of showing yellow?
 (iv) Which spinner has one chance in three of showing yellow?
 (v) Which spinner has one chance in four of showing red?
 (vi) Which spinner has the greatest chance of showing red?

**4.** Order each of the events below from least likely to most likely:
 (i) A die is to be thrown.
   (a) The number showing will be even.
   (b) The number showing will be larger than 4.
   (c) The number showing will be less than 6.
 (ii) One card is to be chosen at random from these six.
   (a) The card will be a 2.
   (b) The card will be a 7.
   (c) The card will be greater than a 3.

**5.** The jar shown contains red, blue and green marbles. When a marble is taken from the bag, the chances of obtaining each of the three colours are shown on the probability scale below.

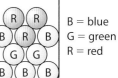

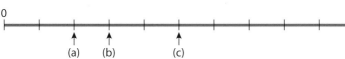

Link each colour to either (a), (b) or (c).

**6.**

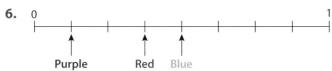

In a game, Todd spins an arrow.
The arrow stops in one of sixteen equal sectors of a circle.
Each sector of the circle is coloured.
The probability scale above shows how likely it is for the arrow to stop on any one colour.

How many sectors are
 (i) coloured red          (ii) coloured blue          (iii) coloured purple?

# Section 8.3 Probability and equally likely outcomes

Before you can start a certain game, you must throw a die and get a six.

The act of throwing a die is called a **trial**.

The numbers 1, 2, 3, 4, 5 and 6 are all the possible **outcomes** of the trial.

The list of all possible outcomes is called a **sample space**.

The desired result is called an **event**.

If you require an even number when throwing a die, then the **events** or **favourable outcomes** are the numbers 2, 4 and 6.

> The result we want is called an **event** or **favourable outcome**.

## Equally likely outcomes

Two events are **equally likely** if they each have the same chance of happening.

The chance of getting a red with this spinner is the same as the chance of getting a blue. Getting a red and getting a blue are **equally likely**.

The chances of getting a red or getting a blue with this spinner are **not** equally likely. The probability of getting a red when this spinner is spun is one chance in four.

We write this as Probability (red) $= \frac{1}{4}$.
This is shortened to P(red) $= \frac{1}{4}$.

> For **equally likely outcomes**, the probability of event $E$ occurring is given by
>
> $$P(E) = \frac{\text{Number of favourable outcomes}}{\text{Number of possible outcomes}}$$

For the spinner on the right,

P(green) $= \frac{1}{5}$, because 1 of the 5 sections is green

P(yellow) $= \frac{2}{5}$, because 2 of the 5 sections are yellow.

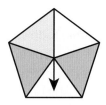

**Example 1**

Below is a number of lettered tiles.

P A R A L L E L O G R A M

One of these tiles is selected at random.
Work out the probability of getting:
  (i)   an A          (ii)  an L          (iii)  an O
  (iv)  an A or an L    (v)   an A or an O    (vi)  an L or an O.

  (i)   There are 3 tiles lettered A out of the 13 tiles.

$$P(A) = \frac{\text{number of As}}{\text{total number}} = \frac{3}{13}$$

 (ii)  $P(L) = \frac{\text{number of Ls}}{\text{total number}} = \frac{3}{13}$

 (iii) $P(O) = \frac{1}{13}$

 (iv)  $P(A \text{ or } L) = \frac{\text{number of As} + \text{Ls}}{\text{total number}} = \frac{6}{13}$

 (v)   $P(A \text{ or } O) = \frac{4}{13}$          (vi)  $P(L \text{ or } O) = \frac{4}{13}$

## Exercise 8.3

**1.** (i)  State the sample space for each of these spinners:

   (a) 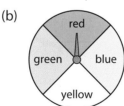          (b) 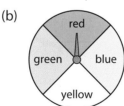          (c)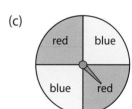

   (ii)  For each of the spinners, write down the probability that the pointer ends on red.

**2.** What is the probability of getting a 6 on each of these spinners?

   (i) 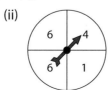          (ii) 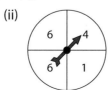          (iii)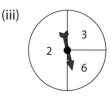

What is the probability of getting a 2 or a 6 on spinner (iii)?

**3.** A fair die is rolled.
   What is the probability of getting

   (i)   a 5                                    (ii)  a 1 or a 2
   (iii)  4 or more                          (iv)  an odd number
   (v)   less than 3                         (vi)  a prime number?

**4.** Here is a selection of shapes.

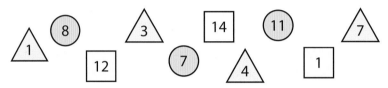

   One of these shapes is chosen at random.
   Work out the probability that the shape will be:

   (i)   a square            (ii)  a triangle          (iii)  a square or a triangle
   (iv)  an odd number       (v)   a 2-digit number     (vi)  a green odd number.

**5.** A letter is chosen at random from the word *PROBABILITY*.
   Write down the probability that it will be

   (i)  *A*          (ii)  *B*          (iii)  *I*          (iv)  a vowel       (v)  a *B* or an *I*.

**6.** For each of the following unbiased spinners, find the probability that the outcome
   of one spin will be a four.

   (i)                                  (ii)                                 (iii)

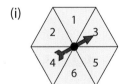  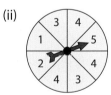  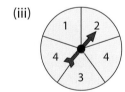

**7.** A dart board has 36 sectors, labelled 1 to 36.
   Determine the probability that a dart thrown
   at the board hits:

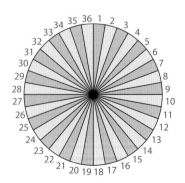

   (i)   a multiple of 4
   (ii)  a number between 6 and 9 inclusive
   (iii)  a number greater than 20
   (iv)  9
   (v)   a multiple of 13
   (vi)  an odd number that is a multiple of 3.

8. A standard pack of cards has 4 suits: hearts (♥), diamonds (♦), clubs (♣) and spades (♠).
   There are 13 cards in each suit and 52 cards altogether.

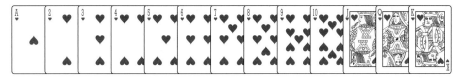

   The first of these cards is called an **Ace**. The last three cards are the *picture* or *court* cards: the **Jack**, the **Queen** and the **King**.

   From the 13 cards shown above, one card is to be chosen at random.
   What is the probability that the card chosen will be:
   (i)   the 7                (ii)  the Ace              (iii) a picture card
   (iv)  a heart              (v)   a spade              (vi)  either a 9 or a 10?

9. From a standard pack of 52 cards, a card is chosen at random.
   What is the probability that the card will be:
   (i)   a diamond            (ii)  a red card           (iii) a black card
   (iv)  a 3                  (v)   a picture card        (vi)  either an Ace or a King?

10. A box contains twelve green marbles, six blue marbles and eight white marbles.
    A marble is selected by a blind-folded person.
    What is the probability that the marble selected is:
    (i)   green or white               (ii)  blue or white
    (iii) not green                    (iv)  orange?

11. A square dart board is divided into sixteen smaller squares. Fourteen of the squares are painted as shown.
    (i)  What colour(s) should the two remaining squares be painted so that the probability of landing on red is $\frac{3}{8}$ and it is impossible to land on black?
    (ii) What colour(s) should the two remaining squares be painted so that the probability of landing on red is twice the probability of landing on blue?

| red | yellow | red | blue |
|-----|--------|-----|------|
| white | red | white | blue |
| red | blue | white | red |
| white | yellow | ? | ? |

12. What is the probability that the pointer of these spinners lands in the blue section?

    (i)                    (ii)                   (iii)                  (iv)

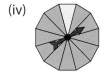

13. Design a spinner for which the probability of the pointer landing on the blue section is:
    (i) half
    (ii) less than half
    (iii) three times as likely as on red.

14. Assuming that a person is equally likely to be born on any day of the week or in any month of the year, what is the probability that a randomly-chosen person has his/her birthday
    (i) on a Tuesday
    (ii) on a Saturday or Sunday
    (iii) in January or February
    (iv) in a month ending in y?

15. A bag contains five red discs with the numbers 1 to 5 painted on them and seven blue discs painted with the numbers 1 to 7. If a disc is chosen at random, what is the probability of choosing
    (i) a red disc
    (ii) a disc numbered 3
    (iii) a disc numbered 6
    (iv) the blue disc numbered 1
    (v) an even-numbered disc
    (vi) an odd-numbered disc?

    Explain why the probabilities in (v) and (vi) sum to 1.

16. In a pre-election poll of 400 people, 120 supported the A party, 140 supported the B party and the rest were undecided. If a person is selected at random from this group, what is the probability that they:
    (i) support the A party
    (ii) support the B party
    (iii) support a party
    (iv) are undecided?

17. At the end of a Summer Camp, 50 boys and girls were asked to name their favourite game at the camp. The results are given in the table below:

| | Tennis | Basketball | Volleyball | Totals |
|---|---|---|---|---|
| **Girls** | 15 | 10 | 5 | |
| **Boys** | 6 | 12 | 2 | |
| **Totals** | | | | |

    (i) Copy and complete the totals in this two-way chart.
    (ii) If a person was selected at random from the group of 50, calculate the probability that the person
       (a) was a boy
       (b) was a girl who named tennis as her favourite game
       (c) named basketball as her/his favourite game.

    If a girl was selected, find the probability that she had named volleyball as her favourite game.

**18.** Of 100 tickets sold in a raffle, Luke bought 10, Heather bought 5 and Alan bought 1.
A ticket was chosen at random to determine who won the only prize.
What is the probability that the prize was won by:

(i) Alan                 (ii) Luke

(iii) Heather         (iv) none of these three people?

How many of the 100 tickets would I need to buy for the probability of my winning to be:

(v) $\frac{3}{10}$          (vi) 0.2          (vii) 25%          (viii) 100%?

**19.** There are 8 counters in a box.
The probability of taking a green counter out of the box is $\frac{1}{2}$.
A green counter is taken out of the box and put to one side.
Gerry now takes a counter at random from the box.
What is the probability it is green?

**20.** A game is played by picking a card, without looking, from a pack of 52 playing cards.
The table shows the results of picking various cards.

If Eileen picks a card, what is the probability that she will

(i) lose money                 (ii) win money

(iii) neither win nor lose      (iv) not lose money?

| Card | Result |
|---|---|
| Ace | Win €2 |
| K, Q or J | Win 50c |
| 6, 7, 8, 9, 10 | Break even |
| 2, 3, 4, 5 | Lose 50c |

## Section 8.4 Two events – Use of sample spaces / tree diagrams / two-way tables

When a die is thrown and a coin is tossed, the set of possible outcomes is as follows:

{H1, H2, H3, H4, H5, H6, T1, T2, T3, T4, T5, T6}.

This set of possible outcomes is called a **sample space**.

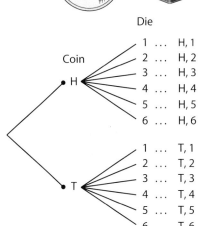

Die

Sample spaces can be created using tree diagrams or two-way tables as we have seen in the last section.

Using the sample space above, we can write down the probability of getting a head and a 6, for example.

$P(H, 6) = \frac{1}{12}$ … there are 12 possible outcomes

The probability of a head and an even number can be found by counting the required outcomes.
These are H2, H4 and H6.

∴    $P(H$ and even number$) = \frac{3}{12} = \frac{1}{4}$

**151**

An experiment such as throwing two dice has a large number of possible outcomes, so we need to set out the sample space in an organised way, as shown in the following example.

---

### Example 1

If two dice are thrown and the scores are added, set out a sample space giving all the possible outcomes. Now find the probability that
- (i) the total is exactly 7
- (ii) the total is 4 or less
- (iii) the total is 11 or more
- (iv) the total is a multiple of 5.

The sample space is set out on the right.
There are 36 outcomes.

(i) There are 6 totals of 7.
$$\Rightarrow \quad P(7) = \frac{6}{36} = \frac{1}{6}$$

(ii) There are 6 totals of 4 or less.
$$\Rightarrow \quad P(4 \text{ or less}) = \frac{6}{36} = \frac{1}{6}$$

(iii) There are 3 totals of 11 or more.
$$\Rightarrow \quad P(11 \text{ or more}) = \frac{3}{36} = \frac{1}{12}$$

(iv) The multiples of 5 are 5 and 10.
There are 7 totals of 5 or 10.
$$\Rightarrow \quad P(\text{multiple of 5}) = \frac{7}{36}$$

Total = 4 or less (red)

|   | 1 | 2 | 3 | 4 | 5 | 6 |
|---|---|---|---|---|---|---|
| **1** | 2 | 3 | 4 | 5 | 6 | 7 |
| **2** | 3 | 4 | 5 | 6 | 7 | 8 |
| **3** | 4 | 5 | 6 | 7 | 8 | 9 |
| **4** | 5 | 6 | 7 | 8 | 9 | 10 |
| **5** | 6 | 7 | 8 | 9 | 10 | 11 |
| **6** | 7 | 8 | 9 | 10 | 11 | 12 |

Total = 7 (green)

---

## Exercise 8.4

**1.** These are the possible outcomes when a coin is tossed twice:

*HH, HT, TH, TT*

Write down the probability of getting
- (i) 2 tails
- (ii) 2 heads
- (iii) a head and a tail.

**2.** When these two spinners are spun and the scores are added, you get the results shown on the right.

**Number on 1st spinner**

| Number on 2nd spinner |   | 1 | 2 | 3 | 4 |
|---|---|---|---|---|---|
|   | **1** | 2 | 3 | 4 | 5 |
|   | **2** | 3 | 4 | 5 | 6 |
|   | **3** | 4 | 5 | 6 | 7 |
|   | **4** | 5 | 6 | 7 | 8 |

Use the table to write down the following probabilities:
- (i) the total score is 6
- (ii) the total score is an odd number
- (iii) the total score is 7 or more
- (iv) the total score is 2 or 3.

3. A fair three-sided spinner has sections labelled
   2, 4 and 6.
   The spinner is spun once and a fair
   six-sided die is rolled once.

The number that the spinner lands
on is added to the number that the
dice shows. This gives the score.

Copy and complete the table to show all
possible scores.

Use the table to write down the probability
that the score is

  (i)  4         (ii)  5

(iii)  7       (iv)  9 or more

 (v)  5 or less   (vi)  a multiple of 4

**Die**

|  | + | 1 | 2 | 3 | 4 | 5 | 6 |
|---|---|---|---|---|---|---|---|
| **Spinner** | 2 | 3 |  |  |  |  |  |
|  | 4 |  |  |  |  |  |  |
|  | 6 |  |  |  |  |  | 12 |

4. Karl has two fair spinners, numbered as shown.
   He spins them and finds the **product** of the
   two scores.
     (i)  Copy and complete the grid to show all
        possible outcomes (products) of the two spins.
   (ii)  What is the probability that the product is
        (a)  12
        (b)  greater than 10
        (c)  a multiple of 3?

  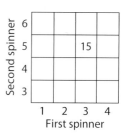

5. The ace, king, queen and jack of clubs and the
   ace, king, queen and jack of diamonds are put
   into two separate piles. The sample space
   diagram shows all the possible outcomes when
   a card is taken from each pile.

Write down the probability that
  (i)  both cards will be kings
 (ii)  one card will be a club
(iii)  only one of the cards will be a queen
(iv)  the cards will make a matching pair
 (v)  at least one of the cards will be a queen
(vi)  neither card will be a jack.

**6.** Three fair coins are tossed.
Using a tree diagram make a sample space
for all the possible outcomes.

Now write down the probability
that the outcome will be

   (i)  three heads

   (iii)  no heads

   (ii)  two heads and one tail (in any order)

   (iv)  at least one head.

**7.** Two dice are thrown and the scores obtained
are added. The resulting outcomes are
shown in the given sample space.
Find the probability that the sum of
the two numbers is

   (i)  9

   (iii)  3 or less

   (ii)  10

   (iv)  10 or 11.

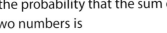

| | | | | | | |
|---|---|---|---|---|---|---|
| 6 | 7 | 8 | 9 | 10 | 11 | 12 |
| 5 | 6 | 7 | 8 | 9 | 10 | 11 |
| 4 | 5 | 6 | 7 | 8 | 9 | 10 |
| 3 | 4 | 5 | 6 | 7 | 8 | 9 |
| 2 | 3 | 4 | 5 | 6 | 7 | 8 |
| 1 | 2 | 3 | 4 | 5 | 6 | 7 |
| | 1 | 2 | 3 | 4 | 5 | 6 |

**8.** Chloe is playing a word game and chooses
both a vowel and a consonant at random
from her letters.

   (i)  Show all the possible choices she can make using a tree diagram.

   (ii)  What is the probability of choosing A and R?

   (iii)  What is the probability of choosing I and L?

   (iv)  Work out the probability of choosing I and not choosing L.

**9.** Bag A contains 2 red beads and 1 white bead.
Bag B contains 2 white beads and 1 red bead.
A bead is drawn at random from each bag.

Copy and complete the table to show all
the possible pairs of colours.

   (i)  Find the probability that both beads
     are red.

   (ii)  Find the probability that the two beads
     are the same colour.

   (iii)  Find the probability that the pair of beads will be different in colour.

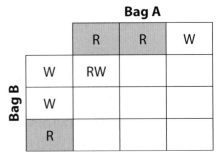

**Bag A**

| Bag B | R | R | W |
|---|---|---|---|
| W | RW | | |
| W | | | |
| R | | | |

**10.** A red car (R), a blue car (B) and a green car (G) are parked on a narrow driveway,
one behind the other.

   (i)  List all the possible orders in which the three cars could be parked.

The cars are parked on the driveway at random.

   (ii)  What is the probability that the blue car is the first on the driveway?

**11.** Mark did a project on language choices in 5th year in his school.

He collected the following information:

The 125 students in 5th year studied either French, German or Spanish.
22 girls studied French. There were 70 girls in total.
25 boys did German. There were 42 students in the Spanish class of which 12 were boys.

He then used a two-way table to present his results.

|        | French | German | Spanish | Total |
|--------|--------|--------|---------|-------|
| **Boys** | ( )  | 25     | 12      | ( )   |
| **Girls** | 22  | ( )    | ( )     | 70    |
| **Total** | ( )  | ( )    | 42      | 125   |

(a) Fill in the missing numbers to complete the table.

(b) How many students studied French in 5th year?

(c) How many boys were in 5th year?

(d) What fraction of the students studied German.

(e) If a student was selected at random from 5th year what is the probability that the student;
   (i) studied French,
   (ii) was a girl who studied Spanish,
   (iii) was a boy who studied German?

# Section 8.5 Estimating probability from experiments

## Doing an experiment

Suppose I wanted to estimate the probability of a drawing pin landing 'point upwards' when dropped onto a hard surface.

Is it **equally likely** that the point lands upwards or downwards?

Since we are not sure that each event is equally likely, we cannot calculate the exact probability of the event happening.

But we can get an **estimate of the probability** by doing an **experiment**.

To find an estimate of the probability that a drawing pin lands 'point upwards', we could toss the pin 500 times and record the number of times it finishes 'point upwards'.

If the drawing pin landed 'point upwards' 350 times in 500 tosses, we could then write down an **estimate** of the probability.

$$\text{Experimental probability (point upwards)} = \frac{\text{Number of 'point upwards'}}{\text{Total number of tosses}}$$
$$= \frac{350}{500} = \frac{35}{50} = \frac{7}{10}$$

In general, if we need a more accurate estimate of the probability of some event happening, we increase the number of trials or experiments conducted.

---

**Example 1**

The table below shows the results in Division One of a football league.

| Home wins | Away wins | Draws |
|:---------:|:---------:|:-----:|
| 24 | 10 | 6 |

Use the data in this table to estimate the probability of getting the following results in a randomly selected match taking place in the next round of fixtures.

(i) a home win     (ii) an away win     (iii) a draw

(i) There were 24 home wins out of 40 matches.

$$\text{Estimated probability of home win} = \frac{24}{40} = \frac{6}{10} = \frac{3}{5}$$

(ii) $\text{Estimated probability of away win} = \frac{10}{40} = \frac{1}{4}$

(iii) $\text{Estimated probability of a draw} = \frac{6}{40} = \frac{3}{20}$

---

## Relative frequency

We can also describe the $\dfrac{Number\ of\ successes}{Total\ number\ of\ trials}$ as the **relative frequency** of that outcome.
In all experiments as the total number of trials increases the relative frequency (or experimental probability) gives a better estimate of the true probability.

$$\text{Relative frequency} = \frac{Number\ of\ successes}{Total\ number\ of\ trials} = \text{Experimental probability}$$

## Example 2

A fair six-sided die has its faces painted red, white or blue.

The die is thrown 36 times

Here are the results.

Based on the results, how many faces are painted each colour?

| Colour | Frequency |
|--------|-----------|
| Red    | 7         |
| White  | 11        |
| Blue   | 18        |

The relative frequency for the Blue face is $\dfrac{18}{36} = \dfrac{1}{2}$ ∴ half the faces $\left(\dfrac{1}{2} \times 6 = 3\right)$, must be blue.

The relative frequency for the White face is $\dfrac{11}{36} \cong \dfrac{1}{3}$ ∴ one third of the faces $\left(\dfrac{1}{3} \times 6 = 2\right)$, must be white.

The relative frequency for the Red face is $\dfrac{7}{36} \cong \dfrac{1}{6}$ ∴ one sixth of the faces $\left(\dfrac{1}{6} \times 6 = 1\right)$, must be red.

## Exercise 8.5

1. Shane tosses a fair coin six times. He gets a head four times. Shane says that if he tosses it another six times, he will get four heads again. Explain why Shane could be wrong. If the coin is tossed 100 times, how many heads should Shane expect?

2. Jane and Nicky both did the 'dropping a drawing pin' experiment. Here are their results.

Jane
| Trials     | 20 |
|------------|----|
| 'Point up' | 10 |

Nicky
| Trials     | 100 |
|------------|-----|
| 'Point up' | 75  |

Another drawing pin is dropped.
   (i)   For Jane, what is the probability of getting 'point up'?
   (ii)  For Nicky, what is the probability of getting 'point up'?
   (iii) Whose result is likely to be more reliable? Explain your answer.

3. 50 cars are observed passing the school gate.
   15 of these cars are red.
   Use these results to estimate the probability that the next car to pass the school gate will be red.

**4.** Eric is a goalkeeper. His manager records the number of shots he saves.

| | Tally | Frequency |
|---|---|---|
| **Saves** | ЖЖ ЖЖ ЖЖ ЖЖ ЖЖ IIII | 29 |
| **Doesn't save** | ЖЖ ЖЖ ЖЖ I | 16 |

Estimate the probability that Eric saves the next shot.
Give your answer as a decimal, correct to one decimal place.

**5.** Ciara surveyed the colours of vehicles passing her home. Here are her results.

| Colour | Red | Black | Silver | Green | White | Other |
|---|---|---|---|---|---|---|
| **Frequency** | 6 | 10 | 24 | 4 | 12 | 8 |

Calculate an estimate of the probability that the next vehicle to pass will be silver.

**6.** Eoin is carrying out the experiment 'dropping a spoon'.
He records whether the spoon lands up or down.

Up

Down

(i) Copy and complete this table of Eoin's results.

| Number of drops | 5 | 10 | 20 | 25 | 50 | 100 |
|---|---|---|---|---|---|---|
| **Number of times landed up** | 3 | 7 | 11 | 15 | 32 | 63 |
| **Probability** | 0.6 | 0.7 | | | | |

(ii) What do you think would be a reasonable estimate for the probability
of this spoon landing up?
Give your answer as a decimal, correct to 1 decimal place.

**7.** A fair six-sided die has its faces painted either red (R),
blue (B) or white (W).
The dice is thrown 36 times.

Here are the results.

| | | | | | | | | |
|---|---|---|---|---|---|---|---|---|
| B | B | R | W | B | W | B | R | W |
| B | R | W | R | B | B | W | W | B |
| W | B | B | R | W | B | W | W | B |
| B | B | R | B | B | W | R | W | B |

Copy and complete the table below for these results.

| Outcome | Tally | Frequency |
|---|---|---|
| Red | | |
| White | | |
| Blue | | |
| Total | | 36 |

(i) Use these results to estimate the probability that the next throw will be red.

(ii) Estimate the probability that the next throw will be white.

(iii) Based on these results, how many faces do you think are painted blue?

8. A biased dice is cast 1000 times and the results recorded.

Biased means not fair.

| Number on dice | 1 | 2 | 3 | 4 | 5 | 6 |
|---|---|---|---|---|---|---|
| Frequency | 60 | 196 | 84 | 148 | 162 | 350 |

Use the results to estimate the probability of obtaining a six when the dice is cast again. Give your answer as a decimal.

9. Sean collected the results of 40 *Rovers* home games.
Estimate the probability that in their next home game:

| Won | 18 |
|---|---|
| Lost | 10 |
| Drawn | 12 |

(i) they will win
(ii) they will lose.

For *Rover's* next 40 home games, the results were as follows:
Using all 80 results, estimate the probability of *Rovers*

| Won | 24 |
|---|---|
| Lost | 10 |
| Drawn | 6 |

(iii) winning their next home game
(iv) drawing their next home game.

Would you expect these probabilities to be more accurate than those based on the first 40 matches? Why?

10. The results from 40 spins of a numbered spinner are:

2 1 4 3 2 1 3 4 5 2 1 2 2 3 2 1 2 4 5 2
1 5 3 4 2 3 3 3 2 4 2 3 4 2 1 5 3 3 5 3

Make out a frequency table to show this data.
Use the table to estimate the probability of getting a 2 with the next spin.

11. A bag contained coloured beads. Darren randomly selects a bead and then replaces it. He does this 60 times. Here are the results.

| Colour | White | Green | Blue |
|---|---|---|---|
| Frequency | 10 | 30 | 20 |

Estimate the probability that on his next draw he will select
(i) a white bead
(ii) a green bead
(iii) a white bead or a blue bead.

**12.** Kathy is recording in which direction cars go when they reach a T-junction in the road near her school.

She writes right (R) or left (L) for each car. Here are her results in order.

```
R  R  L  R  L  R  R  L  L  L  R  R  R  L  L  R  L
R  L  R  L  R  L  L  R  R  R  R  R  L  L  R  L  R
L  R  R  R  L  R  R  L  R  R  R  L  L  R  R  R
```

Estimate the probability of the next car turning right after the following numbers of results (write each answer as a decimal);
   (i)   after the first 10 cars have passed
   (ii)  after 20 cars have passed
   (iii) after 50 cars have passed.

Kathy's local council have also carried out a survey at this junction. They observed over 1000 cars and estimated that the probability of a car turning right is 0.62.
   (iv)  Do you think Kathy's results agree with this?
   (v)   Whose estimate do you think is more accurate, Kathy's or the council's? Explain your answer.

**13.** In an experiment Tom drops 12 drawing pins onto a hard floor. He does the experiment 10 times and counts how many pins land 'point up' each time. His results were

| Number of the 12 drawing pins that landed 'point up' | | | | | | | | | |
|---|---|---|---|---|---|---|---|---|---|
| 3 | 5 | 6 | 2 | 4 | 7 | 3 | 3 | 4 | 5 |

   (i)   Use Tom's data to work out the probability that a *single* drawing pin will land 'point up'.
   (ii)  Tom continues the experiment until he has dropped the 12 drawing pins 100 times. About how many drawing pins in total would you expect to land 'point up'?

**14.** Rachel, Barry and Leanore each rolled a different die 360 times.
The results are shown in the given table. Only one of the dice was fair.
Whose was it? Explain your answer.

| Number | Rachel | Barry | Leanore |
|---|---|---|---|
| 1 | 27 | 58 | 141 |
| 2 | 69 | 62 | 52 |
| 3 | 78 | 63 | 56 |
| 4 | 43 | 57 | 53 |
| 5 | 76 | 56 | 53 |
| 6 | 67 | 64 | 5 |

# Test yourself 8

1. A bag contains 50 marbles: 20 are red, 12 are pink and 18 are black.
   What is the probability that a marble selected at random is:
   - (i) red
   - (ii) pink
   - (iii) not black?

2. The first 100 vehicles to pass a checkpoint gave the results in the table. If these figures truly represent the traffic at any time passing this checkpoint, determine the probability that the next vehicle will be:
   - (i) a car
   - (ii) a motorcycle
   - (iii) a bus
   - (iv) *not* a car
   - (v) *not* a car or truck

| Type of vehicle | Frequency |
| --- | --- |
| Cars | 70 |
| Trucks | 15 |
| Motorcycles | 10 |
| Buses | 5 |

3. Raffle tickets are numbered 1 to 300. Lucy buys five tickets and gets the numbers 8, 9, 10, 11 and 12. Robbie buys five tickets and gets the numbers 18, 29, 182, 207, 234. One ticket is chosen at random.
   Is Lucy or Robbie more likely to have the winning number?
   Explain your answer.

4.

A        B        C

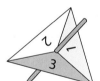 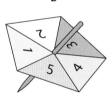 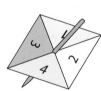

For which of these spinners is the probability of spinning a 3 equal to:
   - (i) 20%
   - (ii) 25%
   - (iii) $\frac{1}{3}$?

5. Silvia has cards numbered 1, 2, 3, 4 and 5. She puts several cards in a bag.
   She takes out a card at random, records the number on the card, and then replaces it in the bag.
   The table shows her results.

| Number on card | 1 | 2 | 3 | 4 | 5 |
| --- | --- | --- | --- | --- | --- |
| Tally | ⦀⦀ ⏐ | ⏐⏐⏐ | ⏐⏐ | ⦀⦀ ⏐⏐⏐ | ⦀⦀ |
| Frequency | | | | | |

Copy the table and complete the last row.
   - (i) How many times did Silvia take a card out of the bag?
   - (ii) Which number did she take out most often?
   - (iii) Estimate the probability that the next card Silvia picks has the number 2 on it.

**6.** Tom has a four-sided die.
He rolls the die 100 times.
The table shows the outcomes.
Is the dice fair? Explain your answer.

| Outcome | 1 | 2 | 3 | 4 |
|---|---|---|---|---|
| **Frequency** | 18 | 44 | 19 | 19 |

**7.** A bag contains two red counters, three blue counters and three green counters.
A counter is taken out of the bag at random.
Find, as a fraction, the probabilities of these outcomes:
  (i)  a red counter     (ii)  a blue counter
(iii)  a green counter   (iv)  either a red or a blue counter.
Add together your answers for (i), (ii) and (iii).
Explain your result.

**8.** An ordinary pack of playing cards is shuffled well and a card is drawn out.
Determine the probability that it is:
  (i)  a red card                   (ii)  the ace of spades
(iii)  a number less than ten and greater than four
(iv)  a black picture card        (v)  an ace
(vi)  a number between four and ten inclusive.

**9.** One ball is selected at random from the bag shown and
then replaced. This procedure is done 400 times.
How many times would you expect to select:
  (i)  a blue ball
 (ii)  a red ball?

**10.** In an experiment a gardener plants 40 daffodil bulbs of which 36 grew to produce
flowers. Use these results to estimate the probability that his next daffodil bulb will
grow to produce a flower.

**11.** Ava spins a coin and rolls a die.
Some of the possible outcomes
are shown in the table.
Copy and complete the table.
  (i)  What is the total number
      of outcomes?
 (ii)  What is the probability of
      getting a head and a 5?
(iii)  What is the probability of getting a tail and a number less than 4?
(iv)  What is the probability of getting a 2?

**Die**

| Coin | 1 | 2 | 3 | 4 | 5 | 6 |
|---|---|---|---|---|---|---|
| H | H, 1 | H, 2 | | | | |
| T | | | | T, 4 | | T, 6 |

**12.** The probability that a biased die will land '3 up' is 0.4.
Mark rolls the biased dice 200 times.
Work out an estimate for the number of times that the die will land '3 up'.

**13.** 100 students go on a school trip.
On the trip they each have a drink of water,
orange juice or milk.
24 out of the 57 boys drank milk.
27 girls drank water.
A total of 24 students drank orange juice,
$\frac{1}{3}$ of these are girls.

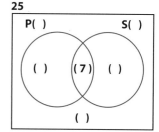

Copy and complete the two-way table.

|  | Milk | Water | Orange Juice | Totals |
|---|---|---|---|---|
| **Boys** | 24 | ( ) | ( ) | 57 |
| **Girls** | ( ) | 27 | ( ) | ( ) |
| **Totals** | ( ) | ( ) | 24 | 100 |

Find (a) the probability that a student chosen at random from the group is drinking water.
(b) the probability that a boy chosen at random from the group is drinking water.

**14.** Dave sent out a questionnaire to his class of 25 students to find out if they had travelled to Spain(S) or Portugal(P)
He discovered:
15 students visited Portugal
11 students visited Spain
7 students visited both Portugal and Spain.

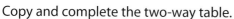

(a) Copy and complete the Venn diagram he drew of his results.

(b) How many students did not visit either Spain or Portugal?

If one of the students is chosen at random what is the probability that the student:
(i) visited Spain only
(ii) visited Spain
(iii) visited Spain and Portugal
(iv) did not visit Spain or Portugal?

# Assignment:

Compare the relative frequency (experimental probability) and true (or theoretical) probability.

If a fair die is rolled, we know that each face is equally likely to occur.
The probability of each face occurring is $\frac{1}{6} \approx 0.167$.
This is the true (or theoretical) probability.

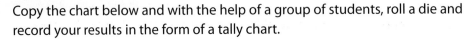

Copy the chart below and with the help of a group of students, roll a die and record your results in the form of a tally chart.

Every 30 throws find the experimental probability of each number occurring on the die. Correct your answers to three places of decimals.

Add the sets of 30 throws together until the die is rolled 120 times.

| Number of rolls | 1 | 2 | 3 | 4 | 5 | 6 |
|---|---|---|---|---|---|---|
| 30 | | | | | | |
| Experimental Probability | $= \dfrac{(\ )}{30}$ | $= \dfrac{(\ )}{30}$ | $= \dfrac{(\ )}{30}$ | $= \dfrac{(\ )}{30}$ | $= \dfrac{(\ )}{30}$ | $= \dfrac{(\ )}{30}$ |
| 30 (60) | | | | | | |
| Experimental Probability | $= \dfrac{(\ )}{60}$ | $= \dfrac{(\ )}{60}$ | $= \dfrac{(\ )}{60}$ | $= \dfrac{(\ )}{60}$ | $= \dfrac{(\ )}{60}$ | $= \dfrac{(\ )}{60}$ |
| 30 (90) | | | | | | |
| Experimental Probability | $= \dfrac{(\ )}{90}$ | $= \dfrac{(\ )}{90}$ | $= \dfrac{(\ )}{90}$ | $= \dfrac{(\ )}{90}$ | $= \dfrac{(\ )}{90}$ | $= \dfrac{(\ )}{90}$ |
| 30 (120) | | | | | | |
| Experimental Probability | $= \dfrac{(\ )}{120}$ | $= \dfrac{(\ )}{120}$ | $= \dfrac{(\ )}{120}$ | $= \dfrac{(\ )}{120}$ | $= \dfrac{(\ )}{120}$ | $= \dfrac{(\ )}{120}$ |

Compare the experimental probability to the theoretical probability as the number of times the die is rolled is increased.

Write a conclusion:

# Statistics 2

## In this chapter, you will learn to:

- find the mode of a data set,
- find the median of a data set,
- calculate the mean of a data set,
- identify an outlier,
- use the range to show how spread out a data set is,
- select the correct average to compare two sets of data,
- find a missing piece of data from a set if you know the mean,
- read data from a frequency table,
- calculate the mean and mode from a frequency table.

## Section 9.1  Summary statistics

Summary statistics is information that gives a quick and simple description of collected data.

Our course includes measures of **average** which give information about the centre of the data (central tendency) and **range** which gives information about the spread (variability) of the data.

### Averages

When we look for an average, we are trying to find a **single** or **typical value** that will represent the **many values** we have collected.

The idea of an average is extremely useful because it enables us to compare one set of data with another by comparing just two values – their averages.
The most commonly-used averages in statistics are the **mode**, the **median** and the **mean**.
In this section we will deal with the first two of these, the mode and the median.

### 1.  The mode

The mode is the value that occurs most often in the data. The mode is particularly relevant when one value appears much more often than the other values. The mode is often called the **modal value**.

---

**Example 1**

Find the mode of each data set:

(i) 7, 9, 8, 7, 12, 10, 7, 11, 8

(ii) red, blue, yellow, blue, green, yellow, blue, red, blue, yellow, red, blue

(i) The mode is 7 because it appears more often than any other value.

(ii) In the data set there are

3 reds, 5 blues, 3 yellows, 1 green

The mode is blue as it occurs most often.

---

## 2. The median

To find the median of a list of numbers, put the numbers in order of size, starting with the smallest. The median is the middle number.

---

**Example 1**

Find the median of each of these arrays of numbers:

(i) 2, 5, 3, 4, 5, 8, 7, 9, 6

(ii) 12, 15, 13, 9, 7, 15

(i) We rewrite the numbers in order of size.

2, 3, 4, 5, 5, 6, 7, 8, 9

The middle number is 5, so 5 is the median.

(ii) Again, we rewrite the numbers in order of size

7, 9, 12, 13, 15, 15

Here there are 6 numbers, so there are two middle numbers,

12 and 13.

The median is $\frac{1}{2}(12 + 13)$

$$= \frac{1}{2}(25) = 12\frac{1}{2}$$

**Note:** When there is an even number of numbers, the median is

$\frac{1}{2}$ [Sum of the two middle numbers]

---

## Exercise 9.1

**1.** Find the mode of each of these sets:

(i) 7, 8, 3, 7, 5, 6, 3, 7, 2

(ii) 15, 12, 16, 19, 12, 14, 16, 12

(iii)  5.6, 5.4, 5.7, 5.5, 5.7, 5.6, 5.7

(iv)  bus, car, bus, walk, car, bus, cycle, car, bus, bus, walk, cycle, car, walk, bus

**2.** Write down the mode for each set of data:

(i)  10, 1000, 100, 1000, 10, 10, 1000, 10, 1000, 100, 10

(ii)  sun, snow, sun, fog, rain, snow, fog, rain, sun, cloud, sun, rain

(iii)  $\frac{1}{2}$, $\frac{1}{4}$, $\frac{3}{4}$, $\frac{1}{4}$, 1, $\frac{1}{4}$, $\frac{3}{4}$, 1, 0, $\frac{1}{4}$, 0, $\frac{1}{4}$, $\frac{3}{4}$, $\frac{1}{2}$, 1, $\frac{1}{4}$, $\frac{1}{2}$

**3.** The mode of these numbers is 5. Find the value of *.

2, 3, 7, 5, 2, 6, *, 5, 3

**4.** The girls in one class were asked how much time they spend on homework each week. The results are shown in this bar chart.

(i)  How many girls spend 3 hours on homework?

(ii)  What is the modal number of hours?

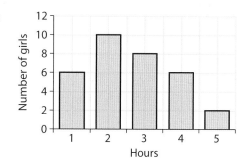

**5.** Explain why there is no single mode in the following set of data:

2, 1, 3, 4, 6, 4, 1, 3, 0, 2, 6, 0

**6.** Joan did a survey to find the shoe sizes of pupils in her class. The bar chart illustrates her data.

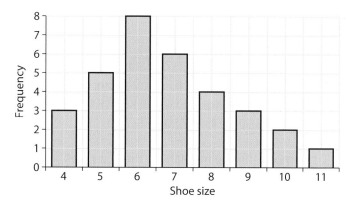

(i)  How many pupils are there in Joan's class?

(ii)  What is the modal shoe size?

(iii)  Can you tell from the bar chart which shoe sizes are the boys and which are the girls in her class?

(iv) Joan then decided to draw a bar chart to show the shoe sizes of the boys and the girls separately. Do you think that the mode for the boys and the mode for the girls will be the same as the mode for the whole class? Explain your answer.

**7.** What is the median height of this group of friends?

180 cm    163 cm    151 cm    180 cm    175 cm    171 cm    158 cm

**8.** Find the median of each set of numbers:
   (i)   3, 4, 6, 6, 7, 8, 9
   (ii)  12, 12, 13, 14, 14, 15, 15, 16, 17
   (iii) 3.2, 3.5, 3.5, 3.6, 3.6, 3.7, 3.8

**9.** Rewrite each of the following sets of data in order of size and then write down the median of each set.
   (i)   6, 8, 3, 9, 8, 5, 7, 2, 8
   (ii)  24, 23, 19, 27, 26, 20, 25, 23, 25
   (iii) 3.5, 3, 3.7, 3.7, 3.9, 3.5, 3.6, 3.8, 3.9

**10.** By finding half the sum of the two middle numbers, write down the median of this set of data:

   7, 10, 9, 13, 12, 9, 11, 14

**11.** Find the median of each of these sets of data:
   (i)   9 cm, 12 cm, 4 cm, 8 cm, 7 cm, 5 cm, 3 cm, 10 cm
   (ii)  23 kg, 15 kg, 19 kg, 34 kg, 16 kg, 26 kg, 18 kg, 27 kg
   (iii) €10, €5, €8, €5.50, €4, €7.50, €6, €9

**12.** Work out (i) the mode (ii) the median for this data set.

   5, 7, 9, 9, 8, 7, 9, 10, 12, 11, 9, 9, 5

**13.** In this set of data, the mode is 9.

   7, 4, 3, 3, 12, 9, $x$, 10, 9

   (i)  Find the value of $x$.
   (ii) What is the median of the set?

**14.** The bar chart on the right
shows the test scores of a group
of pupils.

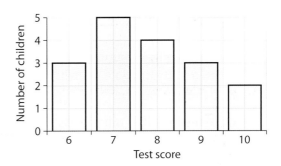

 (i) What is the modal test
score?

 (ii) How many pupils were in
the group?

 (iii) List all the scores in order
of size.

 The first four are listed for you.

 6, 6, 6, 7, ...

 Now write down the median test score.

## Section 9.2 The mean

The **mean** of the numbers

 4, 5, 7, 9, 10

$$\text{Mean} = \frac{\text{Sum of the numbers}}{\text{Number of numbers}}$$

is the sum of these numbers divided by the number of numbers.

$$\therefore \quad \text{Mean} = \frac{4 + 5 + 7 + 9 + 10}{5} = \frac{35}{5} = 7$$

In everyday language the word 'average' is generally used instead of 'mean'.
The mean is a very important value in statistics as it takes into account all the values in
the set of data.

---
**Example 1**

In five basketball matches Joan scored 16 points, 10 points, 22 points,
18 points and 24 points. Calculate her mean score for the five matches.

$$\text{Mean} = \frac{16 + 10 + 22 + 18 + 24}{5} = \frac{90}{5} = 18 \text{ points}$$

---

If the mean of three numbers is 9, it follows that the sum of the three numbers is 27,
since $27 \div 3 = 9$.

---

**Example 2**

The mean of four numbers is 7.
When a fifth number is added, the mean of the five numbers is 9.
Find the fifth number.

If the mean of four numbers is 7, then the sum of the four numbers is
$4 \times 7$, i.e. 28.
The mean of five numbers $= 9 \Rightarrow$ sum of the five numbers $= 45$ ... $5 \times 9 = 45$
∴   the fifth number $= 45 - 28$
$$= 17$$

---

## Extreme values

Here are the marks scored by six pupils in a maths test:
   26, 35, 34, 46, 52, 95

The mean mark is $\dfrac{26 + 35 + 34 + 46 + 52 + 95}{6} = \dfrac{288}{6} = 48$

Notice that four out of the six students are below the mean mark.
This is caused by one mark, i.e. 95, which is much higher than all the other marks.

Such a mark is generally known as an **outlier** or **extreme value**. When an outlier exists, the mean may not fully represent the set of data given. This happens, in particular, when the number of data items is small.

## Exercise 9.2

**1.** Find the mean of each of these sets of data.
   (i)  2, 4, 5, 6, 8
   (ii)  3, 7, 8, 10, 11, 15
   (iii)  14, 17, 21, 13, 6, 13
   (iv)  1, 0, 5, 7, 17, 12

**2.** Ava's marks in six subjects were  47, 68, 62, 76, 59  and  54.
   Find her mean mark.

**3.** A snooker player scored 208 points in 8 visits to the table.
   What was his average number of points per visit?

**4.** Five girls had these sums of money:
   €3.80, €8.30, €2.40, €5.70  and  €11.30.
   Work out the mean sum of money.

5. Find the mean of the numbers  6,  8,  9,  10,  12.
   If a sixth number, zero, is added to these five numbers, find the mean of the six numbers.

6. The mean of four numbers is 9.
   Find the sum of the four numbers.

7. The mean of three numbers is 8.
   (i)   What is the sum of the three numbers?
   (ii)  If two of the numbers are 6 and 7, find the third number.

8. The mean of four numbers is 9.
   (i)   What is the sum of the four numbers?
   (ii)  If three of the numbers are 6, 11 and 14, find the fourth.

9. The mean of four numbers is 7. Three of the numbers are 3, 5 and 9.
   Find the fourth number.

10. The three sides of this triangle have a mean length of 10 cm.
    Find the length of the side [AC].

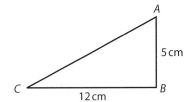

11. The mean of three numbers is 8. When a fourth number is added, the mean becomes 9.
    Find the fourth number.

12. In the first three frames of a snooker match, a player got a mean score of 27 points.
    In the fourth frame he scored 19 points. Find his mean score for the four frames.

13. The mean of three numbers is 10. The numbers 6 and 4 are added to these
    numbers. Now find the mean of the five numbers.

14. The mean of seven numbers is 12.
    One of the numbers is removed.
    Find its value if
    (i)    the mean of the remaining numbers is reduced to 11
    (ii)   the mean of the remaining numbers is unchanged
    (iii)  the mean of the remaining numbers is increased to 14.

15. The average (mean) price of five packets of biscuits is €1.80.
    The prices of two of the packets are €2.10 and €1.71.
    The other three packets are all the same price.
    Find this price.

**16.** Find the mean of these numbers:

   1, 4, 7, 8, 10

   Now increase each number by 4.

   Find the mean of these new numbers.

   Now complete this sentence:

   'When you increase each number in a set by 4, the mean is increased by ...'

**17.** Find the mean of the numbers 1, 4, 7, 8, 10.

   Multiply each number by 5.

   Now find the mean of these numbers.

   What have you discovered?

**18.** A darts player had an average score of 26 in six consecutive throws.

   Calculate his total score for the six throws.

   After his next throw, his average for the seven throws was 24.

   Find his score for the seventh throw.

**19.** Write down five numbers so that:

   the mean is 7

   the median is 6

   the mode is 4.

   ☐ ☐ ☐ ☐ ☐

**20.** The table shows the marks which ten students obtained in Mathematics, English, and Science in their first-year examinations.

| Student | Ava | Barry | Cliona | Derek | Emma | Finn | Gerry | Helen | Ian | Jack |
|---|---|---|---|---|---|---|---|---|---|---|
| **Mathematics** | 45 | 56 | 47 | 77 | 82 | 39 | 78 | 32 | 92 | 62 |
| **English** | 54 | 55 | 59 | 69 | 66 | 49 | 60 | 56 | 88 | 44 |
| **Science** | 62 | 58 | 48 | 41 | 80 | 56 | 72 | 40 | 81 | 52 |

   (i) Calculate the mean mark for Mathematics.

   (ii) Calculate the mean mark for English.

   (iii) Calculate the mean mark for Science.

   (iv) Which student obtained a mark closest to the mean in Science?

   (v) How many students were above the mean mark in Mathematics?

# Section 9.3 The range – variability

The **range** for a set of data is the highest value of the set minus the lowest value.

For the data     3, 7, 9, 15, 21, 28

Range $= 28 - 3$

$= 25$

> The range is largest value minus smallest value.

The range shows how **spread out** a set of data is.
It is very useful when comparing two sets of data.

> The marks, out of 20, scored by Ava and Sean in 6 spelling tests are given below:
>
>
>      **Ava:**    12, 10, 18, 14, 8, 10
>
>      **Sean:**   12, 10, 16, 13, 11, 10
>
> For **Ava:**     Mean $= \frac{72}{6} = 12$;    Range $= 18 - 8 = 10$
>
> For **Sean:**    Mean $= \frac{72}{6} = 12$;    Range $= 16 - 10 = 6$

Notice that the mean mark for both is the same but Sean's marks have a smaller range. Since Sean's marks are less spread out, it shows that Sean's results are more **consistent** than Ava's.

This spread-out nature of Ava's marks compared to Sean's marks illustrates the **variability** of data and how important it can be when comparing two data sets.

The **range** is generally used as a measure of variability as it is easy to find and easy to understand.

## Comparing data

To compare two sets of data, we use the **range** and one of the averages we have studied – the **mean**, the **mode** or the **median**.

In the example above comparing Ava's and Sean's marks, we used the range and the mean.

## Investigation:

Find a set of five numbers with mean 6, median 5 and range 4.

Compare your set of numbers with other students in the class.

Is your set unique?

## Exercise 9.3

1. Find the range for each of the following sets of data:
   (i)   3, 7, 6, 8, 12, 6, 14
   (ii)  18, 27, 36, 19, 21, 42, 20
   (iii) €8, €7, €16, €14, €23, €15

2. A golfer's scores in 6 rounds of golf were:

   75, 84, 92, 79, 85, 77

   (i)  Find her mean score for the 6 rounds.
   (ii) What was the range of her scores?

3. Find the range for each of these sets of data:
   (i)  1.7, 2.3, 0.6, 0.8, 2.1, 1.9, 2.4
   (ii) 6, −1, 0, 3, −2, 4, −3, 1

4. Ann's marks in six maths tests were

   54, 82, 65, 72, 38, 66.

   John's marks in the same six tests were

   58, 62, 51, 66, 71, 64.

   (i)  Find the range of marks for Ann and for John.
        Use your results to find which of the two had the more consistent marks.
   (ii) Which of the two had the higher mean mark?

5. In a golf competition between two clubs, the captain had to choose between Emer and Anna to play in the first round. In the previous eight rounds their scores were as follows:

   Emer:   80, 73, 72, 88, 86, 90, 75, 92
   Anna:   88, 84, 79, 85, 76, 85, 87, 80

   (i)   Calculate the mean score for each golfer.
   (ii)  Find the range of scores for each golfer.
   (iii) Which golfer would you choose to play in the competition?
         Explain your answer. (**Note:** In golf, the lower the score, the better.)

**6.** This table gives the times spent on facebook by six girls on two nights.
  (i) What is the modal time spent on facebook over both nights?
  (ii) What is the modal time spent on Wednesday?
  (iii) What is the range of the times spent on Wednesday?
  (iv) What is the range of the times spent per night over the two days?

**Time spent on facebook**

| Wednesday | Thursday |
|-----------|----------|
| 50 min | 60 min |
| 45 min | 45 min |
| 50 min | 30 min |
| 50 min | 45 min |
| 30 min | 90 min |
| 45 min | 75 min |

**7.** Here are the points scored by the Leinster and Munster rugby teams over six consecutive matches.

**Leinster:** 23, 14, 35, 18, 28, 34    **Munster:** 22, 25, 19, 27, 31, 26

  (i) Find the mean number of points for each team.
  (ii) Find the range of scores for each team.
  (iii) If you were coaching another team, which of these two teams would you like to play against? Explain your answer.

**8.** The range of nine numbers on a card is 60.
One number is covered by a piece of blu-tack.
What could that number be?
  [There are two possible answers.]

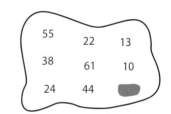

**9.** There were seven people sleeping in a tent.
The mean age of the people was 20 and
the range of their ages was 7.
Write each statement below, and then write
next to it whether it is *True*, *Possible* or *False*.

  (i) The oldest person in the tent was 7 years older than the youngest.
  (ii) The youngest person in the tent was 18 years old.
  (iii) Every person in the tent was 20 years old.

**10.** There were ten children on a coach journey. The mean age of the children was 11 and the range of their ages was 4. Write each statement below and then write next to it whether it is *True, Possible* or *False*.

   (i) The youngest child was 9 years old.

   (ii) Nine of the children were 11 years old.

   (iii) All the children were at least 10 years old.

**11.** Derek has five cards, each of which has a positive whole number printed on it.

Three of the cards have the number 8 written on them.

Without knowing the numbers on the other two cards, is it possible to find the value of

   (i) the median         (ii) the mode         (iii) the mean?

If the mean of the five cards is 8, give two numbers that could be on the other two cards.

Now give two different numbers that could be on the cards.

What are the numbers on these two cards if their range is 12 and the mean of the five cards is still 8?

# Section 9.4 Which average to use

The three averages – the **mean**, the **mode**, and the **median** – are all useful but, depending on the data, one may be more suitable than the other two.

We try to select the 'average' that is most representative of a set of data.

If you use the wrong average, your results may lead to an incorrect conclusion.

Here are the times taken by six people to solve a puzzle:

     12 sec, 15 sec, 11 sec, 16 sec, 18 sec, 60 sec.

The mean time $= \dfrac{12 + 15 + 11 + 16 + 18 + 60}{6}$

$$= \frac{132}{6} = 22 \text{ seconds}$$

The median time: 11, 12, $\boxed{15, 16,}$ 18, 60

$= \frac{1}{2}(15 + 16)$

$= 15.5$ seconds

Which of these two averages is the more suitable?

The mean time is 22 seconds.

Five of the six people take a shorter time than this mean (due to the outlier, 60).

The median, 15.5 seconds, is more typical of the data set and so the median is the more suitable average in this case.

## Example 1

Here are the marks obtained by a group of 10 students in a geography test.

6, 7, 83, 84, 85, 86, 86, 87, 88, 89

Find     (i) the mean     (ii) the median.

State which of these averages best represents the data?

(i)   Mean $= \dfrac{6 + 7 + 83 + 84 + 85 + 86 + 86 + 87 + 88 + 89}{10}$

$\qquad = \dfrac{701}{10}$

$\qquad = 70.1$

(ii)   The median $= \dfrac{85 + 86}{2} = 85.5$

In the data, eight out of the ten marks are in the eighties.
Since the mean is only 70.1, the median is a more suitable average.

The **mode** is most useful when one value appears much more often than any other.
However, if the data is too spread out the mode may not be suitable.
Consider this set of data: 12, 3, 7, 3, 14, 15, 18, 20.
Here the mode is 3, but it is not very representative of all the other numbers in the set because it is the lowest value.
In this case the mode is not a suitable average.
Now consider these colours of dresses in a shop window:
blue, red, green, blue, black, silver, red, blue, white, black, blue, silver, red, blue
Here the mode is blue as it occurs more frequently than any other colour.

> For **categorical data**, such as the colours of dresses listed above, the **mode** is the **only** average that can be used.

## Exercise 9.4

**1.** The numbers of computers in eight classrooms are

3, 15, 1, 2, 1, 30, 2, 1.

(i)   What is the median number of computers?

(ii)   What is the modal number of computers?

(iii)   Why would the mean not be a sensible average for this data?

**2.** The teacher in charge of an outdoor pursuits centre has
10 pairs of boots.
The sizes of the boots are as follows:

4, 7, 5, 5, 3, 10, 8, 5, 5, 8

The teacher calculates the median, the mode, the mean
and the range.

  (i)  Which of them will tell her how spread out the boot sizes are?
 (ii)  Find the (a) mean (b) mode (c) median.
(iii)  Which of the three averages best represents the data?

**3.** For the set of numbers below, find the mean and the median.

1, 3, 3, 3, 4, 6, 99

Which average best describes the set of numbers?

**4.** Sixteen teenagers were asked to state their favourite colour.
These are the results:

blue, green, purple, black, purple, pink, white, blue, yellow, pink, black,
green, orange, green, black, black

State clearly, with reasons, which is the best average to use for the favourite colour
of the teenagers.

Why can you not find the mean of the favourite colours?

**5.** Jack and Daniel are backpacking in Australia and have recorded these daily
temperatures for a week.

| Day | 1 | 2 | 3 | 4 | 5 | 6 | 7 |
|---|---|---|---|---|---|---|---|
| Midday temperature (°C) | 32 | 30 | 30 | 28 | 33 | 31 | 30 |

 (i)  Find the mean midday temperature.
(ii)  Give a reason why the mean is appropriate for this data.

**6.**  (i)  Find the mean of this set of numbers:

37, 26, 37, 18, 18, 20, 26, 18, 37, 37, 18

(ii)  Why is the mode a bad choice of average in this case?

**7.** In March, Rachel and Dave sold five different types of jacket in their clothes shop
and in the amounts shown.

| Jacket | Leather | Suede | Denim | PVC | Cotton |
|---|---|---|---|---|---|
| Amount sold | 45 | 17 | 64 | 28 | 52 |

 (i)  Find the modal type of jacket sold.
(ii)  Why is the mode appropriate for this data?

8. Customers at a roller-skating rink can hire skates.
   The first seven customers on Monday morning take the following skate sizes.

   7, 5, 6, 9, 8, 10, 5

   (i) For the seven customers, find
   
   (a) the median skate size
   
   (b) the modal skate size.

   (ii) The manager is going to buy some new skates.
   He knows the median and modal skate size for 700 customers.
   Which of the values would be the more useful to him?
   Explain your answer.

9.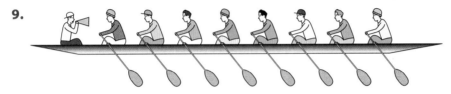

   The weights, in kilograms, of a boat crew are

   96, 86, 94, 96, 91, 95, 90, 96, 43.

   (i) Calculate
   
   (a) their median weight
   
   (b) the range of their weights
   
   (c) their mean weight.

   (ii) Which of the two averages, mean or median, best typifies the data above?
   Give a reason for your answer.

## Section 9.5 Frequency tables

The number of children in each of 50 families in a certain district was recorded in the following way:

1, 3, 4, 3, 2, 2, 4, 2, 6, 7, 6, 2, 4, 5, 5, 4, 3, 4, 3, 2, 1, 6, 2, 5, 1,
4, 4, 4, 3, 5, 3, 6, 2, 4, 5, 7, 2, 4, 3, 5, 5, 3, 3, 4, 1, 2, 5, 3, 4, 4

This list would be much more useful and easier to read if it was presented in the form of a table, as shown below.

| Number of children per family | 1 | 2 | 3 | 4 | 5 | 6 | 7 |
|---|---|---|---|---|---|---|---|
| Number of families | 4 | 9 | 10 | 13 | 8 | 4 | 2 |

The table above is called a **frequency table** or **frequency distribution**.

This table shows the number of families (i.e. the *frequency*) with 1 child, 2 children and so on.

For example, there are 13 families with 4 children per family.

## Mean and mode of a frequency distribution

The frequency table below shows the numbers of children aged from 2 to 7 living on a certain road.

| Age | 2 | 3 | 4 | 5 | 6 | 7 |
|---|---|---|---|---|---|---|
| **Number of children** | 1 | 3 | 5 | 10 | 8 | 3 |

From the table it can be seen that the **mode** or **modal age** is 5 as it occurs more often than any other age.

To find the **mean** age of the children from the table, we perform these operations:

> **1.** Find the sum of all the ages of the children.
> **2.** Find the total number of children.
> **3.** Divide the sum of the ages by the number of children.

**1.** To find the sum of the ages, we multiply each age by the number of children of that age and add up the results.

$$\text{Sum of ages} = (1 \times 2) + (3 \times 3) + (5 \times 4) + (10 \times 5) + (8 \times 6) + (3 \times 7)$$
$$= 2 + 9 + 20 + 50 + 48 + 21$$
$$= 150$$

**2.** The number of children is $1 + 3 + 5 + 10 + 8 + 3 = 30$.

**3.** The mean age $= \dfrac{\text{Sum of all the ages}}{\text{Number of children}} = \dfrac{150}{30} = 5$

$\therefore$ the mean $= 5$

---

**Example 1**

A road-check on 30 motor vehicles yielded the following record of the number of occupants each carried:

2, 1, 3, 4, 5, 3, 2, 1, 2, 3, 1, 1, 2, 4, 6, 5, 4, 2, 2, 1, 1, 2, 4, 6, 5, 2, 6, 2, 5, 3

Make out a frequency table for the above data and hence find the mean and mode of the distribution.

| Number of occupants per vehicle | 1 | 2 | 3 | 4 | 5 | 6 |
|---|---|---|---|---|---|---|
| **Number of vehicles** | 6 | 9 | 4 | 4 | 4 | 3 |

$$\text{Mean} = \frac{(6 \times 1) + (9 \times 2) + (4 \times 3) + (4 \times 4) + (4 \times 5) + (3 \times 6)}{6 + 9 + 4 + 4 + 4 + 3}$$

$$= \frac{90}{30} = 3$$

Mode $= 2$, as 2 occurs with the greatest frequency.

## Exercise 9.5

1. Thirty students in a class were given a test which was marked out of 10.
   The results of the test are shown below:

   4, 6, 7, 5, 9, 8, 6, 4, 3, 5, 6, 9, 8, 7, 6, 10, 1, 3, 6, 7, 9, 8, 5, 3, 2, 4, 7, 9, 10, 5

   Copy and complete this frequency table: (Note; a tally chart can be inserted into this table if required)

   | Marks per student | 1 | 2 | 3 | 4 | 5 | 6 | 7 | 8 | 9 | 10 |
   |---|---|---|---|---|---|---|---|---|---|---|
   | Number of students | | | 3 | | | | | | | |

   From the table, write down the number of students who got
   
   (i)   5 marks          (ii)   8 marks          (iii)   10 marks.
   
   What mark was got most frequently?

2. The following frequency table shows the number of people per car passing a certain point on the road in a five-minute period.

   | Number of people per car | 1 | 2 | 3 | 4 | 5 | 6 |
   |---|---|---|---|---|---|---|
   | Number of cars | 8 | 12 | 7 | 6 | 2 | 1 |

   Use the frequency table to answer these questions:

   (i)   How many cars had three people in them?
   (ii)   How many cars had only 1 person in them?
   (iii)   How many cars had 5 people or more in them?
   (iv)   How many cars were in the survey?
   (v)   What percentage of the cars had 2 people in them?

3. A factory produces 50 television sets per day.
   Tests at the end of one Tuesday gave rise to
   the following data:

   | Number of faults per set | 0 | 1 | 2 | 3 | 4 | 5 | 6 |
   |---|---|---|---|---|---|---|---|
   | Number of sets | 1 | 8 | 12 | 11 | 9 | 5 | 4 |

   (i)   How many sets had no fault?
   (ii)   How many sets had 6 faults?
   (iii)   What was the modal number of faults?
   (iv)   What was the total number of faults recorded in all the sets?
   (v)   Find the mean number of faults per set.

4. The table below shows the numbers of goals scored in a number of matches on a Sunday morning.

| Goals scored | 1 | 2 | 3 | 4 | 5 | 6 |
|---|---|---|---|---|---|---|
| Number of matches | 14 | 16 | 8 | 8 | 6 | 8 |

   (i)   In how many matches were 6 goals scored?
   (ii)  What was the modal number of goals scored?
   (iii) What was the total number of goals scored?
   (iv)  Find the mean number of goals scored.
   (v)   Work out the greatest number of matches which could have ended in a draw.

5. Find the mean of the given frequency distribution.

| Number | 1 | 2 | 3 | 4 | 5 | 6 |
|---|---|---|---|---|---|---|
| Frequency | 9 | 9 | 6 | 4 | 7 | 3 |

   This distribution has two modes. What are they?

6. The following table gives the numbers of children aged one to six years living on a certain road:

| Age in years | 1 | 2 | 3 | 4 | 5 | 6 |
|---|---|---|---|---|---|---|
| Number of children | 14 | 16 | 8 | 8 | 6 | 8 |

   (i)   Find the total number of children aged 1 to 6 living on the road.
   (ii)  How many of these children are aged 2 years or less?
   (iii) What percentage of these children are aged 3 years or more?
   (iv)  What is the mode of the distribution?
   (v)   Calculate the mean of the distribution.

7. A road-check on 50 motor vehicles yielded the following record of the number of occupants in each:

   3, 2, 1, 5, 2, 1, 2, 3, 4, 6, 2, 4, 5, 6, 2, 1, 2, 3, 4, 3, 2, 1, 1, 4, 1,
   3, 2, 1, 4, 3, 2, 1, 2, 3, 1, 4, 2, 3, 4, 1, 2, 1, 4, 5, 1, 2, 3, 2, 4, 2

   (i)   Construct a frequency table to illustrate the data.
   (ii)  What is the modal number of occupants per car?
   (iii) What percentage of the cars had 5 occupants or more?

8. A group of 50 people were asked to count the number of coins they had in their pockets. The results are shown in the following frequency table.

| Number of coins | 0 | 1 | 2 | 3 | 4 | 5 | 6 |
|---|---|---|---|---|---|---|---|
| Number of people | 2 | 8 | 9 | 13 | 8 | 7 | 3 |

   Calculate the mean number of coins per person.

**9.** The following frequency table shows the number of goals scored in 60 football matches.

| Goals scored | 1 | 2 | 3 | 4 | 5 | 6 |
|---|---|---|---|---|---|---|
| **Number of matches** | 15 | 14 | 9 | 6 | 10 | 6 |

  (i)   Find the mean number of goals scored per match.

 (ii)   What was the modal number of goals scored?

(iii)   In what percentage of the matches were 3 or 4 goals scored?

(iv)   Find the greatest number of matches which could have ended in a draw.

**10.** The marks of 36 students in third-year are given below:

     31  49  52  79  40  29  66  71  73  19  51  47  81  67  40  52  20  84

     65  73  60  54  60  59  25  89  21  91  84  77  18  37  55  41  72  38

Copy and complete the grouped frequency table below:

| Marks | 1–20 | 21–40 | 41–60 | 61–80 | 81–100 |
|---|---|---|---|---|---|
| **Number of students** | | | | | |

  (i)   How many students scored between 21 and 60 inclusive?

 (ii)   What is the modal class?

(iii)   Which class had the second largest number of students?

(iv)   Name one disadvantage of a grouped frequency table.

# Test yourself 9

1. A rugby team played 10 games.
   Here are the numbers of points the team
   scored.

   12  22  14  11  7  18  22  14  36  14

   (i)   Write down the mode.
   (ii)  Work out the range.
   (iii) Work out the mean.
   (iv)  Work out the median.

2. Paul got these marks in three tests:   72, 80 and 82
   He had one more test to sit.
   He wanted an average of 80 for the four tests.
   What mark must he get in the fourth test?

3. (i)  The number of safety matches in ten different boxes were as follows.

       48     47     47     50     46     50     49     49     47     51

       Find the modal number of matches in a box.
   (ii) The mean of three numbers is 8. Two of the numbers are 8 and 10.
        Find the third number.

4. The table shows the scores achieved by 20 students who played a game.

   | Score     | 0 | 1 | 2 | 3 | 4 | 5 |
   |-----------|---|---|---|---|---|---|
   | Frequency | 3 | 5 | 6 | 2 | 3 | 1 |

   Calculate the mean score for the 20 students.

5. Find the mean, median and mode of this set of numbers:

       1,  1,  2,  3,  3,  3,  4,  6,  40

   Which of these averages best represents this data?
   Comment on your answer.

6. Here are five number cards.

   (i) Show how you could choose three of these cards so that the mean of the three
       numbers is bigger than the median.

(ii) Now pick another three cards to make the median bigger than the mean.

(iii) Finally, choose three cards where the mean and the median are equal.

7. The bar graph shows a survey on the number of children per family.

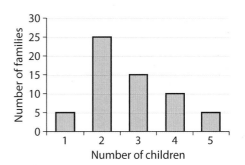

   (i) How many families participated in the survey?

   (ii) How many children were there altogether?

   (iii) Calculate the mean number of children per family.

   (iv) If 1 more family of 4 children were to participate in the survey, how would the mean be affected?

8. Last April, a certain garage sold five different types of cars. The numbers sold were:

| Car | Prestige | Sports | Ordinary | Coupe | 4 × 4 |
|---|---|---|---|---|---|
| **Number sold** | 12 | 8 | 23 | 2 | 5 |

   (i) Find the modal type of car sold.

   (ii) Why is the mode appropriate for this data?

9. (i) Find three numbers with a range of 6, a median of 8 and a mean of 8.

   (ii) Find three numbers with a mode of 4, a median of 4 and a mean of 5.

   (iii) Three people have a mean age of 25.
   The range of the ages is 8 years and the median is 27.
   How old is each person?

10. There are 10 houses in Barrack Street.
   On Monday, the numbers of letters delivered to the houses are:

   0   2   5   3   34   4   0   1   0   2

   Calculate the mean, mode and median of the number of letters.
   Which of the three averages best reflects the data?

11. The mean number of lollies in a bag should be 35. The quality control person took a sample of ten bags to check that this was the case.
    In the first nine bags there were 35, 42, 31, 43, 36, 33, 32, 31, 35.

    (i) What was the total number of lollies in the first nine bags?
    (ii) What was the mean number of lollies in the first nine bags?
    (iii) How many lollies must be in the tenth bag so that the mean number of lollies for the ten bags is 35?

12. Here are some sets of numbers. Add on another number to each set to obtain the median given on the right.

    | | | | Hint: you need to make 5 the middle number. |
    |---|---|---|---|
    | (i) | 1, 8, 5, 2: | median 5 | ← |
    | (ii) | 8, 4, 5, 3, 8, 4, 2, 9: | median 4 | |
    | (iii) | 7, 4, 3, 6, 2, 6, 8, 4: | median 5 | |

13. On the first five days of his holiday, David drove an average of 256 kilometres per day and on the next three days he drove an average of 172 kilometres per day.

    (i) What is the total distance that David drove in the first five days?
    (ii) What is the total distance that David drove in the next three days?
    (iii) What is the mean distance travelled per day, by David, over the eight days?

14. A die was thrown 30 times. The results are recorded below.

    | Score | 1 | 2 | 3 | 4 | 5 | 6 |
    |---|---|---|---|---|---|---|
    | Frequency | 3 | 4 | 6 | 8 | 7 | 2 |

    Find the mean score.

15. Here are the scores of three students in a computer game:

    Tim:    47, 51, 36, 78, 43, 20, 39, 27
    Frank:  35, 38, 42, 55, 28, 43, 61, 54
    Derek:  45, 51, 57, 44, 50, 48, 43, 49

    (i) Which student was least consistent?
        Give a reason for your answer.
    (ii) One of the students scored 75 in his next game.
        His range is now 32. Who was it?

**16.** The weekly wages of the employees of a fast-food takeaway are listed below:

€300, €250, €240, €220, €200, €1050.

Find   (i)   the mean wage
         (ii)  the median wage.

Why can't you find the mode?
Which of the averages – mean or median – best represents the 'typical' wage?

**17.** The range for eight numbers is 40 and seven of these numbers are shown.
Find two possible values for the missing number.

| 27 | 5 | 33 | 42 |
|----|----|----|----|
| 11 |    | 13 | 19 |

## Assignment:

By collecting data from your class using a suitable questionnaire, find the mean, mode and median of your class for each of the following:

(a)  How many phone-calls each student makes per day.
(b)  How far each student lives from the school.
(c)  How long each student spends on homework each evening.
(d)  Each student's favourite colour.

Present your findings in the form of a chart:

Suggestions for collecting the data:

(a)  use phone records
(b)  use Goggle maps
(c)  ask each student to average the time spent on homework for the last 3 or 4 days

**Question:** Did any of the answers result in data for which you could not find some of the central tendencies? Which one and why? Explain.

# Geometry 1: Triangles and Quadrilaterals

## From first year, you will recall how to:

- recognise an acute, obtuse or reflex angle,
- identify vertically opposite, corresponding, alternate and interior angles,
- tell the difference between a line, line segment and ray,
- identify the interior and exterior angles in a triangle.

## In this chapter, you will learn to:

- find missing angles on straight lines, in triangles and compound shapes,
- identify the properties of a quadrilateral,
- understand and use the Theorem of Pythagoras,
- investigate shapes and make observations and deductions,
- understand specific terms related to Geometry such as theorem and converse.

## Section 10.1  Revision of lines and angles

The diagrams below will help you recall some of the facts and terms you will have met in your study of geometry so far.

### 1.  Lines

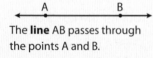

The **line** AB passes through the points A and B.

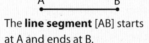

The **line segment** [AB] starts at A and ends at B.

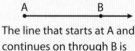

The line that starts at A and continues on through B is called the **ray** [AB.

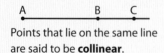

Points that lie on the same line are said to be **collinear**.

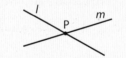

The lines l and m **intersect** at the point P.

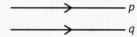

Lines that never meet are said to be **parallel lines**.

## 2. Angles

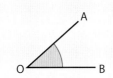

The angle above is written ∠AOB (or ∠BOA).

The angle above is called a **right angle**.
A right angle = 90°.

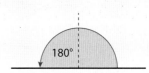

A half a revolution makes a **straight angle**.
A straight angle = 180°.

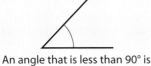

An angle that is less than 90° is called an **acute angle**.

An angle between 90° and 180° is called an **obtuse angle**.

An angle between 180° and 360° is called a **reflex angle**.

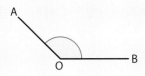

The shaded angle, which is less than 180°, is generally referred to as an **ordinary angle**.

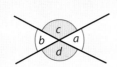

**Vertically opposite angles** are equal in measure.

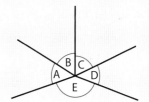

Angles at a point add up to **360°**.

## 3. Parallel lines and angles

Angles formed when a straight line crosses a pair of parallel lines have the following properties:

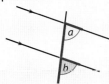

**Corresponding angles** are equal. So, $a = b$. You can find them by looking for an 'F shape'.

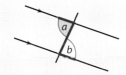

**Alternate angles** are equal. So, $a = b$.
Look for a 'Z shape'.

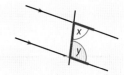

The **interior angles** $x$ and $y$ sum to 180°.
So, $x + y = 180°$.

**Note:**   For proofs of Theorems see Chapter 25 Geometry 3.

189

## Exercise 10.1

**1.** Describe in words each of the following diagrams:

(i)   (ii)   (iii)

**2.** Find the measure of the angle marked with a letter in each of the following diagrams:

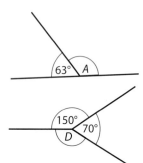 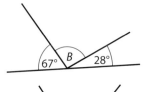 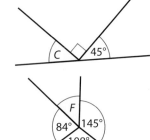

**3.** Work out the angles marked with a letter in each of the following diagrams:

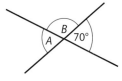 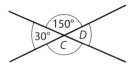 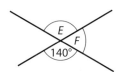

 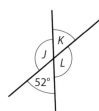 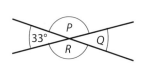

**4.** In each of the following diagrams, write down the number of the angle that **corresponds** to the shaded angle. (Arrows indicate parallel lines.)

(i) 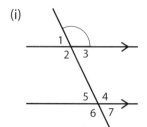  (ii) 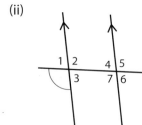  (iii)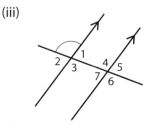

**5.** In each of the following figures, write down the number of the angle which is alternate to the shaded angle:

(i)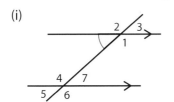

(ii)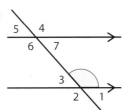

(iii)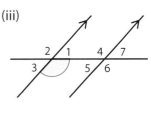

**6.** Write down the sizes of the angles marked with letters in each of the following diagrams, where arrows indicate parallel lines.

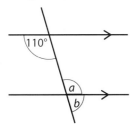

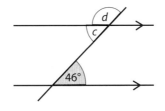

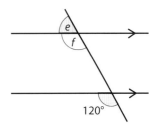

**7.** In each of the following, work out the size of the angle marked with a letter. Arrows indicate parallel lines.

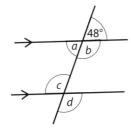

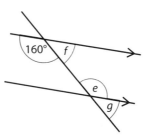

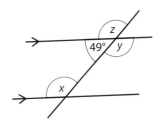

**8.** Find the value of the lettered angles *a*, *b*, *c*, *d*, *e* and *f*, giving reasons for each answer.

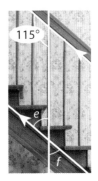

9. Find the sizes of the angles marked
   $a, b, c, d, e, f$ and $g$ in the given figure,
   where arrows indicate parallel lines.

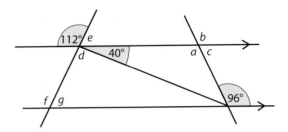

10. Find the measures of the angles marked with
    letters in the given diagram, where the arrows
    indicate parallel lines.

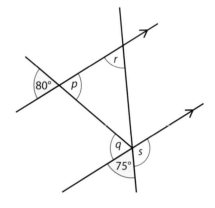

# Section 10.2  Angles of a triangle

The diagrams below will help you recall some important facts about the angles of a triangle.

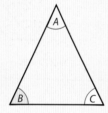

The angles of a triangle sum to 180°.
$$|\angle A| + |\angle B| + |\angle C| = 180°$$

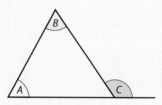

The **exterior angle** of a triangle is equal to the sum
of the interior opposite angles.
$$|\angle C| = |\angle A| + |\angle B|$$

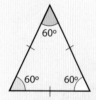

An **equilateral triangle** has
   3 equal sides
   3 equal angles.
   Each angle is 60°.

An **isosceles triangle** has
   2 equal sides
   base angles equal.

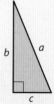

A **right-angled triangle** has
an angle of 90°.
$$a^2 = b^2 + c^2$$

It is stated in the box above that in an isosceles triangle, the angles opposite the equal sides are also equal.

Conversely, it can be shown that if a triangle contains two equal angles, then that triangle is isosceles.

## *Investigation:*

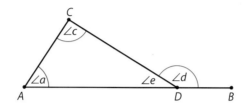

Investigate the diagram above and then copy and complete the following three lines of geometry.

**1.** $\angle a + \angle c + \angle e = ($    $)°$... because _____.

**2.**    $\angle d + \angle e = ($    $)°$... because _____.

**3.** $\therefore \angle($   $) + \angle($   $) = \angle($   $)$

In this diagram, $\angle d$, is called an _____ angle.

In this diagram, $\angle a$, $\angle c$, $\angle e$ are called _____ angles.

In words, you have shown that the _____ angle is equal to the sum of the _____ and _____ angles.

---

**Example 1**

Find the measure of the angle marked $x$ in the given triangle.

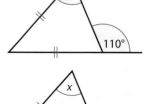

The angle marked $y$ is $180° - 110° = 70°$.
But angle $x =$ angle $y$ ... isosceles triangle
$\therefore$ $|\angle x| = 70°$

## Exercise 10.2

**1.** For each triangle below, name:
   (i)  the exterior angle
   (ii) the two interior opposite angles to the exterior angle.

(a)

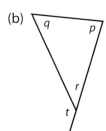

(b)

(c)

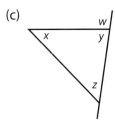

**2.** Find the measure of the angle marked with a letter in each of these triangles:

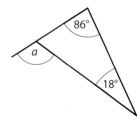

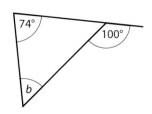

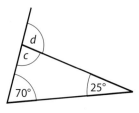

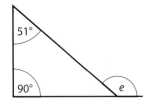

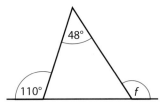

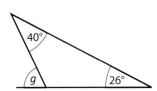

**3.** In the following triangles, equal sides are marked.
   Find the measure of the angle marked with a letter in each triangle:

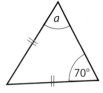

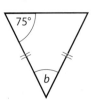

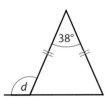

**4.** Work out the sizes of the missing angles in each of these isosceles triangles:

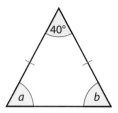   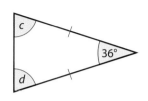   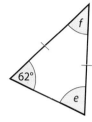

**5.** Find the size of the angle marked with a letter in the following figures:

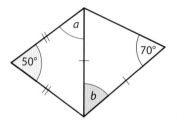   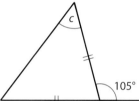   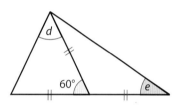

**6.** Calculate the size of each angle marked with a letter:

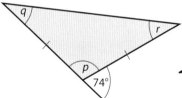   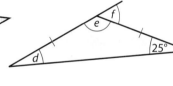   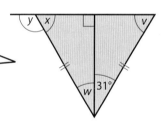

**7.** Find the measure of the angles marked *a* and *b* in the given triangle where equal sides are marked.

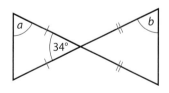

**8.** In each of the following triangles, the arrows indicate that the lines are parallel. Find the measure of each angle marked with a letter.

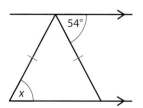   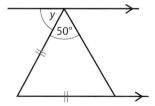   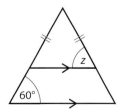

**9.** Find the value of *x* and the value of *y* in each of the following where the arrows indicate parallel lines.

(i)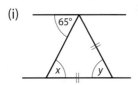

(ii)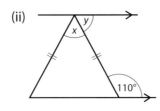

(iii)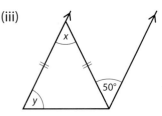

# Section 10.3  Quadrilaterals

A figure which has four sides is called
a **quadrilateral**.
In the quadrilateral shown, the sides have different
lengths and the angles have different sizes.

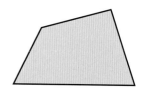

However, there are quadrilaterals with special properties which you should recognise.
Some of these special quadrilaterals are shown below.

## A parallelogram
In a parallelogram,
> the opposite sides are parallel
> the opposite sides are equal in length
> the opposite angles are equal.

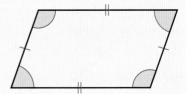

## A rectangle
In a rectangle,
> each pair of opposite sides are parallel and
equal in length
> all four angles are right angles.

## A rhombus
In a rhombus,
> there are 4 equal sides
> opposite sides are parallel
> opposite angles are equal.

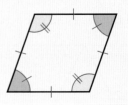

## A square

In a square,

> all four sides are the same length
> opposite sides are parallel
> all four angles are right angles.

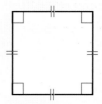

In the given parallelogram, $A$ and $B$ are called
**interior angles** as they add up to 180°.

*Proof:*        $\angle E = \angle A$  … alternate angles

$\angle E + \angle B = 180°$  … straight angle

$\therefore$    $\angle A + \angle B = 180°$

Similarly,    $\angle B + \angle C = 180°, \angle A + \angle D = 180°$   and   $\angle C + \angle D = 180°.$

**Note :**    $\therefore \angle A + \angle B + \angle C + \angle D = 180° + 180° = 360°$

## The angles of a quadrilateral

The quadrilateral shown is divided
into two triangles.
The angles in each triangle add up
to 180°.

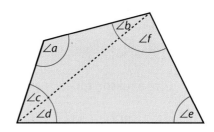

$\angle a + \angle c + \angle b = 180°.$

$\angle d + \angle e + \angle f = 180°.$

$\therefore$   $\angle a + \angle b + \angle c + \angle d + \angle e + \angle f = 360°$

Thus the angles in a
quadrilateral add up to 360°.        The interior angles in a quadrilateral add up to 360°.

## Diagonals

In the special quadrilaterals shown below, the diagonals bisect each other.

| Square | Rectangle | Parallelogram | Rhombus |
|---|---|---|---|
|  | 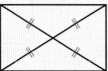 | 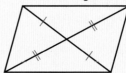 | 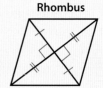 |
| Diagonals are equal and bisect each other at right angles. | Diagonals are equal and bisect each other. | Diagonals bisect each other. | Diagonals bisect each other at right angles. |

**Theorem**   The diagonals of a parallelogram bisect each other.

---

### Example 1

In the given parallelogram ABCD,
$|\angle BAD| = 115°$ and $|\angle BDC| = 28°$.
Find   (i)  $|\angle BCD|$      (ii)  $|\angle ABD|$
        (iii)  $|\angle ADC|$     (iv)  $|\angle DBC|$
Give a reason for each answer.

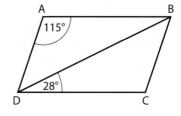

(i)  $|\angle BCD| = 115°$ ... opposite angles are equal
(ii)  $|\angle ABD| = 28°$ ... alternate angles
(iii)  $|\angle ADC| = 180° - 115°$ ... interior angles sum to 180°
            $= 65°$
(iv)  $|\angle DBC| = 180° - 115° - 28°$ ... $|\angle BCD| = 115°$ from (i) above
            $= 37°$

---

## Exercise 10.3

**1.** A, B, C and D are the four angles in the given
   parallelogram.
   (i)  Name two pairs of equal angles.
   (ii)  How many degrees are there in the angles
        A + B?

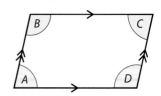

**2.** Find the angle marked with a letter in each of the following parallelograms:

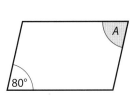 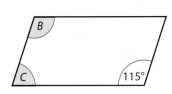 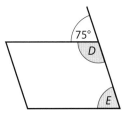

**3.** Find the size of the angle marked with a letter in each of these parallelograms:

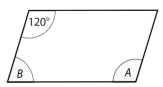 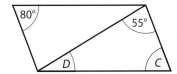 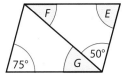

**4.** Find the values of x and y in the given parallelogram.

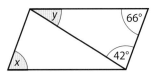

**5.** Find the measure of the angle marked with a letter in these parallelograms:

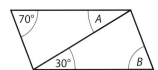 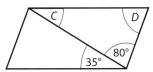 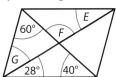

**6.** Find the value of the angle marked x in each of the following parallelograms:

(i) 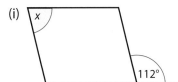  (ii) 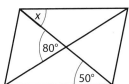  (iii)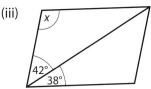

**7.** Find the size of the angle marked with a letter in each of these parallelograms:

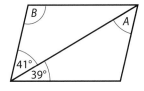 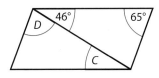 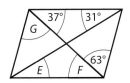

**8.** ABCD is a parallelogram with the diagonals
intersecting at the point O.
Write down the length of
   (i)  [OB]         (ii)  [AB]
   (iii)  [AC]       (iv)  [BC]

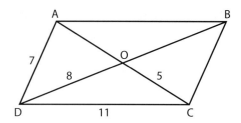

**9.** ABCD is a parallelogram with the
diagonals intersecting at the point O.

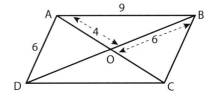

Write down the length of
   (i)  [DO]    (ii)  [OC]    (iii) [DC]    (iv)  [BC].
Now name an angle equal in measure to
   (v)  ∠AOD  (vi)  ∠DAB  (vii)  ∠BDC  (viii)  ∠CAB

**10.** In the given parallelogram all the sides are equal,
as marked.
Calculate the values of $x$, $y$, $z$ and $r$.

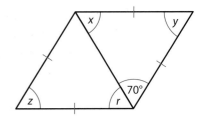

**11.** Copy the given diagram and mark in
these angles:

$$|\angle BDC| = 23°, |\angle DAX| = 75°, |\angle DCB| = 118°.$$

Now find $|\angle AXD|$.

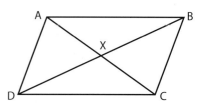

**12.** Find the size of the angle marked with a letter in each of these figures.

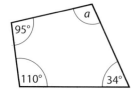

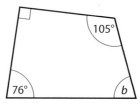

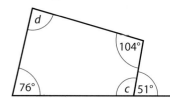

**13.** In the given parallelogram ABCD, parallel
lines are drawn, as shown.
Find the values of the angles
marked *x*, *y* and *z*.

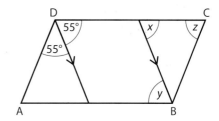

**14.** A square, rectangle, parallelogram and rhombus are shown below.
They are numbered 1, 2, 3, and 4.

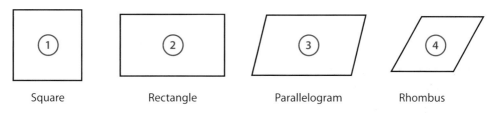

| Square | Rectangle | Parallelogram | Rhombus |

Which of these four shapes will **always** have these properties?
(The third one is done for you.)
- (i)   All angles are the same size.
- (ii)  Opposite angles are equal.
- (iii) All sides are equal in length.
- (iv)  Opposite sides are equal.
- (v)   Opposite sides are parallel.
- (vi)  Both diagonals are equal in length.
- (vii) The diagonals bisect each other.
- (viii) The diagonals intersect at right angles.

**15.** Find the value of *x* in each of the diagrams below:

(i)      (ii)      (iii)

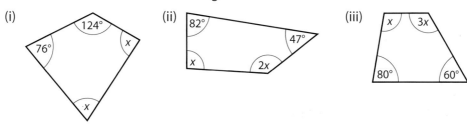

## Investigation:

Find the unknown angle in each of the following triangles.
Copy the box below and match the letter of the angle to the correct given angle
to answer this riddle.
How do you make varnish vanish?

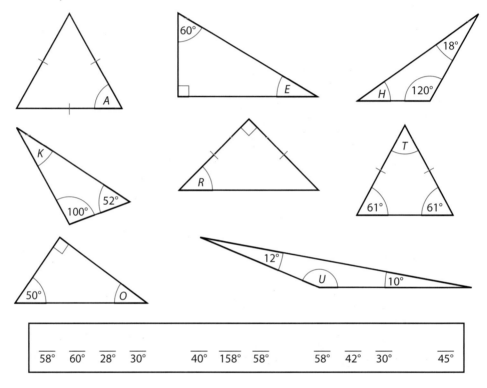

| 58° | 60° | 28° | 30° | | 40° | 158° | 58° | | 58° | 42° | 30° | | 45° |
|-----|-----|-----|-----|--|-----|------|-----|--|-----|-----|-----|--|-----|

## Section 10.4  The Theorem of Pythagoras

The diagram on the right shows a right-angled triangle
of sides 3, 4 and 5 cm.

Squares are drawn on each of the three sides.

By counting the number of cm² in each of these
squares, you will notice that the area of the square
on the **hypotenuse** is 25 cm², while the other two
squares have areas 16 cm² and 9 cm².

This diagram illustrates that the square on the
hypotenuse is equal to the sum of the squares on
the other two sides.

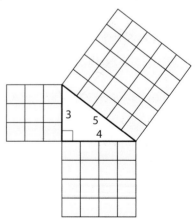

This important theorem is called the *Theorem of Pythagoras*.
Pythagoras was a Greek philosopher and mathematician who died about 500 BC.
The first formal proof of the theorem is attributed to him, although there is evidence that the theorem was well known to the Chinese and Egyptians hundreds of years before.
The Egyptian surveyors knew that a rope containing 12 equally-spaced knots could be used to form a right-angled triangle. They used this for marking fields and squaring buildings.

In a right-angled triangle, the square on the hypotenuse is equal to the sum of the squares on the other two sides.

The Theorem of Pythagoras.

The Theorem of Pythagoras can be expressed very neatly through algebra, as shown.

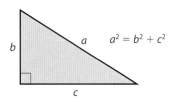

$$a^2 = b^2 + c^2$$

The converse of the Theorem of Pythagoras is also true. It states that:

If the square of one side of a triangle is equal to the sum of the squares of the other two sides, then the angle opposite the first side is a right angle.

Converse of the Theorem of Pythagoras.

The triangle shown is right angled since

$$10^2 = 8^2 + 6^2,$$

i.e.   $100 = 100$

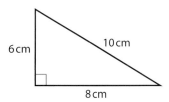

---

**Example 1**

Find the lengths of the sides marked *x* in the following right-angled triangles.

(i)

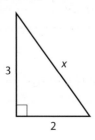

(ii)

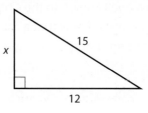

By Theorem of Pythagoras:

(i)    $x^2 = 3^2 + 2^2$

       $= 9 + 4$

   $\therefore \ x^2 = 13$

   $\therefore \ \ x = \sqrt{13}$

   $\therefore \ \ x = 3.6$

(ii)         $15^2 = 12^2 + x^2$

     $\therefore \ \ 225 = 144 + x^2$

   $225 - 144 = 144 + x^2 - 144$

           $x^2 = 81$

       $\therefore \ \ \ x = \sqrt{81}$

       $\therefore \ \ \ x = 9$

## Exercise 10.4

**1.** Write down the length of the hypotenuse in each of these triangles:

(i)

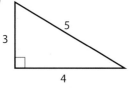

(ii)

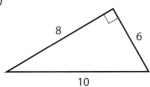

(iii)

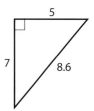

**2.** Use the *Theorem of Pythagoras* to find the area of the square marked with a letter in each of these figures:

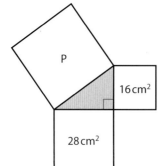

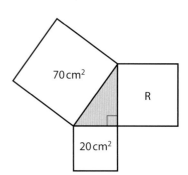

**3.** Find the length of the side marked with a letter in each of these triangles:

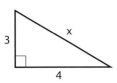 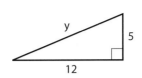 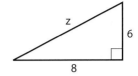

**4.** Find the length of the side marked with a letter in each of these triangles.
(You may leave your answer in $\sqrt{\phantom{x}}$ form.)

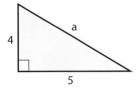 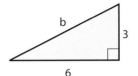 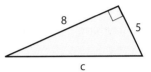

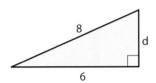 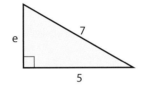 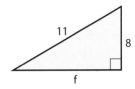

**5.** Find the length of the diagonal in each of these squares.
(You may leave your answer in $\sqrt{\phantom{x}}$ form.)

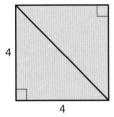 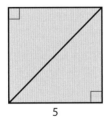 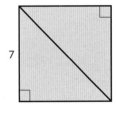

**6.** Calculate the length of the diagonal of the
given rectangle.

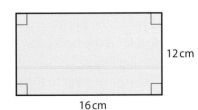

**7.** A windowsill in an office building is 12 m above the ground.
The top of a 13 m long ladder is resting against the windowsill.
How far out from the wall of the office building, is the
foot of the ladder?

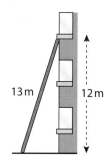

13 m    12 m

**8.** A new section of road cuts off one of the
dangerous right-angled bends on a
country lane.
To the nearest 10 metres, how much shorter
is the new section of road?

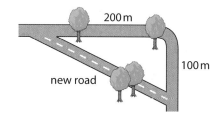

200 m

100 m

new road

**9.** The size of a rectangular television screen is determined
by the length of the diagonal.
The screen size of this television is 54 centimetres.
If the height of the screen is 26 cm, what is the width?
Give your answer correct to 1 decimal place.

54 cm

**10.**

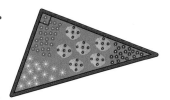

Hannah put a wooden edging around this triangular
garden.
She used a 10 m length of wood for the longest side
and a 6 m length for the shortest side.
What total length of wood did Hannah use?

**11.** A helicopter flew 24 km to the west, then
15 km to the north.
How far is the helicopter then from its
starting point?
Give your answer to the nearest kilometre.

**12.** Use the Theorem of Pythagoras to find the value of $a$ and the value of $b$ in the given right-angled triangle.

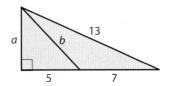

**13.** Alan wanted to find the width of Lake Como. He placed a stake at $Z$ so that $|\angle YXZ| = 90°$. He found $|XZ|$ to be 450 m long and $|YZ|$ to be 780 m long.
What is the distance between $X$ and $Y$?
Give your answer correct to the nearest metre.

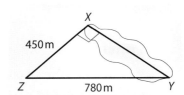

**14.** By checking whether the square of the largest number is equal to the sum of the squares of the other two numbers, state if each of the following obeys Pythagoras's theorem.
   (i)  6, 8, 10      (ii)  7, 11, 12      (iii)  5, 12, 13      (iv)  4, 6, 8

**15.** Mia wants to cross a river 50 m wide. She rows her boat directly across the river but the current takes her boat downstream and she lands on the other side 120 m further down than she wanted.
Use the Theorem of Pythagoras to find out what distance she travelled.

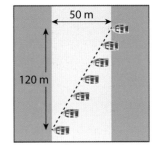

## Investigation:

The **converse** is the result of reversing a conditional statement.
By copying and completing the table below, investigate the converse of each of the following statements. State whether each converse is True or False.

| Statement | True or False |
|---|---|
| **1.** In an equilateral triangle, the three sides have the same length. | |
| **Converse:** If a triangle has three equal sides, then… | |
| **2.** In a right-angled triangle, $a^2 = b^2 + c^2$. | |
| **Converse:** In a triangle if $a^2 = b^2 + c^2$, then … | |
| **3.** If it is raining outside, then the grass is wet. | |
| **Converse:** If the grass is wet outside, then… | |

The Theorem of Pythagoras is very useful when we need to check if a door-frame is 'square' or the walls of a room are perpendicular to one another. Since for every right-angled triangle $a^2 = b^2 + c^2$, where $b$ and $c$ are the two sides of the right-angle and $a$ is the longest side (hypotenuse)

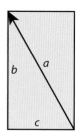

### Conversely:

If $a^2 = b^2 + c^2$, then $b$ and $c$ must be at right-angles to one another.
Investigate any door frame. Measure $a$, $b$ and $c$ accurately. Check if $a^2 = b^2 + c^2$.
Repeat for other door openings and rooms. Copy and complete the following chart.
Note; correct each answer for (i) $a^2$ (ii) $b^2 + c^2$ to 2 significant figures.
Compare your results with other groups.

| Opening | $a$ | $b$ | $c$ | $b^2 + c^2$ | $a^2$ |
|---------|-----|-----|-----|-------------|-------|
|         |     |     |     |             |       |
|         |     |     |     |             |       |
|         |     |     |     |             |       |

# Test yourself 10

1. Find the size of each angle marked with a letter in the figures below, where the arrows indicate parallel lines:

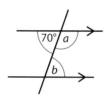
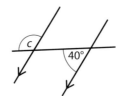
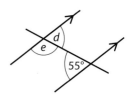

2. Find the size of the angle marked with a letter in each of these triangles:

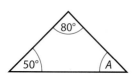
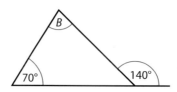
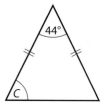

3. Find the values of a, b and c in the following figures:

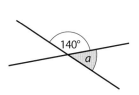 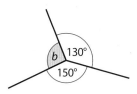 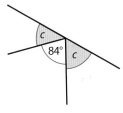

4. Find the measures of the angles marked *a* and *b* in the triangles below, where equal sides are marked.

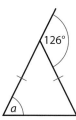 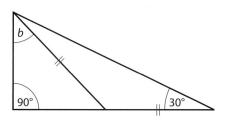

5. Find the measure of each angle marked with a letter in the following parallelograms:

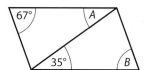 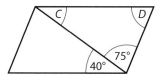 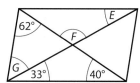

6. In the given figure, equal sides are indicated. Find the sizes of the angles marked *a* and *b*.

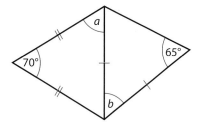

7. Find the third side in each of these right-angled triangles:

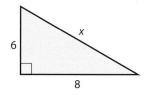 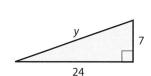 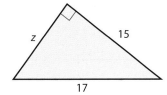

**8.** Find the measure of each angle marked with a letter in each of the following figures, where the arrows indicate parallel lines.

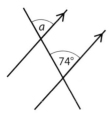 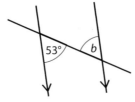 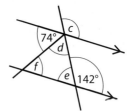

**9.** Find the value of *x* in the given triangle.
What can be deduced about the triangle?

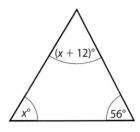

**10.** Find the value of *a* and the value of *b* in each of these triangles:

(i) 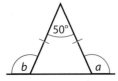  (ii) 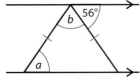  (iii)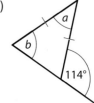

**11.** In the diagram on the right the arrows indicate that the lines are parallel.
Calculate the measures of the angles *A* and *B*.

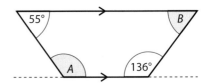

**12.** In the given triangle, $|PQ| = |PR| = |RS|$.
If $|\angle QPR| = 40°$, find the value of *x*.

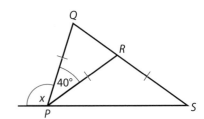

# Assignment:

Each student in your group should draw a
different triangle extending each side to form
3 exterior angles.
Measure each angle $\angle a$, $\angle b$, $\angle c$.
Find the sum of $\angle a + \angle b + \angle c$.
Compare results.
What conclusion can you make?
**Conclusion:**

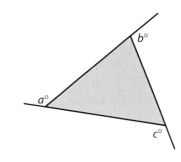

Repeat the procedure with any quadrilateral.
Measure each angle $\angle a$, $\angle b$, $\angle c$, $\angle d$.
Find the sum of $\angle a + \angle b + \angle c + \angle d$.
Compare results.
What conclusion can you make?
**Conclusion:**

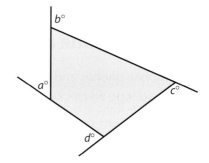

From your results suggest a value for the sum of the exterior angles of *any*
polygon.
Draw a large hexagon and measure the exterior angles and by calculating their
sum test your conclusions. Write a report on your investigations.

# Time and Speed

## *In this chapter, you will learn to:*

- understand the 24-hour clock,
- add and subtract time,
- convert between seconds, minutes and hours,
- read and interpret timetables,
- calculate speed, distance or time when given the other two variables,
- solve problems involving time, distance and speed.

## Section 11.1  Time and timetables

Although mobile phones and electronic devices use the 24-hour clock, it is important to be able to read time on clocks and timing devices which still use 12-hour clock time.

The clock on the right shows the time to be 9.20.

This could be either 9.20 a.m. or 9.20 p.m..

When we give a time containing a.m. or p.m., we are expressing it in **12-hour clock time**.

The letters **a.m.** are used to indicate times between midnight and midday.

Times between noon and midnight are indicated by **p.m.**.

> a.m.   stands for *ante meridiem* – before midday
> p.m.   stands for *post meridiem* – after midday

The **24-hour clock** is another way of telling the time.

This method uses 4 digits, e.g. 10.24.

The first two digits give the hour after midnight and the second two digits give the number of minutes after the hour.

The table below shows times expressed in 12-hour and 24-hour clock times.

| 24-hour clock | 04.00 | 06.00 | 08.00 | 10.00 | 12.00 | 14.00 | 16.00 | 18.00 | 20.00 |
|---|---|---|---|---|---|---|---|---|---|
| 12-hour clock | 4 a.m. | 6 a.m. | 8 a.m. | 10 a.m. | 12 noon | 2 p.m. | 4 p.m. | 6 p.m. | 8 p.m. |

In most bus, airport and train timetables, for example, the decimal point in the 24-hour time is omitted and 21.16 is written as 21 16.

When subtracting 'times', it is important to remember the connection between minutes and hours as the next example shows.

**Subtracting times**

2 hr 23 min ⟶ 1 hr  83 min
−45 min            −45 min
                   1 hr  38 min

---

**Example 1**

A film begins at 20.45 and ends at 22.14. How long does it last?

To calculate, we subtract 20.45 from 22.14 as follows:

   22.14
−20.45

When subtracting a larger number of minutes from a smaller number, change the top line by adding 60 to the minutes and then taking away one hour as follows:

$$\frac{22.14}{-20.45} = \frac{21.74}{-20.45} \quad \text{... 14 minutes after 10 p.m. = 74 minutes after 9 p.m. (22.00 = 10 p.m.)}$$
          1.29

The film lasts 1 hour 29 minutes.

---

## Exercise 11.1

1. How many minutes are there in each of these?

   (i) $\frac{1}{2}$ hour     (ii) $\frac{1}{4}$ hour     (iii) $\frac{2}{5}$ hour     (iv) $1\frac{3}{4}$ hours     (v) $\frac{7}{10}$ hour.

2. Add each of the following:

   (i)   hr   min
       4    12
       3    46

   (ii)   hr   min
       4    38
       3    46

   (iii)   hr   min
       1    29
       3    53

**3.** How many minutes from 7.20 a.m. to 8.00 a.m.?

How many hours and minutes from 8.00 a.m. to 3.40 p.m.?

Now find how many hours and minutes there are between 7.20 a.m. and 3.40 p.m.

**4.** How many hours and minutes from

    (i)  8.30 a.m. to 11.45 a.m.        (ii)  12.30 p.m. to 7 p.m.

    (iii)  7.40 a.m. to 3.30 p.m.        (iv)  10.10 a.m. to 6.40 p.m.

    (v)  8.45 a.m. to 3.50 p.m.        (vi)  11.50 a.m. to 7.45 p.m.?

**5.** Subtract the following:

| (i) | hr | min | | (ii) | hr | min | | (iii) | hr | min |
|---|---|---|---|---|---|---|---|---|---|---|
| | 4 | 53 | | | 3 | 12 | | | 5 | 35 |
| | 2 | 17 | | | 1 | 46 | | | 3 | 54 |

**6.** Write the following in 24-hour clock time:

    (i)  6 a.m.      (ii)  10.45 a.m.      (iii)  4 p.m.      (iv)  5.20 p.m.

    (v)  7.30 p.m.      (vi)  8.45 a.m.      (vii)  12 midday      (viii)  11.40 p.m.

    (ix)  3.15 a.m.      (x)  3.15 p.m.

**7.** Write the following using a.m. or p.m.:

    (i)  11.40      (ii)  15.35      (iii)  12.20      (iv)  00.30      (v)  22.15

    (vi)  04.20      (vii)  10.35      (viii)  14.30      (ix)  18.45      (x)  23.12

**8.** Express each of these in 24-hour clock time:

    (i)             (ii)             (iii)             (iv)

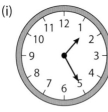 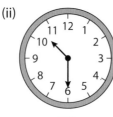 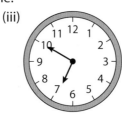 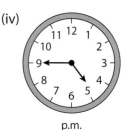

    a.m.                  p.m.                  a.m.                  p.m.

**9.** How many hours and minutes from

    (i)  10.35 to 14.45        (ii)  12.48 to 16.20        (iii)  10.36 to 18.45

    (iv)  8.15 to 10.52        (v)  02.10 to 17.40        (vi)  14.42 to 18.10?

**10.** The times shown on the clocks below give hours, minutes and seconds.
Match the times on the clocks to the digital times in the blue boxes:

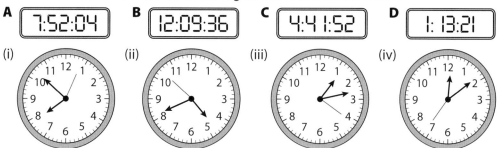

**A** `7:52:04`   **B** `12:09:36`   **C** `4:41:52`   **D** `1:13:21`

(i)   (ii)   (iii)   (iv)

**11.** A woman works from 08.45 to 12.30 and from 13.45 to 17.15 for five days each week.
Calculate how many hours she works in the week.

**12.** A play started at 8.20 p.m. and lasted 2hr 35 min. At what time did it finish?

**13.** A train leaves Tralee at 10.52 and arrives in Dublin at 14.40.
How long does the journey take?

**14.** A turkey needs to be cooked and ready for dinner
at 18.30.
The cooking time is 28 minutes per kg, plus an extra
20 minutes.
If the turkey weighs 8 kg, what is the latest time it
should be put in the oven?

**15.** The following is an extract from the Dublin to Westport train timetable:

|  |  | **Train 1** | **Train 2** |
|---|---|---|---|
| **Dublin Heuston** | dep. | 08 30 | 17 10 |
| **Athlone** | arr. | 10 08 | 18 43 |
| **Athlone** | dep. | 10 10 | 18 45 |
| **Claremorris** | arr. | 11 25 | 20 08 |
| **Claremorris** | dep. | 11 44 | 20 11 |
| **Westport** | arr. | 12 05 | 20 38 |

(i) How long does it take *Train 1* to go from Dublin to Westport?

(ii) For how long does *Train 1* stop in Claremorris?

(iii) After the short stop, how long does it take *Train 2* to go from Athlone to
Westport?

(iv) Which is the faster train from Dublin to Athlone?

(v) How long does it take *Train 1* to go from Dublin to Claremorris?

(vi) For how long does *Train 2* stop in Athlone?

(vii) If I arrive at Heuston Station in Dublin at 07 52, how long do I have to wait for *Train 1* to depart for Westport?

(viii) Which is the faster train from Dublin to Westport?

16. Fill in the shaded spaces marked A, B, C, D, E and F below:

| Train | Time of departure | Time of arrival | Time taken |
|---|---|---|---|
| 1 | 08 43 | 10 54 | A |
| 2 | B | 12 17 | 2 h 40 min |
| 3 | 15 30 | C | 1 h 54 min |
| 4 | 23 17 | 05 18 | D |
| 5 | 06 23 | E | 4 h 12 min |
| 6 | F | 12 15 | 2 h 54 min |

17. A car journey began at 10 40 and finished at 13 25.

(i) How long did the journey take?

(ii) If the car uses 6 litres of petrol per hour and each litre costs €1.65, calculate the cost of the petrol for the journey, correct to the nearest euro.

## *Investigation:*

By copying and completing the following table, investigate parts of an hour in fraction and decimal forms.

| Minutes | Parts of an hour | | Minutes | Parts of an hour | |
|---|---|---|---|---|---|
| | Fraction | Decimal | | Fraction | Decimal |
| 6 minutes | $\frac{6}{60} = \frac{1}{10}$ | 0.1 | | $\frac{2}{5}$ | |
| | | 0.2 | 30 minutes | | |
| | $\frac{3}{10}$ | | | | 0.6 |
| 15 minutes | | | | $\frac{2}{3}$ | |
| | | 0.3$\dot{3}$ | | | 0.75 |
| | | | 50 minutes | | |

**18.** Convert each of the following times to hours and minutes:

    (i) 3.5 hours    (ii) 2.1 hours    (iii) 0.75 hours   (iv) 4.6 hours    (v) $1.\dot{6}\dot{6}$ hours

**19.** On sports day, the rota for supervising a carpark was divided equally between 5 students.

    The carpark opened at 9 a.m. and closed at 3 p.m.

    Find how long each student supervised the carpark in (i) decimal form (ii) in hours and minutes.

**20.** Jessica and Sophie do laps of a park to train for a cross country race.

    Jessica does a lap in 15 minutes and Sophie does a lap in 18 minutes.

    If they both start their training together at 2 p.m., when will they next be together at the start?

**21.** Fiacra and Pat start their exercise routine in their local gym at 10 00 on Saturday morning and meet in the café when they are finished.

    (i)   How long is each exercise routine, give your answers in hours?

    (ii)   Who will be first in the café and how long, in minutes, will they be waiting?

| Fiacra | | Pat | |
|---|---|---|---|
| Bench presses | 0.2 hours | Bench presses | 0.1 hours |
| Rowing machine | 0.25 hours | Rowing machine | 0.1 hours |
| Leg press | 0.1 hours | Leg press | 0.1 hours |
| Push down | 0.2 hours | Push down | 0.2 hours |
| Pull down | 0.2 hours | Pull down | 0.2 hours |
| Rest | 0.1 hours | Rest | 0.25 hours |
| Swimming | 0.4 hours | Swimming | $0.\dot{3}\dot{3}$ hours |
| Rest | 0.1 hours | Rest | 0.25 hours |
| Treadmill | 20 minutes | Treadmill | 18 minutes |
| Cross-Country Skiing Simulator | 0.3 hours | Cross-Country Skiing Simulator | 18 minutes |
| Rest(shower) | 10 minutes | Rest(shower) | 15 minutes |

# Section 11.2 Speed – Distance – Time

If a car travels 100 km in 2 hours, then we say that the **average speed** of the car for the journey is 50 kilometres per hour (written as 50 **km/hr**).

Again, if a train does 300 km in 3 hours, its average speed is 100 km/hr.

In each of these examples, the average speed $= \dfrac{\text{distance travelled}}{\text{time taken}}$.

The examples above could also be used to show that

(i) Time $= \dfrac{\text{Distance}}{\text{Speed}}$ 　　　　　　　(ii) Distance = Speed × Time

The triangle on the right below could help you to remember the formulae given.

Speed $= \dfrac{\text{Distance}}{\text{Time}}$

Time $= \dfrac{\text{Distance}}{\text{Speed}}$

Distance = Speed × Time

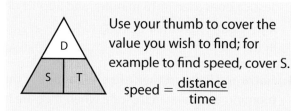

Use your thumb to cover the value you wish to find; for example to find speed, cover S.

speed $= \dfrac{\text{distance}}{\text{time}}$

---

### Example 1

A train travels a journey of 210 km in $2\frac{1}{2}$ hours. Find its average speed.

Average speed $= \dfrac{\text{Distance}}{\text{Time}} = \dfrac{210}{2\frac{1}{2}} = \dfrac{210 \times 2}{2\frac{1}{2} \times 2} = \dfrac{420}{5} = 84$

∴ the average speed = 84 km/hr.

---

### Example 2

A motorist travelled 500 kilometres in six hours.
Her average speed for the first two hours was 100 km/hr.
Find her average speed, in kilometres per hour, for the last four hours.

Distance travelled in the first 2 hours is 100 km × 2 = 200 km. … Distance = Speed × Time

Therefore she travelled 300 km in the last 4 hours.

Average speed $= \dfrac{\text{Distance}}{\text{Time}}$

$= \dfrac{300}{4}$ … 500 km − 200 km = 300 km and 6 hr − 2 hr = 4 hr.

$= 75$

∴ average speed for the last 4 hours = 75 km/hr.

To convert from km/hr to m/s, first convert to **m/hr** then m/s.

To convert from m/s to km/hr, first convert to **m/hr** then km/hr.

|  | 1 km = 1 000 m |  | 1 hour = 3 600 s |
|---|---|---|---|
| 18 km/hr ⟶ m/s | 18 km/hr = | 18 × 1 000 m/hr = | $\dfrac{18\,000}{3\,600}$ = 5 m/s |
|  | 1 hour = 3 600 s |  | 1 km = 1 000 m |
| 10 m/s ⟶ km/hr | 10 m/s = | 10 × 3 600 m/hr = | $\dfrac{36\,000}{1\,000}$ = 36 km/hr |

## Exercise 11.2

**1.** How far will a vehicle travel
   - (i)  in 3 hours at an average speed of 80 km/hr
   - (ii)  in 4 hours at an average speed of 65 km/hr
   - (iii)  in $2\frac{1}{4}$ hours at an average speed of 88 km/hr
   - (iv)  in $\frac{3}{4}$ hour at an average speed of 96 km/hr?

**2.** Find the time taken to travel
   - (i)  210 km at an average speed of 70 km/hr
   - (ii)  200 km at an average speed of 80 km/hr
   - (iii)  20 km at an average speed of 60 km/hr
   - (iv)  48 km at an average speed of 64 km/hr.

**3.** Find the average speed, in km/hr, of a car if it does
   - (i)  250 km in 5 hours
   - (ii)  120 km in 2 hours
   - (iii)  90 km in $1\frac{1}{2}$ hours
   - (iv)  175 km in $2\frac{1}{2}$ hours
   - (v)  25 km in $\frac{1}{2}$ hour
   - (vi)  90 km in 40 mins.

**4.** A racing car completes a 15 km lap of a track in 5 minutes. Express the average speed in km/hr.

**5.** How long would it take a cyclist to travel 45 km at an average speed of 18 km/hr?

**6.** A car is driven on a motorway for $2\frac{1}{4}$ hours at an average speed of 84 km/hr. How far does the car travel in that time?

**7.** The distance from Tralee to Dublin is 312 km. If a motorist completes the journey in 4 hr 20 min, find her average speed in km/hr.

8. A train leaves Dublin at 0925 and reaches Cork at 1210.
   If the journey is 286 km long, find the average speed of the train.

9. A speedboat travels at 60 km/hr for two hours and then at 90 km/hr for one hour.
   Find its average speed over the three hours.

10. A journey takes 3 hours at an average speed of 120 km/hr.
    How long, in hours, would the journey take if the average speed was reduced to
    80 km/hr?

11. A trip of 276 km began at 1040 hrs and ended on the same day at 1430 hrs.
    Find the average speed in km/hr.

12. It takes 4 hours and 20 minutes to travel a journey at an average speed of 120 km/hr.
    How many hours and minutes will it take to travel the same journey if the average
    speed is reduced to 100 km/hr?

13. A motorist travelled 320 km in five hours.
    Her average speed for the first 160 km was 80 km/hr.
    What was her average speed for the second 160 km?

14. A distance of 18 km is travelled in 25 minutes.
    Find the average speed in metres per second.

15. A professional cyclist started a journey of 56 km at
    1015 hours and finished the journey at 1135 hours.
    Calculate the average speed of the cyclist in km/hr.

16. A distance of 600 metres is travelled in 30 seconds.
    Find the average speed in km/hr.

17. Express 72 km/hr in metres per second.

18. Express 400 metres per minute in km/hr.

19. Express 15 metres per second in kilometres per hour.

20. A car journey of 559 kilometres took 6 hours and 30 minutes.
    (i)  Calculate the average speed, in km/hr, for the journey.
    (ii) If the average petrol consumption for the journey was 8.3 km per litre,
         calculate the number of litres used, correct to the nearest litre.
    (iii) Find the cost of the petrol used if each litre cost €1.70.

**21.** The table on the right shows the times taken by some very fast animals to travel the distances given.
Arrange the animals in order, starting with the fastest.

| Animal | Time taken | Distance in metres |
|---|---|---|
| Cheetah | 18 seconds | 500 m |
| Racehorse | 16 seconds | 300 m |
| Antelope | $4\frac{1}{2}$ min | 6 000 m |
| Deer | 42 min | 32 000 m |

**22.** A jogger sets out at midday to run to the next village, a distance of 12 km.
She wants to arrive at this village at 1330 hours.
At what average speed should she jog?

**23.** Complete the following table:

| | | |
|---|---|---|
| 20 m/s | (        ) m/hr | (        ) km/hr |
| 25 m/s | (        ) m/hr | (        ) km/hr |
| 50 m/s | (        ) m/hr | (        ) km/hr |

**24.** Complete the following table:

| | | |
|---|---|---|
| 72 km/hr | (        ) m/hr | (        ) m/s |
| 54 km/hr | (        ) m/hr | (        ) m/s |
| 120 km/hr | (        ) m/hr | (        ) m/s |

## Investigation:

Estimate the width of the road close to your school over which many students cross.

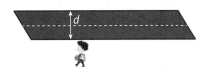

In the school yard mark out this distance(d).

Using a stopwatch find the average time in seconds a student needs to cross to the other side.

Check the speed limit on the road. Copy and complete the table below to calculate the 'safe distance' needed to cross in front of a car assuming the car fails to slow down.

| Speed limit (km/hr) | Speed limit (m/s) | Safe distance (m) = Speed (m/s) × time (s) |
|---|---|---|
| 50 km/hr | | |
| 60 km/hr | | |

Measure out the safe distances in the school yard for the different speed limits.

# Test yourself 11

**1.** Express each of the times shown in the 24-hour clock time.

(i)

a.m.

(ii)

p.m.

**2.** Find the time taken for a journey of 100 km at an average speed of 80 km/hr.

**3.** A school's lessons begin at 9.00 a.m. and end at 3.40 p.m. with an hour's break at lunchtime and 20 minutes break mid-morning.
If there are 8 lessons of equal length, how long is a lesson?

**4.** How many hours and minutes from

(i) 9.15 a.m. to 12.30 p.m.

(ii) 09.35 to 18.10?

**5.** A coach left Dublin at 09.45 and reached Limerick at 12.15.

(i) How long did the journey take?

(ii) If the length of the journey is 220 km, find the average speed of the coach in km/hr.

**6.** A girl jogs for 24 minutes at an average speed of 15 km/hr.
How far does she travel?

**7.** A television film started at 10.15 p.m. and lasted for 2 hours and 35 minutes.
At what time did the film finish?

**8.** A bus travels for two hours at an average speed of 90 km/hr and then for a further hour at a speed of 60 km/hr.
Find

(i) the total distance travelled

(ii) the total time taken

(iii) the average speed of the bus for the whole journey in km/hr.

**9.** Find the distance covered by an aircraft travelling at 600 km/hr for 3 hours and 36 minutes.

**10.** Write the following times in 24-hour clock time:

(i) 6.15 a.m.        (ii) 1.45 p.m.        (iii) 9.52 p.m.        (iv) 12.15 a.m.

**11.** A motorist travels at an average speed of 60 km/hr for $2\frac{1}{4}$ hours.
If his car has an average fuel consumption of 1 litre of petrol per 15 km,
find how many litres of fuel are used.

**12.** A *Luas* left Tallaght at 09.45 and reached Abbey Street at 10.25.

  (i)  How long did the journey take?

  (ii)  If the length of the journey is 13 km, find the average speed of the
*Luas* in km/hr.

**13.** John travelled by car from Tralee to Galway.
He left Tralee at 09.45 and arrived in Galway at 12.57.

  (i)  How long did it take John to travel from Tralee to Galway?
Give your answer in hours and minutes.

  (ii)  The distance from Tralee to Galway is 200 km.
Calculate John's average speed in km/hr.

  (iii)  John had estimated it cost 22 cents per km to drive his car.
How much did it cost him to drive his car from Tralee to Galway?

**14.** At the Olympic Games, a swimmer completed the 1500 m freestyle race in
15 minutes. Express this speed in km/hr.

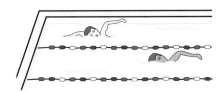

**15.** The Grand Old Duke of York, he had ten thousand men, he marched them up to the
top of the hill . . .
By 2 p.m., they were one third of the way up.
By 4 p.m., they were three quarters of the way up.
When did they set out?

**16.** A *TGV* travels 567 km from Bordeaux to Paris at an average speed of 252 km/hr.
Find the arrival time in Paris, if it leaves Bordeaux at 14.10.

**17.** In a Grand Prix, the winning car passed the chequered
flag 0.3 seconds ahead of the next car.
Both cars were travelling at 84 m/s.
What was the distance between the two cars?

# Assignment:

In groups, plan a school trip with your class.

The trip must include the use of at least one mode of transport: plane – train – bus.

You must research:

1. places of interest to visit.
2. best and most efficient ways to travel to your destination.
3. timetables/calendars to decide dates and start / finish times.
4. costs involved in travelling to and visiting your destination.
5. possible discounts for groups.

Present your plan as a series of bullet points on a large poster, or as a digital presentation, to your class. Compare plans and decide as a class which trip you would like to go on.

# Simultaneous Equations

# chapter 12

## From first year you will recall how to:

- add and subtract like terms,
- multiply algebraic terms by a constant,
- form and solve equations,
- use algebra to solve word problems.

## In this chapter, you will learn to:

- multiply equations by a constant,
- add or subtract equations,
- solve a pair of equations with two variables,
- interpret the point of intersection of two lines,
- create two equations with two unknowns from a word problem.

## Section 12.1  Simultaneous equations

Consider the equation

$$3x + y = 9.$$

The values $x = 2$ and $y = 3$ satisfy this equation.

The values $x = 1$ and $y = 6$ also satisfy the equation.

In fact, there are many pairs of values for $x$ and $y$ which satisfy the equation.

Now we take a second equation

$$2x - y = 1.$$

The values $x = 2$ and $y = 3$ satisfy this equation also.

Thus, the values $x = 2$ and $y = 3$ satisfy both equations

$$3x + y = 9 \text{ and } 2x - y = 1.$$

Only **one** set of values for $x$ and $y$ will satisfy a pair of simultaneous equations.

> When two equations are both satisfied by the same values for $x$ and $y$, they are said to be simultaneous equations.

Solving a pair of simultaneous equations involves finding the values of $x$ and $y$ that make both equations true.

---

**Example 1**

Investigate whether $x = 6$ and $y = 2$ are the correct solutions for these simultaneous equations:

$$x + y = 8 \quad \ldots \text{①}$$
$$x + 2y = 10 \quad \ldots \text{②}$$

We substitute 6 for $x$ and 2 for $y$ in each equation:
Equation ①:  $6 + 2 = 8$    i.e. $8 = 8$; … correct
Equation ②:  $6 + 2(2) = 10$  i.e. $10 = 10$; … correct
Since $x = 6$ and $y = 2$ satisfy both equations, they are the correct solutions.

---

**Exercise 12.1**

For each of the following pairs of simultaneous equations, solutions are given.
Check if each solution is correct.

**1.** $x + y = 8$
$x - y = 4$
**Solution:** $x = 6, y = 2$

**2.** $2x + y = 11$
$x - 2y = 3$
**Solution:** $x = 5, y = 1$

**3.** $3x + 2y = 11$
$2x - 3y = 3$
**Solution:** $x = 3, y = 1$

**4.** $4x - y = 5$
$2x + 3y = 8$
**Solution:** $x = 2, y = 3$

**5.** $3x - y = 4$
$2x + y = 8$
**Solution:** $x = 2, y = 4$

**6.** $3x + y = 14$
$2x - y = 6$
**Solution:** $x = 4, y = 2$

**7.** $x + 2y = 4$
$x - y = 5$
**Solution:** $x = 2, y = 1$

**8.** $2x + 3y = 3$
$x - 4y = 7$
**Solution:** $x = 3, y = -1$

**9.** $2x - y = -8$
$x + 2y = 10$
**Solution:** $x = -2, y = 4$

**10.** $2x + y = -5$
$x - 2y = 5$
**Solution:** $x = -1, y = -3$

# Section 12.2  Solving simultaneous equations

There are many ways of solving simultaneous equations.
One method is called the **elimination method**.
In this method, we 'eliminate' one of the variables.

This method is investigated below.

## *Investigation:*

$5x + 3y = 23$

$2x - 3y = 5$     are simultaneous equations.

We can illustrate them using scales.

On the red scales $5x + 3y$ balances 23

On the green scales $2x - 3y$ balances 5

Investigate what would happen if we add the left-hand sides and the right-hand sides to a new blue scales.

  (i)   Would the blue scales balance?

 (ii)   What are the totals on each side of the blue scales.

(iii)   How can you use these totals to find a value for $x$?

(iv)   How can you use the value of $x$ to find a value for $y$?

From the 'investigation' above, it can be seen that it is easy to solve simultaneous equations when one of the variables can be eliminated by adding or subtracting the two equations.

If a variable cannot be eliminated by simply adding or subtracting, then we have to multiply one or more of the equations by a number to make the elimination possible.

---

### Example 1

Solve the simultaneous equations   $\begin{aligned} x + 2y &= 10 \\ 2x - y &= 5 \end{aligned}$

(To solve these equations, we must make the number of $x$'s or the number of $y$'s equal. We then add or subtract as necessary.

For convenience, we will call the first equation ① and the second equation ②.)

Equation ①:        $x + 2y = 10$

Equation ② × 2:    $4x - 2y = 10$

Adding:            $5x \quad = 20$

           $\therefore \quad x = 4$

Substituting $x = 4$ in ① we get:   $4 + 2y = 10$

                     $2y = 6$

            $\therefore \quad y = 3$

The solution is $x = 4$ and $y = 3$.

(Note: It is important to check that $x = 4$ and $y = 3$ satisfy both equations.)

---

**Example 2**

Solve these simultaneous equations
$$2x - 5y = 9$$
$$3x + 2y = 4$$

We number the equations $\quad 2x - 5y = 9 \quad$ ①
① and ② for convenience. $\quad 3x + 2y = 4 \quad$ ②

We now multiply equation ① by 3 and equation ② by 2 to equate the number of $x$'s.

① × 3: $\quad 6x - 15y = 27$
② × 2: $\quad\; 6x + 4y = 8$

Subtract: $\quad -19y = 19$
$$19y = -19 \;\; \dots \text{ multiply both sides by } -1$$
$$y = -1$$

We now substitute $-1$ for $y$ in equation ①

$$2x - 5y = 9$$
$$y = -1 \;\; \Rightarrow \;\; 2x + 5 = 9$$
$$\Rightarrow \;\; 2x = 4 \;\; \Rightarrow \;\; x = 2$$

∴ $x = 2$ and $y = -1$ are the solutions.

---

## Exercise 12.2

Solve the following simultaneous equations:

**1.** $x + y = 9$
$\quad x - y = 3$

**2.** $2x + y = 8$
$\quad 3x - y = 2$

**3.** $2x - y = 4$
$\quad x + y = 5$

**4.** $3x + y = 7$
$\quad x + y = 5$

**5.** $4x + y = 17$
$\quad 2x + y = 11$

**6.** $x + 2y = 4$
$\quad x - y = 1$

**7.** $x + 2y = 7$
$\quad 2x + y = 8$

**8.** $2x - 3y = 1$
$\quad 2x + 5y = 9$

**9.** $2x + 3y = 3$
$\quad x - 4y = 7$

**10.** $2x - y = -8$
$\quad\; x + 2y = 6$

**11.** $4x - y = 10$
$\quad\; x - y = 1$

**12.** $4x - y = -9$
$\quad\; 2x - 3y = -7$

**13.** $3x - y = 3$
$\quad\; x + 3y = 11$

**14.** $2x + y = -2$
$\quad\; x + 3y = 9$

**15.** $2x - 3y = 14$
$\quad\; 2x - y = 10$

**16.** $3x + 4y = 5$
$\quad\; 2x - 3y = 9$

**17.** $3x + y = 5$
$\quad\; 5x - 4y = -3$

**18.** $2x - y = 12$
$\quad\; 3x + 2y = 11$

**19.** $3x + 4y = 10$
$4x + y = 9$

**20.** $3x - 2y = 13$
$4x + 3y = 6$

**21.** $3x + 5y = 6$
$2x + 3y = 5$

**22.** $4x + 3y = 19$
$3x - 2y = -7$

**23.** $2x - 5y = 1$
$5x + 3y = 18$

**24.** $3x = 5y + 13$
$2x + 5y = -8$

**25.** $x + 2y = 13$
$3x = 5y + 6$

**26.** $7x + 2 = 2y$
$3x = 14 - y$

**27.** $2x - 5y = 3$
$x = 3y + 1$

**28.** $3x = 22 + 2y$
$5y = 2x$

**29.** $2x - 3y = 8$
$3x + 4y = -22$

**30.** $2x - 5y = 22$
$3x + 7y = 4$

# Section 12.3  Problems leading to simultaneous equations

In a later chapter, you will discover that equations such as $y = 2x + 4$ and $x + y = 5$ represent straight lines.

*Investigation:*

Copy and complete the table below.

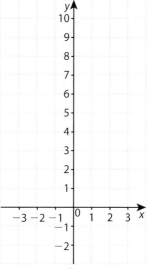

| x | −3 | −2 | −1 | 0 | 1 | 2 | 3 |
|---|----|----|----|---|---|---|---|
| A | $y = 2x + 4$ | | | | | | |
| B | $y = 1 - x$ | | | | | | |

Plot the set of points for A and B.

Join all the points for each line A and B.

Write down the point of intersection of the two lines.

$A: y = 2x + 4 \Rightarrow 2x - y = -4$

$B: y = 1 - x \Rightarrow x + y = 1$

Solve the simultaneous equations A and B using the 'adding or subtracting' method in the last exercise.

What conclusions can you draw from your investigation about the point of intersection and the solution of the simultaneous equations.

From the 'investigation' above, you should have discovered that two simultaneous equations may be solved by drawing graphs of the two equations (lines) and then reading the x-value and y-value of their point of intersection.

## Using simultaneous equations to solve problems

Simultaneous equations are particularly useful for solving problems which have two unknowns. Generally, two different pieces of information enable us to write down two equations.

The following examples illustrate this procedure.

---

### Example 1

The sum of two numbers is 19.
When twice the second number is taken from three times the first number, the result is 22.
Find the two numbers.

Let $x$ and $y$ be the numbers.

| | |
|---|---|
| Equation ①: | $x + y = 19$ |
| Equation ②: | $3x - 2y = 22$ |

| | |
|---|---|
| Equation ① $\times$ 2: | $2x + 2y = 38$ |
| Equation ②: | $3x - 2y = 22$ |
| Adding | $5x \quad\;\; = 60$ |
| | $x \quad\;\; = 12$ |

Substituting 12 for $x$ in equation ①, we get:
$$12 + y = 19$$
$$y = 19 - 12$$
$$y = 7$$

The two numbers are 12 and 7.

---

### Example 2

Tickets to a movie cost either €8 or €10.
If 300 tickets were sold and the total amount of money collected was €2640, how many of each type of ticket were sold?

Let $x$ = number of €8 tickets sold, and
$\quad\;\; y$ = number of €10 tickets sold.

| | | |
|---|---|---|
| ① | Total number of tickets: | $x + y = 300$ |
| ② | Total amount of money collected: | $8x + 10y = 2640$ |

| | |
|---|---|
| ① $\times$ 8: | $8x + 8y = 2400$ |
| ②: | $8x + 10y = 2640$ |
| Subtracting | $-2y = -240$ |
| $\Rightarrow$ | $2y = 240$ |
| $\Rightarrow$ | $y = 120$ |

Substituting 120 for $y$ in equation ①, we get:

$$x + y = 300$$
$$y = 120:\quad x + 120 = 300$$
$$x = 180$$
$$\therefore\quad x = 180 \text{ and } y = 120$$

∴ 180 €8 tickets and 120 €10 tickets were sold.

## Exercise 12.3

**1.** The sum of two numbers is 41 and their difference is 5. Find the numbers.

**2.** The sum of two numbers is 12. Twice one of the numbers added to three times the other is 31. Find the two numbers.

**3.** The sum of two numbers $x$ and $y$ is 50. When twice $y$ is taken from four times $x$, the result is 8. Find the value of $x$ and the value of $y$.

**4.** Find two numbers such that the first added to three times the second is 31, while three times the first less twice the second is 16.

**5.** The sum of two numbers is 9. If twice the first number is added to three times the second, the answer is 15. Find the two numbers.

**6.** The difference of two numbers is 7. When three times the smaller number is taken from twice the larger, the result is 11. Find the two numbers.

**7.** The sum of two numbers is 8. When four times the second number is taken from three times the first number, the result is 3. Find the two numbers.

**8.** Examine the rectangle shown and write down two equations in $x$ and $y$.

Now solve these equations to find the value of $x$ and the value of $y$.

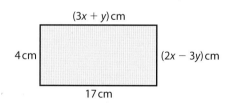

$(3x + y)$ cm

4 cm

$(2x - 3y)$ cm

17 cm

**9.** Three nuts and six bolts have a combined weight of 72 g. Four nuts and five bolts have a combined weight of 66 g. Find the combined weight of one nut and one bolt.

**10.** All weights in these balance
pictures are in grams.
   (i)  Find the weight of a cherry.
   (ii) What is the weight of a pear?

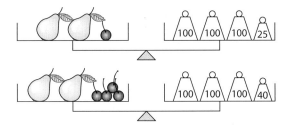

**11.** Three chocolate bars and four chocolate eggs weigh 465 grams.
Three chocolate bars and two chocolate eggs weigh 315 grams.
   (i)  Which of these pairs of equations is correct for the chocolate bars and eggs?

**A**
$3b + 2e = 465$
$3b + 4e = 315$

**B**
$b + 4e = 465$
$b + 2e = 315$

**C**
$3b + 4e = 465$
$3b + 2e = 315$

   (ii) Solve the pair of simultaneous equations that is correct to find the values
of $b$ and $e$.

**12.** A farmer has horses and turkeys. In total, there are 32 heads and 98 legs.
   (i)  If there are $x$ horses and $y$ turkeys, explain why:
        (a)  $x + y = 32$        (b)  $4x + 2y = 98$
   (ii) How many horses and how many turkeys does the farmer have?

**13.** The given diagram shows the graphs
of the lines $x - y = 1$ and $x + 2y = 4$.
   (i)  Write down the coordinates of the point
of intersection of the two lines.
   (ii) Solve the simultaneous equations
$x - y = 1$ and $x + 2y = 4$.
   (iii) Explain the connection between your
answers in (ii) to the answer you found
in (i) above.

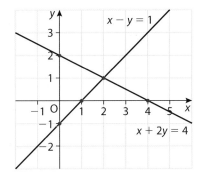

**14.** A sketch of the lines $2x + y = 6$
and $x + y = 5$ is shown.
Use the sketch to write down the point
of intersection of the two lines.
Now use simultaneous equations to
verify your answer.

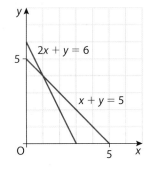

# Test yourself 12

1. Solve these simultaneous equations: $3x + y = 13$
$2x - y = 2$

2. Aisling and Zoe buy some flowers.
Aisling buys a rose and a lily.
These cost her €10.70.
Zoe buys a rose and 3 lilies.
These cost her €14.50.
What is the cost of a lily?

3. Solve the equations: $3x + 2y = 17$
$x - y = 4$

4. The diagram shows a rectangle, not drawn to scale.
All sides are measured in centimetres.
   (i) Write down a pair of simultaneous equations in $a$ and $b$.
   (ii) Solve your pair of simultaneous equations to find $a$ and $b$.

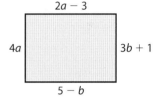

5. Solve these simultaneous equations: $2x - y = 5$
$x - 2y = 4$

6. The weight of a blue brick is $b$ grams.
The weight of a red brick is $r$ grams.

   4 blue bricks and 3 red bricks weigh 58 grams.
   5 blue bricks and 6 red bricks weigh 86 grams.
   (i) Write two equations to represent these diagrams.
   (ii) Solve the equations to find the weight of a blue brick and the weight of a red brick.
   (iii) Find the total weight of 3 blue bricks and 6 red bricks.

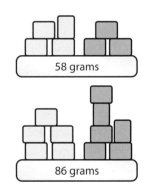

7. Solve the simultaneous equations:
$$5x = 4y + 10$$
$$2x - 3y = -3$$

8. The shape ABCD is a parallelogram.
Write two equations in $x$ and $y$ and solve them to find their values.

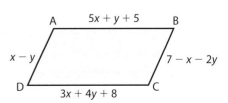

**9.** (i) Show that the points (0, 4), (1, 5.5), (2, 7) satisfy the equation $y = 1.5x + 4$ and (0, 2), (1, 4), (2, 6) satisfy the equation $y = 2x + 2$.

   (ii) Plot the points on a scaled grid, where $0 < x < 8$ and $0 < y < 12$.

   (iii) Using a ruler join the points and hence find the point of intersection of the two lines.

   (iv) Solve the equations to verify your result.

## Assignment:

Ava and Sean were asked to solve the simultaneous equations:

A: $y = 2x + 10$

B: $y = 4x + 2$

They decided to find the point of intersection, where the two lines meet.

Ava said that the points;

$(-5, 0), (-4, 2), (-3, 4), (-2, 6)$ were on line A.

Sean said that the points;

$(-2, -6), (-1, -2), (0, 2), (1, 6)$ were on line B.

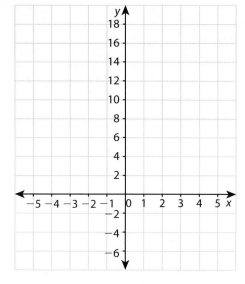

A: Copy the grid that Ava and Sean had started onto a large sheet of paper and plot the points for A and B carefully. Using a ruler extend each line until they intersect.

B: Write down the point of intersection in the form of $(x, y)$.

C: By substitution show that this point is on (i) $y = 2x + 10$ and (ii) $y = 4x + 2$

D: Rewriting the equations as (i) $2x - y = -10$ (ii) $4x - y = -2$ use the elimination method to solve the equations and so verify the answer they got.

# Quadratic Equations

# chapter 13

## From first year, you will recall how to:

- solve linear equations,
- rearrange equations,
- use algebra techniques to solve word problems.

## In this chapter, you will learn to:

- solve a quadratic equation using factors,
- create a quadratic equation from a word problem,
- interpret the point of intersection of a quadratic curve and the $x$-axis.

## Section 13.1 Solving quadratic equations using factors —

Equations such as $x^2 - 4x + 3 = 0$ or $x^2 - x - 3 = 0$ contain a term in $x^2$.
These are called **quadratic equations**.

Take the equation $x^2 - 5x + 6 = 0$.

When $x = 2$, then $x^2 - 5x + 6$ becomes
$$(2)^2 - 5(2) + 6, \text{ i.e. } 4 - 10 + 6 = 0$$

When $x = 3$, then $x^2 - 5x + 6$ becomes
$$(3)^2 - 5(3) + 6, \text{ i.e. } 9 - 15 + 6 = 0$$

When $x = 2$ or $x = 3$, both sides of the equation are zero.
When this happens, we say that $x = 2$ and $x = 3$
are **solutions** or **roots** of the equation.

> The **roots** of an equation are the values of $x$ which satisfy the equation.

### Multiplication by zero —————————————

Any number multiplied by zero is zero.
For example, $4 \times 0 = 0$ or $0 \times 6 = 0$.
This illustrates a very important property of real numbers which is given below.

Thus, if $(x - 3)(x + 5) = 0$, then $x - 3 = 0$ or $x + 5 = 0$
i.e. $x = 3$ or $x = -5$

> If the product of two numbers is zero,
> then at least one of them must be zero.
> e.g. if $ab = 0$, then $a = 0$ or $b = 0$.

## Steps for solving quadratic equations

> ❯ If necessary, rearrange the equation with one side being **zero**.
> ❯ Factorise fully the other side.
> ❯ Let each factor equal zero.
> ❯ Solve the resulting simple equations.

---

**Example 1**

Solve the equation $x^2 - 2x - 8 = 0$.

$x^2 - 2x - 8 = 0$
$(x + 2)(x - 4) = 0$ … factorise the left-hand side
∴ $(x + 2) = 0$ or $(x - 4) = 0$
∴ $x = -2$ or $x = 4$

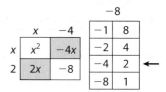

---

**Example 2**

Solve the equation $x^2 - 5x = 0$.

In this equation, there is no number term.
$x^2 - 5x = 0$
$x(x - 5) = 0$ … factorise
∴ $x = 0$ or $(x - 5) = 0$
∴ $x = 0$ or $x = 5$

|   | $x$ | $-5$ |
|---|-----|------|
| $x$ | $x^2$ | $-5x$ |

---

**Example 3**

Solve the equation $x^2 - 25 = 0$.

(Here we use the *difference of two squares* to factorise $x^2 - 25$.)
$x^2 - 25 = 0$
$x^2 - (5)^2 = 0$
$(x + 5)(x - 5) = 0$
∴ $(x + 5) = 0$ or $(x - 5) = 0$
∴ $x = -5$ or $x = 5$

|   | $x$ | $+5$ |
|---|-----|------|
| $x$ | $x^2$ | $+5x$ |
| $-5$ | $-5x$ | $-25$ |

## Exercise 13.1

Solve the following quadratic equations:

**1.** $(x - 2)(x - 3) = 0$      **2.** $(x - 2)(x - 5) = 0$      **3.** $(x - 2)(x + 3) = 0$

**4.** $(x - 4)(x + 5) = 0$      **5.** $(x + 2)(x + 6) = 0$      **6.** $x(x - 4) = 0$

**7.** $x(x + 5) = 0$      **8.** $(x - 3)(x + 3) = 0$      **9.** $(x + 7)(x - 7) = 0$

**10.** $x^2 + 3x + 2 = 0$      **11.** $x^2 + 5x + 6 = 0$      **12.** $x^2 + 6x + 8 = 0$

**13.** $x^2 + 7x + 10 = 0$      **14.** $x^2 + 7x + 12 = 0$      **15.** $x^2 + 12x + 27 = 0$

**16.** $x^2 + 11x + 28 = 0$      **17.** $x^2 + 12x + 35 = 0$      **18.** $x^2 + 14x + 48 = 0$

**19.** $x^2 - 5x + 6 = 0$      **20.** $x^2 - 8x + 15 = 0$      **21.** $x^2 - 10x + 16 = 0$

**22.** $x^2 - 9x + 14 = 0$      **23.** $x^2 - 10x + 21 = 0$      **24.** $x^2 - 10x + 24 = 0$

**25.** $x^2 - 12x + 27 = 0$      **26.** $x^2 - 12x + 32 = 0$      **27.** $x^2 - 16x + 48 = 0$

**28.** $x^2 - x - 12 = 0$      **29.** $x^2 - 3x - 10 = 0$      **30.** $x^2 + 3x - 28 = 0$

**31.** $x^2 - 5x - 24 = 0$      **32.** $x^2 + 5x - 36 = 0$      **33.** $x^2 - x - 72 = 0$

**34.** $x^2 - 3x - 54 = 0$      **35.** $x^2 + 15x + 44 = 0$      **36.** $x^2 - 7x - 60 = 0$

**37.** $x^2 - 16 = 0$      **38.** $x^2 - 25 = 0$      **39.** $x^2 - 64 = 0$

**40.** $x^2 - 1 = 0$      **41.** $x^2 - 121 = 0$      **42.** $x^2 - 81 = 0$

**43.** $x^2 - 3x = 0$      **44.** $x^2 + 4x = 0$      **45.** $x^2 - 8x = 0$

**46.** $x^2 + 9x = 0$      **47.** $x^2 - 14x = 0$      **48.** $x^2 + 7x = 0$

**49.** $x^2 + 7x = 30$      **50.** $x^2 - 10x = 24$      **51.** $x^2 + 4x - 12 = 0$

**52.** $x^2 - 6x - 16 = 0$      **53.** $x^2 - 11x + 28 = 0$      **54.** $x^2 = 100$

**55.** $x^2 - 11x = 0$      **56.** $x^2 - 10x = -9$      **57.** $x^2 - 9x = 52$

# *Investigation:*

Quadratic equations usually have two solutions.

The solutions of $x^2 - 2x - 8 = 0$ are $x = -2$ and $x = 4$
The solutions of $x^2 - 5x = 0$ are $x = 0$ and $x = 5$
The solutions of $x^2 - 25 = 0$ are $x = -5$ and $x = 5$

Verify each of the above.

Solve the equations (a) $x^2 + 10x + 25 = 0$   (b) $x^2 + 8x + 16 = 0$

Investigate what is unusual about these quadratic equations.

# Section 13.2 Problems leading to quadratic equations

When a problem expressed in words is changed into a mathematical sentence, it often results in a quadratic equation.

To find the equation to represent a problem,

> where relevant, draw a diagram and put all the information you are given on it

> use $x$ to represent the unknown you are asked to find

> look for the information in the question to form an equation in $x$

> solve the equation to find the value or values for $x$; you may sometimes have to reject a negative answer.

---

**Example 1**

The sum of a number and its square is 30.
Find two numbers which satisfy this condition.

Let $x$ be the number.

Equation:  $x + x^2 = 30$  … the square of $x$ is $x^2$
$x^2 + x = 30$  … rearrange
$x^2 + x - 30 = 0$  … subtract 30 from
both sides
$(x + 6)(x - 5) = 0$
$x + 6 = 0$  or  $x - 5 = 0$
$\therefore \quad x = -6$  or  $x = 5$

The two numbers are $-6$ and 5.

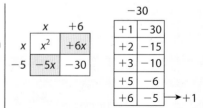

---

## Example 2

The length of a rectangle exceeds its breadth by 6 cm.
If the area of the rectangle is 160 cm², find its length and breadth.

Let the breadth of the rectangle be $x$ cm.

∴ The length is $(x + 6)$ cm.

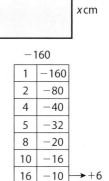

Area = 160 cm²

$$\therefore \quad x(x + 6) = 160 \quad \ldots A = \ell \times b$$
$$x^2 + 6x = 160$$
$$x^2 + 6x - 160 = 0$$
$$(x - 10)(x + 16) = 0$$
$$x - 10 = 0 \text{ or } x + 16 = 0$$
$$x = 10 \text{ or } x = -16$$

Naturally in this case, we reject the negative number $-16$, as a rectangle cannot have a negative breadth,

$$\therefore \quad x = 10$$

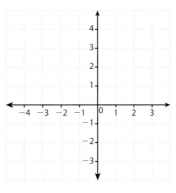

∴ the length, $(x + 6)$ cm = 16 cm and the breadth, $x$ cm = 10 cm

## *Investigation:*

Examine the curve, $y = x^2 + x - 2$

Show that if $x = -3$, then $y = 4$

Repeat for each of the following:

If $x = -2$, then $y = 0$
If $x = -1$, then $y = -2$
If $x = 0$, then $y = -2$
If $x = 1$, then $y = 0$
If $x = 2$, then $y = 4$

Copy the grid onto a large sheet and plot
the points, $(-3, 4), (-2, 0), (-1, -2), (0, -2), (1, 0), (2, 4)$

This curve is called a **parabola.** All quadratics when plotted form similar curves.

Factorise $x^2 + x - 2$ and then solve the equation $x^2 + x - 2 = 0$

Investigate the link between the solution and the graph you have drawn.

What conclusion can you make about the roots of a quadratic equation and the graph of a quadratic equation?

## Exercise 13.2

1. The sum of a positive number $x$ and its square is 42. Find the number.

2. I think of a positive number $x$. When I subtract four times the number from its square, the result is 21. Find the number.

3. One positive number is 4 bigger than another number.
   If the product of the two numbers is 45, find these numbers.

4. Think of a positive number $x$. When twice the number is added to its square, the result is 48. Find the number.

5. One positive number is 3 bigger than another number.
   When the larger number is added to the square of the smaller one, the result is 33.
   Find the two numbers.

6. When four times a positive number is taken from its square, the result is 60.
   What is this number?

7. When a number, $x$, is added to its square, the answer is 72.
   Write an equation in $x$ and solve it to find two numbers.
   Verify that both numbers satisfy the equation.

8. The area of the given rectangle is 77 cm². 
   Form an equation in $x$ and solve it to 
   find the value for $x$.
   Hence find the length and breadth of 
   the rectangle.

   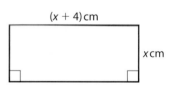

9. A rectangle has length 3 cm greater than its width.
   If it has an area of 28 cm², find the dimensions of the rectangle.

10. The area of a triangle is half the length 
    of the base multiplied by the perpendicular height.

    (i) Express the area of this triangle in terms of $x$.
    (ii) If the area of the triangle is 40 square units, 
    form an equation in $x$ and hence solve it to find its value.

    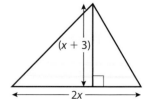

**11.** The area of the given rectangle is 63 cm². Form an equation in $x$ and solve it to find its value.

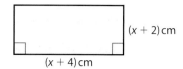

$(x + 2)$ cm

$(x + 4)$ cm

**12.** If you add 3 to a certain number and multiply the result by 4, you will get the same answer by adding 7 to the square of the number.
Find two numbers that satisfy these conditions.

**13.** A square room of side $x$ metres is partly covered by a rectangular carpet, as shown. If the area of the room not covered by the carpet is 16 m², write an equation in $x$ and solve it to find the value of $x$.

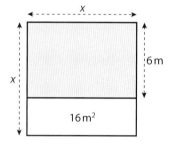

$x$

6 m

$x$

16 m²

**14.** Alan is x years old. His mother's age is the square of his age.
If Alan's father is five years older than his mother, and the sum of all three ages is 60 years, how old is Alan?

**15.** Write down the roots of the equation $x^2 + 2x - 3 = 0$ by referring to the graph shown.

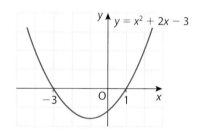

$y = x^2 + 2x - 3$

**16.** Which of the two graphs on the right gives the solutions to the equation $x^2 + 5x - 6 = 0$ ?
Explain your answer.

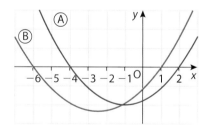

# Test yourself 13

**1.** Solve these equations:

    (i) $(x + 3)(x - 4) = 0$         (ii) $x^2 - 12x + 35 = 0$

**2.** The area of this rectangle is 7 cm².

    (i) Form an equation, in terms of $x$,
and show that it can be written as
$x^2 + 2x - 15 = 0$

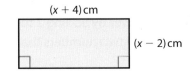

    (ii) Solve this equation to find the dimensions of the rectangle.

**3.** Solve these equations:

    (i) $x^2 + 5x = 0$         (ii) $x^2 - 9x + 8 = 0$

**4.** When twice a certain number is added to the square of the number, the result is
120. Write an equation in $x$ and solve it to find two such numbers.
Verify your answer in each case.

**5.** Solve each of these equations:

    (i) $x^2 + 3x - 40 = 0$         (ii) $x^2 - 144 = 0$

**6.** Each of the following equations has either $x = 2$ or $x = 3$ as a solution.
Which of them has both $x = 2$ and $x = 3$ as solutions?

    Ⓐ $3x + 5 = 4x + 2$     Ⓑ $2(2x - 4) = 3(2x - 4)$     Ⓒ $x^2 - 5x + 6 = 0$

    Ⓓ $(x + 1)^2 = (5 - x)^2$     Ⓔ $\dfrac{1}{x} + \dfrac{1}{2x} = \dfrac{1}{2}$

**7.** Solve these equations:

    (i) $(x + 8)(x - 3) = 0$         (ii) $x^2 - 5x - 14 = 0$

**8.** When five times a certain positive number is taken from its square, the result
is 36. Write an equation in $x$ and solve it to find the number.

**9.** Which one of the graphs below shows the solution of the equation
$(x - 4)(x - 7) = 0$?

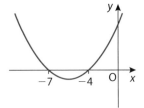 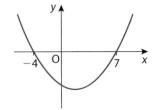 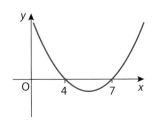

# Assignment:

A ball is hit directly upwards and its height (H), measured in metres, is given by the equation,

$$H = 16t - 4t^2$$

where $t$ is measured in seconds.

The graph of this equation tracks the height of the ball in terms of time and is shown below.

Copy the graph onto a sheet.

Solve the equation

$$0 = 16t - 4t^2$$

and mark your solutions onto the graph.

Explain why you chose the points you did.

By factorising, solve the harder equations:

    (i)    $12 = 16t - 4t^2$

    (ii)   $16 = 16t - 4t^2$

and mark your solutions onto the graph.

(Note: each of these equations should be simplified first before factorising.)

Explain how you could use the graph to solve each of the equations above quickly.

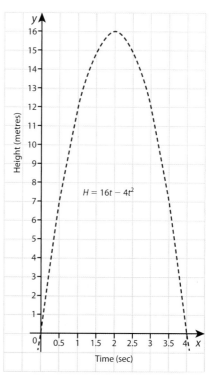

# Chapter 14 Coordinate Geometry – The Line

## *From first year, you will recall how to:*

- use a coordinated plane,
- locate the midpoint of a line segment,
- find the slope of a line segment,
- Identify a positive or negative slope.

## *In this chapter, you will learn to:*

- calculate the distance between two points,
- identify parallel lines using their slopes,
- create the equation of a line,
- find the slope of a line from its equation,
- name the $y$-intercept of a line from its equation,
- draw the graph of a line segment,
- locate the point of intersection between two lines,
- verify that a point in on a line.

## Section 14.1 The coordinated plane

The set of points on a flat surface is called a **plane**.

As stated in *Text & Tests 1*, the French mathematician Rene Descartes drew lines perpendicular to one another on a plane and so formed a grid which enabled him to locate any point on that plane.

The plane so structured is called a coordinated or Cartesian plane.

The horizontal axis is called the ***x*-axis**.

The vertical axis is called the ***y*-axis**.

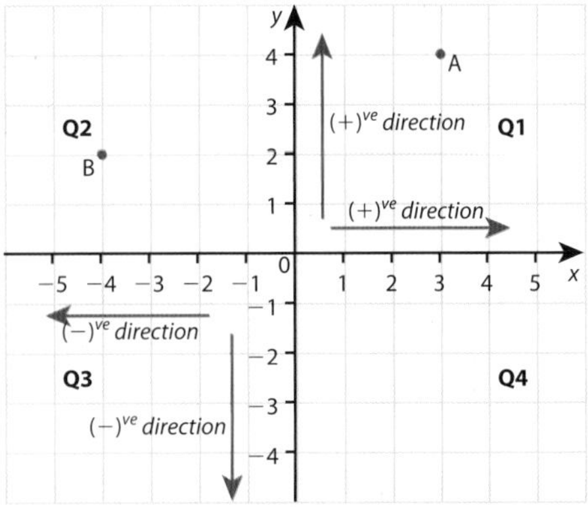


These two axes divide the plane into four **quadrants**.

Where the axes meet is called the **origin**($O$).

The point A(3, 4) is found 3 units to the right and 4 units up. A is therefore in the *first* quadrant.

The point B(−4, 2) is found 4 units to the left and 2 units up. B is in the *second* quadrant.

Each point on the plane has an *x* and a *y* coordinate, written as *(x, y)*.

## Exercise 14.1

**1.** Write down the coordinates of each of the
points marked in the coordinated plane
on the right:

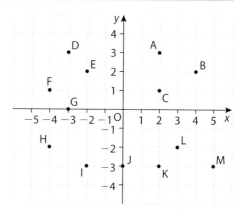

**2.** Draw a grid similar to that shown above and mark in the following points:
    (i) A(3, 4)    (ii) B(−1, 3)    (iii) C(4, −3)    (iv) D(−4, −3)    (v) E(1, −3)

**3.** The four quadrants are shown on the right.
In which quadrant does each of the
following points lie?
    (i) (3, 5)
    (ii) (−2, −3)
    (iii) (1, −4)
    (iv) (−3, 1)
    (v) (3, −3)
    (vi) (−1, −3).

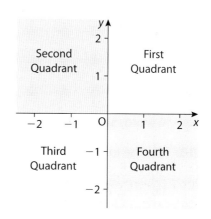

**4.** On which axis does each of these points lie?
    (i) A(4, 0)    (ii) B(0, 2)    (iii) C(0, −3)    (iv) D(−4, 0)    (v) E(−1, 0)

**5.** Write down the coordinates of
the points A, B and D on the
given grid.

If ABCD is a rectangle, write
down the coordinates of the
point C.

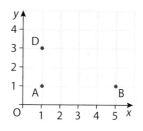

**6.** Draw an x-axis and y-axis from 0 to 5.
   (i)  Plot the points (2, 1), (5, 1) and (5, 4). These are three corners of a square.
   (ii) What are the coordinates of the fourth corner of the square?

**7.** (i)  Plot these points on a number plane:
           $(1, -1), (1, 3), (3, 3), (3, -1)$.
     (ii)  By joining the points in order and then back to the first point again, what type
           of figure is formed?
     (iii) What are the lengths of the sides of this figure?
     (iv)  What is its perimeter?
     (v)   What is its area?

**8.** This triangle has been formed by joining the
   points shown.
     (i)   What is the height $h$ of this triangle?
     (ii)  What is the length of the base $b$?
     (iii) Work out the area of this triangle?

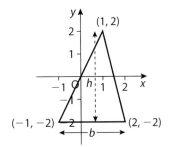

**9.** Plot the following sets of points:
     (i)   (2, 1), (3, 2), (4, 3), (5, 4), (6, 5)
     (ii)  $(-1, 4), (0, 2), (1, 0), (2, -2), (3, -4)$
     (iii) $(-2, -2), (-1, -1), (0, 0), (1, 2), (2, 4)$

   State if each set of points is collinear.
   In words state the rule that connects the collinear points.

**10.** Plot the following sets of collinear points and join the points to form a straight line.
     (i)   $(-3, 9), (2, 8), (7, 7), (12, 6)$
     (ii)  $(-2, 2), (2, 5), (6, 8), (10, 11)$

   In the case of each set of points write down the coordinates of another point on
   each line.

**11.** Plot the set of points formed in this grid.
   Join the points to form a straight line.
   Name point where the line crosses the x-axis.
   Write down the coordinates of one other point on the line.

| x | −3 | −2 | −1 | 0 | 1 | 2 | 3 |
|---|---|---|---|---|---|---|---|
| y | −5 | −3 | −1 | 1 | 3 | 5 | 7 |

## Section 14.2 Revision of midpoint of a line segment

The midpoint of an interval [AB] is the halfway position in the interval.

The halfway point of the interval between −6 and 4 is the average of these two numbers.

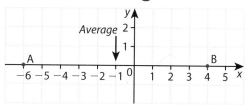

i.e. $\dfrac{-6 + 4}{2} = -1$

To find the midpoint of a line segment AB, where A = (−6, 3) and B = (4, 9), add the x-coordinates and divide by 2, then add the y-coordinates and divide by 2.

$$\therefore Midpoint = \left( \frac{-6 + 4}{2}, \frac{9 + 3}{2} \right) = (-1, 6)$$

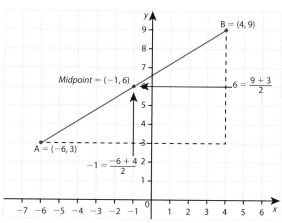

Note: −1 is halfway between −6 and 4

6 is halfway between 3 and 9

In general terms if $(x_1, y_1)$ and $(x_2, y_2)$ are the end points of a line segment then the

midpoint $(x, y) = \left( \dfrac{x_1 + x_2}{2}, \dfrac{y_1 + y_2}{2} \right)$

**In words**; To find the **midpoint** of a line segment,

add the two x-coordinates and divide by 2,

add the two y-coordinates and divide by 2.

**Midpoint $(x, y) = \left( \dfrac{x_1 + x_2}{2}, \dfrac{y_1 + y_2}{2} \right)$**

247

### Example 1

Write down the coordinates of the points A, B, and C.

Use the coordinates to find the midpoint of the line-segments AB, and BC.

A = (4, 3), B = (10, 1), C = (6, −1)

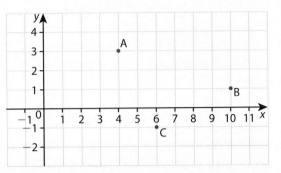

Let $(x_1, y_1) = (4, 3)$ and $(x_2, y_2) = (10, 1)$ ∴ Midpoint of AB $= \left(\dfrac{4 + 10}{2}, \dfrac{3 + 1}{2}\right) = (7, 2)$

Let $(x_1, y_1) = (10, 1)$ and $(x_2, y_2) = (6, -1)$ ∴ Midpoint of BC $= \left(\dfrac{10 + 6}{2}, \dfrac{1 + (-1)}{2}\right)$

$= (8, 0)$

## Exercise 14.2

**1.** What number is halfway between
  (i)  4 and 10
  (ii)  −2 and 6
  (iii)  −10 and −4
  (iv)  4 and −6

**2.** In the following intervals find the halfway point.
  (i)  1, 8
  (ii)  0, 10
  (iii)  −5, 3
  (iv)  −6, −2
  (v)  −6, 12

**3.** A(2, 6), B(4, 2) and C(8, 4) are three points, as shown.

Find the midpoints of each of these line segments:
  (i)  [AC]
  (ii)  [CB]
  (iii)  [AB].

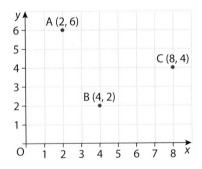

Find the coordinates of the midpoints of the line segments joining the following pairs of points:

**4.** (6, 2) and (−2, 0)

**5.** (−3, 4) and (1, −2)

**6.** (0, 7) and (4, 3)

**7.** (1, −3) and (3, 5)

**8.** (−3, 0) and (1, 6)

**9.** (4, −3) and (2, −3)

**10.** In the given diagram, M(4, 3) is the midpoint of the line segment joining A(1, 1) and B. By trial and error, find the coordinates of the point B.

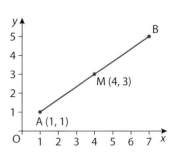

**11.** Show that the midpoint of the line segment joining A(4, −3) and B(−4, 7) lies on the y-axis.

**12.** Find the coordinates of the centre, O, of the given circle.

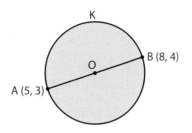

**13.** The given figure shows a parallelogram ABCD.
   (i) Find the coordinates of the midpoint of [AC].
   (ii) Verify that the midpoint of [AC] is also the midpoint of [BD].

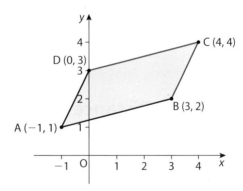

**14.** A ladder DC leans against a vertical wall as shown.
   Using the coordinates of D and C prove that the midpoint of the ladder is (3, 6).

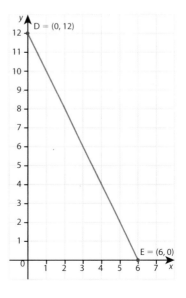

249

**15.** In the diagram C(10, 7) is the midpoint of the line segment AB.

If A has coordinates (5, 9) find the coordinates of B by trial and error.

Using the midpoint formula verify your answer using the coordinates of A and B.

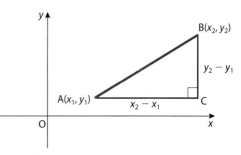

A = (5, 9)

C = (10, 7)

B

**16.** If (8, 3) is the midpoint of (13, 6) and (3, $k$), find the value of $k$.

**17.** (9, 2) are the coordinates of the midpoint of the line segment from (3, 1) to ($t$, 3). Find the value of $t$.

**18.** The coordinates of the ends of a diameter of a circle are (−1, 6) and (7, 2). Find the coordinates of the centre of the circle.

**19.** (i)  Find the midpoint of the points A(−3, 11) and B(−9, −1) and call the point C.
    (ii)  Find the midpoint of the points D(5, 9) and E(11, 1) and call the point F.
    (iii)  Find the midpoint of the line segment CF.

## Section 14.3  Distance between two points

The given diagram shows the points    A($x_1$, $y_1$)   and   B($x_2$, $y_2$).

$|BC| = y_2 - y_1$     and     $|AC| = x_2 - x_1$

Using the Theorem of Pythagoras:

$$|AB|^2 = |AC|^2 + |BC|^2$$
$$= (x_2 - x_1)^2 + (y_2 - y_1)^2$$
$$\therefore \quad |\mathbf{AB}| = \sqrt{(\mathbf{x_2} - \mathbf{x_1})^2 + (\mathbf{y_2} - \mathbf{y_1})^2}$$

The distance between A($x_1$, $y_1$) and B($x_2$, $y_2$) is
$$|AB| = \sqrt{(x_2 - x_1)^2 + (y_2 - y_1)^2}$$

---

**Example 1**

Find the distance between the points A(3, 2) and B(7, 5).

$$|AB| = \sqrt{(x_2 - x_1)^2 + (y_2 - y_1)^2}$$
$$= \sqrt{(7 - 3)^2 + (5 - 2)^2}$$
$$= \sqrt{(4)^2 + (3)^2}$$
$$= \sqrt{16 + 9}$$
$$= \sqrt{25}$$
$$= 5$$

Let $(3, 2)$ and $(7, 5)$
$\downarrow$ $\downarrow$
$(x_1, y_1)$ $(x_2, y_2)$

> The distance between the points A and B is written as $|AB|$.

---

## Exercise 14.3

Find the distances between the following pairs of points:

**1.** (2, 1) and (5, 4)   **2.** (1, 2) and (6, 4)   **3.** (3, 1) and (4, 5)

**4.** (3, 5) and (4, 7)   **5.** (2, −1) and (3, 5)   **6.** (4, 3) and (−2, 5)

**7.** (3, 0) and (7, 2)   **8.** (−1, 4) and (2, 1)   **9.** (3, −2) and (−2, 4)

**10.** (−6, 1) and (1, −4)   **11.** (0, −3) and (4, −5)   **12.** (−1, 5) and (2, 3)

**13.** A(1, 1), B(5, 1) and C(3, 6) are the vertices of a triangle.
Show that $|AC| = |BC|$.

**14.** Show that (2, 1) is the same distance from (5, 3) as it is from (−1, −1).

**15.** Use the given diagram to write down
the coordinates of A, B, C and D.
   (i)  Write down the length of [DA].
   (ii)  Show that $|CD| = |BA|$.
   (iii)  Investigate if the midpoint of [AC]
       is the same as the midpoint of [DB].

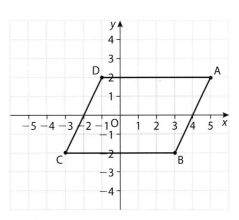

**16.** The points A(1, 2), B(2, 3) and C(3, 1) are the vertices of a triangle.
Find |AB|, |BC| and |AC|.
Which two sides have the same length?
Describe the triangle ABC.

**17.** The given figure shows the line
segment joining C(3, 1) and D(10, 4).
The Theorem of Pythagoras states
that $d^2 = \ell^2 + h^2$.
Use this theorem to find |CD|,
leaving your answer in $\sqrt{\phantom{x}}$ form.
Now use the formula $\sqrt{(x_2 - x_1)^2 + (y_2 - y_1)^2}$
to find |CD|.
You should find both answers to be the same.

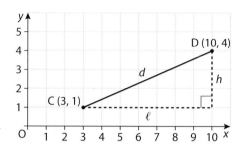

**18.** A sheet of wood 3.7 m by 3.7 m is
needed in *Room R*.
The door of the room is 3 m high
and 2 m wide.
John says that the sheet could fit
in the door if it is held diagonally.
Use the grid and given diagram to
investigate if the sheet can be
brought through the door.

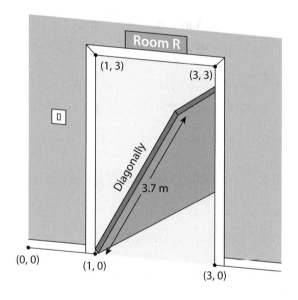

# Section 14.4 Revision of slope of a line segment

The slope of a line is a measure of how steep it is.

In the diagram the slope of AB is greater than the slope of AC.

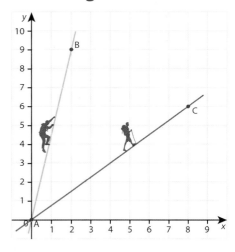

The slope is calculated by dividing the change in $y$(**Rise**) by the change in $x$(**Run**) for each segment.

Consider the segment AB;

Rise $= 9$ and Run $= 2$ $\therefore$ Slope $= \dfrac{\text{Rise}}{\text{Run}} = \dfrac{9}{2} = 4.5$

Consider the segment AC;

Rise $= 6$ and Run $= 8$

$\therefore$ Slope $= \dfrac{\text{Rise}}{\text{Run}} = \dfrac{6}{8} = 0.75$

In general, the slope of a line joining the points $(x_1, y_1)$ and $(x_2, y_2)$ is given by

$$m = \frac{y_2 - y_1}{x_2 - x_1}$$

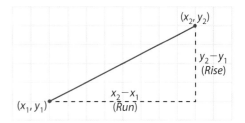

$$\text{Slope } m = \frac{y_2 - y_1}{x_2 - x_1} = \frac{\text{Rise}}{\text{Run}} = \frac{\text{Change in } y}{\text{Change in } x}$$

Moving from left to right if the line is going up then the slope is *positive*.

If the line is not going up or down (i.e. horizontal) then the slope is *zero*.

Moving from left to right if the line is going down then the slope is *negative*.

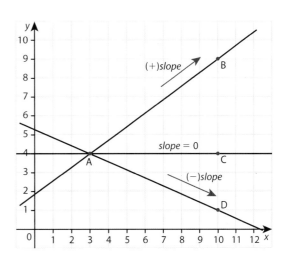

## Parallel lines

The lines AB and CD both have the same slope $\frac{3}{2}$.

These lines are parallel.

Arrows are used to show that two lines are parallel.

Parallel lines have equal slopes.

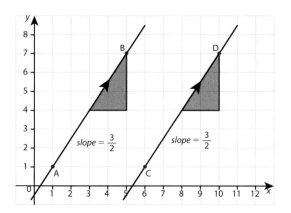

---

### Example 1

Write down the coordinates of the points A, B and C.

Using the coordinates find the slope of the line
(i)  AC        (ii)  AB.

Using the slope formula show that the slope of BC is zero.

$A = (6, 10)$, $B = (11, 2)$ $C = (1, 2)$

Let $(x_1, y_1) = (1, 2)$ and $(x_2, y_2) = (6, 10)$

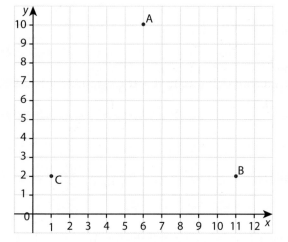

Slope of AC $= \dfrac{y_2 - y_1}{x_2 - x_1} = \dfrac{10 - 2}{6 - 1} = \dfrac{8}{5} = 1.6$

Let $(x_1, y_1) = (11, 2)$ and $(x_2, y_2) = (6, 10)$

Slope of AB $= \dfrac{y_2 - y_1}{x_2 - x_1} = \dfrac{10 - 2}{6 - 11} = \dfrac{8}{-5} = -1.6$

Let $(x_1, y_1) = (1, 2)$ and $(x_2, y_2) = (11, 2)$

Slope of BC $= \dfrac{y_2 - y_1}{x_2 - x_1} = \dfrac{2 - 2}{11 - 1} = \dfrac{0}{10} = 0$

Notice that the slope of AC is **positive** as it is rising as we go from left to right and the slope of AB is **negative** as it is going down as we go from left to right.

## Exercise 14.4

**1.** State whether each of the following has a positive or negative slope.

(i)

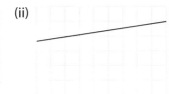

(ii)

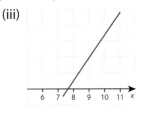

(iii)

(iv)

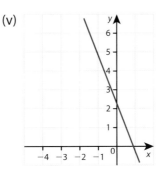

(v)

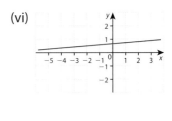

(vi)

**2.** Calculate the slope of each the following line segments using the grid provided:

(i)

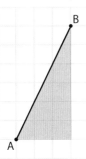

(ii)

(iii)

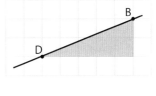

**3.** Using the coordinates given calculate (a) Rise (b) Run for the segments AB
Use these values to find the slope of each line segment.

(i)

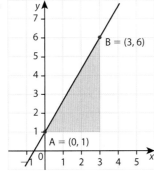

(ii)

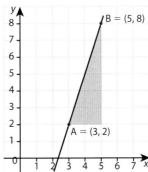

(iii)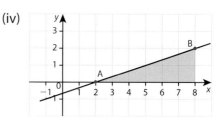

(iv)

4.  (i)   Which of the lines AB, CD or EF has a negative slope?
    (ii)  Write down the coordinates of the points A, B, C, D, E and F.
    (iii) Using the formula,

    $$m = \frac{\text{Change in } y}{\text{Change in } x}$$

    find the slope of the line segments AB, CD and EF.

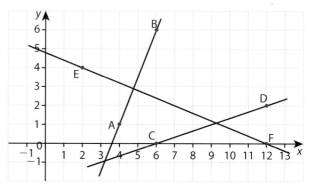

5.  (i)   How do you check if lines are parallel?
    (ii)  Prove that AB is parallel to CD
    (iii) If A is joined to C and B is joined to D, a quadrilateral is formed. Find the slopes of the line segments AC and BD.
    What does your answer tell you about the quadrilateral ABCD?

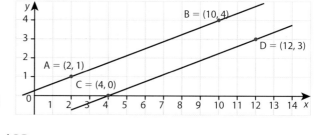

6.  If $A(x_1, y_1) = (3, 2)$ and $B(x_2, y_2) = (6, 14)$, find the slope of AB.

7.  If $C(x_1, y_1) = (4, 6)$ and $D(x_2, y_2) = (-1, -4)$, find the slope of CD.

8.  Find the slopes of the lines through each pair of points:
    (i)   (1, 2) and (3, 4)    (ii)  (0, 4) and (1, 8)    (iii) (2, −4) and (6, 6)
    (iv)  (−2, 0) and ( 3, 2)    (v)   (8, 6) and (1, −1)    (vi)  (−2, −4) and (2, 4)

9. Using the coordinates given in the diagram, show that ABCD is a parallelogram.

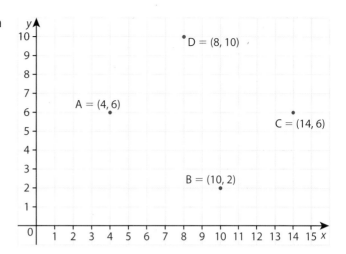

10. Show that the line through A(1, 1) and B(5, −1) is parallel to the line through C(4, 4) and D(8, 2).

Lines with the same slope are parallel.

11. Find (i) the slope of the line through A(2, 4) and B(1, 1)
(ii) the slope of the line through C(4, 1) and D(3, −2).
What can you say about the two lines?

12. The given diagram shows three lines *a*, *b*, and *c*.
Match the lines with these slopes:

    2,      $\frac{1}{2}$,      1.

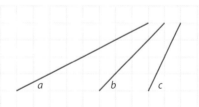

13. By measuring the rise and the run using the millimetre scale on a ruler, find the slope of each of the following inclines.

14. (i) Write down the coordinates of the points A, B, C and D.
    (ii) Find the slopes of the lines through
        (a) AB
        (b) BC
        (c) CD
        (d) AD.

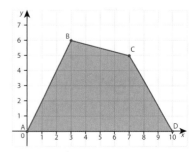

**15.** A ski jump consists of two parts
(i) the descent (ii) the lift.
In the diagram find:

(a) the slope of the descent DB

(b) the slope of the lift CE.

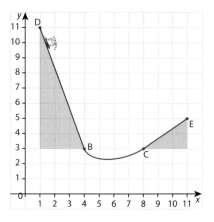

# Investigation:

Investigate any slope in the school grounds or on a driveway at home.

Use a long measuring tape (or string) and a small level.

Measure the distance '$\ell$' which is the **Run** then measure '$h$', the **Rise**.

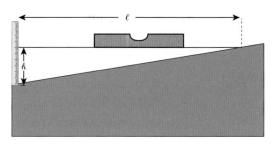

Make sure that the string or tape is kept horizontal using the level and the metre-stick is vertical.

The slope is calculated from, $m = \dfrac{\text{Rise}}{\text{Run}}$.

Compare your answers with other groups.

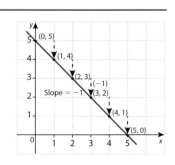

Investigate why a hill on a road may have a negative and positive slope at the same time?

**Note:** the slope of a line(road) is often called the *gradient* of the line(road).

# Section 14.5 The equation of a line

The diagram on the right shows that the points (0, 5), (1, 4), (2, 3), (3, 2), (4, 1) and (5, 0) are all in the same straight line.

Notice that the y-coordinate decreases by 1 as the x-coordinate increases by 1.

The slope $m = \dfrac{0-5}{5-0} = -1$

For all points, $(x, y)$ on this line
$$y = -x + 5$$

We also note that the line crosses the y-axis at $y = 5$ i.e. the point $(0, 5)$

$y = -x + 5$ is called the **equation** of the line.

## The equation of a line in the form $y = mx + c$

The equation of the line through the points, AB, is given by

$$y = 2x + 1$$

This line has a slope $m = \dfrac{5 - 1}{2 - 0} = 2$

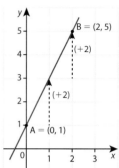

We note that this line crosses the y-axis at $(0, 1)$

Where a line crosses the y-axis is called the y-**intercept**.

When a line is written in the form $y = mx + c$, it is said to be expressed in a **slope-intercept** form.

> For any line in the form $y = mx + c$,
> (i) the slope of the line is $m$
> (ii) the point where it crosses the y-axis is $(0, c)$

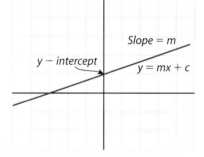

---

### Example 1

Find the slope and y-intercept of these lines:
(i) $y = 3x + 4$
(ii) $y = -2x - 1$

(i) $y = 3x + 4$: slope $= 3$; y-intercept is 4
(ii) $y = -2x - 1$: slope $= -2$; y-intercept is $-1$

---

### Example 2

Write the equation of the following lines:
(i) slope $= 3$, y-intercept $= 6$
(ii) slope $= -2$, y-intercept $= 4$
(iii) slope $= \dfrac{1}{3}$, y-intercept $= -5$

(i) $m = 3, c = 6 \therefore y = mx + c = 3x + 6$
(ii) $m = -2, c = 4 \therefore y = mx + c = -2x + 4$
(iii) $m = \dfrac{1}{3}, c = -5 \therefore y = mx + c = \dfrac{1}{3}x - 5$

Examine the graphs of the lines:

$y = x + 5; \quad y = x + 1; \quad y = x - 4.$

Each line has a slope of 1.

$\therefore$ They are parallel lines.

Each line has a different $y$-intercept.

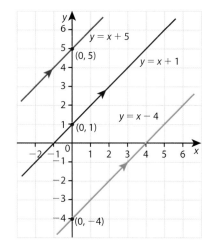

## Exercise 14.5

1. Write down the slope of each of these lines:
   (i)  $y = 2x + 3$
   (ii)  $y = 3x + 6$
   (iii)  $y = 2x - 1$
   (iv)  $y = 5x + 2$
   (v)  $y = -x + 4$
   (vi)  $y = -3x - 2$

2. Write down the coordinates of the point where each of the lines in Question 1 above intersects the $y$-axis.

3. For each of the following lines, write down
   (i)  the slope of the line
   (ii)  the point at which it crosses the $y$-axis.

   (a)  $y = 3x + 1$
   (b)  $y = 2x - 4$
   (c)  $y = -3x + 5$

4. The slope of each of these lines is given.
   Write the equation of each line in the form $y = mx + c$.

   (i)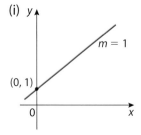

   (ii)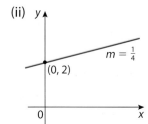

   (iii)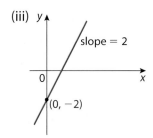

**5.** For the given line, write down
   (i) the slope of the line
   (ii) the coordinates of the point at which
         the line crosses the $y$- axis
   (iii) the equation of the line in the form
         $y = mx + c$.

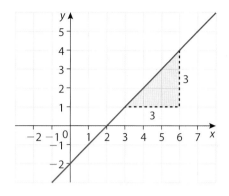

**6.** By reading off the slope and the $y$-intercept, write down the equations of the
following lines in the form $y = mx + c$.

(a) 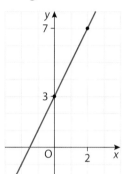     (b) 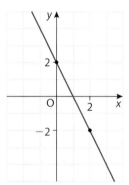     (c)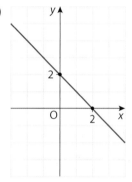

**7.** By finding the slope and $y$-intercept,
write down the equation of the
given line.

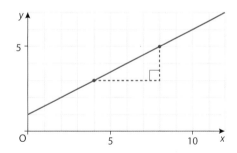

**8.** The equations of six lines are given below:

a: $y = 2x - 3$          c: $y = x + 3$          e: $y = -\frac{1}{2}x + 4$

b: $y = \frac{1}{2}x + 5$          d: $y = -2x - 4$          f: $y = 2x - 2$

   (i) Which two lines are parallel?
   (ii) Which line has a slope of $\frac{1}{2}$?
   (iii) Which line crosses the $y$-axis at $(0, -4)$?
   (iv) At what point does the line marked $a$ cross the $y$-axis?
   (v) What is the slope of the line $c$?

**9.** (i) Using the shaded triangle find the slope of line L.
(ii) What is the y-intercept of the line L.
(iii) Find the equation of L.
(iv) K is parallel to L, find the equation of K.

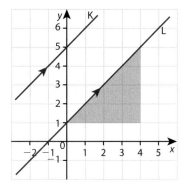

# Section 14.6 The equation of a line containing $(x_1, y_1)$ with slope $m$

If we know a point $(x_1, y_1)$ on a line and its slope $m$, the equation of the line is:

$$y - y_1 = m(x - x_1)$$

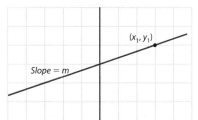

$Slope = m$  $(x_1, y_1)$

## Example 1

Find the equation of the line which has a slope of 2 and which contains the point (3, 1).

The equation is   $y - y_1 = m(x - x_1)$
$y - 1 = 2(x - 3)$
$y - 1 = 2x - 6$
$y = 2x - 6 + 1$
$y = 2x - 5$

$m = 2$
$(x_1, y_1) = (3, 1)$

[Note: The equation may also be written in the form $2x - y - 5 = 0$.]

## Given two points on a line

If we are given two points on a line but no slope, we first find the slope of the line through the two given points. We then use this slope and any **one** of the two points to find the equation of the line.

### Example 2

Find the equation of the line which passes through the points $(-2, 1)$ and $(1, 5)$.

$$m = \frac{y_2 - y_1}{x_2 - x_1} = \frac{5 - 1}{1 + 2} = \frac{4}{3}$$

$$\begin{array}{cc} (x_1, y_1) & (x_2, y_2) \\ \downarrow & \downarrow \\ (-2, 1) & (1, 5) \end{array}$$

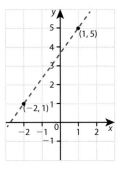

We will now use this slope and the point $(-2, 1)$.

Equation: $y - y_1 = m(x - x_1)$ $\qquad m = \frac{4}{3} \quad (-2, 1)$

$$y - 1 = \tfrac{4}{3}(x + 2) \qquad\qquad\qquad \downarrow$$

$$y - 1 = \frac{4x}{3} + \frac{8}{3} \qquad\qquad\qquad (x_1, y_1)$$

$$y = \frac{4x}{3} + \frac{8}{3} + 1$$

$$y = \frac{4x}{3} + \frac{8}{3} + \frac{3}{3}$$

$$y = \frac{4x}{3} + \frac{11}{3} \quad \text{is the required equation}$$

**Note:** we could have simplified the answer above as follows:

$y - 1 = \tfrac{4}{3}(x + 2)$
$3y - 3 = 4(x + 2)$    …multiplying both sides by 3
$3y - 3 = 4x + 8$
$-4x + 3y - 11 = 0$
$4x - 3y + 11 = 0$ is the **standard form** of the equation of the line.

## Exercise 14.6

Use the formula $y - y_1 = m(x - x_1)$ to find the equation of each of the lines below.
Give each equation in the form $y = mx + c$.

1. Slope $= 2$; point $= (1, 3)$
2. Slope $= 3$; point $= (5, 2)$
3. Slope $= 4$; point $= (1, 4)$
4. Slope $= -2$; point $= (4, 3)$
5. Slope $= 3$; point $= (-3, 2)$
6. Slope $= 4$; point $= (-3, 4)$
7. Slope $= -2$; point $= (-1, 3)$
8. Slope $= 3$; point $= (-1, -3)$
9. Slope $= -4$; point $= (0, -2)$
10. Slope $= 2$; point $= (-2, 0)$

**11.** Slope $= \frac{2}{3}$; point $= (1, 2)$

**12.** Slope $= \frac{1}{3}$; point $= (-3, 2)$

**13.** Slope $= \frac{5}{2}$; point $= (1, -2)$

**14.** Slope $= -\frac{3}{4}$; point $= (0, 3)$

**15.** Find the slope of the line containing A(1, 2) and B(2, 5).
Now use this slope and the point A(1, 2) to find the equation of the line.
Now use the slope and the point B(2, 5) to find the equation of the line.
(Both your answers should be the same.)

**16.** A(2, $-1$) and B(4, 5) are two points. Find
   (i)  the slope of AB
   (ii)  the equation of AB.

**17.** Find the slope and hence the equation of the line through the given pairs of points:
   (i)   $(-1, 3)$ and $(1, 7)$
   (ii)  $(1, -2)$ and $(2, 3)$
   (iii) $(-2, 1)$ and $(-3, 5)$
   (iv)  $(2, -3)$ and $(5, 2)$

**18.**  (i)  Write down the coordinates of the points A, B and C.
   (ii)  Find the slopes of the lines passing through
      (a)  AB
      (b)  BC
   (iii)  Find the equation of the line passing through
      (a)  AB
      (b)  BC

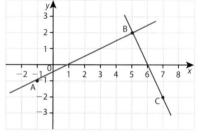

**19.** A($-1$, 3) and B(2, 1) are two points. Find
   (i)  the slope of AB
   (ii)  the equation of AB

**20.** Find the equation of the line which passes through the points $(-4, 1)$ and $(0, 5)$.

**21.** Find the equation of the line through the origin (0, 0) with slope $= -2$.

**22.** Find the midpoint of the line segment R($-1$, 3) and S(5, 5).
Now find the equation of the line through the midpoint of [RS] with slope $= 4$.

**23.** Write each of the following equations in the form $y = mx + c$, hence find the slope and intercept value of each.
   (a)  $4x + y - 3 = 0$
   (b)  $6x + 2y - 5 = 0$
   (c)  $x + 2y - 10 = 0$

# Section 14.7 Graphing lines

## 1. Lines parallel to the *x*-axis or *y*-axis

The lines $x = 2$ and $x = 4$ are shown.

Notice that the *x*-value of each point on the line $x = 4$ is 4.

Similarly, the *x*-value of each point on the line $x = 2$ is 2.

All lines with equations of the form $x = a$ will be parallel to the *y*-axis.

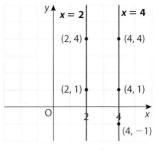

The diagram on the right shows the line $y = 2$.

Again, notice that the *y*-value of each of the points on this line is 2.

All lines with equations of the form $y = a$ will be parallel to the *x*-axis.

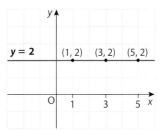

## 2. Graphing lines

To graph the line $y = 2x + 1$, we need to know at least two points on the line.

The *y*-intercept is $+1$, so $(0, 1)$ is one point on the line

The slope $m = 2 = \frac{2}{1}$, for each unit to the right the line moves up 2 units.

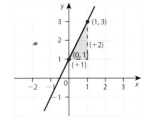

Starting at $(0, 1)$, moving 1 unit to the right and 2 units up, $\therefore$ the point $(1, 3)$ is also on the line.

Also, when $x = 1$, $y = 2(1) + 1 = 3$.

---

**Example 1**

Draw the line $y = \frac{3}{2}x - 2$
The *y*-intercept $= -2$, so $(0, -2)$ is a point on the line.
The slope $m = \frac{3}{2}$, for each 2 units to the right the line moves up 3 units.
$\therefore (2, 1)$ is also a point on the line.

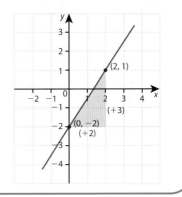

---

A second point on the line could also be found by finding the point where the line crosses the x-axis.

Take the line $y = 2x - 8$.
We know that the y-intercept is $-8$,
$\therefore (0, -8)$, is a point on the line.

On the x-axis all points have $y = 0$.

Given the line $y = 2x - 8$,
when $y = 0$,  $0 = 2x - 8$
$\therefore 2x = 8$
$x = 4$

$\therefore$ a second point on the line is $(4, 0)$

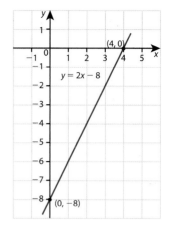

A table of points can also be made as shown.
Given $y = 2x - 8$, five points on the line are
$(0, -8), (1, -6), (2, -4), (3, -2), (4, 0)$

| $x$ | 0 | 1 | 2 | 3 | 4 |
|---|---|---|---|---|---|
| $y = 2x - 8$ | $-8$ | $-6$ | $-4$ | $-2$ | 0 |

## Exercise 14.7

1. Write down the equations of the lines marked $a$ to $d$ on the given diagram.

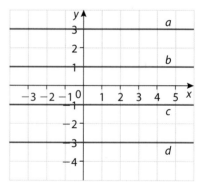

2. Write down the equations of the lines marked $e$, $f$, $g$ and $h$ in the given diagram.

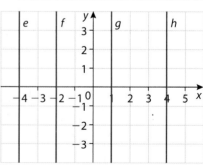

3. Draw a coordinate grid with the x-axis and y-axis each labelled from $-5$ to 5.
   On the grid draw and label these lines:

   (i) $x = 5$  (ii) $x = -2$  (iii) $y = 2$  (iv) $y = -3$

**4.** Write down the equations of the
lines marked Ⓐ to Ⓕ on the given
diagram.

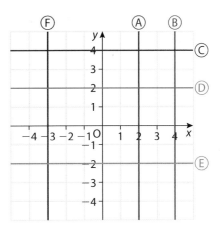

**5.** (i) What is the equation of the *x*-axis?
(ii) What is the equation of the *y*-axis?

**6.** $y = 2x - 4$ is the equation of a line.
(i) If $x = 0$, find the value for *y*.
Now write down the coordinates of the point at which the line crosses the
*y*-axis.
(ii) If $y = 0$, find the value for *x*.
Now write down the coordinates of the point at which the line crosses the *x*-axis.

**7.** Find the coordinates of the point where each of these lines cuts the *x*-axis:

(i) $y = x + 2$        (ii) $y = 3x - 6$        (iii) $y = \frac{1}{2}x + 3$

**8.** Find the coordinates of the point where each of these lines cuts the *y*-axis:

(i) $y = 2x - 3$        (ii) $y = x + 5$        (iii) $y = 3x - 4$

**9.** Find the points at which the line $y = 2x - 5$ intersects the *x*-axis and *y*-axis.
Now draw a sketch of the line.

**10.** Find the points at which the following lines intersect the *x*-axis and *y*-axis.
Hence draw a sketch of each line.

(i) $y = x + 3$        (ii) $y = 4x + 2$        (iii) $y = 6x - 6$

**11.** Find the points at which the line $y = \frac{3}{2}x - 3$ intersects the *x*-axis and *y*-axis.
Now draw a sketch of the line and mark in the coordinates of the points where the
line crosses the *x*-axis and *y*-axis.

**12.** $\ell$ is the line $y = \frac{1}{2}x - 2$ and it cuts the $x$-axis at the point K.

   (i) Find the coordinates of K.

   (ii) $\ell$ intersects the $y$-axis at P. Find the coordinates of P.

   (iii) Find the slope of the line PK.

   (iv) Find the length of [PK].

**13.** Which of the three lines below intersects

   (i) the $x$-axis at $(2, 0)$              (ii) the $y$-axis at $(0, -1)$?

     A: $y = \frac{1}{2}x + 2$     B: $y = 2x - 1$     C: $y = 2x - 4$

**14.** By finding where the line crosses the $x$-axis and $y$-axis, match each of these equations with the correct graph:

   (i) $y = -x + 3$           (ii) $y = x - 3$           (iii) $y = 2x - 3$

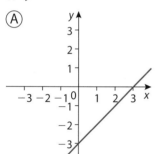 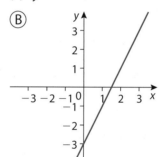 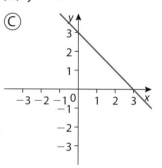

# Section 14.8  Intersection of lines

A sketch of the lines $y = -x + 4$ and $y = \frac{1}{3}x$ is shown on the right.

The point of intersection of the two lines can be read from the diagram.

This point is $(3, 1)$.

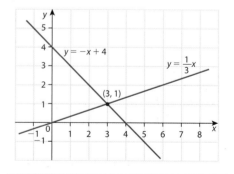

At the point of intersection of the two lines the $(x, y)$ values are the same.

Using algebra, if $y = -x + 4$ and $y = \frac{1}{3}x$

then   $\frac{1}{3}x = -x + 4$   ...at the point of intersection

     $x = -3x + 12$ ...multiplying both sides by 3

     $4x = 12$

      $x = 3$

  If $x = 3$ then $y = -3 + 4 = 1$

  $(x, y) = (3, 1)$ is the point of intersection.

Note: If the lines are given in standard form, we can use **simultaneous equations** as in **Chapter 12** to solve them and find the point of intersection.

**To verify that a point is on a given line**

To investigate if the point (3, 11) is on the line $y = 4x - 1$, we substitute 3 for $x$ and 11 for $y$ in the equation.

$y = 4x - 1$

Let $x = 3$ and $y = 11$

Test; $11 = 4(3) - 1$

$\qquad 11 = 11$ …which is true

> If a point is on a line, then the coordinates of the point will satisfy the equation of the line.

$\therefore$ we say that (3, 11) **satisfies** the equation $y = 4x - 1$.

However $(-2, 5)$ is not on the line $\qquad y = -2x + 5$

$$\text{since } 5 \neq -2(-2) + 5.$$

---

**Example 1**

Is (i) $(2, 3)$ (ii) $(-4, 1)$ on the line $y = -2x + 7$?

(ii) $(2, 3)$: Here we substitute 2 for $x$ and 3 for $y$ in the equation
$\qquad y = -2x + 7$
$\qquad 3 = -2(2) + 7 = 3$
$\qquad \therefore (2, 3)$ is on the line because $(2, 3)$ satisfies the equation.

(ii) $(-4, 1)$: $\quad y = -2x + 7$
$\qquad\qquad 1 \neq -2(-4) + 7$
$\qquad\qquad 1 \neq -1$
$\qquad\qquad \therefore (-4, 1)$ is not on the line because $(-4, 1)$ does not satisfy the equation.

---

**Exercise 14.8**

**1.** Use the diagram on the right to write down the point of intersection of the lines

$\qquad y = -x + 4$ and $y = 2x + 1$

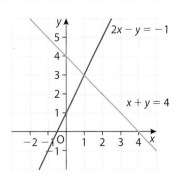

**2.** The diagram shows three lines **A**, **B** and **C**.
The equations of the lines are:

**A:** $y = -x + 3$    **B:** $y = 2x$    **C:** $y = \frac{1}{2}x - \frac{3}{2}$.

Use the diagram to write down the
point of intersection of these lines

(i) $y = -x + 3$   and   $y = 2x$

(ii) $y = \frac{1}{2}x - \frac{3}{2}$   and   $y = -x + 3$

(iii) $y = 2x$   and   $y = \frac{1}{2}x - \frac{3}{2}$

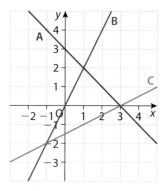

**3.** Using the one diagram, sketch the lines
$$y = -x + 5 \quad \text{and} \quad y = -\tfrac{1}{4}x + 2$$
Use your sketch to write down the point of intersection of the two lines.

**4.** On the same pair of axes, sketch the lines
$$y = -x + 3 \quad \text{and} \quad y = 2x - 3$$
From your graph, write down the point of intersection of the two lines.

**5.** By graphing the two lines $y = -x + 5$ and $y = 2x - 4$, find the coordinates of their point of intersection.

**6.** Show that the point $(2, 1)$ is on the line $y = 3x - 5$.

**7.** Verify that the point $(2, -3)$ is on the line $y = x - 5$.

**8.** Show that $(-3, 1)$ is not on the line $3y = x + 1$.

**9.** Investigate if $(2, 0)$ is on the line $y = 2x + 3$.

**10.** Show that $(-3, 1)$ is on the line $4y = -2x - 2$.

**11.** If $(1, 4)$ is on the line $y = -2x + k$, find the value of $k$.

**12.** If $(2, -3)$ is on the line $ky = x + 7$, find the value of $k$.

**13.**  (i) Find the value of $k$ if the line $ky = -2x + 8$ contains the point $(3, 1)$.
  (ii) If $(1, t)$ lies on the line $y = 2x + 3$, find the value of $t$.

**14.** Using algebra find the point of intersections of the following pairs of lines

(i) $y = 3x - 2$   and   $y = x + 3$

(ii) $y = -x + 2$ and $y = 3x - 2$

On separate axes draw each pair of lines.

## Test yourself 14

**1.** A$(-2, 4)$ and B$(1, 5)$ are the two points.
   (i)  Find the slope of AB.     (ii)  Find the equation of the line AB.

**2.** The equation of the line $\ell$ is $y = 2x - 4$.
   The line $\ell$ intersects the $x$-axis at P and the $y$-axis at Q.
   (i)  Find the coordinates of P and Q.
   (ii)  Find the length of the line segment [PQ].

**3.**  (i)  Find the coordinates of M, the midpoint of the line segment joining
      A$(-1, 6)$ and B$(5, -6)$.
      On which axis does M lie?
  (ii)  P$(6, 2)$, Q$(-1, 3)$ and R$(1, -3)$ are three points.
      Show that $|PQ| = |PR|$.

**4.**  (i)  Write down the slope of the given line $k$.
  (ii)  Write the equation of $k$ in the form $y = mx + c$.

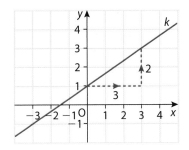

**5.** Four lines $\ell, m, n, k$ are shown in the given figure.
Name the line that is represented by each of these equations:
  (i)  $x = 4$
  (ii)  $x = -3$
  (iii)  $y = 3$
  (iv)  $y = -2$

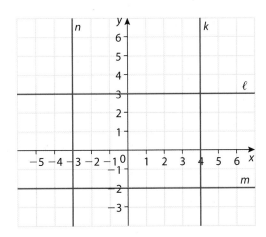

**6.** Find the slope of the line $k$ whose equation is $y = 3x - 2$.
Now find the equation of the line through $(2, -1)$ and which has the same slope as $k$.

**7.** A(5, 4) is shown in the diagram.

   (i) Plot the point B(1, 2) on a copy of this diagram and then find the slope of AB.

   (ii) Find the equation of AB.

   (iii) The line AB intersects the $x$-axis at the point C. Find the coordinates of C.

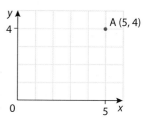

**8.** The diagram shows two lines $\ell_1$ and $\ell_2$.

   (i) Which line has a positive slope?

   (ii) Find the slope of $\ell_2$.

   (iii) Find the equation of $\ell_1$.

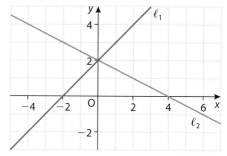

**9.** Write all these equations in the form $y = mx + c$.

       **A:** $y + 4 = 3x$      **B:** $y - 2x = 5$      **C:** $2y = 4x + 6$

   (i) Which line has a slope of 3?

   (ii) Which two lines are parallel?

   (iii) Which line intersects the $y$-axis at (0, 5)?

   (iv) Which line intersects the $x$-axis at $\left(-2\frac{1}{2}, 0\right)$?

**10.** Find the equation of the line shown. Give your answer in the form $y = mx + c$.

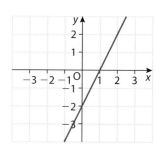

**11.** The equations of the lines $\ell$, $m$, $n$ and $p$ are given on the right.
Say if each of the following is true or false.
Explain each answer.

   (i) $p$ intersects the $x$-axis at $(-3, 0)$.

   (ii) $n$ is parallel to the $y$-axis.

   (iii) $\ell$ intersects the $y$-axis at $(0, -5)$.

   (iv) the slope of the line $m$ is $-3$.

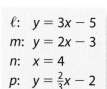

$\ell$: $y = 3x - 5$
$m$: $y = 2x - 3$
$n$: $x = 4$
$p$: $y = \frac{2}{3}x - 2$

# Assignment:

1. On a large sheet of squared paper, make a grid and select 4 points to form a parallelogram.

2. On the poster, label the points you have chosen.

   On a separate sheet of paper, find:
   (i) the length of each line segment using $|AB| = \sqrt{(x_2 - x_1)^2 + (y_2 - y_1)^2}$

   (ii) the slope of each line segment using $\text{slope}_{AB} = m = \dfrac{y_2 - y_1}{x_2 - x_1}$

   (iii) the equation of each line segment using $y - y_1 = m(x - x_1)$

   Write all your results on the parallelogram as shown.
   Compare your results with other groups in the class.

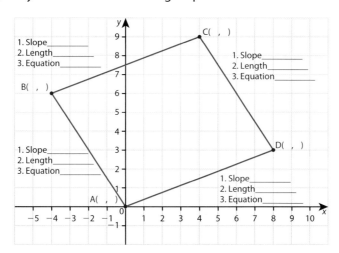

# Statistics 3

*From first year, you will recall how to:*

- draw and interpret line plots,
- draw and interpret bar charts,
- draw and interpret stem and leaf plots,
- understand the key of a stem and leaf plot,
- use bar charts to measure frequency.

*In this chapter, you will learn to:*

- draw and interpret pie charts,
- draw and interpret histograms,
- understand the differences between bar charts and histograms,
- select the most appropriate graph or chart for a given set of data,
- evaluate the effectiveness of a graph or chart,
- identify misleading graphs or charts.

## Section 15.1  Revision of line plots and bar charts

### 1. Line plots

The following data shows the daily maximum temperatures (in °C) in Barcelona during the month of June.

```
27   28   26   25   26   27   22   30   28   29
28   26   24   22   28   24   27   29   28   27
19   25   26   29   29   26   28   28   31   25
```

These temperatures are shown in the **line plot** below:

Each temperature is represented by a dot

Temperature (°C)

The **range** is 19°C to 31°C, i.e., 12°C.
The **mode** is 28°C as it occurs most frequently.

19°C is referred to as an **outlier** as it is significantly different from the rest of the scores. The temperatures are bunched or **clustered** between 25°C and 29°C.

## 2. Bar charts

**Bar charts** are a simple but effective way of displaying data.

A bar chart consists of a series of bars of the same width, drawn either vertically or horizontally from an axis.

The heights (or lengths) of the bars always represent the frequencies.

The bars are generally separated by narrow gaps of equal width.

The bar chart below shows the numbers of text messages received by a group of students on a particular Saturday.

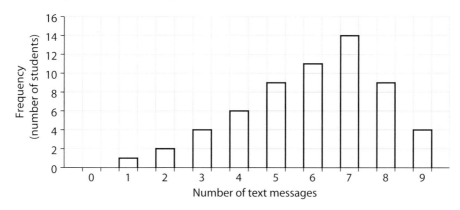

The total number of students =

$$1 + 2 + 4 + 6 + 9 + 11 + 14 + 9 + 4 = 60.$$

The total number of text messages received was $= (1 \times 1) + (2 \times 2) + (4 \times 3) + (6 \times 4) + (9 \times 5) + (11 \times 6) + (14 \times 7) + (9 \times 8) + (4 \times 9) = 358$

The modal number of texts is 7 and the range is 1 to 9, i.e. 8 texts

The mean number of texts per student

$= \dfrac{358}{60} = 6$ (corrected to the nearest whole number)

## Exercise 15.1

**1.** The line plot below illustrates the number of goals scored per match by a hockey team.

Goals scored

    (i)  How many matches has the team played?

    (ii)  Which number of goals scored is the mode?

    (iii)  What is the range of the number of goals scored?

    (iv)  What percentage of their matches were scoreless?

**2.** The daily maximum temperatures (in °C) at the Eiffel Tower during April are shown in this line plot:

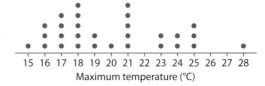

    (i)  What is the mode?

    (ii)  What is the outlier?

    (iii)  On how many days was the maximum temperature 25°C?

    (iv)  On what percentage of days did the maximum temperature drop below 20°C?

    (v)  If a day is selected at random, what is the probability that the maximum temperature is less than 18°C?

**3.** This line plot shows the scores (out of 50) of a group of students in a maths exam:

    (i)  Which score was the most common?

    (ii)  How many students scored 34?

    (iii)  How many students scored 45 or more?

    (iv)  What percentage of students scored 35 or less?

    (v)  If a student was selected at random, what is the probability that he scored 40?

**4.** This bar chart shows the number of pictures remembered by each student in a memory experiment.

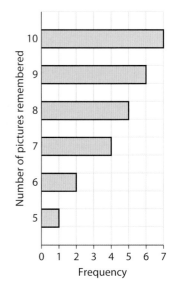

    (i)  How many students took part in the experiment?

    (ii)  What is the modal number of pictures remembered?

    (iii)  How many students remembered less than 7 pictures?

    (iv)  What is the range of the number of pictures remembered?

    (v)  What is the median number of pictures remembered?

**5.** The bar chart shows the numbers of hours spent on homework each week by a group of second-year students.

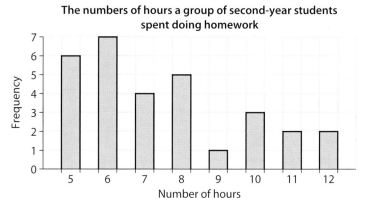

The numbers of hours a group of second-year students spent doing homework

  (i)   How many students spent 6 hours doing homework?
 (ii)   What was the greatest number of hours a student spent doing homework?
(iii)   How many students spent less than 7 hours doing homework?
(iv)   How many students spent more than 10 hours doing homework?
 (v)   How many students were surveyed?
(vi)   What percentage of students spent 8 hours doing homework?
(vii)  If a student is selected at random, what is the probability that the student spent 10 hours doing homework?

**6.** Six coins were tossed 30 times and the number of heads showing each time was recorded.
The results are shown in the given bar chart.

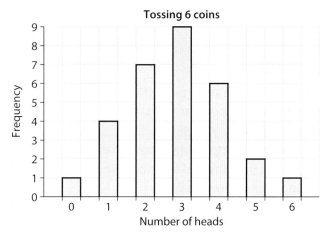

Tossing 6 coins

    (i)  How many times were 4 heads showing?
    (ii)  What was the modal number of heads showing?
    (iii)  If, for a particular toss, there were 2 heads, how many tails showed?
    (iv)  Write down the experimental probability of getting 4 heads.

**7.** The numbers of goals scored in a series of football matches is represented in the bar chart shown on the right.

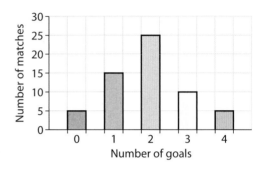

    (i)  How many matches were played?
    (ii)  Calculate the total number of goals scored.
    (iii)  Calculate the mean number of goals scored per match, correct to one decimal place.

**8.** A group of 20 male and 20 female teenagers were asked their opinion on whether physical education should be compulsory.
The results are displayed in this double-column bar chart.

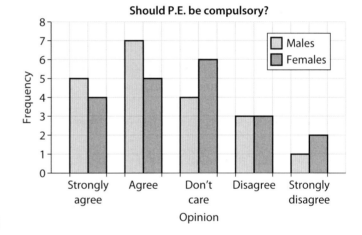

Should P.E. be compulsory?

    (i)  How many females strongly agree with compulsory physical education?
    (ii)  How many males strongly agree with compulsory physical education?
    (iii)  What is the total number of teenagers who strongly disagree with compulsory physical education?
    (iv)  If a teenager was selected at random, what is the probability that the student strongly agreed that physical education should be compulsory?
Give your answer as a decimal.

## *Investigation: Question 8 extension*

Design a questionnaire to collect opinion on the following questions:

(i) Should P.E. be compulsory? and

(ii) Should a school uniform be compulsory?

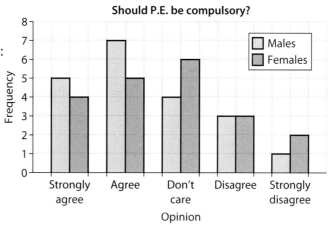

Should P.E. be compulsory?

Use the categories,

       Strongly agree – Agree – Don't care – Disagree – Strongly disagree,

(as in question 8).

Present your findings as a comparative bar chart (male v female or Junior v Senior) for each question.

Describe how your findings differ from the chart in question 8.

# Section 15.2 Pie charts

Another way of showing information in diagram form is by using a **pie chart**.

A pie chart is generally used when we want to show how a given quantity is shared out or divided into different categories. The 'pie', or circle represents the total quantity and each 'slice' or **sector** represents the size of the share. The size of each 'slice' or sector is in proportion to the size of the angle at the centre of the sector.

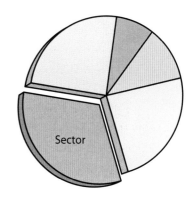

The angle at the centre of a circle or pie is 360°.

A half share will have an angle $\frac{1}{2} \times 360° = 180°$.

The diagram on the right shows how different shares are represented by sectors in a pie chart.

If the fraction of a share is $\frac{1}{6}$, the angle at the centre is found by getting $\frac{1}{6}$ of 360°.

$\frac{1}{6}$ of 360° = 360° ÷ 6 = 60°.

Similarly, if the fraction is $\frac{1}{10}$, the angle at the centre is $\frac{1}{10}$ of 360° = 36°.

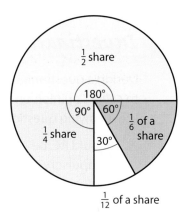

| Sector | Fraction | Degrees | Percentage |
|--------|----------|---------|------------|
| | 1 | 360° | 100% |
| | $\frac{1}{2}$ | $\frac{360°}{2} = 180°$ | 50% |
| | $\frac{1}{4}$ | $\frac{360°}{4} = 90°$ | 25% |
| | $\frac{1}{8}$ | $\frac{360°}{8} = 45°$ | 12.5% |
| | $\frac{1}{3}$ | $\frac{360°}{3} = 120°$ | 33.3% |
| | $\frac{1}{6}$ | $\frac{360°}{6} = 60°$ | 16.6% |

## Example 1

120 first-year girls were asked to name their favourite sport. The results are shown in the given pie chart.

How many girls named

(i) tennis

(ii) athletics

(iii) hockey

(iv) netball

as their favourite sport?

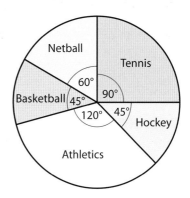

Here we express each of the angles in the sectors required as a fraction of 360°.

(i) **Tennis:** 90° ; $\dfrac{90°}{360°} = \dfrac{1}{4}$ and $\dfrac{1}{4}$ of 120 = 30

∴ 30 girls named tennis

(ii) **Athletics:** 120° ; $\dfrac{120°}{360°} = \dfrac{1}{3}$ and $\dfrac{1}{3}$ of 120 = 40

∴ 40 girls named athletics

(iii) **Hockey:** 45° ; $\dfrac{45°}{360°} = \dfrac{9}{72} = \dfrac{1}{8}$ and $\dfrac{1}{8}$ of 120 = 15

∴ 15 girls named hockey

(iv) **Netball:** 60° ; $\dfrac{60°}{360°} = \dfrac{1}{6}$ and $\dfrac{1}{6}$ of 120 = 20

∴ 20 girls named netball

## Example 2

In a survey, 72 people were asked what type of heating they had in their homes. The results are given in the table below:

| Type of heating | Oil | Gas | Electricity | Solid fuel |
|---|---|---|---|---|
| **Number of households** | 30 | 24 | 12 | 6 |

Draw a pie chart to illustrate this information.

The angle in each sector is found as follows:

**Oil:** $\dfrac{30}{72} = \dfrac{5}{12}$ and $\dfrac{5}{12}$ of $360° = \dfrac{5}{\underset{1}{\cancel{12}}} \times \dfrac{\overset{30}{\cancel{360}}}{1} = 150°$

**Gas:** $\dfrac{24}{72} = \dfrac{1}{3}$ and $\dfrac{1}{3}$ of $360° = 120°$

**Electricity:** $\dfrac{12}{72} = \dfrac{1}{6}$ and $\dfrac{1}{6}$ of $360° = 60°$

**Solid fuel:** $\dfrac{6}{72} = \dfrac{1}{12}$ and $\dfrac{1}{12}$ of $360° = 30°$

The results are represented by the pie chart on the right.

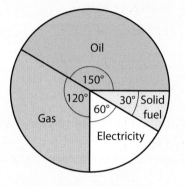

## Exercise 15.2

**1.** A pie chart is shown on the right.
  (i)   What percentage is yellow?
  (ii)  What fraction is yellow?
  (iii) What percentage is red?
  (iv)  What fraction is red?

  The pie chart represents 12 coloured counters.
  (v)   How many of the counters are yellow?
  (vi)  How many of the counters are red?

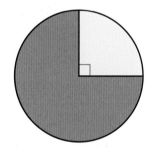

**2.** The contents of a box of mixed sweets are shown in this pie chart.

  (i)   What percentage are fruit chews?
  (ii)  What fraction are toffees?
  The box contains 60 sweets.
  (iii) How many toffees are there?
  (iv)  How many chocolates are there?

**Contents of a box of mixed sweets**

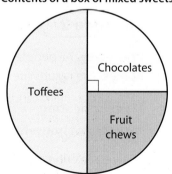

3. The pie chart on the right shows the different types
   of accommodation in a holiday village.
   If the total number of 'units' in the village was 600, find

   (i)   the number of apartments in the village
   (ii)  the number of mobile homes in the village
   (iii) the number of caravans in the village
   (iv)  the angle in the sector representing tents.

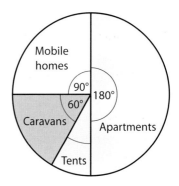

4. Find the value of x in each pie chart shown.
   (i) 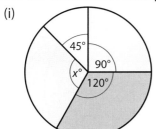  (ii) 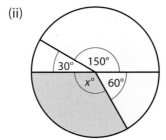  (iii)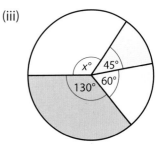

5. On returning to Dublin, 240 holiday makers were
   asked to name the countries they had visited.
   The results are shown in the pie chart on the right.
   (i)   What is the size of the angle marked $x°$?
   (ii)  How many people visited Portugal?
   (iii) Which country was visited by the most people?
   (iv)  Which country was visited by $\frac{1}{4}$ of the people
         questioned?
   (v)   Which two countries combined accounted
         for one half of the holiday makers questioned?

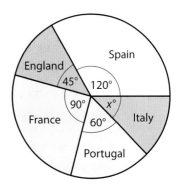

6. The pie chart shows the results of a student poll on preferences
   for a field trip.
   (i)   Use a protractor to find the size of the angle representing
         the **Museum**.
   (ii)  Work out the size of the angle representing the **Zoo**.
   (iii) If 72 students were polled how many voted to go to
         the Museum?

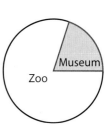

**7.** One hundred and eighty women were asked how many children they had in their families. The results are shown in the pie chart on the right.

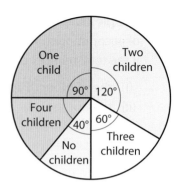

   (i)  How many families had two children?

   (ii)  How many families had no children?

   (iii)  How many families had three children?

   (iv)  What is the angle in the sector representing four children?

   (v)  How many families had four children?

**8.** A packet of breakfast cereal weighing 600 g contains 4 ingredients as follows:

| Oats | Barley | Wheat | Rye |
|------|--------|-------|-----|
| 150 g | 100 g | 75 g | 275 g |

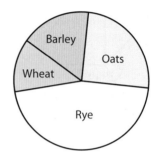

In the pie chart on the right, find the angle in the sector representing

   (i)  oats

  (ii)  wheat

 (iii)  rye.

**9.** Sixty people were asked how they generally travel to work and the results are given in the following table:

| Transport | Bus | Car | Train | Walk | Bicycle |
|-----------|-----|-----|-------|------|---------|
| **Number of people** | 20 | 15 | 12 | 8 | 5 |

   (i)  Calculate the angle in each of the sectors.

  (ii)  Draw a pie chart to illustrate the data.

**10.** Some senior citizens were asked about their favourite pets. The results are shown in the pie chart.

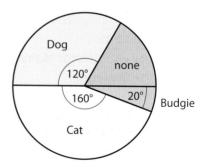

   (i)  What fraction of the citizens liked a dog best?

If 30 people chose dog,

  (ii)  how many people were asked altogether?

 (iii)  how many people chose a cat as their favourite pet?

 (iv)  how many chose a budgie as their favourite pet?

**11.** This pie chart represents the colours of eyes in a group of
children. The angles for blue, green and hazel are
shown in the chart.

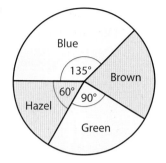

  (i)   What is the angle in the sector representing
        brown?

 (ii)   If there are 30 children with green eyes,
        how many in total are in the group?

(iii)   How many children have blue eyes?

**12.** There are 36 students in A-major Music School.

$\frac{1}{2}$ of the 16 women play the violin.

$\frac{2}{3}$ of the 18 piano players are men.

4 men play the guitar.

Copy and complete the chart.
Draw a pie-chart to compare
the total number of students playing
the different instruments.

|        | Women | Men | Total |
|--------|-------|-----|-------|
| Violin |       |     |       |
| Piano  |       |     |       |
| Guitar |       |     |       |
| Total  |       |     |       |

**13.** A shop that sells mobile phones noted the colours of the phones sold in one month.
The owner of the shop wanted to draw a pie chart to show the results.
Find the values of the angles marked A, B, C and D in the table below.

| Mobile phone colour | Number of mobile phones | Pie chart angle |
|---------------------|-------------------------|-----------------|
| black               | 75                      | A               |
| yellow              | 5                       | B               |
| grey                | 25                      | C               |
| blue                | 15                      | D               |
| **Total**           | **120**                 | **360°**        |

Draw a circle of radius 4 cm.
Represent the information in the table above on your pie chart.

**14.** Which of these sets of data are very suitable to display on a pie chart?
  (i)   The countries chosen by people in which to go on a skiing holiday.
 (ii)   The midday temperatures taken in a seaside resort over a 30-day period.
(iii)   The favourite colour named by each student in a class of 30.
(iv)    The marks (out of 100) scored by the students in first-year.
 (v)    The proportion of people who had chosen hotel, camping or self-catering for
        their most recent holiday.

**15.** These pie charts show the types of cards on sale in two stationery shops.

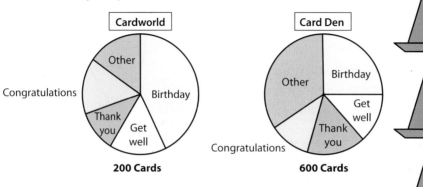

Cardworld had 200 cards and *Card Den* had 600 cards.
  (i) Approximately how many birthday cards were at *Card Den*?
  (ii) Jenny thought that the pie charts above showed there were more *Congratulations* cards at *Cardworld* than at *Card Den*.

Explain why the pie charts show that this is not so.

**16.** The pie chart shows the proportion of the staff in Company A who work in sales / office / support / workshop when the workforce totalled 260 employees on 1st June 2017.
  (i) Using a protractor find the size of the angles in
     (a) workshop (b) office (c) support.
  (ii) Find the number of people who worked in
     (a) workshop (b) office (c) support (d) sales.
  [Give each answer correct to the nearest whole number]

**Workforce 2017**

## Section 15.3  Stem and leaf plots

A **stem and leaf plot** is a very useful way of presenting data. It is useful because it shows all the original data and also gives you the overall picture or shape of the distribution.

It is similar to a horizontal bar chart, with the numbers themselves forming the bars.

Stem and leaf diagrams are suitable only for small amounts of data.

If data consists of 2 digits, the first digit is used as the stem and the second digit as the leaf.

The number 42 is written as 4|2.

A typical stem and leaf diagram is shown below.

| Stem | Leaf |
|------|------|
| 0 | 6 9 |
| 1 | 2 5 ⑦ ← ———————— This represents 17. |
| 2 | 3 3 6 8 |
| 3 | 0 2 7 |
| 4 | 1 2 6 |
| 5 | 3 |

Key: 3|2 = 32

You must always add a key to show how the stem and leaf combine.

The data represented above is:

6, 9, 12, 15, 17, 23, 23, 26, 28, 30, 32, 37, 41, 42, 46, 53

Notice that all the numbers are in order of size, starting with the smallest and finishing with the largest.

This is called an **ordered** stem and leaf plot.

## Example 1

Use a stem and leaf plot to show the following ages of the 21 musicians in an orchestra:

| 25 | 35 | 28 | 47 | 52 | 33 | 50 | 28 | 33 | 35 | 48 |
|----|----|----|----|----|----|----|----|----|----|----|
| 55 | 29 | 50 | 39 | 41 | 32 | 29 | 56 | 26 | 35 | |

(i)  What is the mode of the data?
(ii)  What is the median age?

The ages range from 25 to 56.
We write 2, 3, 4 and 5 down the first column to make the stem.
The leaves are the single digits written next to the stem:
25 is shown by writing a 5 next to the 2 stem.

| Stem | Leaf |
|------|------|
| 2 | 5 8 8 9 9 6 |
| 3 | 5 3 3 5 9 2 5 |
| 4 | 7 8 1 |
| 5 | 2 0 5 0 6 |

This is an **unordered** stem and leaf plot.

In a stem and leaf plot, the numbers must align beneath one another.

It is more useful to rearrange the scores so they are in order, from smallest to largest. This results in an **ordered** stem and leaf plot.

| Stem | Leaf |
|------|------|
| 2 | 5  6  8  8  9  9 |
| 3 | 2  3  3  5  5  5  9 |
| 4 | 1  7  8 |
| 5 | 0  0  2  5  6 |

Key: 3|2 = 32

(i)  The mode is 35 as it occurs most frequently.
(ii)  The median is the value that is halfway through the distribution.
      There are 21 values altogether.
      The median value is the 11th value.
      This value is 35, i.e. the median is 35.

## Exercise 15.3

**1.** The stem and leaf diagram below shows the ages, in years, of 25 people who wished to enter a 10 km walking competition.

| Stem | Leaf |
|------|------|
| 1 | 4  4  6  9 |
| 2 | 1  3  7  7  7  8 |
| 3 | 3  6  6  7  9 |
| 4 | 0  2  3  3  8  8 |
| 5 | 1  3  4  7 |

Key: 1|6  means 16 years old

(i)    How many people were less than 20 years old?
(ii)   Write down the modal age.
(iii)  How many people were between 35 and 45 years old?
(iv)   What was the median age?
(v)    What percentage of people were under 20 years of age?

**2.** The stem and leaf plot below shows the times, in seconds, taken by a group of first-year pupils to complete a 200-metre race.

| Stem | Leaf |
|------|------|
| 2 | 6  8  9 |
| 3 | 1  5  6  8  9 |
| 4 | 0  2  5  5  8  9 |
| 5 | 1  3  6  7 |
| 6 | 2  5  7  8 |
| 7 | 0  1 |

Key: 4|0 = 40 seconds

(i) What was the fastest time recorded?

(ii) How many pupils ran the race in less than 40 seconds?

(iii) How many pupils took part in the race?

(iv) What was the time of the 8th fastest pupil?

(v) What was the time of the 3rd slowest pupil?

(vi) What was the difference between the times of the fastest and slowest pupils?

(vii) If a time of 45 seconds or less qualifies a pupil for a further race, how many pupils qualified?

**3.** Here are the marks of 20 students in a maths test displayed in a stem and leaf diagram.

(i) What is the lowst mark?

(ii) What is the difference between the lowest and highest marks?

(iii) If marks between 40 and 60 inclusive achieve grade C, how many got this grade?

(iv) What percentage of the students got a mark between 50 and 60?

| stem | leaf |
|------|------|
| 2 | 6  8 |
| 3 | 3  7  9 |
| 4 | 0  5  7  8 |
| 5 | 3  5  7  9 |
| 6 | 1  2  4  8 |
| 7 | 1  3  5 |

Key: 5|3 = 53

**4.** The stem and leaf diagram on the right shows the marks obtained by a group of students in a Spanish test.

(i) How many students took this test?

(ii) How many students got between 70 and 79 marks?

(iii) What is the range of the marks obtained?

(iv) Find the median mark.

(v) What percentage of students got a mark between 70 and 80 inclusive?

| stem | leaf |
|------|------|
| 5 | 1  4  6 |
| 6 | 2  3  3  6 |
| 7 | 2  3  5  7  8 |
| 8 | 0  0  2  4  6  6 |
| 9 | 3  4 |

Key: 7|3  means 73 marks

**5.** This stem-and-leaf plot shows the height, in centimetres, of 22 women at a gym.

(i) What is the range of the heights of the women?

(ii) How many women are more than 170 cm in height?

(iii) How many women are between 150 cm and 160 cm, inclusive, in height?

| stem | leaf |
|------|------|
| 14 | 7  8  8 |
| 15 | 0  1  2  3  6  6  8 |
| 16 | 1  5  8  9  9  9 |
| 17 | 2  3  3  5 |
| 18 | 1  1 |

Key: 14|7 = 147 cm

(iv) What is the median height of the women?

(v) What is the ratio of women under 150 cm to women over 180 cm?

**6.** The number of points scored per match by the *Dragons* basketball team are shown below:

| 85 | 67 | 56 | 69 | 99 | 97 | 59 | 65 | 84 | 97 |
|----|----|----|----|----|----|----|----|----|----|
| 49 | 72 | 89 | 78 | 66 | 81 | 92 | 88 | 53 | 73 |

Copy and complete the stem and leaf plot on the right.

(i) Write down the range of the scores.

(ii) Find the median score.

(iii) In how many matches did the *Dragons* score 80 points or more?

(iv) In what percentage of their matches did the *Dragons* score less than 70 points?

| Stem | Leaf |
|------|------|
| 4 | 9 |
| 5 | 3 6 |
| 6 | |
| 7 | |
| 8 | |
| 9 | |

**7.** Twenty four pupils were asked how many CDs they had in their collection. The results are shown below:

| 23 | 2 | 18 | 14 | 7 | 4 | 25 | 21 | 32 | 26 | 31 | 6 |
|----|---|----|----|---|---|----|----|----|----|----|---|
| 17 | 6 | 18 | 19 | 31 | 21 | 12 | 1 | 0 | 8 | 14 | 15 |

(i) Draw a stem and leaf diagram to represent this information.

(ii) How many pupils had more than 20 CDs?

(iii) What percentage of the pupils had between 10 and 20 CDs in their collections?

(iv) What is the median number of CDs in the collections?

(v) What is the mean number of CDs in the collections? Give your answer to the nearest whole number.

**8.** The stem and leaf diagram on the right shows the marks achieved by 20 students in a test.

(i) Write down the range of the marks.

(ii) If students who got 65 marks or more achieved a grade C, how many students got this grade?

(iii) What percentage of students got 70 marks or more?

(iv) Find the median mark.

(v) Calculate the mean mark.

| stem | leaf |
|------|------|
| 2 | 2 |
| 3 | 4 6 |
| 4 | 2 7 9 |
| 5 | 3 4 5 8 9 |
| 6 | 0 2 6 7 |
| 7 | 2 6 7 |
| 8 | 1 4 |

Key: 4|2 − 42 marks

**9.** There are 15 children in a play group. The weight of each child (in kg) is shown in the table below.

| 39 | 19 | 39 | 20 | 37 |
|----|----|----|----|----|
| 27 | 28 | 45 | 26 | 38 |
| 17 | 39 | 19 | 35 | 49 |

| Stem | Leaf |
|------|------|
| 1 | |
| 2 | |
| 3 | |
| 4 | |

Key 2|6 =

  (i) Complete the stem and leaf diagram shown.
 (ii) Find the median weight of the children.
(iii) Find the range of the children's weights.
(iv) If the sum of the children's weight is 477 kg find the mean weight of each child.
 (v) During the next six months each child gains 5 kg in weight. Find the new mean weight of the children.
(vi) Work out the new sum of the children's weights.

# Section 15.4 Histograms

One of the most common ways of representing a frequency distribution is by means of a **histogram**.

Histograms are very similar to bar charts but there are some important differences:
> there are no gaps between the bars in a histogram
> histograms are used to show **continuous data**
   e.g. a continuous time interval from 0 to 25 minutes
      where the time is broken into **classes**, $0 \leqslant t < 5$ min, $5 \leqslant t < 10$ min, etc.

This means that the number at the **end** of each category is included in the next category. 5 min is included in the second category.

**Note:** for histograms, the area of each bar or rectangle represents the frequency. However, with bars of equal width (as in our course), the heights of the bars represent the frequency.

When the class intervals are equal, drawing a histogram is very similar to drawing a bar chart.

## Example 1

Fifty children were asked to solve a puzzle.
The table below records the time, in minutes, taken by the children.
Draw a histogram of this data.

| Time (in mins) | 0–5 | 5–10 | 10–15 | 15–20 | 20–25 |
|---|---|---|---|---|---|
| Number of children | 6 | 10 | 16 | 12 | 6 |

Note: 0–5 means all the values from 0 up to but not including 5, $0 \leqslant t < 5$.

All the groups have the same interval of 5 minutes.
To draw the histogram, you start by drawing the two axes.

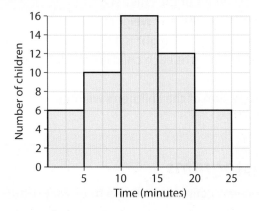

The horizontal axis shows the time. Each group or class is 5 minutes.
The vertical axis is labelled 'Number of children'.
We now draw the rectangles or bars for each class.
Notice that the heights of the bars represent the frequencies.
The **modal class** is (10–15) minutes because there are more children in this class than any other class.

## Exercise 15.4

1. A supermarket opens at 08:00.
   The histogram opposite shows
   the times that employees arrive
   for work.
   (i) How many employees
   arrive before 07:30?
   (ii) How many employees
   arrive after 08:00?

   Note: 07:20–07:30 means
   07:20 $\leqslant t <$ 07:30

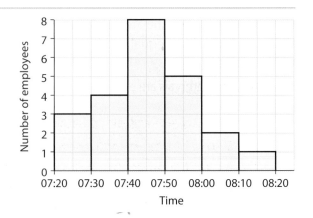

   (iii) How many employees arrive between 07:30 and 08:00?

   (iv) What is the modal class?

   (v) Find the total number of employees turning up for work.

**2.** The histogram shows information about the weights of 100 people.

   (i) How many people weigh between 60 kg and 70 kg?

   (ii) How many people weigh 70 kg or more?

   (iii) What is the modal class?

Note: 50–60 means 50 kg $\leqslant W <$ 60 kg

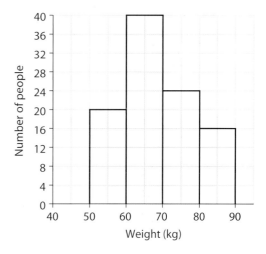

**3.** The histogram on the right shows the distances, in kilometres, travelled to work by people in an office block.

   (i) How many people travelled between 6 km and 9 km to work?

   (ii) How many people had to travel more than 9 km?

   (iii) What is the modal class?

   (iv) What is the total number of people included in the survey?

Note: 0–3 means 0 km $\leqslant D <$ 3 km

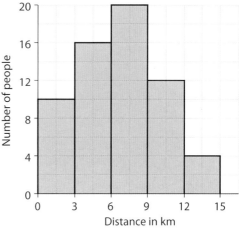

**4.** A Garda officer recorded the speeds of cars passing a school.

The table below shows the speeds that he recorded.

| Speed (in km/hr) | 20–30 | 30–40 | 40–50 | 50–60 |
|---|---|---|---|---|
| **Number of cars** | 8 | 20 | 16 | 12 |

Note: 20–30 means all the values from 20 up to 30 but not including 30

   (i) Draw a histogram to illustrate this data.

   (ii) How many cars were travelling at less than 40 km/hour?

   (iii) If the speed limit was 55 km/hr, what is the maximum number of cars that could have exceeded this limit?

**5.** The histogram shows the number of people who used a snack bar before lunch one weekday.

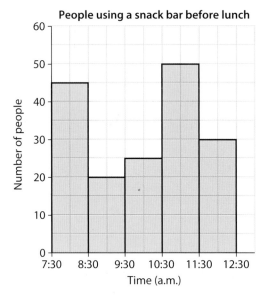

People using a snack bar before lunch

Note: 7:30–8:30 means $07:30 \leqslant t < 08:30$

(i) At what time do you think the snack bar opened?

(ii) How many people used the snack bar during the first hour?

(iii) Why do you think that the people used the snack bar at this time?

The snack bar had another busy hour.

(iv) When was it busy again?

(v) Why do you think that the snack bar was busy for a second time?

**6.** *AB United* played 28 matches away from home last season.
The table below gives the distances travelled to these matches.

| Distance (in km) | 0–20 | 20–40 | 40–60 | 60–80 |
|---|---|---|---|---|
| Number of matches | 6 | 10 | 8 | 4 |

[0–20 means $\geqslant 0$ to $<20$]

(i) Draw a histogram to illustrate this data.

(ii) For how many of the matches did they travel less than 40 km?

(iii) What was the modal distance–class travelled?

(iv) At the end of the season, the club realised that they had drawn half of the matches and had lost one third of the matches that involved journeys of 40 km or more.

How many of these matches did they win?

**7.** The histogram below shows the times taken by a group of pupils to complete a puzzle.

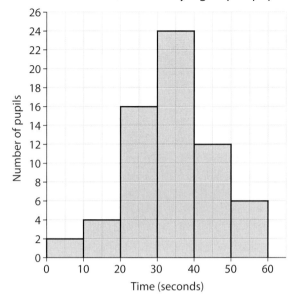

(i) How many pupils took between 20 and 30 seconds to complete the puzzle?

(ii) How many pupils completed the puzzle?

(iii) What is the modal class?

(iv) What is the greatest number of pupils that could have completed the puzzle in less than 25 seconds?

**8.** The histogram below shows the ages of people living in a village.

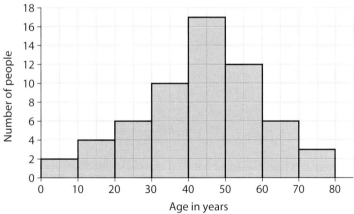

Note: 0–10 means $0 \leqslant t < 10$

(i) How many people are aged under 30 years?

(ii) How many people live in the village?

(iii) Which interval contains 20% of the people?

(iv) If a person is selected at random, what is the probability that he/she is aged between 60 and 70 years?

(v) What is the greatest number of people who could be older than 55 years?

**9.** The following is a record of the lengths, in centimetres, of 40 guinea pigs.

21  22  11  16  22  13  11  25  9  17  21  24  27  25  12  14  8  12  6  17
23  7  12  26  14  8  12  26  17  19  23  29  21  19  26  26  18  21  13  9

(i) Copy and complete the following frequency table.

| Lenght (*l* cm) | Tally | Frequency |
|---|---|---|
| $5 \leqslant l < 10$ | | |
| $10 \leqslant l < 15$ | | |
| $15 \leqslant l < 20$ | | |
| $20 \leqslant l < 25$ | | |
| $25 \leqslant l < 30$ | | |

(ii) Draw a histogram to represent this information.
(iii) What is the modal class for length of guinea pigs?
(iii) How many guinea pigs were under 20 cm in length?

## Section 15.5  Misleading graphs

Because graphs and tables are based on information gathered and presented, people tend to believe the impressions they give. However, graphs can be used by unscrupulous people to give a false or misleading impression.

The following three graphs were used by *Munchies* dog food to compare its sales figures to those of *Doggo's* dog food.

We will use these graphs to highlight some of the more common ways of drawing graphs that may be used to give a false impression.

**1.** This graph does not have a scale on the vertical axis. You cannot tell how big the difference is between *Munchies* sales and *Doggo's* sales.

The vertical axis must be labelled.

Sales of dog food

Doggo's   Munchies

**2.** This graph shows only **part** of a scale.
The scale does not start at 0.
This makes the difference between *Munchies* sales
and *Doggo's* sales look much bigger than it actually is.

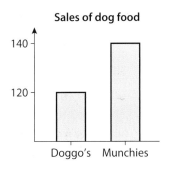

Sales of dog food

> If an axis does not start from zero, or the zero is
> put in the wrong place, it can mislead people.

**3.** This graph uses pictures instead of columns.
The *Munchies* dog is twice as tall as the
*Doggo's* dog, but it is also twice as wide,
making it seem much bigger (four times
bigger).

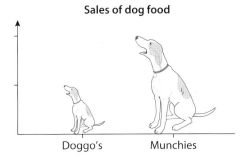

Sales of dog food

> Using area or volume will mislead
> when only height is needed.

**4.** This graph shows the information correctly.
The scale is regular and begins at 0.
Notice that the difference in sales figures is
not as large as it seemed in the misleading
graphs on the previous page.

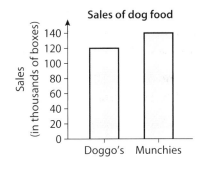

Sales of dog food

## Exercise 15.5

**1.** (i) How many times
greater is the
height of box 2
than the height
of box 1?
(ii) How many times
greater is the
area of box 2
than the area of box 1?

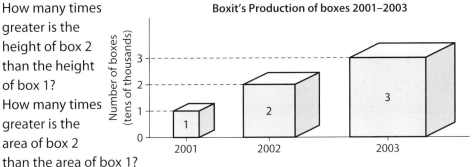

Boxit's Production of boxes 2001–2003

(iii) How many times greater is the volume of box 2 than the volume of box 1?

(iv) How many times greater is the height of box 3 than the height of box 1?

(v) How many times greater is the area of box 3 than the area of box 1?

(vi) How many times greater is the volume of box 3 than the volume of box 1?

(vii) Draw a vertical bar chart to represent the information shown here.

- Box 2 is meant to represent twice what box 1 represents, but it appears to be 8 times as big.
- Box 3 is meant to represent 3 times what box 1 represents, but it appears to be 27 times as big.

**2.** Give one reason why the graph on the right is misleading.

**3.** Describe the misleading or poor features of each of the following graphs:

(i)

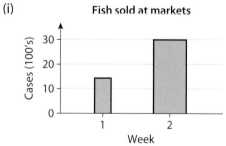

(ii)

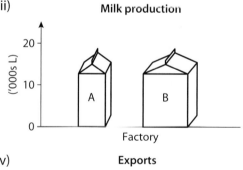

(iii)

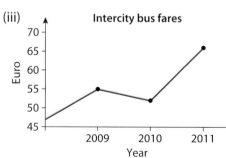

(iv)

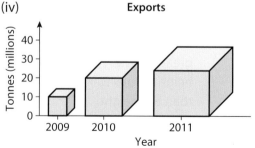

**4.** The bar chart on the right gives the correct representation of the sales of three soft drinks.

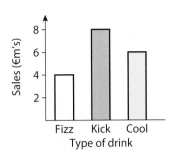

The company produced the following graph to represent the sales.

Name two ways in which this graph is misleading.

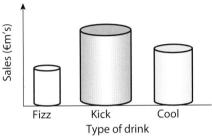

**5.** The Government released the following graph showing the increase in employment in the tourism industry over recent years.
   (i) Explain why the graph is misleading.
  (ii) Redraw the graph in a way that more accurately indicates the increase in employment.

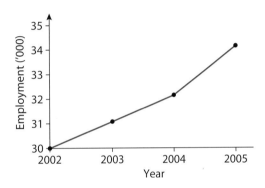

# Test yourself 15

**1.** The bar chart below shows the day of birth for a group of children.

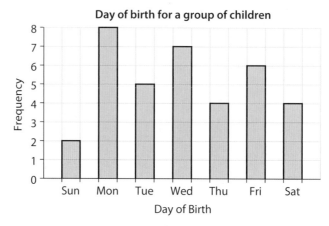

**Day of birth for a group of children**

    (i)  How many children are there in the group?

   (ii)  On which day were one sixth of the children born?

  (iii)  In which two consecutive days was there the highest number of births?

  (iv)  Give one reason why you think the births were low on the Sunday.

**2.** The data below shows the ages of 20 employees in a business.

| 19 | 17 | 26 | 33 | 31 | 41 | 41 | 27 | 25 | 28 |
|----|----|----|----|----|----|----|----|----|----|
| 40 | 31 | 29 | 29 | 39 | 26 | 36 | 26 | 35 | 38 |

    (i)  Construct a stem and leaf diagram to show these ages.

   (ii)  What is the modal age?

  (iii)  What is the range of the ages of the employees?

  (iv)  What percentage of the employees were 25 years of age or younger?

**3.** This dot plot shows the scores of a group of students in a maths exam:

Score

    (i)  Which score was the most common?

   (ii)  How many students scored 34?

  (iii)  How many students scored 45 or more?

  (iv)  Convert this information to a grouped frequency table.
Use class intervals of (30–34), (35–39), (40–44) and (45–49).

**4.** Neil records the number of emails he receives every day for 35 days.
The data he collects is shown in the stem and leaf diagram.

```
0 | 6 7 9 9
1 | 4 7 7 8 8 9 9
2 | 2 3 5 5 6 7 8 9 9 9
3 | 1 5 6 6 6 6 7
4 | 3 6 8 9
5 | 2 3 3
```
Key: $3|1 = 31$

   (i)   Write down the mode of the data.
   (ii)  Find the median.
   (iii) On how many days did he receive more than 30 emails?
   (iv)  Write down the range of the data.

**5.** The pie chart shows how 120 pupils in first-year
travel to school.
   (i)   How many pupils walk to school?
   (ii)  What is the value of the angle marked x°?
   (iii) How many pupils cycle to school?
   (iv)  What percentage of the pupils travel by bus?

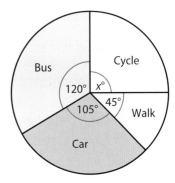

**6.** The histogram below shows information about the training times taken by some
100 m runners before the Olympic Games.
   (i)   Write down the reason
         why there are no gaps
         between bars.
   (ii)  Write down the number
         of runners that took
         between 10 and
         12 seconds.
   (iii) Work out the number
         of runners that took
         12 seconds or more.
   (iv)  Work out how many
         runners there were altogether.

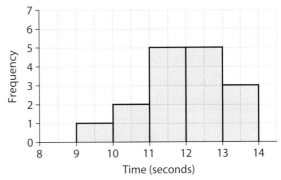

Note: 9–10 means $9s \leqslant t < 10s$

**7.** A total of 25 adults sat a Driver Theory Test.
Their results are shown in the line plot below.

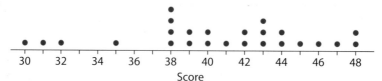

Score

(i) Find the highest and the lowest scores from this line plot.
(ii) Find the number of adults who got 35 marks or below.
(iii) If 35 marks is the pass score, find the percentage that passed.

**8.** The favourite colours of a group of 72 school children are shown in the
following table:

| Favourite colour | Red | Blue | Green | Purple | Others |
|---|---|---|---|---|---|
| Number of students | 24 | 18 | 15 | 9 | 6 |

(i) If the information is represented by a pie chart, work out the angle in each sector.
(ii) Draw a pie chart to illustrate the data.
(iii) Name another diagram that could be used to illustrate this information.

**9.** A class of 20 students took an online test. The time it took each student to complete
the test is shown in minutes.

    12    19    14    46    9    21    12    20    5    18
    13    12    17    6    23    29    5    16    15    27

(i) Represent the data on a stem-and-leaf diagram.
(ii) Find the range of the data.
(iii) Find the mode of the data.

**10.** This pie chart shows how the cost of a holiday
was shared between various items.
The flights cost €300.
(i) Calculate the total cost of the holiday.
(ii) (a) Calculate the size of the angle
which represents the cost of
the hotel.
(b) Calculate the cost of the hotel.

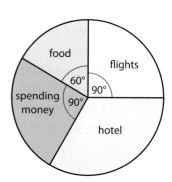

**11.** The president of a college sent a questionnaire to each head of department. One of the questions was as follows:

> How many hours do you think you are working each week?

The results are shown in the table.
 (i)   Draw a histogram to represent this data.
 (ii)  What is the greatest number who could have worked more than 43 hours?
 (iii) Is the given data discrete or continuous?
 (iv)  In which interval do you think the median lies?
       Give a reason for your answer.

| Hours worked each week, $t$ | Number of heads of department |
|---|---|
| $30 \leqslant t < 35$ | 2 |
| $35 \leqslant t < 40$ | 3 |
| $40 \leqslant t < 45$ | 8 |
| $45 \leqslant t < 50$ | 6 |
| $50 \leqslant t < 55$ | 1 |

## Assignment:

Using a group of 5 students, complete the following chart showing the **average** number of hours spent for each of the following activities during a school weekday.

(Note: for exercising include walking to and from school and in school.)

| Activity | Sleeping | School&Homework | Eating | Exercising | Leisure | Total |
|---|---|---|---|---|---|---|
| hours |  |  |  |  |  | 24 hours |

Using the data from this chart, design a bar chart and a pie chart to present this data.

State which chart you think is most effective in presenting this information.

Compare your results with other groups in your class.

# 16 Number 2 – Indices
## – Standard Form

*From first year, you will recall how to:*

- round a number to a give number of decimal places,
- round a number to a given number of significant figures.

*In this chapter, you will learn to:*

- multiply and divide numbers in index form,
- evaluate powers raise to further powers,
- write a number in standard form,
- convert a number in standard form into decimal form,
- perform operations on numbers in standard form,
- correctly use the calculator to carry out multiple procedures at once.

## Section 16.1  The laws of indices

$2^3 = 2 \times 2 \times 2 = 8$

$2^3$ is called '2 cubed' or '2 to the power of 3'.

3 is the **power** or **index** which tells us how many times the number 2 is multiplied by itself.

> **Power** is another word for **index**.

### 1. Multiplication

$$4^2 \times 4^3 = (4 \times 4) \times (4 \times 4 \times 4)$$
$$= 4^5$$

Similarly, $x^2 \times x^3 = (x \times x) \times (x \times x \times x) = x^5$

So,     $x^2 \times x^3 = x^{2+3} = x^5$

> To **multiply** powers of the same number, **add** the indices.

### 2. Division

$$\frac{3^5}{3^2} = \frac{3 \times 3 \times 3 \times 3 \times 3}{3 \times 3} = 3^3$$

Similarly, $\dfrac{x^5}{x^2} = \dfrac{x \times x \times x \times x \times x}{x \times x} = x^3$

> To **divide** powers of the same number, **subtract** the indices.

Thus,     $\dfrac{x^5}{x^2} = x^{5-2} = x^3$

## 3. A power to a power

Consider $(2^3)^2$.

$(2^3)^2 = 2^3 \times 2^3$

$\qquad = 2^{3+3} = 2^6$

Similarly, $(x^2)^4 = x^2 \times x^2 \times x^2 \times x^2$

$\qquad\qquad = x^{2+2+2+2}$

$\qquad\qquad = x^8$

Thus, $\qquad (x^2)^4 = x^{2 \times 4} = x^8$

> To **raise** a power to a further power, **multiply** the indices.

## 4. The meaning of $a^{\frac{1}{2}}$

We use the laws of indices to show that $2^{\frac{1}{2}} = \sqrt{2}$.

$2^{\frac{1}{2}} \times 2^{\frac{1}{2}} = 2^{\frac{1}{2} + \frac{1}{2}} = 2^1 = 2$.

Also, $\sqrt{2} \times \sqrt{2} = 2$.

This shows that $2^{\frac{1}{2}} = \sqrt{2}$.

Thus (i) $25^{\frac{1}{2}} = \sqrt{25} = 5$ (ii) $81^{\frac{1}{2}} = \sqrt{81} = 9$.

> $2^{\frac{1}{2}} = \sqrt{2}$

**Note :** All of these rules are contained on page 21 of the 'formulae and tables' booklet.

## *Investigation:*

Copy and complete the following using the rules of indices.

$$\frac{5 \times 5 \times 5 \times 5}{5} = \frac{5^4}{5} = 5^3 = 125$$

$$\frac{5 \times 5 \times 5 \times 5}{5 \times 5} = \frac{5^{()}}{5^{()}} = 5^{()} = (\quad)$$

$$\frac{5 \times 5 \times 5 \times 5}{5 \times 5 \times 5} = \frac{5^{()}}{5^{()}} = 5^{()} = (\quad)$$

$$\frac{5 \times 5 \times 5 \times 5}{5 \times 5 \times 5 \times 5} = \frac{5^{()}}{5^{()}} = 5^{()} = (\quad)$$

Since this pattern would be the same if any other number (other than 5) was chosen, what deduction can you make based on the last line?

**Deduction:**

## Example 1

Express each of the following as a single number:

(i) $2^2 \times 2^3$   (ii) $\dfrac{3^7}{3^3}$   (iii) $(3^2)^3$   (iv) $(3 \times 5)^2$

(i) $2^2 \times 2^3 = 2^{2+3} = 2^5 = 2 \times 2 \times 2 \times 2 \times 2 = 32$

(ii) $\dfrac{3^7}{3^3} = 3^{7-3} = 3^4 = 3 \times 3 \times 3 \times 3 = 81$

(iii) $(3^2)^3 = 3^{2 \times 3} = 3^6 = 3 \times 3 \times 3 \times 3 \times 3 \times 3 = 729$

(iv) $(3 \times 5)^2 = 15^2 = 15 \times 15 = 225$

## Order of operations

When performing operations containing powers, brackets, multiplication and division, the correct order of operations is given on the right.

**Order of operations**
1. Brackets
2. Indices or square roots
3. Multiplication and division
4. Addition and subtraction

## Example 2

Find the value of $12(5 - 3) + 3 \times 2^2 - 4\sqrt{25}$.

$12(5 - 3) + 3 \times 2^2 - 4\sqrt{25} = 12(2) + 3 \times 4 - 4 \times 5$ ... brackets, indices and square roots first

$= 24 + 12 - 20$ ... multiplication

$= 36 - 20$ ... addition and subtraction

$= 16$

## Exercise 16.1

**1.** Write each of these in index form:

(i) $2 \times 2 \times 2$   (ii) $5 \times 5 \times 5 \times 5$   (iii) $6 \times 6 \times 6 \times 6 \times 6$

(iv) $a \times a \times a$   (v) $k \times k \times k \times k$   (vi) $(-2) \times (-2) \times (-2)$

**2.** Write each of these as a single number without a power:
   (i)  $3^2$         (ii)  $2^3$         (iii)  $4^3$         (iv)  $10^3$         (v)  $(-2)^4$

**3.** Write each of the following as a single number to a power:
   (i)  $3 \times 3$         (ii)  $6 \times 6 \times 6$         (iii)  $3^2 \times 3^3$         (iv)  $5^4 \times 5^2$
   (v)  $5 \times 5^2$         (vi)  $3^4 \times 3^3$         (vii)  $5 \times 5^2 \times 5^3$         (viii)  $2^4 \times 2 \times 2^3$

**4.** Find the missing power in each of these:
   (i)  $2^\square = 8$         (ii)  $3^\square = 27$         (iii)  $2^\square = 16$         (iv)  $10^\square = 100$
   (v)  $6^\square = 36$         (vi)  $5^\square = 125$         (vii)  $10^\square = 1000$         (viii)  $2^\square = 32$

**5.** Work out the value of each of these:
   (i)  $3 \times 2^2$         (ii)  $2 \times 3^2$         (iii)  $4 \times 2^3$         (iv)  $2 \times 5^2$
   (v)  $2^2 \times 3^2$         (vi)  $2 \times 6^2$         (vii)  $4^2 \div 2$         (viii)  $4^3 \div 2^2$

**6.** Evaluate each of these:
   (i)  $(-2)^2$         (ii)  $(-3)^3$         (iii)  $-2 \times (-3)^2$         (iv)  $4 \times (-2)^3$

**7.** Write each of these in the form  $a^n \times b^n$:
   (i)  $2 \times 2 \times 3 \times 3$         (ii)  $3 \times 3 \times 4 \times 4 \times 4$         (iii)  $5 \times 5 \times 5 \times 3 \times 3$
   (iv)  $4 \times a \times a \times 4$         (v)  $3 \times a \times a \times a \times 3^2$         (vi)  $5^2 \times 5a^2 \times a$

**8.** Express as a single number to a power:
   (i)  9         (ii)  25         (iii)  27         (iv)  1000         (v)  81         (vi)  64

**9.** Express as a single number in index form:
   (i)  $\dfrac{5^4}{5^2}$         (ii)  $\dfrac{3^5}{3}$         (iii)  $\dfrac{7^5}{7^3}$         (iv)  $\dfrac{3^8}{3^4}$         (v)  $\dfrac{5^8}{5}$         (vi)  $\dfrac{7^6}{7^4}$

**10.** Find the value of each of these:
   (i)  $8 \times 10^2$         (ii)  $1.5 \times 10^2$         (iii)  $7.6 \times 10^3$         (iv)  $0.3 \times 10^3$         (v)  $0.07 \times 10^2$

**11.** Simplify each of these and express your answer as a whole number:
   (i)  $\dfrac{2^4 \times 2^2}{2^3}$         (ii)  $\dfrac{4^3 \times 4}{4^2}$         (iii)  $\dfrac{3^7 \times 3}{3^6}$         (iv)  $\dfrac{7^6 \times 7^2}{7^5}$

**12.** Write each of these as a whole number:
   (i)  $(2^2)^2$         (ii)  $(2^2)^3$         (iii)  $(3^2)^2$         (iv)  $(2^3)^2$         (v)  $(10^2)^2$

**13.** State whether each of the following statements is true or false:
   (i)  $5^2 = 5 \times 2$         (ii)  $3^2 > 2^3$         (iii)  $2^6 < 5^2$         (iv)  $3^4 < 6^2$

**14.** Express as a single number:

    (i) $(2 \times 3)^2$    (ii) $(4 \times 2)^2$    (iii) $(2 \times 5)^2$    (iv) $(\frac{1}{3} \times 9)^2$    (v) $\left(\dfrac{20}{5}\right)^3$

**15.** Express each of these as a single number:

    (i) $\sqrt{9}$      (ii) $3\sqrt{4}$      (iii) $\sqrt{81}$      (iv) $2\sqrt{64}$

    (v) $\sqrt{9} \times \sqrt{36}$    (vi) $6\sqrt{4}$    (vii) $\dfrac{\sqrt{36}}{\sqrt{4}}$    (viii) $\dfrac{2\sqrt{144}}{\sqrt{36}}$

    (ix) $\dfrac{\sqrt{81} \times \sqrt{4}}{\sqrt{9}}$    (x) $\dfrac{6\sqrt{49}}{14}$

**16.** Find the value of each of these:

    (i) $2^2 + \sqrt{25}$    (ii) $3^3 \times 4 + \sqrt{36}$    (iii) $3 \times 2^3 + 2\sqrt{25}$    (iv) $2^3(\sqrt{81} - 7)$

**17.** Find the value of each of these:

    (i) $4^{\frac{1}{2}}$    (ii) $9^{\frac{1}{2}}$    (iii) $100^{\frac{1}{2}}$    (iv) $\dfrac{64^{\frac{1}{2}}}{4^{\frac{1}{2}}}$    (v) $\dfrac{144^{\frac{1}{2}}}{16^{\frac{1}{2}}}$

**18.** Evaluate each of the following:

    (i) $3(2^2 + \sqrt{16})$              (ii) $3 \times 2^2 - 3 \times \sqrt{9}$

    (iii) $4 \times \sqrt{25} + 2^2(\sqrt{4} + 2)$    (iv) $\sqrt{25} \times 2^2 + 2(\sqrt{16} - 2)$

    (v) $2^4 + 3 \times 4^2 - \sqrt{144}$       (vi) $2^2 \times 3 + \dfrac{3 \times \sqrt{36}}{9}$

**19.** Find the value of the index $n$ in each of these:

    (i) $4^n = 16$    (ii) $2^n = 8$    (iii) $3^n = 27$    (iv) $2^2 \times 2^4 = 2^n$

    (v) $3^4 \times 3^n = 3^7$    (vi) $3^5 \times 3^n = 3^8$    (vii) $\dfrac{5^4 \times 5^2}{5^n} = 5^3$    (viii) $64 = (4 \times 2)^n$

**20.** Copy and complete these:

    (i) $3^2 \times 5^3 \times 5^4 \times 3^6 = 3^\square \times 5^\square$    (ii) $2 \times 9^2 \times 2^5 \times 9^3 = 2^\square \times 9^\square$

    (iii) $4^7 \times 3^\square \times 4 \times 3^2 = 3^{10} \times 4^\square$    (iv) $3^4 \times 11^\square \times 3^\square \times 11^5 = 3^5 \times 11^8$

**21.** Which of these statements is false?

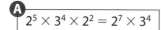  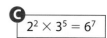

  **Ⓐ** $2^5 \times 3^4 \times 2^2 = 2^7 \times 3^4$    **Ⓑ** $5^2 \times 6^3 \times 5^4 \times 6 = 5^6 \times 6^4$    **Ⓒ** $2^2 \times 3^5 = 6^7$

**22.** If $a = 4$ and $b = 3$, find the value of the following:

    (i) $a^2 + 2b$    (ii) $\sqrt{a} + b^2$    (iii) $2a + b^2$    (iv) $\sqrt{a^2 + b^2}$

    (v) $2a^2 + b$    (vi) $2b^2 + 3\sqrt{a}$    (vii) $a^2b - 2b$    (viii) $\dfrac{2a + 3\sqrt{a}}{b^2 - 2}$.

# Section 16.2  Numbers in standard form

If you use your calculator to perform the operation  60 000 $\times$ 4 600 000, the screen will display the number  $2.76 \times 10^{11}$.

This represents the number 2.76 multiplied by 10 eleven times.

The number  $2.76 \times 10^{11}$  is written in **scientific notation** or **standard form**.

Standard form is a convenient kind of shorthand for writing very large and very small numbers.

*Definition*  A number in the form  $a \times 10^n$, where  $1 \leqslant a < 10$, and $n$ is an integer, is said to be expressed in scientific notation or standard form.

**Example**  $6.8 \times 10^4$

This part is written as a number between 1 and 10.

This part is written as a power of 10.

Here are some numbers written in standard form:

  (i)  $450 = 4.5 \times 100 = 4.5 \times 10^2$
 (ii)  $5000 = 5 \times 1000 = 5 \times 10^3$
(iii)  $64\,000 = 64 \times 1000 = 6.4 \times 10\,000 = 6.4 \times 10^4$
(iv)  $380\,000 = 3.8 \times 10^5$

Notice that if you move the decimal point

  (i)  1 place to the **left**, multiply by $10^1$
 (ii)  2 places to the **left**, multiply by $10^2$
(iii)  3 places to the **left**, multiply by $10^3 \ldots$

 On your calculator, there is an  EXP  or  $\times 10^x$  key which stands for 'exponential' or 10 to any power.

To change the number  $2.54 \times 10^3$  to decimal form, key in  2.54  EXP  3  = .

The calculator will display 2540.

## Adding and subtracting numbers in standard form

To add or subtract numbers expressed in standard form, convert each number to a decimal number and then perform the addition or subtraction.

You may also use a calculator, as shown in the following example.

### Example 1

Express in standard form: $1.84 \times 10^2 + 8.7 \times 10^3$.

$1.84 \times 10^2 = 184$ and $8.7 \times 10^3 = 8700$

$\therefore \quad 1.84 \times 10^2 + 8.7 \times 10^3 = 184 + 8700$

$$= 8884$$
$$= 8.884 \times 10^3$$

 Key in $1.84 \boxed{\times 10^x} 2 + 8.7 \boxed{\times 10^x} 3 \boxed{=}$

The result displayed is 8884 which is $8.884 \times 10^3$.

## Multiplying and dividing numbers in standard form

To multiply (or divide) numbers expressed in standard form, first multiply (or divide) the 'a parts' and then multiply (or divide) the numbers expressed as powers of 10.

The calculator is particularly useful in these operations.

Thus, $(2.6 \times 10^2) \times (5.5 \times 10^3) = (2.6 \times 5.5) \times (10^2 \times 10^3)$

$$= 14.3 \times 10^{2+3}$$

> This number ('a part') must be less than 10.

$$= \boxed{14.3} \times 10^5$$
$$= 1.43 \times 10^6$$

### Example 2

Express $(3.6 \times 10^5) \div (1.2 \times 10^3)$ in standard form.

$(3.6 \times 10^5) \div (1.2 \times 10^3) = \dfrac{3.6 \times 10^5}{1.2 \times 10^3}$

$$= \dfrac{3.6}{1.2} \times \dfrac{10^5}{10^3}$$

$$= 3 \times 10^{5-3} = 3 \times 10^2$$

**Example 3**

There are $7.4 \times 10^5$ new computers made each month.
During the same period $5.9 \times 10^4$ are destroyed.
Find the increase in the number of computers per year.
Increase per month $= 7.4 \times 10^5 - 5.9 \times 10^4$
$\qquad\qquad\qquad = 681\,000 = 6.81 \times 10^5$ ...calculator
Increase per year $= 12 \times 6.81 \times 10^5 = 8172\,000 = 8.172 \times 10^6$

**Note:** $7.4 \times 10^5 = 74.0 \times 10^4$
$\qquad \therefore 74.0 \times 10^4 - 5.9 \times 10^4 = 68.1 \times 10^4 = 6.81 \times 10^5$

## Exercise 16.2

**1.** Which of the following numbers are written in scientific notation?
    (i) $2.4 \times 10^2$     (ii) $0.8 \times 10^4$     (iii) $27.4 \times 10^3$     (iv) $8.9 \times 10^4$

**2.** Write each of the following as a decimal number:
    (i) $2 \times 10^2$     (ii) $3.4 \times 10^2$     (iii) $5.7 \times 10^3$     (iv) $2.84 \times 10^4$
    (v) $5.81 \times 10^2$     (vi) $2.94 \times 10^3$     (vii) $1.837 \times 10^4$     (viii) $9.843 \times 10^3$

**3.** Explain why $30 \times 10^3$ is not written in standard form.

**4.** Write each of these numbers in standard form:
    (i) 28     (ii) 64     (iii) 80     (iv) 150     (v) 467

**5.** Express these numbers in standard form:
    (i) 400     (ii) 650     (iii) 2000     (iv) 2700     (v) 6920

**6.** Express these numbers in the form $a \times 10^n$, where $1 \leqslant a < 10, n \in N$;
    (i) 7800     (ii) 946     (iii) 15\,400     (iv) 38\,900

**7.** Express each of these in scientific notation:
    (i) 2400     (ii) 12\,800     (iii) $80 \times 10^2$     (iv) $12.9 \times 10^3$

**8.**  (i) Add 643 and 78 and express your answer in scientific notation.
    (ii) Multiply 320 by 0.8 and express your answer in scientific notation.

**9.** Write each of the following as a single whole number:
    (i) $3 \times 10^2 + 2.8 \times 10^2$         (ii) $1.4 \times 10^2 + 3.7 \times 10^2$
    (iii) $5.4 \times 10^3 + 9.6 \times 10^3$       (iv) $4.7 \times 10^3 + 8.3 \times 10^3$

**10.** Express $6.8 \times 10^3 - 5.2 \times 10^2$ in the form $a \times 10^n$, where $1 \leqslant a < 10, n \in N$.

Add or subtract each of the following and express your answer in standard form:

**11.** $5 \times 10^2 + 8.9 \times 10^2$

**12.** $6.87 \times 10^2 + 1.92 \times 10^2$

**13.** $9.4 \times 10^3 - 6.4 \times 10^2$

**14.** $1.8 \times 10^3 - 9.4 \times 10^2$

Write each of the following as a single whole number:

**15.** $(4 \times 10) \times (3 \times 10^2)$

**16.** $(1.4 \times 10^2) \times (5 \times 10)$

**17.** $(3.8 \times 10^2) \times (4 \times 10^2)$

**18.** $(5.3 \times 10^2) \times (2 \times 10^7)$

Express each of the following as a single number expressed in scientific notation:

**19.** $(6 \times 10^2) \times (4 \times 10^2)$

**20.** $(5 \times 10^2) \times (3 \times 10^3)$

**21.** $(7 \times 10^2) \times (8 \times 10^4)$

**22.** $(1.5 \times 10^2) \times (5 \times 10^3)$

Simplify each of the following and express your answer in scientific notation:

**23.** $\dfrac{5 \times 10^3}{2 \times 10^2}$

**24.** $\dfrac{8 \times 10^6}{4 \times 10^3}$

**25.** $\dfrac{7.2 \times 10^4}{6 \times 10^2}$

**26.** $\dfrac{9.5 \times 10^4}{5 \times 10}$

**27.** The Earth's diameter is $1.27 \times 10^4$ km and the diameter of Mars is $6.8 \times 10^3$ km.

    (i) Which planet has the larger diameter?

    (ii) What is the difference between their diameters?

    (iii) What is the total if the two diameters are added? Give your answer in standard form.

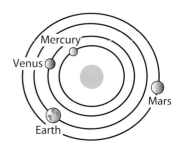

**28.** This table shows the lengths of five well-known rivers.

    (i) In kilometres, the length of the Nile is 6650 km. Write the lengths of the other rivers in kilometres.

    (ii) Express the length of the Congo in scientific notation.

| River | km (thousands) |
|---|---|
| Nile | 6.65 |
| Yangtze-Kiang | 6.3 |
| Congo | 4.7 |
| Danube | 2.84 |
| Seine | 0.78 |

    (iii) Express the length of the Seine in scientific notation.

    (iv) What is the missing number in this statement?

        'The length of the Congo is about ☐ times the length of the Seine.'

**29.** (a) If $speed = \dfrac{distance}{time}$, write an equation for time in terms of distance and speed.

(b) The closest star to our sun is Proxima Centauri.

It is 40 000 000 000 000 000 metres away from the Earth
  (i) Write this distance in standard form.
  (ii) Light travels at a speed of $3 \times 10^8$ m/s. How many seconds does it take for light to travel from Proxima Centauri to Earth.
  Give your answer in standard form correct to 1 decimal place.

**30.** Cylinder A has a volume of $1.7 \times 10^{12}$ cm$^3$

Cylinder B has a volume of $7.4 \times 10^{13}$ cm$^3$
  (i) If 1 litre = 1000 cm$^3$ write the capacity of each cylinder in litres.
  Cylinder B is full of liquid.
  (ii) How many A-cylinders can be filled from cylinder B?

## Section 16.3 Using the calculator

### 1. Powers and roots

The examples below show the procedures for finding powers and roots of numbers on your calculator.

| Operation | Example |
|---|---|
| (i) To find the **square root** of a number, use the $\boxed{\sqrt{\phantom{x}}}$ key. | To find $\sqrt{28}$, key in $\boxed{\sqrt{\phantom{x}}}$ 28 $\boxed{=}$<br>The result is 5.29. |
| (ii) To find the **square** of a number, use the $\boxed{x^2}$ key. | To find $24^2$, key in 24 $\boxed{x^2}$ $\boxed{=}$<br>The result is 576. |
| (iii) To find $8^5$ (or any power), use the $\boxed{x^\blacksquare}$ key. | To find $8^5$, key in 8 $\boxed{x^\blacksquare}$ 5 $\boxed{=}$<br>The result is 32768. |
| (v) To find the reciprocal of a number, use the $\boxed{x^{-1}}$ key. | To find $(0.125)^{-1}$, key in 0.125 $\boxed{x^{-1}}$<br>The result is 8. |

### 2. Operations on the calculator

When using your calculator to find the value of $\dfrac{14 \times 15}{50 - 29}$, always check the screen of the calculator to make sure that the correct digits and operations are keyed in before pressing '=' e.g.

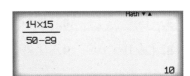

---

### Example 1

Use your calculator to evaluate $\dfrac{12.42 \times 23.47}{13.48 + 5.73}$, correct to two decimal places.

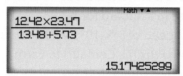

The result is 15.17425 …

Answer = 15.17

---

### Example 2

Use your calculator to find the value of $\dfrac{3}{17.4} + 2\sqrt{74}$, correct to 2 decimal places.

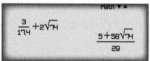   Pressing S ⇔ D key gives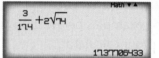

The result is 17.3770 …

Answer = 17.38

---

## Exercise 16.3

**1.** Write down the reciprocal of each of these numbers:

(i)  4 (ii)  12 (iii)  $\frac{1}{3}$ (iv)  $\frac{2}{5}$ (v)  $\frac{5}{4}$

**2.** Use your calculator to find the value of each of these, correct to two decimal places.

(i)  $\frac{1}{9}$ (ii)  $\frac{1}{12}$ (iii)  $\frac{1}{23}$ (iv)  $\frac{1}{12.6}$ (v)  $\frac{3}{8.9}$

Use your calculator to find the value of each of the following:

**3.** $(15)^2$    **4.** $(34)^2$    **5.** $(6.3)^2$    **6.** $(12.4)^2$    **7.** $(32)^2$

**8.** $(26.1)^2$    **9.** $(1.8)^2$    **10.** $(0.9)^2$    **11.** $(9.2)^2$    **12.** $(0.54)^2$

Evaluate each of the following, correct to 1 decimal place:

**13.** $\sqrt{12}$    **14.** $\sqrt{54}$    **15.** $\sqrt{158}$    **16.** $\sqrt{923}$    **17.** $\sqrt{58.5}$

**18.** $\sqrt{98.62}$    **19.** $\sqrt{1596}$    **20.** $\sqrt{2348}$    **21.** $\sqrt{0.84}$    **22.** $\sqrt{0.68}$

Evaluate these correct to 2 decimal places, where necessary:

**23.** $3\sqrt{48}$      **24.** $5\sqrt{105}$      **25.** $3 \times (18)^2$      **26.** $23 \times (4.8)^2$

**27.** $6\sqrt{96.4}$      **28.** $0.7 \times (5.6)^2$      **29.** $68 \div \sqrt{14}$      **30.** $2.5 \times (4.3)^2$

**31.** Use your calculator to verify that $\dfrac{48 \times 64}{16 + 24} = 76.8$.

**32.** Use your calculator to evaluate each of these, correct to one decimal place:

(i) $\dfrac{12.4 \times 5.9}{(3.7 \times 2.5)}$      (ii) $\dfrac{42.3 + 18.4}{16.7 \times 0.4}$      (iii) $\dfrac{81.73 - 21.4}{3.87 \times 1.25}$

**33.** Evaluate each of these correct to 2 decimal places:

(i) $\dfrac{32}{14^2}$      (ii) $\dfrac{\sqrt{26}}{4}$      (iii) $\dfrac{2 \times \sqrt{40}}{3}$      (iv) $\dfrac{(12.8)^2}{3.7}$      (v) $\dfrac{15.4}{\sqrt{38}}$

# Section 16.4 Significant figures – Approximation

There are many occasions when it is either desirable or necessary to **round off** large or small numbers to a reasonable degree of accuracy. If there were 12 946 people at a football match, it would be reasonable to state that the attendance was about 13 000. We say that 13 000 is given 'correct to the nearest thousand'.
Similarly, 1.823 could be rounded off to 1.8.

With the widespread use of calculators, it is important that we have some idea or estimate of the answer we expect to get. Then we will know whether the answer shown on the calculator is reasonable or not. To make a rough estimate of a calculation, we generally give decimals correct to 1 or 2 decimal places and we round whole numbers to the nearest 10, 100 or 1000, as appropriate.

## 1. Decimal places

When writing a decimal correct to a given number of decimal places, count each digit, including zero, after the decimal point. If the last digit is 5 or more, increase the previous digit by 1. If the last digit is 4 or less, leave the previous digit as it is.

Thus, 6.8537 = 6.854, correct to 3 decimal places
           = 6.85, correct to 2 decimal places
           = 6.9, correct to 1 decimal place.

## 2. Significant figures

If the attendance at a football match was 34 176, it would be reasonable to write down 34 200 or 34 000 or even 30 000.

34 200  is written correct to 3 significant figures.
34 000  is written correct to 2 significant figures
30 000 is written correct to 1 significant figure.

When expressing a whole number correct to a given number of significant figures, zeros at the end of the number are not counted but must be included in the final result. All other zeros are significant.

Thus, 52 764 = 52 760, correct to 4 significant figures
                 = 52 800, correct to 3 significant figures
                 = 53 000, correct to 2 significant figures
                 = 50 000, correct to 1 significant figure.

The number  70 425 = 70 400, correct to 3 significant figures.
Notice here that the zero between the 7 and 4 is significant, but the two final zeros are not.

If a number is less than 1, then the zeros immediately after the decimal point are not significant.

Thus,  (i)  0.07406 = 0.0741, correct to 3 significant figures.
         (ii)  0.00892 = 0.0089, correct to 2 significant figures.

Here are some numbers written correct to 1 significant figure:

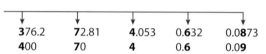

| 376.2 | 72.81 | 4.053 | 0.632 | 0.0873 |
| 400 | 70 | 4 | 0.6 | 0.09 |

## Exercise 16.4

**1.** Write each of the numbers correct to the nearest 10:

(i)  84          (ii)  97          (iii)  31          (iv)  128          (v)  434

**2.** Write these numbers to the nearest 100:

(i)  283          (ii)  134          (iii)  675          (iv)  1852          (v)  7355

**3.** Write these numbers to the nearest 1000:

(i)  796          (ii)  2359          (iii)  9215          (iv)  17 592          (v)  28 199

**4.** Write each of these numbers correct to one decimal place:

(i)  1.37          (ii)  12.32          (iii)  0.48          (iv)  12.06          (v)  0.678

**5.** How many significant figures are there in each of these numbers?

(i)  60          (ii)  240          (iii)  700          (iv)  2500          (v)  31 800

**6.** Round these numbers to one significant figure:

    (i)  68       (ii)  41       (iii)  326       (iv)  587       (v)  2851

**7.** Round these numbers to two significant figures:

    (i)  584       (ii)  989       (iii)  2926       (iv)  5884       (v)  24 676

**8.** Write a headline for each of these stories, with each number rounded to one significant figure.

    (i)  5182 people join a protest march.

    (ii)  38 426 people attend an open-air concert.

**9.** Round these numbers to two significant figures:

    (i)  0.473       (ii)  0.06312       (iii)  2.384       (iv)  0.669       (v)  54.839

**10.** To what number is the arrow pointing?

    Now write this number

    (i)  correct to 2 significant figures

    (ii)  correct to 1 significant figure.

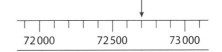

**11.** Round each number correct to one significant figure and hence make an estimate of each of these:

    (i)  $\dfrac{56 \times 18}{28}$       (ii)  $\dfrac{19.48 + 43.2}{10.4 \times 2.8}$       (iii)  $\dfrac{183 \times 46.4}{77.4}$

**12.** Round all the numbers to the nearest whole number and hence estimate the answer to each of these:

    (i)  $\dfrac{2.75 \times 8.34}{5.24 + 2.74}$       (ii)  $\dfrac{0.73 \times 12.42}{1.75 + 2.38}$       (iii)  $\dfrac{6.28 + \sqrt{4.3}}{0.65 \times \sqrt{8.57}}$

**13.** By rounding numbers less than 1 correct to one decimal place and other numbers to one significant figure, make a rough estimate of these calculations:

    (i)  $\dfrac{807}{391.3 \times 0.37}$       (ii)  $\dfrac{31.69 \times 6.25}{0.473}$       (iii)  $\dfrac{324 \times 2.76}{196 \times 0.54}$

## *Investigation:*

When numbers are rounded before a final calculation, there is a percentage error in the result.

Copy and complete the following table to calculate the percentage error when each of the following sums is rounded before the final calculation.

| | Value Correct to 1 decimal place | Numbers corrected to 1 significant figure | Value | Percentage difference |
|---|---|---|---|---|
| $\dfrac{807}{391.3 \times 0.37}$ | 5.6 | $\dfrac{800}{400 \times 0.4}$ | 5.0 | $\dfrac{(5.6 - 5)}{5.6} \times \dfrac{100}{1} \% = 11\%$ |
| $\dfrac{31.69 \times 6.25}{0.473}$ | | | | |
| $\dfrac{324 \times 2.76}{196 \times 0.54}$ | | | | |

## Test yourself 16

**1.** The attendance at a football match was 46 374.

    Write this number correct to

      (i) the nearest 100    (ii) the nearest 1000    (iii) the nearest ten thousand.

**2.** Find the value of each of these:

      (i) $3 \times 4^2$       (ii) $3^2 \times 4 - \sqrt{16}$       (iii) $2^3 \times 3^2$.

**3.** (i)   Write 7400 in scientific notation.

    (ii)  Express $1.8 \times 10^2 + 6.7 \times 10^3$ as a single whole number.

**4.** Put $2^5$, $3^4$, $4^2$ and $\sqrt{144}$ in order of size, starting with the smallest.

**5.** Find $x$ in the following:

    (i)   $100 = 10^x$     (ii)  $36 = 6^x$     (iii)  $x^3 = 27$     (iv)  $x^4 = 16$

**6.** Write   (i) $4 \times 10^2$     (ii) $7.3 \times 10^3$ as single numbers.

    Now write $(4 \times 10^2) + (7.3 \times 10^3)$ as a single number in scientific notation.

7. Find the value of each of these:
   (i)  $4 \times 5^2 - 3 \times 4$   (ii)  $5\sqrt{16} + 2 \times (6)^2$

8. (i)  Write $2.83 \times 10^3$ as a single number.
   (ii)  Write 7930 in scientific notation.

9. Which two of the following have the same value?
   (i)  $2^4$   (ii)  $64^{\frac{1}{2}}$   (iii)  $4\sqrt{16}$   (iv)  $2 \times \sqrt{9}$   (v)  $\dfrac{8^2}{\sqrt{4}}$

10. Express as a single number $\dfrac{2 \times 3^2 + 2^4}{2^2 \times 5 - 3}$

11. By rounding each number to the nearest 100, find an estimate of the value of
   $$\frac{236 \times 453}{202 \times 149}$$

12. Express $6.8 \times 10^2$ and $9 \times 10^3$ as whole numbers.
   Hence express $6.8 \times 10^2 + 9 \times 10^3$ in the form $a \times 10^n$,
   where $1 \leqslant a < 10, n \in N$.

13. Find the value of each of these:
   (i)  $3\sqrt{25} - 2^2 \times 3$   (ii)  $\dfrac{3^4}{3^2}$

14. Simplify each of these:
   (i)  $\dfrac{x^2 \times x^4}{x^3}$   (ii)  $2a^2 \times 4a^3$   (iii)  $\dfrac{4a^3 \times 3a^4}{2a^2}$

15. Use your calculator to evaluate the following correct to 2 decimal places:
   $$\tfrac{4}{17} + (18.3)^2 - 3\sqrt{47}.$$

16. Find the value of $2^3 + 4\sqrt{9} - 16^{\frac{1}{2}} + 3^2 \times 2\sqrt{25}.$

17. (i)  Write $3.74 \times 10^3$ as a whole number.
   (ii)  Express 5820 in standard form.

18. Use your calculator to evaluate, correct to two decimal places:
   $$\frac{14.8}{27.3} + 3 \times (2.9)^2 - \sqrt{38}.$$

19. Sort these into four matching pairs.

**A** $4 \times 10\,000$   **B** $4.7 \times 10\,000\,000$   **C** $4.7 \times 10^6$   **D** $47 \times 100\,000$

**E** $400 \times 1000$   **F** $40 \times 10^3$   **G** $0.47 \times 10^8$   **H** $4 \times 10^5$

# Assignment:

Copy and complete a large poster of this 'doubling' chart.

Martha wins a lottery prize.

She is given the options of:

A: €10 000 now

Or

B: €10 now and this amount 'doubling' each week for 10 weeks.

| Power of 2 | | Answer |
|---|---|---|
| $2^1$ | 2 | 2 |
| $2^2$ | $2 \times 2$ | 4 |
| $2^3$ | $2 \times 2 \times 2$ | 8 |
| $2^4$ | | |
| $2^5$ | | |
| $2^6$ | | |
| $2^7$ | | |

Predict which option will give Martha the biggest prize.

By copying and completing the following chart, decide which option is best.

| Week | 1 | 2 | 3 | 4 | 5 | 6 | 7 | 8 | 9 | 10 |
|---|---|---|---|---|---|---|---|---|---|---|
| **Prize** | €10 | €20 | | | | | | | | |
| **Total** | €10 | €30 | | | | | | | | |

# chapter 17

# Circles and Cylinders

## In this chapter, you will learn to:

- use the irrational number, $\pi$,
- find the area and circumference of a circle or sector,
- solve problems involving circular shapes,
- calculate the volume of a cylinder,
- calculate missing dimensions on a cylinder when given the volume,
- solve problems involving partial, or multiple cylinders and rectangular solids.

## Section 17.1  The circumference of a circle

The **circle** on the right was drawn by placing the point of a compass at O.

The point O is called the **centre** of the circle.

The line that traces the circle is called the **circumference**.

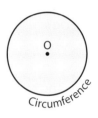

The terms that we will use when dealing with circles are given in the diagrams below:

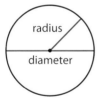

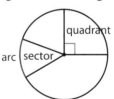

### Length of circumference

> Mark a point on the circumference of a 20 cent coin.
> Place the coin on the ruler with the mark pointing to the scale, as shown.
> Roll the coin along the ruler until the mark returns again to the scale.

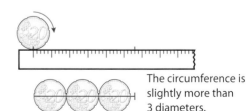

The circumference is slightly more than 3 diameters.

> Read the length of the circumference from the ruler and you will find that it is a little more than three times the length of the diameter.

The number by which we multiply the diameter to get the circumference is represented by the greek letter $\pi$ (pronounced 'pie').

$\pi$ has no exact decimal or fraction value.

However, when using decimals, we generally use **3.14** as an approximate value.

When using fractions, we use $\frac{22}{7}$ as an approximate value.

> Approximate values for $\pi$
>
> $\pi = 3.14$  or  $\pi = \frac{22}{7}$

*Circumference of a circle*

> The length of the circumference of a circle is
>
> $$2\pi r \quad \text{or} \quad \pi d$$
>
> where  $r$ = radius  and  $d$ = diameter

 The $\pi$ key on your calculator gives a more exact value than 3.14 or $\frac{22}{7}$. When using your calculator, you should use this key unless told otherwise.

## Perimeter of a sector

A **sector** is part of a circle that is bounded by two radii and an arc.

To find the arc length, $\ell$, of a sector, we divide the angle in the sector by 360° to get a fraction.

Then we find this fraction of the circumference.

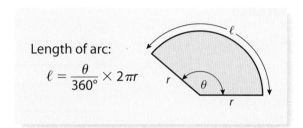

Length of arc:

$$\ell = \frac{\theta}{360°} \times 2\pi r$$

---

**Example 1**

Find the length of the circumference of this circle using 3.14 as an approximation for $\pi$.

Circumference $= 2\pi r$
$\qquad = 2 \times 3.14 \times 12$ ... $r = 12$
$\qquad = 75.36\,\text{cm}$
$\qquad = 75.4\,\text{cm}$, correct to 1 decimal place

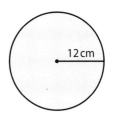

---

**Example 2**

The diagram on the right shows a sector of a circle of radius 21 cm.
Find the length of the perimeter of this figure.
Use $\frac{22}{7}$ as an approximation for $\pi$.

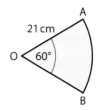

The perimeter consists of the arc AB and two radii.
$60° = \frac{1}{6}$ of $360°$, so the arc AB is $\frac{1}{6}$ of the circumference.
Length of arc AB $= \frac{1}{6} \times 2\pi r$
$\qquad\qquad\qquad = \frac{1}{6} \times \frac{2}{1} \times \frac{22}{7} \times \frac{21}{1}$
$\qquad\qquad\qquad = 22\,\text{cm}$
Total perimeter $= 22 + 21 + 21 = 64\,\text{cm}$

---

## Exercise 17.1

**1.** Name the feature shown, in red, on each circle.

(i)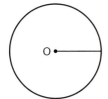

(ii)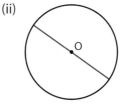

(iii)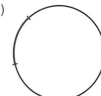

(iv)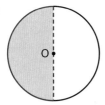

(v)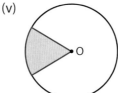

**2.** Calculate the circumference of each of these circles, using $\pi = 3.14$.

(i) 10 cm  (ii) 4 cm  (iii) 12 cm  (iv) 9 cm

**3.** Using the approximation $\pi = \frac{22}{7}$, find the circumference of each circle:

(i) 14 cm  (ii) 21 cm  (iii) 35 cm  (iv) 14 cm

**4.** Using the $\pi$ key on your calculator, find the circumference of each of these circles. Give each answer correct to 1 decimal place.

(i) 8 cm  (ii) 21 cm  (iii) 11 cm  (iv) 18 cm

**5.** Using 3.14 as an approximate value for $\pi$, calculate the lengths of the circumferences of these circles.

(i) radius = 13 cm    (ii) diameter = 30 cm    (iii) radius = 40 cm

**6.** Find the length of the arc AB in each of these sectors, taking $\pi = \frac{22}{7}$.

(i) A, 21 cm, B    (ii) A, 45°, 14 cm, B    (iii) A, 120°, 28 cm, B

**7.** Find the perimeters of these shapes, taking $\pi = \frac{22}{7}$.

(i)

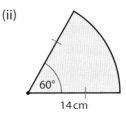

28 cm

(ii)

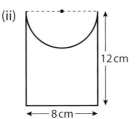

60°

14 cm

(iii)

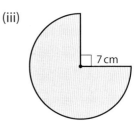

7 cm

**8.** Find the perimeter of each of these shapes.
Give each answer correct to the nearest whole number.

(i)

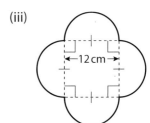

4 cm

9 cm

(ii)

12 cm

8 cm

(iii)

12 cm

**9.** Taking $\pi = 3.142$, work out the perimeter of the given shaded figure, correct to the nearest cm.

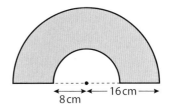

8 cm  16 cm

**10.** Which is the shorter path from A to B

(i) along the 4 semicircles, or
(ii) along the larger semicircle ?

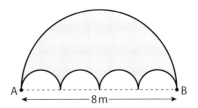

A  8 m  B

**11.** Tape has been placed along all lines of this indoor hockey pitch.
How much tape was used?
Give your answer correct to the nearest metre.

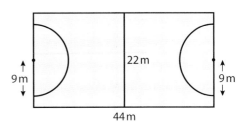

9 m  22 m  9 m

44 m

12. Kevin's dad has a measuring wheel. The radius of the
    wheel is 12 cm.

    (i)  Find the circumference of the measuring wheel in
         metres, correct to two decimal places.
    (ii) Kevin and his dad use this to measure the length
         of the school football pitch.
         The counter shows a reading of 106 revolutions.
         How long is the pitch?
         Give your answer to the nearest metre.

## Section 17.2  The area of a circle

If the 12 sectors of the circle below are cut neatly, they can be formed into a 'parallelogram',
as shown.

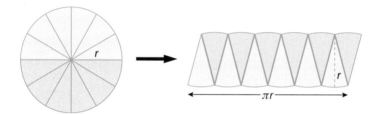

Explain why the length of the parallelogram is $\pi r$ and its height is $r$.

What is the area of the parallelogram?

Explain why the area of the circle is $\pi r^2$.

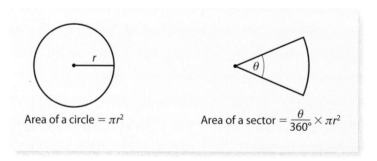

Area of a circle $= \pi r^2$        Area of a sector $= \dfrac{\theta}{360°} \times \pi r^2$

**Example 1**

(i) Find the area of a circle of radius 14 cm. (Take $\pi = \frac{22}{7}$)

(ii) Find the radius of a circle of area 1386 cm².
Use the $\pi$ key on your calculator and give your answer correct to the nearest whole number.

(i) Area $= \pi r^2$

$= \frac{22}{7} \times 14^2$

$= 616 \text{ cm}^2$

(ii) $\pi r^2 = 1386$

$r^2 = \frac{1386}{\pi}$

$r^2 = 441.178$

$r = \sqrt{441.178} = 21.004$

$r = 21 \text{ cm}$

## Exercise 17.2

**1.** Find the area of each of these circles, using $\pi = 3.14$.

(i)
10 cm

(ii)
4 cm

(iii)
12 mm

(iv)
9 cm

**2.** Using the approximation $\pi = \frac{22}{7}$, find the area of each circle:

(i)
14 cm

(ii)
21 cm

(iii)
35 m

(iv)
14 cm

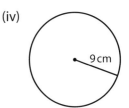

**3.** Use the $\pi$ key on your calculator to find the area of each of these circles, correct to 1 decimal place:

(i)
8 cm

(ii)
21 cm
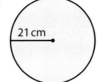

(iii)
11 cm

(iv)
18 mm

**4.** What fraction of the area of a complete circle is each of these sectors?

(i) 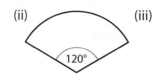  (ii)   (iii) 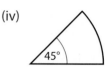  (iv)

**5.** Using $\pi = \frac{22}{7}$, find the area of each of these sectors:

(i)   (ii)   (iii)

**6.** Using $\pi = 3.14$, find the area of each of these shapes.

(i) 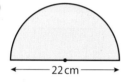  (ii) 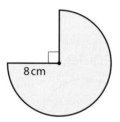  (iii)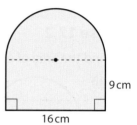

Give each answer correct to one place of decimals.

**7.** The area of each circle below is given in terms of $\pi$.
Find the length of the radius of each circle.

(i) 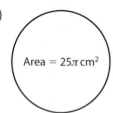  (ii)   (iii)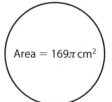

**8.** The area of a circle is 154 cm². Taking $\pi = 3.14$, find, correct to the nearest cm

(i) the length of the radius  (ii) the length of the circumference.

**9.** Write down the formula for the length of the circumference of a circle.
The circumference of a circle is 88 cm. Taking $\pi = 3.14$, find, correct to the nearest whole number.

(i) the length of the radius  (ii) the area of the circle.

**10.** (i) Write down the length of the side of the given square.

   (ii) Taking $\pi = 3.14$, find the area of the shaded part of the figure, correct to the nearest $cm^2$.

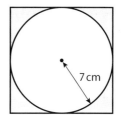

7 cm

**11.** The circumference of a circle is 220 cm.

   Taking $\pi = 3.14$, find, correct to the nearest whole number.

   (i) the radius          (ii) the area of the circle.

**12.** Work out the area of each of these figures.

   Take $\pi = 3.14$ and give each answer correct to the nearest $cm^2$.

(i)

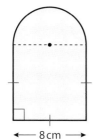

8 cm

(ii)

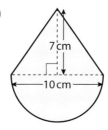

7 cm

10 cm

(iii)

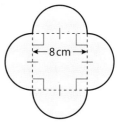

8 cm

**13.** Work out the area of the shaded region between the given pair of circles.

   Take $\pi = 3.142$ and give your answer correct to two decimal places.

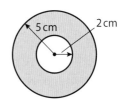

5 cm        2 cm

**14.** A circle was cut out of the square, as shown in the diagram.

   Using $\pi = 3.14$, the area of the circle was found to be $28.26 \ cm^2$.

   (i) What was the side length of the square?

   (ii) What area of cardboard was left after the circle had been removed?

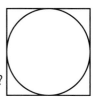

*Investigation:*

Sometimes the word 'circle' is used when we mean 'disc' and sometimes we use the word 'disc' when we mean 'circle'.

Research the words disc and circle and write a clear definition of each.

# Section 17.3 Cylinders

## Volume of a cylinder

The cylinder on the right has a circular top and base, and vertical sides.
The volume of this cylinder is the area of the base multiplied by its height.

∴   volume $= \pi r^2 h$

---

**Example 1**

Find the volume taking $\pi = \frac{22}{7}$.

Volume $= \pi r^2 h$

$= \pi \times 7^2 \times 24$ ... $r = \frac{14\,\text{cm}}{2}$, i.e. 7 cm

$= \dfrac{22}{\cancel{7}_1} \times \dfrac{\cancel{7}^1}{1} \times \dfrac{7}{1} \times \dfrac{24}{1}$

Volume $= 3696 \text{ cm}^3$

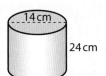

14 cm

24 cm

---

**Example 2**

The volume of a cylinder is 1232 cm³.
If its height is 8 cm, find the length of its radius taking $\pi = 3.14$.
Give your answer correct to the nearest centimetre.

Volume $= 1232 \text{ cm}^3 \Rightarrow \pi r^2 h = 1232$

$$3.14 \times r^2 \times 8 = 1232$$

$$r^2 = \frac{1232}{3.14 \times 8} = 49.04$$

$$r = \sqrt{49.04} = 7.0029$$

The radius $= r = 7$ cm

---

## Exercise 17.3

1. Taking $\pi = 3.14$, find the volume of each of the cylinders shown below:
   (Correct each answer to the nearest whole number)

(i)

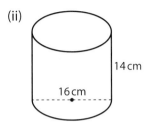

12 cm

7 cm

(ii)

14 cm

16 cm

(iii)

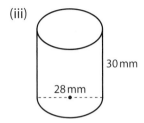

30 mm

28 mm

2. A standard cylinder is cut in half and used as a drinking trough for sheep.
   Write a formula for the volume of the half-cylinder.
   Use your formula to find the volume of the half-cylinder shown.
   Take, $\pi = 3.14$.

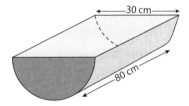

30 cm

80 cm

3. Taking $\pi = 3.14$, find the volume of each of these cylinders.
   Give your answers correct to the nearest whole numbers.

(i)

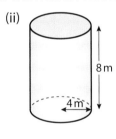

30 cm

24 cm

(ii)

8 m

4 m

(iii)

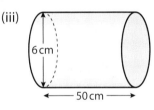

6 cm

50 cm

4. Taking $\pi = 3.14$, find the volume of the cylinder shown on the right.

   If 1 litre = 1000 cm³, find the capacity of the cylinder, correct to the nearest litre.

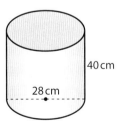

40 cm

28 cm

**5.** The figure on the right shows a solid
cylinder cut along its diameter.
Taking $\pi = 3.14$, find the volume of the figure in cm³.

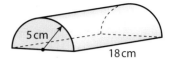

**6.** The volume of the given cylinder is $350\pi$ cm³.
   (i) Write down the formula for the volume of
      a cylinder.
   (ii) Write in all the known values in the formula,
      given that the height is 14 cm.
   (iii) Now find the length of the radius of the cylinder.

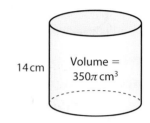

**7.** The two given cylinders have the same
volume.
Find the height, $h$ cm, of the cylinder on
the right.
All dimensions are in centimetres

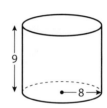
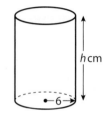

**8.** The volume of a cylinder is $288\pi$ cm³.
If the height of the cylinder is 8 cm, find its radius.

**9.** The volume of a cylinder is $360\pi$ cm³.
If the radius of the cylinder is 6 cm, find its height.

**10.** At Cathy's party 50 glasses of Cola were filled.
Each cylindrical glass of radius 3.5 cm was filled
to a height of 6 cm. $[\pi = 3.14]$
How many litre bottles of Cola were bought for the party?

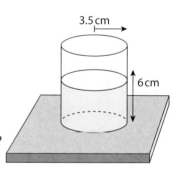

**11.** The volume of a cylinder is 1848 cm³.
If the height of the cylinder is 12 cm, find its radius, taking $\pi = 3.14$.

**12.** A hole of radius 4 cm is bored through this
rectangular solid, as shown.
Using the $\pi$ key on your calculator, find the
volume of the remaining solid, correct to
the nearest cm³.

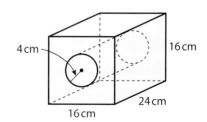

**13.** A cylindrical metal pipe has an external diameter
of 6 cm and an internal diameter of 4 cm, as shown.
The pipe is 1 m long.
Taking $\pi = 3.14$, find

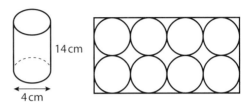

(i) the volume of the pipe in cm³

(ii) the mass of the pipe, in kg, if 1 cm³ of the metal has a mass of 9 g.

**14.** A cylindrical pencil holder has a diameter
4 cm and height 14 cm. Taking $\pi = 3.14$,
find the volume of the holder in cm³.

Eight pencil holders are packed tightly
into a rectangular box as shown.
Find the volume of this box in cm³.

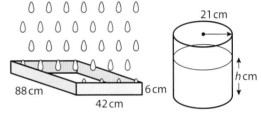

**15.** Rain falls into a flat rectangular
container 88 cm by 42 cm by 6 cm.
When the container is full, it is
poured into an empty cylinder of
radius 21 cm. The depth of water
in the cylinder is $h$ cm.
Find the value of $h$, correct to the nearest cm.
Take $\pi = 3.14$.

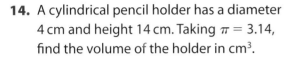

## Test yourself 17

**1.** Find  (i) the circumference
(ii) the area
of the given circle. Take $\pi = \frac{22}{7}$.

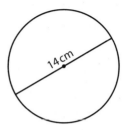

**2.** Using $\pi = 3.14$, find the volume of the given cylinder, correct to the nearest whole number.

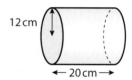

**3.** The figure shown on the right has a semicircular end.
Using $\pi = \frac{22}{7}$, find the area of the figure in cm².

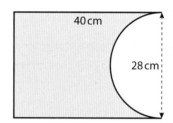

**4.** The diagram shows a quadrant, AOB, of a circle of radius 14 cm.
Taking $\pi = \frac{22}{7}$, find the area of the shaded portion of the figure.

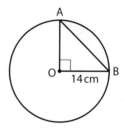

**5.** The given figure consists of a square and a semicircle. Taking $\pi = 3.14$, find correct to 1 decimal place,

(i) the area of the figure
(ii) the perimeter of the figure.

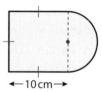

**6.** A Christmas cracker has length 25 cm and diameter 5 cm. A box contains 10 identical crackers arranged in two layers, as shown.
What is the volume of the box?

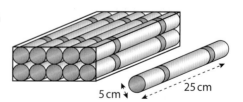

7. Find the area of the shaded part of the given
   diagram if the radius of the larger circle is
   10 cm and the radius of the smaller circle
   is 5 cm.
   Take $\pi = 3.14$.

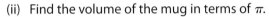

8. A cylindrical water tank has internal
   diameter 40 cm and height 50 cm.
   A cylindrical mug has internal diameter
   8 cm and height 10 cm.

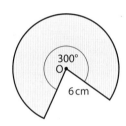
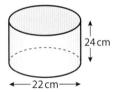

   (i)   Find the volume of the tank
         in terms of $\pi$.
   (ii)  Find the volume of the mug in terms of $\pi$.
   (iii) How many mugs can be filled from a full tank?

9. What fraction of a full circle is shown?
   Taking $\pi = 3.14$, find the area of this sector.

10. Taking $\pi = 3.14$, find the volume of the given
    cylinder, correct to the nearest $cm^3$.
    If  1 litre $= 1000\,cm^3$, find the capacity of this
    cylinder correct to the nearest litre.

11. Circular tops for yoghurt cartons are cut from a strip of metal foil as shown below.
    The radius of each top is 4 cm.
    The gap between each top is 1 cm.
    The gap between each top and the
    edge of the strip is also 1 cm.

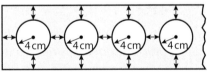
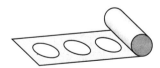

    (i)  How many tops can be cut from a
         strip of foil 7.02 metres long?
    (ii) Find the area of the remainder of the
         strip is $cm^2$, correct to the nearest whole number.

**12.** A cylindrical tank has radius 10 cm, as shown. If the volume of the cylinder is 4400 cm³, find the height, $h$, of the tank. Take $\pi = \frac{22}{7}$.

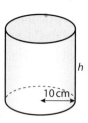

**13.** (i) Calculate the perimeter of this semi-circle.
   (ii) Calculate the area of the triangle.
   (iii) If the triangle is cut from the semi-circle what area is remaining correct to 1 place of decimals? Take $\pi = 3.14$.

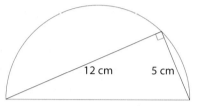

## Assignment:

A new food product is to be sold in cylindrical cans measuring 7 cm in diameter and 10 cm in height.

Each can will have an average weight of 400 g.

You are asked by the manager to design a large cardboard box to hold as many cans as possible.

By law each box can weigh no more than 25 kg.

In your group design a rectangular box for this task.

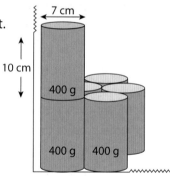

Draw a diagram indicating the length, width and height of the box and the number of cans it is to hold.

Calculate the total surface area of card needed for your box assuming an extra 10% of cardboard is needed for overlapping.

Compare your results with other groups.

# Geometry 2: Triangles and Circles

# chapter 18

## In this chapter, you will learn to:

- identify if two triangles are identical using the 4 tests of congruency,
- prove geometric properties using congruent triangles,
- identify two triangles as similar by comparing their angles,
- find missing sides in similar triangles using ratio,
- justify that an angle inside a semicircle is a right angle,
- find a variety of missing angles within circles.

## Section 18.1 Congruent triangles

Two shapes are said to be **congruent** if they have the **exact same size and shape**.
One shape may be thought of as being an exact copy or duplicate of the other.
The following diagrams illustrate some pairs of congruent shapes, even though some of these shapes are turned over or upside down.

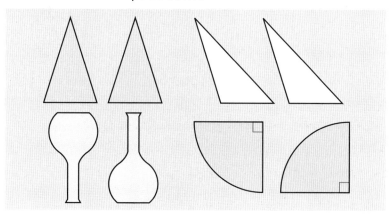

The two triangles below are congruent because all the angles and sides of one triangle are exactly the same as the angles and sides of the other triangle.

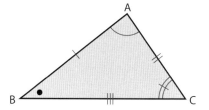
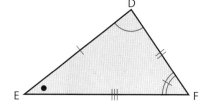

The angles marked with the dot • are called **corresponding** angles.
Similarly, the sides [AC] and [DF] are corresponding because they are opposite
corresponding angles.

Sometimes it is not very obvious
that two triangles are
congruent.

Take, for example, these
two triangles.

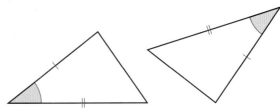

These two triangles are in
fact congruent but it is not immediately obvious.

## Tests for congruent triangles

To help us identify congruent triangles, at least **one** of the following conditions must be
found to exist:

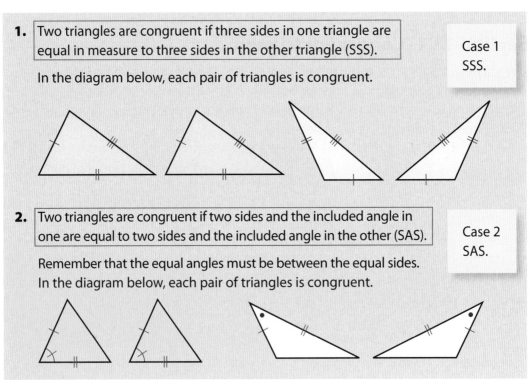

**1.** Two triangles are congruent if three sides in one triangle are
equal in measure to three sides in the other triangle (SSS).

Case 1
SSS.

In the diagram below, each pair of triangles is congruent.

**2.** Two triangles are congruent if two sides and the included angle in
one are equal to two sides and the included angle in the other (SAS).

Case 2
SAS.

Remember that the equal angles must be between the equal sides.
In the diagram below, each pair of triangles is congruent.

3. | Two triangles are congruent if two angles and the side between them are equal in measure in each (ASA). | Case 3 ASA.

In the diagram below, each pair of triangles is congruent.

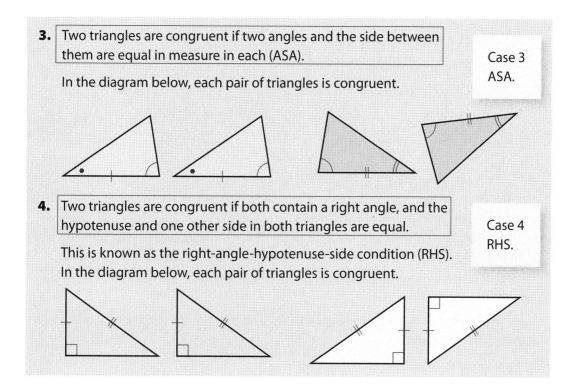

4. | Two triangles are congruent if both contain a right angle, and the hypotenuse and one other side in both triangles are equal. | Case 4 RHS.

This is known as the right-angle-hypotenuse-side condition (RHS). In the diagram below, each pair of triangles is congruent.

## Corresponding sides and angles

The two triangles below are congruent (ASA).

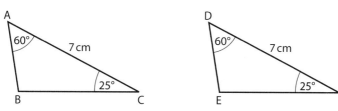

The side [DE] corresponds to the side [AB] as they are both opposite the 25° angle.

Similarly, [EF] corresponds to [BC] as they are both opposite the 60° angle.

The angle ABC corresponds to the angle DEF as they are both opposite the side of length 7 cm.

**Note:** If the triangles ABC and DEF are congruent, it can be written as △**ABC** ≡ △**DEF**.

## Example 1

Explain why the two triangles shown are congruent.

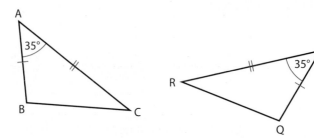

The triangles are congruent because two sides and the included angle in one triangle are equal to two sides and the included angle in the other triangle.

Many geometry theorems and other geometric problems are solved by showing that two triangles are congruent.

The worked example below shows how congruent triangles can be used to prove a very important property of equilateral triangles.

## Example 2

Given the triangle ABC in which
$|AC| = |AB|$ and [AD] bisects $\angle CAB$.
Prove that $|\angle ACD| = |\angle ABD|$.

In the triangles ACD and ABD,
$\quad\quad |AC| = |AB|$ ... given
$\quad\quad |AD| = |AD|$ ... common side
$\quad\quad |\angle CAD| = |\angle BAD|$ ... given [AD] is bisector of $\angle CAB$
$\therefore\quad \triangle ACD \equiv \triangle ABD$ ... SAS
$\therefore\quad |\angle ACD| = |\angle ABD|$ ... corresponding angles, both opposite [AD].

**Note:** For proofs of Theorems see Chapter 25 Geometry 3.

## Exercise 18.1

**1.** Write down the letters of the pairs of shapes that are congruent.

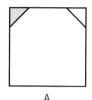 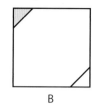 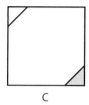 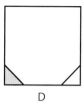

      A              B              C              D

**2.** Name all the shapes that are congruent to the green shape.

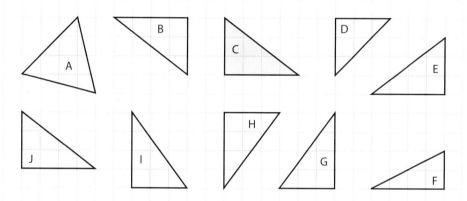

**3.** The given triangles ABC and DEF are congruent.
Which side corresponds to
  (i) [AB]     (ii) [EF]
 (iii) [AC]    (iv) [DE]?

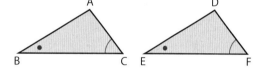

**4.** The two given triangles are congruent.
   (i) Which side corresponds to [XZ]?
  (ii) Which side corresponds to [LN]?
 (iii) Which angle corresponds to ∠XYZ?
 (iv) Which angle corresponds to ∠LMN?

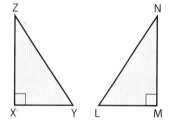

**5.** These two triangles are congruent.
The equal angles are marked.
   (i) Which side corresponds to [MN]?
  (ii) Which side corresponds to [AG]?
 (iii) Which side corresponds to [LM]?

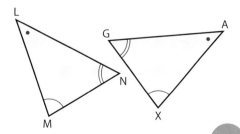

6. Explain why the two triangles
   shown are congruent.

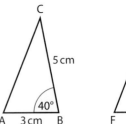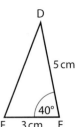

7. State why each of the following pairs of triangles are congruent, using SSS, SAS,
   ASA or RHS as reasons for your answers:

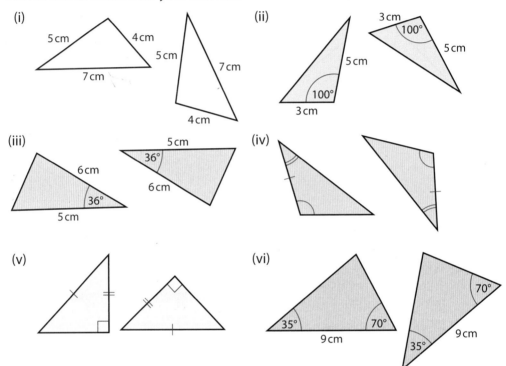

(i)

(ii)

(iii)

(iv)

(v)

(vi)

8. Which two of these triangles are congruent to each other?
   Give a reason for your answer.

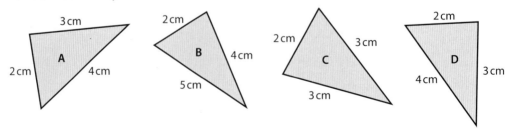

9. Explain why the two triangles ABD and ADC on the right are congruent.

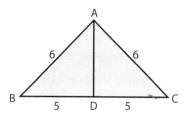

10. Are the triangles ABD and BCD on the right congruent?
    Give a reason for your answer.

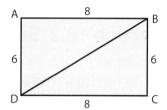

11. Explain why the triangles AOB and COD are congruent.

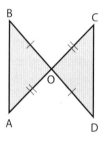

12. Explain why the two triangles shown below are congruent.

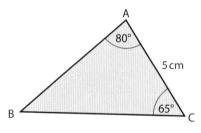 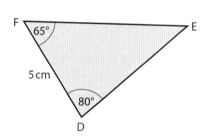

    (i)   Which side corresponds to [BC]?
    (ii)  Which side corresponds to [DE]?
    (iii) Find |∠DEF|.

13. These triangles are congruent.
    Write down the values of x and y.

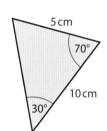 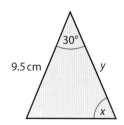

**14.** ABCD is a parallelogram.

Show that the triangles ABC and ACD are congruent.

Hence explain why the angles ABC and ADC are equal in size.

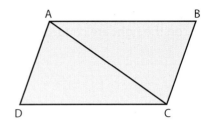

## Section 18.2 Similar triangles

The shapes A and B are similar.
All the corresponding angles are the same and all the sides in shape B are twice as long as the corresponding sides in shape A.

When two figures are **similar**,
> their **shapes** are the **same**
> their **angles** are **equal**
> corresponding **lengths** are in the **same ratio**.

All the sides in figure B are $1\frac{1}{2}$ times longer than the corresponding sides in figure A.

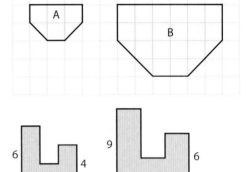

## Investigation:

Investigate the squares A, B and C in the diagram.

Copy and complete the following ratios of the sides using the grid provided.

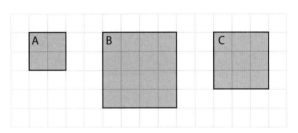

| A : B | A : C | C : B |
|-------|-------|-------|
|       |       |       |

If the length of the side of square A is 6 cm find the length of the side of B and C.

| B | C |
|---|---|
|   |   |

If the length of the diagonal of B is 17 cm, find the length of the diagonals of A and C.

| A | C |
|---|---|
|   |   |

## Similar triangles

 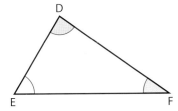

Similar triangles have the same shapes but different sizes.

The triangles ABC and DEF above have equal angles.
Notice that they have the same shape but are different in size.

These triangles are said to be **similar** or **equiangular triangles**.

Equiangular means all the corresponding angles are equal.

The sides [BC] and [EF] are said to be **corresponding sides** since they are opposite equal angles.

The sides [AB] and [DE] are also corresponding.

Since each side in the triangle DEF is twice the length of the corresponding side in the triangle ABC, we say that the sides are in the **same ratio** or are **proportional**.

In the triangles above, $|AB|$ is half $|DE|$.

Similarly, $|BC| = \frac{1}{2}|EF|$ and $|AC| = \frac{1}{2}|DF|$.

Thus, $\dfrac{|AB|}{|DE|} = \dfrac{|BC|}{|EF|} = \dfrac{|AC|}{|DF|} = \dfrac{1}{2}$

This important result for similar triangles is stated in the theorem on the right.

**Theorem**

If two triangles ABC and DEF are similar, then their sides are proportional, in order,

$$\frac{|AB|}{|DE|} = \frac{|BC|}{|EF|} = \frac{|AC|}{|DF|}$$

The **converse** of this theorem is also true.

If the sides of two triangles are proportional, in order, then the triangles are similar.

**Note:** Two triangles are similar if two angles in one triangle are equal to two angles in the other triangle. The triangles are equiangular or similar because the third angles must be equal.

### Example 1

The given triangles ABC and DEF are similar.
Find the lengths of the sides
  (i)  [DE]
  (ii) [DF].

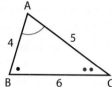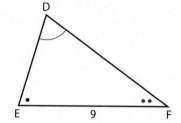

  (i)  [DE] corresponds to [AB].
      Each side of the triangle DEF is $1\frac{1}{2}$ times the length of the corresponding
      side in the triangle ABC since 9 is $1\frac{1}{2}$ times 6.

$$\therefore \quad |DE| = 1\frac{1}{2}|AB|$$
$$|DE| = 1\frac{1}{2}(4) = 6$$

  (ii) $|DF| = 1\frac{1}{2}|AC|$
      $|DF| = 1\frac{1}{2}(5) = 7\frac{1}{2}$

### Example 2

  (i)  Show that triangle ABC is similar to triangle EFG.
  (ii) Find the length of side [FG].

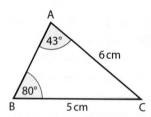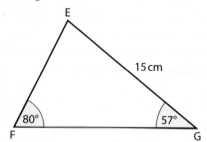

  (i)  Find the missing angles:

$$|\angle ACB| = 180° - 80° - 43° = 57°$$
$$|\angle FEG| = 180° - 80° - 57° = 43°$$

   Since each triangle has angles measuring 80°, 57° and 43°, the triangles
   are similar.

  (ii) [FG] corresponds to the side [BC]  ... opposite equal angles

   Since $|EG| = 2\frac{1}{2}|AC| \Rightarrow |FG| = 2\frac{1}{2}|BC|$  ... 15 cm = 6 cm $\times \left(\frac{5}{2}\right)$
$$= 2\frac{1}{2}(5 \text{ cm})$$
$$|FG| = 12.5 \text{ cm}$$

## Exercise 18.2

1. In the given figures, each side in PQRS is twice the length of the corresponding side in KLMN.

   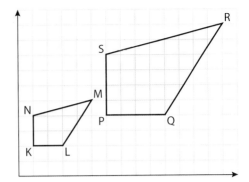

   (i) What side corresponds to [NM]?
   (ii) What side corresponds to [QR]?
   (iii) If $|KL| = 4$, find $|PQ|$.
   (iv) If $|NM| = 8.2$, find $|SR|$.
   (v) If $|QR| = 15$, find $|LM|$.

2. The triangles ABC and DEF are similar.

   (i) Complete this ratio:
   $$|BC| : |EF| = 6 : 12 = \ldots : \ldots$$
   (ii) If $|AC| = 7.2$, find $|DF|$.
   (iii) If $|DE| = 8$, find $|AB|$.

   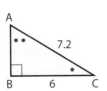
   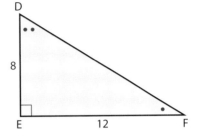

3. The given triangles are similar. Find the lengths of the sides marked $x$ and $y$.

   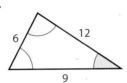
   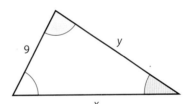

4. The shapes in (i) and (ii) below are similar. Find the lengths of the sides marked with letters.

   (i)
   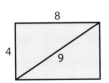
   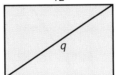

   (ii)

   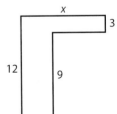

5. The two given triangles are similar.

   (i) Copy and complete this statement:
   'Each side of the bigger triangle is … times the length of the corresponding side of the smaller triangle'.
   (ii) Find the values of $x$ and $y$.

   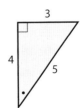
   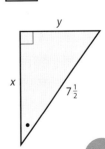

347

**6.** Explain why the triangles ABC and DEF are similar.
Find the values of x and y.

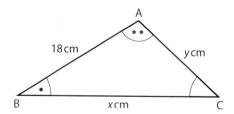 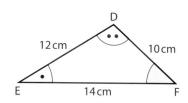

**7.** The triangles ABC and PQR are similar.
In the triangle PQR, which side
corresponds to

  (i) [AB]

  (ii) [AC]

  (iii) [BC]?

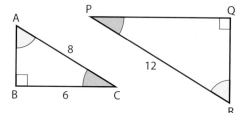

If |AC| = 8, |PR| = 12 and |BC| = 6,
find |PQ|.

**8.** The triangles DEF and KLM are
similar.

  (i) Which side corresponds
to [DF]?

  (ii) Which side corresponds
to [ML]?

  (iii) Find |KM|.

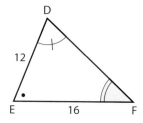 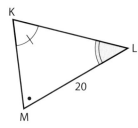

**9.**

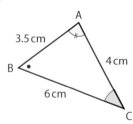 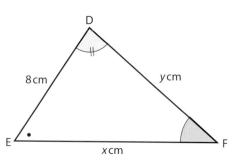

  (i) Explain why the triangles ABC and DEF are similar.

  (ii) Which side of the triangle DEF corresponds to the side [AC]?

  (iii) Find the values of x and y.

**10.** Which of these *shape families* are always similar?

  (i) all squares    (ii) all rectangles

  (iii) all parallelograms    (iv) all circles

  (v) all equilateral triangles    (vi) all isosceles triangles

**11.** When James planted a tree 5 m from a window, the tree just blocked from view a building 50 m away.
If the building was 20 m tall, how tall was the tree?

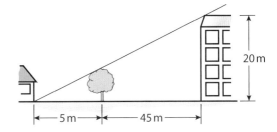

## Section 18.3  Angles and circles

The diagrams below will help remind you of the meanings of the terms frequently used when dealing with circles.

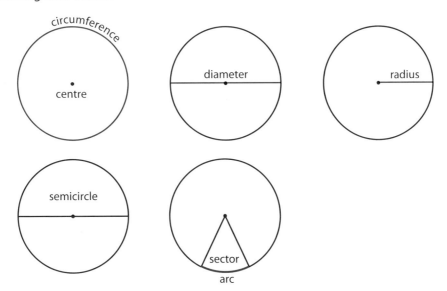

## 1.  The angle in a semicircle

The shaded angle shown is called the **angle in a semicircle** because [AB] is a diameter. We will show below that the angle in a semicircle is a **right angle**.

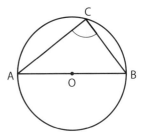

# *Investigation:*

Using compass and paper (or computer software), draw a circle of any radius.

Pick **any** 4 points on the circumference of the semi-circle and join the points to both ends of the diameter.

Using a protractor, measure the angles at the points C, D, E and F.
Consulting other classmates about their results, write a conclusion.

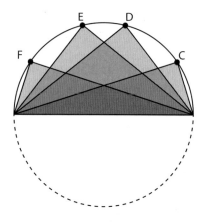

## Explanation

In the given circle,

$$|OB| = |OA| = |OC| = \text{radius}.$$

The angles marked $x$ are equal because the triangle AOB is isosceles.

Similarly, the angles marked $y$ are equal.

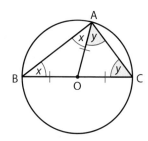

$2x + 2y$ make up the three angles of the $\triangle$ABC.

$$\therefore \quad 2x + 2y = 180°$$
$$\therefore \quad 2(x + y) = 180°$$
$$\therefore \quad |\angle x| + |\angle y| = 90°$$

Thus, $\quad |\angle BAC| = 90°.$

> The angle in a semicircle is a right angle.

## Converse

The angle ACB is said to be standing on the chord [AB].
If $|\angle ACB| = 90°$, then [AB] is a diameter of the circle.

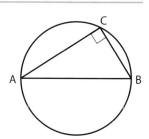

## Example 1

Find the value of *x* in the given diagram where O is the centre of the circle.

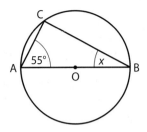

$$|\angle ACB| = 90° \quad \text{… the angle in a semicircle}$$
$$\angle x + 55° = 90° \quad \text{… } 180° \text{ in a triangle}$$
$$\angle x = 90° - 55°$$
$$\angle x = 35°$$

## Example 2

A, B and C are three points on a circle with centre O.
If $|\angle OCB| = 65°$, find

(i) $|\angle OBC|$     (ii) $|\angle AOB|$     (iii) $|\angle OBA|$.

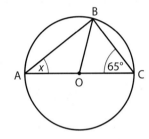

(i) The triangle OCB is isosceles since $|OC| = |OB| = \text{radius}$.
$$\therefore |\angle OBC| = |\angle OCB| = 65°$$

(ii) $|\angle BOC| = 180° - 65° - 65°$
$$\therefore |\angle BOC| = 50°$$
$$\therefore |\angle AOB| = 180° - 50° = 130°$$

(iii) Since $|OA| = |OB| = \text{radius}, |\angle OAB| = |\angle OBA| = x$
$$\therefore x + x + 130° = 180° \quad \text{… } |\angle AOB| = 130° \text{ … from (i) above}$$
$$2x = 50°$$
$$x = 25°$$
$$|\angle OBA| = 25°$$

## Exercise 18.3

**1.** In the given circle, O is the centre.
   If the diameter of the circle is 10 cm, find
   (i) |AB|          (ii) |DC|
   (iii) |OA|          (iv) |OC|
   What type of triangle is AOD?

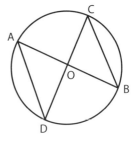

**2.** [AB] is a diameter of the given circle.
   (i) Explain why ∠ACB is a right angle.
   (ii) Find |∠CAB|.
   (iii) Describe the triangle ABC in two ways.

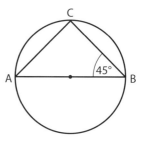

**3.** Find the value of $x$ in each of these circles where O is the centre:

(i)
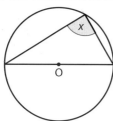

(ii)
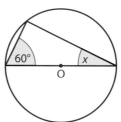

(iii)
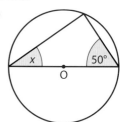

**4.** Write down the sizes of the angles marked with a letter in each of the following circles with O as centre:

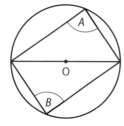

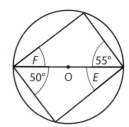

**5.** Find the values of $x$ and $y$ in each of the following circles with O as the centre:

(i)
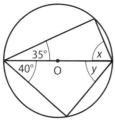

(ii)
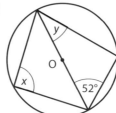

(iii)
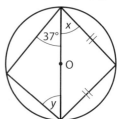

**6.** In the given circle, O is the centre.

    (i)   Why is $|OA| = |OB|$?

    (ii)  What is $|\angle ABC|$?

    (iii) What is $|\angle ABO|$?

    (iv) Now find $|\angle OBC|$.

    (v)  Explain why the triangle OBC is isosceles.

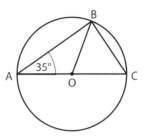

**7.** In the given circle, O is the centre and $|\angle AOC| = 120°$. Explain why $|OB| = |OC|$.

Now find

    (i)  $|\angle COB|$

    (ii) $|\angle OCB|$

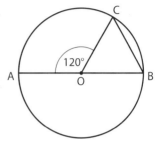

**8.** Find the values of $x$ and $y$ in each of the following diagrams, where O is the centre of the circle.

(i) 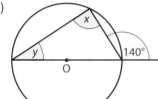    (ii) 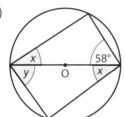    (iii)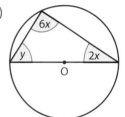

**9.** Find the value of the angle marked $x$ in each of these circles with O as centre:

(i) 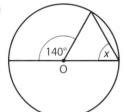    (ii) 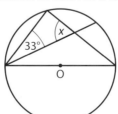    (iii)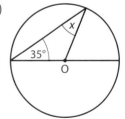

**10.** What sort of triangle is ABC if O is the centre of the circle?

    If $|AC| = 8$ and $|BC| = 6$, find $|AB|$.

Now write down the length of the radius of the circle.

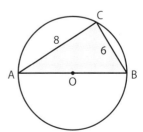

**11.** [AB] is the diameter of a circle of centre O.

$$|OC| = 10 \text{ cm} \quad \text{and} \quad |\angle CAB| = 30°$$

Write down

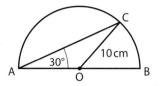

(i) |AB|        (ii) |∠OCA|

(iii) |∠ACB|     (iv) |∠OCB|

**12.** OAB is a quarter circle with O as centre.
OXYZ is a rectangle.

If |XZ| = 8 cm, write down (by examining
the diagram) the length of the radius of
the circle.

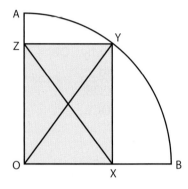

# Test yourself 18

**1.** Find the values of *x*, *y* and *z* in these circles where O is the centre:

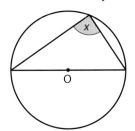 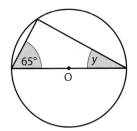 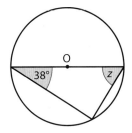

**2.** Which two of the following triangles are congruent? Give a reason for your answer.

(i) 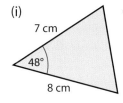    (ii) 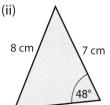    (iii) 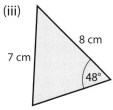    (iv)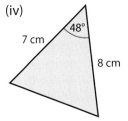

**3.** Find the values of *x* and *y* in the given circle with O as centre.

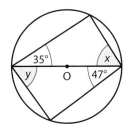

**4.** Two of these triangles are congruent. Which two? Give the reason.

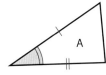 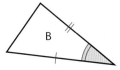 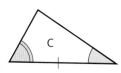

**5.** Explain why the two triangles shown are congruent.

6. In the given figure, O is the centre of the circle.
   Find the values of *a* and *b*.
   Explain your answers.

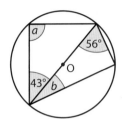

7. In the given circle, O is the centre, $|\angle ACD| = 65°$ and $|AB| = |BC|$.

   (i) Name two right angles in the figure.
   (ii) Find $|\angle BAC|$.
   (iii) Find $|\angle BAD|$.

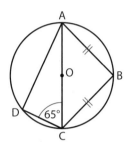

8. In the given triangles, the marked angles are equal.

   (i) Explain why the two triangles are similar.
   (ii) Find the values of *x* and *y*.

9. Find the values of *x* and *y* in each of the following circles with O as centre:

   (i)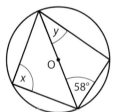
   (ii)
   (iii)

10. Explain why the triangles ABE
    and BCD are congruent.

    (i) Which side matches [BE]?
    (ii) Which side matches [CD]?
    (iii) Which angle matches $\angle AEB$?

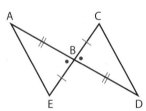

# Assignment:

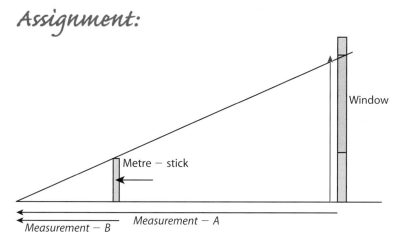

Window

Metre − stick

Measurement − B    Measurement − A

Using the light of a classroom window, a large triangle is made by the wall / window, floor and the ray of light from the top of the window.

Measure from the wall to the point on the floor where the image of the top of the window ends. *Measurement – A.*

Holding a metre-stick vertically to the floor, move it along the floor until the image of the top of the metre-stick corresponds to the image of the top of the window.

Measure from the bottom of the metre-stick to end of the shadow. *Measurement – B.*

Show mathematically that the height of the window $= \dfrac{A}{B}$

By calculation, find the height of the window.

By measuring the height of the window, check the accuracy of your calculation.

Write a report on your results.

**Note:** This method can be adapted to estimate the height of trees or school buildings once a shadow and level ground can be found to create similar triangles.

# Patterns and Sequences

## In this chapter, you will learn to:

- identify a number pattern or sequence,
- use a term-to-term rule,
- describe a sequence in words,
- predict future terms in a repeating pattern,
- identify a linear sequence,
- find the $n$th term of a linear sequence,

- create a linear sequence from shapes,
- identify a quadratic sequence,
- identify an exponential sequence,
- graph linear, quadratic and exponential sequences.

## Section 19.1  Sequences

Whole numbers can produce some very interesting patterns when some basic operations are applied to them. Patterns exist all around us in the real world if we know where to look.

**Number patterns** can be simple like these:

1, 3, 5, 7, 9, …  This pattern is formed by 'adding 2 to the previous number'.

2, 6, 18, 54, …  This pattern is formed by 'multiplying the previous number by 3'.

10, 7, 4, 1, −2, …  This pattern is formed by 'subtracting 3 from the previous number'.

Here is another simple pattern:

0, 4, 8, 12, 16, 20, 24, 28, 32, 36, 40, 44, …  'add 4 to the previous number'

However, if we take the last digit in each of the numbers above, we get another pattern which is as follows:

0, 4, 8, 2, 6, 0, 4, 8, 2, 6, 0, 4, …

The first pattern continues on with each number 4 bigger than the number before it.
The second pattern is a little more complex.
The numbers repeat in **blocks** of 5 with a particular pattern in each block.

In the year 1200 AD, Leonardo Fibonacci of Pisa discovered a sequence of numbers that is very common in nature.

As the new branches form, the following pattern is created
1, 1, 2, 3, 5, 8, 13, 21, …
(count the number of 'new branches' at each level)

Each number after the first is obtained by adding the two previous numbers.

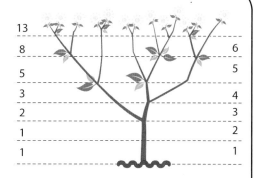

The number patterns above are called **sequences**.
A sequence is a set of numbers in a particular order.

    1, 3, 5, 7, 9, … is a sequence

1st term   4th term   the dots indicate that the sequence continues on.

Each number is called a **term**.
Each number's place in the sequence is called its **position**.

The pattern below creates the sequence 3, 6, 9, 12, 15…

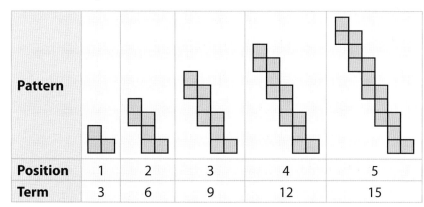

The terms form the sequence.

| Pattern | | | | | |
|---|---|---|---|---|---|
| **Position** | 1 | 2 | 3 | 4 | 5 |
| **Term** | 3 | 6 | 9 | 12 | 15 |

The fifth term is 15. It is made of 15 squares.
The pattern increases by 3 each time.
∴ the sixth pattern in the sequence is made of 18 squares.
Thus, the sixth term in the sequence is 18.

The **term-to-term rule** describes how to get from one term to the next.

The term-to-term rule for 4, 8, 12, 16, 20, … is 'add 4'.
The term-to-term rule for 2, 6, 18, 54, … is 'multiply by 3'.
The term-to-term rule for 30, 25, 20, 15, … is 'subtract 5'.

A sequence can be **described in words** by giving the first term and then the term-to-term rule.

---

### Example 1

(i) A sequence starts at 7 and increases in steps of 4.
   Write down the first six terms of the sequence.

(ii) Describe in words this sequence:
   27, 24, 21, 18, …

(i) The first six terms of the sequence are: 7, 11, 15, 19, 23, 27.

(ii) The sequence begins at 27 and goes down in steps of 3.

---

### Exercise 19.1

1. Write down the next four terms of each of these sequences:

   (i) 3, 5, 7, 9, 11, …     (ii) 2, 5, 8, 11, 14, …     (iii) 4, 8, 12, 16, 20, …
   (iv) 20, 18, 16, 14, …     (v) 50, 45, 40, 35, …     (vi) 12, 8, 4, …

2. Write down the next three terms in each of these sequences:

   (i) 1, 2, 4, 8, …     (ii) 2, 6, 18, …     (iii) 3, 9, 27, …
   (iv) 1, 4, 9, 16, …     (v) $\frac{1}{3}$, 1, 3, …     (vi) $\frac{1}{2}, \frac{2}{3}, \frac{3}{4}, …$

3. Look at this sequence:

   4, 7, 10, 13, …

   The rule to find the next term of this sequence is *add 3 to the previous term*.
   Write down the next three terms in this sequence.

4. Write down the first four terms of these sequences:

   (i) Start with 2 and count forwards in steps of 4.
   (ii) Start with 5 and count forwards in steps of 3.
   (iii) Start with 3 and count forwards in steps of 5.
   (iv) Start with 30 and count back in steps of 4.
   (v) Start with $-10$ and count forwards in steps of 3.

**5.** Describe in words the rule for each of these sequences:

    (i)  3, 6, 9, 12, …        (ii)  −8, −4, 0, 4, …        (iii)  10, 15, 20, 25, …

    (iv)  16, 14, 12, 10, …    (v)  −6, −3, 0, 3, …      (vi)  $2, 3\frac{1}{2}, 5, 6\frac{1}{2}, …$

**6.** For each of these sequences, the first four terms and the rules are given.
Write down the next three terms of each sequence.

    (i)  2, 4, 6, 8, …      Add 2 to the last term.

    (ii)  2, 4, 6, 10, …    Add the previous two terms together.

    (iii)  2, 4, 8, 16, …    Double the last term.

    (iv)  2, 4, 10, 28, …   Multiply the last term by 3 and then take off 2.

**7.** A sequence begins  3, 4, 6, 10, …
The rule for continuing the sequence is

> Double the last number and subtract 2.

What is the next number in this sequence?

**8.** The first term of a sequence is 5.
The term-to-term rule is 'add 6'.

    (i)  What is the second term of the sequence?

    (ii)  What is the fifth term?

**9.** Copy and complete this table:

| 1st term | Term-to-term rule | 2nd, 3rd, 4th and 5th terms |
|:---:|:---:|:---:|
| 8 | +5 | |
| | +4 | 9, 13, 17, 21 |
| | | 12, 15, 18, 21 |
| 0 | −3 | |
| −12 | | −7, −2, 3, 8 |

**10.** The sixth term of a sequence is 11.
The term-to-term rule is 'subtract 3'.

    (i)  What is the fifth term of the sequence?

    (ii)  What is the first term?

**11.** Here are three sequences:

    (a)  7, 14, 21, 28, …     (b)  6, 11, 16, 21, 26, …   (c)  3, 7, 11, 15, 19, …

What goes in the box in each of the following?

(i)   In sequence (a), the terms of the sequence are multiples of ☐.

(ii)  In sequence (b), the terms are all ☐ more than a multiple of ☐.

(iii) In sequence (c), the terms are all ☐ less than a multiple of ☐.

**12.** In the sequence shown below, you add the previous two numbers to get the next number.

   ...   5   8   13   21   ...   ...

(i)  Write down the next two numbers of the sequence.

(ii) Write down the number that came before 5.

**13.** Here is the rule for finding a term in a sequence.

   | Multiply the previous term by 3 and add 2. |

   The first three terms in the sequence are 2, 8 and 26.
   Work out the next two terms.

**14.** Each term in the sequence of patterns below is the number of squares in the pattern.
   Copy and complete the shaded boxes below.

| Pattern | | | | | |
|---|---|---|---|---|---|
| Position | 1 | 2 | 3 | | |
| Term | 5 | 8 | | | |

**15.** Write down the first six terms of this sequence.

> I am thinking of a sequence.
> The third term is 4.
> The rule is 'multiply by 2'.

**16.** The rule for a sequence is 'multiply the previous term by 2 and add 1'.
   The first term of the sequence is 3.

(i)  Write down the second term.

(ii) Work out the sixth term.

**17.** In each of the sequences below, the difference between the terms is constant.
Copy each sequence and fill in the missing numbers.

(i)  4, 6, ——, ——, ——, 14, ...

(ii)  25, ——, 19, ——, 13, 10, ...

(iii)  1, ——, 11, ——, 21, ——, ...

(iv)  ——, 10, ——, ——, 19, ——, ...

## *Investigation:*

Investigate the number patterns below.

Copy each pattern and add the next line without using a calculator.

Using a calculator, check that your answer is correct.

| Number Pattern 1 | Number Pattern 2 | Number Pattern 3 |
|---|---|---|
| $1 \times 9 + 2 = 11$ | $3 \times 11 = 33$ | $9 \times 1 = 9$ |
| $11 \times 9 + 2 = 101$ | $33 \times 11 = 363$ | $9 \times 12 = 108$ |
| $111 \times 9 + 2 = 1001$ | $333 \times 11 = 3663$ | $9 \times 123 = 1107$ |
| $1111 \times 9 + 2 = 10001$ | $3333 \times 11 = 36663$ | $9 \times 1234 = 11106$ |
|  |  |  |

In groups, try to create your own pattern. Compare results.

# Section 19.2  **Repeating patterns**

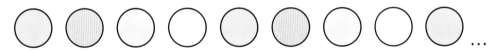

The pattern of the coloured circles above is green, pink, blue, yellow, green, pink, ...
The pattern repeats in blocks of 4.
The pattern of green circles is 1, 5, 9, ...
The pattern of yellow circles is 4, 8, 12, ...

What colour is the 35th circle?
Since the pattern repeats every 4 circles, we find how many blocks of 4 there are in 35
and then see how many circles are left over.

$35 \div 4 = 8$  and remainder 3

When the remainder is 3, we look for the colour of the 3rd circle in the block of 4.

This colour is blue. Therefore, the 35th circle is blue.

## Example 1

A repeating pattern is made up of letters as follows:

| A | B | C | D | E | A | B | C | D | E | A |

...

(i) What is the 25th letter?
(ii) What is the 43rd letter?
(iii) What is the 61st letter?

  (i) The pattern repeats in blocks of 5.
     To find the 25th letter, divide 25 by 5.
     $25 \div 5 = 5$, i.e. five complete blocks.
     The 25th letter is therefore the last letter in the block.
     Thus, the 25th letter is E.

 (ii) The 43rd letter is $43 \div 5$. This is 8 and remainder 3.
     Remainder 3 means it is the 3rd letter in the block.
     This letter is C.
     The 43rd letter is C.

(iii) The 61st letter is $61 \div 5$. This is 12 and remainder 1.
     Remainder 1 means the first letter in the block.
     The 61st letter is A.

## Investigation:

A gardener has
100 flowers.
He wants to plant
them in pots (in
groups of 3) along a driveway.

Show that if he uses the pattern shown he will have flowers left over.

In groups, design a pattern he might use so as not to have any flowers left over.

(Note the pattern must repeat after every 3 pots).

Compare your pattern with other groups in the class.

## Exercise 19.2

**1.** Here is a repeating pattern of geometric shapes:

□ ○ △ ▭ □ ○ △ ▭ ...

(i) What are the next two shapes?
(ii) List the positions of the first three circles. Is there a pattern?
(iii) Which shape forms the pattern  3, 7, …?
(iv) What is the 21st shape?
(v) What is the 37th shape?
(vi) If the 61st shape is a square, what is the 62nd shape?

**2.** Here is a repeating pattern of coloured tiles:

□ □ ▨ ▨ □ □ ▨ ▨ □ □ ...

(i) What is the next colour in the pattern?
(ii) What colour is the 30th tile?
(iii) What colour is the 48th tile?
(iv) If the 63rd tile is red, what colour is the 65th tile?
(v) Write down the pattern formed by the blue tiles.
(vi) In what position is the 6th blue tile?

**3.** The pattern below is the multiples of 6.

6, 12, 18, 24, 30, 36, 42, 48, 54, 60, 66, 72, …

The last digit in each number forms this pattern:

6, 2, 8, 4, 0, 6, 2, 8, 4, 0, 6, 2, …

Notice that this is a repeating pattern.

(i) What are the next two numbers of this pattern?
(ii) What is the 24th number of this pattern?
(iii) What is the 51st number of this pattern?
(iv) What is the position of the fifth 8 of this pattern?

**4.** Here is a repeating pattern of geometric shapes.

○ ▱ ◠ □ △ ○ ▱ ◠ □ △ ...

(i) What is the next shape in the pattern?
(ii) List the positions of the first three triangles.
Now write down the position of the fourth triangle.

(iii) What is the 26th shape?

(iv) What is the 38th shape?

(v) Which shape forms the sequence 3, 8, 13, ... ?

**5.** Write down the first ten multiples of 8.

(i) Show that the last digits of these multiples form a repeating pattern.

(ii) After how many digits does the pattern start repeating?

(iii) What number appears in the 100th position in the pattern?

## Section 19.3 Linear sequences

Look at this sequence:

12, 9, 6, 3, ...      The term-to-term rule is '−3' or 'subtract 3'.

When the term-to-term rule involves adding or subtracting a constant (a fixed number), it is known as a **linear sequence**.

> A **linear sequence** is formed by adding or subtracting a fixed number from a starting number.

Here are some examples of linear sequences:

(i) 5, 8, 11, 14, ... the constant difference is +3.

(ii) 24, 20, 16, 12, ... the constant difference is −4.

The following sequences are not linear because the term-to-term rule does not involve adding or subtracting a constant.

(i) 2, 4, 8, 16, 32, ...      The term-to-term rule is ×2.

(ii) 27, 9, 3, 1, $\frac{1}{3}$, ...      The term-to-term rule is ÷3.

### How to find any term of a linear sequence

We can calculate the value of a term from its position in the sequence by using a **position-to-term rule**. This helps us to avoid having to add or subtract the constant a lot of times.

**Question:** What is 20th term of the sequence 7, 10, 13, 16, 19, 22, ... ?

We could keep adding 3 until we got to the 20th term; however, this is very time consuming and impractical if we need to find a term a large distance along the sequence.

Examine how the following sequence is formed:

Rule: | Position | $\longrightarrow$ | $\times 3$ | $\longrightarrow$ | $+4$ |

| **Position** | 1 | 2 | 3 | 4 | 5 | ...$n$ |
|---|---|---|---|---|---|---|
| **Term** | $(3 \times 1) + 4$ | $(3 \times 2) + 4$ | $(3 \times 3) + 4$ | $(3 \times 4) + 4$ | $(3 \times 5) + 4$ | ...$(3n + 4)$ |
| | 7 | 10 | 13 | 16 | 19 | |

If we call the general term '$n$', then $n$th term of this sequence is given by;

$$T_n = n \boxed{\times 3} + \boxed{4}$$

$$\therefore T_n = 3n + 4$$

$\therefore$ the 20th term is $T_{20} = 3(20) + 4 = 64$.

The position-to-term rule is generally called the $n$th **term** rule.

The position-to-term rule for a sequence can be given by writing an expression for $T_n$, the $n$th term.

When we know $T_n$ we can write down any term of the sequence.

---

**Example 1**

The $n$th term of a sequence is given by $T_n = 3n - 4$.
(i) Write down the first three terms of the sequence and also $T_{20}$.
(ii) Explain why the sequence is linear.

(i) $T_n = 3n - 4$
$T_1 = 3(1) - 4 = 3 - 4 = -1$ ... substitute 1 for $n$.
$T_2 = 3(2) - 4 = 6 - 4 = 2$
$T_3 = 3(3) - 4 = 9 - 4 = 5$
$T_{20} = 3(20) - 4 = 60 - 4 = 56$

The first three terms are $-1, 2, 5$ and $T_{20} = 56$.

(ii) Since the difference between the terms is a constant, i.e. 3, the sequence is linear.

---

## Working backwards

If we know the rule for any sequence we can work backwards as follows:
Starting with the number 3, the rule 'subtract 2 and then multiply by 4', gives the sequence

$$3, 4, 8, 24, 88, \dots$$

Given any starting number then the rule is;

Starting number ⟶ Subtract 2 ⟶ Multiply by 4    e.g. $(8 - 2) \times 4 = 24$.

If we need to find a number that went before in this sequence, we work backwards ...

The original number ⟵ Add 2 ⟵ Divide by 4 (**Start**)

If we start with 24, $24 \div 4 = 6$ then $6 + 2 = 8$, the number before 24.

---

### Example 2

Gary made a sequence of numbers using the rule 'multiply by 3, then add 1'.

He wrote his sequence as ▩, ▩, $22, 67, 202, \ldots$ but some ink spilled on the first two terms.

Find the first two terms.

Working backwards the rule is 'subtract 1 then divide by 3'

Starting with 22, $22 - 1 = 21$ then $21 \div 3 = 7$

Starting with 7, $7 - 1 = 6$ then $6 \div 3 = 2$

His sequence was $2, 7, 22, 67, 202, \ldots$

---

### Exercise 19.3

**1.** The $n$th terms of some sequences are given.
   Write out the first four terms of each sequence.

   (i)  $T_n = 2n$
   (ii)  $T_n = 3n + 1$
   (iii)  $T_n = 4n - 3$
   (iv)  $T_n = 2n + 5$
   (v)  $T_n = 5n - 4$
   (vi)  $T_n = 7 - 2n$

**2.** Explain why each of these sequences is linear:

   (i)  $6, 10, 14, 18, \ldots$
   (ii)  $1, 6, 11, 16, \ldots$
   (iii)  $20, 17, 14, 11, \ldots$

**3.** The $n$th term of a sequence is $T_n = 2n + 3$.

   (i)  Write down the first five terms of the sequence.
   (ii)  Find $T_{20}$ and $T_{100}$.
   (iii)  Explain why the sequence is linear.

**4.** If $T_n = 2n - 6$, show that $T_1 + T_5 = 0$.

5. Write out the first four terms of the sequence given by $T_n = n^2 + 1$.
   Is the sequence linear? Explain your answer.

6. The *n*th term of a sequence is $3n + 2$.
   (i) Write down the first six terms of the sequence.
   (ii) Calculate the 100th term.

7. Linear sequences can be found on this grid.
   Two are highlighted on the diagram.

   | 44 | 34 | 24 | 14 | 4  | 3  | 6  | 9 | 12 |
   |----|----|----|----|----|----|----|---|----|
   | 40 | 30 | 5  | 20 | 10 | 11 | 5  | 8 | 1  |
   | 44 | 37 | 30 | 23 | 16 | 9  | 2  | 7 | 3  |
   | 4  | 11 | 23 | 21 | 22 | 12 | 1  | 6 | 9  |
   | 1  | 7  | 26 | 20 | 28 | 9  | 8  | 5 | 0  |
   | 3  | 31 | 10 | 15 | 34 | 30 | 12 | 4 | 8  |
   | 36 | 6  | 11 | 13 | 40 | 0  | 1  | 3 | 2  |

   (i) Write down each of these two sequences, starting with the smallest number in each case.

   (ii) Find seven more linear sequences that have four terms or more.

8. Examine the number of sides used for each group of triangles.

    ,  ,  ,  , …

   Copy and complete the given table of values which shows how the number of sides used is related to the number of triangles.

   | Number of triangles | 1 | 2 | 3 | 4 | 5 |
   |---------------------|---|---|---|---|---|
   | Number of sides     | 3 | 5 |   |   |   |

   Explain why the sequence formed by the number of sides is linear.

9. Lucille made a sequence using the rule 'multiply by 2 then subtract 2'.
   Find *x*, and *y*, if the first six terms of her sequence were: *x*, *y*, 10, 18, 34, 66, …

10. A rule 'subtract 3 then divide by 2' is used to write a sequence of numbers.
    If 17 is the second term of the sequence, find (i) the first term (ii) the third term.

11. Max made a sequence of numbers using the rule 'multiply the last term by 2 then subtract 1'.
    If the 11th term is 3073, use the information above to find the 10th and 9th terms.

12. Part of a sequence is …, 4, 7, 11, 18, … .
    The rule for this sequence is 'add together the last two numbers to find the next number'.
    (i) Write down two numbers that come after 18 in this sequence.
    (ii) Write down two numbers that come before 4 in this sequence.

# Section 19.4  Finding the *n*th term, $T_n$, of a linear sequence

To find the *n*th term of a linear sequence, we look at the differences between terms.

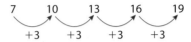

The sequence is linked to 3-times tables because the terms go up in 3s.
So 3*n* will be part of the *n*th term.
$T_n$ will be  3*n* $\pm$ some number.

To work out what to add to or subtract from 3*n*, we compare the terms of $T_n = 3n$ with the given sequence:

If $T_n = 3n$, then sequence is 3, 6, 9, 12, 15, … compare this sequence with the given sequence 7, 10, 13, 16, 19, …

We can see that, 4, needs to be added to each term of the sequence, $T_n = 3n$, to get our given sequence.

∴ $T_n = 3n$, is the *n*th term of the sequence 3, 6, 9, 12, 15, …

∴ $T_n = 3n + 4$, is the *n*th term of the sequence 7, 10, 13, 16, 19, …

---

**Example 1**

Find the *n*th term of the sequence  3, 7, 11, 15, …

In the sequence  3, 7, 11, 15, …, the difference between the terms is +4.
So  $T_n = 4n \pm$ some number.
If  $T_n = 4n$, then  $T_1 = 4(1) = 4$.
What do I need to add to or subtract from 4 in order to get the first term, i.e. 3, of the given sequence?
I need to subtract 1, since  $4 - 1 = 3$.
So  $T_n = 4n - 1$.

**Note:** It is only necessary to compare the first term of each sequence but it is good practice having found $T_n$ to check $T_2$, $T_3$ for example.

**Note:** A second method to find the $n$th term is to set up a table format as the next example indicates.

---

**Example 2**

Find the $n$th term of the sequence 1, 4, 7, 10, 13, …

Hence work out $T_{20}$ of the sequence.

| | $T_1$ | $T_2$ | $T_3$ | $T_4$ | $T_5$ | $...T_n$ |
|---|---|---|---|---|---|---|
| Sequence | 1 | 4 | 7 | 10 | 13 | |
| | | +3 | +3 | +3 | +3 | |
| | 3 | 6 | 9 | 12 | 15 | $+3n$ |
| | 1 | 4 | 7 | 10 | 13 | $+3n - 2$ |

From the table we can see that $(-2)$ needs to be subtracted from the terms of $+3n$ to form the given sequence.

$\therefore T_n = 3n - 2$

$\therefore T_{20} = 3(20) - 2 = 60 - 2 = 58$

---

**Example 3**

The $n$th term of a sequence is given by $T_n = 5n - 4$.
Which term of the sequence is 21?

Let $T_n = 21$
$\therefore 5n - 4 = 21$
$\quad\quad 5n = 25$
$\quad\quad\ n = 5$

Thus, 21 is the 5th term of the sequence.

## Exercise 19.4

**1.** A given sequence is 5, 9, 13, 17, ...

    (i) Write down the constant difference between the terms.

    (ii) If $T_n = \square n \pm$ a number, what number goes in the box?

    (iii) Now find an expression for $T_n$, the $n$th term.

    (iv) Write down the value of $T_{20}$.

**2.** Each of the following sequences is linear.

By finding the constant difference between the terms in each sequence, write down the number in the red box for $T_n$ in each case:

    (i) 2, 5, 8, 11, ... ;    $T_n = \square n \pm$ ?    (ii) 3, 7, 11, 15, ... ;    $T_n = \square n \pm$ ?

    (iii) 6, 12, 18, 24, ... ;    $T_n = \square n \pm$ ?    (iv) 5, 10, 15, 20, ... ;    $T_n = \square n \pm$ ?

**3.** Complete $T_n$, the $n$th term, for each of the following:

(i)

| Position | 1 | 2 | 3 | 4 | 5 |
|---|---|---|---|---|---|
| Term | 3 | 6 | 9 | 12 | 15 |

$$T_n = \square n$$

(ii)

| Position | 1 | 2 | 3 | 4 | 5 |
|---|---|---|---|---|---|
| Term | 4 | 7 | 10 | 13 | 16 |

$$T_n = \square n + 1$$

(iii)

| Position | 1 | 2 | 3 | 4 | 5 |
|---|---|---|---|---|---|
| Term | 5 | 10 | 15 | 20 | 25 |

$$T_n = \square n$$

(iv)

| Position | 1 | 2 | 3 | 4 | 5 |
|---|---|---|---|---|---|
| Term | 3 | 8 | 13 | 18 | 23 |

$$T_n = \square n - \square$$

(v)

| Position | 1 | 2 | 3 | 4 |
|---|---|---|---|---|
| Term | 7 | 9 | 11 | 13 |

$$T_n = \square n + \square$$

(vi)

| Position | 1 | 2 | 3 | 4 | 5 |
|---|---|---|---|---|---|
| Term | 5 | 9 | 13 | 17 | 21 |

$$T_n = \square n + \square$$

**4.** Find an expression for the $n$th term of each of these sequences:

    (i) 5, 7, 9, 11, ...        (ii) 5, 8, 11, 14, ...        (iii) 6, 10, 14, 18, ...

**5.** Find an expression for the $n$th term of this sequence:

        7, 11, 15, 19, ...

Use the expression for the $n$th term to find $T_{10}$ and $T_{20}$.

**6.** Find an expression for the $n$th term of the sequence:

        8, 12, 16, 20, ...

Now find the value of    (i) $T_{10}$    (ii) $T_{30}$.

Use the expression for $T_n$ to find which term of the sequence is 80.

**7.** Consider the sequence  12, 10, 8, 6, … .

   (i)  What is the term-to-term rule for this sequence?

   (ii)  If $T_n = \boxed{\phantom{x}}\, n \pm$ a number,  what number goes in the box?

   (iii)  Use this to find an expression for $T_n$.

   (iv)  Find $T_{10}$ of the sequence.

   (v)  Which term of the sequence is $-14$?

**8.** Find an expression for the $n$th terms of these sequences:

   (i)  $-3, 0, 3, 6, 9, …$        (ii)  $20, 15, 10, 5, …$

## *Investigation:*

Copy and complete (in a different colour) the following linear sequences.

State the rule needed for each sequence.

Draw a large chart of your results.

|   |   |    |    |    |   |    | Rule |
|---|---|----|----|----|---|----|------|
| **A** | 6 |    | 12 | 15 |   | 21 |      |
| **B** |   | 40 | 32 |    |   | 8  |      |
| **C** | 3 |    |    | 15 |   | 23 |      |
| **D** |   | 5  |    |    |   | 25 |      |

# Section 19.5  Linear sequences formed from shapes

So far in this chapter we have dealt mainly with number patterns.

In this section we will examine some geometric figures and the patterns they form.

**Example 1**

The figure on the right shows some
photo frames made with rods.

1 photo      2 photos      3 photos

   (i)  Draw the frame that holds 4 photos.

   (ii)  How many rods are there in the frame that holds 5 photos?

   (iii)  Find an expression for the number of rods in the $n$th frame.

   (iv)  Which frame uses 41 rods?

(i) This is the frame that holds 4 photos:

(ii) The sequence is 3, 5, 7, 9, 11, …
Therefore, the 5th frame has 11 rods.

(iii) The difference between the terms is $+2$.
Thus, the $n$th term will be $2n \pm$ a number.
If $T_n = 2n$, $T_1 = 2$ and so 1 must be added to get the first term 3.
$\therefore T_n = 2n + 1$

(iv) Let $T_n = 41 \Rightarrow 2n + 1 = 41$
$$2n = 40$$
$$n = 20$$
The 20th frame uses 41 rods.

## Exercise 19.5

**1.** Here is a pattern made from sticks.

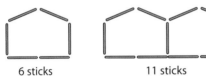

6 sticks        11 sticks

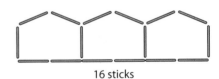

16 sticks

  (i) Draw the 4th pattern in this sequence.
  (ii) Write down the sequence of numbers generated by the sticks in the first six patterns.
  (iii) Show that the number of sticks in the $n$th pattern is given by $T_n = 5n + 1$.
  (iv) How many sticks are required for the 20th pattern?
  (v) For which pattern are 51 sticks required?

**2.** Here are three diagrams made with triangles.

Diagram 1      Diagram 2      Diagram 3

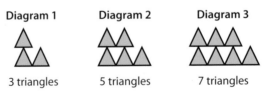

3 triangles      5 triangles      7 triangles

  (i) Draw diagram 4.
  (ii) How many triangles will be in diagram 7?
  (iii) Find an expression for the number of triangles in the $n$th diagram.
  (iv) Which diagram will contain 33 triangles?

**3.** Complete the table of values for this sequence of matchstick patterns.

| Number of squares | 1 | 2 | 3 | 4 | 5 |
|---|---|---|---|---|---|
| Number of matchsticks | 4 | 7 | | | |

   (i)  How many matchsticks are required for the 6th pattern?

  (ii)  Find an expression in $n$ for the number of matchsticks in the $n$th pattern.

 (iii)  Use the expression found to ascertain the number of matchsticks required for the 50th pattern.

**4.** Here is a pattern made with matchsticks.

 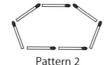 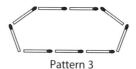

         Pattern 1          Pattern 2          Pattern 3

   (i)  How many matchsticks will be in Pattern 5?

  (ii)  Find an expression for the number of matchsticks in the $n$th pattern.

 (iii)  In which pattern are there 51 matchsticks?

**5.** Here is another pattern made with matchsticks.

 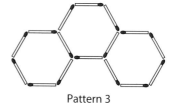

      Pattern 1          Pattern 2          Pattern 3

   (i)  How many matchsticks will there be in pattern 4?

  (ii)  What is the term-to-term rule for the pattern?

 (iii)  How many matchsticks will there be in the $n$th pattern?

 (iv)  Which pattern will contain exactly 66 matchsticks?

  (v)  Will any pattern use exactly 88 matchsticks?

# Section 19.6 Other sequences

## Quadratic sequences

1, 4, 9, 16, 25, ... is the sequence of square numbers.

Since $T_1 = 1^2, T_2 = 2^2, T_3 = 3^2, ..., T_n = n^2$.

Sequences that have an $n$th term containing $n^2$ as the highest power are called **quadratic sequences**.

Let us examine the first seven terms of the sequence $T_n = n^2$.

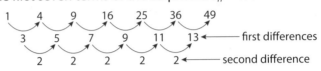

Notice that the **second difference** is a constant, i.e. 2.

Quadratic sequences always have a **constant** second difference.

Now we will examine the sequence 1, 6, 15, 28, 45, ... by finding the first and second differences:

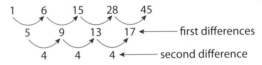

Here again the second differences are all the same, i.e. 4.

*Quadratic sequences*

In a quadratic sequence, the second difference between the terms is always constant.

---

**Example 1**

By finding the second difference between the terms, investigate if the sequence 2, 5, 10, 17, 26, ... is quadratic.

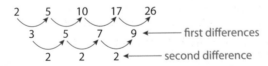

Since the second difference is constant (i.e. 2), the sequence is quadratic.

---

## Example 2

Find the next two terms of the quadratic sequence 5, 7, 10, 14, ... by finding the first and second differences.

In the given sequence, the difference between the terms is increasing by 1 each step.

The next two terms are $(14 + 5)$ and $(19 + 6)$.

∴   the next two terms are 19 and 25.

## *Investigation:*

Copy and complete the table below showing how to form a quadratic sequence, whose first two terms are 3, 7 and which has a second difference of 5.

| Sequence | 3 | | 7 | | ( ) | | ( ) | | ( ) | | ( ) | | ( ) |
|---|---|---|---|---|---|---|---|---|---|---|---|---|---|
| **First diff** | | ( ) | | ( ) | | ( ) | | ( ) | | ( ) | | ( ) | | |
| **Second diff** | | | 5 | | 5 | | 5 | | 5 | | 5 | | | |

∴ The sequence is 3, 7, ….

## Exponential sequences

Here is a special type of sequence formed by the powers of 2:

$2^1, 2^2, 2^3, 2^4, 2^5$ ...   or   2, 4, 8, 16, 32, ...

Notice that the values of the terms increase very quickly.
This is an example of an **exponential sequence**.

If $T_n = 3^n$, then the sequence is

$3^1, 3^2, 3^3, 3^4, 3^5, ...$   or   3, 9, 27, 81, 243, ...

Exponent is another word for power.

In everyday language, **exponential growth** is used to indicate 'very fast growth'.

When the sequence 2, 4, 8, 16, ... is plotted on a graph, it can be seen that the curve rises very steeply.

Using the rule $y = 2^x$

when $x = 1$, $y = 2$,

when $x = 2$, $y = 4$,

when $x = 3$, $y = 8$ etc.

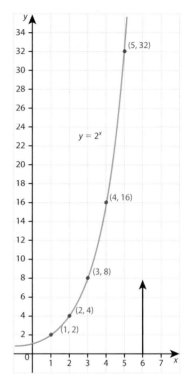

## *Investigation:*

Investigate the graph of $y = 2^x$.

By studying the pattern of numbers, find the value of $y$ when $x = 6$.

Design a poster with scaled axes to show $y = 2^x$, $0 \leq x \leq 6$

## Exercise 19.6

**1.** The $n$th term of a sequence is given by $T_n = n^2 + 3$.
Write out the first five terms of this sequence.
By finding the second difference between these terms, explain why the sequence is quadratic.

**2.** Work out the first four terms of each of these quadratic sequences:
   (i) $T_n = n^2 + 1$          (ii) $T_n = n^2 - 2$          (iii) $T_n = 2n^2 - 1$

**3.** Find the first and second differences between the terms of these sequences.
Hence state if each sequence is quadratic.
   (i) 3, 4, 6, 9, 13, ...          (ii) 3, 6, 11, 18, 27, ...          (iii) 2, 7, 14, 23, 34, ...

**4.** By examining the pattern in the first differences, write down the next two terms of each of these sequences:
   (i) 6, 8, 12, 18, 26, ...          (ii) 4, 7, 12, 19, 28, ...

**5.** Here are the first 3 diagrams
of a matchstick pattern.
  (i)  How many matchsticks
       will there be in
       Diagram 4?
  (ii) Using the sequence
       formed, write down
       the number of
       matchsticks in Diagram 5.
  (iii) Explain why the sequence is quadratic.

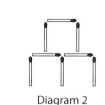
Diagram 1

Diagram 2

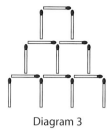
Diagram 3

**6.** Here are the first three terms of an exponential sequence: 3, 9, 27, ...
  (i)  Write out the next three terms.
  (ii) Investigate if the second difference between the terms is a constant.

**7.** Write down the first six terms of the sequence, given that $T_n = 2^n$.
Describe the sequence you have found.

**8.** Work out the first four terms of the sequence defined by $T_n = 3(2^n)$.
By finding the second differences between the terms, show that the sequence is
not quadratic.

## Section 19.7 Graphing linear sequences

Here is a linear pattern: 1, 4, 7, 10, 13, ...
It can be seen that $T_1 = 1, T_2 = 4, T_3 = 7, ...$

These may be written as ordered pairs as follows:
  $(T_1, 1), (T_2, 4), (T_3, 7), (T_4, 10), ...$

On the right, we have plotted the terms
on the horizontal axis and the values of
the terms on the vertical axis.
When the term and its value are plotted,
and the points joined, the result is a
**straight line**.

This illustrates why the sequence is
called **linear**.

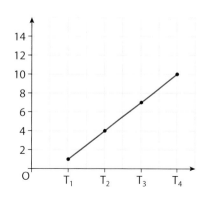

## Exercise 19.7

**1.** The diagram below shows the fare structures of two taxi companies, A and B.

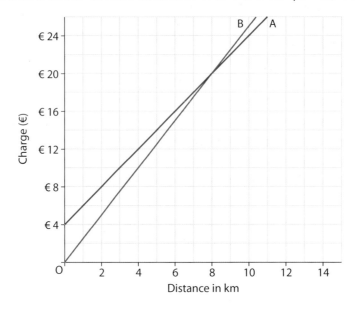

Use the graph to find

   (i)   how much Company A charges for a journey of 10 km
  (ii)   how far you could travel with Company B for €16
 (iii)   the distance for which both companies charge the same amount
 (iv)   the difference in the charges when the distance is 4 km.

**2.** The table on the right shows the first
four terms of a sequence and the values
of these terms.

| Term | 1 | 2 | 3 | 4 |
|------|---|---|----|----|
| Value | 4 | 7 | 10 | 13 |

Putting the terms on the horizontal axis and the values on the vertical axis, draw a
graph of the sequence.
Explain why the sequence is linear.

**3.** If $T_n = 2n + 1$, write out the first five terms of the sequence.
Illustrate this sequence on a graph, putting the term numbers on the horizontal axis.
Describe the graph you have drawn.

**4.** A fast-growing plant is 4 cm in height when purchased.
It grows 2 cm per day each day afterwards.
Copy and complete the table on the right showing
the height of the plant during its first seven days.

| Day | Height (cm) |
|-----|-------------|
| 1 | 4 |
| 2 | 6 |
| 3 | 8 |
| ...... | ...... |

  (i)   Draw a graph to show the height of the plant
        for Day 1 ..... Day 7.
  (ii)  How many days will it take for the plant to
        reach a height of 30 cm?
  (iii) The plant will stop growing when it reaches a height of 60 cm.
        How many days will this take?

**5.** The graph on the right shows a
plumber's charges when called out
to do a repair job on a boiler.

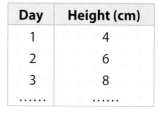

  (i)   What is the initial or 'call out' charge?
  (ii)  How much does he charge for a
        job that lasts for $3\frac{1}{2}$ hours?
        (Include 'call out' charge.)
  (iii) If he charges €135 in total,
        how many hours, roughly,
        has he worked?
  (iv)  Use the sequence of charges
        for 1 hour, 2 hours, 3 hours, ...
        to find approximately what the
        charge would be for 8 hours work.

**6.** The table on the right shows the total
amounts of money Cara has saved after
weeks 1, 2, 3, ....
Draw a graph to illustrate these savings,
putting the week number on the x-axis.

| Week number | Amount saved |
|-------------|--------------|
| 1 | €10 |
| 2 | €20 |
| 3 | €30 |
| 4 | €40 |
| 5 | €50 |
| ...... | ...... |

  (i)   Use the pattern to find the amount
        she will have saved at the end of the
        10th week.
  (ii)  Use the graph to find at the end of which
        week she will have saved €80.

**7.** One candle is 50 cm long and burns at the rate of 5 cm/hour.
A second candle is 40 cm long and burns at the rate of 2 cm/hour.

Make an enlarged copy of this grid and mark
on it the height of each candle after 2 hours,
4 hours, 6 hours, 8 hours and 10 hours.

Draw two lines to show the rates at which
the candles burn.

Use the graph to estimate after how many
hours of burning both candles are the same
length.

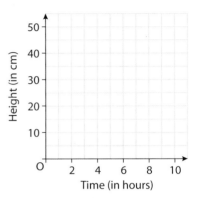

**8.** This pattern is made from cubes.
The outside faces of the cubes in each block are painted.

   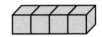

The table below shows the number of faces painted in each block.

| Block number ($n$) | 1 | 2 | 3 | 4 |
|---|---|---|---|---|
| Number of painted faces | 6 | 10 | 14 | 18 |

(i)   Explain why the sequence formed by the numbers of faces painted forms a
       linear sequence.
(ii)  Now find an expression for the $n$th term of the sequence.
(iii) Draw a graph of the sequence, putting the block numbers on the
       horizontal axis.
(iv)  Copy and complete this sentence:
       "The graph of a linear sequence is always a … ."

# Test yourself 19

1. Find the missing number in each of these sequences:

   (i)  3, 7, 11, ☐, 19, …     (ii)  10, 6, 2, ☐, −6, …     (iii)  4, 12, 36, ☐, …

2. A sequence begins  1, 2, 6, 16, …
   Here is the rule to continue the sequence:

   > Add the previous two numbers together, then multiply the answer by two.

   Work out the next two terms of the sequence.

3. The first two terms of a sequence are  3, 9, … .
   (i)  If the sequence is linear, write down the next three terms.
   (ii)  If the sequence is quadratic, write down what the next three terms could be.
   (iii)  If the sequence is exponential, write down the next three terms.

4. Here is a repeating pattern of coloured tiles:

   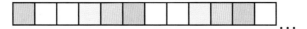

   (i)  What are the colours of the next two tiles?
   (ii)  Write down the sequence formed by the positions of the yellow tiles in the pattern.
   (iii)  In what position is the 10th yellow tile?
   (iv)  What is the colour of the 72nd tile?

5. By finding the second difference between the terms, investigate if the sequence  1, 6, 12, 19, 27, …  is quadratic.
   Explain your result.

6. Kevin has €20 saved. He gets €7 a week for doing jobs at home.
   He spends €2 on sweets every week and saves the rest in a piggybank.
   (i)  How much money, in total, has he saved at the end of week 1?
   (ii)  Complete the table below to show how his savings grow in the first five weeks.

   |       | Week 1 | Week 2 | Week 3 | Week 4 | Week 5 |
   |-------|--------|--------|--------|--------|--------|
   | €20   |        | €30    |        |        |        |

   (iii)  Write down a formula (in words) to represent the amount he has saved at the end of each week.

(iv) Kevin would like to buy a mobile phone costing €100. Use your formula to find out for how many weeks he needs to save in order to have enough money to buy the phone.

(v) Imagine Kevin stopped buying the sweets after five weeks.
How much could he then save each week after that?

(vi) Kevin thinks he can now buy his phone three weeks sooner with the extra savings. Do you agree with Kevin? Explain your answer.

**7.** What number goes in the box in each of these sequences?

(i) 10, 7, 4, 1, ☐, ...

(ii) −2, 1, ☐, 7, ...

(iii) 81, 27, ☐, 3, ...

(iv) 3, 5, 9, ☐, 23, ...

**8.** Look at these matchstick shapes.

5 matchsticks

9 matchsticks

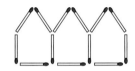

(i) Copy and complete the table below:

| Shape number | 1 | 2 | 3 | 4 | 5 |
|---|---|---|---|---|---|
| Number of matchsticks | 5 | 9 | ... | ... | ... |

(ii) How many matchsticks are there in Shape 7?

(iii) Find an expression for the number of matchsticks in Shape *n*?

(iv) Use this expression for the *n*th term to find which shape contains exactly 101 matchsticks.

**9.** Which **one** of the following sequences is linear?

(i) 6, 4, 0, ...

(ii) −3, −1, 3, 6, ...

(iii) −5, −3, −1, 1, ...

**10.** A sequence of numbers begins 36, 20, 12, 8, ...
The rule for the sequence is 'add 4 to the previous term and then halve the result'.

(i) Work out the next three terms.

(ii) Is the sequence linear? Explain your answer.

(iii) Is the sequence quadratic? Explain your answer.

**11.** Maurice wins a prize in a local lottery and is given two options.
Option A: €1000 cash today
or
Option B: Take €2 today, and double the amount of the previous day, each day for a total of 9 days.
Explain, giving your reasons, which option Maurice should pick.

**12.** Look at the sequence of these triangle patterns:

   (i)  Draw the next triangle in the sequence.
  (ii)  How many dots will there be in the 5th pattern?
 (iii)  Find an expression for the $n$th term for this sequence.
 (iv)  Use the expression for the $n$th term to find which pattern has 63 dots.

## Assignment:

  1 fold      2 folds     3 folds

Imagine a very, very, large sheet of paper.

With your group, copy and complete the following table showing the number of layers of paper in the pile after each fold.

| Folds | 1 | 2 | 3 | 4 | 5 | 6 | 7 | ...$n$ |
|---|---|---|---|---|---|---|---|---|
| **Number of layers** | 2 | 4 | 8 | | | | | |
| **Number of layers as $2^{(\ )}$** | $2^{(\ )}$ | $2^{(\ )}$ | $2^{(\ )}$ | $2^{(\ )}$ | $2^{(\ )}$ | $2^{(\ )}$ | $2^{(\ )}$ | $2^{(\ )}$ |

Write a formula for the number of layers in $n$ folds of the large sheet.

> Number =

Write an estimate from your group for the height of the pile after **50 folds** if a ream of this paper (500 sheets) has a height of 5cm.

> Estimate:

Using a calculator and the $x^{(\ )}$ key find:
  (i)  the number of sheets in the pile after 50 folds.
 (ii)  the height of the pile given that 500 sheets has a height of 5 cm.
(iii)  Compare your answer with other groups.

**Question:** What difference would it have made if the paper was folded only 49 times?

Decide on a suitable title for this assignment.

# Algebra 2: Inequalities – Algebraic Fractions

## *From first year, you will recall how to:*

- identify natural numbers, integers and real numbers,
- add and subtract fractions,
- solve a linear equation,
- substitute values into an expression.

## *In this chapter, you will learn to:*

- use dots to represent numbers from *N* and *Z* on a number line,
- use a solid line to represent numbers from *R* on a number line,
- plot inequalities on a number line,
- solve algebraic inequalities and graph the solution,
- add and subtract algebraic fractions,
- solve equations involving fractions,
- create and solve word problems resulting in equations with fractions,
- simplify algebraic fractions.

## Section 20.1  Plotting numbers on the number line

In your study of numbers so far, you will have dealt with **natural numbers** and **integers**. These numbers are described again below and illustrated on the number line.

1. **Natural numbers** are the counting numbers starting at 1.
   They are denoted by the capital letter **N**.

   $N = 1, 2, 3, 4, 5, \ldots$

   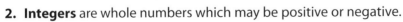

   The arrow indicates that the dots continue indefinitely.

2. **Integers** are whole numbers which may be positive or negative.
   They are denoted by the capital letter **Z**.
   The integers are illustrated here on the number line.

   $Z = \ldots, -3, -2, -1, 0, 1, 2, 3, \ldots$

   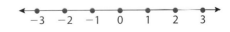

3. **Real numbers** describe all the numbers on the number line.
   These numbers include natural numbers, integers, fractions, decimals and numbers such as $\sqrt{5}, \sqrt{7}, \pi, \ldots$

   Since every number on the number line is a real number, we say that real numbers 'fill' the number line. For this reason, real numbers are represented on the number line by a heavy or 'bold' line as shown below.
   The capital letter **R** is used to denote the set of real numbers.

## Inequalities

The speed limit for cars driving in a city is generally 50 km/hr.
This could be written as speed $\leqslant 50$ or $S \leqslant 50$.
This means that $S$ could be 48, 46, 42, 40, ...
The statement $S \leqslant 50$ is an example of an **inequality**.

$x + 3 = 7$ is an example of an **equation** since one side is *equal* to the other.
However, $x + 3 > 7$ is an example of an **inequality** since one side is **not equal** to the other side.

Here are the four inequality signs we will use:

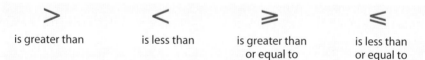

| $>$ | $<$ | $\geqslant$ | $\leqslant$ |
|---|---|---|---|
| is greater than | is less than | is greater than or equal to | is less than or equal to |

**Note:** Always read from left ⟶ to right when using inequalities.

We will now use these inequality signs to show how different numbers can be shown on the number line.

## 1. Natural numbers

The inequality $x \geqslant 4, x \in N$ means that $x$ may be any whole number greater than or equal to 4, i.e. 4, 5, 6, 7, ...
These are represented on the number line below:

## 2. Integers

The inequality $x > -2, x \in Z$ represents all the integers greater than $-2$,
i.e. $-1, 0, 1, 2, 3, \ldots$
These are represented on the number line below:

## 3. Real numbers

The inequality $x \leqslant 3, x \in R$ is the set of all real numbers less than or equal to 3.
The inequality $x \leqslant 3$ is represented on the number line as follows:

The 'bold' line indicates that all the points on the line are included and the closed
circle at 3 shows that the number 3 is **included**.

The inequality $x > -2, x \in R$ is shown below.
The 'empty' circle at $-2$ is used to show that $-2$ is **not included**.

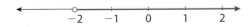

## Changing the order in an inequality

It is clear that $7 > 4$ but $4 < 7$.
This illustrates that when the two parts of an inequality are interchanged, the inequality
sign must also be changed.

Thus,    (i) if $8 > 3$, then $3 < 8$      (ii) if $x \geqslant 5$, then $5 \leqslant x$.

## Exercise 20.1

**1.** State whether each of the following is true or false:
    (i)   $3 \in N$        (ii)   $4 \in Z$        (iii)   $-5 \in N$        (iv)   $2.5 \in R$
    (v)   $-3\frac{1}{2} \in N$      (vi)   $0.5 \in N$      (vii)   $2\frac{3}{8} \in R$      (viii)   $\sqrt{17} \in R$

**2.** Insert $>$ or $<$ in each of the boxes below:
    (i)   $6 \boxed{>} 4$        (ii)   $-5 \boxed{<} 2$        (iii)   $6 \square -2$        (iv)   $-4 \square 3$

**3.** Write a mathematical sentence for each of these:
    (i)   $x$ is less than 4                 (ii)   2 is greater than $-3$
    (iii)   the speed limit ($S$) is 40 km/hr     (iv)   $b$ is less than or equal to $-5$
    (v)   the minimum age ($A$) is 18         (vi)   the maximum age ($A$) is 60

**4.** If $x \in N$, state the values $x$ may have in each of the following inequalities:

(i) $x < 4$      (ii) $x \leqslant 5$      (iii) $x < 6\frac{1}{2}$

(iv) $x > 2$ and $x < 7$      (v) $x \geqslant 1$ and $x \leqslant 4$      (vi) $x \geqslant 2$ and $x < 8$

**5.** If $x \in Z$, state the values $x$ may have in each of the following inequalities:

(i) $x \geqslant -2$ and $x \leqslant 1$      (ii) $x \geqslant 0$ and $x \leqslant 4$      (iii) $x \geqslant -3$ and $x \leqslant 0$

(iv) $x \geqslant -4$ and $x < 1$      (v) $x > -5$ and $x < 2$      (vi) $x > -2\frac{1}{2}$ and $x < 3\frac{1}{4}$

**6.** Graph each of the following inequalities on the number line:

(i) $x \geqslant 3, x \in N$      (ii) $x \leqslant 4, x \in N$      (iii) $x > 3, x \in N$

(iv) $x \leqslant 2, x \in Z$      (v) $x \geqslant -3, x \in Z$      (vi) $x > -2, x \in Z$

**7.** Choose one of $x = 3, x \leqslant 3, x < 3, x > 3$ or $x \geqslant 3$ to describe each graph below, where $x \in R$.

(i)

(ii)

(iii)

(iv)

**8.** Write the inequality represented by each of these number lines:

(i)

(ii)

(iii)

(iv)

(v)

(vi)

**9.** Graph each of the following on the number line:

(i) $x \geqslant 1, x \in R$      (ii) $x \geqslant -3, x \in R$      (iii) $x \leqslant 4, x \in R$

(iv) $x > 3, x \in R$      (v) $x < -1, x \in R$      (vi) $x < 4, x \in R$

**10.** Write each of the following statements as a mathematical sentence. Let $n$ stand for the number in each case.

(i) I have at least 6 shirts in my wardrobe.

(ii) The temperature in a fridge must be 5°C or less.

(iii) Hand baggage must not exceed 10 kg.

(iv) Gillian has more than 5 DVDs.

**11.** When asked, Peter said he had $x$ video games where, $5 < x \leqslant 15$. Describe, using the words maximum and minimum, the number of games Peter might have had.

**12.**

**A** There are at most 5 students in this room with black hair.

**B** Thomas has more than 5 computer games

**C** I'm sure I did not even get 5 marks in my maths test.

**D** I have at least 5 pens in my bag.

Connect one of the above statements with one of the following:

$b > 5$     $b \geqslant 5$     $b < 5$     $b \leqslant 5$

# Section 20.2  Solving inequalities

Here are scales that show  $10 > 8$.

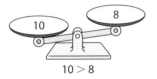

$10 > 8$

Would the scales stay as they are if

> the same amount is added to both sides
> the same amount is subtracted from both sides
> the mass on each side is doubled
> the mass on each side is halved ?

The answer to each question is 'yes'.

The answers to the four questions above illustrate two very important results for inequalities:

*Rules for inequalities*

1.  An inequality remains true when the same number is added to or subtracted from both sides.

2.  An inequality remains true when both sides are multiplied or divided by the same **positive** number.

Here are some numerical examples:

We know that the inequality      **6 > 4**

Add 4 to both sides:            $10 > 8$ ... true

Subtract 3 from both sides:      $3 > 1$ ... true

Multiply both sides by 3:        $18 > 12$ ... true

Divide both sides by 2:          $3 > 2$ ... true

## Multiplication by a negative number

Consider again the inequality $6 > 4$.
Multiply both sides by $-2$: $\quad -12 > -8$ … false … as $-12 < -8$.

This illustrates that the inequality sign must be changed (i.e. reversed) when both sides of an inequality are multiplied or divided by the same **negative** number.

(i) $2 < 5$,
 but $2 \times (-2) > 5 \times (-2)$,
 i.e. $-4 > -10$

(ii) $8 > 6$, but $\dfrac{8}{-2} < \dfrac{6}{-2}$,
 i.e. $-4 < -3$.

> If both sides of an inequality are multiplied or divided by the same negative number, the inequality sign must be reversed.

---

### Example 1

Solve the inequality $5x - 3 \geqslant 12, x \in N$ and graph the solution on the number line.

$$5x - 3 \geqslant 12$$
$$5x \geqslant 12 + 3 \quad \text{…add 3 to both sides}$$
$$5x \geqslant 15$$
$$x \geqslant 3 \quad \text{…divide both sides by 5}$$

The solution is graphed on the number line below.

---

### Example 2

Solve the inequality $10 - 2x > 2, x \in R$ and graph the solution on the number line.

$$10 - 2x > 2$$
$$10 - 10 - 2x > 2 - 10 \quad \text{…subtract 10 from each side}$$
$$-2x > -8$$
$$-x > -4 \quad \text{…divide each side by 2}$$
$$x < 4 \quad \text{…multiply both sides by } -1 \text{ and change direction of inequality.}$$

## Exercise 20.2

**1.** Which of the following inequalities are equivalent to $a \geqslant 10$?

**Ⓐ** $a - 5 \geqslant 5$  **Ⓑ** $2a \geqslant 20$  **Ⓒ** $a + 5 \geqslant 5$  **Ⓓ** $\frac{1}{2}a \geqslant 5$  **Ⓔ** $a + \frac{1}{2} \geqslant 10\frac{1}{2}$

**2.** Which of the following inequalities are equivalent to $m < 3$?

**Ⓐ** $m + 2 < 5$  **Ⓑ** $2m < 4$  **Ⓒ** $3 > m$  **Ⓓ** $8 > m + 5$  **Ⓔ** $6 > 2m$

Solve the following inequalities and graph the solution on the number line in each case:

**3.** $x - 1 \leqslant 4, x \in N$

**4.** $3x - 2 \leqslant 10, x \in N$

**5.** $4x - 5 \leqslant 11, x \in N$

**6.** $3x + 5 \leqslant 14, x \in N$

**7.** $2x + 5 \leqslant 1, x \in Z$

**8.** $3x - 5 \leqslant 7, x \in Z$

**9.** $3x - 1 < -10, x \in Z$

**10.** $5x - 2 \leqslant 8, x \in Z$

**11.** $3x - 8 \leqslant 7, x \in R$

**12.** $2x + 2 \leqslant 8, x \in R$

**13.** $5x + 7 < 17, x \in R$

**14.** $3 - x \leqslant 4, x \in R$

**15.** $5 - 2x \geqslant -7, x \in R$

**16.** $1 - 5x > -14, x \in R$

**17.** $3x + 1 \geqslant 2x + 2, x \in R$

**18.** $4x + 2 \leqslant 2x + 8, x \in R$

**19.** $4x - 5 \leqslant x + 7, x \in R$

**20.** $2x - 1 < x + 2, x \in R$

**21.** $3x - 7 \geqslant x - 1, x \in R$

**22.** $5x + 7 < 3x + 3, x \in Z$

**23.** $1 - 2x \leqslant 5, x \in R$

**24.** $4 - 3x \geqslant 13, x \in R$

**25.** (i) For the set of values $x \leqslant 1$, which of the numbers in the bubble are values of $x$?

(ii) Which are values of $n$ for the set $n > 3$?

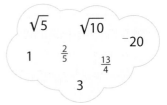

$\sqrt{5}$  $\sqrt{10}$  $^-20$  $1$  $\frac{2}{5}$  $\frac{13}{4}$  $3$

**26.** If we know that $x > 3$, decide if each of the following is

● **always** true   or   ● **sometimes** true   or   ● **never** true

(i) $x > 4$  (ii) $x > 2$  (iii) $x > -1$  (iv) $x < 1$

(v) $x + 5 > 8$  (vi) $x - 1 < 4$  (vii) $2x > 3$  (viii) $3x + 1 > 10$

## Section 20.3 Adding algebraic fractions

To add $\frac{3}{4} + \frac{4}{5}$, we first find the LCM of 4 and 5, i.e. 20.

We now express each fraction with 20 as denominator.

$$\therefore \quad \frac{3}{4} + \frac{4}{5} = \frac{5(3)}{20} + \frac{4(4)}{20} = \frac{15}{20} + \frac{16}{20} = \frac{15 + 16}{20} = \frac{31}{20} = 1\frac{11}{20}$$

Similarly, $\frac{6}{7} - \frac{2}{3} = \frac{3(6) - 7(2)}{21} = \frac{18 - 14}{21} = \frac{4}{21}$

Algebraic fractions can be added or subtracted in the same way as numerical fractions.

---

**Example 1**

Express each of these as a single fraction:

(i) $\frac{x}{4} + \frac{x}{6}$ 　　　(ii) $\frac{x + 3}{5} + \frac{x - 1}{3}$

(i) $\frac{x}{4} + \frac{x}{6}$

The smallest number into which 4 and 6 divide (LCM) is 12.

$$\frac{x}{4} + \frac{x}{6} = \frac{3(x)}{12} + \frac{2(x)}{12} = \frac{3x + 2x}{12} = \frac{5x}{12}$$

(ii) $\frac{x + 3}{5} + \frac{x - 1}{3}$

The smallest number into which 5 and 3 divide is 15.

$$\therefore \quad \frac{x + 3}{5} + \frac{x - 1}{3} = \frac{3(x + 3)}{15} + \frac{5(x - 1)}{15}$$

$$= \frac{3x + 9}{15} + \frac{5x - 5}{15}$$

$$= \frac{3x + 9 + 5x - 5}{15} = \frac{8x + 4}{15}$$

---

**Example 2**

Express as a single fraction: $\frac{5x - 3}{2} - \frac{2x + 1}{3}$

The LCM of 2 and 3 is 6.

$$\frac{5x - 3}{2} - \frac{2x + 1}{3} = \frac{3(5x - 3) - 2(2x + 1)}{6}$$

$$= \frac{15x - 9 - 4x - 2}{6} = \frac{11x - 11}{6}$$

LCM is the lowest common multiple.

## Exercise 20.3

Express each of the following as a single fraction:

**1.** $\frac{1}{2} + \frac{2}{3}$

**2.** $\frac{3}{4} + \frac{3}{5}$

**3.** $\frac{5}{12} + \frac{2}{12} + \frac{1}{12}$

**4.** $\frac{7}{8} - \frac{3}{4}$

**5.** $\frac{x}{2} + \frac{x}{3}$

**6.** $\frac{x}{5} + \frac{x}{3}$

**7.** $\frac{3x}{4} + \frac{5x}{2}$

**8.** $\frac{3x}{5} + \frac{2x}{3}$

**9.** $\frac{x}{4} - \frac{x}{6}$

**10.** $\frac{x}{2} - \frac{x}{5}$

**11.** $\frac{7x}{5} - \frac{x}{2}$

**12.** $\frac{3x}{4} - \frac{2x}{5}$

**13.** $\frac{x+1}{2} + \frac{x}{2}$

**14.** $\frac{x+1}{2} + \frac{x+4}{2}$

**15.** $\frac{x+4}{3} + \frac{2x+1}{3}$

**16.** $\frac{3x-4}{5} + \frac{5x-2}{5}$

**17.** $\frac{3x-2}{4} + \frac{5x+6}{4}$

**18.** $\frac{2x+1}{3} + \frac{2x-3}{3}$

**19.** $\frac{2x+1}{3} + \frac{x+4}{2}$

**20.** $\frac{2x-1}{3} + \frac{x+2}{4}$

**21.** $\frac{2x-1}{6} + \frac{x-3}{4}$

**22.** $\frac{5x-1}{5} - \frac{x}{2}$

**23.** $\frac{3x-2}{3} - \frac{x+4}{2}$

**24.** $\frac{5x-3}{4} - \frac{2x+1}{3}$

**25.** $\frac{2x+1}{3} - \frac{2x-1}{4}$

**26.** $\frac{7x-2}{7} - \frac{x-5}{14}$

**27.** $\frac{2x-1}{12} - \frac{3x-4}{6}$

**28.** $\frac{3x-1}{2} + \frac{2x-6}{5}$

**29.** $\frac{3x+1}{4} - \frac{2x-3}{6}$

**30.** $\frac{2x-3y}{3} - \frac{x-2y}{5}$

**31.** $\frac{2x-3}{2} + \frac{x-1}{4} - \frac{5}{6}$

**32.** $\frac{x-6}{3} + \frac{3}{4} - \frac{3x-4}{2}$

## Section 20.4 Solving equations involving fractions _____

Consider the equation $\frac{x-1}{5} = 4$.

To get rid of the fraction, we multiply both sides by 5.

$$\therefore \frac{^1\cancel{5}(x-1)}{\cancel{5}_1} = 4 \times 5$$

$$x - 1 = 20$$

$$x - 1 + 1 = 20 + 1$$

$$x = 21$$

> If an equation contains more than one fraction, we multiply each part by the lowest common multiple (LCM) of the denominators.

---

**Example 1**

Solve each of these equations:

(i) $\dfrac{3x}{4} - \dfrac{x}{2} = 3$

(ii) $\dfrac{2x - 5}{3} = \dfrac{x - 2}{2}$

(i) The LCM of 4 and 2 is 4.
Multiply each term by 4.

$$\dfrac{4(3x)}{4} - \dfrac{4(x)}{2} = 3 \times 4$$

$$3x - 2x = 12$$

$$x = 12$$

(ii) The LCM of 3 and 2 is 6.
Multiply each term by 6.

$$\dfrac{6(2x - 5)}{3} = \dfrac{6(x - 2)}{2}$$

$$2(2x - 5) = 3(x - 2)$$

$$4x - 10 = 3x - 6$$

$$4x - 3x - 10 = 3x - 3x - 6$$

$$x - 10 = -6$$

$$x - 10 + 10 = -6 + 10$$

$$x = 4$$

**Note:** the introduction of brackets in the example above.

---

**Example 2**

Solve the equation: $\dfrac{3x - 1}{6} - \dfrac{x - 3}{4} = \dfrac{4}{3}$

The LCM of 6, 4 and 3 is 12.
We now multiply each term by 12.

$$\dfrac{12(3x - 1)}{6} - \dfrac{12(x - 3)}{4} = \dfrac{12(4)}{3}$$

$$2(3x - 1) - 3(x - 3) = 4(4)$$

$$6x - 2 - 3x + 9 = 16$$

$$3x + 7 = 16$$

$$3x + 7 - 7 = 16 - 7$$

$$3x = 9$$

$$x = 3$$

## Exercise 20.4

Solve the following equations:

**1.** $\dfrac{x}{2} = 3$

**2.** $\dfrac{x}{4} = 5$

**3.** $\dfrac{2x}{3} = 6$

**4.** $\dfrac{3x}{5} = 3$

**5.** $\dfrac{2x}{3} = \dfrac{14}{3}$

**6.** $\dfrac{2x}{5} = \dfrac{6}{5}$

**7.** $\dfrac{x}{2} = \dfrac{6}{4}$

**8.** $\dfrac{2x}{9} = \dfrac{2}{3}$

**9.** $\dfrac{3x}{4} = \dfrac{9}{2}$

**10.** $\dfrac{5x}{3} = 10$

**11.** $\dfrac{3x}{8} = \dfrac{3}{2}$

**12.** $\dfrac{x-3}{2} = 4$

**13.** $\dfrac{3x-1}{4} = 4$

**14.** $\dfrac{2x+1}{5} = 1$

**15.** $\dfrac{4x-3}{7} = 3$

**16.** $\dfrac{3x-1}{4} = 8$

**17.** $\dfrac{4x+2}{7} = 2$

**18.** $\dfrac{3x-2}{3} = \dfrac{16}{3}$

**19.** $\dfrac{x-3}{3} = \dfrac{x-2}{4}$

**20.** $\dfrac{4x-7}{6} = \dfrac{x+2}{4}$

**21.** $\dfrac{x-1}{2} = \dfrac{2x+1}{5}$

**22.** $\dfrac{x}{2} + \dfrac{x}{3} = 5$

**23.** $\dfrac{x}{3} + \dfrac{x}{6} = 2$

**24.** $\dfrac{x}{2} + \dfrac{2x}{5} = \dfrac{9}{2}$

**25.** $\dfrac{x}{3} - \dfrac{x}{5} = \dfrac{4}{3}$

**26.** $\dfrac{x}{3} - \dfrac{x}{12} = \dfrac{1}{4}$

**27.** $\dfrac{2x}{3} - \dfrac{x}{4} = \dfrac{5}{6}$

**28.** $\dfrac{3x}{4} - \dfrac{x}{2} = 3$

**29.** $\dfrac{x}{3} + \dfrac{2x}{5} = \dfrac{11}{15}$

**30.** $\dfrac{3x}{4} - \dfrac{5x}{8} = \dfrac{1}{2}$

**31.** $\dfrac{3x}{4} - \dfrac{2x}{3} = \dfrac{1}{4}$

**32.** $\dfrac{3x}{2} + \dfrac{2x}{3} = 13$

**33.** $\dfrac{2x}{3} - \dfrac{x}{4} = \dfrac{5}{2}$

**34.** $\dfrac{5x}{6} - \dfrac{x}{2} = 3$

**35.** $\dfrac{3x}{4} - \dfrac{2x}{3} = \dfrac{5}{12}$

**36.** $\dfrac{4x}{5} - \dfrac{x}{2} = \dfrac{3}{4}$

**37.** $\dfrac{2x-1}{5} = \dfrac{x}{3} + \dfrac{1}{3}$

**38.** $\dfrac{2x+3}{5} + \dfrac{x}{2} = 6$

**39.** $\dfrac{x+1}{4} - \dfrac{x}{3} = \dfrac{1}{12}$

**40.** $\dfrac{2x-1}{3} + \dfrac{x}{4} = \dfrac{6}{4}$

**41.** $\dfrac{x+4}{3} - \dfrac{x}{4} = 2$

**42.** $\dfrac{x}{5} - \dfrac{3}{2} = \dfrac{x-3}{6}$

**43.** The diagram shows an isosceles triangle ABC.

If $|AB| = |AC|$,

   (i)  write down an equation in terms of $x$

  (ii)  work out the length of [AB].

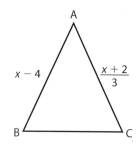

# Section 20.5 Solving problems involving fractions ———

The ability to change a problem expressed in words into a mathematical sentence is very important in mathematics.

You will already have changed statements like that shown on the right into mathematical sentences.

> I think of a number.
> I take off 5.
> I multiply the result by 3.
> My answer is 21.
> What is my number?

Discuss which one of these equations you should use to solve this puzzle.

$$3x - 5 = 21$$   $$3(x - 5) = 21$$   $$x - 5 \times 3 = 21$$

In this section we will deal with some simple problems that involve the use of fractions.

---

**Example 1**

If the sum of a quarter of a number and a fifth of the same number is 18, find the number.

Let $x$ be the number.

$\frac{1}{4}$ of the number $= \frac{x}{4}$        $\frac{1}{5}$ of the number $= \frac{x}{5}$

The equation is: $\frac{x}{4} + \frac{x}{5} = 18$

Multiply each term by 20, the LCM of 4 and 5.

$$\frac{20(x)}{4} + \frac{20(x)}{5} = \frac{20(18)}{1}$$
$$5x + 4x = 360$$
$$9x = 360$$
$$x = 40$$

The required number is 40.

---

## Exercise 20.5

1. The sum of a number and half the number is 12. Find the number.

2. If the sum of half a number and a third of the same number is 15, find the number.

3. The sum of half and three quarters of a certain number is 20. What is this number?

4. When half a certain number is taken from three quarters of the number, the result is 5. Find the number.

5. One sister is 5 years older than her brother. If the sister's age is divided by 4, the answer is 3. Find the age of her brother.

6. When 5 is added to a number and the result is divided by 4, the answer is 3. Work out what this number is.

7. When 3 is taken from four times a certain number and the result is divided by 7, the answer is 3. Find the number.

8. When two thirds of a certain number is taken from three quarters of the number, the answer is 2. Find the number.

9. Jamie says that he has €x in his pocket. If he adds €8 to what he has and divides by 3, he would get the same answer as he would get if he halved the amount he had in his pocket. Find how much money Jamie has in his pocket.

10. Sandra is 3 years older than Izzy. When one sixth of Sandra's age is taken from one third of Izzy's age, the result is 2. Find their ages.

## Section 20.6  Simplifying algebraic fractions

The fraction $\frac{8}{12}$ can be simplified by dividing the numerator and denominator by 4, as shown.

$$\frac{{}^{2}\cancel{8}}{{}_{3}\cancel{12}} = \frac{2}{3}$$

Similarly, the algebraic fraction $\frac{4ab}{2b}$ can be simplified by dividing the numerator and denominator by any common factors.

Thus, $\dfrac{4ab}{2b} = \dfrac{{}^{2}\cancel{4} \times a \times \cancel{b}^{1}}{{}_{1}\cancel{2} \times \cancel{b}_{1}} = \dfrac{2 \times a}{1} = 2 \times a = 2a$

---

**Example 1**

Simplify each of the following:

(i) $\dfrac{9x^2y}{3x}$

(ii) $\dfrac{12a^3b}{ab^2}$

(i) $\dfrac{9x^2y}{3x} = \dfrac{{}^3\cancel{9} \times \cancel{x}^1 \times x \times y}{{}_1\cancel{3} \times \cancel{x}_1}$

$= 3xy$

(ii) $\dfrac{12a^3b}{ab^2} = \dfrac{12 \times a \times a \times \cancel{a}^1 \times \cancel{b}^1}{{}_1\cancel{a} \times b \times \cancel{b}_1}$

$= \dfrac{12a^2}{b}$

---

## Using factors to simplify algebraic fractions

The expression $\dfrac{x^2 - 4}{x + 2}$ can be simplified by first factorising the numerator and then dividing above and below by a common factor.

$$\frac{x^2 - 4}{x + 2} = \frac{\cancel{(x + 2)}^1 (x - 2)}{\cancel{(x + 2)}_1} = x - 2$$

---

**Example 2**

Simplify   (i) $\dfrac{5a - 10b}{2a - 4b}$

(ii) $\dfrac{a^2 + 2a}{a^2 + 3a + 2}.$

(i) $\dfrac{5a - 10b}{2a - 4b} = \dfrac{5\cancel{(a - 2b)}^1}{2\cancel{(a - 2b)}_1}$

$= \dfrac{5}{2}$

(ii) $\dfrac{a^2 + 2a}{a^2 + 3a + 2} = \dfrac{a\cancel{(a + 2)}^1}{\cancel{(a + 2)}_1(a + 1)}$

$= \dfrac{a}{a + 1}$

---

**Note:** To simplify algebraic fractions it is important to fully factorise the numerator and denominator. In chapter 4 the following methods were outlined:

(i) $3x - 12y = 3(x - 4y)$

(ii) $3xs + 6xt + ys + 2yt = (3x + y)(s + 2t)$

(iii) $x^2 - 36 = (x - 6)(x + 6)$

(iv) $x^2 - 4x - 5 = (x + 1)(x - 5)$

## Exercise 20.6

**1.** Simplify each of the following algebraic fractions:

(i) $\dfrac{10ab}{2b}$  (ii) $\dfrac{8xy}{4x}$  (iii) $\dfrac{15cd}{5d}$  (iv) $\dfrac{18ab}{6a}$

(v) $\dfrac{8x^2y}{4xy}$  (vi) $\dfrac{16b^2c}{2c}$  (vii) $\dfrac{14x^3y}{2x^2y}$  (viii) $\dfrac{28ab^2}{7ab}$

**2.** Simplify these expressions:

(i) $\dfrac{3}{x} \times \dfrac{4x}{9}$  (ii) $\dfrac{km}{4n} \times \dfrac{2n}{m}$  (iii) $\dfrac{ab}{3} \times \dfrac{6b}{a}$  (iv) $\dfrac{2ab \times 6a}{3a}$

(v) $\dfrac{x}{3} \div \dfrac{x}{6}$  (vi) $\dfrac{3}{2x} \div \dfrac{1}{3x}$  (vii) $\dfrac{3ab^2}{2} \div \dfrac{ab}{6}$  (viii) $\dfrac{8a \times 3ak}{2a \times 6k}$

**3.**

| A | E | G | L | M | N | O | P | R |
|---|---|---|---|---|---|---|---|---|
| $2b$ | $4bc$ | $bc^2$ | $4d$ | $cd$ | $2b^2$ | $3bd$ | $3c$ | $2b^2d$ |

Simplify each expression below as far as you can.
Use the code above to find a letter for each expression.

Rearrange each set of letters to spell a fruit.

(i) $\dfrac{8cd}{2c}$ $\quad$ $\dfrac{12bc}{3}$ $\quad$ $\dfrac{15cd}{5d}$ $\quad$ $\dfrac{4bc}{2c}$ $\quad$ $\dfrac{9c^2b}{3cb}$

(ii) $\dfrac{18b^2d}{6b}$ $\quad$ $\dfrac{10ab^2}{5a}$ $\quad$ $\dfrac{20b^2c^2}{5bc}$ $\quad$ $\dfrac{12cd^5}{3cd^4}$ $\quad$ $\dfrac{5c^2d}{5c}$

Simplify each of the following, using factors where necessary:

**4.** $\dfrac{6(a + b)}{3}$  **5.** $\dfrac{4x + 4y}{4}$  **6.** $\dfrac{12(a + b)}{3(a + b)}$

**7.** $\dfrac{3(x + y)}{6x + 6y}$  **8.** $\dfrac{4a - 8b}{3(a - 2b)}$  **9.** $\dfrac{3x + 12}{x(x + 4)}$

**10.** $\dfrac{2a - 3b}{6a - 9b}$  **11.** $\dfrac{3(x + y)(x + y)}{3x + 3y}$  **12.** $\dfrac{x(x - 2y)}{3x - 6y}$

**13.** $\dfrac{2x + 4y}{x^2 + 2xy}$  **14.** $\dfrac{x + 2y}{(x + y)(x + 2y)}$  **15.** $\dfrac{x^2 - y^2}{2(x + y)}$

**16.** $\dfrac{x + 3}{x^2 + 6x + 9}$  **17.** $\dfrac{x^2 + 5x + 4}{x + 1}$  **18.** $\dfrac{x^2 - 2x - 3}{2(x - 3)}$

**19.** $\dfrac{x + 4}{x^2 + 2x - 8}$  **20.** $\dfrac{x^2 + 2x - 24}{x - 4}$  **21.** $\dfrac{x^2 - x}{x - 1}$

**22.** $\dfrac{x^2 - 9}{x^2 - x - 6}$  **23.** $\dfrac{x^2 + 3x - 10}{x^2 - 4}$  **24.** $\dfrac{x^2 + 4x - 5}{x - 1}$

**25.** $\dfrac{3(x^2 - 4y^2)}{9(x + 2y)}$  **26.** $\dfrac{x^2 - 2x - 15}{4x + 12}$  **27.** $\dfrac{x^2 + 2x - 35}{x^2 - 25}$

## Test yourself 20

1.  (i)  For what values of $x$ is $2x - 3 \leqslant 7, x \in N$?

    (ii)  Express as a single fraction $\dfrac{x + 3}{4} + \dfrac{2x}{3}$.

2.  (i)  Simplify $\dfrac{5ab}{c} \times \dfrac{ac}{10b}$.

    (ii)  Solve the equation $\dfrac{2x}{5} = 4$.

3.  If $x \in N$, state the values $x$ may have in each of the following:

    (i)  $x \leqslant 6$          (ii)  $x \geqslant 2$ and $x < 9$          (iii)  $2x + 1 < 13$.

4.  (i)  Solve the following inequality and graph the solution on the number line:

    $3x - 2 \geqslant 4, x \in N$

    (ii)  List all the integers, $x$, for which $x^2 < 17$.

5.  (i)  Express as a single fraction $\dfrac{2x + 3}{3} + \dfrac{x - 1}{2}$

    (ii)  Using your answer to (i) solve the equation $\dfrac{2x + 3}{3} + \dfrac{x - 1}{2} = 4$

    (iii)  Verify your answer.

6.  (i)  Use factors to simplify $\dfrac{x^2 - x - 6}{x + 2}$

    (ii)  Hence, solve the equation, $\dfrac{x^2 - x - 6}{x + 2} = 2$.

7.  Simplify each of these:

    (i)  $\dfrac{6x^2y}{3xy}$          (ii)  $\dfrac{10x}{7} \times \dfrac{14y^2}{5xy}$

8.  Solve the following inequality and graph the solution on the number line:

    $3x - 7 \geqslant x - 3, x \in R$.

9.  Solve the equation $\dfrac{3x}{4} - \dfrac{5x}{8} = \dfrac{3}{8}$.

10.  Write down the inequality represented by each of the following number lines, where $x \in Z$ in each case:

    (i)          (ii)

**11.** Solve each of these equations:

(i) $\dfrac{2x + 1}{3} = 7$

(ii) $\dfrac{4x + 4}{3} = \dfrac{3x - 1}{2}$

**12.** Simplify each of these:

(i) $\dfrac{11a^2b}{33ab^2}$

(ii) $\dfrac{x^2 + 3x - 18}{x + 6}$

**13.** Solve this inequality and graph your solution on the number line:

$$4x + 2 \leqslant -10, x \in Z.$$

**14.** Express as a single fraction $\dfrac{2x + 4}{3} - \dfrac{x - 6}{4}$.

**15.** One number is 5 bigger than another number. When twice the smaller number is added to two thirds of the bigger number, the result is 14.
Find the two numbers.

**16.** (i) If $x \in Z$, state the values $x$ may have for this inequality:

$$x \geqslant -3 \text{ and } x < 3.$$

(ii) Write down all the values of $x$ for which $4x - 5 < x + 10, x \in N$.

**17.** Use factors to simplify $\dfrac{x^2 + 3x - 10}{x - 2}$ and hence solve $\dfrac{x^2 + 3x - 10}{x - 2} = 6$.
Verify your answer.

**18.** The equal sides in this triangle are marked.
Write an equation in $x$ and solve it to find its value.
Hence find the length of the equal sides.

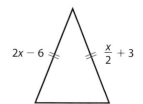

## Assignment:

Draw a large poster comparing two methods for solving the inequality, $7 - 3x \leqslant 1$, by (A) keeping the variable on the left-hand side and solving or (B) bringing the variable to the right-hand side and solving.

Add a note on each line to explain the procedure.

| Method A | Method B |
|---|---|
| $7 - 3x \leqslant 1$ | $7 - 3x \leqslant 1$ |

# chapter 21

# Functions

## In this chapter, you will learn to:

- understand the terms input and output in relation to a function,
- recognise that a function is a rule that produces one output value only for each input value,
- use the terms domain, range, co-domain and couple when describing functions,
- calculate missing operations in a function,
- draw and understand mapping diagrams,
- correctly identify a function,
- understand the notation used to write functions,
- evaluate functions for given values.

## Section 21.1  Functions

Each term in the number sequence below is found by adding 4 to the previous term:

3    7    11    15    19

+4   +4   +4   +4    … 'Add 4' is the **rule** for finding the next term.

Now consider this sequence:

2    6    18    54

×3   ×3   ×3    … Here the rule is 'multiply by 3'

The next number in the sequence is  54 × 3, i.e. 162.
When the operation '×3' is applied to 54, we get 162.
We use the words **input** for 54 and **output** for 162.

The chain of diagrams below shows how we can find the output if we are given the input by means of a **function machine** or **flowchart**.

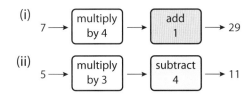

(i)
7 → [multiply by 4] → [add 1] → 29    If the input is 7, the output is  7 × 4 + 1 = 29.

(ii)
5 → [multiply by 3] → [subtract 4] → 11    If the input is 5, the output is 5 × 3 − 4 = 11.

If we call the input number $x$ and the output number $y$, we can then write the 'rule' in terms of $x$ and $y$.

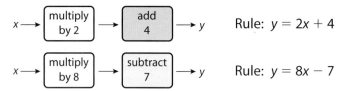

The rule for this function machine is 'multiply by 3, then add 2'.

We can write this as $x \times 3 + 2 = y$ or $y = 3x + 2$.

Here are the rules for these function machines:

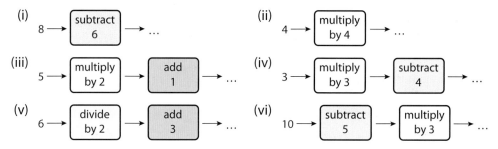

Rule: $y = 2x + 4$

Rule: $y = 8x - 7$

The rule $y = 2x + 4$ may also be written as $x \rightarrow 2x + 4$.

## Exercise 21.1

**1.** Find the output for each of these:

(i) 8 → subtract 6 → ...

(ii) 4 → multiply by 4 → ...

(iii) 5 → multiply by 2 → add 1 → ...

(iv) 3 → multiply by 3 → subtract 4 → ...

(v) 6 → divide by 2 → add 3 → ...

(vi) 10 → subtract 5 → multiply by 3 → ...

**2.** Describe in **words** the rule for each function machine in Question **1.** above.

**3.** Find the outputs for these:

(i) 3, 7, 8 → multiply by 2 → subtract 4 → ...

(ii) 2, 1, 0 → add 4 → multiply by 2 → ...

**4.**

$x$ → add 2 → multiply by 3 → $y$     is a function machine.

Use a copy of this table and fill in the values for $y$.

| $x$ | 1 | 2 | 3 | 4 | 5 |
|-----|---|---|---|---|---|
| $y$ |   |   |   |   |   |

Write in words what this function machine does.

**5.** Write the rules for these function machines as $y = \ldots$

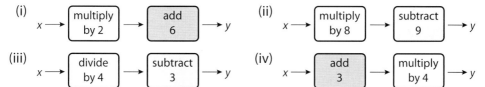

(i)
$x \rightarrow$ [multiply by 2] $\rightarrow$ [add 6] $\rightarrow y$

(ii)
$x \rightarrow$ [multiply by 8] $\rightarrow$ [subtract 9] $\rightarrow y$

(iii)
$x \rightarrow$ [divide by 4] $\rightarrow$ [subtract 3] $\rightarrow y$

(iv)
$x \rightarrow$ [add 3] $\rightarrow$ [multiply by 4] $\rightarrow y$

**6.** Write the rules for these function machines in the form $x \rightarrow \ldots$

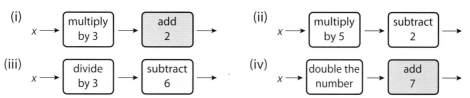

(i)
$x \rightarrow$ [multiply by 3] $\rightarrow$ [add 2] $\rightarrow$

(ii)
$x \rightarrow$ [multiply by 5] $\rightarrow$ [subtract 2] $\rightarrow$

(iii)
$x \rightarrow$ [divide by 3] $\rightarrow$ [subtract 6] $\rightarrow$

(iv)
$x \rightarrow$ [double the number] $\rightarrow$ [add 7] $\rightarrow$

**7.** Find the missing operation in each of these:

(i)
$3 \rightarrow$
$5 \rightarrow$ [?]
$8 \rightarrow$
$\rightarrow 15$
$\rightarrow 25$
$\rightarrow 40$

(ii)
$9 \rightarrow$
$1 \rightarrow$ [?]
$15 \rightarrow$
$\rightarrow 13$
$\rightarrow 5$
$\rightarrow 19$

(iii)
$24 \rightarrow$
$16 \rightarrow$ [?]
$100 \rightarrow$
$\rightarrow 6$
$\rightarrow 4$
$\rightarrow 25$

**8.** Find the missing operations in these function machines:

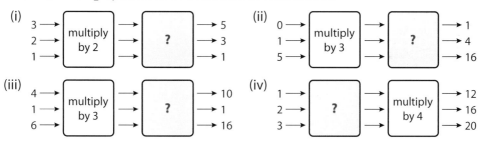

(i)
$3 \rightarrow$
$2 \rightarrow$ [multiply by 2] $\rightarrow$ [?]
$1 \rightarrow$
$\rightarrow 5$
$\rightarrow 3$
$\rightarrow 1$

(ii)
$0 \rightarrow$
$1 \rightarrow$ [multiply by 3] $\rightarrow$ [?]
$5 \rightarrow$
$\rightarrow 1$
$\rightarrow 4$
$\rightarrow 16$

(iii)
$4 \rightarrow$
$1 \rightarrow$ [multiply by 3] $\rightarrow$ [?]
$6 \rightarrow$
$\rightarrow 10$
$\rightarrow 1$
$\rightarrow 16$

(iv)
$1 \rightarrow$
$2 \rightarrow$ [?] $\rightarrow$ [multiply by 4]
$3 \rightarrow$
$\rightarrow 12$
$\rightarrow 16$
$\rightarrow 20$

**9.** What numbers went into each of these function machines?

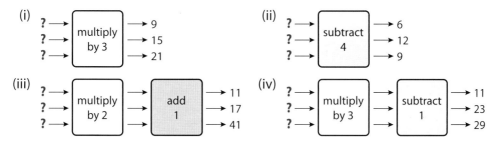

(i)
$? \rightarrow$
$? \rightarrow$ [multiply by 3]
$? \rightarrow$
$\rightarrow 9$
$\rightarrow 15$
$\rightarrow 21$

(ii)
$? \rightarrow$
$? \rightarrow$ [subtract 4]
$? \rightarrow$
$\rightarrow 6$
$\rightarrow 12$
$\rightarrow 9$

(iii)
$? \rightarrow$
$? \rightarrow$ [multiply by 2] $\rightarrow$ [add 1]
$? \rightarrow$
$\rightarrow 11$
$\rightarrow 17$
$\rightarrow 41$

(iv)
$? \rightarrow$
$? \rightarrow$ [multiply by 3] $\rightarrow$ [subtract 1]
$? \rightarrow$
$\rightarrow 11$
$\rightarrow 23$
$\rightarrow 29$

## Section 21.2  Mapping diagrams

Consider this function machine:  ... ⟶ | multiply by 3 | ⟶ | subtract 4 | ⟶ ...

We will input all the numbers from the set  {1, 3, 5, 7, 9}  into the function machine.

The output numbers are:  {−1, 5, 11, 17, 23}.

The set of input numbers is called the **domain.**

The set of output numbers is called the **range.**

The input numbers and output numbers can be represented by a special type of diagram called a **mapping diagram.**

Each input number is mapped onto its corresponding output number.

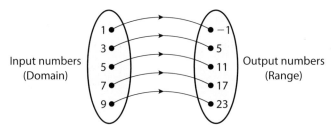

In the mapping diagram above, notice that there is one and **only one output number for each input number.**

> In mathematics, we use the word **function** for any rule that produces one output value only for each input value.

## Notation for a function

Consider this rule for a function:  "Double the number and add 4".

If we input $x$, the output will be  $2x + 4$.

The rule for this function may be written in any one of these three ways:

- (i)  $f(x) = 2x + 4$
- (ii)  $f: x \rightarrow 2x + 4$
- (iii)  $y = 2x + 4$.

These three notations tell us that if the input is 3, the output ($2x + 4$) is  $[(2 \times 3) + 4]$, i.e. 10.

This can be written as  $f(3) = 10$.

## The codomain

Take the two sets A = {1, 2, 3} and B = {1, 3, 5, 7, 9, 11}.
If we are asked to list the couples of the function $f: x \rightarrow 2x - 1$,
where the input numbers come from set A and the output
numbers come from set B, we could set up a mapping
diagram as follows:

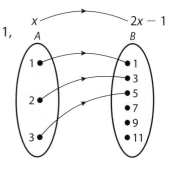

The couples are (1, 1), (2, 3) and (3, 5).

The set A is the **domain**, i.e. {1, 2, 3}.

The **range** is {1, 3, 5}.

The set B is called the **codomain**,
that is, the set of allowable
outputs.

∴ the codomain = {1, 3, 5, 7, 9, 11}.

The set of inputs is called the **domain**.

The set of outputs is called the **range**.

The set of possible outputs is called the **codomain**.

---

( **Example 1** )

A function $f$ is defined as $f: x \rightarrow 3x - 2$.
The domain of $f$ is {0, 1, 2, 3, 4}.
Represent $f$ on a mapping diagram and write out the couples generated.
What is the range of $f$?

| x | 3x − 2 | f(x) |
|---|--------|------|
| 0 | 0 − 2 | −2 |
| 1 | 3 − 2 | 1 |
| 2 | 6 − 2 | 4 |
| 3 | 9 − 2 | 7 |
| 4 | 12 − 2 | 10 |

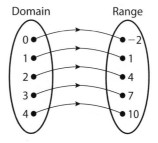

The couples are: {(0, −2), (1, 1), (2, 4), (3, 7), (4, 10)}.
The range is {−2, 1, 4, 7, 10}.

## Identifying functions

When a function is represented by a mapping diagram, each element of the domain
maps onto **one and only one** element of the range.

Consider these two mapping diagrams:

(i)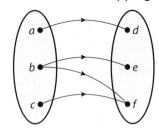
(ii)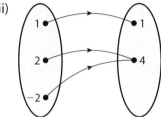

Diagram (i) is not a function because the element *b* is paired with 2 elements (*e* and *f*) in the range.

Diagram (ii) is a function because each element in the domain is mapped onto one and only one element in the range.

## Couples

We have already seen that a function can be written as a set of **couples** or **ordered pairs**, i.e. (input, output).

When a function is written as a set of couples, no two distinct couples will have the same input.

➤ {(1, 4), (2, 5), (3, 6), (4, 7)} is a function as no two couples have the same input.

➤ {(2, 7), (3, 8), (3, 9), (4, 12)} is **not** a function as the input 3 has two different outputs.

## Exercise 21.2

**1.** Use the given mapping diagram to write down

   (i)   the domain
   (ii)  the range
   (iii)  the set of couples formed
   (iv)  the rule that gives the outputs.

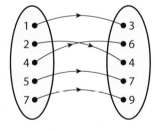

**2.** Copy and complete the mapping diagrams below. Write down the domain and range of each function.

(i)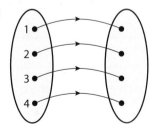
(ii)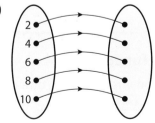

          Rule:  Add 5
                              Rule:  $x \rightarrow 2x + 1$

**3.** State whether each of the following mapping diagrams represents a function.
Give a reason for your answer in each case:

(i)
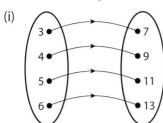

(ii)
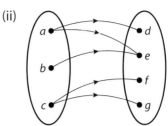

(iii)
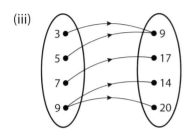

(iv)
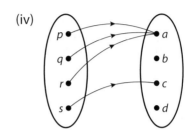

**4.** Say why the following set of couples is a function:

$\{(1, 7), (2, 8), (3, 9), (4, 10)\}$.

**5.** Say why the following set of couples is not a function:

$\{(2, 5), (3, 6), (5, 8), (2, 10)\}$.

**6.** Investigate if each of these sets of couples represents a function.
If it is not a function, state the reason why.

   (i)  $\{(0, 0), (1, 1), (2, 4), (3, 9), (4, 16)\}$
  (ii)  $\{(-2, 1), (-1, 3), (-2, 5), (1, 6), (2, 9)\}$
 (iii)  $\{(-3, 4), (0, 7), (2, 9), (4, 11)\}$

**7.** The flowchart $x \longrightarrow$ [add 3] $\longrightarrow$ [multiply by 2] $\longrightarrow y$ shows how to find the output ($y$)

for any input ($x$).

Express this in the form $y = \ldots\ldots$.

Use this function to find the values
of the outputs in the given table.

| Input (x) | Output (y) |
|-----------|------------|
| 1 | |
| 2 | |
| 3 | |
| 4 | |
| 5 | |

**8.** For each of the mapping diagrams below, write down

    (i)  the domain      (ii)  the range      (iii)  the codomain.

    (a)                                        (b)

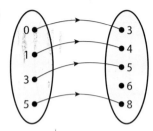

**9.** The rule for a function is: 'Multiply by 2 and add 3'.
If the domain of the function is {0, 1, 3, 5}, write down

    (i)  the range
    (ii)  the couples generated.

**10.** A function $f$ is defined as $f: x \rightarrow 3x - 1$.
The domain of the function is {1, 2, 4, 6}.
Write down the range of the function.

**11.** A function $f$ is defined as $f(x) = 4x - 5$.
The domain of the function is {−2, 0, 2, 4}.

    (i)  What is the range of $f$?
    (ii)  Write $f$ as a set of couples.

**12.** Make a copy of this table.
Fill it in for the function machine shown below.

| $x$ | 1 | 2 | 3 | 4 | 5 |
|---|---|---|---|---|---|
| $y$ | | | | | |

$x \longrightarrow$ [multiply by 2] $\longrightarrow$ [add 7] $\longrightarrow y$

Write the function in the form $y = \ldots\ldots$ .

**13.** This is a function machine:
Write the function in the form
$f(x) = \ldots\ldots$ .

$x \longrightarrow$ [multiply by 4] $\longrightarrow$ [add 10] $\longrightarrow y$

If the input is 5, what is the output?
Use the function rule to find the input when the output is 22.

**14.** $x \longrightarrow$ [multiply by 2] $\longrightarrow$ [add 4] $\longrightarrow y$ describes a function.

Copy the table on the right and fill in
the missing input and output numbers.

| Input ($x$) | Output ($y$) |
|---|---|
| 3 | |
| −2 | |
| | 14 |
| | −8 |

## Section 21.3 Notation for functions

We have already seen that a function can be written in any of these ways:

(i) $f(x) = 3x - 2$        (ii) $f : x \rightarrow 3x - 2$        (iii) $y = 3x - 2$

In each case, the output is $(3x - 2)$ when the input is $x$.

The notation **f(3)** is used to represent the output number when 3 is the input number.
If $f(x) = 3x - 2$
then $f(3) = 3(3) - 2 = 9 - 2 = 7$.

While $f(x)$ is generally used to describe a function, other letters such as $g(x)$ and $h(x)$ are used when we are dealing with more than one function.

---

**Example 1**

The functions $f$ and $g$ are defined as follows
$$f : x \rightarrow x + 5 \quad \text{and} \quad g : x \rightarrow x^2 - 1.$$
Find   (i) $f(3)$   (ii) $f(-4)$   (iii) $3f(-2)$   (iv) $g(4)$   (v) $g(-3)$

(i)   $f(x) = x + 5$            (ii)     $f(x) = x + 5$
     $f(3) = 3 + 5 = 8$                 $f(-4) = -4 + 5 = 1$

(iii)     $f(x) = x + 5$        (iv)   $g(x) = x^2 - 1$
    $3f(-2) = 3(-2 + 5)$           $g(4) = 4^2 - 1 = 16 - 1 = 15$
          $= 3(3) = 9$

(v)     $g(x) = x^2 - 1$
    $g(-3) = (-3)^2 - 1 = 9 - 1 = 8$

---

**Example 2**

$f(x) = 3x - 4$ defines a function.

(i)   If $f(x) = 5$, find the value of $x$.
(ii)   If $f(a) = 11$, find the value of $a$.

(i)       $f(x) = 3x - 4$        (ii)       $f(a) = 3a - 4$
    $\therefore \ 3x - 4 = 5$              $\therefore \ 3a - 4 = 11$
         $3x = 9$                  $3a = 15$
          $x = 3$                   $a = 5$

## Exercise 21.3

**1.** If $f(x) = 3x$, find
    (i) $f(1)$        (ii) $f(3)$        (iii) $f(4)$        (iv) $f(6)$        (v) $f(-2)$

**2.** If $f(x) = 2x + 3$, find
    (i) $f(2)$        (ii) $f(3)$        (iii) $f(5)$        (iv) $f(0)$        (v) $f(-3)$

**3.** If $f(x) = 3x - 1$, find
    (i) $f(1)$        (ii) $f(2)$        (iii) $f(4)$        (iv) $f(5)$        (v) $f(-1)$

**4.** If $f(x) = x^2 - 3$, find
    (i) $f(0)$        (ii) $f(1)$        (iii) $f(2)$        (iv) $f(-2)$        (v) $f(-4)$

**5.** If $f(x) = 5 - 2x$, find
    (i) $f(0)$        (ii) $f(2)$        (iii) $f(-3)$        (iv) $f(-\frac{1}{2})$        (v) $f(k)$

**6.** If $f(x) = 5x - 2$, solve the following equations:
    (i) $f(x) = 8$                (ii) $f(x) = 3$                (iii) $f(k) = -12$

**7.** If $f(x) = 2x - 5$, find
    (i) $f(3)$      (ii) $f(0)$      (iii) $f(1) + f(4)$      (iv) $2f(-3)$      (v) $f(3) + f(-3)$

**8.** If $f(x) = 3x - 2$ and $g(x) = 2 - 4x$, solve the following equations:
    (i) $f(x) = 4$            (ii) $g(x) = -10$           (iii) $g(x) = f(4)$

**9.** If $f(x) = 5x - 2$ and $x \in \{1, 2, 3, 4\}$, write down the four couples of the function.

**10.** A function is defined by $f : x \rightarrow x^2 + 3x - 2$. Find
    (i) $f(1)$        (ii) $f(2)$        (iii) $f(3)$        (iv) $f(0)$        (v) $f(-2)$

**11.** A function is defined by $f(x) = 5x - 4$.
    If the domain of $f$ is $\{0, 1, 2, 3, 4\}$, find the range of $f$.

**12.** $g : x \rightarrow 3x + 4$ is a function.
    (i) Find $g(4)$.        (ii) If $g(x) = 10$, find $x$.        (iii) If $g(k) = -2$, find $k$.

**13.** If $h(x) = 3x - 5$ which *one* of the following is not a couple of the function?
    (i) $(2, 1)$        (ii) $(4, 7)$        (iii) $(2, -1)$        (iv) $(0, -5)$

**14.** The domain of the function $f : x \rightarrow x^2 - 3x + 4$ is $\{-2, -1, 0, 1, 2\}$.
    (i) List the five couples of the function.
    (ii) Write down the range of the function.

## Test yourself 21

1. If $f(x) = 3x - 2$, find
   (i) $f(2)$    (ii) $f(0)$    (iii) $f(-2)$    (iv) $2f(2) + 3f(-1)$.

2. For the set of couples $\{(2, 3), (3, 6), (4, 8), (5, 18)\}$, write down
   (i) the domain    (ii) the range

3. $f(x) = 4x - 3$ defines a function.
   (i) Find $f(-2)$.
   (ii) If $f(x) = 9$, find the value of $x$.
   (iii) If $f(k) = -7$, find the value of $k$.

4. Use a copy of this table.
   Fill it in for the function machine,

   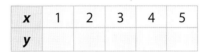

   | $x$ | 1 | 2 | 3 | 4 | 5 |
   |-----|---|---|---|---|---|
   | $y$ |   |   |   |   |   |

5. State whether each of these mapping diagrams represents a function, giving a reason for your answers:
   (i)
   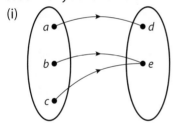
   (ii)
   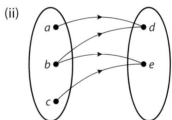

6. A function is defined by $f: x \rightarrow 4x - 5$.
   (i) Find $f(3)$ and $f(10)$.
   (ii) Find the value of $k$ when $f(10) = kf(3)$.

7. A function $f$ is defined by $f: x \rightarrow 5x - 1$.
   If the domain of $f = \{0, 1, 2, 3\}$, find the range of $f$.

8. State why the set of couples $\{(1, 3), (2, 7), (3, 10), (1, 12)\}$ is not a function.

9. $f(x) = ax - 6$ is a function.
   If $f(2) = -2$, find the value of $a$.

10. What operation does the question mark stand for in the given function machine?

    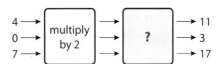

**11.** $f(x) = 3x - 4$ defines a function.
If the domain of $f$ is $\{-3, -2, -1, 0\}$,
what is the range of $f$?

**12.** The cost €$C$ of hiring a taxi is given by $C = 5k + 3$, where $k$ is the number of kilometres travelled.
   (i)  Find the cost of hiring a taxi for a journey of 8 kilometres.
   (ii)  If the cost of a journey was €23, how long was the journey?

**13.** Find the output number for each input number in the function machines below:

   (i)  $2, 0, -3, 7$   →   [multiply by 3] → [add 4] → $—, —, —, —$

   (ii)  $9, 5, 0, -3$   →   [subtract 4] → [multiply by 2] → $—, —, —, —$

**14.** A function is defined as $f : x \rightarrow 4x - 2$.
Copy the mapping diagram and fill in
the missing numbers $a$, $b$ and $c$.

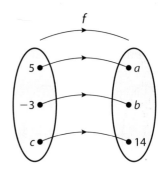

**15.** If $f(x) = 2x - 3$ and $g(x) = 3 - 5x$, solve these equations:
   (i)  $f(x) = 7$
   (ii)  $g(x) = -7$
   (iii)  $f(x) = g(-3)$.

**16.** A function $f$ is defined by $f : x \rightarrow 5x - 3$.
Copy and complete these three couples of $f$:
      $(1, *), \ (3, *), \ (0, *)$.

**17.** A function machine and three output numbers are given below.
Find the three input numbers.

   $—, —, —$  →  [subtract 4] → [multiply by 3] → $3, 12, 24$

**18.** The function $f$ is defined by $f(x) = 7 - 3x$.
If $f(24) = kf(-2)$, find the value of $k$.

## *Assignment:*

By copying the sets below, make a mapping poster for the given functions (use different colours for each mapping).

Beneath each one, emphasise the range and the codomain of each function.

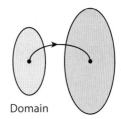

Domain

Mapping

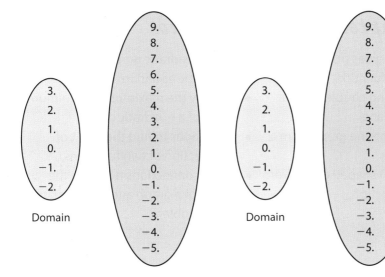

Rule: $f(x) = x^2$

Range = {       }

Codomain = {       }

Rule: $f(x) = x + 2$

Range = {       }

Codomain = {       }

# Graphing Functions

22

## From first year, you will recall how to:

- draw x and y axes, and label the origin,
- plot points onto a coordinated plane.

## In this chapter, you will learn to:

- input various values from a given domain into a function,
- plot the resulting couples onto a coordinated plane,
- create a straight-line graph from a linear function,
- create a ∪ or ∩ shaped graph from a quadratic function,
- use a quadratic graph to solve a quadratic equation,
- identify the maximum or minimum point of a quadratic graph,
- use graphs to find the point of intersection of two functions,
- make connections between the shape of a graph and an associated word problem.

## Section 22.1  Graphing linear functions

Consider the function  $f(x) = x + 3$.
This function can be written as a set of couples by taking different values for $x$.

$f(1) = 1 + 3 = 4 \Rightarrow (1, 4)$  is one couple.
$f(2) = 2 + 3 = 5 \Rightarrow (2, 5)$  is another couple.

Other couples are  $(0, 3), (-3, 0), \ldots$

When these couples are plotted and joined, they will form a line as shown.

Since the graph of  $f(x) = x + 3$  is a line, we say that $f(x)$ is a **linear function**.

A line is the most straightforward function to graph as we need only two points to plot it.

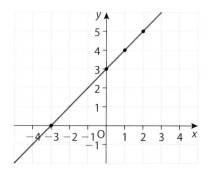

Usually we are given the **domain** in which to draw any function.
The domain  $x = -2$  to  $x = 3$, both included, is written as  $-2 \leqslant x \leqslant 3$.

416

When plotting a line, two points are sufficient to enable us to plot it, but we generally take three points in case any errors are made.

---

**Example 1**

Graph the function $f(x) = 2x - 4$ in the domain $-1 \leqslant x \leqslant 4$.
Use your graph to find
(i) $f(3)$      (ii) the value of $x$ for which $f(x) = -2$.

To find three points, we generally select the smallest and largest $x$-values in the given domain and one value for $x$ in between those two.

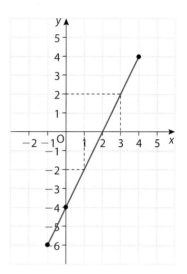

| $x$ | $2x - 4$ | $y$ |
|-----|----------|-----|
| $-1$ | $-2 - 4$ | $-6$ |
| $0$ | $0 - 4$ | $-4$ |
| $4$ | $8 - 4$ | $4$ |

The three points are $(-1, -6)$, $(0, -4)$ and $(4, 4)$.
Join these points to give a line.

(i) $f(3)$ represents the $y$-value when $x = 3$.
From the graph, this is 2, i.e. $f(3) = 2$.

(ii) $f(x) = -2 \Rightarrow y = -2$
The value of $x$ in the graph when $y = -2$ is $x = 1$.

---

*Remember*

**Horizontal lines,** i.e. lines parallel to the $x$-axis are written as $y = ?$

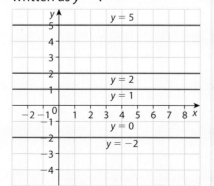

**Vertical lines,** i.e. lines parallel to the $y$-axis are written as $x = ?$

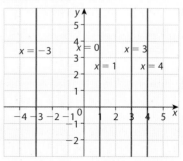

417

### The intercept method for drawing a line

If the equation of a line is in a form such as $3x - 4y = 12$, it is more convenient to find the two points where the line intersects the x-axis and y-axis.

$3x - 4y = 12$

$x = 0 \Rightarrow 0 - 4y = 12 \Rightarrow y = -3$

    $\therefore$ $(0, -3)$ is one point on the line.

$y = 0 \Rightarrow 3x = 12 \Rightarrow x = 4$

    $\therefore$ $(4, 0)$ is a second point on the line.

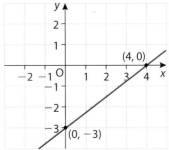

These points are joined to give the required line.

This method is generally called the **intercept method**.

### Exercise 22.1

**1.** Copy and complete the table on the right and use the table to draw the graph of the line $y = 2x - 3$ in the domain $-1 \leqslant x \leqslant 4$.

| x | 2x − 3 | y |
|---|--------|---|
| −1 | | |
| 0 | | |
| 1 | | |
| 2 | | |
| 3 | | |
| 4 | | |

**2.** Copy and complete the table on the right and hence draw the graph of the function $f(x) = 3x - 4$ in the domain $-1 \leqslant x \leqslant 3$.

| x | 3x − 4 | y |
|---|--------|---|
| −1 | | |
| 0 | | |
| 3 | | |

**3.** The equation of a line is $f(x) = 2x - 1$.
Find $f(1), f(2)$ and $f(3)$ and write down three points on the line.
Hence draw the graph of the line.

**4.** $f(x) = 3x - 2$ is the equation of a line.
Find $f(0), f(1)$ and $f(2)$ and hence draw the graph of the line.

**5.** $f(x) = 3x - 4$ is the equation of a line.
Find $f(1), f(2)$ and $f(3)$.
Plot the three points and hence draw the graph of the line.

**6.** Draw the graph of the function $f(x) = 6 - x$ in the domain $0 \leqslant x \leqslant 6$ by finding only three points on the line.

**7.** Draw the graph of the function $f(x) = 2x - 2$ in the domain $-2 \leqslant x \leqslant 3$.

**8.** Copy and complete the table on the right and hence draw the graph of the function $f(x) = 4 - 2x$ in the domain $0 \leqslant x \leqslant 3$.

| x | 4 − 2x | y |
|---|--------|---|
| 0 |        |   |
| 1 | 4 − 2  | 2 |
| 2 |        |   |
| 3 |        |   |

**9.** Draw the graph of $f(x) = 6 - 2x$ in the domain $0 \leqslant x \leqslant 5$.

**10.** Draw the graph of the line $f(x) = 3x - 5$ in the domain $0 \leqslant x \leqslant 3$.

**11.** A student is heating a liquid according to the formula $T = 2t + 10$, where T is measured in °C on the y-axis, and t is measured in minutes on the x-axis. Plot a graph of the temperature of the liquid over the first 5 minutes. What was the starting temperature of the liquid?

**12.** Pat's taxis charge customers using the formula $C = 3m + 4$, where C is the charge in euro and is measured on the y-axis, and m is the number of kilometres travelled and is measured on the x-axis. Draw a graph of this function. From the graph find the charge for a   (i)  4 km journey   (ii)  12 km journey.

**13.** Lucille plotted a graph for her experiment with Temperature on the y-axis and Time on the x-axis. Show that the rule for her graph is given by; $T(°C) = 18 - 4t$, where t is measured in minutes.

   (i)   What temperature did she record at the start of the experiment?
   (ii)  How long did it take for the temperature to go to 'freezing' point (0°C)?
   (iii) List two points on her graph.

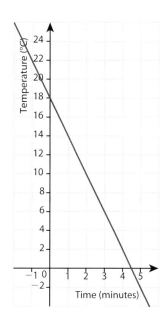

By finding the couples (∗, 0) and (0, ∗), sketch each of the following lines:

**14.** $y = 4 - x$      **15.** $y = x - 6$      **16.** $y = 2x + 4$      **17.** $2y = x + 2$

**18.** Drawn on the right is the graph of a function $y = f(x)$.

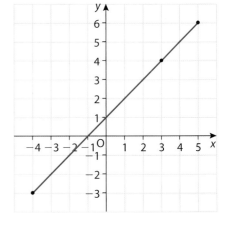

Use this graph to write down

  (i) $f(3)$      (ii) $f(0)$      (iii) $f(-4)$

  (iv) the value of $x$ when $f(x) = -2$

  (v) the value of $x$ when $f(x) = 6$.

**19.** On the same diagram, draw the lines $y = 5 - x$ and $y = 2x - 4$, in the domain $0 \leqslant x \leqslant 4$.

Use your graph to write down the point of intersection of the two lines.

## Investigation:

Caitlin's science project was to measure the height of a sunflower plant every week as it grew from a seed. On weeks 4 and 5 the school closed for holidays and she was not able to take measurements.

The graph of her results was as follows:

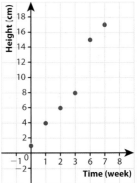

| Time (week) | 0 | 1 | 2 | 3 | 6 | 7 |
|---|---|---|---|---|---|---|
| Height (cm) | 1 | 4 | 6 | 8 | 15 | 17 |

Investigate her results and spot her mistake.

Draw a graph correcting her mistake.

Is the height of the plant a linear function of time?

Explain your answer.

# Section 22.2 Graphs of quadratic functions

The curve on the right is called a **parabola**.
The name parabola comes from the Greek word for
throw, because when a ball, for example, is thrown
high in the air, its path makes a parabolic shape.

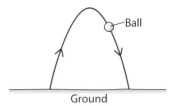

Suspension bridges, such as the
**Golden Gate Bridge** in San Francisco,
form parabolic curves.

The simplest quadratic function is $y = x^2$.
Its graph can be drawn from a table of values from $x = -3$ to $x = 3$.

| x | −3 | −2 | −1 | 0 | 1 | 2 | 3 |
|---|----|----|----|---|---|---|---|
| y | 9  | 4  | 1  | 0 | 1 | 4 | 9 |

The points shown on this curve are:
$(-3, 9), (-2, 4), (-1, 1), (0, 0), (1, 1), (2, 4), (3, 9)$.

When these points are joined, a smooth curve
called a parabola is formed.
Notice that the curve is symmetrical about the $y$-axis.
Hence the $y$-axis is called **the axis of symmetry**.

The function shown above may be written in one of
these three ways:

(i) $y = x^2$      (ii) $f(x) = x^2$      (iii) $f : x \rightarrow x^2$

A function in the form $f(x) = ax^2 + bx + c$, where $a, b$ and $c$ are constants and $a \neq 0$,
is called a **quadratic function**.
It is called a quadratic function because it contains a term in $x^2$.

To draw the **graph of a quadratic function**, we take a given number of $x$-values
(domain) and find the corresponding $f(x)$-values (or $y$-values) and then plot the resulting
points.
The domain values are usually written in the form; **$-2 \leqslant x \leqslant 3$**.

The steps used in drawing a quadratic graph are given in the following example.

---

**Example 1**

Draw the graph of the quadratic function $f(x) = x^2 - 2x - 3$ in the domain $-2 \leqslant x \leqslant 4$.

We set out a table of ordered pairs as follows:

| $x$ | $x^2 - 2x - 3$ | $y$ |
|-----|----------------|-----|
| $-2$ | $4 + 4 - 3$ | $5$ |
| $-1$ | $1 + 2 - 3$ | $0$ |
| $0$ | $0 + 0 - 3$ | $-3$ |
| $1$ | $1 - 2 - 3$ | $-4$ |
| $2$ | $4 - 4 - 3$ | $-3$ |
| $3$ | $9 - 6 - 3$ | $0$ |
| $4$ | $16 - 8 - 3$ | $5$ |

Plotting these ordered pairs, we get the following curve:

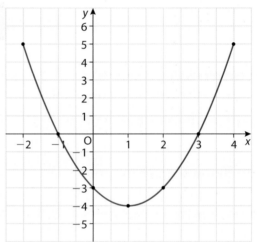

The ordered pairs found are:

$(-2, 5), (-1, 0), (0, -3), (1, -4),$
$(2, -3), (3, 0), (4, 5).$

---

## Graphing functions when the coefficient of $x^2$ is negative

If the coefficient of $x^2$ is negative in a quadratic function, e.g. $f(x) = -3x^2 + 4$, then the graph of the function will take the shape shown on the right.

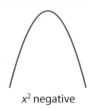

$x^2$ negative

**Example 2**

Draw the graph of the function $f(x) = -x^2 + 3x + 4$ in the domain $-2 \leqslant x \leqslant 5$.

The table of values is set out below:

| $x$ | $-x^2 + 3x + 4$ | $y$ |
|---|---|---|
| $-2$ | $-4 - 6 + 4$ | $-6$ |
| $-1$ | $-1 - 3 + 4$ | $0$ |
| $0$ | $0 + 0 + 4$ | $4$ |
| $1$ | $-1 + 3 + 4$ | $6$ |
| $2$ | $-4 + 6 + 4$ | $6$ |
| $3$ | $-9 + 9 + 4$ | $4$ |
| $4$ | $-16 + 12 + 4$ | $0$ |
| $5$ | $-25 + 15 + 4$ | $-6$ |

The required points are:
$(-2, -6), (-1, 0), (0, 4), (1, 6), (2, 6),$
$(3, 4), (4, 0), (5, -6)$.

The graph of the function is shown below:

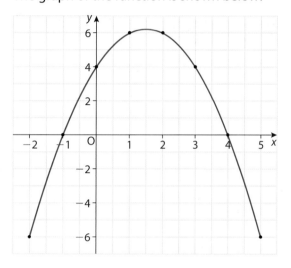

## Forming a table of values using a calculator

A scientific calculator can also be used to form a table of values for a given function.
e.g. $f(x) = x^2 + x - 4$, in the domain, $-3 \leqslant x \leqslant 4$

**Press mode** on the calculator, a window opens with 4 options.

**Press 3** for table and $f(x)$ appears on the screen.

The variable '$x$' is added to the function line by **Pressing Alpha** then **)** keys.

Now the main keys for '$x^2$', $+$, $-$, etc are used to complete the function.

The domain of the function is entered by **Pressing the '='** key. The calculator asks for the lowest value to **Start?** $(-3)$

**Pressing '='** again the calculator asks for the highest value to **End?** (4).

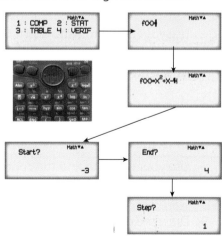

Finally **Pressing '='**, the calculator asks what **Step?** we want to use between (−3) and (4) and the default 1 means the calculator will find values of the function for $x = -3, -2, -1, 0, 1, 2, 3, 4$.

**Pressing '='** now a table of values is created in column form.

The points on the curve are:

$(-3, 2), (-2, -2), (-1, -4), (0, -4), (1, -2), (2, 2), (3, 8), (4, 16)$.

## Exercise 22.2

**1.** Complete the table on the right and hence draw the graph of the function  $f(x) = x^2 - 4$ in the domain $-3 \leqslant x \leqslant 3$.

| x | x² – 4 | y |
|---|--------|---|
| −3 | | |
| −2 | | |
| −1 | | |
| 0 | | |
| 1 | | |
| 2 | | |
| 3 | | |

**2.** Draw the graph of the function  $f : x \rightarrow x^2 - 4x$  in the domain $-1 \leqslant x \leqslant 4$.

**3.** Draw the graph of the function  $g(x) = x^2 + x - 2$  in the domain $-3 \leqslant x \leqslant 3$.

**4.** Draw the graph of the function  $f(x) = 2x^2 - x - 3$  in the domain $-2 \leqslant x \leqslant 3$.

**5.** Draw the graph of the function  $f(x) = 2x^2 + 3x - 4$  in the domain  $-3 \leqslant x \leqslant 2$.

**6.** Draw the graph of the function  $h(x) = 2x^2 - 5x - 3$  in the domain  $-2 \leqslant x \leqslant 4$.
Use your graph to write down the coordinates of the points at which the graph crosses the x-axis.
Now write down the coordinates of the point where the graph crosses the y-axis.

**7.** Draw the graph of the function  $y = -x^2$  in the domain  $-2 \leqslant x \leqslant 2$.

**8.** Draw the graph of the function  $f : x \rightarrow -x^2 + 2x + 3$  in the domain  $-2 \leqslant x \leqslant 4$.
Use your graph to find the coordinates of the points where the graph crosses the x-axis.

**9.** Draw the graph of the function  $f : x \rightarrow -2x^2 + x + 3$  in the domain  $-2 \leqslant x \leqslant 3$.
Write down the values of x at which the curve crosses the x-axis.

**10.** Graph the function $f(x) = -2x^2 + 7x - 3$ in the domain $-1 \leqslant x \leqslant 4$.

(i) Use the graph to write down the coordinates of the points at which the graph intersects the x-axis.

(ii) Write down the coordinates of the point where the graph crosses the y-axis.

## Section 22.3 Using quadratic graphs

### 1. Solving the equation $f(x) = 0$

The graph on the right shows the curve $f(x) = x^2 - 2x - 3$ intersecting the x-axis at A and B.

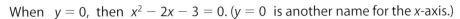

The x-values of these points are the roots of the associated quadratic equation
$$x^2 - 2x - 3 = 0.$$
Why is this?

$f(x) = x^2 - 2x - 3$ may be also written as $y = x^2 - 2x - 3$.

When $y = 0$, then $x^2 - 2x - 3 = 0$. ($y = 0$ is another name for the x-axis.)

Thus the solution of the equation $x^2 - 2x - 3 = 0$, gives the x-values of the points at which $y = x^2 - 2x - 3$ meets $y = 0$ i.e. where the curve crosses the x-axis.

The values are $x = 3$ and $x = -1$ (when $y = 0$).

### 2. Solving the equation $f(x) = k$, where $k \in R$

The graph of the function $f(x) = x^2 - 3x$ is drawn below.

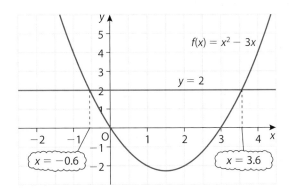

This graph can be used to solve the equation $f(x) = 2$ (or $y = 2$) by drawing the line $y = 2$ and then reading from the graph the x-values of the points where the line $y = 2$ intersects the curve.

These values are $x = -0.6$ or $x = 3.6$.

## 3. Finding $f(k)$ from a graph

The graph of the function $f(x) = x^2 + 5x - 1$ is shown.

To find $f(-4)$, we draw the broken line $x = -4$ and then read the $y$-value of the point where this line intersects the curve.

This $y$-value is $-5$.

Thus, $f(-4) = -5$.

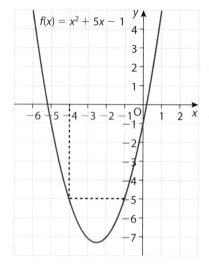

## 4. Intersecting graphs

Graphed below are the functions

$$f(x) = x^2 \text{ (i.e. } y = x^2 \text{)} \text{ and } g(x) = x + 2 \text{ (i.e. } y = x + 2 \text{)}$$

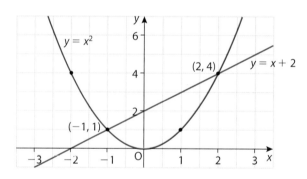

Notice that the curve $f(x)$ and the line $g(x)$ intersect at the points $(-1, 1)$ and $(2, 4)$.

We will now solve the equation $f(x) = g(x)$ to find the points of intersection.

$$\text{i.e.} \quad x^2 = x + 2$$
$$\rightarrow x^2 - x - 2 = 0$$
$$\rightarrow (x + 1)(x - 2) = 0$$
$$\rightarrow x + 1 = 0 \text{ or } x - 2 = 0$$
$$\therefore x = -1 \text{ or } x = 2$$

Notice that these are the *x*-values of the points where the two graphs intersect.

*Remember*

> When we solve the equation $f(x) = g(x)$, we are finding the *x*-values of the points of intersection of the graphs $y = f(x)$ and $y = g(x)$.

## 5. Axis of symmetry

The diagram on the right is the graph of the function $y = x^2 - 2x - 3$.

The broken red line is called the **axis of symmetry** of the curve.

The curve will fold onto itself across this line.

The equation of this axis of symmetry is $x = 1$.

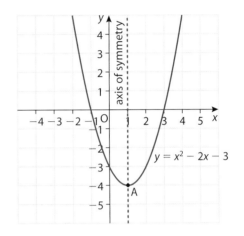

*Remember*

1. **To find $f(x)$ given $x$,** ↓, draw a line vertically from the given value of *x* on the *x*-axis until it intersects the curve, then horizontally until it intersects the $f(x)$ axis.

2. **To find $x$ given $f(x)$,** ⟶, draw a line parallel to the *x*-axis at the given value of $f(x)$, until it intersects the curve and then vertically until it intersects the *x*-axis.

   (Note: this results in two answers normally)

## Exercise 22.3

**1.** The curve on the right is the graph of the function

$$y = x^2 - 4x + 3.$$

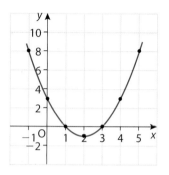

From the graph, write down

- (i) the coordinates of the points where the curve crosses the x-axis
- (ii) the value of y when x = 2
- (iii) the values of x when y = 8
- (iv) the equation of the axis of symmetry of the curve.

**2.** The curve on the right is the graph of the function

$$f(x) = x^2 - 1.$$

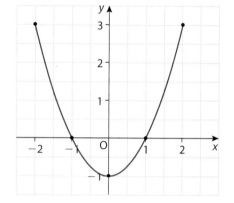

Use the graph to find

- (i) the values of x when f(x) = 0
- (ii) the values of x when f(x) = 3
- (iii) the value of f(x) when x = 2
- (iv) the value of f(x) when x = 0.
- (v) the coordinates of the minimum point of the curve.

**3.** The graph of f(x) = $x^2 - 2x - 5$
is given on the right.
Use the graph to estimate

- (i) the values of x for which f(x) = 0
- (ii) the values of x for which f(x) = 6
- (iii) the value of f(-3)
- (iv) the value of f(1)

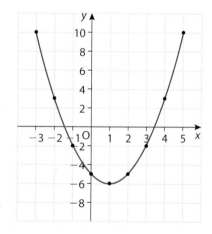

**4.** Drawn below is the graph of the function:

$f: x \rightarrow 3 + 2x - x^2$ for $-2 \leqslant x \leqslant 4, x \in R$.

Use the graph to write down

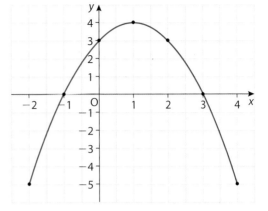

   (i)  the roots of the equation $f(x) = 0$

  (ii)  the values of $x$ for which $f(x) = 3$

 (iii)  the values of $x$ for which $f(x) = -2$

 (iv)  the value of $f(2)$

  (v)  the value of $f(-1\frac{1}{2})$

 (vi)  the equation of the axis of symmetry of the curve.

(vii)  the coordinates of the maximum point of the curve.

**5.** A baker making cakes finds that her profit per hour €$P$, is given by the quadratic equation €$P = 20x - x^2$, where $x$ is the number of cakes baked per hour. Use the graph to find:

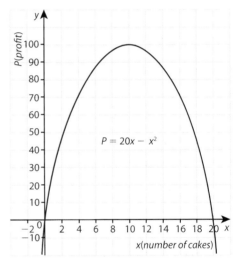

   (i)  the values of $x$ at which she makes no profit.i.e. €$P = 0$

  (ii)  the values of $x$ at which she makes a profit of €84 per hour.

 (iii)  the baker's maximum profit per hour.

 (iv)  how many cakes must be baked per hour to maximise her profit?

Use algebra to verify your answers to (i) and (ii).

**6.** The graphs of the functions $f(x) = x^2$ and $g(x) = 2x + 3$ are shown below.

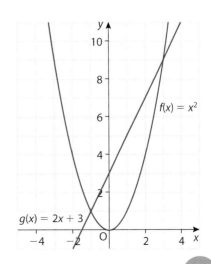

   (i)  Write down the coordinates of the points where the curve and line meet.

  (ii)  Solve the equation $x^2 = 2x + 3$.

 (iii)  What is the connection between the answers in (i) and (ii) above?

 (iv)  Explain the meaning of the equation $f(x) = g(x)$.

**7.** Drawn on the right are the graphs of
$f(x) = x^2 - 2x$ and $g(x) = x - 1$
in the domain $-1 \leqslant x \leqslant 3$.

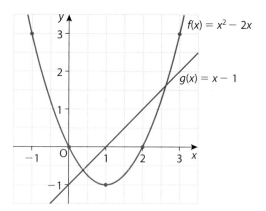

Use the graph to write down
  (i)   the values of $x$ for which $f(x) = 0$
  (ii)  the values of $x$ for which $f(x) = 3$
  (iii) the value of $x$ for which $g(x) = 0$
  (iv)  the value of $x$ for which $g(x) = 2.5$
  (v)   the values of $x$ for which $f(x) = g(x)$
  (vi)  the equation of the axis of
         symmetry of the curve.

**8.** Drawn below are the graphs $f(x) = x^2 + x - 6$ and $g(x) = 3x - 3$.

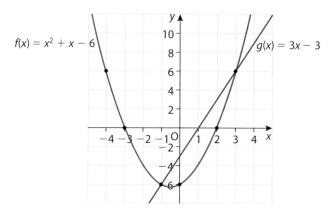

Use the graph to estimate
  (i)   $f(-2)$
  (ii)  $g(3)$
  (iii) the values of $x$ for which $f(x) = 0$
  (iv)  the values of $x$ for which $f(x) = 4$
  (v)   the value of $x$ for which $g(x) = 0$
  (vi)  the values of $x$ for which $f(x) = g(x)$.

Solve algebraically the equation $f(x) = g(x)$.
Explain the connection between the values for $x$ you have just found and the values
for $x$ in (vi) above.

**9.** Using the same axes and the same scales, graph the functions

$f: x \rightarrow x^2 + 3x - 3$ and $g: x \rightarrow x - 2$ in the domain $-4 \leqslant x \leqslant 2, x \in R$.

Use the graph to estimate
   (i)   the values of $x$ for which $x^2 + 3x - 3 = 0$
   (ii)  the values of $x$ for which $x^2 + 3x - 3 = -2$
   (iii) the values of $x$ for which $f(x) = g(x)$.

**10.** On the right is the graph of the function
$f(x) = -x^2 + 4x + 12$.

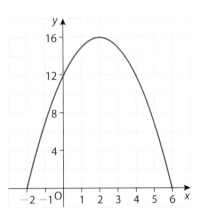

$f(x)$ represents the number of taxis at a
taxi-rank from 10 a.m. $(x = -2)$ to 6 p.m. $(x = 6)$.
Each unit on the $x$-axis represents one hour
and each unit on the $y$-axis represents one taxi.

Use the graph to estimate
   (i)    the number of taxis at the rank at 12 noon
   (ii)   the times when there were 14 taxis at the rank
   (iii)  the times when there were no taxis at the rank
   (iv)   the number of hours when there were 10 taxis or more at the rank
   (v)    the greatest number of taxis at the rank during this period.

## Test yourself 22

1. Draw the graph of the function $f(x) = 3x - 1$ in the domain $-2 \leqslant x \leqslant 3$.
   Use your graph to estimate
   (i) $f(-1.5)$      (ii) the value of $x$ when $f(x) = 3.5$.

2. Copy and complete the table on the
   right for the function $f(x) = 2x^2 + 3x - 6$.

   Hence draw the graph of the function
   in the domain $-4 \leqslant x \leqslant 3$.

   Use your graph to estimate
   (i) the values of $x$ when $f(x) = 0$
   (ii) the values of $x$ when $f(x) = -3$
   (iii) the value of $f(1.5)$.

   | x | 2x² + 3x − 6 | y |
   |----|----|----|
   | −4 | | |
   | −3 | 18 − 9 − 6 | 3 |
   | −2 | | |
   | −1 | | |
   | 0 | | |
   | 1 | | |
   | 2 | 8 + 6 − 6 | 8 |
   | 3 | | |

3. Draw the graph of $f(x) = 2x - 5$ in the domain $0 \leqslant x \leqslant 5$.

4. The graph of $y = x^2 - 2x$ has
   been drawn on the given grid.

   Use the graph to find estimates
   for the solutions of these
   equations:
   (i) $x^2 - 2x = 0$
   (ii) $x^2 - 2x = 3$.

   Write down the equation of
   the axis of symmetry of the
   curve.

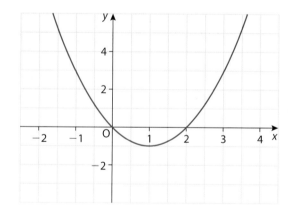

5. $x - 2y = 6$ is the equation of a line.
   If $x = 0$, find the value of $y$.
   If $y = 0$, find the value of $x$.
   Plot the two points you have found and draw the graph of the line $x - 2y = 6$.

6. Draw the graph of the function $f : x \to x^2 + 2x - 4$ in the domain $-4 \leqslant x \leqslant 2, x \in R$.
   Use your graph to find
   (i) $f(0.5)$
   (ii) the values of $x$ when $f(x) = 0$
   (iii) the values of $x$ for which $f(x) = 3$.

**7.** The graph of the function $f(x) = 2x + 5$ is shown.

Use the graph to write down

  (i) $f(0)$    (ii) $f(1)$    (iii) $f(-1)$
  (iv) the value of $x$ when $y = 3$
  (v) the value of $y$ when $x = -2.5$.

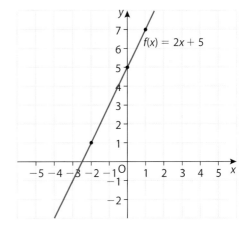

**8.** Which sketch graph fits which equation?
Give reasons for your answers.

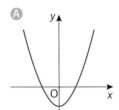    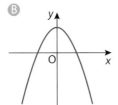    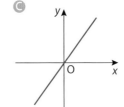

$$y = 2x$$

$$y = x^2 - 2$$

$$y = 2 - x^2$$

**9.** Copy and complete the table on the right and hence draw a graph of the function $f(x) = 3 - 2x$ in the domain $-1 \leqslant x \leqslant 3$.

| $x$ | $3 - 2x$ | $y$ |
|-----|----------|-----|
| $-1$ |          |     |
| $0$  |          |     |
| $3$  |          |     |

**10.** Draw the graph of the function $f: x \rightarrow 6x - x^2$ in the domain $0 \leqslant x \leqslant 6$.

$f(x)$ represents the height above ground, in metres, reached by a golf ball from the time it was struck $(x = 0)$ to the time it hit the ground $(x = 6)$.

If each unit on the $x$-axis represents 1 second and each unit on the $y$-axis represents 5 metres, use your graph to estimate
  (i) the greatest height reached by the golf ball
  (ii) the height of the golf ball after $1\frac{1}{2}$ seconds
  (iii) after how many seconds the ball was 10 metres above ground (two times)
  (iv) after how many seconds the ball reached its maximum height.

## Assignment:

Ella and Sean were given 28 m of mesh to fence off a class garden.

One side of the garden had to be against the school wall as shown.

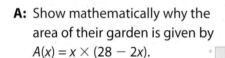

**A:** Show mathematically why the area of their garden is given by $A(x) = x \times (28 - 2x)$.

**B:** What is the meaning of $A(x)$?

**C:** Using a calculator copy and complete the table for values of $A(x)$ up to $x = 16$.

| x | 0 | 2 | 4 | 6 | 8 | 10 | 12 | 14 | 16 |
|------|---|---|---|----|---|----|----|----|----|
| A(x) | | | | 96 | | | | | |

**D:** Explain why $x = 16$ m is significant.

**E:** Plot the values of $A(x)$ on a large grid as shown.

**F:** From your graph, answer the following:

(i) What conclusions can you make from the graph when $x = 0$ m or 14 m?

(ii) What is the area of the garden when $x = 7$ m?

(iii) For what values of $x$ will the area be 70 m²?

(iv) What is the maximum possible area of the garden?

(v) What are the dimensions of the garden of maximum area?

# Trigonometry

# chapter 23

## In this chapter, you will learn to:

- use the Theorem of Pythagoras,
- identify the three sides of a right-angled triangle,
- use the three trigonometric ratios: Sin, Cos and Tan,
- apply inverse trigonometric functions to find missing angles,
- solve right-angled triangles,
- use trigonometry to solve real life problems.

## Section 23.1  The Theorem of Pythagoras

In Chapter 10, you learned about the Greek mathematician Pythagoras and his theorem about right-angled triangles. This theorem is given below.

### Theorem of Pythagoras

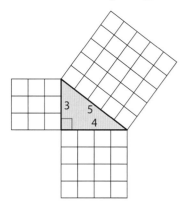

The square on the hypotenuse of a right-angled triangle is equal to the sum of the squares on the other two sides.

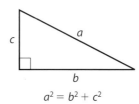

$$a^2 = b^2 + c^2$$

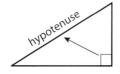

The **hypotenuse** is opposite the right angle.

---

**Example 1**

Find the area of the square marked $A$ in the given figure.

$A = 64 \text{ cm}^2 + 36 \text{ cm}^2$
$A = 100 \text{ cm}^2$

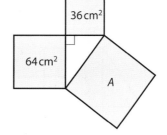

## Example 2

Find the length of the side marked x in each of these right-angled triangles:

(i)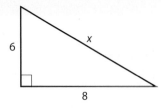

(ii)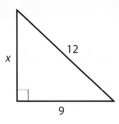

(i)  $x^2 = 8^2 + 6^2$

   $= 64 + 36$

   $x^2 = 100$

   $x = \sqrt{100} = 10$

(ii)  $12^2 = 9^2 + x^2$

   $144 = 81 + x^2$

   $144 - 81 = x^2$

   $63 = x^2$

   $x^2 = 63$

   $x = \sqrt{63}$

The answer $\sqrt{63}$ is said to be in **surd** form.

## Exercise 23.1

**1.** Find the area of the shaded square in each of the following right-angled triangles:

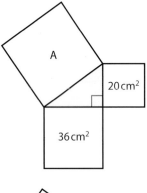

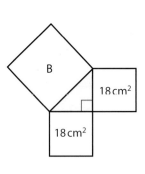

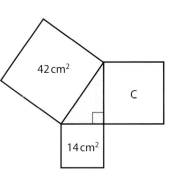

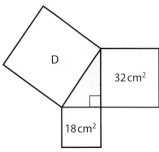

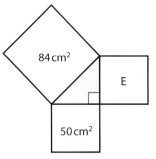

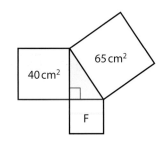

**2.** Find the length of the hypotenuse in each of the following right-angled triangles:

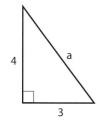
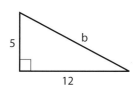
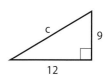

**3.** Find the length of the side marked with a letter in each of the following right-angled triangles:
(You may leave your answers in surd form.)

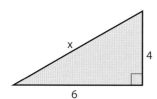
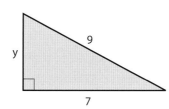
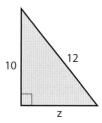

**4.** Find the length of the side marked with a letter in each of these triangles:
(Give each answer correct to one decimal place.)

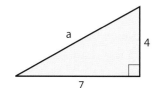
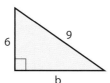
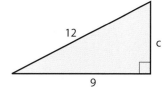

**5.** Find the length of the hypotenuse in each of these triangles:
(Give each answer correct to 1 decimal place.)

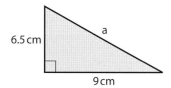
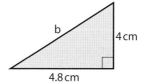
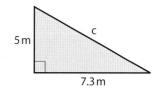

**6.** Use the Theorem of Pythagoras to determine whether each of these triangles is right-angled:

(i)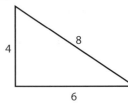

(ii)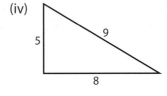

> If a triangle is right-angled, the square on the hypotenuse must be equal to the sum of the squares on the other two sides.

(iii)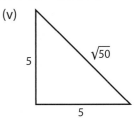

(iv)

(v)

**7.** Name the hypotenuse in the given triangle.
Now find the length of the side [BC].

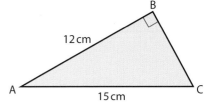

**8.**

A vertical tree 16 metres tall casts a shadow that is 14 metres in length. What is the distance from the top of the tree to the tip of the shadow, represented by the line marked, $\ell$?
(Give your answer to the nearest metre.)

**9.** The size of a television screen is the length of its diagonal.
The size of this television screen is 80 cm.
If the height of the screen is 42 cm, find the width of the screen in centimetres, correct to the nearest whole number.

**10.** Seven lengths of wood are needed to make this gate.
Find the total length of wood needed, giving your answer in metres, correct to one decimal place.

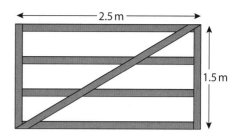

# Section 23.2  Sides of a right-angle triangle

The **hypotenuse**, the **opposite side** and the **adjacent side** have all been labelled in the two triangles below for the angle A and the angle B.

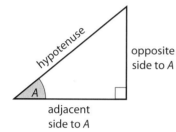

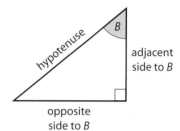

---

**Example 1**

For the angle A in the given figure, write down
(i)  the length of the opposite side
(ii)  the length of the adjacent side
(iii)  the fraction $\dfrac{\text{opposite side}}{\text{hypotenuse}}$.

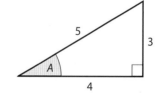

(i)  Opposite side to angle A is 3.  (ii)  Adjacent side is 4.

(iii)  $\dfrac{\text{opposite side}}{\text{hypotenuse}} = \dfrac{3}{5}$.

---

## Exercise 23.2

**1.** Write down the length of the hypotenuse in each of the following triangles:

(i)

(ii)

(iii)

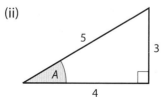

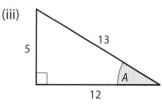

2. Write down the length of the side adjacent to the angle *A* in each of the triangles in Question 1 above.

3. Write down the length of the side opposite the angle *A* in each of the triangles in Question 1 above.

4. Write down the length of the hypotenuse in each of the triangles below:

(i) 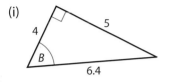  (ii) 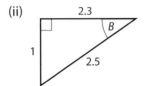  (iii)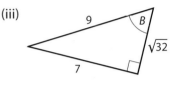

5. Write down the length of the side opposite the angle *B* in each of the triangles in Question 4 above.

6. Write down the length of the side adjacent to the angle *B* in each of the triangles in Question 4 above.

7. In relation to the angle *A* in the given triangle, express as a fraction the length of

   (i) $\dfrac{\text{opposite side}}{\text{hypotenuse}}$   (ii) $\dfrac{\text{adjacent side}}{\text{hypotenuse}}$ .

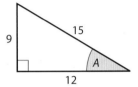

8. In relation to the angle *B* in the given triangle, express as a fraction the length of

   (i) $\dfrac{\text{opposite side}}{\text{adjacent side}}$   (ii) $\dfrac{\text{opposite side}}{\text{hypotenuse}}$ .

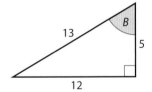

# Section 23.3 Sine, Cosine and Tangent ratios

## The sine ratio

The three triangles below are all different sizes but each contains an angle marked A which is the same size in all the triangles.

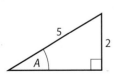   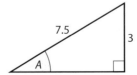   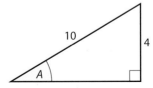

In each triangle, the length of the side opposite the angle A and the length of the hypotenuse are given.

In each triangle, the ratio $\dfrac{\text{opposite side}}{\text{hypotenuse}}$ is the same, that is 0.4.

The ratio $\dfrac{\text{opposite side}}{\text{hypotenuse}}$ is called the **sine** of the angle.

**sin** is used for **sine**.

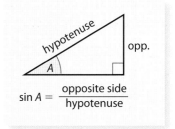

$$\sin A = \frac{\text{opposite side}}{\text{hypotenuse}}$$

## The cosine ratio

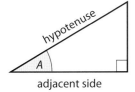

In the given right-angled triangle, the ratio

$$\frac{\text{adjacent side}}{\text{hypotenuse}}$$

is called the **cosine** of the angle A.

**cos** is used for **cosine**.

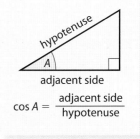

$$\cos A = \frac{\text{adjacent side}}{\text{hypotenuse}}$$

## The tangent ratio

In the given right-angled triangle, the ratio

$$\frac{\text{opposite side}}{\text{adjacent side}}$$

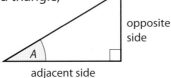

is called the **tangent** of the angle A.
**tan** is used for **tangent**.

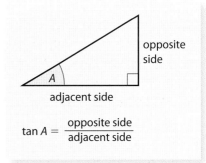

$$\tan A = \frac{\text{opposite side}}{\text{adjacent side}}$$

---

**Example 1**

Find the values of sin A, cos A and tan A in the given right-angled triangle.

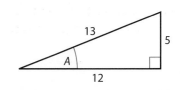

$$\sin A = \frac{\text{opposite}}{\text{hypotenuse}} = \frac{5}{13}$$

$$\cos A = \frac{\text{adjacent}}{\text{hypotenuse}} = \frac{12}{13} \qquad \tan A = \frac{\text{opposite}}{\text{adjacent}} = \frac{5}{12}$$

## *Investigation:*

Although page 16 of the 'formulae and tables' booklet contains the ratios for sin, cos and tan we need, a personalised mnemonic (silent *m*) can be a great memory aide.

Besides the well-known great chief, Soh-Cah-Toa, devise a mnemonic for your group.

Compare results.

## Exercise 23.3

**1.** Write down the value of sin *A* in each of the following triangles:

(i)　　　　　　　　　(ii)　　　　　　　　　(iii)

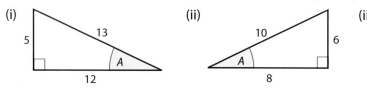
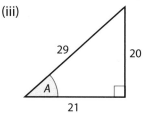

**2.** Write down the value of cos *A* in each of the triangles in Question 1.

**3.** Find the value of tan *A* in each of the triangles in Question 1.

**4.** Find the value of sin *B* in each of the triangles below:

(i)　　　　　　　　　(ii)　　　　　　　　　(iii)

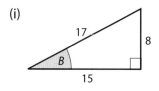
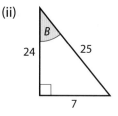
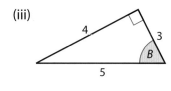

**5.** Write down the value of cos *B* in each of the triangles in Question 4.

**6.** Write down the value of tan *B* in each of the triangles in Question 4.

**7.** From the given triangle, write down the value of

   (i)  sin $A$            (ii)  cos $B$

  (iii)  tan $A$           (iv)  cos $A$

   (v)  tan $B$           (vi)  sin $B$.

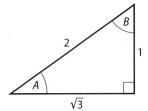

**8.** Use the Theorem of Pythagoras to find the length of the side marked $x$ in the given triangle.

Now write down the value of

   (i)  sin $A$

  (ii)  cos $A$

 (iii)  tan $A$.

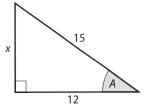

## Section 23.4  Using your calculator to find ratios

The value of the sine, cosine and tangent of any angle can be found by using an electronic calculator. When using a calculator make sure that it is in **degree mode.**

---

### Example 1

Use your calculator to find, correct to two decimal places, the value of

   (i)  sin 58°           (ii)  cos 74°           (iii)  tan 37°.

   (i)  Key in $\boxed{\text{sin}}$ $\boxed{5}$ $\boxed{8}$ $\boxed{=}$         The answer is 0.8480 = 0.85.

  (ii)  Key in $\boxed{\text{cos}}$ $\boxed{7}$ $\boxed{4}$ $\boxed{=}$        The answer is 0.2756 = 0.28.

 (iii)  Key in $\boxed{\text{tan}}$ $\boxed{3}$ $\boxed{7}$ $\boxed{=}$        The answer is 0.7536 = 0.75.

---

### How to find the angle when given its sin, cos or tan

When you use your calculator you will find that sin 60° = 0.8660.
If you are asked the question, 'What angle has a sine of 0.8660?', of course the answer is 60°.

If we are given  sin $A$ = 0.8660, we use the $\boxed{\text{sin}^{-1}}$ key on the calculator to find the value of the angle $A$.

The $\boxed{\text{sin}^{-1}}$ key is found by keying in $\boxed{\text{SHIFT}}$ $\boxed{\text{sin}}$.

So to find the angle $A$ when sin $A = 0.8660$, key in

$\boxed{\text{SHIFT}}\ \boxed{\text{sin}}\ \boxed{\bullet}\ \boxed{8}\ \boxed{6}\ \boxed{6}\ \boxed{0}\ \boxed{=}$

Your answer is $59.99° = 60°$, correct to the nearest degree.

---

**Example 2**

(i) If sin $A = 0.5786$, find $A$ correct to the nearest degree.
(ii) If tan $B = 1.8453$, find $B$ correct to the nearest degree.

(i) sin $A = 0.5786$
To find $A$, key in $\boxed{\text{SHIFT}}\ \boxed{\text{sin}}\ \boxed{\bullet}\ \boxed{5}\ \boxed{7}\ \boxed{8}\ \boxed{6}\ \boxed{=}$.
The result is $35.35° = 35°$, correct to the nearest degree.

(ii) tan $B = 1.8453$
To find $B$, key in $\boxed{\text{SHIFT}}\ \boxed{\text{tan}}\ \boxed{1}\ \boxed{\bullet}\ \boxed{8}\ \boxed{4}\ \boxed{5}\ \boxed{3}\ \boxed{=}$.
The result is $61.55° = 62°$, correct to the nearest degree.

---

## Exercise 23.4

Use your calculator to find the value of each of the following, correct to 4 decimal places:

1. sin 34°
2. sin 74°
3. sin 12°
4. cos 28°
5. tan 56°
6. tan 74°
7. tan 18°
8. sin 67°
9. cos 80°
10. tan 19°
11. sin 54°
12. cos 58°
13. tan 68°
14. tan 32°
15. sin 18°
16. cos 63°

17. Find the angle $A$ in each of the following, correct to the nearest degree:
    (i) sin $A = 0.7453$      (ii) sin $A = 0.2154$      (iii) sin $A = 0.8416$
    (iv) sin $A = 0.5129$      (v) sin $A = 0.1684$      (vi) sin $A = 0.9154$.

18. Find the angle $B$ in each of the following, correct to the nearest degree:
    (i) cos $B = 0.4587$      (ii) cos $B = 0.7416$      (iii) cos $B = 0.2153$.

19. Find the angle $C$ in each of the following, correct to the nearest degree:
    (i) tan $C = 0.5286$      (ii) tan $C = 1.4251$      (iii) tan $C = 2.4127$.

20. Find the angle $A$ in each of the following, correct to the nearest degree:
    (i) tan $A = 2.0416$      (ii) sin $A = 0.7463$      (iii) cos $A = 0.4197$

21. Verify that          (i) sin 27° = cos 63°          (ii) sin 51° = cos 39°.

**22.** Use your calculator to find the value of these, correct to 2 decimal places:

(i) $3 \times \sin 54°$    (ii) $5 \times \cos 14°$    (iii) $7 \times \tan 44°$    (iv) $8 \times \sin 55°$.

**23.** Look at the triangle on the right and say which ratio $\frac{3}{5}$ represents.

Express $\frac{3}{5}$ as a decimal and then find the value of
the angle $A$, correct to the nearest degree.

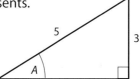

**24.** What ratio does $\frac{7}{10}$ represent?

Find the size of the angle $A$ correct to the nearest degree.

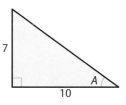

**25.** Using your calculator find the value of each of the following correct to the nearest
degree:

(i) $\sin^{-1}\left(\frac{1}{5}\right)$    (ii) $\cos^{-1}\left(\frac{2}{3}\right)$    (iii) $\tan^{-1}\left(\frac{8}{9}\right)$

**26.** What ratio does $\frac{3}{14}$ represent?

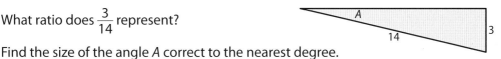

Find the size of the angle $A$ correct to the nearest degree.

**27.** Using the measurements on the triangle and the $(\tan^{-1})$ key on
your calculator find:

(i) $|\angle A|$    (ii) $|\angle B|$    (iii) $|\angle(A + B)|$

Suggest another method of finding $|\angle(A + B)|$.

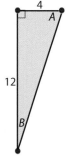

# Section 23.5  Finding sides and angles of a triangle

If we know the angles and one side of a right-angled
triangle, we can then find the lengths of the other sides.

For example, we could calculate the height of a
tree if we know the angle to the top of the tree
as well as the distance from the base of the tree.

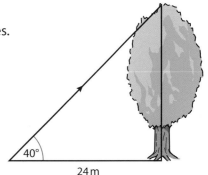

## Example 1

Find the value of the side marked *x* in the
given triangle.
Give your answer correct to 1 decimal place.

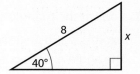

In relation to the angle 40°, we have the **opposite** side and the **hypotenuse**
which gives us the **sine** ratio.

$$\frac{x}{8} = \sin 40°$$

$$\frac{x}{8} = 0.6428 \quad \text{... (to find sin 40°, key in } \boxed{\sin}\,\boxed{4}\,\boxed{0}\,\boxed{=}.$$

$$x = 8 \times 0.6428 \quad \text{... multiply both sides by 8}$$

$$x = 5.1, \text{ correct to 1 decimal place.}$$

## Example 2

Find the length of the side marked *y* in the
given triangle.
Give your answer correct to 1 decimal place.

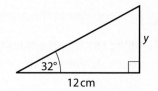

$$\frac{y}{12} = \tan 32° \quad \text{... } \tan = \frac{\text{opposite}}{\text{adjacent}}$$

$$\frac{y}{12} = 0.6249$$

$$y = 12 \times (0.6249) \quad \text{... multiply both sides by 12}$$

$$y = 7.499$$

$$y = 7.5 \text{ cm}$$

**Example 3**

Find the measure of the angle $A$ in the given triangle.
Give your answer correct to the nearest degree.

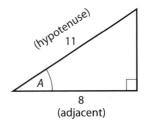

Relative to the angle $A$, we have the adjacent side and the hypotenuse.

$$\cos A = \tfrac{8}{11}$$
$$A = \cos^{-1}\left(\tfrac{8}{11}\right)$$

$$\frac{\text{adjacent}}{\text{hypotenuse}} = \cos A$$

To find $A$, key in $\boxed{\text{SHIFT}}\ \boxed{\cos}\ \boxed{(\tfrac{\square}{\square})}\ \boxed{8}\ \boxed{\downarrow}\ \boxed{11}\ \boxed{=}$

This gives $A = 43.34°$.
$A = 43°$, correct to the nearest degree

## Exercise 23.5

**1.** Which ratio (sine, cosine or tangent) would you use to find $x$ in each of these triangles?

(i)　　　　　　(ii)　　　　　　(iii)　　　　　　(iv)

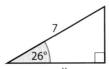
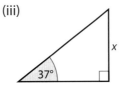
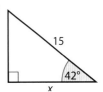

**2.** Use the sine ratio to find the length, correct to one decimal place, of the side marked $x$ in each of these triangles:

(i)　　　　　　　　(ii)　　　　　　　　(iii)

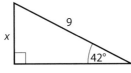

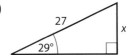

**3.** Use the tangent ratio to find the length of the side marked with a letter in each of these triangles. Give each answer correct to one decimal place.

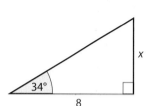

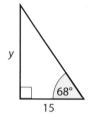

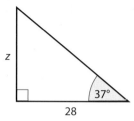

**4.** Use the cosine ratio to find, correct to the nearest whole number, the length of the side marked *a* in each of these triangles:

(i)

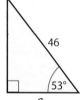

(ii)

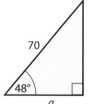

(iii)

**5.** Find the length of the side marked with the letter *x* in each of these triangles:
Give your answers correct to one decimal place.

(i)

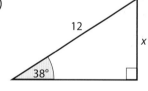

(ii)

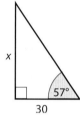

(iii)

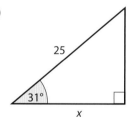

**6.** Find in metres, correct to the nearest whole number, the height of the office block shown.

**7.** A ladder 8 m in length is placed at an angle of 60° against a vertical wall. How far is the foot of the ladder from the wall?

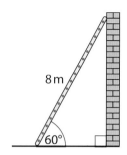

**8.** Jack is fishing from the straight bank of a river. He lets out 18 m of line and this is carried down stream so that the line makes an angle of 22° with the bank where Jack is standing.
What is the shortest distance from the hook to the bank?
Give your answer in metres, correct to one decimal place.

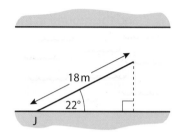

**9.** Find the height of the church tower in the given diagram.

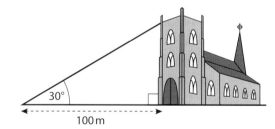

Give your answer correct to the nearest metre.

**10.** In the given triangle ABC, $|AB| = 10$ and $|\angle BAC| = 41°$.
Find, correct to 1 decimal place
(i) $|BC|$
(ii) $|AC|$.

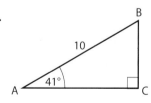

**11.** Which trigonometric ratio links 5, 8 and $B$ in the given right-angled triangle?
Use this ratio to find the measure of the angle $B$, correct to the nearest degree.

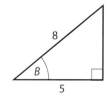

**12.** Find the angle marked with a letter in each of these triangles.
Give each angle correct to the nearest degree.

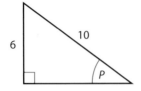 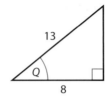 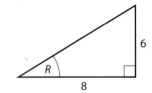

**13.** Find the measure of the angle between the kite-line
and the ground in the given figure.
Give your answer correct to the nearest degree.

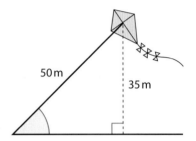

**14.** A plane, which took off from Dublin Airport, had gained a height of 1.8 km after it
had travelled 8 km.

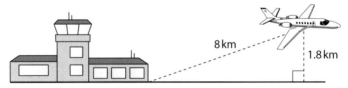

At what angle was the plane climbing?
Give your answer correct to the nearest degree.

# Section 23.6  Using trigonometry to solve problems

Today, trigonometry is used by engineers, architects and surveyors who need to work
out relationships between distances and angles.

In this section we will use trigonometry to solve
some very simple problems involving right-
angled triangles.

Some of the terms we will use are explained
below.

An **angle of elevation** is an angle formed by a
horizontal line and the line of sight above
the horizontal line.

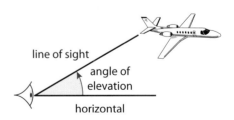

When we look down at something, the angle between the horizontal line and the direction in which we are looking is called the **angle of depression**.

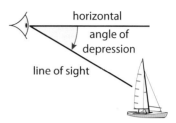

*Investigation:*

Using a clinometer, find the angle of elevation ($a°$) to the top of a wall of the school.

Measure your distance ($d$) to the wall in metres, correct to 1 place of decimals.

Measure the height ($h$) of your eye to the ground, correct to 1 place of decimals.

Repeat from different positions from the wall.

Based on the diagram $H = x + h$

Write a formula for $x$ in terms of $\tan a°$ and $d$.

$\therefore$ $x =$

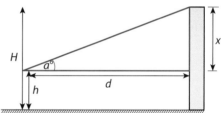

Using this formula, copy and complete the following table.

| Angle | | | |
|-------|--|--|--|
| **x** | | | |
| **h** | | | |
| **H** | | | |

Average height $H =$

A **clinometer** is often used to measure angles of elevation or depression. The clinometer shown above is being used to measure an angle of elevation as the observer is looking upwards.

**Example 1**

From a point P on level ground, the angle of elevation
of the top of a tower is 42°. If P is 40 metres from
the foot of the tower, find $h$, the height of the
tower, correct to the nearest metre.

$$\frac{h}{40} = \tan 42° \quad \Rightarrow \quad \frac{h}{40} = 0.9004$$

$$h = 40 \times 0.9004$$

$$\therefore \quad h = 36 \text{ metres}$$

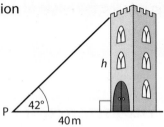

### Exercise 23.6

**1.** When the angle of elevation of the sun is 22°,
the length of the shadow cast by a tower is 15 m.
Find the height $h$ of the tower, in metres,
correct to one decimal place.

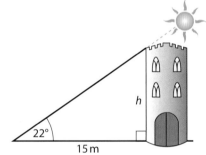

**2.** From a point on the ground 200 m from
the middle of the base of the Eiffel Tower,
the angle of elevation of the top is 58°.
Use this information to find the height of
the tower, correct to the nearest metre.

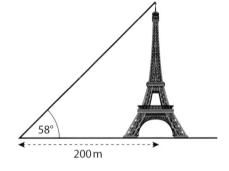

**3.** A boy is flying a kite from a string of length 30 m.
If the string makes an angle of 71° with the ground,
find the height $h$ of the kite, correct to the nearest
metre.

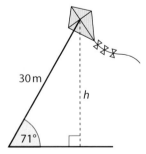

**4.** When the angle of elevation of the sun is 42°,
a tree casts a shadow 14 m long on level ground.
Find the height of the tree, correct to the nearest
integer.

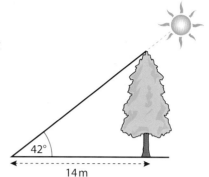

42°

14 m

**5.** The distance from the roof of an office block to the point C on level ground is 40 m.
If $|\angle ACB| = 32°$, find correct to the nearest metre,
(i) the height of the block        (ii) the length [BC].

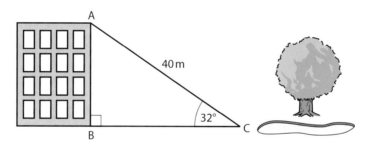

A

40 m

32°

B    C

**6.** Daniel lies down 25 m away from his house, which is built on flat ground. He uses a
clinometer to measure the angle between the ground and the top of his house.
The angle is 20°.

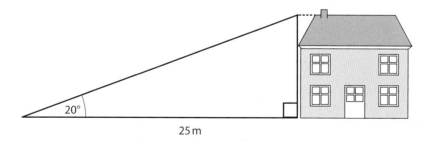

20°

25 m

Estimate the height of Daniel's house, correct to the nearest metre.

**7.** A ladder of length 5 metres rests against a wall so
that the base of the ladder is 3 m from the wall.
Find the angle between the ladder and the ground,
correct to the nearest degree.

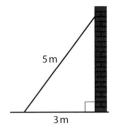

**8.** From the top of a rig 80 m high,
the angle of depression of a
boat at sea is 25°.
Explain why the shaded angle
is also 25°.
Now find the distance from the
middle of the base of the rig to
the boat.
Give your answer correct to
the nearest metre.

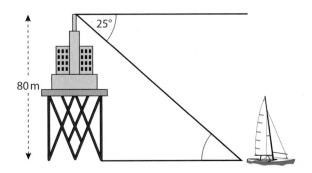

## Test yourself 23

**1.** In the given triangle, write down
   (i)   the length of the hypotenuse
   (ii)  the length of the side adjacent to the angle *A*.
   (iii) the value of sin *A*
   (iv)  the value of tan *A*.

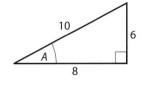

**2.** Use the diagram on the right to write down
   (i)   cos 60°
   (ii)  sin 30°
   (iii) tan 60°.

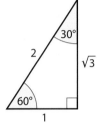

**3.** Use the *Theorem of Pythagoras* to find the length of
the side marked *x* in the given right-angled triangle.
Use the length found to write down the value of
(i) sin *A*          (ii) cos *A*          (iii) tan *B*.

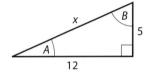

**4.** Andy stands at A, directly under the
end of a crane.
From A, he walks 12 m to B. At B, he
measures the angle of elevation of
the end of the crane as 70°.
How high is the end of the crane, *h*?
Give your answer correct to the
nearest metre.

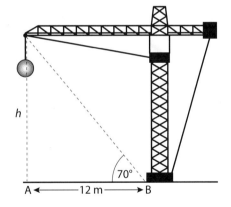

**5.** Find, correct to one decimal place,
the length of the side marked *y* in
the given triangle.

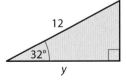

**6.** A playground slide has a 6 m sloped side.
It makes an angle of 52° with the ground, as shown.
How high is the top of the slide above the ground?
Give your answer in metres, correct to
one decimal place.

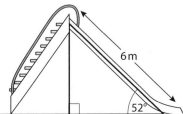

7. (i) If cos A = 0.5592, find A correct to the nearest degree.
   (ii) A wire runs from the top of a pole 10 metres in
        height to the ground.
        The end of the wire is 15 m from the
        bottom of the pole.
        What angle does the wire make with
        the ground?
        Give your answer correct to the nearest degree.

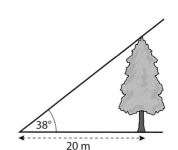

10 m

15 m

8. The angle of elevation of a tree top is 38° when
   measured from a point 20 m from its base.
   Find the height of the tree in metres,
   correct to one decimal place.

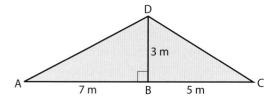

38°

20 m

9. A see-saw is made from a 4-metre plank of wood,
   pivoting about the middle on a stand.
   The piece of wood makes an angle of 30° with
   the ground when one side of the see-saw is touching the ground.
   How high is the top of the pivot stand?

10. The diagram shows a roofing frame
    ADC with BD perpendicular to AC.
    (i) Find |AD|, in metres, correct to
        one decimal place.
    (ii) Find the size of the angle
         BAD correct to the nearest degree.

D

3 m

A     7 m     B     5 m     C

11. A flagpole is on the top of a building. From the point D,
    4 m from the base of the building, Joanne measures
    the angles of elevation of the top, A, and the
    bottom, B, of the flagpole. Her measurements
    are shown on the diagram.
    (i) Find the length |AC|.
    (ii) Find the length |BC| and hence the height of
         the flagpole.
         Give each answer in metres, correct
         to one decimal place.

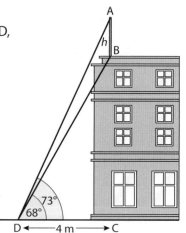

A

h B

73°
68°

D ←— 4 m —→ C

# Assignment:

1. On a large sheet of squared paper, scale axes from 0 to 1 as shown.

2. Using a compass, draw a quarter circle.

3. Using a protractor centred at the origin, mark the position of 4 angles, e.g. 20°, 40°, 60°, 80°.

4. Draw the line segment OD, OE, OF, OG

5. Using a ruler or setsquare, measure the perpendicular height of each point D, E, F, G.

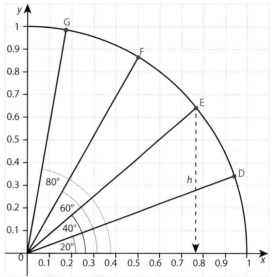

6. Copy and complete the table below.

7. Use a calculator to fill out the second line of the table.

Correct all readings to 2 places of decimals.

| Angle | D | 20° | E | 40° | F | 60° | G | 80° |
|---|---|---|---|---|---|---|---|---|
| **sin of the angle** | | | | | | | | |
| **Perpendicular height (h)** | | | | | | | | |

Compare your results with other students in your class.

Draw a large poster of your results.

Write a conclusion for this assignment.

# Drawing and Interpreting Real-life Graphs

## From first year, you will recall how to:

- draw *x* and *y* axes, and label them,
- plot points onto a coordinated plane.

## In this chapter, you will learn to:

- draw distance-time graphs,
- read information from a distance-time graph,
- recognise a directly proportional graph as a straight line through the origin,
- draw directly proportional graphs,
- interpret information from directly proportional graphs,
- compare graphs that represent liquid being poured at a steady rate into various containers,
- interpret graphs that represent a variety of real-world scenarios.

## Section 24.1  Distance–time graphs

❯ A **distance–time graph** (or travel graph) is a special type of line graph used to describe a journey.

❯ The vertical axis represents the distance from a certain point, while the horizontal axis represents time.

The distance–time graph below shows the journey of a cyclist who set out from town *A*.

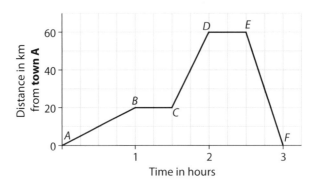

(i) From *A* to *B*, he cycled a distance of 20 km in 1 hour.

(ii) At B, he stopped for half an hour which is represented by [*BC*].

(iii) At *C*, he took a lift on a lorry and travelled to *D*, a distance of 40 km. This part of the journey took half an hour.

(iv) He then rested for half an hour. This is represented by [*DE*].

(v) He then took a train back to the town he had originally left and completed the 60 km return journey in half an hour. This is represented by [*EF*].

(Note that both *A* and *F* represent town *A*.)

*Distance–time graphs*

› A change in steepness represents a change in speed.
› The steeper the line, the faster the speed.
› The flatter the line, the slower the speed.
› A horizontal line indicates that the person or object is stopped.

The formulae that connect distance (D), time (T) and average speed (S) are given on the right.

$$D = S \times T \qquad S = \frac{D}{T} \qquad T = \frac{D}{S}$$

## Exercise 24.1

**1.** The distance–time graph given shows Olivia's 3-hour journey.

   (i) How far did she travel in the first hour?

   (ii) For how long was she stopped?

   (iii) How far did she travel in the third hour?

   (iv) What was the total length of the journey?

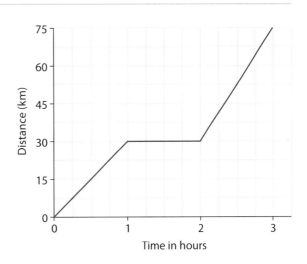

**2.** The graph below shows Mr. Desmond's journey from Town A to Town B and back.

(i) Find the distance travelled in the first two hours.

(ii) Find his average speed for these two hours.

(iii) For how long did he rest?

(iv) How long did the return journey take?

(v) What was his average speed on the return journey?

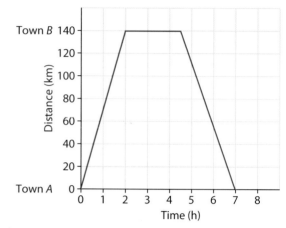

**3.** This travel graph gives the distance of a boy from home.

(i) When did the boy leave home? When did he return?

(ii) How far was he from home at 1.00 p.m.?

(iii) At what times was he 15 km from home?

(iv) At what times did he rest?

(v) When was he travelling most quickly?

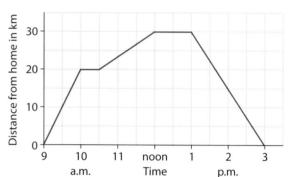

**4.** The travel graph shows the distance of a cyclist from his home between the times of 10. a.m. and 4.30 p.m.

(i) How far does the cyclist travel in the first 2 hours?

(ii) How far from home is he when he stops to rest?

(iii) At what time does he commence the return journey?

(iv) At 3.00 p.m. his speed changes. Does it increase or decrease? How can you tell without calculating the actual speeds?

(v) How far does he travel altogether?

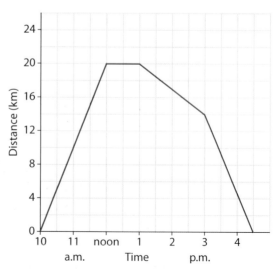

**5.** The graph shows the journey taken by Joseph to cycle from Town *P* to Town *Q*.

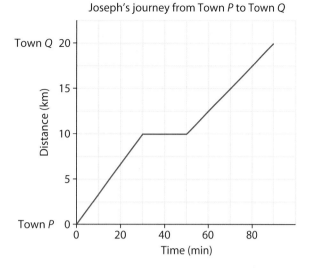

Joseph's journey from Town *P* to Town *Q*

Use the graph to find
- (i) the time taken to travel from Town *P* to Town *Q* including rest time
- (ii) what is the length of his rest
- (iii) the distance from Town *Q* when he stopped to rest.
- (iv) What was his average speed for the part of the journey before he took a rest?

**6.** Match the graph to the story.

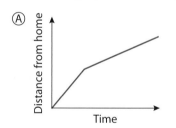
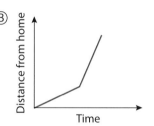
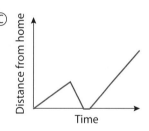

- (i) I am walking steadily to school. After a while, I meet a friend and we walk together. We walk slower than when I was by myself.
- (ii) I am part-way to school when I remember that I have left my homework at home. I run back home to get it and then run to school.
- (iii) I start to walk to school, then I accept a ride with a friend.

**7.** The given distance–time graph shows the journey from his office undertaken by a sales representative to the countryside.

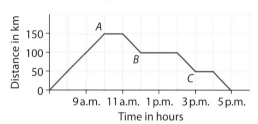

- (i) At what time did he leave his office?
- (ii) How far did he travel to Town *A*?
- (iii) What was his average speed for this leg of the journey?
- (iv) How far is it from Town *A* to Town *B*?
- (v) He had his lunch in Town *B*. How long did it last?
- (vi) What was his overall average speed, excluding the breaks?

461

**8.** The graph shows the journeys of two motorists, Conor and Adam. They are travelling on the same road and in the same direction, leaving town *A* at 9.00 a.m.

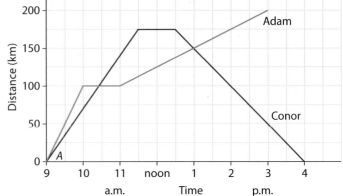

(i) Who travels faster in the first hour?

(ii) How many times do they pass each other?

(iii) At what time do they pass each other for the second time?

(iv) How far apart are they at 3.00 p.m.?

(v) How far does each man travel altogether?

**9.** Use the graph below to answer the following question.

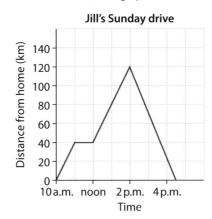

Jill's Sunday drive

Write a paragraph to describe Jill's journey to and from her destination, including:

(i) her departure and arrival times

(ii) when and where the rest stop is taken

(iii) the time spent driving

(iv) her average speed for the return part of the journey.

**10.** The graph shows the journeys of two tourists and gives their distances from their hotel.

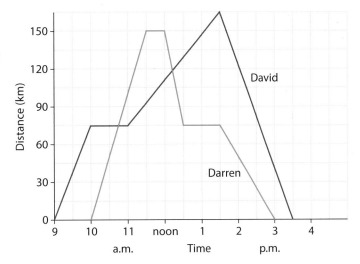

   (i) How far is David from the hotel when Darren starts his journey?

   (ii) At approximately what times do their paths cross?

   (iii) At what time does David begin his return journey?

   (iv) How far is Darren from his hotel when David begins his return journey?

   (v) Who returns to the hotel first?
   What time elapses before the other tourist arrives?

# Section 24.2 Directly proportional graphs

Lucy is paid for the hours that she works at the rate of €12 per hour.
If she works 2 hours, she is paid €12 × 2 = €24.
If she works 5 hours, she is paid €12 × 5 = €60.

The hours worked and the pay received are said to be **directly proportional**.

When two quantities are in direct proportion, a graph is particularly useful for illustrating how one quantity increases (or decreases) relative to the second quantity.

> Directly proportional graphs are always straight lines through the origin.

**Example 1**

The graph below shows the relationship between kilograms and pounds.

Use the graph to approximately convert

  (i)  20 pounds to kilograms (kg)
 (ii)  14 pounds to kilograms
(iii)  4 kg to pounds
(iv)  7.5 kg to pounds.

From the graph,

  (i)  20 pounds = 9.1 kg
 (ii)  14 pounds = 6.4 kg
(iii)  4 kg = 8.8 pounds
(iv)  7.5 kg = 16.5 pounds

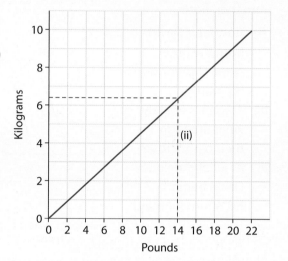

## Exercise 24.2

**1.** In which of these graphs is *h* directly proportional to *t*?

(i)  *h*

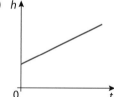

(ii)  *h*

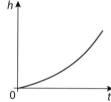

(iii)  *h*

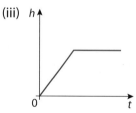

(iv)  *h*

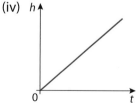

Explain your answers.

**2.** The graph below shows the relationship between kilometres and miles.

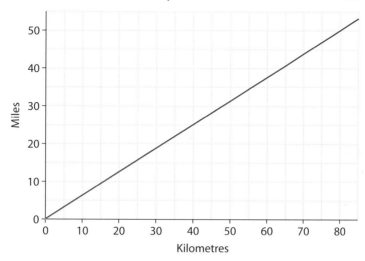

Use the graph to convert approximately

(i) 60 km to miles

(ii) 80 km to miles

(iii) 30 miles to km

(iv) 15 miles to km.

Is the given graph a directly proportional one?

**3.** The graph below shows the relationship between degrees Celsius (°C) and degrees Fahrenheit (°F).

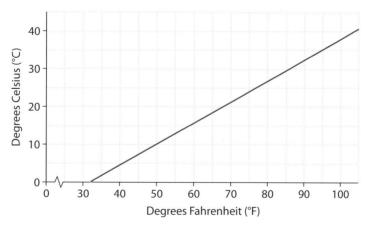

Is this a directly proportional graph? Explain your answer.

Use the graph to convert approximately

(i) 35°C to Fahrenheit

(ii) 15°C to Fahrenheit

(iii) 50°F to Celsius

(iv) 100°F to Celsius.

If the temperature in a city on a particular day ranges between 55°F and 90°F, express this range in °C.

**4.** Television repair charges depend on the length of time taken for the repair, as shown on the graph.

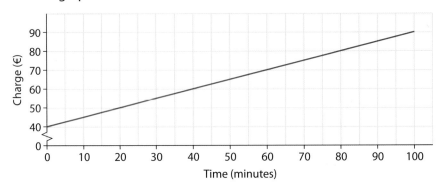

(i) What is the charge for a repair that took 60 minutes?

(ii) What is the charge for a repair that took 30 minutes?

(iii) If the charge was €80, how long did the repair take?

(iv) If the charge was €60, how long did the repair take?

The standing charge is the basic charge before the time charge is added.

(v) What is this standing charge?

**5.** The graph below shows the typical weight for a man of medium build and given height.

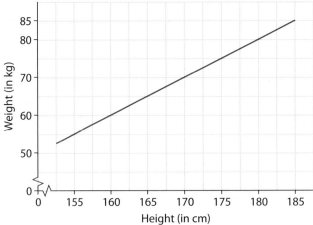

Use the graph to estimate:

(i) the weight of a man whose height is 165 cm

(ii) the weight of a man whose height is 175 cm

(iii) the height of a man whose weight is 78 kg.

If a group of men are all between 160 cm and 170 cm in height, what is the range of their weights likely to be?

**6.** The graph below can be used to convert between litres and pints.

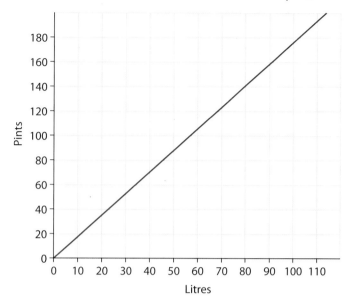

(i) Use the graph to find the number of pints equivalent to 90 litres.

(ii) Use the graph to find the number of litres equivalent to 80 pints.

(iii) A petrol tank contains 95 litres of fuel.

Use the graph to express this in pints, correct to the nearest 10 pints.

(iv) The average yearly milk-yield for a dairy cow in Ireland is roughly 10 000 pints.

Use your graph to convert this figure to litres, correct to the nearest 1000 litres.

**7.** The given diagram shows that the length of the shadow cast by a tree at midday is directly proportional to the height of the tree.

(i) What is the length of the shadow when the tree is 8 m in height?

(ii) By using two points on the line, find the equation of the line in terms of $s$ and $h$.

(iii) Use the equation you have found to write down the length of the shadow when the tree is 15 metres in height.

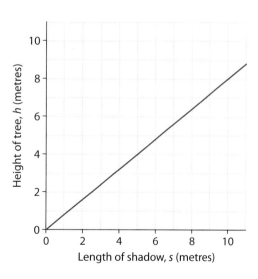

**8.** The graph on the right represents taxi fares for journeys of up to 9 km.

  (i)  What is the fare for a journey of 5 km?

 (ii)  What is the fare for a journey of 9 km?

(iii)  The taxi fare for a certain journey is €21. What is the length of this journey?

(iv)  Suggest a reason why the graph does not pass through the origin.

**Taxi fares**

**9.** This graph shows how much petrol two cars consume.

——————— David's car

– – – – – – – – Stephen's car

  (i)  David's car travelled 80 km. How much petrol did it use?

 (ii)  Stephen's car used 9 litres of petrol one day. How far did it go?

(iii)  How much more petrol does Stephen's car use than David's car when each car travels 60 km?

(iv)  Is each line graph directly proportional? Explain your answer.

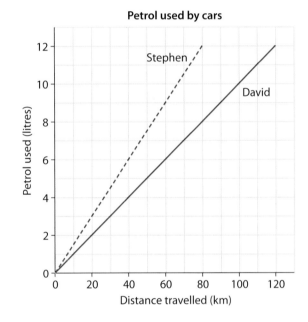

**Petrol used by cars**

 (v)  Find the equation of the broken red line in the form $y = mx$. Now use this equation to find the number of litres used when the car travels 300 km.

# Section 24.3 Real-life graphs

When water is poured into the vessel below **at a steady rate**, the water will rise in the vessel also at a steady rate.
The graph of the water's height as time passes is shown on the right below.

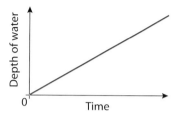

The graph is a straight line because the water rises at a **constant rate**.

The thinner the container, the steeper the graph.

You can see the differences in the graphs of the containers below.
They all have the same height.

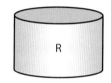
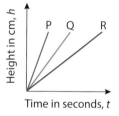

Containers with sides that bulge out have a curved line graph. They may start steeply, get less steep and then get steep again.

The graph of the water's height for the given container is shown on the right.
The top part of the graph is a straight line because the water rises at a constant rate due to the uniform shape of the container at the top.

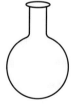
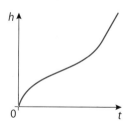

**Example 1**

Match these containers to their graphs when they are filled with liquid at a constant rate.

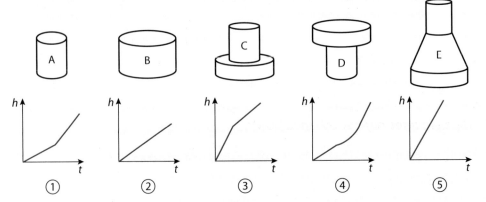

A is matched to ⑤ since A has straight parallel sides and is thin. It rises faster than container B.

B is matched to ② since B has straight parallel sides but is wider than A.

C is matched to ① since C is initially wide with straight sides and then narrow with straight sides – hence two line segments.

D is matched to ③ since D is initially narrow with straight sides and then wide with straight sides.

E is matched to ④ since E has three distinct sections which can be identified on the graph.

## Exercise 24.3

**1.** Which of these best describes what this graph tells us?

   (i)   The pulse rate is steady, then decreases, then is steady.
   (ii)  The pulse rate increases, then stops, then decreases.
   (iii) The pulse rate increases, then stays steady, then decreases with time.

**2.** Water is added to the tank shown at a steady rate.
Which graph best represents the increase in the water level *h*?

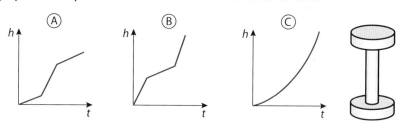

**3.** Here are three different-shaped bowls.

(i) Which description of filling the bowls with water goes with which bowl?
   (a) *The water level goes up fast at first and then suddenly goes up more slowly.*
   (b) *The water level goes up slowly at first, then changes to go up more quickly.*
   (c) *The water level starts by going up quickly, but gets slower and slower.*

(ii) Which graph goes with which bowl?

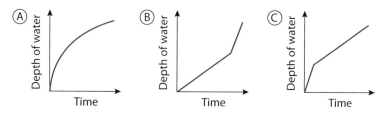

**4.** There are three routes from Appleville to Peartown.
Match the route descriptions to the appropriate *distance–time graphs*:

   *Route A:*    A two-lane highway direct with a maximum speed limit of 110 km/hour. A thirty minute wait at bridge-works.

   *Route B:*    A winding mountain road with steep gradients and curves requiring you to travel at a constant slower speed.

   *Route C:*    A two-lane highway with a maximum speed limit of 110 km/hour and then a winding detour to avoid bridge-works.

(i) Distance / Time

(ii) Distance / Time

(iii) Distance / Time

**5.** This graph shows the temperatures in a greenhouse during 24 hours in summer.

**Greenhouse temperature**

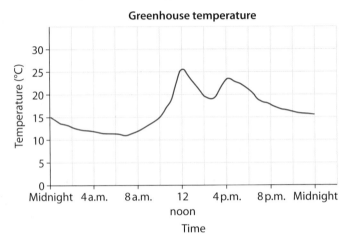

The temperature in a greenhouse falls during the night and rises during the day. There are windows in this greenhouse to help keep the temperature down when it gets too hot.

(i) At roughly what time in the morning does the temperature in the greenhouse start to go up?

(ii) About when during the day is the temperature going up fastest?

(iii) About when is it going down fastest?

(iv) Because it was getting too hot, the gardener opened the windows in the greenhouse. Later she closed them again.
   (a) At about what time do you think she opened the windows?
   (b) Roughly when did she close them?

(v) What was the highest temperature in the greenhouse during the day?

(vi) What was the lowest temperature in this 24-hour period?

**6.** (i)   (ii)   (iii)   (iv)

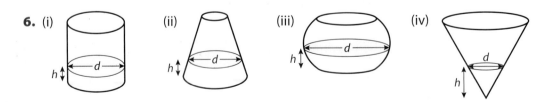

These containers are being filled with liquid.
The graphs below show how the diameter of the surface of the liquid changes as the height of the liquid increases.
Which graph belongs to which container?

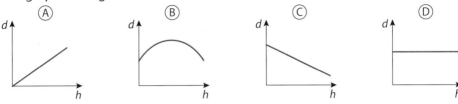

7. Match the graph to the story.

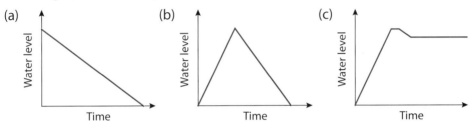

   (i)   I fill a bucket with water. After a few minutes, my dog drinks some of the water. I decide to leave the water in the bucket in case he wants a drink later.
   (ii)  I quickly fill a bucket with water but the bucket is spilt over and the water runs out.
   (iii) I start with a full bucket of water and pour the water steadily over my seedlings until the bucket is empty.

8. The graph gives the shortest braking distances that should be between cars at different speeds.

   (i)   Ed is driving in bad weather at 60 km per hour. What is the shortest distance he should be from the car in front?
   (ii)  Fay is driving in good weather at 90 km per hour. What is the shortest distance she should be from the car in front?
   (iii) Mr Shaw is driving 70 metres behind another car. The weather is bad. What is the fastest he should be driving?

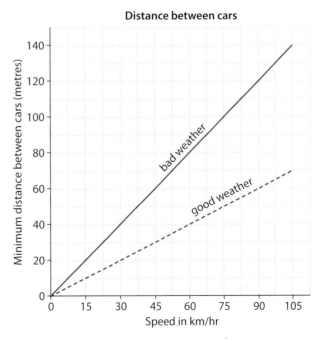

Distance between cars

# Assignment A:

On a large sheet of squared paper, draw and scale axes as shown.

Using a lab digital thermometer, measure and record the temperature in a specific spot in the classroom or corridor each hour on a particular day of the month.

Plot your results on the graph and date the graph.

Repeat the procedure in a month's time using the same graph.

Write a report on the fluctuations in temperature that occur on a daily and monthly basis.

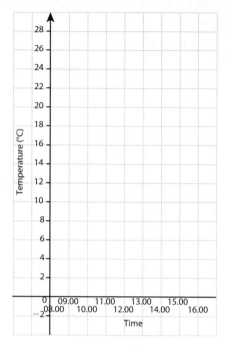

# Assignment B:

In a fitness test, a student runs from a baseline in the gym to a halfway line and back again.

This is called a lap.

The result of student A's test is shown.

Answer the following questions about his test:

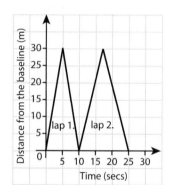

**1.** How far is the baseline from the halfway line?

**2.** How long did each lap take?

**3.** Write down the average speed of the student for each lap in m/s.

**4.** How does the graph show that the student is running at a constant rate during each lap?

Using a stopwatch and a fixed distance in the gym, draw a real-life fitness graph of each student in your group. Find out how many laps each student can complete in 40 seconds.

Draw a graph for each student, indicating the number of laps completed in 40 seconds and the average speed for each lap.

# chapter 25

# Geometry 3: Transformations – Constructions – Proofs

## From first year, you will recall how to:

- construct an image using translations,
- identify axes and centres of symmetry,
- construct an image using axial and central symmetry,
- bisect an angle and line segment,
- draw parallel and perpendicular lines,
- divide a line segment into 3 equal parts.

## In this chapter, you will learn to:

- perform a rotation of given points and objects,
- construct different types of triangles including SSS, SAS, ASA and RHS,
- construct rectangles,
- display an understanding of the proofs of theorems.

## Section 25.1 Transformation geometry

The figure marked A in the diagram below has been moved to different positions. All the figures have the same shape and size. Some are upside-down and some are back-to-front.

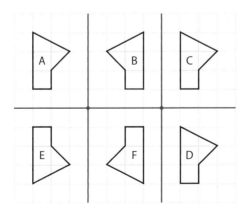

Each of the figures B, C, D, E and F is an **image** of the figure A under a **transformation**.
The original figure A is called the **object**.
The new position is called the **image**.
In this chapter we consider four transformations.
These are **translations**, **axial symmetry**, **central symmetry** and **rotation**.

## Translations

A translation is movement in a straight line.
It may also be described as a 'sliding movement'.

The shape A on the left has been moved in the
direction PQ and by a distance equal to |PQ|.
The translation PQ is written $\overrightarrow{PQ}$.

The image of the given figure is found by
moving 4 units to the right and 3 units up.
Notice that the size and shape of the figure
is unchanged.

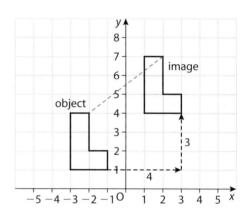

Here is the image of a line segment [AB]
under the translation $\vec{t}$.
The image is labelled **A′B′**.

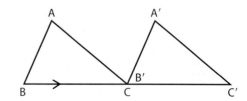

The image of the triangle ABC under the
translation $\overrightarrow{BC}$ is shown on the right.
The image is A′B′C′.

## Exercise 25.1

1. Describe the translation that maps the blue shape onto the red shape in each of the following. Use words such as right, left, up and down.

(i)  (ii)  (iii)

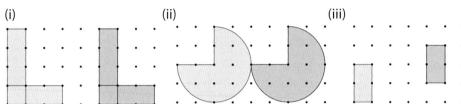

(iv)  (v)  (vi)

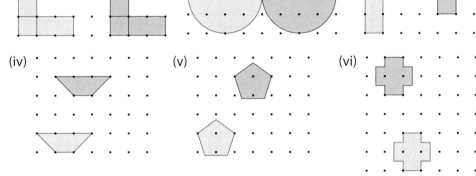

2.

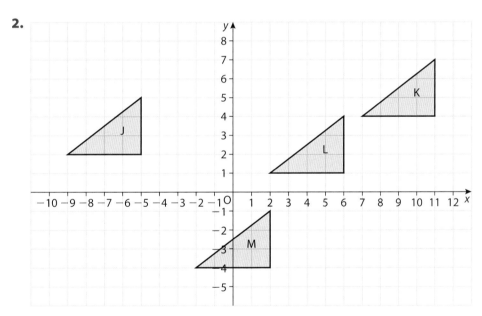

Describe fully the translation that maps
   (i)   shape L onto shape K
  (ii)   shape J onto shape L
  (iii)   shape M onto shape L
  (iv)   shape J onto shape M
   (v)   shape L onto shape M.

**3.** Construct the image of the letter T
under the given translation $\overrightarrow{AB}$.

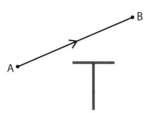

**4.** Draw the triangle ABC twice and
construct its image under

    (i)  $\overrightarrow{BC}$                    (ii)  $\overrightarrow{AC}$.

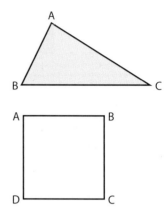

**5.** ABCD is a square, as shown.
Copy the diagram and draw a rough
sketch of the image of ABCD

    (i)  under $\overrightarrow{AB}$            (ii)  under $\overrightarrow{DB}$.

**6.** ABCD is a rectangle with the diagonals
intersecting at the point O.
Find each of the following:

    (i)  the image of A under $\overrightarrow{DC}$

    (ii)  the image of [AB] under $\overrightarrow{BC}$

    (iii)  the image of D under $\overrightarrow{OB}$

    (iv)  the image of [DC] under $\overrightarrow{DA}$.

**7.** ABCD and ABEC are parallelograms.
Under the translation $\overrightarrow{CE}$, write down
the image of

    (i)  the point A      (ii)  [AD]

    (iii)  △ADC      (iv)  [AC].

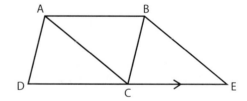

**8.** In the given figure, ABCD is a square
and BECD is a parallelogram.

    (i)  What is the image of [BD] under $\overrightarrow{DC}$?

    (ii)  What is the image of C under $\overrightarrow{DB}$?

    (iii)  What is the image of △ABD under $\overrightarrow{BE}$?

    (iv)  Of what point is B the image under $\overrightarrow{CE}$?

    (v)  Of what line segment is [BC] its image under $\overrightarrow{DC}$?

    (vi)  Of what triangle is ABD the image under $\overrightarrow{CD}$?

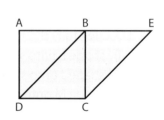

**9.**

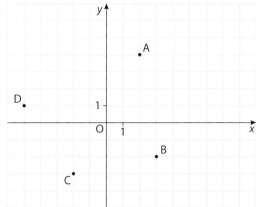

(i)   Write down the coordinates of A, B, C and D.

(ii)  Each point is translated 5 units to the right and 2 units up.
      What are the coordinates of the image points A′, B′, C′ and D′?

# Section 25.2  **Symmetries**

## 1.  **Symmetrical shapes**

Each of the figures below is **symmetrical**.

The broken line(s) in each figure is called an **axis of symmetry**.

A figure will have an axis of symmetry if it can be reflected in a line so that each half of the figure is reflected exactly onto the other half of the figure.

 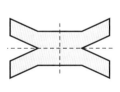  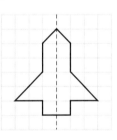

Here are some well-known geometrical figures and their axes of symmetry.

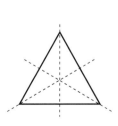 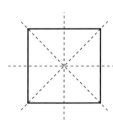 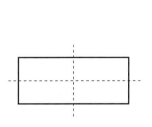 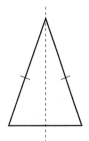

| Equilateral triangle | A square | A rectangle | Isosceles triangle |
| (3 axes of symmetry) | (4 axes of symmetry) | (2 axes of symmetry) | (one axis of symmetry) |

A parallelogram with unequal sides and no right angle has no axis of symmetry.

## 2. Axial symmetry

In the given diagram, the blue figure is the image of the green figure under reflection in the broken line $\ell$.

We name the image figure A'B'C'D'.

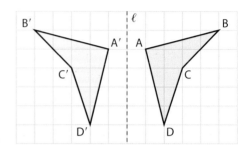

Here is another reflection in the horizontal broken red line.

The word MAM has line symmetry. Can you think of any other words that have line symmetry?

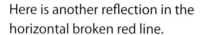

The diagram on the right illustrates how the image of a figure is constructed under reflection in a line.

## 3. Central symmetry

In the diagram on the right, the point A is joined to the point X and produced to A' such that
$$|XA'| = |AX|.$$
We say that the point A' is the image of A under reflection in the point X or **central symmetry** in X.

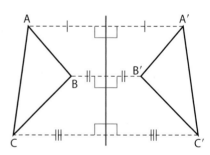

This diagram on the right shows the letter F and its image under central symmetry in the point X.

Notice that the image appears **upside-down and back-to-front** in relation to the given figure.

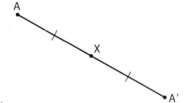

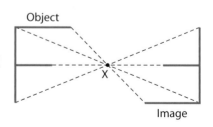

Object

Image

## 4. Centre of symmetry

All the figures below are mapped onto themselves under central symmetry in the point X.

  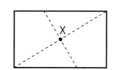 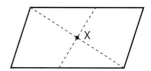

In each case, the point X is the **centre of symmetry**.

## 5. Rotation

This diagram shows the **rotation** of the shape S through $\frac{1}{4}$ of a turn in an anti-clockwise direction.

The point O is called the **centre of rotation**.

There are two directions of rotation:

1. anticlockwise ↺

2. clockwise ↻

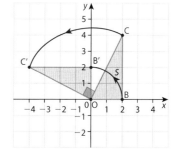

In this diagram, triangle T is rotated through 90°, about the origin O, in a clockwise direction.

When a shape is rotated, its size and shape remain the same but its position on the plane changes.

All points on the shape are turned through the same angle about the same point.

$\angle EOE' = \angle FOF' = 90°$

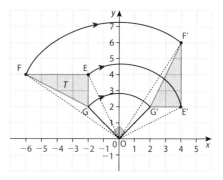

## Exercise 25.2

1. Use a set square and ruler to construct the image of the point X under reflection in the line $\ell$ in each of the following:

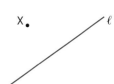

**2.** Use a set square and ruler to draw a rough sketch of the images of these triangles under reflection in the line *m*.

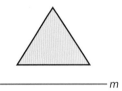 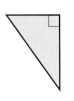 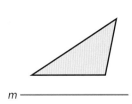

**3.** The rectangle DCFE is the image of the rectangle ABCD under axial symmetry in the line *k*.

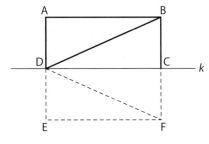

Write down the image of each of the following under reflection in the line *k*.

(i) the point B      (ii) [AB]      (iii) [DB]
(iv) △DCB      (v) △ABD      (vi) [CB]

**4.** Which of the following transformations represent reflection in a line?

(i) 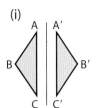  (ii) 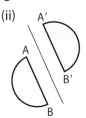  (iii) 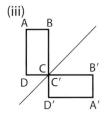  (iv)

**5.** Which of the letters in the word below have an axis of symmetry?

**6.** Sketch the image of the triangle ABC under central symmetry in the point C in each of the following.

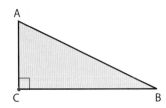      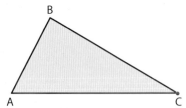

**7.** ABCD is a rectangle with the diagonals intersecting at the point O.

Find the image of each of the following under central symmetry in the point O.

(i)  D                  (ii)  C                  (iii)  [BC]              (iv)  △AOB
(v)  [AO]            (vi)  △ADB           (vii)  [OC]              (viii)  ABCD.

**8.** Which of the four faces shown below could be the image of the face shown on the right under a central symmetry?

Ⓐ      Ⓑ      Ⓒ      Ⓓ

**9.** Which of the four faces in question 8 could be the image of the given face under
(i)  reflection in a vertical line
(ii)  a translation?

**10.** In the diagram on the right, describe fully the single transformation which will map

(i)  shape P onto shape $P_1$
(ii)  shape $P_1$ onto shape $P_2$
(iii)  shape P onto shape $P_2$.

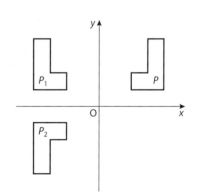

**11.** On the right is a circle of centre C. Name two transformations, each of which maps the circle onto itself.

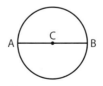

**12.** The diagram on the right shows a pattern and a line *n*.

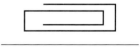

Which one of the following diagrams is the reflection of the pattern in *n*?

A                        B                        C                        D

     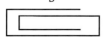     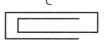

**13.** The diagram on the right shows the
triangle ABC.

The image of ABC under reflection in
the y-axis is A'B'C'.

(i) Find the coordinates of A', B' and C'.

A", B" and C" are the images of A, B and C
under reflection in the x-axis.

(ii) Find the coordinates of A", B" and C".

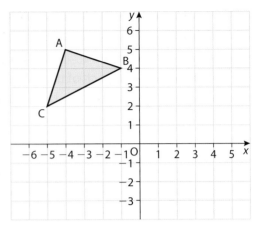

**14.** How many axes of symmetry has each of the following figures?

(i) 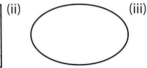 (ii) 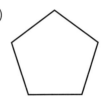 (iii) (iv)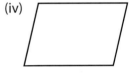

**15.** Which of the figures in question 14 have a centre of symmetry?

**16.**

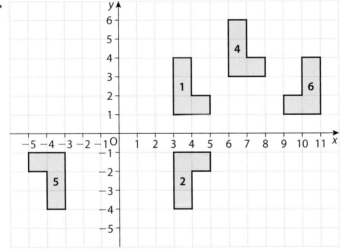

Which of the transformations – axial symmetry, central symmetry, translation or
rotation – will map

   (i)  $L_1$ onto $L_2$           (ii)  $L_1$ onto $L_4$

(iii)  $L_5$ onto $L_2$         (iv)  $L_1$ onto $L_6$

  (v)  $L_1$ onto $L_5$         (vi)  $L_5$ onto $L_4$?

**17.** Copy the diagram of the rectangle and draw its image by a rotation of 180° clockwise about the origin O.

Write down the coordinates of the image of points B, C and D, under this rotation.

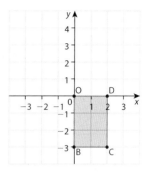

**18.** Describe each of the following rotations:

  (i)   ABC → DEC

  (ii)  ABC → IHC

  (iii) ABC → GFC

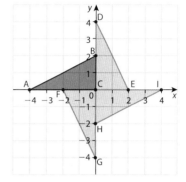

**19.** Copy the following shape onto squared paper.
Draw the new position of the shape after a rotation of:

  (i)   90° clockwise

  (ii)  180°

  (iii) 270° clockwise.

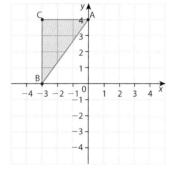

# Section 25.3 Constructions 1

Here are the instruments you will need to do various geometrical constructions.

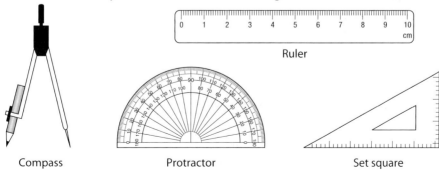

Compass       Protractor       Set square

**Note:** The words 'ruler' and 'straightedge' are used interchangeably.

## 1. Bisector of a given angle using only compass and straightedge

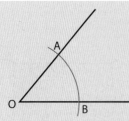 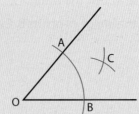 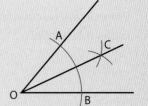

To bisect the given angle, place the point of the compass at O and draw an arc to cut both arms of the angle at A and B.

With the point of the compass at A and with the same radius, draw an arc between the arms of the angle. Repeat at B, cutting the first arc at C.

Join the point O to C. OC is the bisector of the angle AOB.

## 2. How to construct the perpendicular bisector of a line segment

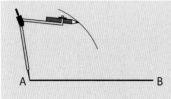 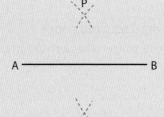 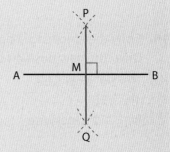

Set your compass to over half the length of [AB]. With A as centre, draw an arc above and below the line.

Keep your compass with the same radius. With B as centre, draw two more arcs. These arcs intersect the first two arcs at P and Q.

Join P and Q. PQ is the perpendicular bisector of [AB]. M is the midpoint of [AB].

## 3. Line perpendicular to a given line $\ell$, passing through a given point on $\ell$

### (i) Using a set square and straightedge

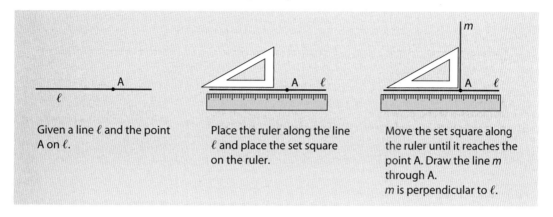

Given a line $\ell$ and the point A on $\ell$.

Place the ruler along the line $\ell$ and place the set square on the ruler.

Move the set square along the ruler until it reaches the point A. Draw the line $m$ through A.
$m$ is perpendicular to $\ell$.

### (ii) Using a compass and straightedge

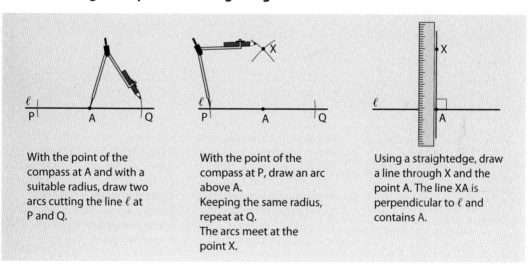

With the point of the compass at A and with a suitable radius, draw two arcs cutting the line $\ell$ at P and Q.

With the point of the compass at P, draw an arc above A.
Keeping the same radius, repeat at Q.
The arcs meet at the point X.

Using a straightedge, draw a line through X and the point A. The line XA is perpendicular to $\ell$ and contains A.

## 4. How to draw a line parallel to a given line, through a given point

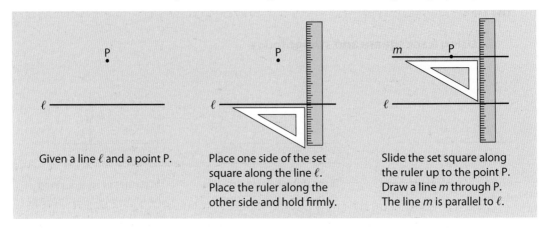

Given a line ℓ and a point P.

Place one side of the set square along the line ℓ. Place the ruler along the other side and hold firmly.

Slide the set square along the ruler up to the point P. Draw a line m through P. The line m is parallel to ℓ.

## 5. Division of a line segment into three equal parts

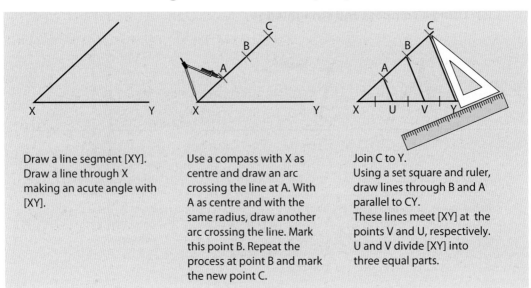

Draw a line segment [XY]. Draw a line through X making an acute angle with [XY].

Use a compass with X as centre and draw an arc crossing the line at A. With A as centre and with the same radius, draw another arc crossing the line. Mark this point B. Repeat the process at point B and mark the new point C.

Join C to Y. Using a set square and ruler, draw lines through B and A parallel to CY. These lines meet [XY] at the points V and U, respectively. U and V divide [XY] into three equal parts.

## 6. Line segment of a given length on a given ray

We use a compass, ruler and straightedge to draw a line segment of a given length on a given ray.

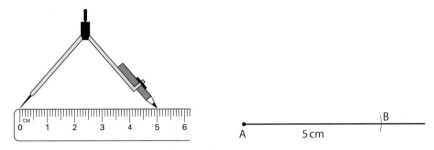

To draw a line segment of 5 cm, we use a compass and ruler to get a radius of 5 cm. We now place the compass at the point A and without changing the radius, draw an arc intersecting the line at B.

[AB] is 5 cm in length.

## 7. Angle of a given number of degrees with a given ray as one arm

We use a protractor to measure angles and draw angles of given sizes. The diagrams below show how to draw an angle of 74°.

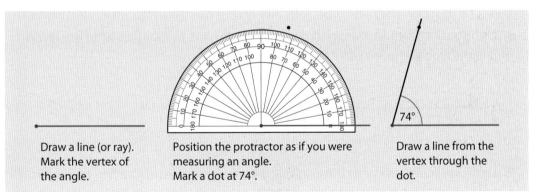

Draw a line (or ray). Mark the vertex of the angle.

Position the protractor as if you were measuring an angle. Mark a dot at 74°.

Draw a line from the vertex through the dot.

## Exercise 25.3

**1.** Using only a compass and straightedge, construct the bisector of each of the angles shown below:

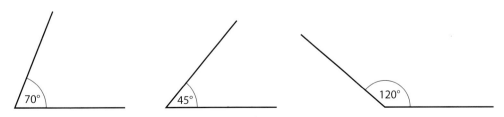

**2.** Use your set square to draw a right angle.
Now use your compass and straightedge to divide the angle into two equal parts.
Use your protractor to verify that each part is 45°.

**3.** Draw a line segment 6 cm in length.
Use your compass and straightedge to construct the perpendicular bisector of this line segment.
Verify that each half is 3 cm in length.

**4.** Draw a line segment 7 cm in length.
Bisect the line and verify that both halves are equal in length.

**5.** Draw a line segment [AB], 8 cm in length.
Use a compass and straightedge to construct the perpendicular bisector of this line segment.
Pick any point on the perpendicular bisector and verify that it is the same distance from A and B.

**6.** Using a set square and straightedge, construct a line perpendicular to the given line through the given point for each of the lines shown below:

**7.** Using diagrams similar to those in question 6 above, construct a line perpendicular to the given line through the given point using only a compass and straightedge.

**8.** Using a set square and straightedge, draw a line through the point P parallel to the line ℓ.

P.

ℓ

**9.** Draw any line segment and plot a point P not on the line.
Now, using a set square and straightedge, draw a line through P parallel to the line segment you have drawn.

**10.** The diagram on the right shows a line segment [AB]
and a line AY in which |AX| = |XY|.
Use your set square and ruler to draw XM parallel to YB.
Verify that M is the midpoint of [AB].

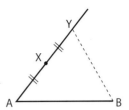

**11.** Draw a line segment 9 cm in length.
Now use your compass, ruler and set square to divide the line into 3 equal parts.
Use your ruler to verify that each part is 3 cm in length.

**12.** Use your protractor to draw an angle of 65° (∠BAC).
Now use a compass and straightedge to construct
the bisector of this angle.
If X is any point on the bisector of the angle BAC and
XB ⊥ AB and XC ⊥ AC, use congruent triangles to
show that |XB| = |XC|.

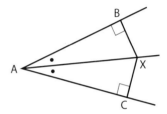

# Section 25.4  **Constructing triangles and rectangles** ———

## 1.  **Triangle given lengths of the three sides**

Make an accurate drawing of triangle ABC with |AB| = 6 cm,
|BC| = 5 cm and |CA| = 4 cm.

Make a rough sketch first, to get an idea of what
your finished drawing should be like.

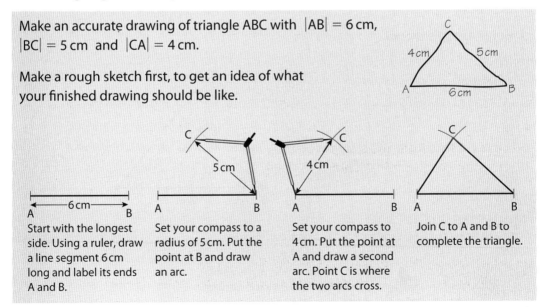

Start with the longest
side. Using a ruler, draw
a line segment 6 cm
long and label its ends
A and B.

Set your compass to a
radius of 5 cm. Put the
point at B and draw
an arc.

Set your compass to
4 cm. Put the point at
A and draw a second
arc. Point C is where
the two arcs cross.

Join C to A and B to
complete the triangle.

## 2. Triangle given side, angle and side measurements

Construct a triangle ABC with [BC] as base,
where |BC| = 4 cm, |AB| = 3 cm and |∠ABC| = 60°.
Measure the side [AC].

A rough sketch is shown on the right.

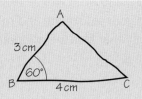

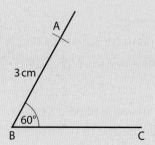

| | | |
|---|---|---|
| Draw a horizontal line and use your compass to mark off 4 cm. This gives the base [BC] = 4 cm. | Use your protractor to measure ∠CBA = 60° and draw the line BA. Place the point of your compass at B and draw an arc using a radius of 3 cm. The point where the arc cuts the line BA gives us the required point A. | Join A to C. ABC is the required triangle. If we measure |AC|, we get 3.6 cm. |

## 3. Triangle given angle, side, angle measures

Construct a triangle ABC with |BC| = 5 cm, |∠ABC| = 40°
and |∠ACB| = 50°.

A rough sketch is shown.

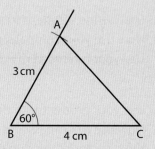

Draw a line segment [BC], 5 cm in length.

Use a protractor to make
|∠ABC| = 40° and |∠BCA| = 50°.
The lines meet at the point A.
ABC is the required triangle.

## 4. Right-angled triangle, given the length of the hypotenuse and one other side

Construct the triangle ABC so that $|\angle ABC| = 90°$, $|BC| = 5$ cm and $|AC| = 6$ cm.

A rough sketch of the triangle is shown.

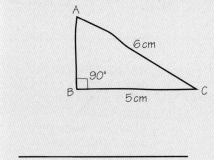

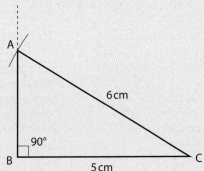

Draw a line segment [BC],
5 cm in length.

Use a protractor to make an angle of 90° at B.
Draw a vertical line BA.
Set your compass to a radius of 6 cm.
With C as centre, draw an arc cutting the vertical line.
Mark this point A and join AC.
ABC is the required triangle.

## 5. Right-angled triangle, given one side and one of the acute angles

Construct the triangle ABC so that the base [BC] = 5 cm, $|\angle ABC| = 90°$ and $|\angle ACB| = 40°$. A rough sketch is shown.

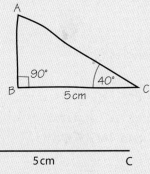

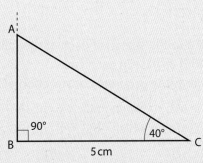

Draw a line segment [BC],
5 cm in length.

Use a protractor to make an angle of 90° at B.
Draw a vertical line BA.
Now use your protractor to make an angle of 40° at C.
Mark the point A where the arm of the angle meets the vertical line.
ABC is the required triangle.

## 6. Constructing rectangles

Construct a rectangle of sides 5 cm and 3 cm in length.

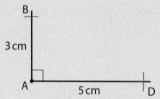

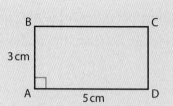

Draw a horizontal line and mark a point A on it. Use a set square or protractor to draw a line perpendicular to the given line at A.

Use a compass to measure 5 cm on the horizontal line and 3 cm on the vertical line. Mark the points D and B, respectively.

Draw a line through B parallel to AD. Draw a line through D parallel to AB. These lines meet at the point C. ABCD is the required rectangle.

## Exercise 25.4

**1.** Draw an accurate construction of each of the following triangles. All construction lines must be shown.

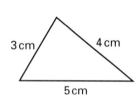

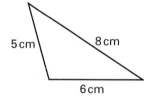

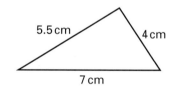

**2.** Draw a rough sketch of each of the following triangles.
Use [BC] as base in each case.
Now draw an accurate construction of each triangle.

   (i)  △ABC in which $|BC| = 6$ cm, $|AB| = 5$ cm and $|AC| = 4$ cm.

  (ii)  △ABC in which $|BC| = 8$ cm, $|AB| = 5.5$ cm and $|AC| = 6$ cm.

**3.** Draw a triangle of sides 3 cm, 5 cm and 6 cm.
Measure the three angles and verify that

   (i)  the smallest angle is opposite the shortest side

  (ii)  the largest angle is opposite the longest side.

**4.** Construct the following triangles based on the dimensions shown in the rough sketches below.

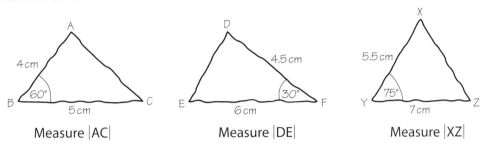

Measure |AC|          Measure |DE|          Measure |XZ|

**5.** Construct a triangle ABC, with [BC] as base, in each of the following cases. (First draw a rough sketch.)
Measure the third side in each triangle.

   (i)  |BC| = 4 cm, |AB| = 3 cm  and  |∠ABC| = 50°.
   (ii) |BC| = 6 cm, |∠BCA| = 60°  and  |AC| = 4.5 cm.

**6.** Draw accurate diagrams of the sketches shown below:

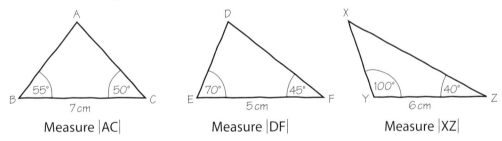

Measure |AC|          Measure |DF|          Measure |XZ|

**7.** Draw an accurate construction of each of the following right-angled triangles:

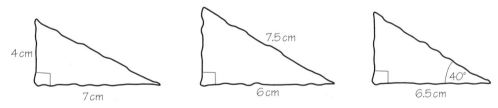

**8.** Construct the triangle DEF with base [EF], in which  |DE| = 5 cm, |EF| = 6.5 cm  and  |∠DEF| = 90°.

**9.** Construct the triangle ABC, with [BC] as base, in which  |BC| = 7 cm, |∠ABC| = 90°  and  |∠ACB| = 50°.
Measure |AC|.

**10.** Draw a rectangle of sides 6 cm and 4 cm in length.
Verify that both diagonals are equal in length.

**11.** Draw a rectangle of sides 70 mm and 45 mm in length.
Measure the length of the diagonal.

**12.** Construct the rectangle ABCD with base [AB] = 7 cm in length, where the area of
the rectangle is 28 cm².

**13.** (i) Draw an accurate plan of this
park, using a scale of 1 cm to 10 m.
(ii) There are two straight paths
in the park, one from Main
Gate to Honeysuckle Gate
and the other from Archway
to Dewdrop Gap.

What is the length, in metres,
of the longer path?

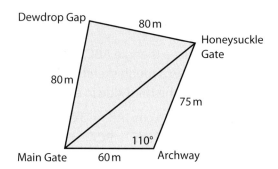

## Section 25.5 Revision of theorems

Students are **not** required to know the full formal proof of these geometry theorems, but
must be able to display an understanding of the theorems and their outcomes.

---

**Theorem 1. To prove that vertically opposite angles are equal.**

If two lines $\ell$ and $m$ cross then:

$\angle A + \angle C = 180°$ ... because $\ell$ is a straight line.
$\angle B + \angle C = 180°$ ... because $m$ is a straight line.
$\therefore \angle A = \angle B$

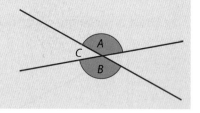

---

**Theorem 2. In an isosceles triangle the angles opposite the equal sides are equal.**

If the angle $\angle BAC$ is bisected by $AP$ then:

1. $\angle BAP = \angle PAC$ ... because $\angle BAC$ is bisected.
2. $|BA| = |AC|$ ... because $\triangle BAC$ is isosceles.
3. $|AP| = |AP|$
$\therefore \triangle BAP$ is congruent to $\triangle PAC$ ... SAS

$\therefore \angle ABP = \angle ACP$

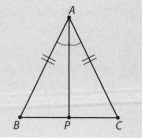

**Conversely: If a triangle has two equal angles it is isosceles.**

If the angle ∠BAC is bisected by AP then:

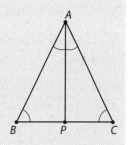

1. ∠BAP = ∠PAC ... because ∠BAC is bisected.
2. ∠ABP = ∠ACP ... because △BAC triangle has two equal angles
∴ ∠APB = ∠APC
3. |AP| = |AP|
∴ △BAP is congruent to △PAC ... ASA

∴ |BA| = |AC|

---

**Theorem 3. If a transversal, *t*, makes equal alternate angles, *A*, on two lines, ℓ and *m*, then the lines, ℓ and *m*, are parallel.**

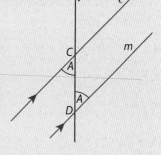

∠A + ∠C = 180° ... because *t* is a straight line.
∠A + ∠D = 180° ... because *m* is a straight line.
∴ ∠D = ∠C
∴ ℓ and *m* are parallel

---

**Conversely: If ℓ and *m*, are parallel then a transversal, *t*, makes equal alternate angles, *A*, with *t*.**

If ℓ and *m* are parallel then:

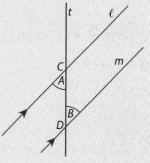

∠D = ∠C
∠A + ∠C = 180° ... because *t* is a straight line.
∠B + ∠D = 180° ... because *m* is a straight line.
∴ ∠B = ∠A

---

**Theorem 4. The angles in any triangle add to 180°**

If ℓ is drawn parallel to the base of the triangle then:

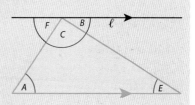

∠B = ∠E ... alternate angles
∠F = ∠A ... alternate angles
∠B + ∠C + ∠F = 180° ... because ℓ is a straight line.

∴ ∠E + ∠C + ∠A = 180°

**Theorem 5. Two lines are parallel if and only if, for any transversal, the corresponding angles are equal.**

The corresponding angles $\angle C$ and $\angle E$ are equal.

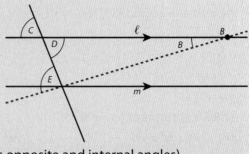

If the lines $\ell$ and $m$ are **not** parallel they must meet at a point (say) $B$.

Since $\angle C = \angle D$ (vertically opposite angles)
$$\angle E = \angle D$$

But   $\angle E = \angle D + \angle B$ (external angle equals opposite and internal angles)

$\therefore \angle B = 0$   $\therefore$ the lines are parallel.

---

**Theorem 6. Each exterior angle of a triangle is equal to the sum of the interior opposite angles.**

If $\angle F$ is the exterior angle then:

$\angle E + \angle F = 180°$   ... because the *base* is a straight line.

$\angle E + \angle C + \angle A = 180°$   ... angles in a triangle add to 180°.

$\therefore \angle F = \angle C + \angle A$

---

**Theorem 9. In a parallelogram, opposite angles are equal.**

In a parallelogram:

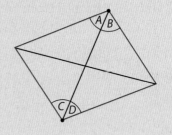

$\angle D = \angle A$   ... alternate angles
$\angle B = \angle C$   ... alternate angles
$\therefore \angle D + \angle C = \angle B + \angle A$
i.e. opposite angles are equal.

---

**Theorem 9. In a parallelogram, opposite sides are equal.**

In a parallelogram $ABCD$:

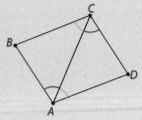

$\angle ACB = \angle CAD$   ... alternate angles
$\angle BAC = \angle ACD$   ... alternate angles
$|AC| = |AC|$
$\therefore \triangle ABC$ is congruent to $\triangle ACD$
$\therefore |CD| = |AB|$ and $|BC| = |AD|$

**Theorem 10. The diagonals of a parallelogram bisect each other.**

In a parallelogram $ABCD$:

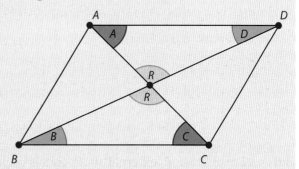

... alternate angles

$\angle B = \angle D$ ... alternate angles

$\angle R = \angle R$

$|AD| = |BC|$ ... $ABCD$ is a parallelogram

$\therefore \triangle ARD$ is congruent to $\triangle RCB$

$\therefore |AR| = |RC|$ and $|DR| = |BR|$

**Theorem 13. If two triangles are similar, then their sides are proportional and in order.**

$\triangle DEF$ is similar to $\triangle ABC$

$\therefore$ all the angles in $\triangle DEF =$ the angles in $\triangle ABC$

$\therefore \dfrac{|DE|}{|AB|} = \dfrac{|EF|}{|BC|} = \dfrac{|DF|}{|AC|}$

$\Rightarrow \dfrac{|AG|}{|AB|} = \dfrac{|GH|}{|BC|} = \dfrac{|AH|}{|AC|}$

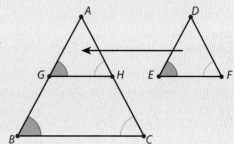

**Theorem of Pythagoras 14. In a right-angled triangle the square of the hypotenuse is the sum of the squares of the other two sides.**

$ABC$ is a right – angled triangle

Let $BD$ be perpendicular to $AC$

$\angle ABC = \angle ADB$, $\angle BAC = \angle BAD$, $\therefore \angle ABD = \angle BDC$

$\therefore \triangle ABC$ is similar to $\triangle ABD$, so their sides are in ratio.

$\therefore \dfrac{|AC|}{|AB|} = \dfrac{|AB|}{|AD|} \Rightarrow |AB|^2 = |AC| \cdot |AD|$

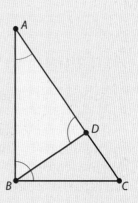

Also $\triangle ABC$ is similar to $\triangle BDC$, so their sides are in ratio.

$\therefore \dfrac{|AC|}{|BC|} = \dfrac{|BC|}{|DC|} \Rightarrow |BC|^2 = |AC| \cdot |DC|$

$\therefore |AB|^2 + |BC|^2 = |AC| \cdot |DC| + |AC| \cdot |AD| = (|AC|)(|DC| + |AD|) = |AC| \cdot |AC| = |AC|^2$

**Theorem 15. If the square of one side of a triangle is the sum of the squares of the other two sides, then the angle opposite the first side is a right-angle.**

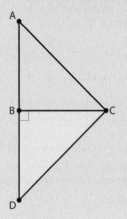

Given that $|AB|^2 + |BC|^2 = |AC|^2$

Draw a right-angled $\triangle BDC$ so that $|DB| = |AB|$

$|DC|^2 = |DB|^2 + |BC|^2$ ...Pythagoras

$|DC|^2 = |AB|^2 + |BC|^2$ ...$|DB| = |AB|$

$\therefore |DC|^2 = |AC|^2$ ...$|AB|^2 + |BC|^2 = |AC|^2$

$\therefore |DC| = |AC|$ and $|BC| = |BC|$ and $|DB| = |AB|$

$\therefore \triangle BDC$ is congruent to $\triangle ABC$

$\therefore \triangle DBC$ is a right-angle.

**Corollary to theorem 12. Each angle in a semi-circle is a right angle.**

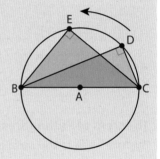

If BC is a diameter of a circle of centre A, then any point on the circumference D forms a right-angled triangle BDC.

If D moves to a new point E, triangle BEC is a right-angle.

**Conversely:** If the angle standing on a chord BC is a right-angle then the chord BC is a diameter.

## Assignment:

Using geometric shapes you have studied and the processes of:
central symmetry – axial symmetry – rotation and translation
design a logo for:

  (i)  A fitness centre.

or

 (ii)  A shipping company.

or

(iii)  A new technology firm.

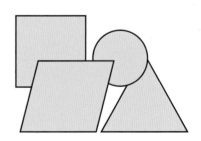

# Answers

## Chapter 1:  Number 1

### Exercise 1.1

1. (i) Y  (ii) N  (iii) N
   (iv) N  (v) N  (vi) Y
2. 5, 10, 15, 20, 25, 30
3. (i) 6, 12, 18, 24, 30, 36, 42, 48
   (ii) 7, 14, 21, 28, 35, 42, 49, 56
   (iii) 42
4. (i) 1, 2, 4, 7, 14, 28
   (ii) 1, 2, 3, 5, 6, 10, 15, 30
   (iii) 1, 3, 5, 9, 15, 45
   (iv) 1, 2, 3, 4, 5, 6, 10, 12, 15, 20, 30, 60
   (v) 1, 2, 3, 4, 6, 8, 9, 12, 18, 24, 36, 72
5. (i) 6  (ii) 6  (iii) 4  (iv) 4
6. 54, 60, 66
7. (i) 2, 3, 5, 7, 11, 13, 17, 19, 23, 29
   (ii) As every other even number has at least 3 factors, e.g. 6, 12
8. 13, 23, 31, 53
9. (i) $2^3 \times 3$  (ii) $2^2 \times 3^2$  (iii) $2 \times 3 \times 7$
   (iv) $2 \times 3 \times 11$  (v) $2^2 \times 5^2$
10. 13, 17, 37
11. 17, 29
12. €3 and €8 (or €6 and €8) (or 'euro'1, 'euro'24, (or 'euro'24, 'euro'24)
13. (1, 4, 18) years or (9, 9, 12) years or (9, 12, 12) years or (4, 4, 18) years or (4, 18, 18) years or (12, 12, 18) years or (12, 18, 18) years  or (1, 1, 36) years or (1, 36, 36) years or (36, 36, 36) years
14. 1 minute (60 sec)

### Exercise 1.2

1. (i) $-7°C, -4°C, 0°C, 3°C, 10°C$
   (ii) $-5°C, -4.5°C, -1°C, 6°C, 7.5°C$
2. (i) $-4°C$  (ii) $-9°C$  (iii) $-2°C$  (iv) $-10°C$
3. (i) 5  (ii) $-1$
   (iii) $-9$  (iv) $-8$
   (v) $-2$  (vi) $-19$
   (vii) $-2$  (viii) 4
4. SUBARU
5. (i) $7, -4$  (ii) $7, -12$
   (iii) $-4, -12$  (iv) $10, -5$
6. (i) $-12$  (ii) $-18$
   (iii) 6  (iv) $-40$
   (v) $-120$  (vi) $-56$

---

(vii) $-24$  (viii) $-48$
7. (i) 2  (ii) $-5$  (iii) $-3$
   (iv) $-7$  (v) 8  (vi) 5
8. (i) $-7$  (ii) 4  (iii) $-9$  (iv) 9
9. (i) SHEEP  (ii) RABBIT  (iii) HAMSTER
10. (i) 19  (ii) 7  (iii) 12  (iv) 14
    (v) 40  (vi) 6  (vii) 15  (viii) 34
    (ix) 58
11. (i) Fine as it is
    (ii) $54 \div (6 + 3) + 2 = 8$
    (iii) $(6 + 34 \div 2 + 3) \div 2 = 13$
    (iv) $42 \div (5 + 2) \times 5 = 30$
    (v) $15 + 4 \times (5 - 5) = 15$
    (vi) $(81 \div 9) \div (2 + 1) = 3$
12. (i) F  (ii) F  (iii) T  (iv) F
13. (i) $+, \div$  (ii) $-, \times$  (iii) $\times, -$
    (iv) $+, \div$  (v) $-, +$  (vi) $-, \div$
14. (i) 8  (ii) 5  (iii) 57  (iv) 1
15. (i) $-5 \times 4 \times -3$ (i.e. 60)
    (ii) $-5 \times 4 \times 3$ (i.e. $-60$)
16. (i) $-2°C$  (ii) 11 : 40 a.m.

### Exercise 1.3

1. (i) $\frac{5}{10}$  (ii) $\frac{3}{12}$  (iii) $\frac{8}{20}$  (iv) $\frac{4}{6}$
2. (i) $\frac{1}{2}$  (ii) $\frac{2}{3}$  (iii) $\frac{3}{4}$  (iv) $\frac{3}{5}$  (v) $\frac{5}{7}$
3. (i) $\frac{5}{3}$  (ii) $\frac{21}{8}$  (iii) $\frac{15}{4}$  (iv) $\frac{28}{5}$  (v) $\frac{61}{8}$
4. (i) $1\frac{3}{5}$  (ii) $5\frac{3}{4}$  (iii) $2\frac{2}{7}$  (iv) $3\frac{1}{4}$  (v) $6\frac{1}{2}$
5. $\frac{9}{2}\left(\text{i.e. } 4\frac{1}{2}\right)$
6. $\frac{8}{7}, \frac{17}{10}, \frac{11}{4}, \frac{15}{5}, \frac{10}{3}$
7. (i) $\frac{6}{7}$  (ii) $\frac{2}{3}$  (iii) $\frac{2}{5}$  (iv) $\frac{1}{4}$
8. (i) 6  (ii) 12  (iii) 18  (iv) 24
9. (i) $\frac{9}{10}$  (ii) $\frac{5}{8}$  (iii) $\frac{7}{12}$  (iv) $1\frac{5}{12}$
   (v) $\frac{13}{18}$  (vi) $1\frac{1}{15}$  (vii) $1\frac{3}{28}$  (viii) $\frac{31}{36}$
10. (i) $\frac{1}{12}$  (ii) $\frac{17}{40}$  (iii) $\frac{7}{30}$  (iv) $\frac{2}{3}$
11. (i) $\frac{1}{10}, \frac{1}{4}, \frac{2}{5}, \frac{1}{2}, \frac{3}{5}$  (ii) $\frac{7}{12}, \frac{5}{8}, \frac{2}{3}, \frac{17}{24}, \frac{3}{4}, \frac{5}{6}$
12. (i) $3\frac{11}{12}$  (ii) $4\frac{3}{10}$  (iii) $6\frac{1}{5}$
    (iv) $4\frac{7}{12}$  (v) $1\frac{3}{10}$  (vi) $2\frac{1}{15}$
    (vii) $\frac{5}{8}$  (viii) $2\frac{1}{6}$
13. (i) $\frac{5}{8}$  (ii) $\frac{2}{7}$  (iii) $\frac{3}{7}$  (iv) $\frac{1}{9}$

(v) $4\frac{2}{3}$    (vi) 6    (vii) $1\frac{1}{2}$    (viii) $\frac{18}{35}$

**17.** (i) $\frac{1}{2}$    (ii) 6    (iii) $\frac{5}{6}$    (iv) $2\frac{5}{8}$

**18.** (i) $\frac{11}{12}$ of 60 (55)    (ii) Both the same (18)

**19.** (i) Ⓐ and Ⓡ, Ⓑ and Ⓠ, Ⓒ and Ⓟ

(ii) $\frac{3}{10}, \frac{5}{12}, \frac{2}{15}$

**20.** GLASGOW     **21.** Ⓒ

**22.** 14 students     **23.** 5 tins

**24.** (i) 48      (ii) 84

**25.** Thirty      **26.** 13

**27.** €81

**28.** (i) $1\frac{3}{4}$ m; $\frac{7}{20}$ m

**29.** $\frac{5}{24}$

**30.** Largest $= \frac{115}{3}\left(3\frac{5}{6} \div \frac{1}{10}\right)$, smallest $= \frac{1}{80}\left(\frac{1}{8} \times \frac{1}{10}\right)$

**31.** $\frac{3}{8}$

**32.** 1215

## Exercise 1.4

**1.** (i) $\frac{4}{5}$    (ii) $\frac{1}{4}$    (iii) $\frac{3}{4}$
(iv) $\frac{7}{20}$    (v) $\frac{1}{20}$

**2.** (i) 0.7    (ii) 0.65    (iii) 0.87
(iv) 0.05    (v) 0.035

**3.** (i) 16   (ii) 134   (iii) 104   (iv) 20

**4.** (i) 7.4   (ii) 3.45   (iii) 0.015   (iv) 0.184

**5.** (i) 0.9    (ii) 6    (iii) 7.2
(iv) 12.3    (v) 16.3

**6.** (i) 9.525    (ii) 0.9525    (iii) 0.9525

**7.** (i) 12    (ii) 27    (iii) 1.2
(iv) 300    (v) 120    (vi) 3
(vii) 0.21    (viii) 0.84

**8.** (a) $= 7.4$,    (b) $= 8.2$,    (c) $= 8.8$,
(d) $= 0.75$,    (e) $= 1.5$,    (f) $= 2.25$

**9.** (i) $\frac{3}{5}$   (ii) $\frac{1}{4}$   (iii) $\frac{3}{4}$   (iv) $\frac{13}{20}$   (v) $\frac{1}{8}$

**10.** (i) 14      (ii) 24
(iii) 27      (iv) 24

**11.** (i) 60      (ii) 30
(iii) 24      (iv) 6

**12.** (i) 75      (ii) 161
(iii) 60      (iv) 210

**13.** 10% of 40 & 5% of 80 ; 30% of 10 & 50% of 6;
20% of 50 & 25% of 40 ; 30% of 50 & 75% of 20

**14.** (i) $\frac{3}{10}$      (ii) 30%
(iii)

**15.** (i) 0.15      (ii) 0.4
(iii) 0.09, 15%, 0.2, $\frac{2}{5}$

**16.** (i) 0.18, $\frac{1}{4}$, 28%, 0.3    (ii) 8%, 0.55, 0.6, $\frac{7}{10}$
(iii) 0.09, $\frac{3}{4}$, 78%, 0.8    (iv) 0.19, 0.4, 48%, $\frac{1}{2}$

**17.**

| Percentage | Fraction | Decimal |
|---|---|---|
| 21% | $\frac{21}{100}$ | 0.21 |
| 57% | $\frac{57}{100}$ | 0.57 |
| 41% | $\frac{41}{100}$ | 0.41 |
| 9% | $\frac{9}{100}$ | 0.09 |
| 3% | $\frac{3}{100}$ | 0.03 |
| 8% | $\frac{8}{100}$ | 0.08 |

**18.** (i) 87.5%, 85%, 80%, 90%, 87.5%
(ii) Business

**19.** (i) 75 m²    (ii) $41\frac{1}{4}$ m²    (iii) 8%

**20.** €239 616

## Exercise 1.5

**1.** (i) 5 : 4    (ii) 3 : 2    (iii) 2 : 5
(iv) 2 : 4 (1 : 2)   (v) $\frac{1}{8}$   (vi) $\frac{1}{4}$
(vii) 12.5%

**2.** (i) 1 : 2    (ii) 1 : 3    (iii) 4 : 5
(iv) 4 : 7    (v) 5 : 4    (vi) 2 : 5
(vii) 5 : 9    (viii) 2 : 3

**3.** (i) 9    (ii) 15    (iii) 6    (iv) 2
(v) 3    (vi) 28

**4.** (i) 1 : 4    (ii) 3 : 14    (iii) 1 : 5

**5.** (i) 1 : 4    (ii) 1 : 2    (iii) 3 : 2    (iv) 6 : 7

**6.** (i) 1 : 10    (ii) 1 : 4    (iii) 10 : 1    (iv) 3 : 4
(v) C     (vi) B

**7.** (i) 2 : 3    (ii) 2 : 3    (iii) 4 : 9

**8.** Lighter

**9.** 320 boys, 240 girls

**10.** Tom – €1050, Gerry – €840

**11.** €40 : €60 : €100

**12.** 75 kg

**13.** €1400

**14.** (i) (a) 750 g    (b) 270 g    (c) 360 g
(ii) 10      (iii) 12

**15.** €73.60

**16.** (i) $13\frac{1}{3}$ km      (ii) 60 km
(iii) 200 km ; 1 hr 15 min

**17.** (i) 9 km    (ii) 126 km
(iii) 10 $\ell$

**18.** Adam – €3240, Emer – €2160; Adam – €3000, Emer – €2400

**19.** 3 : 1

**20.** (i) 45 cm, 20 cm    (ii) 900 cm²
(iii) 30 cm      (iv) 12 : 13

## Test yourself 1

**1.** (i) 24    (ii) 6

**2.** (i)

(ii) $\frac{9}{10}, \frac{4}{5}, \frac{3}{4}, \frac{7}{10}, \frac{13}{20}, \frac{3}{5}$

**3.** €5508

**4.** $\frac{4}{5}$, 80%, 0.8; $\frac{3}{4}$, 75%, 0.75; $\frac{2}{5}$, 40%, $\frac{4}{10}$

**5.** (i) T    (ii) T    (iii) F(32)

**6.** ALBANIA

**7.** (i) 6 ℓ    (ii) 36

**8.** (i) $\frac{1}{4}, \frac{3}{10}, \frac{2}{5}, \frac{1}{2}, \frac{3}{5}$

   (ii) $\frac{1}{2}$, 60%, 0.65, $\frac{2}{3}, \frac{3}{4}, \frac{4}{5}$

**9.** (i) J    (ii) H    (iii) D

   (iv) I    (v) C

**10.** $7\frac{1}{2}$ cups of flour, 5 tsp baking powder,

   $\frac{5}{8}$ litre of milk

**11.** (i) 8%    (ii) 7.5%

**12.** 8400 ppl

**13.** Same (both 24)

**14.** $22\frac{1}{2}$ km

**15.** 28 veggie sausages, 1050 g rice, 7 ℓ water

**16.** (i) (a) correct (ii) (a) correct (iii) (b) correct

**17.** 3 : 11

## Chapter 2: Algebra 1

### Exercise 2.1

**1.** $10x$

**2.** $7a$

**3.** $5a + 8b$

**4.** $6x + 2y$, i.e. $2(3x + y)$

**5.** $15a + 6b$, i.e. $3(5a + 2b)$

**6.** $7x + 5y + 4$

**7.** $7x + 4$

**8.** $4x + 3$

**9.** $8a + 3b + 2$

**10.** $6x + 1$

**11.** $5a + 4b$

**12.** $5ab + 2$

**13.** $3p - q + r$

**14.** $2k + 5$

**15.** $7ab - 3c$

**16.** $4xy + 11z$

**17.** $5ab + 5cd$

**18.** $11x - 8xy$

**19.** $8a + 10$

**20.** $10x^2 + x$

**21.** $-t - 4w$

**22.** $-6h - 9$

**23.** $3m^2 + 2m + 3$

**24.** $11a^2 - a - 1$

**25.** $14a^2 - 11a$

**26.** $7ab - bc$

**27.** (i) $4x + 11$    (ii) $8a - 1$    (iii) $8x + 6$

**28.** $a : x + 2y + z$, $b : 4x + 2y$, $c : 2y + 3z$,
   $d : 4x + 4y + 3z$, $e : 3x - 2y$, $f : 5x - 2y$,
   $g : 8x - 4y$

**29.** (i) $4p + 2$    (ii) 3    (iii) $2x$    (iv) $5x + 4$

**30.** (i) $\boxed{3x + 1}$, $\boxed{x + 3}$

   (ii) $\boxed{3x + 1}$, $\boxed{4 - 2x}$

   (iii) $\boxed{2x}$, $\boxed{4 - 2x}$

   (iv) $\boxed{7 - x}$, $\boxed{x + 3}$

   (v) $\boxed{7 - x}$, $\boxed{3x + 1}$, $\boxed{4 - 2x}$

   (vi) $\boxed{7 - x}$, $\boxed{3x + 1}$, $\boxed{x + 3}$

   (vii) $4x + 10$

**31.** (i) $3b$            (ii) $5w$

   (iii) $4j$          (iv) $3j, 4, 3k$

**32.** $2 - 5d$

**33.** $a : x + y$, $b : 3x - 2y$, $c : 7x - y$

**34.** (i) $x, y$    (ii) $-4$    (iii) two

   (iv) $+3xy$    (v) $+6$

### Exercise 2.2

**1.** (i) $12a$    (ii) $21x$    (iii) $16m$

   (iv) $48a$    (v) $6m^2$    (vi) $6pq$

   (vii) $6k^2$    (viii) $6ab$

**2.** (i) $a^2b$    (ii) $2ab^2$    (iii) $6a^2b^2$

   (iv) $10cd^2e$    (v) $6ab$    (vi) $18abc$

   (vii) $abc$    (viii) $12x^2y$

**3.** (i) $-15x$    (ii) $-14m$    (iii) $12a$

   (iv) $-27m$    (v) $30k$    (vi) $14a$

   (vii) $-2ab$    (viii) $pq$    (ix) $-10mn$

   (x) $6tw$    (xi) $-56xy$    (xii) $-30m^2$

**4.** $11x + 7$        **5.** $8x + 7$

**6.** $13x - 8$        **7.** $x + 2$

**8.** $18x - 20$       **9.** $3x - 14$

**10.** $a - 1$         **11.** $a - 5$

**12.** (i) $4x^2 - 4x - 6$    **13.** $x^2 + x - 24$

**14.** (i) $2x^2 + 7x + 3$    (ii) $3x^2 - 12x - 15$

**15.** $2x^2 + 11x + 12$    **16.** $2x^2 + 11x + 5$

**17.** $3x^2 - 10x - 8$    **18.** $2x^2 + 3x - 9$

**19.** $2x^2 + 6x - 8$    **20.** $2x^2 - x - 3$

**21.** $x^2 - 5x + 6$    **22.** $2x^2 - 7x + 6$

**23.** $4x^2 + 7x - 15$    **24.** $2x^2 - 11x - 6$

**25.** $3x^2 - 13x - 10$    **26.** $2x^2 - 13x + 15$

**27.** $10x^2 + 11x - 6$    **28.** $2x^2 + 7x - 4$

**29.** $2x^2 - 8xy + 6y^2$    **30.** $12x^2 + 5xy - 3y^2$

**31.** $4x^2 - xy - 5y^2$    **32.** $x^2 + 8x + 16$

**33.** $4x^2 + 12x + 9$    **34.** $4x^2 - 4x + 1$

**35.** (i) $8x + 2$    (ii) $3x^2 + 5x - 2$

### Exercise 2.3

**1.** (i) 15    (ii) 9    (iii) 7    (iv) 4

**2.** (i) 10    (ii) 8    (iii) $-10$    (iv) 8

**3.** (i) 8    (ii) 5    (iii) 3    (iv) 3

**4.** (i) 5    (ii) $-18$    (iii) 10    (iv) $-14$

**5.** (i) 9    (ii) 5    (iii) 8    (iv) 6

**6.** (i) 5    (ii) 16    (iii) 35
    (iv) 1    (v) 2    (vi) 21
    (vii) 14    (viii) 19
**7.** (i) 29    (ii) 4
    (iii) 2    (iv) 3
**8.** (i) 9    (ii) 6    (iii) 6
    (iv) 9    (v) 12    (vi) 7
    (vii) 5    (viii) 7

## Exercise 2.4

**1.** (i) 6    (ii) 14    (iii) 7
    (iv) 9    (v) 5    (vi) 8
    (vii) 33    (viii) 15
**2.** (i) 7    (ii) 4    (iii) 10
    (iv) 4    (v) 3    (vi) 6
**3.** (i) $x = 4$    (ii) $x = 9$    (iii) $x = 7$
    (iv) $x = 7$    (v) $x = 7$
**4.** $x = 7$     **5.** $x = 16$     **6.** $x = 7$
**7.** $x = 4$     **8.** $x = 3$     **9.** $x = 7$
**10.** $x = 6$     **11.** $x = 4$     **12.** $x = 5$
**13.** $x = 3$     **14.** $x = 4$     **15.** $x = 1$
**16.** $x = 6$     **17.** $x = -4$     **18.** $x = 4$
**19.** $x = 6$     **20.** $x = 5$     **21.** $x = 2$
**22.** $x = 6$     **23.** $x = 6$     **24.** $x = 14$
**25.** $x = -9$     **26.** $x = 10$     **27.** $x = 2$
**28.** $x = 3$     **29.** $x = 14$     **30.** $x = 3$
**31.** $x = 1$     **32.** $x = 10$     **33.** $x = 2$
**34.** $x = 3$
**35.** (i) $x = 5$     (ii) $x = 5$
**36.** (i) $x = 2$     (ii) $x = 2$
**37.** $x = 7$
**38.** (i) $a = 2$     (ii) $m = 3$
    (iii) $n = 2$     (iv) $a = 2$

## Exercise 2.5

**1.** (i) $3x + 2 = 17; 5$     (ii) $4x + 1 = 13; 3$
    (iii) $3x - 4 = 2x; 4$     (iv) $4(x + 2) = 20; 3$
**2.** $4x + 3 = 3x + 8; 5$
**3.** 2      **4.** 4      **5.** 9
**6.** 15      **7.** $(x + 4); 4, 8$
**8.** (i) $3x$    (ii) $3x + 3$    (iii) $x + 3$
    (iv) $x + 3 + 3x + 3 = 26$
    (v) Martin $= 15$, Eoin $= 5$
**9.** 14      **10.** 6, 11
**11.** (i) $6x + 1$     (ii) 9    **12.** 7
**13.** (i) $(6x + 2)$ cm     (ii) $6x + 2 = 44; x = 7$
**14.** (i) $(4x + 20)°$
    (ii) $4x + 20 = 180°; x = 40°$
**15.** Chair – €50, stool – €40
**16.** $x = 7$     **17.** $x + 5 = 3x - 7; x = 6; 11$ cm
**18.** 10 years old    **19.** 48
**20.** (i) 15    (ii) 9.5    (iii) 10

## Exercise 2.6

**1.** (a) $x + 2$ (b) $x + 3$    **2.** $x + 4$    **3.** $x + 7$
**4.** $2x + 1$     **5.** $3x + 1$     **6.** $x - 2$
**7.** $2x - 4$     **8.** $2x + 1$     **9.** $x - 7$
**10.** $3x - 5$     **11.** $5x + 4$    **12.** $3x - 4$

## Test yourself 2

**1.** (i) $2x + 3$    (ii) $4y + 18$    (iii) $2k + 22$
**2.** (i) 4    (ii) $-6$    (iii) $-3$
    (iv) 22
**3.** (i) $x = 3$    (ii) 7
**4.** (i) $8x + 3$    (ii) $6x - 5$
**5.** A
**6.** (i) $-3$    (ii) 4
**7.** (i) 12    (ii) 4
    (iii) 12    (iv) 2
**8.** (i) $g + 15$    (ii) $12 - t$
**9.** $4(x + 3) = 48; 9$
**10.** (i) $8x - 22$   (ii) $x^2 + 18x$
**11.** (i) A – 52, B – 66, C – 18, D – 32, E – 15, F – 9
    (ii) D     (iii) F     (iv) A and B
**12.** (i) $4a + 4b$ (ii) $2p + q + 2$
**13.** (i) $7 - x$    (ii) $6 - 4k$
**14.** $x = 3; 21$
**15.** (i) $x + 3$    (ii) $2x - 4$
**16.** All $= 21$
**17.** $10(x + 3); 2 - 4x^2$
**18.** (i) €150    (ii) $T = a + 6b$

## Chapter 3: Sets

### Exercise 3.1

**1.** A Venn diagram; $A = \{1, 3, 4, 6, 8\}$; $\#A = 5$
**2.** (i) T    (ii) F    (iii) T    (iv) F
**3.** Is an element of; is not an element of;
    (i) $\in$    (ii) $\notin$    (iii) $\in$    (iv) $\notin$    (v) $\in$
**4.** A and C; both contain exactly the same
    elements
**5.** (i) $\{1, 3, 4, 5, 6, 7\}$     (ii) $\{1, 7, 8, 9, 10, 11\}$
    (iii) $\{1, 7\}$
    (iv) $\{1, 3, 4, 5, 6, 7, 8, 9, 10, 11\}$
**6.** (i) $\{4, 5, 6\}$     (ii) $\{4, 5, 6, 7, 8, 9, 10\}$
    (iii) $\{7, 8\}$     (iv) $\{\}$ ($\varnothing$)
**7.** (i) 7    (ii) 6    (iii) 3    (iv) 10
**8.** U

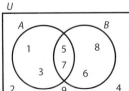

**9.** (i) {a, e, i, o, t, u}  (ii) {o, p, q, r, s, t, u}
(iii) {o, t, u}
(iv) {a, e, i, o, p, q, r, s, t, u}

**10.** (i) {1, 2, 3, 5, 6, 7, 8, 9}
(ii) {1, 5, 6, 8, 9}  (iii) {2, 3, 7}

**11.** (i) {3, 4, 5, 6}  (ii) {3, 4, 8, 9}
(iii) {2, 7, 8, 9, 10}  (iv) {2, 5, 6, 7, 10}
(v) {3, 4, 5, 6, 8, 9}  (vi) {2, 7, 10}

**12.** (i) 7  (ii) 7  (iii) 14
(iv) 11  (v) 3  (vi) 3

**13.** (i) {2, 4, 6, 8, 9, 10}  (ii) {1, 2, 7, 8, 9, 10}
(iii) {1, 3, 4, 5, 6, 7}  (iv) {2, 8, 9, 10}

**14.**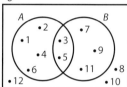

**15.** (i) T  (ii) T  (iii) T
(iv) T  (v) T  (vi) F

**16.** (ii) {e, f, g}  (iii) 1

**17.** Is a subset of; is not a subset of;
(i) ⊂  (ii) ⊂  (iii) ⊄  (iv) ⊄

**18.** (i) {3}, {4}, {5}
(ii) {3, 4}, {3, 5}, {4, 5}
{ }, {3, 4, 5}

**19.** (i) {−2, −1, 0, 1, 2}
(ii) {4, 8, 12, 16, 20}
(iii) {2, 3, 4, 5, 6, 7, 8, 9, 10, 11}

**20.**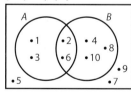

**21.** {5, 6, 7}
**22.** {−2, −1, 0, 1}
**23.**

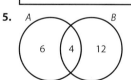

(i) False  (ii) True  (iii) False

## Exercise 3.2

**1.** (i) {1, 2, 4, 5, 7, 8}  (ii) {3, 9, 10}
(iii) {1, 3, 5, 7}  (iv) { }

**2.** (i) {a, c, e}  (ii) {f, g, h}
(iii) {f, g, h, i, j}  (iv) {a, c, e, f, g, h, i, j}

**3.** (i) T  (ii) F  (iii) T  (iv) F
(v) T  (vi) T  (vii) T  (viii) F

**4.** (i) {2, 4, 8, 10}
(ii) {3, 9, 15}; no; set difference is not
commutative

**5.** (i) {5, 6, 8, 12}  (ii) {1, 2, 3, 4, 6}
(iii) {0, 15}  (iv) {5, 6, 8, 10, 12}
(v) {1, 3, 6}  (vi) {1, 2, 3, 8, 10, 12}

**6.** 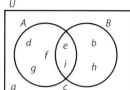 ;  (i) 3
(ii) 4
(iii) 2
(iv) 7

**8.** (i) T  (ii) T  (iii) T  (iv) F  (v) T  (vi) T

**9.** Total = 20

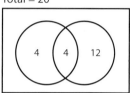

(a) 12  (b) 8  (c) 4

**10.** (i) N – Natural numbers, Z – Integers,
Q – Rational numbers, R – Real

**11.** (i) Students who like apples or bananas
(ii) Students who like apples only.

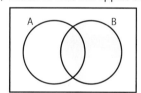

## Exercise 3.3

**1.** (i) 5  (ii) 30  (iii) 11  (iv) 7
**2.** (i) 12  (ii) 11  (iii) 2  (iv) 7
**3.** (i) 40  (ii) 33  (iii) 28  (iv) 14
**4.** 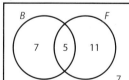 ;  (i) 7
(ii) 7
(iii) 18

**5.**

(i) 23  (ii) 17  (iii) 9  (iv) 31
**6.** (i) 23  (ii) 17  (iii) 9  (iv) 31

**7.** *U*

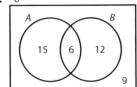

; (i) 33
(ii) 24
(iii) 9

**8.** *U*

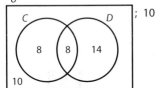

; 10

**9.** (i) 33 (ii) 12 (iii) 16

**10.** *A*

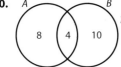

; (i) 4
(ii) 10

**11.** (i) some were in both clubs (ii) 16 (iii) 39
**12.** (i) 6 (ii) 10 (iii) 22
**13.** 32
**14.** *U*

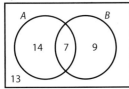

; (i) 7
(ii) 9
(iii) 13

## Test yourself 3

**1.** (i) {2, 3, 4, 5, 7} (ii) {3, 5, 7}
 (iii) {1, 6, 9, 10, 11} (iv) 2
**2.** (i) 7 (ii) 9 (iii) 12 (iv) 8
**3.** (i) {2, 3, 5, 6, 7, 8, 9}
 (ii) {1, 4, 8, 9, 12}
 (iii) {1, 2, 3, 4, 5, 6, 7, 8, 9, 12}
 (iv) {2, 3, 5, 6, 7}

**4.** (i) 30 (ii) 17 (iii) 7
 (iv) 8 (v) 15
**5.** (i) {4} (ii) {2, 3}
 (iii) {1, 2, 3, 4, 8} (iv) {1, 2, 3, 8}
**6.** (iv) is true
**7.** (i) {a, b, c, d, e} (ii) {c, d, g, h}
 (iii) {a, b, c, d, e, g, h, k, l, m}
 (iv) {c, d}
 (v) {g, h, k, l, m}
 (vi) {k, l, m}
**8.** 6

**9.** (i) {2, 4, 5, 6, 8}
 (ii) {2, 3, 4, 5, 6, 7, 8}
 (iii) {3, 7}
 (iv) {2, 5, 8, 9}
**10.** (i) 28 (ii) 12 (iii) 12
**11.** 12, 18
**12.** *U*

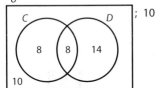

# Chapter 4: Factors

## Exercise 4.1

**1.** (i) 3 (ii) 6
 (iii) 7 (iv) 7
**2.** (i) $4x$ (ii) $3n$ (iii) $5x$
 (iv) $3a$ (v) $3x$ (vi) $2ab$
**3.** $4(x + 2)$ **4.** $6(a + 2b)$
**5.** $7(x + 2y)$ **6.** $11(2a + 3b)$
**7.** $12(x - 2y)$ **8.** $b(a + c)$
**9.** $2a(x + 2y)$ **10.** $x(x + 1)$
**11.** $5x(x - 2)$ **12.** $3a(a + 2)$
**13.** $4x(x - 3)$ **14.** $6b(a - 2c)$
**15.** $7xy(x - 2)$ **16.** $3x^2(2y - 5)$
**17.** $4(x + 4)$ **18.** $6(x + 3y)$
**19.** $10(a - 4b)$ **20.** $a(b + y)$
**21.** $3b(a + c)$ **22.** $2x(y - z)$
**23.** $7x(y + 2z)$ **24.** $5b(a - 3c)$
**25.** $6a(x - 2y)$ **26.** $x(x + 4)$
**27.** $3x(x + 3)$ **28.** $5x(x + 2)$
**29.** $6a(a - 2)$ **30.** $7a(a - 3)$
**31.** $10x(x + 4)$ **32.** $5x(5x - 3)$
**33.** $7x(x - 4)$ **34.** $6x(2x + 3)$
**35.** $5x(3x + 5y)$ **36.** $3x^2(1 - 2y)$
**37.** $x(x^2 + x + 1)$ **38.** $3ab(b - 2)$
**39.** $12xy(1 - 2x)$ **40.** $5x^2(3x - 7)$

## Exercise 4.2

**1.** $(x + 4)(a + b)$ **2.** $(2a + 3)(x + 4)$
**3.** $(y + z)(x + y)$ **4.** $(b + 2c)(a + 3)$
**5.** $(x - 6)(a + 3)$ **6.** $(x + y)(2a - 3b)$
**7.** $(2x - 3)(3x + 1)$ **8.** $(3b - c)(2a - 1)$
**9.** $(a + b)(x + y)$ **10.** $(b + d)(a + c)$
**11.** $(c + 3)(a + b)$ **12.** $(p + q)(m + n)$
**13.** $(2b + 3d)(a + c)$ **14.** $(7x + 3)(a - b)$
**15.** $(c + 2)(a - b)$ **16.** $(c + 2d)(a - b)$
**17.** $(a + b)(2x + 3y)$ **18.** $(4 + a)(x - y)$
**19.** $(3 + x)(a - b)$ **20.** $(a + 4)(x - 2)$

**21.** $(b + d)(2a - c)$    **22.** $(a + b)(2x - y)$
**23.** $(x + b)(x + a)$    **24.** $(a + c)(a - 2b)$
**25.** $(y - z)(4a + x)$    **26.** $(m + n)(3x - a)$
**27.** $(x + z)(x - y)$    **28.** $(2 - c)(x - y)$
**29.** $(3 - b)(x + y)$    **30.** $(5 - c)(a + b)$
**31.** $(x + y)(x - 2)$    **32.** $(a + b)(a - 3)$
**33.** $(a - b)(x - 1)$    **34.** $(y - z)(a - 2b)$
**35.** $(x + 1)(2a - 3b)$    **36.** $(a - 1)(x + 2y)$
**37.** $(a - b)(b + c)$    **38.** $(b + 2d)(a - c)$
**39.** $(a - 3)(b + 3)$    **40.** $(3a + 2b)(x - 2y)$

## Exercise 4.3

**1.** $(x + 2)(x - 2)$    **2.** $(x + 4)(x - 4)$
**3.** $(y + 6)(y - 6)$    **4.** $(y + 10)(y - 10)$
**5.** $(a - 3)(a + 3)$
**6.** (ii) $5(c + d)(c - d)$   (iii) $3(a + 3)(a - 3)$
    (iv) $3(x + 5)(x - 5)$    (v) $12(a + 2)(a - 2)$
**7.** 9200            **8.** 53
**9.** 400             **10.** 109

## Exercise 4.4

**1.** $(x + 2)(x + 1)$    **2.** $(x + 2)(x + 2)$
**3.** $(x + 7)(x + 1)$    **4.** $(x + 3)(x + 2)$
**5.** $(x + 6)(x + 2)$    **6.** $(x + 7)(x + 2)$
**7.** $(a + 4)(a + 3)$    **8.** $(x + 3)(x + 1)$
**9.** $(a + 4)(a + 2)$    **10.** $(a + 6)(a + 3)$
**11.** $(a + 8)(a + 2)$    **12.** $(a + 6)(a + 4)$
**13.** $(x + 8)(x + 3)$    **14.** $(x + 10)(x + 2)$
**15.** $(x + 9)(x + 3)$    **16.** $(x + 11)(x + 2)$
**17.** $(x + 10)(x + 3)$    **18.** $(x + 6)(x + 5)$
**19.** $(x + 11)(x + 3)$    **20.** $(x + 12)(x + 3)$
**21.** $(x + 11)(x + 4)$    **22.** $(x + 5)(x + 4)$
**23.** $(x + 17)(x + 1)$    **24.** $(x + 16)(x + 2)$
**25.** $(x - 3)(x - 1)$    **26.** $(x - 3)(x - 2)$
**27.** $(x - 4)(x - 2)$    **28.** $(x - 4)(x - 1)$
**29.** $(x - 4)(x - 3)$    **30.** $(x - 5)(x - 2)$
**31.** $(x - 7)(x - 2)$    **32.** $(x - 8)(x - 3)$
**33.** $(p - 5)(p - 3)$    **34.** $(x - 6)(x - 3)$
**35.** $(x - 5)(x - 4)$    **36.** $(x - 10)(x - 2)$
**37.** $(x - 7)(x - 5)$    **38.** $(x - 6)(x - 4)$
**39.** $(x - 12)(x - 2)$    **40.** $(x - 9)(x - 3)$
**41.** $(x - 6)(x - 5)$    **42.** $(x - 10)(x - 3)$
**43.** $(x - 15)(x - 2)$    **44.** $(x - 9)(x - 4)$
**45.** $(m - 12)(m - 3)$    **46.** $(x - 9)(x - 5)$
**47.** $(x - 10)(x - 4)$    **48.** $(x - 8)(x - 5)$

## Exercise 4.5

**1.** $(x - 2)(x + 1)$    **2.** $(x - 3)(x + 1)$
**3.** $(x - 4)(x + 1)$    **4.** $(x - 1)(x + 3)$
**5.** $(x - 4)(x + 3)$    **6.** $(x - 3)(x + 4)$

**7.** $(x - 6)(x + 2)$    **8.** $(x - 5)(x + 2)$
**9.** $(x - 10)(x + 1)$    **10.** $(x - 7)(x + 2)$
**11.** $(x - 5)(x + 3)$    **12.** $(x - 2)(x + 9)$
**13.** $(x - 3)(x + 6)$    **14.** $(x - 3)(x + 7)$
**15.** $(x - 6)(x + 4)$    **16.** $(x - 3)(x + 8)$
**17.** $(x - 12)(x + 2)$    **18.** $(x - 6)(x + 5)$
**19.** $(x - 3)(x + 10)$    **20.** $(x - 15)(x + 2)$
**21.** $(x - 4)(x + 7)$    **22.** $(x - 14)(x + 2)$
**23.** $(x - 4)(x + 9)$    **24.** $(x + 3)(x - 12)$
**25.** $(x - 4)(x + 10)$    **26.** $(x - 8)(x + 5)$
**27.** $(x - 20)(x + 2)$    **28.** $(x - 9)(x + 5)$
**29.** $(x - 2)(x + 8)$    **30.** $(x + 4)(x - 12)$
**31.** $(p + 7)(p + 2)$    **32.** $(m - 9)(m - 3)$
**33.** $(x - 4)(x + 6)$    **34.** $(x - 7)(x - 1)$
**35.** $(x - 7)(x - 2)$    **36.** $(x - 8)(x + 4)$
**37.** $(x + 12)(x + 2)$    **38.** $(x - 6)(x + 7)$
**39.** $(x - 5)(x + 10)$    **40.** $(x - 7)(x - 4)$
**41.** $(x - 10)(x + 6)$    **42.** $(s - 12)(s - 5)$

## Test yourself 4

**1.** (i) $9x(x + 4)$          (ii) $5b(a + 3c)$
    (iii) $6a(x - 2y)$      (iv) $6x(x^2 - 3y)$
**2.** (i) $(a + b)(7 + x)$    (ii) $(a - 5b)(a + c)$
**3.** (i) $(x - 5)(x - 11)$   (ii) $16(x - 1)(x + 1)$
**4.** (i) $(p - 2)$         (ii) $(4n + 1)$
    (iii) $(3x - 1)$        (iv) $(d - 3)$
**5.** $(n + 1)$
**6.** (i) $(n + 4)$    (ii) $(n + 6)$     (iii) $(n - 8)$
**7.** (i) $(12 - b)(12 + b)$    (ii) 600
**8.** (i) $(x - 3z)$       (ii) $(x - 3z)$
**9.** (i) $(2a - b)(3x + y)$    (ii) $(x - 6)(x - 9)$
**10.** (i) $6(x - 2)(x + 2)$    (ii) 1080
**11.** (i) $4(2a + 3b - 4c)$    (ii) $6x(x - 3)$
**12.** (i) $(5 + y)(x + y)$    (ii) $(x - 2)(x - 11)$
**13.** (i) $(4 + a)(4 - a)$    (ii) $(x - 5)$

# Chapter 5: Applied Arithmetic

## Exercise 5.1

**1.** €594.90          **2.** €282.12
**3.** €381.26          **4.** €1264.32
**5.** (i) 671      (ii) €140.91
**6.** €347.25          **7.** 480
**8.** €407.33
**9.** D. Maher – €143.35; G. O. Gorman – €198.85
**10.** €65.70
**11.** €205.52
**12.** €94.34
**13.** (i) €25.20    (ii) €39.20    (iii) €17.60
    (iv) €25.20; total cost = €107.20

**14.** €900
**15.** (i) 8     (ii) €640     (iii) 5
**16.** (i) €12.60     (ii) €31.52
**17.** (i) 30c     (ii) 75c     (iii) €1.20
**18.** €15.90
**19.** (i) €2780     (ii) €4320
(iii) €2280     (iv) €5880
**20.** (i) €1152     (ii) €1275.90
(iii) €926.80     (iv) €848; €260 000
**21.** €189.77

## Exercise 5.2

**1.** (i) 0.06     (ii) 0.08     (iii) 0.075     (iv) 0.095
(v) 0.1     (vi) 0.13     (vii) 0.125     (viii) 1.06
(ix) 1.12     (x) 0.84
**2.** (i) 220     (ii) 144     (iii) 260     (iv) 102
**3.** (i) 320     (ii) 18     (iii) 1110     (iv) 15
**4.** (i) €799.50     (ii) €145.20
(iii) €340.50     (iv) €1380
**5.** €119.90     **6.** €200
**7.** €800     **8.** €120
**9.** A: €184.80, B: €368, C: €2.43, D: €30 000,
E: €37.80, F: €10 560, G: €1120
**10.** 25%
**11.** (i) €60     (ii) 10%
**12.** 25%     **13.** €1380
**14.** (i) €600 each     (ii) 15%
(iii) 5%
**15.** €60; €18     **16.** 30%
**17.** (i) €245     (ii) €240
**18.** (i) €920     (ii) €1104
**19.** 20%     **20.** $21\frac{1}{3}$%
**21.** (i) €320     (ii) 17%
**22.** PJ's (€256)

## Exercise 5.3

**1.** (i) €6     (ii) €8     (iii) €8
(iv) €21
**2.** (i) €24     (ii) €52.50     (iii) €85.50
(iv) €132
**3.** (i) €27     (ii) €127.50     (iii) €103.50
(iv) €300
**4.** (i) €324     (ii) €954     (iii) €1664
(iv) €1960     (v) €1207.50     (vi) €748
**5.** (i) €9     (ii) €42     (iii) €96
(iv) €56     (v) €12     (vi) €120

## Exercise 5.4

**1.**

| Year | Principal | Rate | Interest | Final Amount |
|---|---|---|---|---|
| 1 | €400 | 6% | (400 × 0.06) = €24 | €424 |
| 2 | €424 | 6% | (424 × 0.06) = €25.44 | €449.44 |

(i) €49.44     (ii) €449.44
**2.** €133.12     **3.** €92.25
**4.** €188.10     **5.** €57.12
**6.** €178.50     **7.** €126.10
**8.** €305.28     **9.** €162.47
**10.** €224.76     **11.** €122
**12.** €1505.28     **13.** €1736.44
**14.** €1663.20     **15.** €15 540.35
**16.**

| Year | Principal | Rate | Interest | Final Amount | Withdrawal |
|---|---|---|---|---|---|
| 1 | €12 000 | 3% | €360 | €12 360 | |
| 2 | €12 360 | 4% | €494.40 | €12 354.40 | €500 |
| 3 | €12 354.40 | 6% | €471.26 | €13 095.66 | |

**17.** (i) 0.75%     (ii) 0.67%
**18.** (i) 1.2%     (ii) 0.375%
**19.**

| Year | Principal | Rate | Interest | Final Amount |
|---|---|---|---|---|
| 1 | €1200 | 3% | €36 | €1236 |
| 2 | €1236 | 3% | €37.08 | €1273.08 |
| 3 | €1273.08 | 3% | €38.19 | €1311.27 |

## Exercise 5.5

**1.** €730     **2.** €29 729
**3.** €120, €120, €78     **4.** €120.50
**5.** €424     **6.** €136.80
**7.** €5640
**8.** (i) €174     (ii) €876
**9.** (i) €520     (ii) €67.20     (iii) €452.80
**10.** (i) €3240     (ii) €8660     (iii) €42 100
**11.** (i) €703.33     (ii) €3296.67
**12.** €1421.54

## Exercise 5.6

**1.** (i) $435     (ii) 86 250 yen
**2.** (i) $585     (ii) €615.38
**3.** (i) 108 000 yen     (ii) €75
**4.** (i) £960     (ii) €750

5. €400
6. (i) 4900 Canadian dollars    (ii) €4000
7. (i) €250    (ii) €423.53
8. (i) 6900 kr    (ii) €163.04
9. (i) €2868
10. (i) €6737    (ii) 7980 rand
11. 101 600 yen, €16

## Test yourself 5

1. (i) €60    (ii) €7.50
2. 30%
3. €329.69
4. (i) €731.50    (ii) €936
5. 641
6. (i) €24.60    (ii) €8.85
7. €102.40
8. €208
9. €111.24
10. (i) A – €1190, B – €1210
    (ii) €20
11. (i) 72 000 baht    (ii) €55
12. €651.60
13. (i) 14%    (ii) 7%
14. (i) €6880    (ii) €35 120
15. (A), $\times 1.76$ ; (B), $\times 0.76$ ; (C), $\times 1.24$ ;
    (D), $\times 0.24$ ; (E), $\times 1.2$ ; (F), $\times 0.8$
16. (i) €991.20
    (ii) 2250 km
17. €35

## Chapter 6:
## Perimeter – Area – Volume

### Exercise 6.1

1. (i) 46 cm    (ii) 42 cm    (iii) 56 cm
2. (i) 126 cm$^2$    (ii) 104 cm$^2$    (iii) 187 cm$^2$
3. (i) 30 cm    (ii) 36 cm$^2$
4. (i) 36 m$^2$    (ii) 27 m$^2$
5. (i) 20 cm$^2$    (ii) 15 cm$^2$    (iii) 30 cm$^2$
6. (i) 56 cm$^2$    (ii) 120 cm$^2$    (iii) 120 cm$^2$
    (iv) $31\frac{1}{2}$ cm$^2$    (v) 60 cm$^2$    (vi) 240 cm$^2$
7. 100 cm$^2$, 182 cm$^2$, 270 cm$^2$
8. (i) 220 cm$^2$    (ii) 165 m$^2$    (iii) 24 cm$^2$
9. (i) 312 cm$^2$    (ii) 126 cm$^2$
10. (i) 7 cm    (ii) 16 cm    (iii) 22 cm
11. (i) 5 cm    (ii) 12 m    (iii) 25 cm
12. (i) 6 cm    (ii) 7 cm    (iii) 9 cm

13. (i) 10 cm    (ii) 14 cm    (iii) 12 cm
14. (i) 58 cm    (ii) 54 cm    (iii) 58 cm
15. (i) 12 cm$^2$    (ii) 24 cm$^2$    (iii) $x = 8$ cm
16. 20 m$^2$; 25 m$^2$
17. (i) 21 cm$^2$    (ii) 55 cm$^2$    (iii) 165 cm$^2$
18. (i) 3600 cm$^2$    (ii) 2520 cm$^2$
    (iii) 4.5 cm (across); 4 cm (top-to-bottom)

### Exercise 6.2

1. (i) 240 cm$^2$    (ii) 63 cm$^2$    (iii) 165 cm$^2$
2. (i) 60 cm$^2$    (ii) 52.5 cm$^2$    (iii) 30 cm$^2$
3. (i) 6 cm    (ii) 7 cm    (iii) 4.5 cm
4. (i) 126 cm$^2$    (ii) 154 cm$^2$    (iii) 120 cm$^2$
5. (i) 5 cm    (ii) 6.5 cm    (iii) 12 cm
6. 322 cm$^2$; 154 cm$^2$
7. (i) $a : 6$ cm$^2$, $b : 4.8$ cm$^2$, $c : 7.2$ cm$^2$
   (ii) $a : 1.5$ cm, $b : 1.6$ cm, $c : 4$ cm

### Exercise 6.3

1. (i) 24 cm$^3$    (ii) 30 cm$^3$    (iii) 72 cm$^3$
2. (i) 52 cm$^2$    (ii) 62 cm$^2$    (iii) 108 cm$^2$
3. (i) 120 cm$^3$, 164 cm$^2$ (ii) 1368 cm$^3$, 828 cm$^2$
   (iii) 216 cm$^3$, 216 cm$^2$
4. (i) 188 cm$^2$    (ii) 209 cm$^2$
5. (i) 900 cm$^3$    (ii) 368 cm$^3$    (iii) 532 cm$^3$
6. (i) 64 cm$^3$    (ii) 136 cm$^2$
7. (i) 10 cm    (ii) 2.5 cm    (iii) 6 cm
8. (i) 5 cm    (ii) 150 cm$^2$
9. (i) 4 cm    (ii) 64 cm$^3$
10. (i) 19    (ii) 152 cm$^3$
    (iii) 56    (iv) 224 cm$^2$
11. 150
12. 25 cm
13. (i) (a) 2.42 m$^3$    (b) 2420 $\ell$    (ii) 11.44 m$^2$
14. €40 320 000
15. (i)    (ii) 10 left over
16. 64 cm$^3$
17. $\frac{a}{b} = \frac{1}{3}$
18. (i) 6 $\ell$    (ii) 1.6 $\ell$    (iii) 6.75 $\ell$

### Exercise 6.4

1. (i) 1.5 m    (ii) 3.5 m    (iii) 9 m
   (iv) 3.25 m    (v) 6.4 m
2. (i) 80 km    (ii) 6 cm

**3.** (i) 6 m    (ii) 24 m    (iii) 40 m
    (iv) 7.5 m

**4.** (i) 120 cm    (ii) 3.6 m    (iii) 1.35 m

**5.** 6.2 m; 2.7 m

**6.** (i) (a) 400 m      (b) 1 km
     (c) 1.7 km      (d) 2.5 km
   (ii) (a) 50 cm      (b) 20 cm
     (c) 2 m      (d) 135 cm

**7.** (i) 17 km    (ii) 4.4 cm

**8.** (i) 7.52 m    (ii) 2.16 m

**9.** (i) (a) 12 cm      (b) 8.5 cm
   (ii)

**10.** 1 : 40 000; 75 cm

**11.** (i) 1 : 200    (ii) 6 m    (iii) 30 m$^2$

**12.** (i) 50 cm    (ii) 1 : 25

### Test yourself 6

**1.** 44 cm$^2$

**2.** (i) 2880 cm$^3$    (ii) 1288 cm$^2$

**3.** 105 cm$^2$

**4.** 24 cm

**5.** 7 cm

**6.** (i) $b = 30$ cm, $a = 20$ cm    (ii) 24 litres
   (iii) 5200 cm$^2$

**7.** (i) 330 000 cm$^3$    (ii) 330*l*

**8.** face 3

**9.** 99 m$^2$

**10.** (i) 66 cm$^3$    (ii) 8    (iii) 122 cm$^2$
   (iv) 70 cm    (v) 4

**11.** 126 cm$^2$ (9 cm × 14 cm)

**12.** (i) 18 cm$^2$    (ii) 72 cm$^2$    (iii) 54 cm$^2$

**13.** (i) 4 cm    (ii) 252 cm$^3$    (iii) 254 cm$^2$

**14.** (i) 12 m$^2$    (ii) 8 m$^2$
   (iii) €960    (iv) €112

**15.** (i) 1 km    (ii) 14 cm

**16.** (i) 27 cm$^3$    (ii) 3 cm

## Chapter 7: Statistics 1

### Exercise 7.1

**1.** (i) N    (ii) C    (iii) C    (iv) N
   (v) N    (vi) C    (vii) C    (viii) N

**2.** (i) P    (ii) P    (iii) S    (iv) S

**4.** (i) Overlap between 'not very often' and
    'sometimes'; Not specific enough; no time-
    frame provided

**5.** Q(i) is the one to use as Q(ii) is a leading question

**6.** (i) Too personal
   (ii) May cause embarrassment
   (iii) Biased
   (iv) Leading question
   (v) Too personal/embarrassing/shaming
   (vi) Too personal
   (vii) Leading question

**7.** (i) Too personal, first name would suffice
   (ii) 'Often' and 'sometimes' are too vague

**8.** (i) Question is too personal and response boxes
    aren't specific enough/are too subjective

**10.** QA – Too subjective/potentially embarrassing
   QB – Biased question which encourages a
   positive response

**11.** Only members of the club would be likely to
   answer and so answers would be biased.

**12.** How many students use 'Snapchat'

**13.** Everyone would consider themselves normal.
   "On average how many hours sleep do you get
   per night."

**14.** (i)

| 12 | 13 | 14 | 15 | 16 | 17 | 18 |
|----|----|----|----|----|----|----|
| 3  | 6  | 7  | 9  | 5  | 3  | 1  |

   (ii) 6      (iii) 15
   (iv) 18 students are busy preparing for exams.

**15.** (i)

|          | Frequency |
|----------|-----------|
| Bus      | 16        |
| Car      | 27        |
| Lorry    | 13        |
| Van      | 8         |
| Motorbike| 8         |
| Total    | 72        |

   (ii) car
   (iii) Traffic patterns depend on the day and
      time of day.

### Exercise 7.2

**1.** (i) 820      (ii) 40

**2.** (i) Population      (ii) Population
   (iii) Sample      (iv) Sample
   (v) Population

**3.** Sample size 40. 4 would not be representative
   of the group 400 would take too long

4. (i) • People already at a cinema are much more likely to be regular "cinema-goers"
   • No men surveyed
5. These people are likely to be "sporty", i.e. not representative
6. B
7. B; this sample best represents the community at large.
8. Method 2

## Test yourself 7

1. (i) C (ii) N (iii) N (iv) C (v) C (vi) N
2. (i) Primary (ii) Secondary
   (iii) Secondary (iv) Secondary
3. (ii) is better
4. Inherently biased sample as they are clearly 'pro-libraries' people
5. (i) 3.7% (ii) (a) 1999 (b) 2005
   (iii) 2001/2002
6. (i)

| 1 | 2 | 3 | 4 | 5 | 6 |
|---|---|---|---|---|---|
| 8 | 10 | 6 | 3 | 2 | 1 |

   (ii) 20%
   (iii) Each student surveyed was belong to a family.
7. (i) Potentially embarrassing
   (ii) Too personal and assumes car ownership
   (iii) Too personal
8. Far too restricted, 'rush-hour' not included
9. (i) Patently absurd as you can only phone someone if they own a phone!
   (ii) Reliable sample for those who shop at *Zacs Discount* but definitley not adequately representative of the general public
   (iii) Number of issues here; First, the question assumes that you were insulting your neighbours. Second, it is a rude/offensive question. Third, it is the sort of question which may receive a dishonest answer as someone is unlikely to admit to continuing to insult his/her neighbour

## Chapter 8: Probability

### Exercise 8.1

1. 12
2. HH, HT, TH, TT
3. (i) 18 (ii) 6 (iii) 3
4. 36  5. 24  6. 27
7. (i) 36 (ii) 12

8. 12

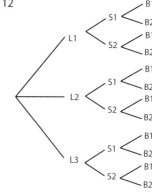

9. (i) four (ii) 128
10.

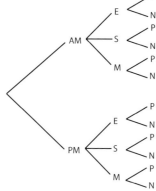

a.m – E – P     p.m – E – P
a.m – E – N     p.m – E – N
a.m – S – P     p.m – S – P
a.m – S – N     p.m – S – N
a.m – M – P     p.m – M – P
a.m – M – N     p.m – M – N

11. (i)

|  | Boys | Girls | Totals |
|---|---|---|---|
| Swimming | 12 | 16 | 28 |
| Tennis | 9 | 13 | 22 |
| Football | 25 | 11 | 36 |
| Totals | 46 | 40 | 86 |

   (ii) 86 (iii) Tennis (iv) Swimming
   (v) $\frac{11}{43}$ (vi) 40%

### Exercise 8.2

1. (i) even chance (ii) certain
   (iii) impossible (iv) unlikely
   (v) likely (vi) even chance
   (vii) likely (viii) unlikely
   (ix) even chance (x) likely/certain

**2.** (i) event 1 : unlikely
   event 2 : even chance
   event 3 : even chance
   event 4 : impossible
   event 5 : certain
 (ii) event 1 : likely
   event 2 : certain
   event 3 : impossible
   event 4 : unlikely
   event 5 : likely

**3.** (i) B  (ii) C  (iii) C  (iv) A  (v) B  (vi) C

**4.** (i) (b), (a), (c)   (ii) (b), (a), (c)

**5.** (a) & green, (b) & red, (c) & blue

**6.** (i) 6   (ii) 8   (iii) 2

## Exercise 8.3

**1.** (i) (a) red, blue
    (b) red, green, yellow, blue
    (c) red, blue
   (ii) (a) $\frac{1}{2}$   (b) $\frac{1}{4}$   (c) $\frac{1}{2}$

**2.** (i) $\frac{1}{4}$   (ii) $\frac{1}{2}$   (iii) $\frac{1}{4}, \frac{3}{4}$

**3.** (i) $\frac{1}{6}$   (ii) $\frac{1}{3}$   (iii) $\frac{1}{2}$
   (iv) $\frac{1}{2}$   (v) $\frac{1}{3}$   (vi) $\frac{1}{2}$

**4.** (i) $\frac{3}{10}$   (ii) $\frac{2}{5}$   (iii) $\frac{7}{10}$
   (iv) $\frac{3}{5}$   (v) $\frac{3}{10}$   (vi) $\frac{3}{10}$

**5.** (i) $\frac{1}{11}$   (ii) $\frac{2}{11}$   (iii) $\frac{2}{11}$
   (iv) $\frac{4}{11}$   (v) $\frac{4}{11}$

**6.** (i) $\frac{1}{6}$   (ii) $\frac{3}{8}$   (iii) $\frac{2}{5}$

**7.** (i) $\frac{1}{4}$   (ii) $\frac{1}{9}$   (iii) $\frac{4}{9}$
   (iv) $\frac{1}{36}$   (v) $\frac{1}{18}$   (vi) $\frac{1}{6}$

**8.** (i) $\frac{1}{13}$   (ii) $\frac{1}{13}$   (iii) $\frac{3}{13}$
   (iv) $1\left(\frac{13}{13}\right)$   (v) $0\left(\frac{0}{13}\right)$   (vi) $\frac{2}{13}$

**9.** (i) $\frac{1}{4}$   (ii) $\frac{1}{2}$   (iii) $\frac{1}{2}$
   (iv) $\frac{1}{13}$   (v) $\frac{3}{13}$   (vi) $\frac{2}{13}$

**10.** (i) $\frac{10}{13}$   (ii) $\frac{7}{13}$   (iii) $\frac{7}{13}$
   (iv) 0

**11.** (i) Red and any other colour which is not red
    or black
   (ii) Red and any other colour which is not red
    or blue

**12.** (i) $\frac{1}{6}$   (ii) $\frac{3}{8}$   (iii) $\frac{1}{6}$   (iv) $\frac{1}{12}$

**14.** (i) $\frac{1}{7}$   (ii) $\frac{2}{7}$   (iii) $\frac{1}{6}$   (iv) $\frac{1}{3}$

**15.** (i) $\frac{5}{12}$   (ii) $\frac{1}{6}$   (iii) $\frac{1}{12}$   (iv) $\frac{1}{12}$
   (v) $\frac{5}{12}$   (vi) $\frac{7}{12}$;
   As every disc has either an odd or an even
   number on it

**16.** (i) $\frac{3}{10}$   (ii) $\frac{7}{20}$   (iii) $\frac{13}{20}$   (iv) $\frac{7}{20}$

**17.** (i)

|  | Girls | Boys | Totals |
|---|---|---|---|
| Tennis | 15 | 6 | 21 |
| Basketball | 10 | 12 | 22 |
| Volleyball | 5 | 2 | 7 |
| Totals | 30 | 20 | 50 |

   (i) (a) $\frac{2}{5}$   (b) $\frac{3}{10}$   (c) $\frac{11}{25}, \frac{1}{6}$

**18.** (i) $\frac{1}{100}$   (ii) $\frac{1}{10}$   (iii) $\frac{1}{20}$
   (iv) $\frac{21}{25}$   (v) 30   (vi) 20
   (vii) 25   (viii) all 100

**19.** $\frac{3}{7}$

**20.** (i) $\frac{4}{13}$   (ii) $\frac{4}{13}$   (iii) $\frac{5}{13}$   (iv) $\frac{9}{13}$

## Exercise 8.4

**1.** (i) $\frac{1}{4}$   (ii) $\frac{1}{4}$   (iii) $\frac{1}{2}$

**2.** (i) $\frac{3}{16}$   (ii) $\frac{1}{2}$   (iii) $\frac{3}{16}$   (iv) $\frac{3}{16}$

**3.** (i) $\frac{1}{18}$   (ii) $\frac{1}{9}$   (iii) $\frac{1}{6}$
   (iv) $\frac{1}{3}$   (v) $\frac{2}{9}$   (vi) $\frac{5}{18}$

**4.** (ii) (a) $\frac{3}{16}$   (b) $\frac{9}{16}$   (c) $\frac{5}{8}$

**5.** (i) $\frac{1}{16}$   (ii) 1   (iii) $\frac{3}{8}$
   (iv) $\frac{1}{4}$   (v) $\frac{7}{16}$   (vi) $\frac{9}{16}$

**6.**

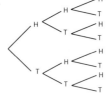

HHH, HHT, HTH, HTT, TTT, TTH, THH, THT;
   (i) $\frac{1}{8}$   (ii) $\frac{3}{8}$   (iii) $\frac{1}{8}$   (iv) $\frac{7}{8}$

**7.** (i) $\frac{1}{9}$   (ii) $\frac{1}{12}$   (iii) $\frac{1}{12}$   (iv) $\frac{5}{36}$

**8.** (i)

   (ii) $\frac{1}{9}$   (iii) $\frac{1}{9}$   (iv) $\frac{2}{9}$

**9.** (i) $\frac{2}{9}$   (ii) $\frac{4}{9}$   (iii) $\frac{5}{9}$

**10.** (i) RBG, RGB, BRG, BGR, GRB, GBR  (ii) $\frac{1}{3}$

**11.** (a)

| | Boys | Girls | Total |
|---|---|---|---|
| **French** | (18) | 22 | (40) |
| **German** | 25 | (18) | (43) |
| **Spanish** | 12 | (30) | 42 |
| **Total** | (55) | 70 | 125 |

　(b) 40　　(c) 55　　(d) $\frac{43}{125}$

　(e) (i) $\frac{8}{25}$　　(ii) $\frac{6}{25}$　　(iii) $\frac{1}{5}$

## Exercise 8.5

**1.** As the two sets of six throws are completely independent. Thus the probability of him getting four heads again is not 1, but $\frac{15}{64}$; roughly fifty

**2.** (i) $\frac{1}{2}$　　(ii) $\frac{3}{4}$

　(iii) Nicky's result; greater number of trials conducted

**3.** $\frac{3}{10}$

**4.** 0.6

**5.** $\frac{3}{8}$

**6.** (ii) 0.6

**7.** (i) $\frac{7}{36}$　　(ii) $\frac{1}{3}$　　(iii) 3

**8.** 0.35

**9.** (i) $\frac{9}{20}$　　(ii) $\frac{1}{4}$　　(iii) $\frac{21}{40}$

　(iv) $\frac{9}{40}$; yes, because there are more games being considered

**10.** $\frac{3}{10}$

**11.** (i) $\frac{1}{6}$　　(ii) $\frac{1}{2}$　　(iii) $\frac{1}{2}$

**12.** (i) 0.5　　(ii) 0.55　　(iii) 0.6
　(iv) yes　　(v) the council's

**13.** (i) $\frac{7}{20}$　　　　(ii) c. 420

**14.** Barry's dice was fair; unlike Rachel's and Leanore's, there is a relatively even spread of outcomes which is what one would expect from a fair dice

## Test yourself 8

**1.** (i) $\frac{2}{5}$　　(ii) $\frac{6}{25}$　　(iii) $\frac{16}{25}$

**2.** (i) $\frac{7}{10}$　　(ii) $\frac{1}{10}$　　(iii) $\frac{1}{20}$
　(iv) $\frac{3}{10}$　　(v) $\frac{3}{20}$

**3.** Both equally likely to have the winning number $\left(\frac{1}{60}\text{ chance}\right)$

**4.** A & (iii), B & (i), C & (ii)

**5.** (i) 24 times　　(ii) 4　　(iii) $\frac{1}{8}$

**6.** Almost definitley unfair; the '2 face' showed way above $\left(\frac{11}{25}\right)$ what the expected frequency of a fair four-sided dice would be $\left(\text{around }\frac{1}{4}\right)$. Also, 100 throws was a fairly large number of trials to conduct and so the results ought to be reliable

**7.** (i) $\frac{1}{4}$　　(ii) $\frac{3}{8}$　　(iii) $\frac{3}{8}$

　(iv) $\frac{5}{8}$; $\frac{8}{8}$ (i.e. 1); there were only three different colour counters in the bag and accordingly the probability has to be 1.

**8.** (i) $\frac{1}{2}$　　(ii) $\frac{1}{52}$　　(iii) $\frac{5}{13}$
　(iv) $\frac{3}{26}$　　(v) $\frac{1}{13}$　　(vi) $\frac{7}{13}$

**9.** (i) 160　　(ii) 240

**10.** 90% chance $\left(\frac{9}{10}\right)$

**11.** (i) 12　　(ii) $\frac{1}{12}$　　(iii) $\frac{1}{4}$　　(iv) $\frac{1}{6}$

**12.** 80

**13.**

| | Boys | Girls | Totals |
|---|---|---|---|
| **Milk** | 24 | (8) | (32) |
| **Water** | (17) | 27 | (44) |
| **Orange Juice** | (16) | (8) | 24 |
| **Totals** | 57 | (43) | 100 |

　(a) $\frac{11}{25}$　　(b) $\frac{17}{57}$

**14.** (a) **25**

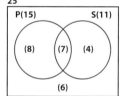

　(b) 6
　(i) $\frac{4}{25}$　　(ii) $\frac{11}{25}$　　(iii) $\frac{7}{25}$　　(iv) $\frac{6}{25}$

# Chapter 9:  Statistics 2

## Exercise 9.1

**1.** (i) 7　　(ii) 12　　(iii) 5.7　　(iv) bus

**2.** (i) 10　　(ii) sun　　(iii) $\frac{1}{4}$

**3.** 5

**4.** (i) 8　　(ii) 2

**5.** Each number appears twice

**6.** (i) 32　　(ii) 6　　(iii) no　　(iv) no

**7.** 171 cm

**8.** (i) 6　　(ii) 14　　(iii) 3.6

**9.** (i) 7　　(ii) 24　　(iii) 3.7

**10.** 10.5

**11.** (i) 7.5 cm (ii) 21 kg (iii) €6.75
**12.** (i) 9 (ii) 9
**13.** (i) 9 (ii) 9
**14.** (i) 7 (ii) 17 (iii) median = 8

## Exercise 9.2

**1.** (i) 5 (ii) 9 (iii) 14 (iv) 7
**2.** 61 **3.** 26
**4.** €6.30 **5.** 9; 7.5
**6.** 36
**7.** (i) 24 (ii) 11
**8.** (i) 36 (ii) 5
**9.** 11 **10.** 13 cm
**11.** 12 **12.** 25
**13.** 8
**14.** (i) 18 (ii) 12 (iii) 0
**15.** €1.73 **16.** 6; 10; increased by 4
**17.** 30 **18.** 156; 12
**19.** 4, 4, 6, 10, 11 or 4, 4, 6, 7, 14, . . . etc.
**20.** (i) 61 (ii) 60 (iii) 59
(iv) Barry (v) 5

## Exercise 9.3

**1.** (i) 11 (ii) 24 (iii) €16
**2.** (i) 82 (ii) 17
**3.** (i) 1.8 (ii) 9
**4.** (i) Ann : 44; John : 20; John is more consistent
(ii) Ann
**5.** (i) Emer : 82; Anna : 83
(ii) Emer : 20; Anna : 12
(iii) Anna
**6.** (i) 45 mins (ii) 50 mins (iii) 20 mins
(iv) 60 mins
**7.** (i) Leinster : $25\frac{1}{3}$; Munster : 25
(ii) Leinster : 21; Munster : 12
**8.** 70 or 1
**9.** (i) True (ii) Possible (iii) False
**10.** (i) Possible (ii) False (iii) Possible
**11.** (i) Yes, 8 (ii) Yes, 8
(iii) No; 8 + 8 or 7 + 9, . . . etc.; 14 + 2

## Exercise 9.4

**1.** (i) 2 (ii) 1
(iii) 6 of the 8 numbers < mean – not representative
**2.** (i) Range
(ii) (a) 6 (b) 5 (c) 5
(iii) Mean, median or mode
**3.** Mean = 17; median = 3; median
**4.** Mode (black)
**5.** (i) 30.57°C
(ii) Data closely bunched

**6.** (i) 26.55 (ii) Mode
**7.** (i) Denim
(ii) It is the only average we can get
**8.** (i) (a) 7 (b) 5
(ii) Mode, though in this instance the mode and median may be one and the same!
**9.** (i) (a) 94 kg (b) 53 kg (c) 87.44 kg
(ii) Median

## Exercise 9.5

**1.** (i) 4 (ii) 3 (iii) 2; 6
**2.** (i) 7 (ii) 8 (iii) 3
(iv) 36 (v) 33.33%
**3.** (i) 1 (ii) 4 (iii) 2
(iv) 150 (v) 3
**4.** (i) 8 (ii) 2 (iii) 180
(iv) 3 (v) 32
**5.** Mean = 3; mode = 1 and 2
**6.** (i) 60 (ii) 30
(iii) 50% (iv) 2 year olds
(v) 3 year olds
**7.** (ii) 2 (iii) 10%
**8.** 3
**9.** (i) 3 (ii) 1 (iii) 25% (iv) 26
**10.** (i) 19 (ii) (41-60) (iii) (61-80)
(iv) one cannot get an exact mean

## Test yourself 9

**1.** (i) 14 (ii) 29
(iii) 17 (iv) 14
**2.** 86
**3.** (i) 47 (ii) 6
**4.** 2
**5.** Mean = 7, median = 3, mode = 3;
median or mode as all but one of the values are below the mean and so the mean is misleading
**6.** (i) 1, 3, 9 or 1, 4, 9 or 3, 5, 9 or 4, 5, 9
(ii) 1, 3, 4 (iii) 1, 5, 9 or 1, 3, 5
**7.** (i) 60 (ii) 165 (iii) 2.75
(iv) The mean would increase very slightly (by 0.02)
**8.** (i) Ordinary
(ii) Not dealing in numbers; so only average we can get
**9.** (i) 5, 8, 11 (ii) 4, 4, 7 (iii) 20, 27, 28
**10.** Mean – 5.1, mode – 0, median – 2; median
**11.** (i) 318 (ii) $35\frac{1}{3}$ (iii) 32
**12.** (i) 5 (ii) 4 (iii) 5
**13.** (i) 1280 km (ii) 516 km
(iii) $224\frac{1}{2}$ km
**14.** 3.6
**15.** (i) Tim, largest range (58) (ii) Derek

**16.** (i) €376.67

(ii) €245; no two values the same; Median

**17.** 45, 2

# Chapter 10: Geometry 1 – Triangles and Quadrilaterals

## Exercise 10.1

**1.** (i) The line segment [AB]

(ii) The line AB

(iii) The ray [BA

**2.** $A = 117°, B = 85°, C = 45°, D = 140°, E = 70°,$ $F = 23°$

**3.** $A = 70°, B = 110°, C = 150°, D = 30°, E = 140°,$ $F = 40°, G = 62°, H = 118°, I = 62°, J = 128°,$ $K = 52°, L = 128°, P = 147°, Q = 33°, R = 147°$

**4.** (i) 4 (ii) 7 (iii) 4

**5.** (i) 7 (ii) 6 (iii) 4

**6.** $a = 110°, b = 70°, c = 46°, d = 134°, e = 60°,$ $f = 120°$

**7.** $a = 48°, b = 132°, c = 132°, d = 132°, e = 160°,$ $f = 20°, g = 20°, x = 131°, y = 131°, z = 131°$

**8.** $a° = 50°$ (alternate), $b° = 130°$ $(a° + b° = 180°)$, $c° = 110°$ (corresponding), $d° = 70°$ $(c° + d° = 180°)$, $e° = 65°$ $(e° + 115° = 180°)$, $f° = 65°$ (vertically opposite angles)

**9.** $a = 96°, b = 96°, c = 84°, d = 72°, e = 68°,$ $f = 112°, g = 68°$

**10.** $p = 80°, q = 80°, r = 75°, s = 105°$

## Exercise 10.2

**1.** (i) (a) $d°$ (b) $t°$ (c) $w°$

(ii) (a) $a°$ and $b°$ (b) $q°$ and $p°$ (c) $x°$ and $z°$

**2.** $a = 104°, b = 26°, c = 85°, d = 95°, e = 141°,$ $f = 118°, g = 66°$

**3.** $a = 70°, b = 30°, c = 40°, d = 109°$

**4.** $a = 70°, b = 70°, c = 72°, d = 72°, e = 62°,$ $f = 56°$

**5.** $a = 65°, b = 40°, c = 52.5°, d = 60°, e = 30°$

**6.** $p = 106°, q = 37°, r = 37°, d = 25°, e = 130°,$ $f = 50°, v = 59°, w = 31°, x = 59°, y = 121°$

**7.** $a = 73°, b = 73°$

**8.** $x = 54°, y = 80°, z = 60°$

**9.** (i) $x = 65°, y = 50°$

(ii) $x = 40°, y = 70°$

(iii) $x = 50°, y = 65°$

## Exercise 10.3

**1.** (i) $A$ & $C$, $B$ & $D$ (ii) 180°

**2.** $A = 80°, B = 115°, C = 65°, D = 105°, E = 75°$

**3.** $A = 120°, B = 60°, C = 80°, D = 45°, E = 75°,$ $F = 55°, G = 55°$

**4.** $x = 66°, y = 72°$

**5.** $A = 30°, B = 70°, C = 35°, D = 65°, E = 28°,$ $F = 112°, G = 52°$

**6.** (i) 68° (ii) 50° (iii) 100°

**7.** $A = 41°, B = 100°, C = 46°, D = 69°, E = 31°,$ $F = 37°, G = 63°$

**8.** (i) 8 (ii) 11 (iii) 10 (iv) 7

**9.** (i) 6 (ii) 4 (iii) 9

(iv) 6 (v) $\angle BOC$ (vi) $\angle BCD$

(vii) $\angle ABD$ (viii) $\angle ACD$

**10.** (i) $x = 70°, y = 40°, z = 40°, r = 70°$

**11.**

**12.** $a = 121°, b = 89°, c = 129°, d = 51°$

**13.** $x = 55°, y = 55°, z = 70°$

**14.** (i) 1, 2 (ii) 1, 2, 3, 4 (iii) 1, 4

(iv) 1, 2, 3, 4 (v) 1, 2, 3, 4 (vi) 1, 2

(vii) 1, 2, 3, 4 (viii) 1, 4

**15.** (i) 80° (ii) 77° (iii) 55°

## Exercise 10.4

**1.** (i) 5 (ii) 10 (iii) 8.6

**2.** $P = 44$ cm$^2$, $Q = 46$ cm$^2$, $R = 50$ cm$^2$

**3.** $x = 5, y = 13, z = 10$

**4.** $a = \sqrt{41}, b = \sqrt{45}, c = \sqrt{89}, d = \sqrt{28}, e = \sqrt{24},$ $f = \sqrt{57}$

**5.** $\sqrt{32}, \sqrt{50}, \sqrt{98}$ **6.** 20 cm

**7.** 5 m **8.** 80 m

**9.** 47.3 cm **10.** 24 m

**11.** 28 km **12.** $a = 5, b = \sqrt{50}$

**13.** 637 m

**14.** (i) Yes (ii) No (iii) Yes (iv) No

**15.** 130 m

## Test yourself 10

**1.** $a = 110°, b = 70°, c = 140°, d = 55°, e = 125°$

**2.** $A = 50°, B = 70°, C = 68°$

**3.** $a = 40°, b = 80°, c = 48°$

**4.** $a = 63°, b = 30°$

**5.** $A = 35°, B = 67°, C = 40°, D = 65°, E = 33°,$ $F = 107°, G = 45°$

**6.** $a = 55°, b = 50°$

**7.** $x = 10, y = 25, z = 8$

**8.** $a = 74°, b = 53°, c = 142°, d = 68°, e = 38°,$ $f = 74°$

**9.** $x = 56$; isosceles $\triangle$

**10.** (i) $a = 115°, b = 115°$

(ii) $a = 56°, b = 68°$

(iii) $a = 48°, b = 66°$

**11.** $A = 125°, B = 44°$ **12.** $x = 105°$

# Chapter 11: Time and Speed

## Exercise 11.1

1. (i) 30    (ii) 15    (iii) 24
   (iv) 105    (v) 42
2. (i) 7 hr 58 min    (ii) 8 hr 24 min
   (iii) 5 hr 22 min
3. 40; 7 hr 40 min; 8 hr 20 min
4. (i) 3 hr 15 min    (ii) 6 hr 30 min
   (iii) 7 hr 50 min    (iv) 8 hr 30 min
   (v) 7 hr 5 min    (vi) 7 hr 55 min
5. (i) 2 hr 36 min    (ii) 1 hr 26 min
   (iii) 1 hr 41 min
6. (i) 06.00    (ii) 10.45    (iii) 16.00
   (iv) 17.20    (v) 19.30    (vi) 08.45
   (vii) 12.00    (viii) 23.40    (ix) 03.15
   (x) 15.15
7. (i) 11.40 am    (ii) 3.35 pm
   (iii) 12.20 pm    (iv) 12.30 am
   (v) 10.15 pm    (vi) 4.20 am
   (vii) 10.35 am    (viii) 2.30 pm
   (ix) 6.45 pm    (x) 11.12 pm
8. (i) 01.25    (ii) 22.30
   (iii) 06.50    (iv) 16.45
9. (i) 4 hr 10 min    (ii) 3 hr 32 min
   (iii) 8 hr 9 min    (iv) 2 hr 37 min
   (v) 15 hr 30 min    (vi) 3 hr 28 min
10. A and (i), C and (ii), D and (iii), B and (iv)
11. $36\frac{1}{4}$ hr (36 hr 15 min)
12. 10.55 pm
13. 3 hr 48 min
14. 14.26
15. (i) 3 hr 35 min    (ii) 19 min
    (iii) 1 hr 53 min    (iv) Train 2
    (v) 2 hr 55 min    (vi) 2 min
    (vii) 38 min    (viii) Train 2 (by 7 min)
16. A – 2 hr 11 min, B – 09.37, C – 17.24,
    D – 6 hr 1 min, E – 10.35, F – 09.21
17. (i) 2 hr 45 min    (ii) €27
18. (i) 3 hr 30 min    (ii) 2 hr 6 min
    (iii) 45 min    (iv) 4 hr 36 min
    (v) 1 hr 40 min
19. (i) 1.2 hr    (ii) 1 hr 12 min
20. 3.30 p.m.
21. (i) F; 2 hrs 21 min P; 2 hrs 23 min    (ii) 2 min

## Exercise 11.2

1. (i) 240 km    (ii) 260 km
   (iii) 198 km    (iv) 72 km
2. (i) 3 hr    (ii) $2\frac{1}{2}$ hr
   (iii) 20 min    (iv) 45 min

3. (i) 50 km/hr    (ii) 60 km/hr
   (iii) 60 km/hr    (iv) 70 km/hr
   (v) 50 km/hr    (vi) 135 km/hr
4. 180 km/hr    5. 2 hr 30 min
6. 189 km    7. 72 km/hr
8. 104 km/hr    9. 70 km/hr
10. $4\frac{1}{2}$ hours    11. 72 km/hr
12. 5 hr 12 min    13. $53\frac{1}{3}$ km/hr
14. 12 m/sec    15. 42 km/hr
16. 72 km/hr    17. 20 m/sec
18. 24 km/hr    19. 54 km/hr
20. (i) 86 km/hr    (ii) 67ℓ    (iii) €113.90
21. Cheetah (100 km/hr), Antelope (80 km/hr),
    Racehorse $\left(67\frac{1}{2}\text{ km/hr}\right)$, Deer (45.7 km/hr)
22. 8 km/hr
23.

| | | |
|---|---|---|
| 20 | 72000 | 72 |
| 25 | 90000 | 90 |
| 50 | 180000 | 180 |

24.

| | | |
|---|---|---|
| 72 | 72000 | 20 |
| 54 | 54000 | 15 |
| 120 | 120000 | $33\frac{1}{3}$ |

## Test yourself 11

1. (i) 02.40    (ii) 22.50
2. 1 hr 15 min
3. 40 min each
4. (i) 3 hr 15 min    (ii) 8 hr 35 min
5. (i) $2\frac{1}{2}$ hr    (ii) 88 km/hr
6. 6000 m
7. 12.50 am
8. (i) 240 km    (ii) 3 hours
   (iii) 80 km/hr
9. 2160 km
10. (i) 06.15    (ii) 13.45
    (iii) 21.52    (iv) 00.15
11. 9 litres
12. (i) 40 min    (ii) $19\frac{1}{2}$ km/hr
13. (i) 3 hr 12 min    (ii) $62\frac{1}{2}$ km/hr
    (iii) €44
14. 6 km/hr
15. 12.24 pm
16. 16.25
17. 25.2 m

# Chapter 12:
# Simultaneous Equations

## Exercise 12.1
1. Correct   2. Correct   3. Correct
4. Incorrect   5. Incorrect   6. Correct
7. Incorrect   8. Correct   9. Incorrect
10. Correct

## Exercise 12.2
1. $x = 6, y = 3$   2. $x = 2, y = 4$   3. $x = 3, y = 2$
4. $1, 4$   5. $3, 5$   6. $2, 1$
7. $3, 2$   8. $2, 1$   9. $3, -1$
10. $-2, 4$   11. $3, 2$   12. $-2, 1$
13. $2, 3$   14. $-3, 4$   15. $4, -2$
16. $3, -1$   17. $1, 2$   18. $5, -2$
19. $2, 1$   20. $3, -2$   21. $7, -3$
22. $1, 5$   23. $3, 1$   24. $1, -2$
25. $7, 3$   26. $2, 8$   27. $4, 1$
28. $10, 4$   29. $-2, -4$   30. $6, -2$

## Exercise 12.3
1. $18, 23$   2. $5, 7$
3. $x = 18, y = 32$   4. $10, 7$
5. $12, -3$   6. $10, 3$
7. $5, 3$
8. $2x - 3y = 4, 3x + y = 17; x = 5, y = 2$
9. nut – 4 g, bolt – 10 g
10. (i) 5 g   (ii) 160 g
11. (i) $C$   (ii) $b - 55$ g, $e - 75$ g
12. (i) (a) Every horse and every turkey has one head
    (b) Every horse has four legs and every turkey has two legs
    (ii) 17 horses, 15 turkeys
13. (i) $(2, 1)$   (ii) $x = 2, y = 1$
14. $(1, 4)$

## Test yourself 12
1. $x = 3, y = 4$
2. €1.90
3. $x = 5, y = 1$
4. (i) $2a + b = 8, 4a - 3b = 1$
   (ii) $a = 2.5, b = 3$
5. $x = 2, y = -1$
6. (i) $4b + 3r = 58, 5b + 6r = 86$
   (ii) blue brick – 10 g, red brick – 6 g
   (iii) 66 g
7. $x = 6, y = 5$
8. $2x - 3y = 3, 2x + y = 7; x = 3, y = 1$

9. (ii)

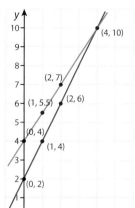

(iii) $(4, 10)$

# Chapter 13:  Quadratic Equations

## Exercise 13.1
1. $x = 2$ or $x = 3$   2. $x = 2$ or $x = 5$
3. $x = 2$ or $x = -3$
4. $4, -5$   5. $-2, -6$   6. $0, 4$
7. $0, -5$   8. $3, -3$   9. $-7, 7$
10. $-2, -1$   11. $-3, -2$   12. $-4, -2$
13. $-5, -2$   14. $-4, -3$   15. $-9, -3$
16. $-7, -4$   17. $-7, -5$   18. $-8, -6$
19. $2, 3$   20. $3, 5$   21. $2, 8$
22. $2, 7$   23. $3, 7$   24. $4, 6$
25. $3, 9$   26. $4, 8$   27. $4, 12$
28. $-3, 4$   29. $-2, 5$   30. $-7, 4$
31. $-3, 8$   32. $-9, 4$   33. $-8, 9$
34. $-6, 9$   35. $-11, -4$   36. $-5, 12$
37. $-4, 4$   38. $-5, 5$   39. $-8, 8$
40. $-1, 1$   41. $-11, 11$   42. $-9, 9$
43. $0, 3$   44. $-4, 0$   45. $0, 8$
46. $-9, 0$   47. $0, 14$   48. $-7, 0$
49. $-10, 3$   50. $-2, 12$   51. $-6, 2$
52. $-2, 8$   53. $4, 7$   54. $-10, 10$
55. $0, 11$   56. $1, 9$   57. $-4, 13$

## Exercise 13.2
1. 6   2. 7   3. $5, 9$
4. 6   5. $5, 8$   6. 10
7. $x^2 + x - 72 = 0; +8, -9$
8. $x^2 + 4x - 77 = 0; x = 7; l = 11$ cm, $b = 7$ cm
9. 7 cm by 4 cm
10. (i) $x^2 + 3x$   (ii) $x = 5$
11. $x = 5$   12. $-1, 5$
13. $x(x - 6) = 16; x = 8$   14. Alan is 5 years old
15. $x = -3, 1$   16. Ⓑ

**Test yourself 13**

1.  (i) $x = -3, 4$   (ii) $x = 5, 7$
2.  (ii) 7 cm by 1 cm
3.  (i) $x = -5, 0$   (ii) $x = 1, 8$
4.  $x^2 + 2x - 120 = 0; -12, 10$
5.  (i) $x = -8, 5$   (ii) $x = -12, 12$
6.  Ⓒ
7.  (i) $x = -8, 3$   (ii) $x = -2, 7$
8.  $x^2 - 5x - 36 = 0; x - 9$
9.  The third graph

# Chapter 14: Coordinate Geometry – The Line

## Exercise 14.1

1.  $A(2, 3), B(4, 2), C(2, 1), D(-3, 3), E(-2, 2),$
    $F(-4, 1), G(-3, 0), H(-4, -2), I(-2, -3),$
    $J(0, -3), K(2, -3), L(3, -2), M(5, -3)$
3.  (i) 1st        (ii) 3rd        (iii) 4th
    (iv) 2nd       (v) 4th         (vi) 3rd
4.  (i) $x$-axis   (ii) $y$-axis   (iii) $y$-axis
    (iv) $x$-axis  (v) $x$-axis
5.  $A(1, 1), B(5, 1), D(1, 3), C(5, 3)$
6.  (ii) $(2, 4)$
7.  (ii) rectangle        (iii) 4 units, 2 units
    (iv) 12 units         (v) 8 square units
8.  (i) 4 units           (ii) 3 units
    (iii) 6 square units
9.  (i) Collinear         (ii) Collinear
    (iii) Not collinear
    (i) add 1 to $x$ and increase $y$ by 1.
    (ii) add 1 to $x$ and decrease $y$ by 2.

10.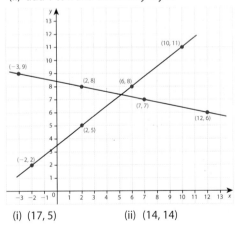
    (i) $(17, 5)$           (ii) $(14, 14)$

11.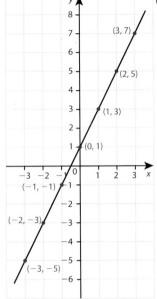
    $(-0.5, 0), (4, 9)$

## Exercise 14.2

1.  (i) 7          (ii) 2          (iii) $-7$
    (iv) $-1$
2.  (i) 4.5        (ii) 5          (iii) $-1$
    (iv) $-4$      (v) 3
3.  (i) $(5, 5)$   (ii) $(6, 3)$   (iii) $(3, 4)$
4.  $(2, 1)$       5.  $(-1, 1)$   6.  $(2, 5)$
7.  $(2, 1)$       8.  $(-1, 3)$   9.  $(3, -3)$
10. $B(7, 5)$      12. $O\left(6\frac{1}{2}, 3\frac{1}{2}\right)$
13. (i) $\left(\frac{3}{2}, \frac{5}{2}\right)$   15. $(15, 5)$
16. $k = 0$        17. $t = 15$    18. $(3, 4)$
19. (i) $C(-6, 5)$   (ii) $F(8, 5)$   (iii) $(1, 5)$

## Exercise 14.3

1.  $\sqrt{18}$        2.  $\sqrt{29}$        3.  $\sqrt{17}$
4.  $\sqrt{5}$         5.  $\sqrt{37}$        6.  $\sqrt{40}$
7.  $\sqrt{20}$        8.  $\sqrt{18}$        9.  $\sqrt{61}$
10. $\sqrt{74}$        11. $\sqrt{20}$        12. $\sqrt{13}$
15. $A(5, 2), B(3, -2), C(-3, -2), D(-1, 2)$
    (i) 6                    (iii) Yes, both $(1, 0)$
16. $\sqrt{2}, \sqrt{5}, \sqrt{5}$; $[BC]$ and $[AC]$; isosceles $\triangle$
17. $\sqrt{58}$
18. No $(\sqrt{13} < 3.7)$

## Exercise 14.4

1.  (i) Positive        (ii) Positive
    (iii) Positive       (iv) Negative
    (v) Negative         (vi) Positive

**2.** (i) 2    (ii) $\frac{-5}{2}$    (iii) $\frac{2}{5}$

**3.** (i) Rise = 5, Run = 3, Slope = $\frac{5}{3}$

   (ii) Rise = 6, Run = 2, Slope = 3

   (iii) Rise = −1, Run = 8, Slope = $\frac{-1}{8}$

   (iv) Rise = 2, Run = 6, Slope = $\frac{1}{3}$

**4.** (i) EF

   (ii) A(4, 1), B(6, 6), C(6, 0), D(12, 2), E(2, 4), F(12, 0)

   (iii) AB$\left(\frac{5}{2}\right)$, CD$\left(\frac{1}{3}\right)$, EF$\left(\frac{-2}{5}\right)$

**5.** (i) same slope

   (iii) AC$\left(\frac{-1}{2}\right)$, BD$\left(\frac{-1}{2}\right)$, ABCD is a parallelogram

**6.** 4

**7.** 2

**8.** (i) 1    (ii) 4    (iii) $\left(\frac{5}{2}\right)$    (iv) $\left(\frac{2}{5}\right)$

   (v) 1    (vi) 2

**9.** slope of AB = $\left(\frac{-2}{3}\right)$, slope of DC = $\left(\frac{-2}{3}\right)$, slope of AD = 1, slope of BC = 1

**11.** They are parallel as they have the same slope (3)

**12.** $a \& \frac{1}{2}, b \& 1, c \& 2$

**13.** Green $\frac{9}{35}$, Blue $\frac{-10}{31}$

**14.** (i) A(0, 0)   B(3, 6)   C(7, 5)   D(10, 0)

   (ii) (a) 2   (b) $\frac{-1}{4}$   (c) $\frac{-5}{3}$   (d) 0

**15.** (a) $\frac{-8}{3}$    (b) $\frac{2}{3}$

## Exercise 14.5

**1.** (i) 2    (ii) 3    (iii) 2

   (iv) 5    (v) −1    (vi) −3

**2.** (i) (0, 3)    (ii) (0, 6)    (iii) (0, −1)

   (iv) (0, 2)    (v) (0, 4)    (vi) (0, −2)

**3.** (a) (i) 3            (ii) (0, 1)

   (b) (i) 2            (ii) (0, −4)

   (c) (i) −3          (ii) (0, 5)

**4.** (i) $y = x + 1$        (ii) $y = \frac{1}{4}x + 2$

   (iii) $y = 2x - 2$

**5.** (i) 1       (ii) (0, −2)    (iii) $y = x - 2$

**6.** $a : y = 2x + 3, b : y = -2x + 2, c : y = -x + 2$

**7.** $y = \frac{1}{2}x + 1$    $(x - 2y + 2 = 0)$

**8.** (i) $a \& f$    (ii) $b$    (iii) $d$

   (iv) (0, −3)    (v) 1

**9.** (i) 1   (ii) 1   (iii) $y = x + 1$   (iv) $y = x + 5$

## Exercise 14.6

**1.** $y = 2x + 1$         **2.** $y = 3x - 13$

**3.** $y = 4x$             **4.** $y = -2x + 11$

**5.** $y = 3x + 11$        **6.** $y = 4x + 16$

**7.** $y = -2x + 1$        **8.** $y = 3x$

**9.** $y = -4x - 2$      **10.** $y = 2x + 4$

**11.** $y = \frac{2}{3}x + \frac{4}{3}$      **12.** $y = \frac{1}{3}x + 3$

**13.** $y = \frac{5}{2}x - \frac{9}{2}$      **14.** $y = -\frac{3}{4}x + 3$

**15.** $3; y = 3x - 1$

**16.** (i) 3              (ii) $y = 3x - 7$

**17.** (i) $y = 2x + 5$       (ii) $y = 5x - 7$

   (iii) $y = -4x - 7$     (iv) $y = \frac{5}{3}x - \frac{19}{3}$

**18.** (i) A(−1, −1), B(5, 2), C(7, −2)

   (ii) slope of AB = $\frac{1}{2}$, slope of BC = −2

   (iii) (a) $2y = x - 1$    (b) $y = -2x + 12$

**19.** (i) $m = -\frac{2}{3}$      (ii) $y = -\frac{2}{3}x + \frac{7}{3}$

**20.** $y = x + 5$

**21.** $y = -2x$

**22.** $(2, 4); y = 4x - 4$

**23.** (a) $y = -4x + 3$, slope = −4, Intercept = 3

   (b) $y = -3x + \frac{5}{2}$, slope = −3, Intercept = $\frac{5}{2}$

   (c) $y = -\frac{x}{2} + 5$, slope = $-\frac{1}{2}$, Intercept = 5

## Exercise 14.7

**1.** $a : y = 3, b : y = 1, c : y = -1, d : y = -3$

**2.** $e : x = -4, f : x = -2, g : x = 1, h : x = 4$

**4.** Ⓐ$: x = 2$, Ⓑ$: x = 4$, Ⓒ$: y = 4$, Ⓓ$: y = 2$, Ⓔ$: y = -2$, Ⓕ$: x = -3$

**5.** (i) $y = 0$           (ii) $x = 0$

**6.** (i) −4; (0, −4)    (ii) 2; (2, 0)

**7.** (i) (−2, 0)   (ii) (2, 0)   (iii) (−6, 0)

**8.** (i) (0, −3)   (ii) (0, 5)   (iii) (0, −4)

**9.** $\left(\frac{5}{2}, 0\right)$, (0, −5)

**10.** (i) (−3, 0), (0, 3)     (ii) $\left(-\frac{1}{2}, 0\right)$, (0, 2)

   (iii) (1, 0), (0, −6)

**11.** (2, 0), (0, −3)

**12.** (i) $K(4, 0)$         (ii) $P(0, -2)$

   (iii) $\frac{1}{2}$            (iv) $\sqrt{20}$

**13.** (i) $C$            (ii) $B$

**14.** (i) & Ⓒ, (ii) & Ⓐ, (iii) & Ⓑ

## Exercise 14.8

**1.** (1, 3)

**2.** (i) (1, 2)    (ii) (3, 0)    (iii) (−1, −2)

**3.** (4, 1)

**4.** (2, 1)

**5.** (3, 2)

**9.** Not on the line

**11.** $k = 6$

**12.** $k = -3$

**13.** (i) $k = 2$         (ii) $t = 5$

**14.** (i) $(x, y) = (2.5, 5.5)$

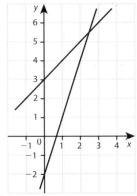

(ii) $(x, y) = (1, 1)$

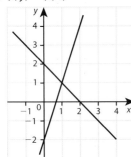

**Test yourself 14**

**1.** (i) $\frac{1}{3}$      (ii) $x - 3y + 14 = 0$

**2.** (i) $P(2, 0), Q(0, -4)$    (ii) $\sqrt{20}$

**3.** (i) $M(2, 0)$; $x$-axis

**4.** (i) $\frac{2}{3}$      (ii) $y = \frac{2x}{3} + 1$

**5.** (i) $k$        (ii) $n$

    (iii) $\ell$       (iv) $m$

**6.** $3$; $3x - y - 7 = 0$

**7.** (i) $\frac{1}{2}$      (ii) $x - 2y + 3 = 0$

    (iii) $(-3, 0)$

**8.** (i) $\ell_1$      (ii) $-\frac{1}{2}$

    (iii) $x - y + 2 = 0$

**9.** $A : y = 3x - 4, B : y = 2x + 5, C : y = 2x + 3$;

    (i) $A$    (ii) $B \& C$    (iii) $B$    (iv) $B$

**10.** $y = 2x - 2$

**11.** (i) F    (ii) T    (iii) T    (iv) F

# Chapter 15: Statistics 3

## Exercise 15.1

**1.** (i) 15               (ii) 1

    (iii) 0 to 5 (i.e. 5)      (iv) 20%

**2.** (i) 18°C      (ii) 28°C      (iii) 3

    (iv) $53\frac{1}{3}\%$      (v) $\frac{4}{15}$

**3.** (i) 42       (ii) 3         (iii) 10

    (iv) 29.2%    (v) $\frac{1}{13}$

**4.** (i) 25      (ii) 10       (iii) 3

    (iv) 5–10 (i.e. 5)       (v) 9

**5.** (i) 7    (ii) 12    (iii) 13    (iv) 4

    (v) 30    (vi) $16\frac{2}{3}\%$ (vii) $\frac{1}{10}$

**6.** (i) 6    (ii) 3    (iii) 4    (iv) $\frac{1}{5}$

**7.** (i) 60    (ii) 115    (iii) 1.9

**8.** (i) 4    (ii) 5    (iii) 3    (iv) 0.225

## Exercise 15.2

**1.** (i) 25%    (ii) $\frac{1}{4}$    (iii) 75%

    (iv) $\frac{3}{4}$    (v) 3    (vi) 9

**2.** (i) 25%    (ii) $\frac{1}{2}$    (iii) 30    (iv) 15

**3.** (i) 300    (ii) 150    (iii) 100    (iv) 30°

**4.** (i) 105°    (ii) 120°    (iii) 125°

**5.** (i) 45°    (ii) 40    (iii) Spain

    (iv) France

    (v) Spain and Portugal

**6.** (i) 70°    (ii) 290°    (iii) 14

**7.** (i) 60    (ii) 20    (iii) 30

    (iv) 50°    (v) 25

**8.** (i) 90°    (ii) 45°    (iii) 165°

**9.** (i) Bus – 120°; Car – 90°; Train – 72°; Walk – 48°;

    Bicycle – 30°

**10.** (i) $\frac{1}{3}$    (ii) 90    (iii) 40    (iv) 5

**11.** (i) 75°    (ii) 120    (iii) 45

**12.**

|       | W  | M  | Total |
|-------|----|----|-------|
| V     | 8  | 4  | 12    |
| P     | 6  | 12 | 18    |
| G     | 2  | 4  | 6     |
| Total | 16 | 20 | 36    |

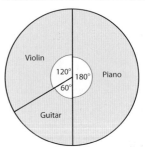

**13.** $A - 225°$; $B - 15°$; $C - 75°$; $D - 45°$

**14.** (i), (iii) and (v)

**15.** (i) 150

**16.** (i) (a) 145° (b) 75° (c) 35°
 (ii) (a) 105 (b) 54 (c) 25 (d) 76

## Exercise 15.3

**1.** (i) 4  (ii) 27 years  (iii) 8
 (iv) 36 years  (v) 16%

**2.** (i) 26 sec  (ii) 8  (iii) 24
 (iv) 39 sec  (v) 68 sec  (vi) 45 sec
 (vii) 12

**3.** (i) 26  (ii) 49  (iii) 8
 (iv) 20%

**4.** (i) 20  (ii) 5  (iii) 43
 (iv) 76  (v) 35%

**5.** (i) 34 cm  (ii) 6  (iii) 7
 (iv) 163 cm  (v) 3 : 2

**6.** (i) 50  (ii) $75\frac{1}{2}$  (iii) 9  (iv) 40%

**7.** (ii) 8  (iii) $33\frac{1}{3}$%  (iv) 16  (v) 15

**8.** (i) 22 to 84 (i.e. range of 62)
 (ii) 7  (iii) 25%  (iv) $58\frac{1}{2}$ marks
 (v) 57.7 marks

**9.** (i)

| 1 | 7 | 9 | 9 | | | |
|---|---|---|---|---|---|---|
| 2 | 0 | 6 | 7 | 8 | | |
| 3 | 5 | 7 | 8 | 9 | 9 | 9 |
| 4 | 5 | 9 | | | | |

Key 2|6 = 26 kg

 (ii) 35 kg  (iii) 32 kg  (iv) 31.8 kg
 (v) 36.8 kg  (vi) 552 kg

## Exercise 15.4

**1.** (i) 3  (ii) 3
 (iii) 17  (iv) 07.40–07.50
 (v) 23

**2.** (i) 40  (ii) 40
 (iii) (60–70) kg

**3.** (i) 20  (ii) 16
 (iii) (6–9) km  (iv) 62

**4.** (ii) 28  (iii) 12

**5.** (i) 7 : 30 am  (ii) 45
 (iii) Breakfast  (iv) 10.30 am–11.30 am
 (v) 'Elevenses'

**6.** (ii) 16  (iii) (20–40) km
 (iv) 2

**7.** (i) 16  (ii) 64
 (iii) (30–40) sec  (iv) 22

**8.** (i) 12  (ii) 60
 (iii) (50–60) years  (iv) $\frac{1}{10}$

(v) 21

**9.** (i)

| Length ($l$ cm) | Tally | Frequency |
|---|---|---|
| $5 \leqslant l < 10$ | | 6 |
| $10 \leqslant l < 15$ | | 10 |
| $15 \leqslant l < 20$ | | 7 |
| $20 \leqslant l < 25$ | | 9 |
| $25 \leqslant l < 30$ | | 8 |

(ii)

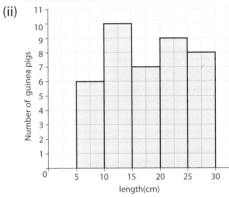

(iii) $10 \leqslant l < 15$  (iv) 23

## Exercise 15.5

**1.** (i) 2  (ii) 4  (iii) 8
 (iv) 3  (v) 9  (vi) 27

**2.** Graph only shows part of the scale

**3.** (i) Area of column for 'fish 2' increased dramatically by larger width
 (ii) Increased width and depth (and by extension, volume) of carton B creates illusion of greater production despite the actual productions being the same
 (iii) Scale doesn't start at 0
 (iv) 'Creative' cubes (area and volume) mislead

**4.** Vertical axis unlabelled; cylinders of varying radii used

**5.** (i) Graph shows only part of the vertical scale

## Test yourself 15

**1.** (i) 36  (ii) Friday
 (iii) Mon, Tues
 (iv) The small sample size of 36

**2.** (ii) 26 years  (iii) 24 years
 (iv) 15%

**3.** (i) 42  (ii) 3
 (iii) 10

**4.** (i) 36 (emails)  (ii) 28 (emails)
 (iii) 14  (iv) 47

**5.** (i) 15  (ii) 90°
 (iii) 30  (iv) $33\frac{1}{3}$%

**6.** (i) As the continuous data is grouped
   (ii) 7             (iii) 8
   (iv) 16

**7.** (i) 48 – highest, 30 – lowest
   (ii) 4             (iii) 88%

**8.** (i) Red – 120°, Blue – 90°, Green – 75°,
    Purple – 45°, Others – 30°
   (iii) A bar chart

**9.** (i)

```
0 | 5  5  6  9
1 | 2  2  2  3  4  5  6  7  8  9
2 | 0  1  3  7  9
3 |
4 | 6
Key 2|0 = 20s
```

   (ii) range = 41 s    (iii) mode = 12 s

**10.** (i) €1200    (ii) (a) 120°    (b) €400

**11.** (ii) 15
   (iii) Number of department heads – discrete,
      number of hours – continuous
   (iv) (40–45) hour interval

# Chapter 16: Indices – Scientific Notation – Reciprocals

## Exercise 16.1

**1.** (i) $2^3$   (ii) $5^4$   (iii) $6^5$   (iv) $a^3$
   (v) $k^4$   (vi) $(-2)^3$

**2.** (i) 9   (ii) 8   (iii) 64   (iv) 1000
   (v) 16

**3.** (i) $3^2$   (ii) $6^3$   (iii) $3^5$   (iv) $5^6$
   (v) $5^3$   (vi) $3^7$   (vii) $5^6$   (viii) $2^8$

**4.** (i) 3   (ii) 3   (iii) 4   (iv) 2
   (v) 2   (vi) 3   (vii) 3   (viii) 5

**5.** (i) 12   (ii) 18   (iii) 32   (iv) 50
   (v) 36   (vi) 72   (vii) 8   (viii) 16

**6.** (i) 4   (ii) −27   (iii) −18   (iv) −32

**7.** (i) $2^2 \times 3^2$   (ii) $3^2 \times 4^3$   (iii) $5^3 \times 3^2$
   (iv) $4^2 \times a^2$   (v) $3^3 \times a^3$   (vi) $5^3 \times a^3$

**8.** (i) $3^2$   (ii) $5^2$   (iii) $3^3$
   (iv) $10^3$   (v) $9^2$ (or $3^4$)   (vi) $8^2$ (or $4^3$)

**9.** (i) $5^2$   (ii) $3^4$   (iii) $7^2$
   (iv) $3^4$   (v) $5^7$   (vi) $7^2$

**10.** (i) 800   (ii) 150   (iii) 7600
   (iv) 300   (v) 7

**11.** (i) 8   (ii) 16   (iii) 9   (iv) 343

**12.** (i) 16   (ii) 64   (iii) 81   (iv) 64
   (v) 10 000

**13.** (i) $F$   (ii) $T$   (iii) $F$   (iv) $F$

**14.** (i) 36   (ii) 64   (iii) 100   (iv) 9
   (v) 64

**15.** (i) 3   (ii) 6   (iii) 9   (iv) 16
   (v) 18   (vi) 12   (vii) 3   (viii) 4
   (ix) 6   (x) 3

**16.** (i) 9   (ii) 114   (iii) 34   (iv) 16

**17.** (i) 2   (ii) 3   (iii) 10   (iv) 4
   (v) 3

**18.** (i) 24   (ii) 3   (iii) 36   (iv) 24
   (v) 52   (vi) 14

**19.** (i) 2   (ii) 3   (iii) 3   (iv) 6
   (v) 3   (vi) 3   (vii) 3   (viii) 2

**20.** (i) 8, 7   (ii) 6, 5   (iii) 8, 8   (iv) 3, 1

**21.** $C$ is false

**22.** (i) 22    (ii) 11    (iii) 17
   (iv) 5    (v) 35    (vi) 24
   (vii) 42    (viii) 2

## Exercise 16.2

**1.** (i), (iv)

**2.** (i) 200   (ii) 340   (iii) 5700
   (iv) 28 400   (v) 581   (vi) 2940
   (vii) 18 370   (viii) 9843

**3.** As the 'a part' (in this case 30) is not a number between 1 and 10. $3 \times 10^4$ is the same number (30 000) written in standard form

**4.** (i) $2.8 \times 10^1$   (ii) $6.4 \times 10$   (iii) $8 \times 10$
   (iv) $1.5 \times 10^2$   (v) $4.67 \times 10^2$

**5.** (i) $4 \times 10^2$   (ii) $6.5 \times 10^2$   (iii) $2 \times 10^3$
   (iv) $2.7 \times 10^3$   (v) $6.92 \times 10^3$

**6.** (i) $7.8 \times 10^3$      (ii) $9.46 \times 10^2$
   (iii) $1.54 \times 10^4$     (iv) $3.89 \times 10^4$

**7.** (i) $2.4 \times 10^3$      (ii) $1.28 \times 10^4$
   (iii) $8 \times 10^3$      (iv) $1.29 \times 10^4$

**8.** (i) $7.21 \times 10^2$    (ii) $2.56 \times 10^2$

**9.** (i) 580          (ii) 510
   (iii) 15 000      (iv) 13 000

**10.** $6.28 \times 10^3$     **11.** $1.39 \times 10^3$

**12.** $8.79 \times 10^2$     **13.** $8.76 \times 10^3$

**14.** $8.6 \times 10^2$      **15.** 12 000

**16.** 7000          **17.** 152 000

**18.** 106 000       **19.** $2.4 \times 10^5$

**20.** $1.5 \times 10^6$      **21.** $5.6 \times 10^7$

**22.** $7.5 \times 10^5$      **23.** $2.5 \times 10$

**24.** $2 \times 10^3$       **25.** $1.2 \times 10^2$

**26.** $1.9 \times 10^3$

**27.** (i) Earth
   (ii) $5.9 \times 10^3$ km (or 5900 km)
   (iii) $1.95 \times 10^4$ km

**28.** (i) Yangtze – 6300 km; Congo – 4700 km;
    Danube – 2840 km; Seine – 780 km
   (ii) $4.7 \times 10^3$ km
   (iii) $7.8 \times 10^2$ km
   (iv) six times

**29.** (a) $time = \frac{distance}{speed}$

(b) (i) $4 \times 10^{16}$ m (ii) $1.3 \times 10^8$ s

**30.** (i) $A = 1.7 \times 10^9\,l$, $B = 7.4 \times 10^{10}\,l$

(ii) 43

## Exercise 16.3

**1.** (i) $\frac{1}{4}$ (ii) $\frac{1}{12}$ (iii) 3

(iv) $\frac{5}{2}$ (v) $\frac{4}{5}$

**2.** (i) 0.11 (ii) 0.08 (iii) 0.04

(iv) 0.08 (v) 0.34

**3.** 225 **4.** 1156

**5.** 39.69 **6.** 153.76

**7.** 1024 **8.** 681.21

**9.** 3.24 **10.** 0.81

**11.** 84.64 **12.** 0.2916

**13.** 3.5 **14.** 7.3

**15.** 12.6 **16.** 30.4

**17.** 7.6 **18.** 9.9

**19.** 40.0 **20.** 48.5

**21.** 0.9 **22.** 0.8

**23.** 20.78 **24.** 51.23

**25.** 972 **26.** 529.92

**27.** 58.91 **28.** 21.95

**29.** 18.17 **30.** 46.23

**32.** (i) 7.9 (ii) 9.1 (iii) 12.5

**33.** (i) 0.16 (ii) 1.27 (iii) 4.22

(iv) 44.28 (v) 2.50

## Exercise 16.4

**1.** (i) 80 (ii) 100 (iii) 30

(iv) 130 (v) 430

**2.** (i) 300 (ii) 100 (iii) 700

(iv) 1900 (v) 7400

**3.** (i) 1000 (ii) 2000 (iii) 9000

(iv) 18 000 (v) 28 000

**4.** (i) 1.4 (ii) 12.3 (iii) 0.5

(iv) 12.1 (v) 0.7

**5.** (i) one (ii) two (iii) one

(iv) two (v) three

**6.** (i) 70 (ii) 40 (iii) 300

(iv) 600 (v) 3000

**7.** (i) 580 (ii) 990 (iii) 2900

(iv) 5900 (v) 25 000

**8.** (i) Roughly 5000 disgruntled farmers descend on *The Dail*

(ii) 40 000 filled the *R.D.S.* for sell-out concert

**9.** (i) 0.47 (ii) 0.063 (iii) 2.4

(iv) 0.67 (v) 55.0

**10.** 72 700; (i) 73 000 (ii) 70 000

**11.** (i) 40 (ii) 2 (iii) 125

**12.** (i) 3 (ii) 3 (iii) $2\frac{2}{3}$

**13.** (i) 5 (ii) 360 (iii) 9

## Test yourself 16

**1.** (i) 46 400 (ii) 46 000

(iii) 50 000

**2.** (i) 48 (ii) 32

(iii) 72

**3.** (i) $7.4 \times 10^3$ (ii) 6880

**4.** $\sqrt{144}$, $4^2$, $2^5$, $3^4$ (12, 16, 32, 81)

**5.** (i) 2 (ii) 2

(iii) 3 (iv) 2

**6.** (i) 400 (ii) 7300; $7.7 \times 10^3$

**7.** (i) 88 (ii) 92

**8.** (i) 2830 (ii) $7.93 \times 10^3$

**9.** (i), (iii) (ie 16)

**10.** 2

**11.** 5

**12.** 680, 9000; $9.68 \times 10^3$

**13.** (i) 3 (ii) 9

**14.** (i) $x^3$ (ii) $8a^5$

(iii) $6a^5$

**15.** 314.56

**16.** 106

**17.** (i) 3740 (ii) $5.82 \times 10^3$

**18.** 19.61

**19.** $A$ & $F$, $B$ & $G$, $C$ & $D$, $E$ & $H$

## Chapter 17: Circles and Cylinders

### Exercise 17.1

**1.** (i) Radius (ii) Diameter (iii) Arc

(iv) Semicircle (v) Sector

**2.** (i) 62.8 cm (ii) 25.12 cm

(iii) 75.36 cm (iv) 56.52 mm

**3.** (i) 88 cm (ii) 132 cm

(iii) 220 cm (iv) 44 cm

**4.** (i) 50.3 cm (ii) 131.9 cm

(iii) 69.1 cm (iv) 56.5 m

**5.** (i) 81.64 cm (ii) 94.2 cm

(iii) 251.2 cm

**6.** (i) 33 cm (ii) 11 cm

(iii) $58\frac{2}{3}$ cm

**7.** (i) 72 cm (ii) $42\frac{2}{3}$ cm

(iii) 47 cm

**8.** (i) 31 cm (ii) 45 cm

(iii) 75 cm

**9.** 91 cm

**10.** Each is the same distance ($4\pi$ m)

**11.** 211 m of tape

**12.** (i) 0.75 m (ii) 80 m

## Exercise 17.2

1.  (i) 314 cm²      (ii) 50.24 cm²
    (iii) 452.16 mm²    (iv) 254.34 cm²
2.  (i) 616 cm²      (ii) 1386 cm²
    (iii) 3850 m²      (iv) 154 cm²
3.  (i) 201.1 cm²     (ii) 1385.4 cm²
    (iii) 380.1 cm²    (iv) 254.5 mm²
4.  (i) $\frac{1}{4}$   (ii) $\frac{1}{3}$   (iii) $\frac{1}{6}$   (iv) $\frac{1}{8}$
5.  (i) 1386 cm²   (ii) 77 cm²   (iii) $821\frac{1}{3}$ cm²
6.  (i) 189.97 cm² (ii) 150.72 cm² (iii) 244.48 cm²
7.  (i) $r = 5$ cm   (ii) $r = 11$ m   (iii) $r = 13$ cm
8.  (i) $r = 7$ cm   (ii) 44 cm
9.  (i) 14 cm      (ii) 616 cm²
10. (i) 14 cm      (ii) 42 cm²
11. (i) $r = 35$ cm   (ii) 3854 cm²
12. (i) 89 cm²     (ii) 74 cm²    (iii) 164 cm²
13. 65.98 cm²
14. (i) 6 cm      (ii) 7.74 cm²

## Exercise 17.3

1.  (i) 1846 cm³      (ii) 2813 cm³
    (iii) 18 463 mm³
2.  $\frac{1}{2}\pi r^2 h$, 28 260 cm³
3.  (i) 54 259 cm³     (ii) 402 m³
    (iii) 1413 cm³
4.  24 640 cm³; 25 $l$
5.  706.5 cm³
6.  (i) $V = \pi r^2 h$     (ii) $350\pi = 14\pi r^2$
    (iii) $r = 5$ cm
7.  16 cm
8.  6 cm
9.  10 cm
10. 12 bottles
11. 7 cm
12. 4938 cm³
13. (i) 1570 cm³      (ii) 14.13 kg
14. 175.84 cm³; 1792 cm³
15. $h = 16$ cm

## Test yourself 17

1.  (i) 44 cm      (ii) 154 cm²
2.  9043 cm³
3.  812 cm²
4.  56 cm²
5.  (i) 139.3 cm²     (ii) 45.7 cm
6.  6250 cm³
7.  235.5 cm²
8.  (i) 20 000$\pi$ cm³    (ii) 160$\pi$ cm³
    (iii) 125
9.  $\frac{5}{6}$; 94.2 cm²

10. 9119 cm³; 9$\ell$
11. (i) 78           (ii) 3099 cm²
12. 14 cm
13. (i) 33.41 cm   (ii) 30 cm²   (iii) 36.3 cm²

## Chapter 18:
## Geometry 2 – Triangles and Circles

## Exercise 18.1

1.  A & D, B & C      2.  B, E, G, H, I, J
3.  (i) [DE]   (ii) [BC]   (iii) [DF]   (iv) [AB]
4.  (i) [MN]   (ii) [YZ]   (iii) ∠MLN (iv) ∠YXZ
5.  (i) [XG]   (ii) [LN]   (iii) [AX]
6.  SAS
7.  (i) SSS      (ii) SAS      (iii) SAS
    (iv) ASA    (v) RHS    (vi) ASA
8.  A & D
9.  SSS
10. Yes; SSS ([BD] is a common side)
11. SAS (|∠AOB| = (|∠COD| . . . vertically opposite
    each other)
12. ASA; (i) [EF]    (ii) [AB]      (iii) 35°
13. $x = 70°, y = 10$ cm
14. SSS; (|∠ABC| = |∠ADC| as they are opposite
    angles in parallelogram)

## Exercise 18.2

1.  (i) [SR]      (ii) [LM]      (iii) 8
    (iv) 16.4     (v) 7.5
2.  (i) 1 : 2     (ii) 14.4     (iii) 4
3.  $x = 13.5, y = 18$
4.  (i) $p = 6, q = 13.5$
    (ii) $x = 9, y = 1$
5.  (i) 1.5      (ii) $x = 6, y = 4.5$
6.  Same shape (i.e. same angles) but different
    sizes; $x = 21, y = 15$
7.  (i) [RQ]     (ii) [RP]     (iii) [QP]; 9
8.  (i) [KL]     (ii) [EF]     (iii) 15
9.  (ii) [DF]    (iii) $x = 13\frac{5}{7}$ cm; $y = 9\frac{1}{7}$ cm
10. (i), (iv), (v)        11. 2 m

## Exercise 18.3

1.  (i) 10 cm       (ii) 10 cm
    (iii) 5 cm        (iv) 5 cm; isosceles
2.  (i) The angle in a semicircle is always 90°
    (ii) 45°      (iii) Right-angled and isosceles
3.  (i) 90°      (ii) 30°      (iii) 40°
4.  $A = 90°, B = 90°, C = 30°, D = 90°, E = 40°,$
    $F = 35°$

**5.** (i) $x = 55°, y = 50°$    (ii) $x = 90°, y = 38°$
   (iii) $x = 45°, y = 53°$
**6.** (i) both radii   (ii) $90°$    (iii) $35°$
   (iv) $55°$    (v) $|OB| = |OC| = $ radius
**7.** (i) $60°$    (ii) $60°$
**8.** (i) $x = 90°, y = 50°$
   (ii) $x = 32°, y = 58°$
   (iii) $x = 15°, y = 60°$
**9.** (i) $x = 70°$   (ii) $x = 57°$   (iii) $x = 35°$
**10.** Right-angled; 10; 5
**11.** (i) 20 cm   (ii) $30°$   (iii) $90°$   (iv) $60°$
**12.** 8 cm

## Test yourself 18

**1.** $x = 90°, y = 25°, z = 52°$
**2.** (i) & (iv); SAS
**3.** $x = 55°, y = 43°$
**4.** A & B (SAS)
**5.** SSS
**6.** $a = 90°, b = 34°$
**7.** (i) $\angle ADC$ & $\angle ABC$    (ii) $45°$
   (iii) $70°$
**8.** (i) equiangular triangles
   (ii) $x = 9, y = 10.5$
**9.** (i) $x = 60°, y = 45°$
   (ii) $x = 90°, y = 32°$
   (iii) $x = 45°, y = 55°$
**10.** SAS; (i) $[BC]$     (ii) $[EA]$
   (iii) $\angle BCD$

# Chapter 19:
# Patterns and Sequences

## Exercise 19.1

**1.** (i) 13, 15, 17, 19    (ii) 17, 20, 23, 26
   (iii) 24, 28, 32, 36    (iv) 12, 10, 8, 6
   (v) 30, 25, 20, 15    (vi) 0, −4, −8, −12
**2.** (i) 16, 32, 64    (ii) 54, 162, 486
   (iii) 81, 243, 729    (iv) 25, 36, 49
   (v) 9, 27, 81    (vi) $\frac{4}{5}, \frac{5}{6}, \frac{6}{7}$
**3.** 16, 19, 22
**4.** (i) 2, 6, 10, 14    (ii) 5, 8, 11, 14
   (iii) 3, 8, 13, 18    (iv) 30, 26, 22, 18
   (v) −10, −7, −4, −1
**5.** (i) 'Add 3 to the previous term'
   (ii) 'Add 4 to the previous term'
   (iii) 'Add 5 to the previous term'
   (iv) 'Subtract 2 from the previous term'
   (v) 'Add 3 to the previous term'
   (vi) 'Add $1\frac{1}{2}$ to the previous term'
**6.** (i) 10, 12, 14    (ii) 16, 26, 42
   (iii) 32, 64, 128    (iv) 82, 244, 730

**7.** 18
**8.** (i) 11      (ii) 29
**9.**

| 1st term | Term-to-term rule | 2nd, 3rd, 4th and 5th terms |
|---|---|---|
| 8 | +5 | 13, 18, 23, 28 |
| 5 | +4 | 9, 13, 17, 21 |
| 9 | +3 | 12, 15, 18, 21 |
| 0 | −3 | −3, −6, −9, −12 |
| −12 | +5 | −7, −2, 3, 8 |

**10.** (i) 14      (ii) 26
**11.** (i) 7      (ii) 1, 5     (iii) 1, 4
**12.** (i) 34, 55    (ii) 3
**13.** 80, 242
**14.** Pattern: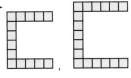

   Position: 4, 5
   Term: 11, 14, 17

**15.** 1, 2, 4, 8, 16, 32
**16.** (i) 7      (ii) 127
**17.** (i) 8, 10, 12    (ii) 22, 16
   (iii) 6, 16, 26    (iv) 7, 13, 16, 22

## Exercise 19.2

**1.** (i) Square, circle
   (ii) 2, 6, 10; Yes, the circle is the second shape in each block of four shapes
   (iii) Triangle      (iv) Square
   (v) Square      (vi) Circle
**2.** (i) Green      (ii) Blue
   (iii) Red      (iv) Blue
   (v) 5, 10, 15, 20    (vi) 30th
**3.** (i) 8, 4      (ii) 4
   (iii) 6      (iv) 23rd
**4.** (i) Circle      (ii) 5, 10, 15; 20
   (iii) Circle      (iv) Semicircle
   (v) Semicircle
**5.** 8, 16, 24, 32, 40, 48, 56, 64, 72, 80;
   (i) 8, 6, 4, 2, 0 , 8, 6, 4, 2, 0
   (ii) 5      (iii) 0

## Exercise 19.3

**1.** (i) 2, 4, 6, 8      (ii) 4, 7, 10, 13
   (iii) 1, 5, 9, 13    (iv) 7, 9, 11, 13
   (v) 1, 6, 11, 16    (vi) 5, 3, 1, −1
**2.** As the difference between the terms is a constant in each sequence
**3.** (i) 5, 7, 9, 11, 13    (ii) $T_{20} = 43, T_{100} = 203$
   (iii) Constant difference is +2

**5.** 2, 5, 10, 17; No, differences between the terms vary

**6.** (i) 5, 8, 11, 14, 17, 20 (ii) $T_{100} = 302$

**7.** (i) 3, 6, 9, 12 etc.

**8.** 7, 9, 11; Difference between terms is a constant (2)

**9.** $x = 4, y = 6$

**10.** (i) 37 (ii) 7

**11.** $10^{th} = 1537, 9^{th} = 769$

**12.** (i) 29, 47 (ii) 1, 3

## Exercise 19.4

**1.** (i) $+4$ (ii) 4
(iii) $Tn = 4n + 1$ (iv) 81

**2.** (i) 3 (ii) 4 (iii) 6 (iv) 5

**3.** (i) 3 (ii) 3 (iii) 5
(iv) 5, 2 (v) 2, 5 (vi) 4, 1

**4.** (i) $T_n = 2n + 3$
(ii) $T_n = 3n + 2$
(iii) $T_n = 4n + 2$

**5.** $T_n = 4n + 3$; $T_{10} = 43, T_{20} = 83$

**6.** $T_n = 4n + 4$;
(i) $T_{10} = 44$ (ii) $T_{30} = 124$; $T_{19}$

**7.** (i) 'Subtract 2 from the previous term'
(ii) $-2$ (iii) $T_n = -2n + 14$
(iv) $-6$ (v) 14th term

**8.** (i) $T_n = 3n - 6$ (ii) $T_n = -5n + 25$

## Exercise 19.5

**1.** (i)

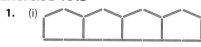

(ii) 6, 11, 16, 21, 26, 31
(iv) 101 (v) 10th

**2.** (i)

(iii) $T_n = 2n + 1$ (iv) Diagram 16

**3.** 10, 13, 16;
(i) 19 (ii) $T_n = 3n + 1$
(iii) 151

**4.** (i) 13 (ii) $T_n = 2n + 3$
(iii) Pattern 24

**5.** (i) 21 (ii) 'Add 5' matchsticks
(iii) $T_n = 5n + 1$ (iii) Pattern 13
(v) No

## Exercise 19.6

**1.** 4, 7, 12, 19, 28; As the 2nd difference is a constant (2)

**2.** (i) 2, 5, 10, 17 (ii) $-1, 2, 7, 14$
(iii) 1, 7, 17, 31

**3.** (i) First differences : 1, 2, 3, 4; Yes, quadratic
Second differences : 1, 1, 1

(ii) First differences : 3, 5, 7, 9; Yes, quadratic
Second differences : 2, 2, 2

(iii) First differences : 5, 7, 9, 11;
Second differences : 2, 2, 2; Yes, quadratic

**4.** (i) 36, 48 (ii) 39, 52

**5.** (i) 24 (ii) 35
(iii) The second difference between the terms (2) is a constant

**6.** (i) 81, 243, 729 (ii) Not a constant

**7.** 2, 4, 8, 16, 32, 64; exponential sequence

**8.** 6, 12, 24, 48

## Exercise 19.7

**1.** (i) €24 (ii) 6.4 km
(iii) 8 km (iv) €2 difference

**3.** 3, 5, 7, 9, 11; a linear graph

**4.**

| Day | Height (cm) |
| --- | --- |
| 4 | 10 |
| 5 | 12 |
| 6 | 14 |
| 7 | 16 |

(ii) 14 days (iii) 29 days

**5.** (i) €30 (ii) €105
(iii) 5 hours (iv) €200

**6.** (i) €100 (ii) Week 8

**7.** 3 hr 20 min

**8.** (i) The term-to-term rule involves adding a constant (i.e. 4)
(ii) $T_n = 4n + 2$ (iv) Straight line

## Test yourself 19

**1.** (i) 15 (ii) $-2$ (iii) 108

**2.** 44, 120

**3.** (i) 15, 21, 27 (ii) 17, 27, 39
(iii) 27, 81, 243

**4.** (i) Yellow, green (ii) 3, 8, 13, 18, . . .
(iii) 48th position (iv) blue

**5.** Quadratic sequence; constant 2nd difference

**6.** (i) €25
(iii) The previous week's savings plus €5
(iv) 16 weeks
(v) €7
(vi) Yes; he will have €101 saved after 13 weeks with the extra savings, enough to buy the €100 phone

**7.** (i) $-2$ (ii) 4
(iii) 9 (iv) 15

**8.** (i) 13, 17, 21 (ii) 29
(iii) $T_n = 4n + 1$ (iv) Shape 25

**9.** (iii)

**10.** (i) $6, 5, 4\frac{1}{2}$ (ii) No; No

**11.** Option B €1022

**12.** (i)

(ii) 15      (iii) $T_n = 3n$

(iv) 21st pattern

# Chapter 20: Algebra 2: Inequalities – Algebraic Fractions

## Exercise 20.1

**1.** (i) T    (ii) T    (iii) F    (iv) T

    (v) F    (vi) F    (vii) T    (viii) T

**2.** (i) $>$    (ii) $<$    (iii) $>$    (iv) $<$

**3.** (i) $x < 4$    (ii) $2 > -3$    (iii) $S \leqslant 40$

    (iv) $b \leqslant -5$    (v) $A \geqslant 18$    (vi) $A \leqslant 60$

**4.** (i) 1, 2, 3           (ii) 1, 2, 3, 4, 5

    (iii) 1, 2, 3, 4, 5, 6    (iv) 3, 4, 5, 6

    (v) 1, 2, 3, 4       (vi) 2, 3, 4, 5, 6, 7

**5.** (i) $-2, -1, 0, 1$     (ii) $0, 1, 2, 3, 4$

    (iii) $-3, -2, -1, 0$    (iv) $-4, -3, -2, -1, 0$

    (v) $-4, -3, -2, -1, 0, 1$

    (vi) $-2, -1, 0, 1, 2, 3$

**7.** (i) $x > 3$         (ii) $x < 3$

    (iii) $x = 3$        (iv) $x \leqslant 3$

**8.** (i) $x \geqslant 1$         (ii) $x \leqslant -1$

    (iii) $x < 4$        (iv) $x > -6$

    (v) $x > 6$        (vi) $x < 2$

       ($x \in R$ in each case)

**10.** (i) $n \geqslant 6$ (ii) $n \leqslant 5$ (iii) $n \leqslant 10$ (iv) $n > 5$

**11.** he had a maximum of 15 and a minimum of 6 games.

**12.** C: $b < 5$, B: $b > 5$, A: $\leqslant 5$, D $\geqslant 5$

## Exercise 20.2

**1.** Ⓐ, Ⓑ, Ⓓ, Ⓔ      **2.** Ⓐ, Ⓒ, Ⓓ, Ⓔ

**3.** $x \leqslant 5$            **4.** $x \leqslant 4$

**5.** $x \leqslant 4$            **6.** $x \leqslant 3$

**7.** $x \leqslant -2$          **8.** $x \leqslant 4$

**9.** $x < -3$         **10.** $x \leqslant 2$

**11.** $x \leqslant 5$         **12.** $x \leqslant 3$

**13.** $x < 2$          **14.** $x \geqslant -1$

**15.** $x \leqslant 6$         **16.** $x < 3$

**17.** $x \geqslant 1$         **18.** $x \leqslant 3$

**19.** $x \leqslant 4$         **20.** $x < 3$

**21.** $x \geqslant 3$         **22.** $x < -2$

**23.** $x \geqslant -2$       **24.** $x \leqslant -3$

**25.** (i) $1, \frac{2}{5}, -20$     (ii) $\sqrt{10}, \frac{13}{4}$

**26.** (i) Sometimes    (ii) Always

    (iii) Always      (iv) Never

    (v) Always      (vi) Sometimes

    (vii) Always     (viii) Always

## Exercise 20.3

**1.** $\dfrac{7}{6}$           **2.** $\dfrac{27}{20}$

**3.** $\dfrac{2}{3}$           **4.** $\dfrac{1}{8}$

**5.** $\dfrac{5x}{6}$          **6.** $\dfrac{8x}{15}$

**7.** $\dfrac{13x}{4}$         **8.** $\dfrac{19x}{15}$

**9.** $\dfrac{x}{12}$          **10.** $\dfrac{3x}{10}$

**11.** $\dfrac{9x}{10}$        **12.** $\dfrac{7x}{20}$

**13.** $\dfrac{2x+1}{2}$      **14.** $\dfrac{2x+5}{2}$

**15.** $\dfrac{3x+5}{3}$      **16.** $\dfrac{8x-6}{3}$

**17.** $2x+1$        **18.** $\dfrac{4x-2}{3}$

**19.** $\dfrac{7x+14}{6}$     **20.** $\dfrac{11x+2}{12}$

**21.** $\dfrac{7x-11}{12}$     **22.** $\dfrac{5x-2}{10}$

**23.** $\dfrac{3x-16}{6}$     **24.** $\dfrac{7x-13}{12}$

**25.** $\dfrac{2x+7}{12}$     **26.** $\dfrac{13x+1}{14}$

**27.** $\dfrac{-4x+7}{12}$    **28.** $\dfrac{19x-17}{10}$

**29.** $\dfrac{5x+9}{12}$     **30.** $\dfrac{7x-9y}{15}$

**31.** $\dfrac{15x-31}{12}$    **32.** $\dfrac{-14x+9}{12}$

## Exercise 20.4

**1.** $x = 6$    **2.** $x = 20$    **3.** $x = 9$    **4.** 5

**5.** 7        **6.** 3          **7.** 3        **8.** 3

**9.** 6        **10.** 6        **11.** 4      **12.** 11

**13.** $5\frac{2}{3}$      **14.** 2        **15.** 6      **16.** 11

**17.** 3       **18.** 6        **19.** 6      **20.** 4

**21.** 7       **22.** 6        **23.** 4      **24.** 5

**25.** 10     **26.** 1        **27.** 2      **28.** 12

**29.** 1       **30.** 4        **31.** 3      **32.** 6

**33.** 6       **34.** 9        **35.** 5      **36.** $2\frac{1}{2}$

**37.** 8       **38.** 6        **39.** 2      **40.** 2

**41.** 8       **42.** 30

**43.** (i) $x - 4 = \dfrac{x+2}{3}$     (ii) 3 units

## Exercise 20.5

1. 8    2. 18    3. 16    4. 20
5. 7 years    6. 7    7. 6    8. 24
9. €16    10. 15 years, 18 years

## Exercise 20.6

1. (i) $5a$    (ii) $2y$    (iii) $3c$
   (iv) $3b$    (v) $2x$    (vi) $8b^2$
   (vii) $7x$    (viii) $4b$

2. (i) $\frac{4}{3}$    (ii) $\frac{k}{2}$    (iii) $2b^2$
   (iv) $4ab$    (v) $2$    (vi) $\frac{9}{2}$
   (vii) $9b$    (viii) $2a$.

3. (i) APPLE    (ii) LEMON/MELON
4. $2(a + b)$    5. $x + y$    6. $4$
7. $\frac{1}{2}$    8. $\frac{4}{3}$    9. $\frac{3}{x}$
10. $\frac{1}{3}$    11. $x + y$    12. $\frac{x}{3}$
13. $\frac{2}{x}$    14. $\frac{1}{x + y}$    15. $\frac{x - y}{2}$
16. $\frac{1}{x + 3}$    17. $x + 4$    18. $\frac{x + 1}{2}$
19. $\frac{1}{x - 2}$    20. $x + 6$    21. $x$
22. $\frac{x + 3}{x + 2}$    23. $\frac{x + 5}{x + 2}$    24. $x + 5$
25. $\frac{x - 2y}{3}$    26. $\frac{x - 5}{4}$    27. $\frac{x + 7}{x + 5}$

## Test Yourself 20

1. (i) $x \leqslant 5$    (ii) $\frac{11x + 9}{12}$
2. (i) $\frac{a^2}{2}$    (ii) $x = 10$
3. (i) 1, 2, 3, 4, 5, 6    (ii) 2, 3, 4, 5, 6, 7, 8
   (iii) 1, 2, 3, 4, 5
4. (i) $x \geqslant 2$
   (ii) $-4, -3, -2, -1, 0, 1, 2, 3, 4$
5. (i) $\frac{7x + 3}{6}$    (ii) $x = 3$
6. (i) $(x - 3)$    (ii) $x = 5$
7. (i) $2x$    (i) $4y$
8. $x \geqslant 2$
9. $x = 3$
10. (i) $x \leqslant 2$    (ii) $x \geqslant -3$
11. (i) $x = 10$    (ii) $x = 11$
12. (i) $\frac{a}{3b}$    (ii) $x - 3$
13. $x \leqslant -3$
14. $\frac{5x + 34}{12}$
15. 4, 9

16. (i) $-3, -2, -1, 0, 1, 2$
    (ii) 1, 2, 3, 4
17. (i) $(x + 5)$    (ii) $x = 1$
18. $2x - 6 = \frac{x}{2} + 3; x = 6; 6$ units

# Chapter 21: Functions

## Exercise 21.1

1. (i) 2    (ii) 16    (iii) 11
   (iv) 5    (v) 6    (vi) 15
2. (i) 'Subtract 6'
   (ii) 'Multiply by 4'
   (iii) 'Multiply by 2, then add 1'
   (iv) 'Multiply by 3, then subtract 4'
   (v) 'Divide by 2, then add 3'
   (vi) 'Subtract 5, then multiply by 3'
3. (i) 2, 10, 12    (ii) 12, 10, 8
4. 9, 12, 15, 18, 21
5. (i) $y = 2x + 6$    (ii) $y = 8x - 9$
   (iii) $y = \frac{x}{4} - 3$    (iv) $y = 4(x + 3)$
6. (i) $x \to 3x + 2$    (ii) $x \to 5x - 2$
   (iii) $x \to \frac{x}{3} - 6$    (iv) $x \to 2x + 7$
7. (i) 'Multiply by 5'    (ii) 'Add 4'
   (iii) 'Divide by 4'
8. (i) 'Subtract 1'    (ii) 'Add 1'
   (iii) 'Subtract 2'    (iv) 'Add 2'
9. (i) 3, 5, 7    (ii) 10, 16, 13
   (iii) 5, 8, 20    (iv) 4, 8, 10

## Exercise 21.2

1. (i) {1, 2, 4, 5, 7}    (ii) {3, 6, 4, 7, 9}
   (iii) {(1, 3), (2, 4), (4, 6), (5, 7), (7, 9)}
   (iv) (i) 'Add 2'
2. (i) Domain – {1, 2, 3, 4}
   Range – {6, 7, 8, 9}
   (ii) Domain – {2, 4, 6, 8, 10}
   Range – {5, 9, 13, 17, 21}
3. (i) Yes
   (ii) No (the element $c$ is paired with two elements in the range)
   (iii) No    (iv) Yes
4. As no two couples have the same input
5. As the input 2 has two different outputs, i.e. 5 and 10
6. (i) Yes
   (ii) No (each element of the domain does not map on to only one element of the range)
   (iii) Yes
7. $y = 2(x + 3)$; 8, 10, 12, 14, 16

**8.** (a) (i) {0, 1, 3, 5}   (ii) {3, 4, 5, 8}
   (iii) {3, 4, 5, 6, 8}
   (b) (i) {−2, 2, 3, 7}   (ii) {−4, 6, 9}
   (iii) {−4, 2, 6, −3, 4, 9}
**9.** (i) {3, 5, 9, 13}
   (ii) {(0, 3), (1, 5), (3, 9), (5, 13)}
**10.** {2, 5, 11, 17}
**11.** (i) {−13, −5, 3, 11}
   (ii) {(−2, −13), (0, −5), (2, 3), (4, 11)}
**12.** 9, 11, 13, 15, 17; $y = 2x + 7$
**13.** $f(x) = 4x + 10$; 30; 3
**14.** 10, 0, 5, −6

## Exercise 21.3

**1.** (i) 3       (ii) 9       (iii) 12
   (iv) 18      (v) −6
**2.** (i) 7       (ii) 9       (iii) 13
   (iv) 3       (v) −3
**3.** (i) 2       (ii) 5       (iii) 11
   (iv) 14      (v) −4
**4.** (i) −3      (ii) −2      (iii) 1
   (iv) 1       (v) 13
**5.** (i) 5       (ii) 1       (iii) 11
   (iv) 6       (v) $5 − 2k$
**6.** (i) $x = 2$   (ii) $x = 1$   (iii) $k = −2$
**7.** (i) 1       (ii) −5      (iii) 0
   (iv) −22     (v) −10
**8.** (i) $x = 2$   (ii) $x = 3$   (iii) $x = −2$
**9.** {(1, 3), (2, 8), (3, 13), (4, 18)}
**10.** (i) 2       (ii) 8       (iii) 16
   (iv) −2      (v) −4
**11.** {−4, 1, 6, 11, 16}
**12.** (i) 16      (ii) $x = 2$   (iii) $k = −2$
**13.** (iii) (2, −1)
**14.** (i) {(−2, 14), (−1, 8), (0, 4), (1, 2), (2, 2)}
   (ii) {14, 8, 4, 2}

## Test Yourself 21

**1.** (i) 4       (ii) −2
   (iii) −8      (iv) −7
**2.** (i) {2, 3, 4, 5}   (ii) {3, 6, 8, 18}
**3.** (i) −11      (ii) $x = 3$
   (iii) $k = −1$
**4.** 9, 11, 13, 15, 17
**5.** (i) Yes      (ii) No
**6.** (i) 7, 35     (ii) $k = 5$
**7.** {−1, 4, 9, 14}
**8.** As the input 1 has two different outputs
**9.** $a = 2$
**10.** 'Add 3'
**11.** {−13, −10, −7, −4}
**12.** (i) €43      (ii) 4 km

**13.** (i) 10, 4, −5, 25   (ii) 10, 2, −8, −14
**14.** $a = 18, b = −14, c = 4$
**15.** (i) $x = 5$       (ii) $x = 2$
   (iii) $x = 10\frac{1}{2}$
**16.** (1, 2), (3, 12), (0, −3)
**17.** 5, 8, 12
**18.** $k = −5$

## Chapter 22: Graphing Functions

### Exercise 22.1

**1.**

| x | 2x − 3 | y |
|---|--------|---|
| −1 | −2 − 3 | −5 |
| 0 | 0 − 3 | −3 |
| 1 | 2 − 3 | −1 |
| 2 | 4 − 3 | 1 |
| 3 | 6 − 3 | 3 |
| 4 | 8 − 3 | 5 |

**2.**

| x | 3x − 4 | y |
|---|--------|---|
| −1 | −3 − 4 | −7 |
| 0 | 0 − 4 | −4 |
| 3 | 9 − 4 | 5 |

**3.** $f(1) = 1, f(2) = 3, f(3) = 5$; (1, 1), (2, 3), (3, 5)
**4.** $f(0) = −2, f(1) = 1, f(2) = 4$
**5.** $f(1) = −1, f(2) = 2, f(3) = 5$; (1, −1), (2, 2), (3, 5)
**8.**

| x | 4 − 2x | y |
|---|--------|---|
| 0 | 4 − 0 | 4 |
| 1 | 4 − 2 | 2 |
| 2 | 4 − 4 | 0 |
| 3 | 4 − 6 | −2 |

**11.**

, 10 °C

T = 2t + 10

**12.**

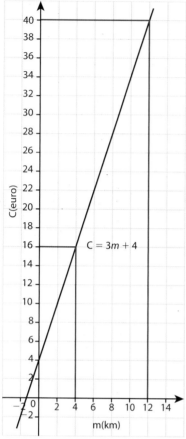

$C = 3m + 4$

(i) €16    (ii) €40

**13.** (i) 18°C    (ii) $4\frac{1}{2}$ min
(iii) (1, 14), (4, 2)

**14.** (4, 0), (0, 4)    **15.** (6, 0), (0, −6)
**16.** (−2, 0), (0, 4)    **17.** (−2, 0), (0, 1)
**18.** (i) 4    (ii) 1    (iii) −3
(iv) −3    (v) 5
**19.** (3, 2)

**Exercise 22.2**

**1.**

| x | x² − 4 | y |
|---|---|---|
| −3 | 9 − 4 | 5 |
| −2 | 4 − 4 | 0 |
| −1 | 1 − 4 | −3 |
| 0 | 0 − 4 | −4 |
| 1 | 1 − 4 | −3 |
| 2 | 4 − 4 | 0 |
| 3 | 9 − 4 | 5 |

**6.** $\left(-\frac{1}{2}, 0\right)$, (3, 0); (0, −3)
**8.** (−1, 0), (3, 0)    **9.** $x = -1, \frac{3}{2}$
**10.** (i) $\left(\frac{1}{2}, 0\right)$, (3, 0)    (ii) (0, −3)

**Exercise 22.3**

**1.** (i) (1, 0), (3, 0)    (ii) −1
(iii) −1, 5    (iv) x = 2
**2.** (i) −1, 1    (ii) −2, 2
(iii) 3    (iv) −1
(v) (0, −1)
**3.** (i) −1.4, 3.4    (ii) −2.4, 4.4
(iii) 10    (iv) −6
**4.** (i) −1, 3    (ii) 0, 2
(iii) −1.5, 3.5    (iv) 3
(v) $-2\frac{1}{4}$    (vi) x = 1
(vii) (1, 4)

**5.** (i) x = 0, 20    (ii) x = 6, 14
(iii) €100 per hour    (iv) 10
**6.** (i) (−1, 1), (3, 9)
(ii) x = −1 or x = 3
(iii) x-values the same
(iv) The x-values of the points where the line
and curve meet
**7.** (i) 0, 2    (ii) −1, 3    (iii) 1
(iv) 3.5    (v) 0.4, 2.6    (vi) x = 1
**8.** (i) −4    (ii) 6    (iii) −3, 2
(iv) −3.7, 2.7    (v) 1
(vi) −1, 3; x = −1 or x = 3
**9.** (i) −3.8, 0.8    (ii) −3.3, 0.3    (iii) −2.4, 0.4
**10.** (i) 12    (ii) 12.30 pm, 3.30 pm
(iii) 10.00 am, 6.00 pm
(iv) 5 hours
(v) 16

**Test Yourself 22**

**1.** (i) −5.5    (ii) 1.5
**2.**

| x | 2x² + 3x − 6 | y |
|---|---|---|
| −4 | 32 − 12 − 6 | 14 |
| −3 | 18 − 9 − 6 | 3 |
| −2 | 8 − 6 − 6 | −4 |
| −1 | 2 − 3 − 6 | −7 |
| 0 | 0 + 0 − 6 | −6 |
| 1 | 2 + 3 − 6 | −1 |
| 2 | 8 + 6 − 6 | 8 |
| 3 | 18 + 9 − 6 | 21 |

(i) −2.6, 1.1    (ii) −2.2, 0.7    (iii) 3

**4.** (i) $x = 0, 2$    (ii) $x = -1, 3; x = 1$
**5.** $-3; 6; (0, -3), (6, 0)$
**6.** (i) $-2.7$    (ii) $-3.2, 1.2$
    (iii) $-3.8, 1.8$
**7.** (i) 5    (ii) 7
    (iii) 3    (iv) $-1$
    (v) 0
**8.** $A$ & $y = x^2 - 2$, $B$ & $y = 2 - x^2$,
    $C$ & $y = 2x$ (coefficient of $x^2$ is positive,
    coefficient of $x^2$ is negative, linear function)
**9.**

| $x$ | $3 - 2x$ | $y$ |
|------|-----------|------|
| $-1$ | $3 + 2$ | 5 |
| 0 | $3 - 0$ | 3 |
| 3 | $3 - 6$ | $-3$ |

**10.** $(0, 0), (1, 5), (2, 8), (3, 9), (4, 8), (5, 5), (6, 0)$;
    (i) 45 m    (ii) 34 m
    (iii) 0.4 sec, 5.6 sec    (iv) 3 sec

# Chapter 23: Trigonometry

## Exercise 23.1

**1.** $A = 56$ cm$^2$, $B = 36$ cm$^2$, $C = 28$ cm$^2$,
    $D = 50$ cm$^2$, $E = 34$ cm$^2$, $F = 25$ cm$^2$
**2.** $a = 5, b = 13, c = 15$
**3.** $x = \sqrt{52}, y = \sqrt{32}, z = \sqrt{44}$
**4.** $a = 8.1, b = 6.7, c = 7.9$
**5.** $a = 11.1$ cm, $b = 6.2$ cm, $c = 8.8$ mm
**6.** (i) Yes    (ii) No    (iii) Yes
    (iv) No    (v) Yes
**7.** $[AC]$; 9 cm    **8.** 21 m
**9.** 68 cm    **10.** 15.9 m

## Exercise 23.2

**1.** (i) 10    (ii) 5    (iii) 13
**2.** (i) 8    (ii) 4    (iii) 12
**3.** (i) 6    (ii) 3    (iii) 5
**4.** (i) 6.4    (ii) 2.5    (iii) 9
**5.** (i) 5    (ii) 1    (iii) 7
**6.** (i) 4    (ii) 2.3    (iii) $\sqrt{32}$
**7.** (i) $\frac{9}{15}\left(\frac{3}{5}\right)$    (ii) $\frac{12}{15}\left(\frac{4}{5}\right)$
**8.** (i) $\frac{12}{5}$    (ii) $\frac{12}{13}$

## Exercise 23.3

**1.** (i) $\frac{5}{13}$    (ii) $\frac{6}{10}$    (iii) $\frac{20}{29}$
**2.** (i) $\frac{12}{13}$    (ii) $\frac{8}{10}$    (iii) $\frac{21}{29}$
**3.** (i) $\frac{5}{12}$    (ii) $\frac{6}{8}$    (iii) $\frac{20}{21}$
**4.** (i) $\frac{8}{17}$    (ii) $\frac{7}{25}$    (iii) $\frac{4}{5}$

**5.** (i) $\frac{15}{17}$    (ii) $\frac{24}{25}$    (iii) $\frac{3}{5}$
**6.** (i) $\frac{8}{15}$    (ii) $\frac{7}{24}$    (iii) $\frac{4}{3}$
**7.** (i) $\frac{1}{2}$    (ii) $\frac{1}{2}$
    (iii) $\frac{1}{\sqrt{3}}$    (iv) $\frac{\sqrt{3}}{2}$
    (v) $\frac{\sqrt{3}}{1}$ ($\sqrt{3}$)    (vi) $\frac{\sqrt{3}}{2}$
**8.** 9; (i) $\frac{9}{15}$    (ii) $\frac{12}{15}$    (iii) $\frac{9}{12}$

## Exercise 23.4

**1.** 0.5592    **2.** 0.9613    **3.** 0.2079
**4.** 0.8829    **5.** 1.4826    **6.** 3.4874
**7.** 0.3249    **8.** 0.9205    **9.** 0.1736
**10.** 0.3443    **11.** 0.8090    **12.** 0.5299
**13.** 2.4751    **14.** 0.6249    **15.** 0.3090
**16.** 0.4540
**17.** (i) 48°    (ii) 12°    (iii) 57°
    (iv) 31°    (v) 10°    (vi) 66°
**18.** (i) 63°    (ii) 42°    (iii) 78°
**19.** (i) 28°    (ii) 55°    (iii) 67°
**20.** (i) 64°    (ii) 48°    (iii) 65°
**22.** (i) 2.43    (ii) 4.85    (iii) 6.76    (iv) 6.55
**23.** Sine; 0.6, 37°
**24.** tan, 35°
**25.** (i) 12°    (ii) 48°    (iii) 42°
**26.** sin, 12°
**27.** (i) 71.56°    (ii) 18.43°    (iii) 90°

## Exercise 23.5

**1.** Sine, cosine, tangent, cosine (from left to right)
**2.** (i) 6.0    (ii) 10.4    (iii) 13.1
**3.** $x = 5.4, y = 37.1, z = 21.1$
**4.** (i) 28    (ii) 47    (iii) 14
**5.** (i) 7.4    (ii) 46.2    (iii) 21.4
**6.** 32 m    **7.** 4 m
**8.** 6.7 m    **9.** 58 m
**10.** (i) 6.6    (ii) 7.5
**11.** Cosine; 51°
**12.** $P = 37°, Q = 52°, R = 37°$
**13.** 44°    **14.** 13°

## Exercise 23.6

**1.** 6.1 m    **2.** 320 m
**3.** 28 m    **4.** 13 m
**5.** (i) 21 m    (ii) 34 m
**6.** 9 m    **7.** 53°
**8.** Alternate angles (with the horizontal || sea
    level); 172 m

## Test Yourself 23

1. (i) 10 (ii) 8
   (iii) 0.6 (iv) 0.75
2. (i) $\frac{1}{2}$ (ii) $\frac{1}{2}$
   (iii) $\sqrt{3}$
3. 13;
   (i) $\frac{5}{13}$ (ii) $\frac{12}{13}$
   (iii) $\frac{12}{5}$
4. 33 m
5. 10.2
6. 4.7 m
7. (i) 56° (ii) 34°
8. 15.6 m
9. 1 metre
10. (i) 7.6 m (ii) 23°
11. (i) 13.1 m (ii) 9.9 m; 3.2 m

## Chapter 24: Drawing and Interpreting Real-life Graphs

### Exercise 24.1

1. (i) 30 km (ii) 1 hour
   (iii) 45 km (iv) 75 km
2. (i) 140 km (ii) 70 km/hr
   (iii) $2\frac{1}{2}$ hr (iv) $2\frac{1}{2}$ hr (v) 56 km/hr
3. (i) 9.00 am; 3.00 pm (ii) 30 km
   (iii) 9.45 am, 2.00 pm
   (iv) 10.00 am–10.30 am, 12.00 pm–1.00 pm
   (v) 9.00 am–10.00 am (20 km/hr)
4. (i) 20 km (ii) 20 km
   (iii) 1.00 pm
   (iv) Increase (the line gets steeper)
   (v) 40 km
5. (i) 90 min (ii) 20 min
   (iii) 10 km (iv) 20 km/hr
6. Ⓐ & (i), Ⓑ & (iii), Ⓒ & (ii)
7. (i) 7.00 am (ii) 150 km
   (iii) 50 km/hr (iv) 50 km
   (v) 2 hours (vi) 50 km/hr
8. (i) Adam (ii) Twice
   (iii) 1.00 pm (iv) 150 km
   (v) Adam – 200 km; Conor – 350 km
9. Jill departed at 10.00 am and reached her destination at 2.00 pm. She stopped to rest once for one hour and she did so 40 km from home on the outbound leg of her journey. She was driving for a total of $5\frac{1}{2}$ hours and her

average speed during this time was 43.6 km/hr. Her average speed for the return part of the journey was faster (48 km/hr).
10. (i) 75 km
    (ii) 10.45 am and 12.15 pm
    (iii) 1.30 pm (iv) 75 km
    (v) Darren; 30 min

### Exercise 24.2

1. (iv)
2. (i) $37\frac{1}{2}$ miles (ii) 50 miles
   (iii) 48 km (iv) 24 km; Yes
3. No; the graph is linear (i.e. a straight line) but it does not pass through the origin and therefore it is not a directly proportional graph
   (i) 95°F (ii) 59°F
   (iii) 10°C (iv) 38°C; 13°C to 32°C
4. (i) €70 (ii) €55
   (iii) 80 min (iv) 40 min
   (v) €40
5. (i) 65 kg (ii) 75 kg
   (iii) 178 cm; between 60 kg and 70 kg
6. (i) 158 pints (ii) 45 litres
   (iii) 170 pints (iv) 6000 litres
7. (i) 10 m (ii) $4s - 5h = 0$
   (iii) $18\frac{3}{4}$ m
8. (i) €12 (ii) €24
   (iii) 8 km
   (iv) There is a minimum charge of €3
9. (i) 8ℓ (ii) 60 km
   (iii) 3ℓ (iv) Yes
   (v) $y = \left(\frac{3}{20}\right)x$ or $\ell = \left(\frac{3}{20}\right)k$; 45ℓ

### Exercise 24.3

1. (iii)
2. Ⓐ
3. (i) (a) & A, (b) & C, (c) & B
   (ii) Ⓐ & B, Ⓑ & C, Ⓒ & A
4. Route A & (iii), Route B & (i), Route C & (ii)
5. (i) 7.00 am
   (ii) From 10.00 am to midday
   (iii) From midday to 2.00 pm
   (iv) (a) Noon (b) 3.00 p.m.
   (v) 26°C
   (vi) 11°C
6. (i) & Ⓓ, (ii) & Ⓒ, (iii) & Ⓑ, (iv) & Ⓐ
7. (i) & (c), (ii) & (b), (iii) & (a)
8. (i) 80 m (ii) 60 m (iii) 52.5 km/hr

# Chapter 25: Geometry 3: Transformations – Constructions

## Exercise 25.1

1. (i) 5 units to the right
   (ii) 4 units to the right
   (iii) 1 unit up and 4 units right
   (iv) 1 unit right and 3 units up
   (v) 2 units right and 3 units up
   (vi) 1 unit left and 4 units up
2. (i) 5 units right and 3 units up
   (ii) 11 units right and 1 unit down
   (iii) 4 units right and 5 units up
   (iv) 7 units right and 6 units down
   (v) 4 units left and 5 units down
6. (i) B　　(ii) [DC]　(iii) O　　(iv) [AB]
7. (i) B　　(ii) [BC]　(iii) △BCE　(iv) [BE]
8. (i) [EC]　　(ii) E　　　(iii) △BEC
   (iv) D　　　(v) [AD]　　(vi) △BEC
9. (i) A(2, 4), B(3, −2), C(−2, −3), D(−5, 1)
   (ii) A′(7, 6), B′(8, 0), C′(3, −1), D′(0, 3)

## Exercise 25.2

3. (i) The point F　　(ii) [EF]
   (iii) [DF]　　　　(iv) △DCF
   (v) △EFD　　　　(vi) [CF]
4. (i) & (iii)
5. M, O, D, A, Y
7. (i) B　　　　　(ii) A
   (iii) [DA]　　　(iv) △COD
   (v) [CO]　　　　(vi) △CBD
   (vii) [OA]　　　(viii) CDAB

8. C
9. (i) D　　　　　　　(ii) A
10. (i) Axial symmetry in $y$-axis
    (ii) Axial symmetry in $x$-axis
    (iii) Central symmetry in the origin or rotation of 180°.
11. Central symmetry in C and axial symmetry in AB
12. D
13. (i) A′(4, 5), B′(1, 4), C′(5, 2)
    (ii) A′′(−4, −5), B′′(−1, −4), C′′(−5, −2)
14. (i) 2　　(ii) 2　　(iii) 5　　(iv) 0
15. (i), (ii), (iv)
16. (i) A.S. (ii) Tr. (iii) A.S. (iv) A.S. (v) C.S.
    (vi) Clockwise rotation (180°) about (1.5, 1)
17. B = (0, 3), C = (−2, 3), D = (−2, 0)
18. (i) Clockwise 90°
    (ii) Clockwise 180°
    (iii) Anticlockwise 90°

## Exercise 25.4

4. |AC| = 4.6 cm, |DE| = 3.1 cm, |XZ| = 7.7 cm
5. (i) |AC| = 3.1 cm　　(ii) |AB| = 5.4 cm
6. |AC| = 5.9 cm, |DF| = 5.2 cm, |XZ| = 9.2 cm
9. |AC| = 10.8 cm
11. 8.3 cm
13. (ii) 111 m